WRITING IN THE SOCIAL SCIENCES
A RHETORIC WITH READINGS

Second Edition

Kristine Hansen
Brigham Young University

Excerpts taken from:

A Rhetoric for the Social Sciences: A Guide to Academic and Professional Communication
by Kristine Hansen

PEARSON
Custom
Publishing

PEARSON CUSTOM PUBLISHING
75 Arlington Street, Suite 300, Boston, MA 02116
A Pearson Education Company

This book is affectionately dedicated,
for the third time,
to my students

CONTENTS

THE RHETORIC

PART I: RHETORIC AND COMPOSING

1 RHETORIC AND THE SOCIAL SCIENCES 5

What is Rhetoric? 6

What are the Social Sciences? 10

The Social Construction of Knowledge 12

The Process of Knowledge-Making Starts with Questions 14

Answers Come from Observation 15

Observation Relies on Methods and Instruments 15

Interpretations of Data Become Claims of Knowledge 16

Claims Are Disseminated for Peer Review 16

How Persuasion Creates Change in Social Sciences 17

The Rhetorical Situation 18

Suggestions for Discussion or Writing 21

References 22

2 THE INDIVIDUAL AND SOCIAL DIMENSIONS OF COMPOSING   23

The Subprocesses of Composing   24
   Common Ways of Prewriting   24
   Specialized Kinds of Prewriting   25
   Drafting   26
   Revising   27
   Editing   27
   Composing with a Computer   28

The Individual Nature of Composing   28
   Composing as an Idiosyncratic Act   28
   Composing as a Private Act   29

The Social Nature of Composing   29
   Language as a Social Medium   29
   The Influence of Audiences   30
   The Social Evolution and Influence of Genres   31
   The Influence of Genres on Writers   33

Composing Collaboratively   34
   Guidelines for Working in Groups   36
   Guidelines for Individuals   38
   Avoiding Plagiarism and Giving Credit   39

Suggestions for Discussion   40

Suggestions for Writing   41

References   42

PART II: PRIMARY AND SECONDARY RESEARCH

3 RESEARCH METHODS, WRITING, AND ETHICS   45

Researching is Part of Writing   45

Methods as Disciplined Inquiry   46

Quantitative and Qualitative Methods   47

Ethical Considerations in Doing Research   50
   Using Human Participants   50
   Institutional Review Boards   51

Research that Qualifies for Exempt Review   54

What Does Not Require IRB Review?   55
   Plagiarism and Fraud   56
   The Consequences of Ethical Lapses   57

Suggestions for Discussion or Writing   57

4 **INTERPRETING DOCUMENTS** 59

Interpretations Depend on Prior Knowledge and Assumptions 60

Statistics Must Also Be Interpreted 61

What Histories Are Made Of 62

Reading Source Documents 64

Writing about Source Documents 66

Suggestions for Research and Writing 68

References 69

5 **INTERVIEWING** 71

Preparing for the Interview 72
Find Informants 72
Contact the Informants 73
Do Necessary Background Research 73
Plan Your Questions 74
Prepare the Materials You Will Need 74

Recording the Interview 74
Notetaking 74
Audiotaping 75
Videotaping 76
Conducting the Interview 76

Moving from Notes or Tape to Text 78
Transcripts 78
Dialogue or Edited Transcript 79
Interview Summary 80
Synthesis 80
Synthesis with Elaboration 81

Suggestions for Research and Writing 81

References 82

6 **OBSERVING** 83

Kinds of Observation 84
Unobtrusive Observation 84
Structured Observation 85
Case Studies 85
Participant Observation 86

Making Observations 88
Define Your Purpose 88
Select People, Setting, and Behavior for Observation 88
Record Data 89

Make Conclusions Reliable   91
Analyzing and Writing About Observations   92
Suggestions for Research and Writing   94
References   95

7 SURVEYING   97

Advantages of Surveying   98
Disadvantages of Surveying   98
Designing a Survey   99
Define Your Purpose   99
Create Demographic Questions   100
Create Fixed-Response Questions   100
Write Open-Ended Questions   101
Write Unambiguous Questions   102
Determine the Order of Questions   103
Write Clear Directions   103

Finding Respondents   104
Random Sampling   105
Convenience Sampling   105
Sample Size   106

Conducting the Survey   106
Analyzing the Data   107
Writing the Report   108
Suggestions for Research and Writing   109
Reference   110

8 EXPERIMENTING   111

The Purpose of Experiments   111
Steps and Considerations in Conducting Experiments   113
Creating Hypotheses   113
Creating Operational Definitions   113
Designing the Experiment and Implementing Controls   114
Selecting Participants   116
Establishing Validity and Reliability   117
Meeting Ethical Standards   118

Writing about Experiments   119
Suggestions for Research and Writing   121
References   122

9 RESEARCHING IN THE LIBRARY AND ON THE INTERNET   123

Why Do Library Research?   124

Finding Information in the Library   125
Locate Search Terms   126
Search Databases and Online Catalogs with Boolean Operators   127
Search for Government Publications   129
Use Interlibrary Loan   129
Ask the Librarian   129

Finding Information on the Internet   130
Use Search Engines and Subject Directories   131
Search Engines   131
Subject Directories   134
Use the Internet for Other Kinds of Research   135

Evaluating Sources   136
How to Evaluate Reliability of Print Sources   136
Political Dimensions of Peer Review   136
Ideological Dimensions of Research Funding   136
How to Evaluate Reliability of Web Sources   140
Source Usefulness   142
Evaluating Books   142
Evaluating Articles   143
Evaluating Web Sites   143

References   144

PART III: ACADEMIC AND PROFESSIONAL GENRES

10 PROPOSALS AND PROSPECTUSES   147

Proposals   148
The IRB Proposal   149

An ORCA Proposal   163

The Prospectus   163
Parts of the Prospectus   167
Organization of the Prospectus   172
Sample Prospectus   173

Suggestions for Writing   179

11 RESEARCH PAPERS 181

Identifying Types of Research Writing 182
  Reviews of Literature 183
  Source-Based Arguments 184
  Empirical Research Papers 185

Planning and Building Your Argument 186
  Outlining 187
  Recording Information 189
    Photocopying 190
    Writing Note Cards 190
    Using a Computer 190
  Using Sources Ethically 191
    Avoiding Plagiarism 191
    Common Knowledge 192
    A Final Caution 192

Drafting Your Argument 194
  Summarizing 194
  Paraphrasing 195
  Quoting 196
    Embedded Quotations 196
    Block Quotations 197
    Quotation within a Quotation 198
    Using Brackets to Add to Quotations 199
    Using Ellipsis to Omit Parts of Quotations 199
    Citing Non-recoverable Sources 200
    Adding Emphasis to Quotations 200
    Changing Capitalization 200
  Including Transitions with Headings 201
  Writing the Introduction and Conclusion 202

Formatting the Final Draft 203

Conclusion 205

Suggestions for Discussion and Writing 205

Reference 206

12 PUBLIC POSITION PAPERS AND OPINION PIECES 207

Writing a Position Paper 209
  Define and Limit the Problem 209
  Research the Problem 210
  Evaluate Possible Solutions 211
  Recommend One or More Solutions 212
  Draft the Position Paper 213

Suggestions for Research and Writing 215

13 ABSTRACTS, CRITIQUES, AND REVIEWS 217

Writing an Abstract 218

Writing a Critique 220

A Caution about Being Tactful *224*

Example of a Student Critique 225

Writing a Review 225

The Facts of Publication *228*
Statement of the Book's Purpose and Scope *229*
Summary of the Book's Contents *229*
Evaluation of Strengths and Weaknesses *229*
General Recommendation *230*

Suggestions for Writing 231

References 231

14 RESUMES 233

Types of Resumes 233

Traditional Resumes 234

Organization of the Traditional Resume *234*
Contents of the Traditional Resume *235*
Design of the Resume *238*
Paper and Printing *240*

Scannable Resumes 243

Design of the Scannable Resume *243*
Organization of the Scannable Resume *244*

Online Resumes 246

In-House Help 247

Suggestions for Writing 247

15 LETTERS AND MEMOS 249

Letters of Application 250

Parts of the Letter *250*
Design of the Letter *253*
Composing Your Letter *254*

Letters of Intent and Personal Statements 258

Importance of the Letter *258*
Generating Substance Through Prewriting *259*
Drafting Around a Theme *264*
Revising and Editing *264*

Memos 265

Composing a Memo *266*

Designing the Memo   266
E-mail Etiquette   269
Suggestions for Writing   270

PART IV: VISUAL AND ORAL RHETORIC

16 BASIC PRINCIPLES OF DOCUMENT DESIGN   273

Enhancing a Document's Readability   273
Page Layout   274
Typography   278
Visual Cues to Text Structure   280
Headings   280
Headings and Professional Style Guides   284
References   289

17 GRAPHICS   291

Graphics As Rhetoric   291
Tables   293
Figures   294
Photographs   295
Line Drawings   295
Maps   296
Diagrams and Flowcharts   296
Graphs   297
Positioning and Labeling Graphics   301
Position Graphics for Easy Viewing   301
Number Graphics for Easy Reference   301
Give Graphics Descriptive Captions   301
Label Parts of Tables and Figures   302
Ethical Issues in Using Graphics   304
Plagiarism   304
Omitting or Misrepresenting Variations in the Data   305
Distorting or Cluttering the Design   306
Conclusion   308
Suggestions for Practice   308
Reference   309

18 ORAL PRESENTATIONS   311

The Tradition of Oral Rhetoric   311

Evaluating the Rhetorical Situation   312
    Defining Your Purpose   312
    Sizing Up Your Audience   313
    Assessing the Context and Environment   313

Organizing Your Presentation   314
    The Beginning   314
    The Middle   317
    The Ending   317

Using Resources Wisely   318
    Time   318
    Environment   319
    Visual Aids   319

Planning for Delivery   324
    Memory Support   324
    Appropriate Dress   325
    Voice Qualities   326
    Nonverbal Communication   327

Rehearsing Your Delivery   328

Suggestions for Discussion and Application   328

PART V: STYLE IN THE SOCIAL SCIENCES

19 INSTITUTIONAL STYLE   333

Why Do Styles Differ?   333

Style in the Social Sciences   334
    The Detached Persona   335
    Jargon: When It Is and When It Isn't   337
    Inclusive and Unbiased Language   341
    References to Participants in Research   344

Conclusion   344

Suggestions for Writing or Discussion   345

References   347

THE READINGS

Journal Article Review   351
    by Michelle Pomeroy

From *Bare Branches: The Security Implications of Asia's Surplus Male Population*   354
    by Valerie M. Hudson and Andrea M. den Boer

"Harlem Town"   378
    by Sarah and A. Elizabeth Delany with Amy Hill Hearth

From *Watching the English: The Hidden Rules of English Behaviour*   388
    by Kate Fox

From *Soul Searching: The Religious and Spiritual Lives of American Teenagers*   402
    by Christian Smith with Melinda Lundquist Denton

"The SPE: What It Was, Where It Came From, and What Came Out of It"   420
    by Philip G. Zimbardo

Three Student Research Papers   434

    "Exploring the Open-Response Task as a Tool for Assessing the Understanding of Fifth-Grade Students in the Content Area of Fractions"   435
        by Heather Bahlmann

    "The Social Problems that Deter Xhosa Women from Marriage and How Education and Westernization Allow Them to Refuse Marriage"   462
        by Colleen Rebecca Johnson

    "Addressing the Causes of Obesity in the United States: American Lifestyle and the Psychology of Health"   477
        by Kemarie Ann Campbell

"Consumer Marriage and Modern Covenant Marriage"   498
    by William J. Doherty

"Abolishing Welfare Won't Stop Poverty, Illegitimacy"   504
    by Elijah Anderson

"Competition in the Classroom: Are We Teaching Kids to be Insecure?"   507
    by Jordan Richardson Cahoon

Book Review of *Bare Branches: The Security Implications of Asia's Surplus Male Population*   510

　　by Rose McDermott

Book Review of *Soul Searching: The Religious and Spiritual Lives of American Teenagers*   514

　　by Jeffrey Jensen Arnett

Book Review of *Code of the Street: Decency, Violence, and the Moral Life of the Inner City*   517

　　by Brad Gunnell

INDEX   519

PREFACE

This second edition of *Writing in the Social Sciences: A Rhetoric with Readings* is the grandchild of my 1998 book, *A Rhetoric for the Social Sciences*. The original grew out of my conviction that students in the social sciences, who constitute the largest number of graduates at Brigham Young University each year, deserved a writing textbook that dealt with the methods of inquiry and invention, the genres, and the stylistic registers that are found in their disciplines. Over nearly twenty years it has been my good fortune and my great pleasure to teach students at BYU majoring in anthropology, archaeology, communications, economics, secondary education, family science, geography, health science, history, international relations, linguistics, political science, psychology, social work, sociology, and a few other fields as well. The research that is done in these fields interests me a great deal, so being able to blend my love for writing and teaching with the subject matter of the social sciences has created the ideal professional opportunity for me.

I have learned a great deal from my students, and I hope that the contents of this book reflect some of that learning as well as the study I have undertaken on my own to stay abreast of new developments in the social sciences and in the teaching of writing. The following changes in this edition are an effort to make the book as current as possible and more serviceable to students and teachers:

- New professional and student models illustrate various methods of inquiry and various genres discussed in Part II and Part III.
- Chapter 9 has been significantly revised with the help of BYU librarians Allyson Washburn and Suzanne Julian.
- Chapter 11 is new and is meant to provide answers to some of the questions I found myself answering again and again in class.
- Various changes throughout the book reflect the fact that we are well into a new digital era when it comes to conducting research, communicating the findings, applying for jobs, and writing in the workplace.
- Various references peculiar to the BYU campus have been updated, e.g., its IRB and ORCA grant requirements and services offered at the Career and Counseling Center.

I want to say a word about why there are so many student and professional models in this book. I believe that learning to write well depends in large measure on reading well-written texts of the kind one is expected to write. Simply describing the features of a desired text is not sufficient for students to learn to produce it. They have to see how others have met the demands of rhetorical situations similar to the ones they face. I believe strongly in the ancient rhetorical practice of imitation, and I commend it to teachers and students alike. I have worked hard to find interesting and provocative professional readings as well as student papers that have broad appeal and that illustrate successful responses to common challenges. I urge all users of this book to read all of the models and notice the way that writers introduce their subjects and state their claims, how they describe their methods, how they organize their evidence, how they construct paragraphs and sentences, how they present data in tables and figures, how they document borrowed information, how they present their own persona and voice in their writing, and how they address their audiences. Taking time to observe these things and then trying to adapt successful strategies to your own writing will prove far more useful than dry and abstract discussions of writing principles.

Like any writer of a textbook, I must gratefully acknowledge the assistance of many others, without whose help it would have been impossible for me to complete this edition. I express deep thanks to the following students, who have allowed their writing to be used as models and who have, in some cases, worked patiently with me during the editing process: Emily Robison Adams, Heather Bahlmann, Warren Brookes, Jordan Cahoon, Kemarie Campbell, Brant Ellsworth, Bradley Gunnell, Spencer James, Colleen Johnson, Sam Lindsey, Ashley Jones Nelson, Michelle Pomeroy, and Jenelle Tittelfitz. I am also grateful to Amy Hurt, whose criticisms improved Chapters 5 and 6, and to many other students whose names I do not know, but whose feedback has come to me via their teachers and has helped me to see ways to improve the book.

I particularly thank my colleagues in the ranks of teaching advanced writing, who have made comments and suggestions over the past few years that have contributed to changes in this edition: Joyce Adams, Ana Preto Bay, John Beeson, Laura Card, Lynne Christy, Nancy Gunn, Sherri Guyon, Matt Haslam, Matt Jackson, Sherland Jackson, Tracy Jackson, Pam Johstoneaux, Sondra Jones, Mary Lee, Danette Paul, Tammy Scofield, Scott Stewart, and Heidi Yates. My colleague Beverly Zimmerman has always been ready to answer my questions and share her knowledge. As noted above, I also owe a great debt to BYU librarians Allyson Washburn and Suzanne Julian, who have helped me bring the chapter on library and Internet research up to date.

My student research assistant, Crystal Roper Lefler, has been invaluable to me in the many chores related to revision—finding and in some cases drafting new material, formatting text, retyping tables, editing, proofreading, tracking correspondence, criticizing my writing, and helping me think through possible changes. Thanks to her, this project was completed with a minimum of stress and on time. I also express gratitude for the interest and support of family and friends who have cheered me on.

With all the help I've had, it doesn't seem possible that there should be any errors or shortcomings in this edition. But I know there will be, and I alone accept responsibility for them. I invite students and teachers to communicate freely with me about any needed changes so that the next edition can be better.

THE RHETORIC

PART

I

RHETORIC
AND COMPOSING

The first two chapters of this book describe how the terms *rhetoric* and *composing* apply to writing in the social sciences. In Chapter 1 you will learn that writing about scientific knowledge is not a simple act of packaging facts in neutral words; instead, social scientists use the art of rhetoric to argue for their claims of knowledge. This does not mean that the documents social scientists write are attempts to manipulate their readers or bamboozle them with fancy words; rather, it means that social scientists often deal with probable and contingent truths. Through the social processes involved in producing new knowledge, social scientists refine their claims to make them as true to the evidence and as persuasive as possible for the audience of their peers. If their claims are to be accepted by the intellectual communities they belong to, social scientists must meet rigorous standards in their research and writing. They must understand their purpose and audience well and know how to use the language conventions that characterize the rhetoric of the social sciences.

In Chapter 2, you will find a brief review of the processes that take place when individuals compose documents, with particular attention given to the specialized kinds of prewriting that social scientists do. Beyond that, you will read about the social dimensions of composing to see how learning to think like a social scientist is connected with learning to write like one. Finally, since many social scientists research and write with their colleagues, you will find some guidelines for researching and writing collaboratively with your fellow students.

1

RHETORIC AND THE SOCIAL SCIENCES

CHAPTER OVERVIEW

After reading this chapter, you should be able to answer the following questions:

1. What is meant by rhetoric?
2. What is meant by social sciences?
3. What does it mean to say that knowledge is socially constructed?
4. In what sense do the social sciences involve rhetoric?
5. How can you as a social scientist use rhetoric persuasively and responsibly both as a professional and as a citizen of your nation and the world?

The title and subtitle of this book yoke two terms—*rhetoric* and *science*—that are generally believed to name things that are incompatible with each other. The word *rhetoric* is in many people's minds a name for "fancy talk," language that uses figures of speech or a flowery style to draw attention to itself. In other people's minds it might be a name for "empty talk" of the type politicians are frequently accused of using. In the view of still others, it is a synonym for "propaganda," deliberately slanted, misleading language that can result in various levels of harm—everything from voting for scoundrels to participating in genocide—when uncritical people believe what they're told. In all of these views, rhetoric is language that masks a lack of real substance in thinking or that distorts what is communicated, drawing attention away from the ideas by clothing them in beguiling dress. At best, rhetoric is thought to be language that attempts to persuade audiences by appealing more to their emotions than to their reasoning ability.

Science, on the other hand, is popularly believed to name both a kind of inquiry and its results; that is, science is a body of facts that have been produced by rigorously controlled methods. When properly carried out, these methods result in the discovery of objective truths. "Objective" means that the truths are independent of the subjective perception of those who discovered them. These facts are usually said to "speak for themselves"; they seem so obvious and logical that the language used to communicate them is also considered objective, neutral, transparent, free from bias or emotion. Thus, scientific language has long been held to be the opposite of rhetoric. In popular thought, rhetoric is meant to persuade, sometimes in an underhanded way, while science merely explains the way things are, with no hidden agendas.

What, then, can rhetoric have to do with science, particularly the social sciences? What can it possibly mean to call this book a rhetoric *for* the social sciences? To answer these questions, it's necessary to provide a more complete understanding of both rhetoric and the social sciences. These fields of study both have long and fascinating histories, too long to cover in detail here, but a brief summary will help to show how the two are compatible, indeed why it is helpful to think of writing in the social sciences as rhetorical. As you read the following, you will see that language—even supposedly neutral scientific language—can't escape being rhetorical. And the consequences of that for you, as a student majoring in the social sciences, are important, because as you will see, studying what makes up rhetoric will help you to be both a more skillful analyst of the rhetoric you read and hear and a more effective practitioner of it yourself.

WHAT IS RHETORIC?

Rhetoric has been defined many ways in its 2500-year-old history. Most of the definitions have been positive, unlike many contemporary understandings of the word. The word comes from the Greek *rhetorike*, the name for the art of oratory, or public speaking. The great philosopher Aristotle, who attempted to catalog so many other fields of learning, also wrote a systematic description of the art of rhetoric. He defined rhetoric as the art of "finding the available means of persuasion" in any situation. His book *Rhetoric* explains how to find and arrange ideas for a speech, how to appeal to various audiences, and how to choose the right style—in short, how to use language skillfully to express one's thoughts so as to win the confidence and assent of others. He recognized that such a powerful art could be used for unethical purposes, but he believed that in itself, the art of rhetoric is neither moral nor immoral. He thought that rhetoric used by a moral person to argue for good purposes would be inherently more persuasive and therefore superior to the rhetoric of an immoral person with evil ends in mind.

Isocrates, a contemporary of Aristotle, also believed that rhetoric should be used for virtuous aims. In the school he kept in Athens, Isocrates taught his students to be effective leaders in public affairs; he also attempted to teach them to be ethical by example and by challenging them to choose good and noble ways of making their arguments effective. Since ancient Athens was a true democracy in which each citizen was expected to participate personally, instead of by electing representatives, a knowledge of rhetoric was paramount for each citizen because making effective speeches was the way to influence the debates of the legislature and the judgments of the courts. (It should be noted here that participation in public life was limited to male citizens; women, slaves, and other non-citizens did not have this opportunity.) All other facets of education were intended to give young men a store of knowledge to draw on in their oratory.

The Roman rhetorician Quintilian extended Isocrates' ideas, declaring that the rhetorician should be a "good man, skilled in speaking." Quintilian laid a foundation for schooling the young in rhetoric and other fields of knowledge that lasted through the Renaissance in Western Europe. Although theories of rhetoric underwent some important changes during and after the Renaissance, the art and practice of rhetoric remained central to education in Europe and America until well into the nineteenth century, when the ideal of the citizen orator began to falter. Skill in oratory began to take a back seat then, as correctness in writing became the new goal in language arts instruction at the university.

If rhetoric was so respectable for centuries, how did it get the bad reputation that it now so often has? Actually, suspicions about rhetoric were voiced almost from the start, most prominently by Aristotle's teacher, Plato. He thought that the art of rhetoric in the hands of an unscrupulous person had the power to make bad ideas seem like good ones; he was also troubled that rhetoric could make merely probable ideas seem like undisputed truths (see *Gorgias*). Plato believed that one must know absolute truths before learning to use rhetoric so that one might never use the art to deceive, either intentionally or unintentionally (see *Phaedrus*). Plato's fears about rhetoric have been justified over the centuries by people such as Hitler, Stalin, Mao Tse Tung, or Senator Joseph McCarthy, who have deceived others through their cunning use of language. As a result, the reputation of rhetoric has always had its shady side. On the other hand, Aristotle's, Isocrates's, and Quintilian's faith in rhetoric as a potentially positive force has also been justified by people such as Abraham Lincoln, Sojourner Truth, Elizabeth Cady Stanton, Winston Churchill, Martin Luther King, Jr., and Pope John Paul II, who have used artfully composed language to inspire their followers in times of crisis and change to achieve goals they believed would make their worlds better.

Although most people would agree that rhetoric based on absolute truth is preferable to rhetoric based on probabilities, they would also have to admit that knowing the truth about everything before advocating a course of action seems hopelessly idealistic, if not impossible—an unaffordable luxury, especially in the face of urgent decisions that we must make collectively all the time. In our shared public life, we have to decide such things as how to vote, spend tax revenues, create and sustain schools and colleges, plan cities and transportation systems, interact with our environment, encourage and maintain healthy families, choose between arguments in a jury trial, help the poor, and deal with lawbreakers. We all respond to rhetoric as citizens of neighborhoods, cities, states, and nations, and we must often do so by the light of what we believe is probably true, rather than what we know for sure. Many of us also use rhetoric in the public sphere as we write letters to the editor, speak out at city council meetings, or urge others to vote for a candidate or an initiative. As a result, it is important to study rhetoric, both to understand how to analyze the rhetoric of others and how to practice the art ourselves.

Rhetoric will be defined in this book as *using words and other symbols skillfully to articulate and advocate your beliefs about something you assume to be true by addressing an audience whom you want to persuade to consider your beliefs, by choice and not coercion, and possibly to cooperate with you in achieving a shared goal.* Let's break that long, complex definition down into six parts:

(1) *Rhetoric is using words and other symbols skillfully to articulate . . .* The key words here are "skillfully," which means using communally accepted conventions of effective form, a pleasing style, and correctness in language; and "to articulate," which means to state what you believe in precise words and clear sentences, arranged in a logical and compelling sequence.

(2) *. . . and to advocate your beliefs . . .* The word "advocate" means that you actively argue for your beliefs, as an attorney argues for a client, using the kinds of logic, reasoning, examples, facts, evidence, statistics, or other data that you and your audience consider valid and trustworthy. But because human beings also have emotions which can be very powerful factors in how we make up our minds about an issue, an effective rhetorician will often advocate a case by appealing to emotions as well as reason. However, an ethical rhetorician will avoid doing so in a manipulative way. Ancient rhetoricians recognized that rhetoric included both appeals to reason (the Greeks called it *logos*) and to emotion (*pathos*).

(3) *. . . about something you assume to be true . . .* This part of the definition allows for either certain or probable knowledge. The key point is that you are convinced something is true or so probable that you are willing to urge that others consider and possibly share your view. In order for that to happen, your own conviction must ring true to your audience. Your listeners or readers must perceive you as a credible and knowledgeable person with their best interests in mind, one who would not willfully mislead them. Your character, as conveyed in your rhetoric, becomes another type of appeal to the audience, in addition to reason and emotion. Presenting yourself as knowledgeable, credible, trustworthy, and well-intentioned is called the ethical appeal, from the Greek *ethos*.

(4) *. . . by addressing an audience whom you want to persuade . . .*
Rhetoric by its very nature is communal; its aim is to construct the broadest possible consensus, encompassing as many members of the addressed audience as possible. Consensus is likely to come about when the rhetor successfully appeals to the needs, values, beliefs, and assumptions of individual members of the audience.

(5) *. . . to consider your beliefs, by choice and not coercion . . .* By using threats, extortion, torture, or some other unethical means of exercising power, you might get others to say they agree with you and to cooperate with you, but you wouldn't be using rhetoric. Rhetoric is language or other symbols used to present a point of view to an audience that is free to choose whether or not to agree with you. The audience has an important role to play in any rhetorical situation: They have to judge not only the soundness and logic of the argument offered them but also the character of the speaker or writer. If their emotions have been appealed to, they must decide if such appeals are fair and well-meant.

(6) *. . . and possibly to cooperate with you in achieving a shared goal.*
Often, the purpose of rhetoric is simply to gain the audience's fair consideration of ideas, and, if possible, their intellectual assent. But it may also be used to go beyond assent, to persuade others to *act* upon their conviction—to vote a certain way, to join a movement, to volunteer for a cause, to make a change in their lives. The stronger and more persuasive your appeals, the more likely it is that people will act to join you in whatever efforts must be made to achieve a goal.

In this book I will maintain that the above definition of rhetoric applies not just to public discourse but to university disciplines as well, the social sciences in particular. Like cities, states, and nations, academic disciplines are communities too—but they are highly specialized ones that people enter by choice rather than by birth or naturalization. As teachers and students, as current and future professionals engaged in understanding the world and creating bodies of knowledge, we use various types of rhetoric all the time to present our claims of knowledge to one another and to urge their acceptance.

Just as founders of the United States agreed long ago to construct a new society on the premises that "all men are created equal" and that power is located ultimately in the people, so academic disciplines are based on assumptions that the members of each discipline accept as valid. Although the rhetoric used in American political life is often scorned, we must not forget that using the power of language to act on each other is our principal way of bringing about change in our society. The goal of most political rhetoric is to help citizens work toward building and maintaining a society that furthers a nation's founding principles—although it's clear that there is often disagreement about how to do that.

Similarly, the rhetoric used in academic disciplines allows members of those disciplines to create and maintain bodies of knowledge erected on their basic assumptions. But members of a discipline also use rhetoric to question, criticize, and revise assumptions, principles, and theories. No university discipline claims to be based on indisputable, absolute truths; in fact, the history of each field of academic study is replete with examples of how the field has changed its basic principles from time to time. Even though the assumptions of a discipline are provisional, they provide a basis for the research, writing, and talk that to a large extent make up the discipline. They enable something like a broad communal conversation to be carried on.

The specialized conversation of academic disciplines brings up another sense in which the word *rhetoric* is used. For centuries, the word has been used as the name for the book in which the art of rhetoric is laid out as an object of study and a guide for practice. Since this book will present practical advice for writing persuasively in the social sciences, it is in that sense a "rhetoric." This book, or rhetoric, will instruct you how to write like a social scientist by teaching you about the genres and styles regularly used in the social sciences. More importantly, it will show you how these genres and styles reflect how social scientists reason and carry out research. The readings at the end of this book will serve as models of various genres and styles. By reading them, you will see how social scientists create written arguments.

WHAT ARE THE SOCIAL SCIENCES?

The social sciences are the fields of learning and research that concern themselves with human behavior, human relationships, and the social, cultural, economic, and political institutions that human beings have created. Considering their broad scope, the social sciences encompass many university disciplines and sub-disciplines. Although they might be named and grouped differently on various campuses, generally they include at least the following six disciplines: anthropology, economics, history, political science, psychology, and sociology. Yet other fields of study are commonly grouped with the social sciences because they also deal with human behavior and institutions. These include communications, education, family science, linguistics, geography, organizational behavior, demography, international relations, counseling, social work, and criminology.

Another way to identify the social sciences is to say what they are *not*. They are not the physical sciences, such as math, physics, or geology; they are not the biological sciences such as agronomy, botany, or zoology; and they are not the humanities and fine arts, such as literature, music, and theater. Yet even this negative definition is in some ways inadequate, as various social sciences might draw on one or more of these areas of learning. Most of the social sciences, for example, make use of mathematical and statistical procedures. Geographers must know something of geology, climatology, and cultural studies. Historians and archaeologists must often understand agronomy or botany to interpret practices or evidence from the past. Cultural anthropologists and sociologists are interested in the role that the humanities play in people's lives. Furthermore, there are cross-disciplinary fields, such as political geography, created when two social sciences intersect, or psychobiology, created when a social science field overlaps with a natural science. Perhaps it is best to focus on what all the social sciences have in common: They all aim to understand humans as individuals and as social beings, using empirical methods, in order to point the way toward solutions for personal and social problems, small and large, that confront us.

The social sciences are all relatively young as university disciplines, most of them having been established as separate fields of study and university departments in the late nineteenth or early twentieth century. This is not to say that prior to that time no one thought about human behavior, relationships, and institutions. But many of the questions that now preoccupy the social sciences were generally treated within the single discipline of philosophy (and they still are, though differently from how they are treated in the social sciences). Then in the seventeenth, eighteenth, and nineteenth centuries the natural sciences arose as powerful fields of study that investigated and explained the natural world with increasingly greater precision, yielding beneficial applications in such fields as medicine and industry. These achievements led some to think that a "science of man" or a "science of society" could also be established. They reasoned that, just as physicists and biologists could explain the laws of nature, and therefore predict and attempt to control the effects of natural processes, so the sciences of humans and society might uncover laws of individual and social behavior that would lead to developing better human beings and more just societies.

Some social scientists now believe that finding social and behavioral laws as consistent and reliable as the laws of nature is a utopian goal, since human beings and their interactions are often unpredictable, being influenced by more variables than one could possibly control. Nevertheless, all social scientists aim to develop the best tools and methods for understanding how individuals and groups think and behave so that they can state or predict with some accuracy the *probable* truth about whatever they might study—the causes of eating disorders, the reasons for voting behavior, the significance of head-hunting among the Ilongot people, the possible outcomes of an international trade alliance, why the sixteenth century was an age of exploration in Europe, why the Bay of Pigs invasion failed, or how to stem the tide of domestic abuse.

This emphasis on the probable, you will note, is consistent with the definition of rhetoric established earlier. If absolute certainty eludes social scientists—and most of them would admit that it does—they find themselves in the predicament that the philosopher Plato most feared in people's learning to use rhetoric. Social scientists have to make the case for what they have discovered based on what is probably true rather than what they know to be absolutely and objectively true. Is this situation as dangerous as Plato feared? If social scientists can't base their claims on absolute truth, will their writing be deceptive and therefore harmful?

The answer is, "It depends." It depends to a great extent on the assumptions that social scientists begin with. In the nineteenth century, there was a group of people who called themselves "scientists" and called their science "phrenology." They believed that they could determine intelligence and character traits from the shape of people's skulls. They developed instruments for measuring the parts of the skull, and they created elaborate, scientific-looking drawings of various skull types, with parts and attributes of each neatly labeled. For a time many people accepted the conclusions the phrenologists came to, which included that some races are inferior because their skulls tended to be formed differently from those of supposedly superior races. Most people today would consider phrenology a pseudo-science because when one examines its tenets and applications carefully, it becomes clear that one of its main purposes was to justify racial segregation and discrimination. This example shows that the assumptions of a group who call themselves scientists may be heavily influenced by political and ideological agendas that are somewhat hidden because the science presents itself as impartial and neutral.

The phrenology example shows there is some danger in proceeding from merely probable assumptions. Nevertheless, current theories of how knowledge is created and disseminated suggest that arguments based on probabilities may not pose a long-term danger, *provided* a scientific community's conversation is open and welcomes any responsible participant. According to these theories, intellectual communities that develop and ratify new claims of knowledge do so by examining, moderating, and even censoring excessive or potentially dangerous claims. These theories contend that knowledge is not so much discovered as it is socially constructed.

THE SOCIAL CONSTRUCTION OF KNOWLEDGE

We often say that knowledge is "discovered," as if it were like an uncharted island where a ship one day lands. After that, the fact of the island's existence and location is known, and the captain of the ship usually gets the credit for discovering it. But if we stop to think about it, the captain must credit the ship-builders who provided a seaworthy ship, and he owes a debt to the map-makers and inventors of the navigational instruments that allowed him to chart a course across the ocean. Nor would he likely have succeeded in getting there alone, so he must credit the crew of the ship whose teamwork kept the ship sailing on course in all kinds of weather. Perhaps he even owes some thanks to unpredictable and seemingly random events, such as a storm that blew the ship off-course for a day or an argument with the ship's mate about what course to steer. Maybe one of these seemingly unrelated events actually contributed to the island's discovery.

The point of this analogy is that no one acts completely alone in establishing a new fact or idea. Knowledge has a powerful social dimension, both in the way it originates and in the way it is disseminated. Even if the ship captain had sailed alone, he would have been dependent on knowledge created earlier by others. More important, he wouldn't be able to establish his discovery of the island as a fact if all he had to offer as proof was his own word. Before the island's existence would be widely accepted as a fact, some kind of evidence would be required that others would find plausible. The captain's private knowledge would likely not count as a fact for anyone else until he could offer descriptions, pictures, artifacts, corroborating testimony, or other convincing evidence that he had made a discovery. Furthermore, he would have to submit his claim of new knowledge to be judged by standards that the community finds acceptable. The ship captain's claims must be persuasive to the audience to whom he makes them.

But this analogy brings up a few interesing observations. First, despite the help that enables the captain to make his claim, in a society that believes in intellectual property, he will generally get all or most of the credit for the discovery. Second, the discovery of an island is important only in a larger political system that values adventurous voyages into the unknown and finds it important to know the location of islands. In some political systems this discovery might be unimportant, particularly if there were no resources or inhabitants on the island to exploit. And third, if there were inhabitants on the island, what about their perspective? What seems a discovery from the captain's point of view might seem like an invasion to the inhabitants. The words "uncharted island" take on a different meaning when you ask, "Uncharted to whom?" Perhaps the island was included on other people's maps long before our hypothetical captain arrived. These points remind us that credit and rewards for knowledge often accrue to those who already have power and status; that what counts as the discovery of an important fact is also socially determined; and that there are ethical questions to be considered in the production of knowledge.

In the social sciences it is in some ways harder to establish convincing claims of knowledge than it is to prove the existence of islands. Islands have a concrete, physical reality that can be empirically demonstrated. Although social scientists also claim an empirical basis for their knowledge, the concepts they deal in are nevertheless usually abstract. The facts that social scientists discuss do not lie about in the physical world, like stones waiting to be stumbled over. They are not discovered in the sense that islands might be. Instead, they are created, constructed, or made. None of these words is meant to imply that there is a basic dishonesty in the facts, ideas, and theories of the social sciences—that they are somehow just fabricated out of thin air. There is a basis for social science concepts, but that basis often lies more in the social organization of the disciplines than in the physical reality of the surrounding world.

Saying this may make it sound like the social sciences are unconcerned with reality. On the contrary, they are very much concerned with reality, but these realities generally take the form of something like an economic trend, a cultural practice, an event in the past, a behavior, or an attitude. Because these realities are abstract, the social sciences must collectively negotiate their understanding and ways of perceiving and describing them—in effect, their ways of making knowledge. This collective negotiation results in the social production of knowledge. It will become clear how knowledge is socially produced as we consider the steps that all social sciences follow in creating and establishing claims of knowledge.

THE PROCESS OF KNOWLEDGE-MAKING STARTS WITH QUESTIONS

The social sciences, like the natural sciences, were organized to answer questions that are of general interest to practitioners of those sciences. Questions are the starting point for all of the social sciences' knowledge-making practices. As the social sciences have grown and developed, the initial questions that were asked have produced answers and theories that in turn have spawned new questions and refinement of the original theories. Thus, previous research affects present research, so much in fact, that a scientist planning to extend an established line of questioning, say on the relationship between parenting and personality, is expected to read all the previous literature on that question and to determine how the new questions relate to already established answers.

The boundaries of disciplines also direct the line of questioning. Most of the social sciences are concerned in some way with the institution of the family, but the questions a sociologist asks about the family might be very different from those an economist asks, which in turn are different from those a historian asks. As Ziman (1968) has noted, each field of science is like a corporate enterprise in which there are general overall goals and purposes, yet much specialization throughout the ranks and divisions of the enterprise. Each person spends his or her time and talents working with colleagues to create and maintain some part of the overall field. Although there may be some friction and disagreement—or sometimes even competition—within a particular field, there is usually general agreement about the overall goals because the research agendas of each science are largely shared by their members. In each field some questions will be considered not worth asking because they seem uninteresting, they appear to already have definitive answers, or it's believed there is no good way of answering them.

Because there is some social pressure to conform to established research agendas, maybe some originality is stifled or some potentially interesting avenues are left unexplored. However, the social influences on the defining of research questions do not necessarily mean that an individual must cease to think critically and independently or give up the freedom to choose *how* to think. There are still ways for independent thinkers to inquire into issues that others consider uninteresting, and such mavericks often ask unusual questions and make surprising claims that persuade others to join them in changing the direction of a field. At such a time, rhetoric becomes an important tool for them to use.

ANSWERS COME FROM OBSERVATION

To answer the questions each social science deems important, individuals must somehow observe the reality that will produce an answer, whether that reality is a past event, a person's behavior, or a political trend. Here the word "observation" is used in the broadest possible sense, to include everything from examining documents to interviewing people to using scales to measure attitudes. But observation itself is also socially influenced in several ways. The reality that the social scientist observes must first be selected or defined as an object for investigation. Some part of reality must be focused on and marked off from other, related phenomena that surround it. Social scientists focus on a reality in the ways their disciplines have taught them to.

Yet even focusing carefully on something does not make it accessible to direct investigation. It is not possible to just "read off" the meaning of any particular object or event simply by looking at it, like reading the label on a can of beans. The phenomenon must be interpreted. This interpretation is socially conditioned because observers view reality from the perspective created by their education, their cultural conditioning, and their personal backgrounds. In addition, observation always takes place from a particular standpoint because an observer can't stand outside of a particular time or space and observe something "as it really is." The act of observing is already the act of interpreting. Also, the interpretation one arrives at will depend on the questions one asks to begin with and on the methods and instruments that one uses to observe with. Since these often come from the intellectual community one belongs to, observation is, like the questions the scientist begins with, also socially influenced.

OBSERVATION RELIES ON METHODS AND INSTRUMENTS

Using methods and instruments with which to observe reality is the third common characteristic of the social sciences' knowledge-making practices. Methods are discipline-sanctioned procedures for answering the questions of interest in that particular discipline. But no method ever just dropped from the sky. All methods are human creations; each method has a history, with a definite beginning and many changes and refinements along the way. So important is method that when social scientists write papers, articles, and books about their findings, they include detailed descriptions of the methods they used. They know that their claims of knowledge will be judged in part by how carefully they followed the procedures and met the standards their field currently considers acceptable. (You will read a great deal more about methods in Part 2.)

INTERPRETATIONS OF DATA BECOME CLAIMS OF KNOWLEDGE

Social scientists use methods to create data, find evidence, or otherwise come up with results that can be interpreted and related to existing knowledge. Although findings sometimes are ambiguous and don't point to any larger conclusions, interpretations of new evidence usually either support or contradict existing claims. In either case, the scientist's goal is to make valid and reliable statements. The validity of an interpretation is established by adequate evidence and sound reasoning about the evidence. Reliability is generally established through separate studies of the same phenomenon that reach similar conclusions, suggesting that the results will hold up over time. In order to make valid and reliable statements, social scientists go through the steps previously described, but they also subject their initial interpretations to careful scrutiny and criticism before disseminating them more widely. Scientists working to answer a particular question often communicate with their colleagues about their research throughout the whole investigation; in this way, they benefit from the advice and criticism of others even before they have written anything for others to read.

CLAIMS ARE DISSEMINATED FOR PEER REVIEW

When investigators have finished their research and have written a paper, an article, or other document, they do not print and disseminate their findings immediately. Most informally seek peer review by asking colleagues to read and criticize early drafts of the document they have written. Besides this informal peer review, each field has more formal ways of conducting peer review of new claims so that they will be as strong as possible before being submitted to the discipline at large. This formal kind of peer review generally takes place in at least two forums that are a part of every social science. In the first, a scientist might read a near-final draft of a paper or present a poster about his or her research at a professional conference or symposium. The questions and comments the audience poses might cause the scientist to rethink and revise some parts of his or her paper. In the second, the scientist sends a draft of a paper to a journal or publisher. The editor then sends the paper to two or more reviewers who read it carefully and recommend publication, revision, or rejection. Very few articles or books are published without some additional revision recommended by the reviewers. Because the reviewers have different backgrounds than the writer, they may have different perceptions of what the writer has observed. By taking the reviewers' positions and perceptions into account, the writer can revise to make the final draft stronger and more acceptable to other members of the field to whom the research is finally disseminated.

What does all of this mean for you? It means that learning to think like a social scientist is a process of socialization into your field's assumptions about what knowledge is and about how to ask the right questions. It is learning to follow methodological procedures and techniques, often using instruments that yield precise results. It is learning to interpret results and make claims that your scientific peers can examine and criticize. Your goal in this process is to do your work so well and present it so persuasively that peers will ratify your claims as valid and reliable. Claims so ratified attain the status of facts. Knowledge-making is a long process, and as you've seen, at every step it is a highly social one.

Because the processes for producing knowledge are social, the objectivity so often claimed by the social sciences is really a kind of *intersubjectivity*. That is, different persons, each with a different subjective consciousness, agree on the interpretation of particular observations. While the facts social scientists agree on don't usually have the same kind of physical status as islands, they are nonetheless true for the discipline that created them. The goal of any science is to achieve the widest possible intersubjective agreement about the facts. This social process of constructing knowledge protects a discipline—and society at large—from whatever dangers might come from the idiosyncratic claims of individuals who want to claim they have discovered some new fact, when in reality they may have some other agenda in mind, such as self-aggrandizement or spreading a bias.

HOW PERSUASION CREATES CHANGE IN SOCIAL SCIENCES

Because knowledge is socially constructed in the way just described, it is fairly "safe" from the claims of cranks and crackpots who might have a pseudo-scientific ax to grind. The social nature of scientific investigation and the peer review system are actually rather conservative elements in the process of knowledge creation, acting to censor unconventional interpretations and claims. On the one hand, this kind of conservatism is good, because it prevents the scientific journals from being clogged with just anything somebody might want to write. On the other hand, this conservatism may make science somewhat resistant and slow to change, even when legitimate scientists make worthwhile claims. Such resistance happens particularly when scientists challenge existing facts. Because many established scientists have invested their careers in building up a body of knowledge, they may sometimes let personal feelings get in the way of dispassionate review of new claims, especially when they can exercise power as a reviewer or editor. Change does occur, but it usually takes time and convincing new evidence, presented with great rhetorical skill, to change previous perceptions and interpretations.

While it is disturbing to think that strongly held personal views or desires to control knowledge, not objectivity and common sense, may sometimes get in the way of establishing claims of new knowledge, it is worth remembering that "objectivity" and "common sense" are often nothing more than the combined beliefs and assumptions of those who have had the power to control which claims were to be admitted to a discipline's body of knowledge. As one example, consider that all of the social sciences were initially developed by men; since women researchers and their assumptions and viewpoints were often excluded from knowledge-making processes in the not-so-distant past, many have argued that the social sciences have had a previously unacknowledged masculine bias. As more women have entered the social sciences, new focuses of research and new frameworks for interpretation have altered these fields somewhat and have generated some lively debates about the nature and status of knowledge. New interpretations and new claims of knowledge coming from a different generation of scientists always have to be negotiated through a rhetorical process that, if successful, enables the discipline to rethink some of its basic positions and then proceed from more acceptable, more valid, more widely held assumptions. As members of a field work through these negotiations, they, like anyone using rhetoric in public life, must remember to demonstrate good will, good faith, and patience in order to avoid the crippling outcomes of acrimony, fragmentation, and silence.

THE RHETORICAL SITUATION

This chapter opened with the claim that the words *rhetoric* and *social science* are compatible. It has focused mainly on demonstrating that social scientists, because of the interpretive nature of their research, need rhetorical skill to make their knowledge claims convincing to their audiences. The premise of this book is that speaking and writing in the social sciences is not simply a matter of packaging "objective" truths in "neutral" language. Because social scientists construct their claims from the methods of observation used in their fields, and because we perceive reality to some extent through socially constructed lenses, communication in the social sciences always has a persuasive dimension; i.e., it is rhetorical. But the rhetorical skill you wield as a social scientist should never be deceptive in the way Plato worried all rhetoric might be; instead, it should be true to the most rigorous standards of inquiry your discipline has formulated and to the highest standards of honesty and respect for others.

Your rhetoric should result from a considered balance and interaction among the various elements that together define any *rhetorical situation*. The rhetorical situation is any situation in which rhetoric is called for—and that includes a great many! An abstract way of thinking about the elements of any rhetorical situation is shown in Figure 1-1 (based on Jakobson 1960). This diagram shows that in any situation in which you use rhetoric, you must consider these six elements:

1. Rhetoric comes from a writer or speaker (called the addresser) who has a purpose in communicating with others. The purpose might be to inform, instruct, persuade, convince, entertain, delight, or otherwise express oneself. Being clear about your purpose is one of the keys for being successful as a rhetor. Just as important, your rhetoric will convey an impression of who you are, as you will create a persona, a role, or a voice in the way you construct your message.

2. Rhetoric is directed toward an audience of readers or listeners (or both, called the addressee). The audience might be large or small; it might be close by or remote in time or space. It might be composed of people who are very knowledgeable about the subject or people who know little about it. They might be well-disposed or ill-disposed toward the subject and its author, or they might be entirely indifferent. Analyzing the characteristics

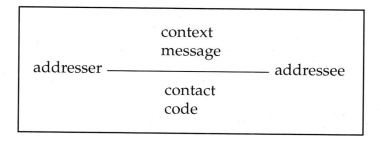

FIGURE 1-1. Jakobson's Model of the Rhetorical Situation

of your audience carefully before you begin to construct a message will enhance your chances of success.

3. Rhetoric is about a message you desire to send to the audience. This message might be about facts, ideas, feelings, impressions, or anything that one human attempts to convey to another through language. Often the hardest part of communication is deciding for yourself what the message is; the very act of attempting to put it into words may help you understand it more clearly and give you the opportunity to shape and re-shape it so that it includes all that you want it to.

4. The message is usually encoded in a natural language, but it might make use of other ways of symbolizing meanings, such as still or moving pictures, graphs, tables, statistics, mathematical equations, etc. Furthermore, the design of a printed message or the delivery of a spoken message is itself a part of the encoding of the message; they are not simply the packaging the message comes in, but part of the message itself.

5. In order for the encoded message to be conveyed to the audience, there must be a form of contact, a connecting medium. In a spoken communication, this medium is either the air conveying sound waves or electronic recording devices. For written messages, the medium might be printed or electronic. In our age, the computer has given us marvelous ways of combining almost all media, so that in a given message, you might see the author of the message, hear the author's voice, and read the author's words.

6. Finally, every communication occurs within a context; in other words, historical, social, cultural, ideological, and personal elements surrounding the communication impinge on the way it is constructed, conveyed, and received. That being the case, there is invariably a certain amount of "slippage" between the way a message might be intended and the way it might be understood. All messages are interpreted in ways influenced by the context, so various members of an audience might construe them somewhat differently. Knowing this, as a social scientist, you will want to take care to understand your audience and the context you share so that you can choose to use language and symbols that will be as unambiguous as possible.

You will note that the code is really the element that ties the other five elements together. This is significant because language, next to emotional bonds, is perhaps the strongest strand in the cord that connects us to others. To a great extent we know each other through the words we share. The way you use language as a writer is a way of conveying something about yourself to an audience who may never have met you. That is, through your writing you may reveal yourself to be educated, witty, friendly, aloof, or any one of many other possible descriptors. The language of much scientific writing doesn't allow for a lot of variation in the persona you can convey. In fact, one of the conventions of scientific writing is to convey the persona of a detached, thoughtful observer who doesn't let emotions get in the way. (More will be said about the writing style of the social sciences and its contribution to persona, or ethos, in Chapter 18.)

The reality that writers aim to share with an audience is also mediated to us in great part by language. What you have learned already about your major discipline has come to you mainly through words that you have read or listened to. These words have shaped your understanding of the realities your discipline examines. As someone now learning to write in your discipline, you must express what you know about reality to your audience through language. You must choose language that is as true to your experiences and observations of reality as you can make it, and as clear to your audience as you can make it. (More will be said in Chapter 2 about how to analyze your audience and judge the best way to construct a message for them.)

Since social scientists deal with issues that affect us all intimately, it is important that you consider carefully who your audience is and how to communicate with not only your peers in the social sciences but with laypersons as well. As citizens we face serious problems in our families, neighborhoods, cities, and nation, and in a world community that is becoming ever more tightly knit through political and trade alliances and through advances in communication and transportation. Therefore, we need whatever expertise social scientists can offer to solve these problems that loom so large. Clear communication is an indispensable part of whatever solutions are offered. Because the members of different scientific communities often speak mostly to each other in their own discipline-specific language, there is a need for all of them to learn to use a more general rhetoric adapted to the ordinary citizen so that they can translate their specialized knowledge for the general public. (See Chapter 12 for guidelines on how to do this.) This book aims to help you acquire the rhetorical skill you will need to make a difference in the world, not only as a professional writing for your peers, but as a citizen who cares about the community you live in and who can apply your expertise to make it better. The centuries-old ideal of the citizen rhetor, espoused by Isocrates and Quintilian, might perhaps be revived if you and fellow social scientists learn to be skilled writers, capable of using the rhetoric not only of professional discourse but of public discourse as well.

SUGGESTIONS FOR DISCUSSION OR WRITING

1. Before you read this chapter, how would you have defined rhetoric? How would you have defined social science? In what ways, if any, has reading this chapter changed your thinking?

2. What is the history of the discipline you are majoring in? When did it become a recognized division of the university? What changes has it undergone in its history? How would you characterize its aims when it first began? Are they the same now? If not, how have they changed?

3. How have your discipline's methods changed over time? Why have they changed? Why would today's researchers find inadequate the methods used by the first practitioners of your discipline?

4. Has there been a time when members of your discipline were divided about some issue, theory, or method? What was the conflict about? How was rhetoric used to resolve it?

5. How would you characterize writing in your field? Do you believe it has a persuasive dimension to it? What sorts of evidence, data, and reasoning count as convincing and logical in your field's writing? How do writers in your field construct an *ethos* (credible persona) in their writing? What kinds of appeal to *pathos* (emotion) are evident in their writing?

REFERENCES

Aristotle. 1926. *Art of Rhetoric*. Translated by J. H. Freese. Cambridge, MA: Harvard University Press.

Isocrates. 1929. *Antidosis*. Translated by George Norlin. Cambridge, MA: Harvard University Press.

Jakobson, Roman. 1960. Linguistics and Poetics. In *Style in Language*, ed. Thomas Sebeok, 350–377. Cambridge, MA: MIT Press.

Plato. 1925. *Gorgias*. Translated by W. R. M. Lamb. Cambridge, MA: Harvard University Press.

Plato. 1914. *Phaedrus*. Translated by H. N. Fowler. Cambridge, MA: Harvard University Press.

Quintilian. 1921. The Institutio Oratoria *of Quintilian*. Translated by H. E. Butler. Cambridge, MA: Harvard University Press.

Ziman, John. 1968. *Public knowledge: An essay concerning the social dimension of science*. London: Cambridge University Press.

2

THE INDIVIDUAL AND SOCIAL DIMENSIONS OF COMPOSING

CHAPTER OVERVIEW

After reading this chapter, you should be able to answer the following questions:

1. What is composing?
2. What are the general steps in the usual process of composing?
3. What are the individual dimensions of composing?
4. What are the social dimensions of composing? How does the notion of *genre* help both readers and writers?
5. What is involved in effective collaboration in research and writing?

Rhetoric of any kind seldom springs fully formed from anyone's mind. In order to be as effective as possible, rhetoric must first be composed. In ancient times, students often composed their speeches mentally because they lacked convenient and inexpensive ways to compose in writing. In modern times, however, most composing is done in writing. *Composing* is the name for the process of writing something—a term paper, a report, a letter, a review, or anything else—from start to finish. Actually, this "process" is really a set of subprocesses that interact with each other and recur in various ways depending on what you are writing about, whom you are writing for, what kind of text you are writing, and your own unique history and preferences as a writer. As you know, composing does not necessarily begin when you first set pen to paper or turn on the computer. Before that point you may engage in a process of thinking, discussing, listing, outlining, researching, gathering data, or otherwise generating ideas and facts to write about. Finding something to say, the first step in composing, was called *invention* by ancient rhetoricians.

Composing continues as you actually write a draft of your paper—that is, as you decide how best to organize the matter of your paper, how to structure paragraphs and sentences, and which words will best express your intentions. (The ancients called dealing with these matters *arrangement* and *style*.) Nor does composing end when you finish a draft. At that point, you often ask others to respond to your ideas and criticize how you've presented them. Then you revise to improve the content and organization of your paper. Finally you edit to make your paper stylistically correct and effective. Even after all of that, you may begin a new process of composing as you attempt to improve your first composition.

Some of these subprocesses of composing can run simultaneously: you can still be generating ideas and gathering information at the same time as you are drafting paragraphs and sentences. One subprocess can be interrupted for another to take place; you might pause in drafting, for instance, to revise and edit sentences and paragraphs already in place. Sometimes you may eliminate one of these composing subprocesses completely, out of choice or necessity; for example, when you write essay exams under time constraints you must do without outside criticism, revision, and editing.

Because of the various combinations and sequences of all the subprocesses that make up composing, it's safe to say that no two acts of composing are the same for two different individuals. They may not even be the same for one person writing two different documents. Because each act of composing and each person is unique, a textbook like this can offer only some observations that may help you reflect on how *you* write and decide whether your individual processes serve you well for all rhetorical situations. Setting aside individual differences, this chapter offers some generalizations and advice that may help you in your writing. You'll find here a brief discussion of the subprocesses of composing, followed by an analysis of both the individual and the social nature of composing. Because collaborative writing is an important feature of writing in many of the social sciences, the chapter ends with advice for working successfully with others to produce jointly composed papers.

THE SUBPROCESSES OF COMPOSING

COMMON WAYS OF PREWRITING

If you took a writing class in your first year at college, your teacher may have used the term *prewriting* to describe a number of activities that you can do to get your mind working on what to write about in a paper and how to organize it. You may have learned of some or all of these common prewriting techniques:

- Incubating
- Brainstorming
- Freewriting
- Questioning
- Discussing
- Clustering
- Outlining

Each of these prewriting techniques can help you get past "being stuck" because each helps you see that you *do* have something to write about. They help you get down on paper some of the thoughts that may be swarming through your mind. Simply getting your mind and your pen or computer cursor moving can help decrease the anxiety you may feel when you are assigned to write. You relax as you start thinking about the connections you can make between the ideas you've generated and captured in your prewriting. You start to see a main point you can argue for and the stance you can take in the paper.

SPECIALIZED KINDS OF PREWRITING

The above prewriting techniques are generally applicable to all forms and fields of writing. Other kinds of prewriting, however, are peculiar to academic writing, especially in the sciences. Though these are not always thought of as belonging to writing, they certainly belong to rhetorical invention—the process of finding something to write about. One such invention technique is keeping an *observation journal, log,* or *research notebook*. Another is using the *research methods* of the social sciences to create data to write about.

Observation journals, logs, and notebooks. The social sciences all depend on some form of observation and on careful recording of the data observed. For example, the historian must observe the previously unnoticed facts or the recurring patterns in the documents he reads in archives and libraries; he can't rely on only his memory to store all the information he discovers, so he keeps a research notebook, an organized card file, or computer files of notes. Similarly, the anthropologist pauses often to take careful field notes of customs and behaviors she observes in the people she lives among, not only noting their actions but also speculating on an interpretation. The psychologist doing repeated laboratory experiments with rats must keep accurate records of the behaviors he observes. The sociologist tape-recording interviews supplements the tapes with notes about the context of each interview and facts about each respondent that she couldn't capture on the tape.

These methods of record-keeping may seem to be more removed from composing than the prewriting techniques described earlier, but they are no less important to successful composing. The social scientist may begin keeping a research journal or log with only a vague idea of what kind of text it will eventually grow into, but without the data recorded there, no paper of great value to other social scientists could be written. In most cases other social scientists expect that professional writing will be based on more than the thoughts in a writer's mind. This audience wants evidence that the observer was systematic and thorough in gathering, analyzing, and interpreting data that will support a claim. Without a research log or notebook to re-read, the social scientist would be less likely to find the themes and patterns that can be discovered in the daily entries. In that sense, some method of regularly recording observations is a kind of prewriting; without it, no findings could be established in a more formal document.

Research methods. In addition to keeping notebooks, logs, or journals, social scientists carry out systematic research using the specialized methods of their disciplines. Because these methods yield findings, evidence, or data that the scientist can then write about, they are also a highly structured form of prewriting. Certain methods have come to be associated with certain kinds of texts: participant observation with the genre called ethnography, experimentation with the experimental research report, observation of selected individuals with the case study. Chapters 3 through 8 discuss particular research methods in detail and illustrate the kinds of texts that result from several of these methods.

DRAFTING

Prewriting is usually followed by drafting. In this step of composing, you take the ideas or data you have invented and determine what interpretation you can support or what claim you can make. Often you state this interpretation or claim directly at the beginning of the draft, and this statement becomes the main point or thesis of your paper. In some kinds of writing, however, the interpretation comes last, as in the discussion section of an experimental research report.

Besides interpreting your data as you draft, you also organize it in a particular sequence, according to the needs of your audience and the type of text you are writing. You organize on two levels:

1. The macro level, i.e., deciding what large "chunks" of information should come before other chunks.

2. The micro level, i.e, what sentences should precede other sentences within paragraphs.

If you experience anxiety about writing, it helps when drafting to remind yourself that nothing has to be perfect the first time. A paper can go through several drafts—and usually should.

REVISING

Once you have a complete draft, the next step is usually to revise. To *re-vise* means to *re-see*. It means to pay attention to the overall structure of a text, considering again your sequencing of ideas, the proportions of space and emphasis you have given to particular points, and the amount of detail you have given in any particular part. When you revise, you do any or all of these three activities:

1. Rearrange
2. Add
3. Delete

A valuable way to revise a draft is to first set it aside for at least a day. Reading it again after you have rested and gained some emotional distance from your paper will help you to view it critically. Another way to evaluate your draft for revision is to let others read it. As they tell you how they viewed your draft, you may see its strengths and flaws more clearly so that you can capitalize on the strengths and eliminate the weaknesses.

EDITING

Theoretically, there is no limit to the number of times you could revise a single paper. Practically, however, there are limits, and the greatest of these is time. Few students have the time to revise a paper more than two or three times, as the term rolls on and other assignments must take precedence. Eventually a deadline comes and you must submit a final paper. But everyone should take the time to edit a paper before handing it in. Editing differs from revising in that it is local, rather than global. In other words, revising improves the macro-structure, and editing the micro-structure. It is usually best to wait until you have made large-scale, global revisions to your paper before you begin to edit. Otherwise, you might end up deleting something you've already spent time editing. After you get the structure the way you want it, you edit to polish the surface of your writing—making sure your sentences are clear and effective, choosing precise words, using appropriate grammar, and spelling and punctuating correctly.

COMPOSING WITH A COMPUTER

The computer has undoubtedly revolutionized most aspects of the writing process. While it may not make drafting any easier (especially if you don't type well), once you have an electronic draft, it is easier to revise because you don't have to retype every new draft. The blinking cursor allows you to add text at any point; the delete function lets you get rid of useless words and sentences with a keystroke; and the cut-and-paste functions permit you to rearrange sentences or whole sections of a paper without the scissors and tape of yesteryear. Spell-checkers make it easier to submit correct copy, and printer programs allow you to use typographical features that can improve the readability of your writing (see Chapter 16).

In some ways computers have made prewriting easier as well. Most libraries now give you access to huge databases, so searching for and retrieving information is more efficient than in the past (see Chapter 9). You can also use your computer like a research notebook, log, or journal to store bits of information that you can later retrieve and insert into a paper you are writing. The Internet can also make composing easier, as you can find some valuable information on the Web. However, it is an act of plagiarism simply to copy and paste text from the Web or use borrowed information without citing the source.

THE INDIVIDUAL NATURE OF COMPOSING

COMPOSING AS AN IDIOSYNCRATIC ACT

So far the subprocesses of composing have been portrayed as if they were the same for everyone. But they are not. In every act of composing, you can exercise some of your unique preferences and habits. For example, some people like to begin composing by sitting alone in the library or another quiet place with a favorite pen and a pad on which to list their thoughts. Others prefer the background noise of a cafeteria and perhaps a conversation to test their ideas, using a napkin or scrap of paper for jotting down good ideas. Still others have become so used to writing with a computer that they can hardly write with pen and paper anymore.

When some people start drafting, they like to work at a neat desk in the early morning, wearing a robe or comfortable sweats, with a favorite beverage beside them. Sometimes these writers have to get other important tasks, like cleaning the apartment, out of the way first so that they can concentrate on writing. Others write best late at night, with music in the background, oblivious to clutter in the room, dishes in the sink, and laundry piling up. Some people need three to four hours of uninterrupted writing time; others can write in twenty-minute snatches.

Some revise as they go, shaping sentences and paragraphs to their satisfaction, even correcting spelling and grammar before proceeding to the next part.

Others pour out words as they come, waiting until later to add, delete, rearrange, and edit. And all of us have our own prose style—a preference for certain words, a typical sentence length or construction, short or long paragraphs, few or many transitional elements. It's important to determine for yourself what times and places, what moods and physical states, what habits and rituals contribute to your productivity as a writer. It's also important to become conscious of style—both your own and others'—because the more aware you are of the stylistic options you have as a writer, the more control you have over shaping your meaning.

COMPOSING AS A PRIVATE ACT

Another sense in which composing is a highly individual act is that some writing is private. It isn't meant for others; it's just for you. You may keep a journal or a diary in which you record your thoughts about your life's experiences and your innermost thoughts and feelings. You may have the vague intention of someday letting family members or close friends read what you've written, but mostly the writing is for your own benefit. Even if you don't keep a journal, you may occasionally write as a way of helping you sort out complex matters—the pros and cons related to a particular decision you must make, for example, or as a way to blow off steam, such as a letter to someone with whom you've just had a heated argument (but which you probably won't mail). Perhaps you make lists that are just for you, of things to do, resolutions for improving your life, books you want to read. Maybe you are a closet poet, someone who loves to write poems or song lyrics you wouldn't dream of showing to others. And maybe you consider private the early writing you do for things that will eventually be read by others. Whatever your reasons for not sharing your writing with others, it's obvious that some pieces of writing are mainly for an audience of one—yourself—and the way you write them is nobody's business but yours.

But most writing is meant to "go public" eventually, and since it will then be read by others, there is automatically a social dimension to it. This social dimension will be explored next because it affects how you compose, particularly how you compose in the social sciences. The more you understand writing as a social transaction, the more successful you will be in participating in the intellectual communities of the social sciences.

THE SOCIAL NATURE OF COMPOSING

LANGUAGE AS A SOCIAL MEDIUM

Just as creating knowledge is a social endeavor (see Chapter 1), so the act of composing is permeated with the influence and the awareness of others.

Writing exists mainly for the purpose of communicating with others, after all, so it would be odd if it were not shaped by communal expectations and norms. Imagine how much more difficult writing and reading would be if there were no standardized spelling, no common agreements about how punctuation marks should be used, no grammar rules, or even conventional forms such as the business letter. Readers can understand writers more readily, writers can compose with greater confidence, editors can improve writing more surely, and typesetters can work more rapidly if there are norms and conventions that everyone understands and agrees on. Thus composing is social in the sense that the written language we use, with all its detailed conventions, is one that we share with others. Composing is social in other senses as well.

THE INFLUENCE OF AUDIENCES

The audience you write for exerts a powerful influence on what and how you write. Audiences can be divided into roughly two general classes: professional and lay audiences. If you have written for one of your professors about their area of expertise (and what student hasn't?), you have written for a professional audience. You know the pressure you feel to include accurate and complete information as well as to write about it in the way you think your professor expects you to—using the right terminology and the form of presentation that will most likely convince the professor that, even though you are a novice, you are beginning to understand the discipline and its norms for communication.

On the other hand, sometimes you are the expert in what you are writing about, and your audience is relatively uninformed about the subject—a lay audience. If you think carefully about how to succeed in communicating with them, you will realize that specialized jargon will not be appropriate, that you may have to use comparisons to familiar things to help them understand difficult concepts, and that the organization of your writing must be appealing and accessible to them. This is not to say that writing for a professional audience should not also be appealing and accessible; rather, it means that the level of language and the organizational conventions you might use would differ if you were planning to publish the same research findings in both a professional publication such as *Journal of Marriage and the Family* and in the popular periodical *Parents' Magazine*.

Audiences can vary widely. Depending on your subject matter and your purpose in writing, you will likely have to consider many of the following audience characteristics that may affect how you address them:

relationship to you	age
purposes for reading your writing	social class
familiarity with the subject	education
opinions and attitudes	religion

political affiliations	disability
geographic location	prejudices
race or ethnicity	gender

The level of complexity of your subject matter, the words you choose, the examples you use, and even how you organize what you write, should all be affected by your audience. The better you understand your audience, the more likely it is that you will make successful choices in writing documents that both inform and persuade your readers.

THE SOCIAL EVOLUTION AND INFLUENCE OF GENRES

Social influences are particularly important when it comes to the form and format of many documents. The social sciences, as noted in Chapter 1, function like highly selective and organized communities. As such they develop *genres*, forms of communication that provide socially constructed ways of dealing with rhetorical situations that occur again and again. For example, experimental psychologists have a recurring need to inform their peers about research they've conducted and to persuade their colleagues that these experiments add something important to the group's existing knowledge. Over the years, the genre of the experimental research report has evolved to the point that it now has seven very predictable features:

1. A title that explains directly and unambiguously what the article is about.
2. An abstract summarizing the basic aim, methods, and findings of the experiment.
3. An introduction that contextualizes the experiment in a review of related literature and states the research focus.
4. A description of the methods used to conduct the experiment.
5. A presentation of the results of the experiment, often including tables and figures.
6. A discussion of the significance of the results.
7. A list of references to articles and books cited in the report.

These various parts of the report are indicated by headings and typographical features (such as italics or boldface print) that help readers identify the parts quickly.

Beyond these standard parts, a typical style of writing is used in experimental reports, a style characterized not only by specialized vocabulary and preferred sentence structures but by the stance the writer takes toward the subject and the audience as well. A psychologist writing an article to publicize experimental findings would be wise to follow all of the above genre conventions.

They not only help readers rapidly locate the information most important to them, but they also show that the writer has internalized a way of thinking, researching, and writing that marks him or her as a member of the scientific community. Being able to use these features of the genre in the expected ways subtly influences the persuasiveness of the claim the writer is making.

Other fields have developed their own genres: case studies, position papers, narratives, ethnographies, and so on. In every discipline, each genre represents the result of an ongoing historical process of standardizing forms of discourse that enable the members of the discipline to establish and debate claims through journals and books. In a way, the members of a discipline carry on a conversation through their writing, and their genre conventions simply make that conversation more understandable to all. All genres are dynamic, however, not static, so every discipline is seeing changes in its forms of discourse, particularly as electronic forums such as e-mail, listservs, and electronic journals become more important as a medium for exchanging ideas.

The genres of each discipline reflect its assumptions about what knowledge is and how it is created: the methods of inquiry used, the kinds of evidence offered, and the presentation of the evidence show how the discipline's claims of truth are created and supported. But just as methods of inquiry shape genres, genres also shape methods. As one example, take anthropology. As it began to establish itself as a significant branch of inquiry, its main rhetorical genre, the ethnography, was shaped by the assumption that an outside observer, the anthropologist, could discover the important cultural practices of a given group of people (usually a "primitive tribe") through a process of neutral observation and then could report these practices in an authoritative manner, using "transparent" language (see Clifford 1986). A sort of imperialist assumption underlay this rhetorical practice: that the culturally superior anthropologist was able to determine and name the significance of the other culture's practices. In a sense, these early ethnographies intellectually "colonized" the natives' culture for consumption by interested readers, usually those back home in the anthropologist's native culture. This kind of genre had a powerful effect on new anthropologists entering the field, because as they read previous ethnographies of this sort, they took these as proper models for their own writing. In just this way, once it is established, a genre shapes future inquiry—until someone begins to question the values and assumptions the genre embodies.

That kind of questioning in the last two or three decades has led some anthropologists to write very different ethnographies from those that were written in the early twentieth century. Many recent ethnographies are characterized by their concern with the ethnographer's subjectivity; with the unavoidably interpretive nature of observation; with what can't be observed and therefore can't be interpreted and recounted; with the constructed nature of the stories the ethnographer tells; and with the role of metaphor, style, and other rhetorical devices used in writing the ethnography. In short, as anthropologists have become more aware of the rhetorical nature of their writing, their writing has become more self-aware and, many would say, more honest. Anthropologists have always tried to make true claims; now they seem to be more conscious that their claims to truth can only be partial and contingent. These changes in the genre of ethnography inevitably shape how the next generation of anthropologists will approach their own inquiry.

This interaction between methods of inquiry and rhetorical genres means that, as a would-be professional in your field, you would do well to learn to read and write as much as you can in your field's genres. But while reading widely in professional journals and imitating what you read may be an important first step, a lot of what you need to know and do will happen naturally as a matter of your being socialized into the field. Gradually, almost without your thinking about it, you will internalize your field's assumptions about knowledge and how it is created.

In that sense, learning to write for a *particular* social science discipline is a process that runs beyond the boundaries of this book or the time you may consciously devote to it in one course. All this book can do is teach you to examine how genres shape and are shaped by the kinds of inquiry your discipline is engaged in, so that you can be more conscious of how to compose its rhetoric successfully, and so that you can become more aware of the assumptions embodied in that rhetoric. These assumptions are not neutral; they reflect the values of the disciplines that created them. Sometimes these values and assumptions are (or perhaps should be) challenged and changed. Anyone who wants to change them, however, must first know the discipline's rhetoric well enough to mount an effective challenge.

THE INFLUENCE OF GENRES ON WRITERS

As you learn to write as a professional in your discipline, the particular subjects you write about and the genres you write in also construct you as a person. In other words, the genres of your field offer you a role to play, a persona to inhabit as you write, and a stance to take toward your audience and the material you are writing about. Even though you are an individual with a unique past and personality, your individuality has been constructed by the various social forces you have encountered in your life—your family, your peer group, your community, schools, church, clubs, teams, the mass media, and many other influences. In each of these networks of relationships with others and with the objects they are interested in, you have occupied a certain position that teaches you how the network uses language, prompting you to use it in certain ways, too. In joining a professional discipline, you enter into yet another network of relationships sustained in large part by the profession's rhetorical practices. You learn to occupy a position in that network and to use its language yourself to join in the conversation that maintains and furthers the discipline's projects. By becoming aware of how the rhetoric of your field constructs your thinking and your professional persona, you are more likely to control the rhetoric. That is, you will be able to speak the language consciously and by choice, rather than letting it "speak you."

COMPOSING COLLABORATIVELY

A final important way in which composing is a social act is that it may be done by more than one person. It is fairly common in some of the social sciences for researchers to work in teams—to collaborate. Perhaps some of your professors have assigned collaborative projects in courses you have taken. It is even more common for professionals outside the academy to collaborate on writing tasks, so it is worth understanding how to do it well, as there is a high possibility you will work and write with others at some point in your life.

Collaboration can lead to some important advantages: the division of labor, a high degree of individual specialization, collective reasoning and decision-making that may be superior to individual thinking, and increased efficiency, resulting in time and money savings. Collaboration also has the potential disadvantages of friction and disagreement among team members, some people not doing their share of the work, incompatibility in writing styles, and—especially for students—difficulty finding time to get together. But these disadvantages need not be part of collaboration if you enter into it understanding the different ways groups can function and if you plan ahead so that you can counteract possible problems.

Researchers (e.g., Ede and Lunsford 1990) who have studied various collaborative groups conclude there is a continuum of possible models with two extremes. At one extreme, the team divides all tasks completely; at the other, the team works together through all phases of the work. As an example of the first, imagine that four students are assigned to conduct an experiment to determine which of two kinds of peanut butter—one expensive and the other less so—students prefer in a blind taste test. They might divide the labor of running and "writing up" the experiment as follows: Anne goes to the library to find related literature that provides a context for the experiment, and she recruits participants for the experiment. Ben purchases the peanut butter and other materials, prepares the laboratory for the taste tests, and administers the samples to the participants. David is at the lab to record the results and then later analyzes the data. Carla leads the team and coordinates the whole process. After that, Anne writes the introduction to the paper and creates the list of references. Ben writes the methods section. David writes the results section, including the tables, and the discussion section. And Carla takes all the parts, blends them into one finished and edited report, then adds the abstract and title.

This example might be an efficient division of labor and use of time, particularly if each team member is doing the tasks for which he or she has a special talent, and if Carla successfully provides the leadership to ensure that the others carry out their roles well. But notice that the final paper might actually be stronger if the whole group, rather than just Carla, got together to join the parts and discuss the best ways of organizing paragraphs or phrasing sentences. Perhaps David, despite skill in creating tables, has overlooked something important that Ben could help him remember; maybe Anne will remember something from reading the previous literature that will strengthen the discussion. In other words, a complete division of labor throughout the whole process may not always result in the best product.

In the other extreme model of collaboration, all of the team members work together through all or nearly all phases of conducting the research and writing the report. This is roughly the model that was used by the four psychologists who wrote the influential book *Women's Ways of Knowing,* Mary Field Belenky, Blythe McVicker Clinchy, Nancy Rule Goldberger, and Jill Mattuck Tarule. For their research, they interviewed 135 women at length, using a set of questions that they had previously constructed together. Usually only one researcher was present at each interview, as the interviews lasted from two to five hours, and they took place in different geographical locations (so in this phase there was some division of labor). Each interview was tape recorded so that the whole team could listen to it. All of the interviews were transcribed, producing five thousand pages of text that each of the researchers read!

To analyze all of this data, the researchers together developed some categories for coding the respondents' statements along certain dimensions; then they read and re-read the transcripts, copying out quotations that illustrated various positions along these dimensions. The authors wrote independently but gathered as often as possible to discuss, to question, to rethink, and to rework each other's drafts. Over a period of five years, they shaped their study into a book. This kind of collaboration is obviously time-consuming, but it can also be very satisfying, especially if the group members enjoy working together and find a creative synergy in the give-and-take of lively discussion about ideas they all care deeply about. Despite the time and effort required, the results of this dialogic form of collaboration are often far superior to what one person working alone could create.

Obviously, there are many ways to combine the two extremes of collaborating: a team can divide some phases of the work of creating and writing a paper but work as a group on other phases. Regardless of how the process is managed, here are some important guidelines for student groups to follow in order to make the experience of collaborating more successful.[1]

---

[1] Adapted from Chapter 2 of *Learning Together: An Introduction to Collaborative Learning* by Tori Haring-Smith. Copyright © 1993 HarperCollins College Publishers. Used by permission of Addison-Wesley Educational Publishers, Inc.

GUIDELINES FOR WORKING IN GROUPS

1. **Keep the group small enough to succeed.** Since academic group projects usually require some meetings outside of class, your chances of coordinating individual schedules are greater if the group is small, usually not larger than four. Having more than three or four people in a group increases the difficulty of finding a time when all the group members are free to meet.

2. **Get acquainted as individuals and determine each other's strengths and weaknesses.** Whether you choose your team members or your teacher assigns you to work together, as a group you need to assess what talents you possess individually and collectively. Don't be shy about stating the special skills you possess: if you're a whiz in statistics, say so; if you can edit and proofread skillfully, everyone will be relieved to hear it. Each member should be equally forthright about any limitations that will affect his or her performance. For example, if you have a heavy course load and a part-time job, you should say so, as this will affect when the group can meet and the number or kinds of tasks you can be responsible for.

3. **Get organized.** It is almost always helpful to choose a leader, someone who will accept the responsibility of keeping the group on task and of monitoring each person's performance. Exchange phone numbers and e-mail addresses at this stage, too, so that you can contact each other when necessary.

4. **Lay the ground rules your group will abide by.** One such rule ought to concern how group meetings will be conducted so that each member will have relatively equal opportunities to speak. Another rule should address what you will do as a group if someone fails to do their assignments on time or adequately, or even fails to do them at all. If your instructor will have you evaluate each other at the end of the collaborative process, he or she will probably provide evaluation criteria. But as a group you can also determine fair standards that you will all apply equally in judging the quality of each other's contributions. Having rules and standards should help everyone proceed from the same assumptions and, later, make judgments about each member's performance, including what to do if someone doesn't do their part. If these prior agreements are in place, judgments are less likely to be taken as personal attacks and more as simply compliance with decisions the group made at the outset. For example, you might decide ahead of time if all group members do their assigned part well by the deadline that you will tell your teacher you all deserve the same grade. However, if someone's part is late, incomplete, or poorly done, the rest of the group will report to the teacher that the offender should receive a lower grade for their work (the severity of the penalty would be determined by agreement among the group members).

5. **Analyze the task you have designed or been assigned to do.** To analyze the task, ask questions such as these: Will you be conducting interviews, an experiment, or a survey? Will you be reading and analyzing documents? Will you be carrying out observations in natural settings? Will you be doing library research? How long will the eventual paper be? Has the teacher specified parts that it must have, or will you determine its organization completely? If you will determine the organization, spend some time thinking about what the eventual document might contain. Break the task into sub-tasks and discuss whether each should be accomplished by an individual, a pair of people, or more. Determine together a fair division of the labor, assigning tasks according to each person's particular abilities and limitations.

6. **Create a schedule for completing the sub-tasks.** Sometimes your teacher may impose a schedule for completing sub-tasks; other times, only a final deadline is given. If there is only a final deadline, set realistic intermediate deadlines that will help you monitor your progress and keep the work moving along at a steady rate. Remember that some delays are inevitable—a book you need will be checked out of the library, a group member may become sick and unable to finish an assignment, or a computer will crash. To help compensate for these setbacks, you can "pad" the schedule with a little extra time to allow you to meet the final deadline without too much stress.

7. **Hold regular meetings during the entire process to evaluate progress.** Your teacher may allow some class time for your group to work on its project, but even so you will probably need to meet at other times to keep the work moving along successfully. The group leader will need to be especially responsible to schedule meetings when all members can attend and to determine whether each person has completed their assignments. At these meetings you can share problems you have encountered and seek the advice of the others. You can also discuss what you have learned so far and begin developing the actual contents and form of the eventual paper.

8. **Draft, revise, and edit the paper as collaboratively as possible.** Once you have collected the data, found the evidence, or otherwise created what you will use in your paper, spend some time discussing as a group what it all means, and what the central arguments will be in your paper. Discuss and agree on how the paper should be organized. Then decide how you will create the first draft: Will you all get together around the computer at someone's apartment with plenty of pizza and soft drinks to keep you going? Will you work individually, each one taking responsibility for a different section? Will some of you work individually, while others work in pairs? Or will you find another solution?

   If you choose to work individually on different sections, arrange for everyone to bring or send computer files at the appointed time to merge the parts. After putting together a draft, send or print each member a copy and allow a day or two for everyone to review it and think about it. Then meet again to discuss how to revise it—what to cut, what to add, how to rearrange—and to focus on the details of editing—sentence structure, word choice, and punctuation. After agreeing on what the final draft should be like, assign one or more members to produce it, making sure that the best proofreader and editor in the group will be available to okay it before submission. Everyone should chip in to cover whatever costs are incurred—for high quality paper, laser printing, color graphics, and binding, for example.

9. **Evaluate the performance of your group and of individual members.** Your teacher may assign each of you to evaluate your group as a whole and each individual in it. In fact, if your teacher will grade your work, his or her evaluation will probably be affected by the way you grade each other. Even if no evaluation has been assigned, you may want to meet as a group one final time and consider how the process and the project might have been improved. This would be particularly important in a course in which your group will do more than one collaborative project. At the very least you should make some mental notes of what was successful and what was not so helpful so that you will be better prepared the next time you collaborate.

GUIDELINES FOR INDIVIDUALS

Besides the preceding advice for the entire group, here are some guidelines for you to follow as an individual so that you can contribute to the progress of any collaborative project you may be part of.

1. **Communicate with group members openly, honestly, and tactfully.** Your ideas are as important as anyone else's, so don't be shy about sharing them. If your other courses demand a lot of your time at the start of the project, you could offer to do more work at the end of the project to compensate. But don't promise to do what you can't possibly accomplish just to make a favorable impression. Tactfully express your concerns rather than attacking a team member's ideas or personality. Don't say bluntly, "That's a bad idea," but explain *why* you are concerned about the idea; for example, say, "That sounds like it will take more time than we have"; or phrase your concern as a question: "Do you think we have time to do all that?"

2. **Listen carefully to other group members.** Listening is more than just being quiet when others are talking. It is concentrating on what they are saying, watching their faces and body movements for clues to their meanings, their attitudes, and their feelings. Paraphrase what someone else has just said by asking, "Do you mean that . . . ?" Paraphrasing is especially important when you are not sure of the other's idea or when you think you may disagree.

3. **Learn and practice the art of negotiation.** Don't automatically shy away from conflicts. Conflicts can be productive if they are followed by negotiation rather than a stalemate or a victory for one side and a defeat for the other. Negotiation resolves conflict by first finding the areas of agreement and disagreement and then by working towards a "win-win" solution acceptable to all. Negotiation requires patience, tact, and skill, as well as a willingness to compromise sometimes in order to help the group reach a consensus. Avoid being so attached to your own ideas that you won't even consider the other person's point of view. In fact, you should try advocating another person's position for a few minutes. This kind of empathetic role-playing can sometimes help you see the value of or at least the reasons for another person's point of view. By negotiating your way through conflicts, you and the other members of your group can all feel as if you "own" the solutions and the final product your group creates.

4. **Be a person whom others can count on.** Everyone's worst fear of collaboration (or worst experience with it) involves someone who is uncooperative or uncommunicative, someone unwilling to do their fair share, someone who agrees and then fails to do their assigned part, or someone who does such a poor job that the other group members feel penalized. Analyze yourself and your past performance in groups and determine if you have a tendency to be that kind of person. If so, it is likely high time to change some of your habits and make a more determined effort to be a team player. If you are someone who has had disastrous experiences working with others, who strongly prefers to work alone, or who has insurmountable difficulties in finding time to be part of a group, consult your teacher about the possibility of working alone or with people you already know and with whom you are likely to work well. Remember that the ability to work well with others is highly valued in the workplace and in graduate and professional schools, so to achieve your educational and career goals, there may not be a better time than now for you to learn how to be an effective collaborator.

AVOIDING PLAGIARISM AND GIVING CREDIT

In addition to full-scale collaborations, composing may have partially collaborative dimensions at any point. Even when you are not working on a jointly authored paper, for example, you would be wise to seek responses from others about your writing. One helpful strategy in prewriting is simply to discuss your ideas with others, such as a friend, a roommate, a mentor, or a tutor in your campus writing center. You can invite these same people to intervene in your composing process at the drafting, revising, and editing stages as well. It is particularly helpful to get a classmate's or tutor's response after you have a complete draft and before you begin to revise. Often, after spending hours on your writing, you are so involved in your ideas, and your paper seems so clear to you that you can't see its flaws. Or you know a part of your paper has problems, but you can't think how to fix them. A careful peer critic or tutor can offer you a reading that reveals where your paper doesn't communicate as well as you want it to. Your teacher may make this kind of review a mandatory part of composing your papers before you submit them for a grade.

In seeking feedback from others about your work, you are participating in a practice that is widespread in all professions. Virtually no professional in the social sciences or other fields publishes writing that hasn't been thoroughly reviewed by peers and then revised for improvement. There is a line to be observed, however, between acceptable and unethical use of others' help in your writing. You should ask others only for advice and instruction, not to do your work for you. As you probably know by now, using someone else's ideas or words without giving them credit is plagiarism. Buying an already written paper or hiring someone to write your papers is a serious breach of honesty that, if discovered, will result not only in academic and professional penalties but, more significantly, in your failure to learn and develop your own abilities to research and write.

You may certainly seek the help of others, however, as long as you accept the final responsibility for each phase of composing any paper you are assigned to write alone. If the form of the paper permits, you should graciously acknowledge the assistance others have given you—for example, in a preface, acknowledgments page, footnote, or letter of transmittal. If someone's contribution to your work turns out to be more significant than simply offering advice and instruction, if they provide you with data to use in your paper, for example, or if they actually write some parts of your paper, it may be more appropriate to consider listing them as a co-author. In all facets of collaborating with others— whether the collaboration is limited or full-scale—respecting others and attending to professional and ethical standards should be uppermost in your thoughts and actions.

SUGGESTIONS FOR DISCUSSION

1. What times and places, habits or rituals seem to contribute to your being able to write well? What happens if you try to write at other times or in other places than the ones you are most comfortable with?

2. What kind of prewriting, if any, do you typically do for a writing assignment? Does it vary with the nature of the assignment? If so, how? What kinds of prewriting described in this chapter were new for you? Which of them would you like to try and why?

3. Have you ever kept a research log or journal? What sorts of things did you write in it? Did any kind of larger paper result from it? If so, describe how you synthesized your entries into a coherent piece of writing.

4. How many drafts of a paper do you typically write? How much and what kind of revising do you do? How confident are you about editing a paper? Do you seek the advice of others before revising and editing?

5. Do you compose with a computer? What advantages do you find to using it? What disadvantages?

6. This chapter stresses that composing has a powerful social dimension to it. Which of the ideas presented here were new for you? Which were most interesting? Reflecting upon past writing experiences, can you see how social factors influenced how you composed? How, if at all, have this chapter and your own reflections changed how you now think about writing?

7. Have you ever been assigned to collaborate with classmates on a paper or project? If so, what were the advantages? What were the disadvantages? What ways can you see to prevent some of the problems often associated with collaboration?

SUGGESTIONS FOR WRITING

To learn more about an important genre in your field and how writers use it to make their rhetoric persuasive, find an article in a major journal in your field, read it carefully, and analyze it by answering questions 1–10 below. If you have already decided on a research topic for your term paper, choose an article that is related to your topic. Hand in this exercise with an attached photocopy of the article you analyzed. For guidance in how to answer the questions, see the student paper by Michelle Pomeroy in the Readings at the end of this book.

1. Who wrote the article? What credentials does (do) the author(s) have? How do the credentials of the author(s) affect the persuasiveness of the article? (Note that the credentials are likely to be in small type at the bottom of the first page or at the end of the article. If the author's credentials are not listed, try doing an online search to see if you can find out more about the author.)

2. What is the title of the article? Does it accurately describe the contents of the article? Why or why not?

3. Does the article have an abstract (a summary of the entire article that follows the title and precedes the introduction)? If so, how well does it summarize the contents of the article? What do you notice about the style of the abstract?

4. What is included in the introduction of the article? Do you find in the introduction a statement of the main point, the thesis, the hypothesis, or the research question the article focuses on? (Note that a thesis is a claim

the author argues for; a hypothesis is a prediction that the author tests using statistics.) Is the main point easy to find? Does it fit with the rest of the article?

5. What kind of research methods (e.g., content analysis, interviews, surveys, experiments, observations, etc.) did the author(s) use to create the information they report in the article? Is a section of the article devoted to the description of the methods? How carefully do they describe the methods they used? Do the methods seem well-chosen to test the hypothesis or answer the research question? Why or why not?

6. What are the main findings of the article? Write a brief summary of the new insights this article contributes to its field. Where are the findings reported? Does the article use tables or graphs to present findings? If so, how do these contribute to the presentation of results? If not, would their addition be helpful? Why or why not?

7. What conclusions or inferences does the article draw from the findings? Are they justified? Notice the language the authors use to discuss the conclusions. How strongly do they assert these conclusions?

8. How convincing do you find the entire article? How much of the article relies on rational arguments for persuasion? How much depends on the credibility and reputation of the author(s)? Does any of it appeal to your emotions? What seems to be the most persuasive appeal?

9. What audience does the article seem to be aimed at? Why do you think so?

10. Write a complete bibliographic reference for the article at the end of your analysis.

REFERENCES

Belenky, Mary Field, Blythe McVicker Clinchy, Nancy Rule Goldberger, and Jill Mattuck Tarule. 1986. *Women's ways of knowing: The development of self, voice, and mind.* New York: Basic Books.

Clifford, James. 1986. Introduction: Partial truths. In *Writing culture: The poetics and politics of ethnography,* ed. James Clifford and George E. Marcus, 1–26. Berkeley: University of California Press.

Ede, Lisa, and Andrea Lunsford. 1990. *Singular texts/plural authors: Perspectives on collaborative writing.* Carbondale and Edwardsville, IL: Southern Illinois University Press.

Haring-Smith, Tori. 1993. *Learning together: An introduction to collaborative learning.* New York: HarperCollins.

Miller, Carolyn. 1984. Genre as social action. *Quarterly Journal of Speech* 70: 151–167.

PART

II

PRIMARY AND SECONDARY RESEARCH

In the next seven chapters you will learn about methods of creating and synthesizing knowledge in the social sciences. Chapter 3 provides an overview of quantitative and qualitative research methods and a discussion of the ethical obligations of the social scientist. Chapters 4 through 8 describe several different methods commonly used in the social sciences. As you read these chapters, you will learn about methods of interpreting documents, interviewing, observing, surveying, and experimenting. It is not possible in a book this size to give more than a brief introduction to each method; it is particularly not feasible to discuss the statistical tests and procedures that are important components of some of these methods. Other courses, both undergraduate and graduate, will provide you with the detailed knowledge about methods and statistics that will enable you to become a full-fledged researcher in the social sciences.

But such courses may often skimp on teaching you how to write about the knowledge you create with methods; they often assume that "writing up" what you know is a simple process of packaging facts in words. In contrast, this book is based on the assumption that "writing up" begins the moment you decide what question you want to answer or what hypothesis you want to test. So Chapters 4-8 focus on analyzing methods as a kind of rhetorical invention and on helping you understand how to create documents in the genres social scientists typically use to present persuasive arguments about the data or evidence these methods produce.

Finally, Chapter 9 outlines principles and processes for finding and evaluating scholarly research in libraries and on the Internet. In our day, we are inundated with more information than we can possibly take in. More than knowing a lot of facts, the hallmark of an educated person today may be knowing where to look for information when you need it and how to evaluate its quality and relevance to your purposes.

3

RESEARCH METHODS, WRITING, AND ETHICS

CHAPTER OVERVIEW

After reading this chapter, you should be able to answer the following questions:

1. In what sense does writing begin with and extend throughout the research process rather than merely follow it?
2. What does it mean to say that methods are "disciplined inquiry"?
3. What is meant by quantitative methods? By qualitative methods? What are the pros and cons of each kind of inquiry?
4. What is an IRB and what is its function?
5. What are the ethical and legal requirements for involving human beings in research?
6. What is plagiarism? What is fraud? Why are these ethical lapses so serious and so detrimental to the scientific enterprise?

RESEARCHING IS PART OF WRITING

The documents that social scientists write are more likely to be persuasive when the scientists have used a method their readers find acceptable. If scientists do not follow the procedures and meet the standards that their colleagues find persuasive, it really won't matter how eloquently they write the final document about their research. Their rhetoric will not be persuasive if the evidence it is based on has been gathered sloppily or interpreted carelessly. Since good writing in the social sciences begins with finding or creating the evidence that will eventually be used in the document, using a research method is a kind of prewriting—yet a highly structured kind, much more rigorous and time-consuming than, say, freewriting or brainstorming.

If you will think of methods in this way, you should be more conscious throughout the research process of the paper you will write. You should begin thinking about the rhetorical situation for this paper even as you plan your research. For example, you should consider your audience from the first: What evidence will be sufficient to persuade them that your conclusions are reasonable and acceptable? What kinds of data will they expect in order to be convinced that your hypothesis was correct? The more you know about what your audience will require as sufficient proof, the more careful you will be as you plan your research, collect evidence or data, and consider plausible interpretations.

You should also be thinking about the genre of the paper you will be writing. What things are usually part of such a paper? A review of literature? Quotations from primary sources? Vivid descriptions? Detailed narratives? Tables and graphs? The results of statistical tests? A bibliography? The better you understand the genre conventions of the paper you will be writing, the more likely it is that you will gather all the information you will need to write it. Instead of thinking of research as something you do first and then "write up" later, you should think of writing as something you are doing all along as you research—from formulating your research hypothesis or question to choosing a method to collecting and interpreting data to proofreading your paper.

METHODS AS DISCIPLINED INQUIRY

A good definition of method would be simply "disciplined inquiry." This definition implies not only that the inquiry is focused and rigorous, but also that it is sanctioned by a discipline. In other words, it meets the discipline's assumptions about what knowledge is and its standards for judging claims of knowledge. The formalization of methods of inquiry is largely responsible for making the sciences what they are today. Although humans have probably always carried out the kinds of experiments that helped them learn how to preserve foods, dye fabrics, or make bricks, for example, it was only in the nineteenth century that the experimental method began to be considered a special form of inquiry that produces a special kind of knowledge called *science*. Before then, the word *science* could be applied to any field of study, including the arts, humanities, and theology; it simply meant *knowledge*. Now, however, we generally consider science a special kind of knowledge that has been created in an especially rigorous way so that its claims will have widespread and long-lasting validity.

When we realize that scientific methods are human inventions and, as such, are not necessarily perfect in revealing all that we would like to know, we start to see that the claims of science also may not be perfect. This does not stop the quest for rigor, however. Methods are constantly refined by repeated use and by the criticism of peers in the scientific community. In this way, scientific methods are always changing in the hope they will yield ever more reliable results. Experimental scientists have refined their method, for example, to remove as much doubt as possible from claims of knowledge by focusing on certain variables in the complex flux of events surrounding them. By controlling other variables and their own biases, experimental scientists attempt to manipulate the selected variables to establish cause-and-effect relationships, and then to state laws that can be used to predict future behavior. As a result of this remarkable endeavor to make experimental inquiry rigorous, the popular view of science is that it is knowledge produced by the experimental method.

However, the experimental method is not the only method of science, especially not the only one used by social scientists. Some social scientists long ago rejected the experiment as the one and only way of establishing valid claims of knowledge. The experiment is simply not appropriate to answer some kinds of questions. Also, because experiments focus on selected variables to study while controlling others, they create artificial situations unlike those that exist naturally. If the object of the social sciences is to describe human behavior, critics claim, then experiments may not be appropriate because, by their design, they may alter the very behavior that is of interest.

Some critics of the experimental method favor studying human behavior in natural, not controlled, settings; they reject the premise of control in favor of observing the multiplicity of factors that influence behavior. Like the experimentalists, their goal is also to question and to observe, to describe, and to generalize. But they have created other methods that will permit them to seek knowledge in the ways they consider most likely to produce meaningful findings. Each of the methods that social scientists have used in the twentieth century is rigorous in its own way, and each produces knowledge that may bear the label of *science* in the honorific sense. Each method has its strengths and its limitations; each is suited to answering some kinds of questions about reality and not others. Each method is reliable to the extent that it represents a discipline's consensus about the most rigorous way to investigate the questions that the discipline pursues. And if a method is followed carefully, the knowledge it produces will be considered valid.

QUANTITATIVE AND QUALITATIVE METHODS

Methods are usually divided into two categories: quantitative and qualitative. As their names imply, quantitative methods yield data that can be expressed numerically, and qualitative methods produce data that must be described by their qualities or distinguishing characteristics. Two methods that are often quantitative are experiments and surveys; two that are generally qualitative are interviews and observations.

But there may be some overlap between these two categories of methods. For example, a questionnaire might ask both multiple-choice and open-ended questions. The answers to the multiple choice questions can be counted and expressed as numbers; then other numerical operations can be performed on those numbers, yielding quantitative data. The answers to the open-ended questions, on the other hand, are qualitative data; they might have to be read several times to see what general patterns or themes emerge. Similarly, observation in natural settings is generally qualitative, with the observer attempting to record and describe what he or she observes. But the observer might also count certain repeated behaviors and then perform additional statistical operations on these data. So a written report of research might contain both quantitative and qualitative results.

Proponents of quantitative methods sometimes assume that these methods are superior because numbers are generally thought to be "hard" and factual, to have a solid and unambiguous meaning. It is often said that numerical data "speak for themselves" and require little or no interpretation the way the "soft" and more "messy" qualitative methods do. Adherents of qualitative methods, on the other hand, often think these methods are superior because of the rich data they produce. For them, the details and the subtle differences in the data are precisely what is most interesting, and they relish examining the data and using their interpretive powers to make sense of it. They might view quantitative methods as too superficial, arguing that, in fact, numbers tell us very little about *why* people act or think as they do; like qualitative data, numbers have to be interpreted in order to be meaningful. Despite these differences of opinion, both kinds of methods are valuable, and social scientists should be aware of the strengths and limitations of each in order to choose methods that are appropriate to answer the kinds of questions they want to ask.

A strength of quantitative methods is that they can be used with a large number of participants. If the participants in an experiment or the respondents to a survey are numerous enough and if they were randomly selected, therefore representative of the larger population from which they are drawn, then the results of the experiment or survey are said to be *generalizable*. That is, even without surveying or experimenting on the whole population, the results will presumably hold true for the whole population the sample represents. Another characteristic of quantitative methods that might be considered a strength or a limitation, depending on your viewpoint, is that experiments and surveys are usually designed and then pilot tested or repeated until all the "bugs" are worked out. With this kind of careful advance planning, surveys and experiments can yield very precise answers to highly focused questions. The data collected can often be quickly analyzed using computer software that will test relationships between any of the variables the researchers are investigating. The significant investment of time to plan and refine the study at the beginning is usually compensated for by speed in obtaining results.

Yet because they often require special equipment, computer time and expertise, or printing and mailing, experiments and surveys may sometimes cost more to conduct than many qualitative studies. Another limitation of quantitative methods stems from the way they transform data into numbers, particularly into means (numerical averages). The emphasis on the mean performance of a group effaces the individuality of the participants. Depth of description may thus be sacrificed to the desire to make broad generalizations.

In contrast, a notable strength of qualitative methods, such as interviews, observations, case studies, and analyses of documents, is that they allow researchers to describe in depth the individuals and circumstances they study. Although qualitative research is also carefully planned, it is not so precisely scripted that the researcher has no chance to pursue interesting questions that may arise during the investigation; qualitative methods offer much opportunity to branch, probe, and question. Rather than attempt to remove or minimize the researcher's subjectivity through rigorous control, qualitative methods actually foreground the subjectivity of the researcher as someone with an active, questioning mind, someone who makes informed decisions throughout the whole process of gathering and interpreting data.

Perhaps a drawback to qualitative research is that it is generally time-consuming to carry out well, so it usually includes fewer participants than surveys and experiments do. Although the texts that result from qualitative methods may contain many interesting observations and valid inferences, because they are typically based on observations of only a few participants, they are usually not considered generalizable to a larger population. Nevertheless, even with few participants, qualitative methods yield much data that must be laboriously recorded and transcribed, read and pondered, coded and categorized. Although qualitative research can often be done locally at little cost, it can also be expensive if it involves travel or special equipment.

It is good to be able to appreciate both qualitative and quantitative methods, for even though you may be inclined in your field to prefer certain methods over others, you will no doubt be influenced all your life by knowledge that is created by both kinds of methods. Understanding all methods, with their strengths and limitations, will help you to be a more critical reader of all kinds of research that you will encounter as a professional or as a citizen. Table 3-1 sums up the differences between quantitative and qualitative methods.

TABLE 3-1. A Comparison of Quantitative and Qualitative Methods

	Types	Advantages	Limitations
Quantitative Methods	Experiments Surveys	Possibility of large sample size Generalizability and breadth High degree of control	Loss of particularity Possibly high costs
Qualitative Methods	Interviews Observations Documents	Rich data Particularity and depth Large scope for interpretation	Low generalizability Overwhelming data Time consumption

ETHICAL CONSIDERATIONS IN DOING RESEARCH

USING HUMAN PARTICIPANTS

Since social scientists are interested in human behavior and human institutions, they must naturally study other human beings when they conduct their experiments, surveys, interviews, or observations. Yet human beings are not like the rocks, plants, or animals that a physical or natural scientist might study. A geologist can climb around on a pile of rocks chipping off pieces to take back to the laboratory anywhere it is legal to do so. An agronomist needn't obtain consent from two strains of corn before cross-breeding them. And a zoologist doesn't worry much about rats' right to privacy (although the zoologist is expected to treat the rats humanely).

Obviously, humans are capable of much more complex kinds of behavior than rocks, corn, and rats. They also have rights and needs that social scientists must respect in their research. In fact, to prevent abuses of human participants in research, laws have been enacted in the United States to prevent physical, social, emotional, mental, or other kinds of harm to any participants in a study and to protect their privacy. Interestingly enough, these laws stem from the Nuremberg trials, held in the aftermath of World War II, to try Nazi party officials and military officers for war crimes. Horrific experiments conducted by the Nazis on human beings had come to light, and it was discovered that people who were forced to participate in these experiments had not been informed of the purpose or the consequences of their participation. The Nuremberg Code of the late 1940s was formulated to prevent future abuses of this kind. The cornerstone of this ten-point code was informed consent by participants. In 1974, the United States developed its own federal policies outlining ethical treatment of human participants in research. In 1979, the Belmont Report, produced for the US Department of Health, Education, and Welfare, focused on three main ethical principles that researchers need to follow when human beings are involved. These are as follows:

- *Respect* for the dignity and autonomy of individuals requires that participants comprehend the nature of the research, give their informed consent, and participate voluntarily.
- *Beneficence* means the researchers do no foreseeable harm to participants and maximize possible benefits while minimizing any possible harm.
- *Justice* requires researchers to recruit participants so that benefits and burdens are distributed fairly across social groups, classes, etc.

INSTITUTIONAL REVIEW BOARDS

In order to insure that research would meet the standards of respect, beneficence, and justice, in the 1970s the US government issued regulations requiring all institutions that receive federal research funds to create and maintain committees that would oversee all research involving human participants. These committees are called Institutional Review Boards for the Protection of Human Subjects—or *IRBs* for short. By now, on all college campuses where any federal funds are used (and that includes campuses where students receive federal grants-in-aid), there is an IRB that is charged with reviewing and approving research with human participants to make sure that it complies with the laws. At Brigham Young University, the IRB is located in the Office of Research and Creative Activities (ORCA). If you decide to conduct research involving human participants, you must comply with applicable policies and procedures of BYU's IRB. Typically, the IRB will require that you submit a formal proposal to conduct research with human participants. The IRB's focus in reviewing your proposal will be mainly on the ethical and legal issues associated with the research project; however, its technical merits are important too, as no research should waste participants' time. You are under an ethical obligation to disclose everything you plan to do in your research and, once your proposal is approved, not to vary from your plan without seeking additional approval for the changes. Those who review your proposal will make sure that you meet four conditions for ethical social science research: confidentiality, informed consent, protection of vulnerable groups, and minimization of risk. (More information about how to fill out an IRB proposal will be given in Chapter 10.)

Confidentiality. First, you must ensure the *confidentiality of human participants.* How you do this depends on the methods you are using. On questionnaires, respondents generally are not asked to give their names, so their anonymity is easily preserved. However, researchers frequently ask respondents to give demographic information about themselves. Sometimes the researchers may know who gave certain answers, but they must ensure that others can't trace any answers to a specific person. Experiments and observations can also be conducted with little or no need to learn participants' names. If names seem necessary when investigators are writing the report of their research, they may use pseudonyms. Reports of interviews are more likely to require names, so the interviewer must determine whether the informants want the interviewer to use their real names or pseudonyms. If at all possible, a report of an interview that created an oral history should include the informant's real name, but only with his or her permission, of course. Interviews with public figures—elected officials or other people who hold a public trust—would also include real names. Interviews conducted for the purpose of identifying attitudes and behavior would more likely use pseudonyms, since *who* said something is not as important as *what* they said.

Informed Consent. Second, human participants involved in research must know enough about the purposes of the study to give their *informed consent* before they participate. If you conduct an experiment, you must create an informed consent document for each participant to read and sign. If you conduct surveys and interviews, you must inform participants of the purposes of the research so that they can choose whether or not to proceed; if they do proceed, they imply their consent by completing the survey or the interview. If you conduct unobtrusive observations of people going about their daily lives (e.g., counting how many people come to a complete stop at a stop sign) you are not required to obtain informed consent. However, if your observation somehow intrudes in a participant's life so that they are aware of it, you must obtain informed consent. Typical elements of informed consent are as follows:

1. Who is conducting the research
2. Purpose or objective of the research
3. How participants are selected
4. Procedures to be used and how long the research will take
5. What the known risks and benefits are
6. Participants' voluntary status and right to withdraw without penalty
7. Promise of confidentiality
8. Name and phone number of contact person for questions related to research. (Usually, the name and phone number of the professor supervising your research should be used for this.)
9. Name, address, and phone number of an IRB contact person for questions related to rights of participants. (At BYU, this is the current chair of the IRB.)
10. Implicit or explicit statement of consent that the participant agrees to; signatures are required for explicit consent.

Protection of Vulnerable Groups. Third, the laws also carefully regulate and insist on strict monitoring of research conducted with the following *vulnerable groups*:

- People who are ill or physically disabled
- People who are institutionalized, including people in hospitals, jails, and prisons
- People who are cognitively impaired
- People under 18 years of age (minors)
- Pregnant women, if the research is likely to do harm to the mother or her baby
- Members of minority groups, when the focus of the research is on their minority status
- People under your supervision or authority, e.g., students whom you teach

It is possible to study vulnerable groups, but the proposed research has to undergo a much more thorough review than research with other groups or individuals not designated as vulnerable.

Minimization of Risk. Fourth, you must be able to show that participants will face little to no risk of physical, social, emotional or other kinds of harm from participating in your research. The nature of the research and the level of risk each participant is exposed to is one factor that determines how carefully a research proposal is reviewed. At BYU, there are three levels of review: exempt, expedited, and full-board review. The differences between these are summarized in Table 3-2.

Note that exempt review does *not* mean that no review is required. It simply means that the research is such that it can be reviewed and approved quickly. Because of time and expertise constraints, students should usually plan research that can be reviewed at the exempt or expedited level. This means the research should involve minimal risk to participants. Experiments are the most

TABLE 3-2. Levels of IRB Review

Type of Review	Level of Risk	Number of Reviewers	Approximate Time Required for Review
Exempt	Minimal	1–2	3–4 days
Expedited	Minimal	2–3	2–3 weeks
Full Board	Minimal	5 or more	2-month minimum

likely to pose some emotional risk because they sometimes temporarily deceive participants. If the participants knew exactly what the investigators were trying to discover, then they might behave in a way that would alter the findings. By creating a ruse, the experimenters are better able to control how the participants act.

While some social scientists have argued that there should be no deception in research, others have maintained that temporary deception may be justified if the knowledge sought is important enough to justify the ruse. The general consensus is that researchers should not tell participants something that is untrue, but they may temporarily withhold some information regarding the aim of the study. If the participants in an experiment are given general, yet still accurate, information, and if participation in the study does not pose a risk of significant harm of any kind, an IRB would likely approve it as meeting ethical standards *provided* the researchers debrief the participants afterward to inform them fully of the purposes of the experiment. Without this debriefing, the participants may incur some psychological harm as a result of believing something about the experiment or about their own behavior that is not completely accurate.

RESEARCH THAT QUALIFIES FOR EXEMPT REVIEW

In order for research with human participants to qualify for exempt status it must meet the following criteria:

- It must be non-therapeutic. That is, it must not be designed to produce a diagnostic, preventive, or therapeutic benefit to the participants.
- The data must be recorded in such a way as to protect the identities of the participants.
- The research must not deal with sensitive or private aspects of the participants' behavior, such as sexual practices or illegal activities. At BYU, this could include inquiries about participants' violations of the Honor Code.
- The research must include no vulnerable populations. However, if you were to administer a questionnaire to 100 first-year students about how they like college life, and if there were in that group one or two pregnant women, and five or ten members of minority groups, your research could qualify as exempt so as long as the questions were not about their vulnerabilities.
- There must be no risk of criminal or civil liability to the investigator or to his or her sponsoring institution in the event that a participant's responses became known outside the boundaries of the research project itself.
- As a result of the preceding restriction about liability, plans for publication must be appropriate to your level of expertise and the nature of the topic.

Since you are a student taking a course at BYU, the university has an interest in making sure that any research you make public would not embarrass the institution or its sponsoring church. Therefore, your intent to publish findings in venues outside the classroom must be stated in the proposal so reviewers can judge how appropriate the research is for public knowledge.

Although all of the preceding may seem like a formidable list of restrictions on research, there is still ample opportunity for you to use various research methods to answer interesting questions and thereby gain valuable practice in researching and writing. As you read the next five chapters, you will begin to think of questions that you can answer using social science methods. You will learn how to plan a research project. If you plan one that includes human participants, you will also need to prepare a proposal and seek approval before proceeding. The campus IRB has a set of instructions and forms for you to fill out as part of a proposal. Chapter 10 presents an example of a complete proposal for research with human participants; by studying it, you will gain a sense of how a researcher must demonstrate compliance with the regulations that govern this kind of research.

WHAT DOES NOT REQUIRE IRB REVIEW?

At this point, you may be thinking, "What can I do without IRB approval?" This is a question often asked, and there are some good answers. Provided the research does not involve vulnerable subjects, sensitive issues, and identification of participants, the following would not require review by the IRB:

1. Students observing, surveying, or interviewing classmates in the class where the research is assigned.
2. Interviews with professors on campus.
3. Interviews with elected officials or others who hold a public trust.

In addition, students are frequently assigned to do projects or papers based on their contacts with other people in service-learning projects, internships, and cooperative learning. These and other such assignments usually do not require IRB approval because these activities usually do not fall under the definition of "research." According to "Guidelines for Defining Public Health Research and Public Health Non-Research," issued by the Centers for Disease Control and Prevention in 1997, "research means a systematic investigation, including research development, testing and evaluation, designed to develop or contribute to generalizable knowledge." Working with your professor or advisor in service-learning or internship situations, you could measure projects and assignments against this definition to determine whether they require IRB review or not.

PLAGIARISM AND FRAUD

In addition to meeting legal and ethical standards that prevent abuse of human participants, researchers in the social sciences must meet other ethical standards common to all professions. Two of the most important are not plagiarizing and not reporting fraudulent research results.

Plagiarism. Social science research usually builds on previous research; in fact, most social science documents review previous studies that attempted to answer questions related to those of the present investigation. Usually, the previous research is presented in summary fashion. Occasionally, however, some studies are reviewed at more length, and it becomes necessary to paraphrase or quote parts of the original research. In such situations, you must be careful to observe all the accepted conventions of paraphrasing, quoting, and documenting the previous research. You are not free to borrow someone's ideas or language without citing the author; if you do so, you are implying that you thought of those ideas and created those words yourself. While it may seem a trivial thing to borrow a few ideas or words without acknowledgment, it is a serious breach of professional integrity; and if it is discovered that you have plagiarized, there are serious consequences, similar to those following from the discovery of fraud.

Fraud. Fraud in social science research is reporting data that are fabricated (not actually obtained through the application of a method) or data that have been altered somewhat in order to provide more clear-cut conclusions. Data might be altered by conveniently leaving out findings that are inconsistent with the hypothesis or by altering numbers in order to obtain a particular level of statistical significance. Some researchers may feel strong pressure to report data that is somewhat or even completely fraudulent, particularly if they have a lot at stake. For example, young researchers just beginning their careers may feel the need to publish as much as possible quickly, so they may cut corners to get results that are publishable; their promotion or grant funding may depend on successful research that finds its way to print quickly. Similarly, students wanting a good grade in a course or trying to complete a thesis for graduation may be tempted to "cook" the data a little to have a more impressive study.

THE CONSEQUENCES OF ETHICAL LAPSES

You should scrupulously avoid plagiarism and fraud in any degree. You may get away with either for a time, but if you plan to make your career as a researcher, you are foolish if you think you will never get caught. As Chapter 1 explained, the social sciences are communal and collaborative enterprises. As members of these fields work to create knowledge that will advance human understanding, each person depends on work that others have done. Each person owes a debt to earlier researchers who have established reliable knowledge and pointed the way to new research; this debt is acknowledged through proper citation of earlier work. Others in your field will have read much of the same research as you, and sooner or later they will realize when you have borrowed information without proper acknowledgment. Your failure to give credit where it is due will result in a weakening of the trust that makes a social enterprise like science possible.

Like plagiarism, fraudulent research weakens trust. Your peers will trust that whatever knowledge they borrow from you or others meets the highest professional standards of using methods and interpreting data. If your peers ignorantly attempt to base new research on earlier fraudulent work, it is like building a house on sand. Far from being small or one-time breaches of honesty, fraudulent studies can have a ripple effect throughout the whole research community. Perhaps this is why the social penalties are so severe when plagiarism and fraud are uncovered: these ethical lapses waste other people's time and often their money, therefore consuming their good will and slowing the progress of the whole community of researchers.

Social scientists whose plagiarism and fraud are discovered face not only the tarnishing of their reputations and the loss of their peers' respect, but also the loss of grant funding and sometimes their jobs as well. Students who plagiarize or commit fraud indicate to their professors that they are not ready to be trusted to enter into the community of professionals. Whatever your status, there is too much at stake to cut corners. It is far better to take the time to meet the ethical standards your field has established because they are there to protect everyone's best interests.

SUGGESTIONS FOR DISCUSSION OR WRITING

1. Have you ever designed a research study before? What method or methods did you use? Did you submit your research proposal to an IRB? Did you carry out the research?

2. Does your major field tend to favor quantitative or qualitative methods? Explain your answer.

3. How much do you know about the development of methods in your discipline? To find out more, find a professional journal that has been published for a long time in your field. Compare early issues of this journal with more recent ones. What do you notice about the development of methods of inquiry?

4. Have you ever been a participant in a research project—an experiment, a survey, an observation? If so, did you give your informed consent prior to participation? What did you experience? Do you feel the ethical standards described in this chapter were met? Why or why not?

5. Has this chapter changed your thinking in any way about the need for ethics in research? For example, do you have a better understanding than previously of why plagiarism is detrimental to scientific work?

4

INTERPRETING DOCUMENTS

CHAPTER OVERVIEW

After reading this chapter, you should be able to answer the following questions:

1. In what ways is reading a kind of disciplined inquiry?
2. Do the facts ever speak for themselves? Do numbers?
3. What is a primary source? A secondary source?
4. What are the general steps in interpreting source documents?
5. What are the general steps in writing a paper based on source documents?

Reading and interpreting documents is the primary method of the historian, who could not write history without diaries, journals, letters, newspapers, magazines, immigration data, military records, parish registers, ships' passenger lists, and other documents from the past from which to cull facts and piece together an argument. But other social scientists may interpret documents as well. For example, political scientists concerned with theories of government, public policy, and social practices also read and interpret documents—constitutions, manifestos, court rulings, laws, census data, or the writings of Machiavelli, John Locke, Alexis de Tocqueville, and James Madison, among others.

Some psychiatrists or psychologists may collect and interpret the writings of clients in therapy. Sociologists also interpret documents that relate to social behavior, a kind of research that is often called *content analysis*. Archaeologists attempt to decipher ancient writings and drawings on papyrus, clay tablets, or canyon walls. Economists may interpret documents composed primarily of numbers, such as gains and losses on the stock exchange, budgets, or reports of the national debt and gross national product. Historians have also become more interested in statistical data, as they attempt to write about common people and their daily lives rather than only about presidents, kings, and generals and the events they participated in.

INTERPRETATIONS DEPEND ON PRIOR KNOWLEDGE AND ASSUMPTIONS

When they interpret documents according to the methodological standards of their disciplines, social scientists are, in effect, practicing a highly specialized kind of reading. Although reading may seem to be a very straightforward activity, one that you have been doing since you were a small child, when you examine what goes into reading like a historian, a political scientist, a psychologist, a sociologist, an economist, or an archaeologist, you start to see what a complex practice reading is. An ordinary citizen simply reading the daily newspaper draws (often unconsciously) on complex cultural knowledge in order to make sense of a story about strife in the Middle East, a description of famine or drought, or a report of the latest medical findings.

When social scientists read the documents of interest to them, they also draw on the assumptions, the accumulated knowledge, and the interpretive practices they have learned in their disciplines, not to mention their own personal backgrounds and experiences. They are able to discern relationships in and draw conclusions from documents that might mean little to the untrained reader. But even training in a particular discipline is no guarantee that all practitioners will see eye to eye on the meaning or relevance of a particular document. Within a discipline, two readers with different theoretical orientations may interpret the same text differently. For example, a historian with a Marxist orientation will read differently from a feminist historian.

Reading is not simply a process of decoding what a text says. If it were, there would be only one meaning for a given document. Yet, as we know, all kinds of documents, from poems and novels to wills and contracts to the U.S. Constitution, have been interpreted differently. Sometimes disputes about interpretation are settled in court, as in the case of wills and contracts. The meaning of various parts of the U.S. Constitution is also often disputed; frequently, the combined interpretation of just a handful of people determines the course of the nation, as in disputes that are resolved by a 5-4 vote of the U.S. Supreme Court. Occasionally, justices of that court have also reversed the decisions of earlier justices; for example, the 1954 *Brown v. Board of Education* ruling overturned an 1896 decision permitting racially segregated schools, thus demonstrating that interpretations may change with the times and the attitudes of the people. Sometimes competing readings of a document never are reconciled, as in the case of literary works. Several interpretations of *Huckleberry Finn* are possible, and one cannot be declared absolutely "right," although some interpretations will be more plausible and persuasive than others.

Different interpretations arise because we bring to our reading, just as we do to our observations of the world, our particular personal history, prior knowledge, theoretical positions, assumptions, biases, and expectations. This is not to say that we can make a document mean anything we want it to—we can't, for example, pretend that Lewis Carroll's poem "Jabberwocky" is a recipe for spaghetti sauce. (Well, we could, but we would not succeed in making anything edible from using it as such, and others might question our sanity.) Despite differences in readers, words do have relatively stable meanings and documents do bear a relationship to the worlds in which they were created and which they represent. Thus, part of reading sensitively involves understanding the context of a document and, if possible, the rhetorical situation that produced it. It helps to know who created the document, who the intended audience was, the purpose of the document, what it has reference to, and the words or other symbols used in it. The more we know about all these factors, the more our interpretation will be shaped by them—pushed in a certain direction. The more reasonable readers possess a similar understanding of a document's context, rhetorical situation, and its language or style, the more likely it is they will interpret it similarly.

STATISTICS MUST ALSO BE INTERPRETED

We often believe that numbers and statistics, unlike documents composed mainly of words, are easier to interpret because numbers are less ambiguous than words. It is true that numbers refer to the size or amount of something; therefore, given precise scales or procedures to follow, two different people asked to weigh, measure, or count the same thing should come up with the same number. Yet the resulting number in itself is often trivial; what the measurement signifies in relationship to other concerns still has to be established.

As an example of how numbers can be interpreted differently, consider Richard Herrnstein and Charles Murray's book *The Bell Curve* (1994), which examined many years of data collected from administering IQ tests to Americans of all races. One of their findings was that, as a group, African Americans have scored an average of 15 points lower on these tests than other racial groups. The authors interpreted this difference as principally due to the genetic inheritance of African Americans rather than to environmental factors. They then concluded that there is little point in spending tax revenues for social programs that attempt to improve education and job preparation for African Americans, because no matter how much was spent, social programs would not raise intelligence, something they viewed as largely inherited.

Other scholars agreed that the 15-point difference in average IQ scores exists, but they interpreted its significance very differently. They point out that a single factor—intelligence—cannot be the sole reason for the differences in test scores and therefore for differences in social and economic matters. A person's environment obviously influences his or her success in life but so do such things as character, personality, motivation, social skills, and common sense. Critics of Herrnstein and Murray noted that IQ tests are often culturally biased and fail to measure various forms of intelligence. They concluded that what the average difference shows, if it shows anything, is that our society should create better ways of educating all its members and preparing them for the labor market (see, for example, Gould 1994; Heckman 1995; Brace 1996). As this example shows, numbers and measurements may be very precise, but they are mute about their meaning in relationship to larger issues and questions. Statistical facts don't necessarily speak for themselves; someone must speak for them, interpreting their significance. Because of their beliefs, assumptions, experience, and training, different people often interpret the same statistic differently.

Although reading and interpreting words and statistics is a fundamental practice in all of the social sciences, it is difficult to generalize about how to do it. Much of what you should do when you interpret documents or other artifacts will depend on the questions you are trying to answer and the quickness of your own mind in identifying a bit of evidence as significant or in perceiving a pattern in a data set. A few guidelines for reading and interpreting historical documents are discussed below.

WHAT HISTORIES ARE MADE OF

A German historian of the nineteenth century declared that the historian's goal is to write about the past *wie es eigentlich gewesen ist*—as it actually was. Contemporary historians have pretty much agreed that it is impossible to do that, for the past is not recoverable in its entirety. A historical document is a *trace* of the past, evidence that something happened, as a contrail in the sky is evidence that a jet plane just flew over. The trace is not the past itself, but it allows you to infer some things about the past. Obviously, the more traces of the past you can find, and the more they say similar things, the more secure you may feel about inferring a conclusion.

But it's also important to keep in mind that each document you examine was itself constructed by someone who was able to record only a fraction of what actually transpired, someone who selected from a multiplicity of events the ones they found important. Not only were particular events selected, they were interpreted by the person who recorded them according to that person's interests, attitudes, and biases. There is no way to get outside of the accounts you read to check their accuracy, to see if they correspond to the reality of the past. You can't check those records' accuracy against the past itself, only against other documents from the same era and other histories of that era.

These two kinds of corroborating sources are usually called primary and secondary. *Primary sources* are those that are closest to the time and the topic under investigation; they include such documents as letters, diaries, journals, memoirs, notes, and statistical data (but they may also include non-documents such as eyewitnesses, photographs, audiotapes, videotapes, and artifacts). *Secondary sources* interpret primary sources. They are books and articles that scholars have written about the traces of the past they have found. Scholars not only create secondary texts; they use each other's books and articles (other secondary sources) to help interpret primary sources.

As a result, a major characteristic of writing that interprets texts is that it is *intertextual*. It makes connections between many texts—between previously unrelated primary sources from the past and the present, between primary and secondary sources, between secondary sources—connections that have never been made before, thus creating a new text, one that is based on all the sources that informed it but one that is also a result of the writers' new interpretive angle, selections, and rhetorical choices. Such a text, far from being like a transparent window revealing the past as it actually was, is more like a web, consisting of strands from other texts, woven together in ways their originators could not have foreseen.

To be persuasive, the writer of a such a text must use the sources in ways his or her peers find acceptable. One reason for the extensive footnotes or endnotes and bibliographies in histories and other interpretive documents is to allow other readers to read the sources themselves and decide if the inferences the writer has made are justifiable. In that sense, documentation is one of the chief rhetorical devices that historians and other scholars use to make their texts persuasive. By citing other reliable sources, they show that they have considered all the available evidence and created their interpretations out of real data, not their imaginations. However, like good fiction writers, they must also be skilled in writing narrative and description so that they are realistic and convincing. They do use their imaginations to envision the past and to create believable scenes of people acting in other times and places, though without going beyond what their sources permit them to say. In other words, they are writing stories—but not fiction.

In the readings at the end of this book, you will find an excerpt from the book *Bare Branches: The Security Implications of Asia's Surplus Male Population* by Valerie Hudson and Andrea Den Boer, two political scientists, who first use a primary source, census data, to show that there is a skewed ratio of male to female births in most parts of China. They attempt to tease out the reasons for the skewness by using their own reasoning and their reading of other primary and secondary sources dealing with demographics in China. Second, Hudson and Den Boer use a wide array of secondary sources, drawn from both science and history, on the nature and behavior of unmarried men to predict that the lopsided male-to-female ratio in China and other Asian countries is likely to lead to crime, social unrest, and perhaps even to warfare in the near future. Although both the census data and the scientific and historical documents were created at other times, for other purposes and other audiences, Hudson and den Boer used them to construct a new document to serve a very different purpose and the needs of other readers interested in issues of global security. Their book caused an international stir when it was published and has been quite controversial because of the inductive leap it makes from the demographic facts to the suggestion that the presence of large numbers of unmarried men in China poses a threat to international security.

In addition, the student research paper by Heather Bahlmann in the readings includes elements of analyzing and interpreting texts—fifth graders' solutions to fraction problems, to be precise. By looking at the students' responses to various problems on a test, Heather and her research associates were able to infer what concepts students understood and didn't understand with regard to fractions. Heather used these analyses to support her contention that open-response tasks in math are an excellent way for teachers to assess student learning and develop instruction to fill in the gaps.

READING SOURCE DOCUMENTS

In interpreting source documents so that you can create your own new text, here are some steps to follow:

Define the question you are trying to answer and limit it to something you can investigate, given constraints of time, budget, location, and availability of sources. As a student you probably don't have the time and resources to spend on a major project such as analyzing census data from several countries, but you can still conduct interesting research in a limited time using resources available in local libraries, archives, and even your own home. For example, say you want to understand some very recent history: how the image of the computer has changed in mass media from a futuristic, science fiction type of invention to a tool that has today become a standard fixture in education, business, and industry, and most people's homes—in fact, something many people carry about with them each day. Suppose you have only about four weeks to research this topic, and you have no funding for travel, long distance calls, or acquiring documents, so your main source of materials to answer this question is your campus and local libraries. In this case, you would probably decide to limit your study to just a few magazines that span a time period you could identify as important for investigating this issue. You might phrase your research questions like this: "How have the covers and full-page ads of *Personal Computing* and *BYTE* magazines changed in the period from 1982 to 2002? What do the images on covers and in ads reveal about the changing conception and role of the computer in American culture?"

Locate suitable materials that preserve traces of the reality (primary documents) or that interpret the reality you are interested in (secondary sources). To begin to answer the above questions, you would check campus and local libraries to see if they have complete collections of the two magazines from the time period you want to review. You could also search library holdings to see what previous work, if any, has already been done on this or related topics. By reading any previous research on the general topic, you could avoid simply repeating an earlier study (though you may want to repeat it if you believe the method of the earlier study had flaws that you can avoid in your research). You could also connect what you learn to what other scholars have already established. This might help you to begin your research with some plausible guesses about what you'd find. Connecting your findings to earlier ones would also shape your paper so that it would contribute to building a body of integrated knowledge on your topic.

Determine the authenticity and reliability of the sources you locate. For historical topics, it's important to determine that the primary documents you are working with are authentic. Some historians have been embarrassed after basing their claims on documents that turned out to be forgeries. You must also determine that the secondary sources you've chosen are reliable, ones that meet high standards for scholarship. (See Chapter 9 for a discussion of how to determine the reliability of sources.) For the computer example, you would want to ask whether the magazines you have chosen to examine represent conceptions of the computer that are typical of the time period you are interested in. If you plan eventually to claim that these two magazines have documented an important shift in society's thinking about the computer, they shouldn't be obscure magazines but mainstream ones that contributed to the shaping of cultural images of the computer. You could check subscription records for the magazines to see how widely read they were, and you could compare them with one another and other computing magazines to see if they all have similar images in them.

Ask the journalist's questions as you read. These questions are *Who? What? Where? When? Why?* and *How?* With reference to our example of images of the computer, you might ask these questions about the images you are looking at: What images are depicted? How are the images created—mostly by words? Or by a combination of words and pictures? Are the pictures drawings, black and white photos, or color photos? What is emphasized? How much text is there in comparison to photos and drawings? What does the text focus on? Who seems to be the audience the covers and ads aim at? Computer hobbyists? Business people? Families? Can you discern a shift in audience from 1982 to 2002? When in the time period you're studying did the mass-produced personal computer appear? How did its appearance affect the images recorded? By asking and answering questions such as these, you will start to see patterns in the evidence and begin to draw inferences that will become a claim to argue for in your paper.

Analyze systematically. Even limiting your examination to a 20-year period, you might not be able to look at all issues of the two magazines. But you could decide to look at every other issue, every fourth issue, or every tenth issue, so that you would be systematically sampling the available data. You should have some reasonable method of selecting and reading the data so that you won't later be accused of simply looking for what you hoped to find while ignoring possible contrary evidence. Full-page ads might appear in several places throughout a magazine, for example, but they are often in the first few pages. To guard against the charge of selecting full-page ads that support your emerging thesis, you might decide to study only the first full-page ad in each issue you examine.

Take notes about what you find and how you interpret it. You should write notes describing what you see, including specific issues and page numbers in your notes so that you can eventually construct the bibliography for your paper. You should also photocopy several representative images to illustrate the trends that you identify. You might even want to construct a table or another way of counting the prevalence of certain repeated images. You would also do well to begin stating tentative interpretations of what these changes in images imply about society's conception of the computer.

WRITING ABOUT SOURCE DOCUMENTS

When you have gathered sufficient evidence to begin writing, follow these steps:

1. OUTLINE A PLAUSIBLE ARGUMENT BY ASKING THE FOLLOWING QUESTIONS:

Who is your audience? Ask yourself questions such as these: Who will read your paper? What do they already know about this topic? Will they be difficult to persuade? What kind of evidence will be most convincing to them?

What claim will the evidence support? Which of the possible ways of interpreting the evidence seems most likely, most believable? State a tentative thesis, keeping in mind that you can alter it later if you feel your claim is too narrow, too broad, or skewed.

What evidence will best illustrate your claim? For the example used here, you will certainly want to describe the overall impression of the many images you looked at and probably include some photocopies that most strikingly illustrate those impressions. If you have come up with some categories of images that change over time, you might consider using a table or a graph to depict the changes. (See Chapter 16 for a discussion of how to place and refer to illustrations in your writing.) If you have used secondary sources, you must also decide what information you will quote, summarize or paraphrase from them. Remember to document any borrowed information.

What is the best way to organize the evidence to support the claim? A common way of organizing historical accounts is chronologically. But you could also organize by categories of images you've discovered, using some chronological organization within categories. You might also discern themes in the material you amass and organize your paper around them.

What documentation will you need? If you have used only primary sources, you would need at least a bibliography of the magazines and the particular issues that you used. If you have used quotations or reproduced images from your sources, you need to indicate with a footnote, endnote, or in-text reference where each borrowed item appeared originally. Any secondary sources used should also be cited in the bibliography.

2. DRAFT YOUR PAPER

Actually, you will probably be drafting as you answer the questions given above. Expect to change your mind several times about what to claim, what to include, and how to organize it. Draft and redraft the paper or parts of it as necessary until you have shaped it to reflect the most plausible claims you can make, given the evidence you have.

3. SEEK FEEDBACK

Once you have a complete draft that you are fairly satisfied with, ask someone whose judgment you trust to read it and respond to its overall effectiveness. Better yet, ask more than one person. Listen carefully to their comments, but don't feel compelled to follow everyone's advice. Let your draft sit a few days and re-read it yourself, critically. You will no doubt see ways to revise it.

4. REVISE AND EDIT YOUR PAPER

Using the responses of others and your own sense of what the paper still needs, rearrange elements of your paper, delete unnecessary or confusing parts, and add details, transitions, and documentation, to make your paper effective and correct.

SUGGESTIONS FOR RESEARCH AND WRITING

1. If your parents or some other family members have saved letters, perhaps from a courtship or a period of military service, obtain and read the letters, looking for one or more themes that you could develop in a paper. Use the letters as primary sources, quoting from them to support your interpretations. If appropriate, locate and use secondary sources that will help illuminate the time period in which the letters were written. Use appropriate citations and provide a bibliography for all your sources.

2. Often when states, communities, or colleges approach an important anniversary (the bicentennial of their founding, for example), they write a history of the time period just ended. If you live in a place where an important anniversary is about to be commemorated, see if you can contribute to writing its history. If someone is coordinating the history, you may be assigned to read and interpret documents that contribute to one part of the total history. On the other hand, if no one is in charge of writing a history, you might volunteer to pore over documents that have been saved and write a brief history of some part of an overall project

3. How has student life changed on your campus in the past 60 years? There is likely to be an archive of student newspapers and yearbooks on campus that you can explore to answer questions that are interesting to you about your parents' and grandparents' college days. Here are some possibilities: What were the important campus issues in the 1950s? How important were sports or the Greek system or queen contests in the 1960s? Have students become more politically aware over the last 20 years? Have students become more career-oriented since 1980?

4. Study magazine ads for a particular kind of product (e.g., alcohol, cigarettes, cars, or headache remedies) over a period of 20–30 years. Note how the ads change, if they do, to appeal to different needs or desires of the consumer. What can you infer about how the ad makers viewed consumers in a particular time period?

5. Television programs are a type of text. They begin as written documents, but the viewer watches a script enacted, rather than reading it. Watch reruns of a particular TV program over a period of several weeks, say *Leave it to Beaver* or *Happy Days,* and study how one character is developed. From that character's words and actions, try to infer what viewers valued in the era when the program was current and popular. Another possibility would be to compare two programs that featured African Americans as the main characters, e.g., *The Fresh Prince of Bel Air* and *The Cosby Show.* How do the characters, the plots, and the values differ between these two shows?

6. Identify one of the oldest of the major journals in your field. Check your library to see if it has the earliest volumes of the journal; skim several early volumes to identify a main research topic then. Read carefully two or three articles that report investigations of that topic. What are the research questions or hypotheses? What methods are used? What are the findings and how are they interpreted? How does the state of knowledge at that time compare to the present understanding of that topic? What can you infer about how your discipline has changed?

REFERENCES

Brace, C. Loring. 1996. Review of *The bell curve: Intelligence and class structure in American life*, by Richard J. Herrnstein and Charles Murray. *Current Anthropology* 37 (February Supplement): S156–S161.

Gould, Stephen J. 1994. Curveball. *New Yorker*. 28 November, 139-149.

Heckman, James J. 1995. Lessons from *The bell curve*. *Journal of Political Economy* 103 (October): 1091–1120.

Herrnstein, Richard J., and Charles Murray. 1994. *The bell curve: Intelligence and class structure in American life*. New York: Free Press.

Hudson, Valerie, and Andrea Den Boer. 2004. *Bare branches: The security implications of Asia's surplus male population*. Cambridge, MA: MIT Press.

5

INTERVIEWING

CHAPTER OVERVIEW

After reading this chapter, you should be able to answer the following questions:

1. Which fields are likely to use interviews as a method of inquiry?
2. What are the steps in preparing for a successful interview?
3. What is involved in tape recording an interview?
4. What are four ways of presenting interview information in a text?
5. What precautions must a researcher take to be sure interviews are ethical?

Interviewing is a widely used method of data-gathering in the social sciences. This method is the primary one of anthropologists, folklorists, and some sociologists; it is also commonly used by political scientists, psychologists, and linguists. Both print and broadcast journalists rely on interviewing as their main way of gathering information for news stories. Interviews can be highly structured, following carefully predetermined questions aimed at gathering precise bits of information; or they can be very open-ended, guided only by a general purpose. Skilled interviewers in most fields learn how to conduct both kinds.

Interviewing is commonly used also to supplement other methods of data-gathering. For example, observational research and experimental research might be followed by an interview in which participants are questioned about the behavior they exhibited. Surveys may be conducted orally, in which case they are a type of interview. The study of documents may also be supplemented with interviews. A researcher can compensate for the gaps in documents by interviewing people who are knowledgeable about whatever time, people, or customs are described in the documents. Since some individuals and groups tend not to create many documents that would tell future generations about them, and since it is impossible to interview the dead, some oral historians work to preserve the history of individuals and groups before they die. For example, many of the Allied soldiers who liberated the Nazi extermination camps in the 1940s have either already died or are now advanced in age. Historians have interviewed many of these former soldiers to create a record of their impressions when they first found the survivors, the bodies, and the ovens at such places as Auschwitz and Buchenwald.

Usually, we think of interviewing only one person—at most two or three people—at a time, but a new type of group interview is emerging as an important research tool. This group interview, called focus group research, is used frequently in marketing, opinion polling, education, social psychology, and law. Focus group research could well be an important method for you to learn about. However, it is fairly difficult for undergraduates to conduct focus group research, given the difficulty of getting several people in one place at the same time and given the typically limited resources students have for funding research projects. Therefore, this chapter will provide basic instructions for conducting interviews only with individuals.

Interviewing is one of the easiest and least expensive methods of research that students can try. But it is not a trivial method by any means, for as this chapter will show, there are a number of things you will need to consider as you plan and conduct an interview in order to have something worth writing about at the end. First, you prepare for the interview and for recording information. Then you conduct the interview itself. Finally, you use the data collected to construct a written record of the interview or contextualize the information from the interview to support the thesis of a broader argument.

PREPARING FOR THE INTERVIEW

An interview will be only as successful as the preparation that precedes it. Begin with the end in mind. Think about your reasons for conducting the interview. What do you want to find out? How will you eventually use the information you obtain? What kind of document will you be writing? Will it be simply a transcript of the interview? Will it be part of a larger research project that includes information from other sources as well? Once you have answered questions like these, you are ready to follow the steps below to prepare for a successful interview.

FIND INFORMANTS

How you find people to interview depends on what you're looking for. Sometimes you may want to know what a particular person thinks—a famous writer, a government official, a successful business executive, a noted scholar. In that case, you simply ask the person for an interview. Other times, you may want to know about a particular topic—events in the past, how to do something, or how people south of the Alleghenies pronounce the word *greasy*. In that case, you must find people who possess the kind of information you want.

Suppose you want to collect information about woodcarving, an art that some of the older men in your community, including your grandfather, practice. Your grandfather would be an obvious person to interview; he might also refer you to others. There are other possible ways to locate woodcarvers whom you could interview: local museums that display carvings, specialty shops that market them, and newspaper ads are all possible ways of getting leads for interviews. Simply asking around is another way to find informants. For example, if you wanted to interview old-timers about the history of a small town, you might stop at the local cafe and ask the regular customers who some likely informants are.

Contact the Informants

If time permits, you can send a letter stating your aims and why you want to interview the person you've contacted. The letter gives the person time to think over the invitation and decide whether they can be helpful to you. Follow the letter with a phone call or visit. If time is more pressing, a telephone call or personal visit may be the first contact. Be prepared to state clearly what you want and why you think that person will be a good informant. Ask a few questions to get acquainted with your informant and find out if he or she really has the kind of information you are looking for and is willing to share the information. If both of you are willing to continue, arrange for a mutually agreeable time and location for the interview. It may be possible to conduct the interview over the telephone if time, distances, or scheduling conflicts prohibit a face-to-face meeting. An e-mail interview is also a possibility.

Do Necessary Background Research

You should come to the interview knowing as much as you can about the informant and the subject you will discuss. If the informant is well known, you may be able to read about him or her in the library or online by finding biographical information, previous interviews, or articles or books they've published. Whenever you can, learn about your informant's background. Learn also the terminology you will need. You should know the basic vocabulary and issues related to the topic of the interview so that you can ask intelligent questions and understand the answers. The interview time will not be as profitably spent as it might be if your informant must give you an introduction to the basic assumptions, ideas, and terms involved. Being interested in and knowledgeable about your informants is a good way to win their trust and confidence.

PLAN YOUR QUESTIONS

Either write your questions out completely or list the topics you want to cover in the interview. But study them long enough that you have them well in mind when you go because you shouldn't let your questions get in the way of having a real conversation. For example, don't plan to simply read from your list mechanically, checking off items on it, as if you can't wait to be finished. Plan to be flexible because in some cases you may want the interview to follow the course suggested by whatever the informant brings up. You will not be able to anticipate all the questions you should ask; therefore, a critical skill to develop as an interviewer is the ability to listen attentively to your informant and follow up interesting or provocative information with questions that draw out a little more information or pursue the implications of what has been said. It can be helpful to conduct a mock interview first, asking a friend to play the role of the informant. By rehearsing your questions in this way, you will feel better prepared when you conduct the real interview.

PREPARE THE MATERIALS YOU WILL NEED

At a minimum, you will need a notebook and pens or pencils to take notes. If it is possible, however, you should plan to record the interview, using audiotape or, in some cases, videotape. You will need to get the prior consent of your informants to use mechanical recording devices; you may also need the approval of an Institutional Review Board (see Chapter 3) and you probably need to have your informant sign a consent form (see Chapter 10). There are potential advantages and drawbacks to all three means of recording the proceedings of the interview, as explained next.

RECORDING THE INTERVIEW

NOTETAKING

Taking notes has the advantage of costing little and perhaps of making informants feel more at ease than they often do in the presence of a tape recorder. But writing while you attempt to be an attentive listener and at the same time think about your next question is difficult at best, and it slows the interview down. There is the possibility that you may not write down as much as you should or that you will write something inaccurately. Oversights and errors such as these obviously will impair the quality of what you eventually write about the interview. However, some interviewers, such as journalists, often cannot use recorders so they practice to become adept at taking notes efficiently.

They sometimes check the accuracy of what they have written by later telephoning their informants to be sure that their written representations of the interview, particularly quotations, are accurate.

AUDIOTAPING

You must decide if it is necessary to make an audiotape by evaluating your purpose in the interview and the necessity of having a complete record of what was said. If your goal is simply to ask someone a few questions to fill a class assignment, and if nothing further will be done with the interview data, making an audiotape may be an elaborate and unnecessary step. On the other hand, if your purpose requires that you be more thorough and careful in recording, consider taping the interview.

Because tapes provide a more complete and permanent record of an interview than notes, they are indispensable for data collection in fields such as folklore, oral history, anthropology, sociology, and linguistic mapping of regional dialects. If you conduct research in one of these fields and particularly if you plan to become a professional, purchasing a good tape recorder could be a wise investment in your future. If you are not ready to make that investment, you can often borrow or rent the recorder; purchasing the tape itself is not a big expense. There are also devices you can attach to a telephone to tape record an interview—which you must only use with the informant's permission, of course.

Once you have the equipment, however, you must familiarize yourself with how to use it and be prepared for the kinds of mechanical failures that can disrupt an otherwise well-planned interview. Edward Ives (1995) suggests you practice using the equipment in mock interviews first. If possible, Ives advises, you should have an external microphone for your recorder because you will be able to position it better to pick up both your informant's and your own voice. Ives also reminds you to check the batteries, microphone, and electrical cord before you go to the interview, and to pack an extension cord in case you will need it. When you start the interview, record a few words; then stop and play them back to be sure the recorder is working before you proceed.

Ives (1995) also suggests you let your informants know at the time you arrange for the interview that you would like to tape it. If they are reluctant, try to reassure and gently persuade them of the value of a taped interview. If they still object, you could pack the recorder along anyway; they may decide to permit you to turn it on once they see how notetaking slows down the process. But if they do still decline to be recorded, you must respect their wishes. Never secretly record an interview.

VIDEOTAPING

What is true of audiotaping is often doubly true of videotaping. A good video camera can be expensive, and learning to use it takes time. The location of the interview also must be conducive to good recording, with adequate lighting and background motion and noise kept to a minimum. You must weigh these considerations against what you gain by having a visual as well as auditory record of the interview. Is it important to capture such things as the informant's facial expressions, gestures, and movements? Will you be trying to interpret these visual cues as well as to analyze the spoken words of the informant?

For many social scientists, the words spoken in the interview are all they want to record. For others, however, videotapes permit them to analyze the participants' nonverbal behavior as well as their words. With videotapes they can view the behavior more than once, and different observers can view the same event. Using categories they have previously agreed on, these observers can code the behaviors they see and calculate a statistic, called interrater reliability, to determine the consistency of the observational analysis (see Chapter 6). More detail about videotaped interviews is beyond the scope of this chapter, so the next section focuses mainly on using audiotape to preserve an accurate record of the interview.

CONDUCTING THE INTERVIEW

Whatever method you choose to record the interview, when you finally come face to face with your informant, you must first set him or her at ease. Some informants may think that their lives are so "ordinary" that no one could possibly be interested in what they have to say. As a result, at first they may not say very much; they may have to warm up to you and the topic first, so be patient if the beginning seems slow and difficult. Others may be a little suspicious of your motives; if so, reassure them of what you said in the initial contact about your aims and about what will eventually be done with the information they give you. Having informants read and sign an informed consent document will also help them understand the purposes and uses of the interview. (See Chapter 3 and Chapter 10 for more information.) Some informants may be nervous about talking into a tape recorder and will "clam up." However, most will probably relax after a few minutes. It may help to let them know you are a little nervous, too.

If you are taping the interview, and if the tape will become part of an archive (as is common in folklore and oral history research), Ives (1995) suggests you let the informant listen to you record your opening statement. Speaking directly into the microphone, state the date and your name. Then state the name of the person you are interviewing and the topic of the interview.

After stating the preliminaries, begin by asking a few easy or general questions. Then you should direct the interview intelligently, using good on-the-spot judgment about where to go next. For example, you could vary the order of questions from what you initially planned. If the informant wants to talk about something that obviously interests him or her, you should probably permit the digression and bring it back to your topic when you can. Shifts and tangents can often be revealing, making you aware of dimensions of the topic that you hadn't considered. Don't be afraid to probe your informant's answers more deeply to get more and better information. Use follow-up questions to get more detail, such as "Where?" "When?" or "Who else was there?" Don't fire these questions too rapidly at the informant, however. Remember that silence can also be probing, so don't rush to fill every silence with more words; give your informant time to think and to answer at length.

Because notes and audiotape have no visual dimension, Ives (1995) notes that you may have to put into words what your informant is showing through gestures. If the informant says, "It was about this big," judge the distance displayed by their hands and say something like, "About four feet tall and two feet wide?" Record accurate information that will help explain a gestured "this" and "that" or "here" and "there." The record you make of the interview is for all the people who will later be interested in it, so try to preserve information they would get if they were present at the interview. However, take special care to be ethical in using the information you have received from the informant. For example, if the informant has said anything about someone else that is potentially harmful to that person, consider whether you should omit the information or disguise the reference by using a pseudonym or a vague description in order to protect the privacy of the person mentioned and to protect your informant from any sort of retaliation.

The length of interviews will vary. One hour is a good rule of thumb, but good information can be collected in less time, depending on your purposes. If you spend longer than an hour or two, you may wear out your welcome and overtax the informant. You may need more than one interview session to get all the information that you want. For example, if you are doing an oral history and your informant turns out to have a wealth of good information to offer, ask if you can come back another time to continue interviewing. Even if you think you have gleaned all you can in one interview, you may realize later that you need a brief follow-up interview, either in person or by telephone, to fill in gaps or answer questions that have arisen since your interview. Your informant may also remember more in the meantime, and you may be pleasantly surprised by what else you will gain from an additional interview.

When you are sure that no more interviews will be necessary, write a thank-you note to your informant to express your gratitude for the time they gave you. Let your informant know where the interview data will be archived, if it will be. If the interview will be published, let them know where and when. If it won't be published, you can at least offer to send a copy of the report you will write.

MOVING FROM NOTES OR TAPE TO TEXT

Immediately after an interview, write complete and careful notes about the circumstances of the interview. Consider what contextual information is important for future readers of the interview to know. For example, you may want to note the surroundings in which the interview took place, what the informant looked like, or who else was present. If you audiotape the interview, include in your notes any information that will help explain any background noises or other voices. If you will be depositing the tape in an archive, you will need to know what requirements the archive has for the notes to accompany the tape. Think of future listeners to the tapes and include in your notes whatever would help them to make better use of it.

After writing notes about the context of the interview, you must consider how to "write up" the interview in a paper that will allow readers to know what went on without actually listening to the tape or trying to reconstruct the interview from your notes. There are basically five ways to make a text out of an interview.

TRANSCRIPTS

The first type of text is a *transcript*—a literal word-by-word rendering of the entire interview, including the "ums" and "ahs," the pauses, the laughter, and the incomplete or convoluted sentences that are a part of any conversation. Transcription of an interview is a time-consuming process but often a necessary one to be sure that no possibly relevant detail is omitted. Transcriptions are seldom published unedited, but they are sometimes considered primary documents, and if they are worthy of preservation, they are often stored in archives along with tapes. Most oral history archives require complete transcripts.

The completeness of the transcription and the extra features it might include depend on how it is to be used. Linguistics research might require a special phonetic alphabet or diacritical marks on words to indicate how they were pronounced; psychological research might require including pauses, laughs, "ums," and "ers." Other non-verbal features can be noted in brackets. Decide how closely the transcript must follow the tape. You may decide to leave out the false starts and "ums," simply noting that you have done so; but generally you would not correct grammar, usage, or sentence structure because these may reveal important things about the informant. Use your judgment as to how to punctuate the transcript. When you are finished transcribing, listen to the tape again and compare it to the transcript. Oral historians sometimes send the informant a copy of the transcript, and ask for it to be returned with corrections noted. For oral history, the corrected transcript becomes the primary document. But folklorists consider the tape the primary document and the transcript as merely supplemental.

DIALOGUE OR EDITED TRANSCRIPT

The second type of text is the *dialogue or edited transcript*. If you edit a transcript, you should include a note at the beginning or end indicating what kinds of editorial changes have been made; you should also note in the text when you have inserted a word or phrase for clarity by including it in brackets. One way to edit a transcript is to write it as a dialogue. On paper, a dialogue looks like the script for a play, with the speaker's name given in boldface or capital letters right before their words. The words following the speakers' names represent essentially what they said in the sequence in which they said it, but the words have been edited to omit the verbal tics such as "uh" and to improve syntax and clarity. The following excerpt from an interview with Mary Field Belenky, one of the four authors of *Women's Ways of Knowing*, shows the dialogue method of presenting an interview (it also presents interesting information about how interviewers and informants can become collaborators). The words of the interviewers (Ashton and Thomas) and the informant (Belenky) in this dialogue are represented by "Q" (for question) and "A" (for answer).

Q. Are you positing a much larger group of collaborators than the four of you who coauthored *Women's Ways?*

A. Absolutely. The women we interviewed were themselves drawn in. A word that seems better than *collaboration* is *dialogue* because it suggests that our so-called research subjects were real participants in the project. In a very real sense they were also, much of the time when we were writing, the audience. Let me tell you about Lillian Rubin's *Worlds of Pain*, a study of lower middle-class marriages—a study that is, like ours, based on interviews. Rubin had a pact with the people that she interviewed: they would review and approve any writing she did before it went to publication. She notes that none of those people had much criticism of her writing, so she didn't change or reedit the work in light of it; but I believe, because she had this pact to give them the work before publishing it, that she wrote *to them* in a way—and it's a beautiful book. Rubin's book was a model for us, even though our sample was too large to promise everybody we would get their permission. But as our book was written, we very much had in mind that it would be read by the people we had interviewed.

Q. So the audience you had in mind as you were writing was a friendly audience, women who could benefit from the information as you organized it?

A. Absolutely. But the information wasn't just what *we* were thinking or organizing; it was also *their* words because we worked from transcripts of the interviews. In fact, when the book first came out many women said that we had given words to things they'd always thought. It seemed funny at first, a backhanded kind of compliment. Here we'd done this extraordinary thing. But giving words to these ideas was exactly what we tried to do, and that's a lot to do. Moreover, I think we ought to teach ourselves and our students that we can have real choices about audience. We all need to understand how writing the same material for different audiences changes the voice. That is very empowering knowledge to have. (Ashton and Thomas 1990, 278–279)

INTERVIEW SUMMARY

The third type of text is one that presents mainly a *summary of the interview* with occasional quoting of the informant's words as they were spoken. This kind of text is commonly found in newspapers and magazines. This way of writing up an interview gives the writer more control of how to sequence the information obtained in the interview. The writer can select from the entire contents of the interview those parts that help him or her to support a particular interpretation or overall claim about the interview. Of course, an ethical interviewer will not deliberately select some kinds of information or distort what was said to present a biased claim that would not be supported by a reading of the entire transcript of the interview. However, the writer's ability to select and determine the order of presentation does mean that the final "write-up" of an interview can be quite different from the interview itself. The student paper entitled "The Social Problems that Deter Xhosa Women from Marriage and How Education and Westernization Allow Them to Refuse Marriage" illustrates summarized interviews with numerous direct quotations to underscore points.

SYNTHESIS

The fourth kind of text is a *synthesis* of interview data, used mainly when the text is based on many interviews, each one aimed at gathering information to answer particular research questions. The writer analyzes the transcripts of all of the interviews, looking for points of similarity and difference and for ways of categorizing the information revealed in all the interviews. The writer then presents the findings in a way that synthesizes many interviews. This type of text is represented in the selection at the end of this book entitled "Harlem Town." The two stories you will read in this selection, one from Sadie Delany and one from Bessie Delany, are the product of many interviews. The researcher, Amy Hill Hearth, stated that she wove these two stories (and others in the book *Having Our Say*) from "thousands of anecdotes that [she] coaxed from the Delany sisters during an eighteen-month period." Hearth further states, "The sequence of stories is mine but the words are all theirs" (xiii). That is, the stories are told from the viewpoint and in the voice of the two sisters that Hearth interviewed, but the sentences have been taken from different places in the many transcripts and synthesized in a way that makes the stories coherent and easy for a reader to follow. In handling her material this way, Hearth followed a common practice in writing oral history.

Synthesis with Elaboration

Another kind of synthesis may be noted in the book *Women's Ways of Knowing* (referred to above in the example of an edited dialogue). The authors of this book interviewed 135 women of all ages and from many walks of life over a period of months. On the basis of all the data collected (5,000 pages of transcripts), the authors concluded that women use five ways of knowing. In discussing each way of knowing, they quote liberally from various interviews, but they elaborate on this primary data with material from secondary sources that help them interpret the primary interviews. For them, the interviews are not just something to report but a way of making a larger claim about women in general, one that they can only make with the help of supporting texts. If you use interviews as a method of inquiry, you will need to think carefully about the best way to "write up" your data depending on your purpose and your audience's needs.

SUGGESTIONS FOR RESEARCH AND WRITING

1. Interview a notable person on your campus or in your community. Do some background research on the person and the contributions for which he or she is noted. Plan some questions that will further illuminate that person's life or achievements and arrange for an interview. After conducting it and writing a report, try to interest your campus or local newspaper in publishing all or part of your interview.

2. Interview one of the professors in your major field to learn more about the field. Ask the professor to describe his or her own education and research in the field. Get the professor's perspective on the major developments in the field during his or her career span. Consider how what you learn from this interview corroborates or contradicts your understanding of the field from the courses you've taken or books you've read. Another possibility in this interview would be to focus on the kinds of writing this professor does: What genres does he or she most often write in? What sort of process does he or she follow? What is hardest about writing? What has become easier? What advice does the professor have for you to help you learn to write in your field?

3. What was happening on your campus fifty years ago? In your community? In the U.S.? Identify some important events or social, cultural, educational, or industrial developments that occurred at that time. Locate a person in

your community who can tell about those events or developments from firsthand experience. Identify some likely informants by asking around, by advertising, or by visiting a senior citizens' center. Then arrange for interviews to collect an oral history concerning the event or development you are interested in.

4. Collect some of your family's history by interviewing your grandparents, aunts, uncles, and parents. Where did your ancestors come from? Where did they first settle? What was life like when your grandparents were growing up? Your aunts, uncles, and parents? What can your grandparents and aunts and uncles tell you about your parents that your parents haven't told you? What are some of the memorable events in your family's history that ought to be recorded for future generations?

5. Identify a local expert on a social problem you are interested in and interview that person to learn how the problem is understood or dealt with locally. For example, if you are interested in the problem of domestic violence, interview the director of a shelter where victims of domestic violence may seek refuge. If you are interested in your community's response to the problem of homelessness, interview the person who directs your city's homeless shelter. As a way of learning about career or volunteer experiences you could have, interview the person in your city or county government who is responsible for low-income housing, the director of a rape crisis center, a worker at a suicide prevention center, or a social worker.

REFERENCES

Ashton-Jones, Evelyn, and Dene Kay Thomas. 1990. Composition, collaboration, and women's ways of knowing: A conversation with Mary Belenky. *Journal of Advanced Composition* 10 (Fall): 275–292.

Belenky, Mary Field, Blythe McVicker Clinchy, Nancy Rule Goldberger, and Jill Mattuck Tarule. 1986. *Women's ways of knowing: The development of self, voice, and mind.* New York: Basic Books.

Delany, Sarah, and A. Elizabeth Delany, with Amy Hill Hearth. 1993. *Having our say: The Delany sisters' first 100 years.* New York: Kodansha International.

Ives, Edward D. 1995. *The tape-recorded interview: A manual for field workers in folklore and oral history.* 2d ed. Knoxville: University of Tennessee Press.

6

OBSERVING

CHAPTER OVERVIEW

After reading this chapter, you should be able to answer the following questions:

1. When does observation become a scientific method?
2. What are four different kinds of observation?
3. What are the steps in performing observational research?
4. How does one typically analyze and write about quantitative observations? About qualitative observations?
5. What ethical issues arise in observational research?

Observing is such a fundamental activity in daily life it may be difficult to think of it as a scientific method. You observe the weather and decide how to dress for the day. You observe your family members' or co-workers' moods and decide whether to treat them with kid gloves or to joke, argue, or have a heart-to-heart talk with them. These kinds of daily observations are valuable on a personal level, but they are not scientific research. Observation becomes a scientific method only when it is purposeful and systematic, when it attempts to analyze and explain phenomena in a way that other scientists find plausible, and when it draws reliable and lasting conclusions.

Imagine you were a personnel manager who observed that your employees seemed to work less enthusiastically on Monday mornings right after the weekly staff meeting. This observation would give you a significant objective for making further observations. You could start to keep systematic notes of what behaviors the employees exhibited and of what was happening in the staff meetings. If you realized that frequently the meetings centered on how the employees were falling short in their work, and then you also observed that these meetings were followed by a lot of time-wasting and grumbling around the office water cooler, you might infer that negative motivational strategies were not successful with your employees. You then would have some good reasons, based on observational data, for trying different incentives to get your employees to work harder.

Observing is really the basis of all methods. In reading documents, you must be observant to notice the details and the connections that reveal something new about your subject. In interviewing, you should observe the person you are interviewing—their face, their gestures, their dress, and their surroundings—for what these tell you that the person's words don't. Surveying and experimenting, the methods discussed in Chapters 7 and 8, are controlled but indirect methods of observation; both use instruments and measurements to make selected observations rigorous and precise. Direct observation of human behavior, even though it is more difficult to control and make precise, is often the best method to use to answer certain kinds of research questions because it occurs in natural settings, unlike experiments. Also, unlike surveys or questionnaires, direct observation does not depend on the observed people's willingness to report their behavior honestly or their ability to remember it accurately.

But direct observation is not without flaws. One obvious flaw is that the observer might be selective in what he or she observes, failing to see or hear something that is critical for understanding the observed phenomenon completely. Our personal background and biases may make us sensitive to perceiving some kinds of data and not others. Another flaw is that our sensory organs—the basic tools of observation—can become tired, overstimulated, or so accustomed to the environment that we fail to notice something important. Even when we augment our senses with instruments such as audio or video recorders, we still have to use our senses to interpret the data recorded. Still another problem is that the act of observing often influences the very behavior that is under investigation. Social scientists have long noted that changes in people's behavior often result simply from the fact that they know they are being observed. Users of observational methods have devised some ways to compensate for these flaws, ways that will be explained later in this chapter.

KINDS OF OBSERVATION

There are many different ways of using observation as a method, but they can be lumped into four categories: unobtrusive observation, structured observation, case studies, and participant observation.

UNOBTRUSIVE OBSERVATION

Unobtrusive observation occurs when the persons being observed don't realize it. The observers simply carry out their observations in natural settings without drawing attention to the fact that they are doing research. For example, researchers who want to learn how children develop the ability to interact with other children could go to a nursery school and observe toddlers at play through a one-way mirror. Because the children don't know they are being observed, they should behave normally, and the researchers should be able to gather data on which to base generalizations helpful for parents, teachers, psychologists, and others who work with children. Unobtrusive observation is ethical as long as there are no physical or emotional risks to the observed persons and no benefits they would be entitled to share in.

STRUCTURED OBSERVATION

Structured observation occurs when participants realize that they are part of an observational study, and the study has been devised to answer questions determined ahead of time. One example of structured observation is a study by sociolinguist Deborah Tannen of differences between males and females in two-person, same-sex conversations. This research was structured in the sense that the eight participants—pairs of friends at four different age levels—were taken to an office in which a video camera was set up. They were then instructed to have a serious or intimate conversation while the camera recorded it and the investigator went away. The setting and the instructions no doubt made it a bit difficult for the participants to perform on demand for the video camera. However, they did not know how the investigator would analyze the videotape. In fact, Tannen did not analyze the tapes in the way she initially expected to, so the observation was unstructured in an important sense. Still, the initial structuring of the observations permitted Tannen to draw her unexpected and interesting conclusions. Another example of structured observation is in Heather Bahlmann's research paper at the end of this book. She videotaped fifth graders solving fraction problems and then analyzed their strategies.

CASE STUDIES

Case studies can be considered a special kind of structured observation. Typically, a case study involves intense observation of one individual—at most very few people—over a long period of time, usually as a part of the individual's clinical treatment for a physical, psychological, or social problem. The observer—who might be a medical doctor, a therapist, or social worker—establishes a high degree of rapport with the observed person, while still remaining detached enough to make objective descriptions of what is observed. The observations may include much more than simply watching a person; interviews, tests, and mental and physical examinations may all be additional means of collecting data that lead to conclusions about the case. Although it may seem that conclusions from individual case studies are not generalizable, many similar cases are often compared to draw inferences that have significance for a broader population. (Because case studies are generally conducted by licensed professionals and require a great deal of time to complete, they are usually not feasible for undergraduate students to undertake, so little more will be said about them.)

PARTICIPANT OBSERVATION

Participant observation is the favored method of cultural anthropologists and sometimes of sociologists and social psychologists. As the name implies, the observer becomes a participant in the phenomena he or she is observing. Anthropologists call this method "ethnographic research" because the end result is a text in the genre called ethnography (from *ethno* meaning "people" and *graphy* meaning "writing"). An anthropologist may not become a complete participant in the culture he or she observes (learning to shrink heads, for example, may be going too far!), but sociologists and social psychologists usually try to participate completely because they are more likely to study people in their own culture. For example, to learn what it means to be homeless in America, some sociologists have assumed the role of a homeless person, living on the streets without access to the comforts of a bed or bathroom, wearing cast-off clothing, and begging for money for food.

One assumption underlying participant observation is that a researcher cannot adequately understand the reality and significance of others' lives without becoming an insider in their daily experiences. Participant observers do not believe, as experimenters do, that researchers must be detached from whatever they study. Another assumption is that the researcher should bring to the study as few preconceived theories as possible. The goal of participant observation is to let understanding emerge from deep involvement in the experience. To gain this understanding, the researcher collects as much data as possible to sort out later, not by using predetermined analytical categories but by finding themes in the material that the researcher believes explain the most about the observed phenomena. Participant observers readily admit the role their subjective perception plays in the construction of the knowledge they finally write about. They do not pretend that knowledge is objective and self-existent because they realize that a different observer would have a different experience and therefore create a different text.

The excerpt from Kate Fox's book *Watching the English: The Hidden Rules of English Behaviour*, reprinted in the Readings section of this book, is based on her participant-observation of the inhabitants of England, augmented by interviews and experiments. It is unusual for an anthropologist to study the behavior and cultural practices of her own people, but Fox believed that alarmists proclaiming the death of Englishness were wrong, that there still were unique features that set British culture apart from other cultures. She set out to derive the unwritten rules which guide the daily behavior of British people in all kinds of practices and situations—their conversation, humor, work, play, food, and dress. The excerpt you will read discusses both her methods and the rules that govern British people's behavior when they use public transportation. As someone who already knew how to participate in British culture without thinking, Fox had to step back from her own behavior and make the familiar strange in order to explain to outsiders what the British do and why they do it. As you will see, this required her to be quite resourceful to deduce the general rule and its exceptions.

Despite the intensive nature of participant observation, there are limits to what participant observation can reveal. One of these limits might come from *ethnocentrism*—the tendency of observers to understand and judge what they observe in terms of their own culture and experience. Assuming that ethnocentrism can be overcome, though, it is still questionable whether a researcher really can "go native," for example in becoming a homeless person, when all the time they know they have a home to return to and a better way of earning an income. On the other hand, there is also a danger that the researcher might begin to identify so completely with the group studied that he or she will lose the ability to think objectively and critically about the experience. Some police undercover agents who have infiltrated the criminal world in order to gather evidence to convict lawbreakers, for example, have been seduced by the lifestyle they have pretended to live and become corrupt themselves.

Another problem is logistical: To provide the deep understanding that it aims for, participant observation usually requires a long period of time, and the massive data that accumulates in such a study can be formidable when the time for analysis arrives. A final problem rises from the ethical questions that may arise: Is it right for someone to beg if they really have the means to provide for themselves? Should participant observers gain entrance into the groups they study by means of a false story about themselves? If they are candid about their true identity, can they really become a part of the group enough to understand it? How does a researcher get the informed consent of those observed?

Kate Fox apparently did not formally seek informed consent from the British commuters that she observed and interviewed and certainly not from the pedestrians she bumped into "accidentally-on-purpose" in her experiments. Her book offers no explanation of whether she completed an IRB proposal before conducting her research. However, it is clear that she had ethical concerns in mind. She does not disclose the names of any of the people she studied (she probably didn't even ask for names), and she explains how she used naturally occurring opportunities in order to break through the privacy barrier of commuters and ask them questions or how she sometimes even disclosed her own identity as a social scientist engaged in research for her book. And even though she often writes about her subject in a lighthearted way, Fox's purpose is clearly serious, as she is not mocking the British but explaining to them and to others the norms that govern behavior. She takes pains to show how her research was methodologically sound and her motives unquestionable.

Questions about ethnocentrism, logistics, and ethics show that observation is not as straightforward or easy as it might seem. But social scientists have developed ways of dealing with many of the concerns that threaten the reliability of the information gained with this method. As you read the following steps for using this method, think about how you could plan observational research to eliminate or compensate for some of its drawbacks.

MAKING OBSERVATIONS

DEFINE YOUR PURPOSE

The first step in any kind of observation is to define your purpose. For some kinds of research you can state a very definite, limited purpose. Suppose you wanted to know, for example, whether male or female students speak out more often in class without first raising their hands. You could state your research question very specifically and answer it with fairly uncomplicated observations. For other kinds of research, such as participant observation, a very general, broadly stated purpose is more typical because the researcher wants to be open to the experience rather than bringing preconceived notions to it. So a very general question such as, "How do the British behave when they ride the train?" is more appropriate as a starting point. In participant observation, the focus of the research can and often does change, becoming more specific as the observer spends more time conducting the research.

SELECT PEOPLE, SETTING, AND BEHAVIOR FOR OBSERVATION

After defining your purpose, you need to decide what person or persons you will observe, where you will observe them, and what behavior you will look for—but not necessarily in that order. As noted already, with participant observation you will know who you want to study and often where, but usually not the particular behaviors you'll watch for. You define your focus more gradually as you become acquainted with the people and surroundings you are in. With unobtrusive observation, it may be best to choose the setting first and then observe the people who happen to be in it. Say you wanted to observe how people react when strangers sit in a vacant seat right next to them rather than choosing one farther away. A public place where there are many people who are not familiar with one another would be the ideal setting for conducting this research—perhaps a library, an airport, or the lobby of a busy public building.

Sometimes it's best to decide first what specific behaviors you will look for. For example, if you wanted to do a structured observation of how a seven-year-old explains a procedure, such as putting together a toy, to a three-year-old, you would have to create a setting that would be conducive to this kind of observation. Then, of course, you would have to find children who could participate in the study. Using children in a study would require full-board clearance from an IRB (see Chapter 3) as well as the people who are entrusted with the children's care. Often the observational research you can do depends on the availability of and access to the kind of people you want to study, as well as access to special settings and equipment that make the observations feasible.

RECORD DATA

After defining your purpose and choosing a setting with people and behaviors to observe, the next step is to devise a way of recording data about your observations. There are several different ways to record data. One thing not to do is simply trust your memory to retain very complex information for very long. Preferably, you should record what you observe as it happens, or very soon afterwards, before proceeding with more observations. Here are some ways to make a record that you can refer to repeatedly as you later analyze your data.

Keep a notebook or log. Writing extensive notes in a log or diary is the preferred recording system of participant observers. Often they can't very well take notes while mingling with the people they are studying, so they find ways to do this privately. Observers watching students in a classroom, say, or children at play could usually write while they are observing without significantly disturbing either the process of observation or the behavior of interest. The notes you take can be of two kinds—descriptive and evaluative. Descriptive notes aim simply to capture the observed behavior as precisely as possible without making judgments about it. Evaluative notes are your first, rough attempts to interpret the meaning of the other notes—to make sense of the data as it grows. Upon reflection, you may change your first interpretations, but capturing your thoughts while observing should stimulate better analytical thinking about the data.

Work with one or more collaborators. Because observing and recording at the same time can prove difficult when complex behaviors are under study, sometimes observers work with collaborators. Usually the collaborators determine ahead of time what the salient items or activities are that they will observe. Suppose you wanted to conduct a study of strangers' reactions when someone takes a vacant seat right next to them rather than choosing one farther away.

This study should include at least two researchers—one to sit by strangers and the other to unobtrusively watch and record the observed person's behavior. For even more control of the accuracy of the observations, still another collaborator could watch and record each interaction from a different vantage point. Then all three of you could compare your observations and determine the most accurate way of describing what happened.

Devise a coding system. If you have determined ahead of time exactly what behaviors you intend to watch for, you can make a simple grid for checking off the behaviors each time they occur. For example, if you wanted to observe whether male or female fourth graders interrupted class discussion more frequently by talking out of turn, you could devise a coding system with two columns, one labeled "Boys" and one labeled "Girls." Each time you observed a boy or girl make a comment without raising a hand first, you would simply make a check in the appropriate column. To track individual boys and girls who talk out of turn, you could make a seating chart and simply make check marks under the students' names each time they exhibited the behavior.

Coding systems for more complex behavior are more difficult to devise. The categories for these coding systems might be based on a review of literature, your hypotheses, or preliminary observations. For example, to devise a coding system for the study of sitting by strangers, you could do some preliminary observations in order to come up with the categories that describe all possible behaviors. Your preliminary observations might show that those whose personal space was invaded by a stranger sitting next to them usually reacted in one or more of several ways. Using this information you could come up with categories for your coding system—for example, "shifts in seat away from intruder," "moves chair," "walks away," "stares at intruder," "makes a comment to intruder," and so on. You might make a grid for recording observations.

Use mechanical recording devices. A final way of recording observations is to use mechanical recording devices such as audiotapes or videotapes. Rather than writing field notes, some participant-observers record their observations by speaking into a tape recorder. Anthropologists make extensive use of audio recorders to capture the language and music of the cultures they study. Social psychologists studying crowd behavior have worn hidden microphones and tape recorders to capture comments from people in the crowd. Audiotapes allow the researcher to listen again and again to what was recorded so they can discern patterns in the data and draw conclusions.

Videotaping observations allows the same opportunity to view the behaviors repeatedly, watching for things that the observer might miss without a permanent record of the event. Both video and audio recordings also allow for multiple trained observers to check the data to see if they discern the same things and draw the same conclusions.

MAKE CONCLUSIONS RELIABLE

Reliability is an important concept in social science research. It means that the findings of a particular study are consistent and stable—likely to be the same if the study were repeated. Some threats to the reliability of observational research have already been noted, such as the tendency of observers to be selective about what they observe or to interpret and judge the behaviors they observe by ethnocentric standards. Social scientists acknowledge that it isn't possible to completely eliminate human frailty and error from observational research, but to ensure that results are as reliable as possible, people who do this kind of research can take the following steps.

Get an adequate sample or provide a thick description. There are human and material limits to how much time you can spend in research, how many people you can observe, and how many different behaviors you can attend to. But readers of your research will not be persuaded that your conclusions are reliable unless the conclusions are based on evidence that appears sufficient and representative. In other words, readers will expect most observational research to be based on an adequate sampling of the entire population you could have observed; or, if sampling is not feasible, readers will expect that conclusions are based on a sustained, in-depth study of the phenomena.

Getting an adequate sample means including enough people in your observation (this depends on the kind of observation you are doing), spending enough time observing, and focusing on a sufficient number of the different kinds of behaviors you are interested in. For example, if you were to do the sitting-by-a-stranger study in 30 minutes one afternoon at a bar and only include five different observations, readers could rightly protest that your conclusions aren't based on enough data to be reliable. They might also point out that the results are probably not representative since a bar is a place where it is perhaps more common for strangers to sit next to each other and a place where you aren't likely to encounter people from all walks of life.

Adequate sampling isn't a critical issue for case studies and participant-observation, however. The length of time spent accumulating data and the depth and insight of the researcher's observations are what count in persuading readers the conclusions are reliable. Ethnographers speak of providing a "thick description," one that may be based on only a few individuals but is nevertheless rich, detailed, and penetrating.

Use multiple observers. Another way of assuring readers that your observations have produced reliable conclusions is to use multiple observers. If at least two people have been trained to observe for the same things and they tend to agree on what happened in the observations, there is less chance that the observations are simply the result of the observer's experience and biases, or that the observations have been tainted by the observer's fatigue or boredom. The technique of using multiple observers is often combined with recording systems such as coding devices and audio- and videotaping so that all observers can independently listen to or watch and code the same observations. If two or more observers independently code behavior the same way, it is more likely that the observations are reliable. There is even a way of calculating what is called "interrater reliability" to get a statistic that shows how often the observers agreed with each other.

However, for case studies and participant observation, multiple observers are usually not considered necessary for reliability. Readers tend to believe the conclusions from these kinds of research in proportion to the writer's skill in providing evidence that he or she has been thorough in gathering data over a long period of time, interpreting it, relating it to other knowledge, and supporting the conclusions drawn.

Triangulate observations with other methods of research. A final way that researchers can increase the reliability of their conclusions is to *triangulate* observation with other methods of answering their questions. The word *triangulation* comes from navigation; it is a method of locating an unknown point by using two known points to create a triangle intersecting all three points. In research, then, triangulation is a way of determining if your conclusions are reliable by comparing them to conclusions from other research methods that you have confidence in. So observational data could be compared to survey and interview data, for example, that sought to answer the same or similar questions. If there is a high degree of correspondence in the results from all three kinds of research, you may feel more confident that the observational data is reliable.

ANALYZING AND WRITING ABOUT OBSERVATIONS

After collecting data through your observations, your next step is to analyze and interpret them carefully so that you can write about your findings. The simpler and the more quantitative your observations were, the more straightforward your analysis will be. For example, if you hypothesized ahead of time that boys in a fourth-grade classroom would speak out more often than girls without raising their hands, then simply counted and compared the number of times both groups exhibited the behavior, you would be able to confirm or reject your hypothesis quickly and report your findings without spending much time on analysis.

On the other hand, if you did a qualitative study of events in a college sorority during Rush Week, acting as a participant-observer, you would usually not have a hypothesis nor would you have data already neatly coded into predetermined categories. Instead, you would need to sift through all of your notes and begin seeking a general focus that would allow you to organize your findings and draw useful conclusions. In either a quantitative or a qualitative study, however, your first goal is to make your analysis illuminate the questions that led you to do the observations. Your second goal is to draw conclusions that provide greater understanding of the people and phenomena you have studied.

Writing about quantitative data is usually a more straightforward rhetorical problem than is writing about qualitative research. Quantitative research typically fits in the genre of the empirical research report. In this genre, the body of the text usually has four main divisions: (1) an introduction that provides a context for the problem (often including a review of related literature) and states the research question or hypothesis; (2) a description of the methods used, including who the participants were and what equipment or instruments were used; (3) a description of the results, which may include tables and graphs to present summaries and analyses of numerical data; and (4) a discussion of the significance of the results. Sometimes the results and the discussion of their significance are combined. This genre is very familiar in the social sciences, and it is popular for reporting quantitative research because it makes very clear to the reader how the writer arrived at conclusions. The reader can easily find the information necessary to judge whether or not the results permit you to draw the inferences you make in the discussion.

Writing about qualitative data is more difficult for reasons already mentioned. There is often so much varied data to be analyzed that it is usually difficult to define a focus that lets you present it all systematically—unless you write a book. Even then, including all the data you've collected in a qualitative report is nearly impossible. Usually the best strategy is to generalize and then illustrate each generalization with some well-chosen details or a telling anecdote. Another strategy is to put some of your data in appendices to your report. Sometimes, some of the data can be quantified, and tables or figures can be devised to summarize it. Because you can't display the entire weight of the evidence nor all of the inferential processes that led you to draw your conclusions, readers may be more skeptical when reading a qualitative report. Your ability to persuade them that your conclusions are valid and reliable rests in large part on your rhetorical skill. You must make your argument as logically as you can and also create an ethos in your text of a credible and careful researcher.

You can easily find models of texts reporting qualitative observations, but they cannot be summarized here as neatly as the typical four-part article reporting quantitative research. In general, however, texts reporting qualitative research also have an introduction that presents a problem or question and then describes related research. They also include some information about methods, though it may not all be summarized in one section of the report. Results and interpretations of results are often intermingled, and they are not necessarily signaled with headings. Instead, unique headings may be used that name categories used in analyzing the data.

SUGGESTIONS FOR RESEARCH AND WRITING

1. Plan some kind of unobtrusive observation that will allow you to make a claim about typical human behavior. For example, this chapter repeatedly used the example of observing what people do when a stranger sits in the chair right next to them, rather than choosing a vacant chair further away. Working with two or three classmates, conduct such a study by sitting next to 30–40 strangers in a public place. Have one or more collaborators unobtrusively observe and record what the people do.

2. Who buys what at the supermarket? After making some initial observations of product displays and customers at a supermarket near where you live, formulate a hypothesis about the type of person who is most likely to buy a certain kind of product. For example, who buys frozen dinners the most—men or women? old or young? What kinds of dinners do they buy? Who buys the tabloids (newspapers that typically have headlines like "Woman gives birth to two-headed child after encounter with space alien") that line the aisle leading to the checkout stand? You could observe by posing as shoppers.

3. Identify one or more words that often have an unusual pronunciation in your region of the country. For example, in some regions, "bell" and "bale" and "hell" and "hail" might be pronounced the same. Plan a structured observation of pronunciation by writing a brief passage that you ask passers-by to stop and read aloud. As they read, notice what pronunciation they give to the target words and make a record. Or choose an object that has various names in your region. For example, a soft drink might be called a "coke" no matter what brand or flavor it is; but perhaps young people are more likely to call it that than older people are. Take the object in question to a busy place and stop people to ask them what they call it. Have a collaborator record answers and ages. See what generalizations you can make based on the data you collect.

4. Cell phones are now widely used at all times and in all places. Some people would like to see legal curbs on their use, and one prohibition frequently proposed is banning drivers from using their phones while driving. The reasons for this proposed ban frequently include the assertion that drivers using cell phones are more likely to violate rules of the road and to cause accidents or at least to disturb the orderly flow of traffic. Evidence to confirm or disprove this reasoning could be collected through observational research. Plan an observational study of drivers in a certain area to see whether those using cell phones do engage in more dangerous driving behavior. For example, you and other observers could station yourselves at stop lights and count the numbers of drivers using cell phones or not using cell phones. Every time you see a risky driving behavior, such as not slowing down adequately to stop for the red light or

not moving forward in a timely manner when the light turns green, you could note whether the driver is distracted by talking on the phone or not. Then by comparing numbers of cell-phone users with numbers of non-users, you would be able to state whether using the phone leads to more risky driving behavior.

REFERENCES

Fox, Kate. 2004. *Watching the English: The hidden rules of English behaviour.* London: Hodder.

Tannen, Deborah. 1990. Gender differences in conversational coherence: Physical alignment and topical cohesion. In *Conversational organization and its development*, ed. Bruce Dorval, 167–180. Norwood, NJ: Ablex.

7

SURVEYING

CHAPTER OVERVIEW

After reading this chapter, you should be able to answer the following questions:

1. What are the advantages and disadvantages of surveying as a method of inquiry?
2. What are the steps in designing a survey?
3. What does it mean to sample a population in a survey? What is the difference between random sampling and convenience sampling?
4. How does a researcher analyze the data from fixed-response questions? From open-ended ones?
5. What ethical issues may arise in survey research? How do you handle them responsibly?

Has a representative of an organization ever called you on the telephone to ask your opinion about a political candidate, a referendum on the ballot, or current issue in your community? Have you ever filled out a form to evaluate a teacher, a product you've purchased, or a service you've received? Has someone ever stopped you on campus, at the mall, or as you've emerged from the voting booth to see if you would answer a few questions about a university policy, about your shopping habits, or about how you just voted? If so, you have been a respondent in a survey.

Surveying is probably the most common method of research that social scientists use, if you include oral surveys along with written ones. Oral surveys can take the form of structured interviews with well-defined questions (called the interview schedule), and they can be conducted on the telephone as well as in face-to-face encounters. Written surveys are frequently called questionnaires. They too can be structured, asking questions that offer only fixed answers for the respondent to choose, or they can be open-ended, permitting respondents to answer as they wish. Questionnaires may be given to respondents in face-to-face settings, mailed to the respondents, or personally delivered to classrooms, homes, and workplaces to be picked up later.

ADVANTAGES OF SURVEYING

Many social scientists favor the survey method because it is the best way to get large numbers of responses in relatively short periods, usually at a reasonable cost. A large set of data is important when researchers want to draw generalizations that are valid for the whole population under investigation. However, many people don't want to take the time to complete a survey, so to get a response rate that is sufficiently large, researchers have to cast a broad net and be persistent. The best way to get people to participate in a survey is to make it short and easy to complete. When a representative sample of an entire population answers a survey, researchers can then generalize the results, making valid claims or predictions about people who didn't even participate in the survey. That is why each time there is a presidential election, the television reporters covering the election can project which candidate has won in each state even when only a small percentage of the voting districts have reported results. If one candidate has a clear majority in those districts, and if the districts are representative of the state as a whole, polling experts can quite accurately predict which candidate will receive the state's electoral votes.

Social scientists, particularly sociologists, also prefer surveying because it is probably the best way to learn about people's attitudes, beliefs, and practices. Researchers assume it is fairly likely that the respondents will answer truthfully, particularly if they are sure that their identity will remain anonymous. For sensitive topics, a written survey is probably more reliable than an oral one, because respondents are more likely to answer questions candidly in writing than they are in a face-to-face interview, in which they might be embarrassed to reveal their true attitudes or opinions. With a written survey respondents are also less likely to answer the way they think the investigator wants them to. Finally, filling out a questionnaire affords the respondent more time to think, and perhaps even to consult with others or to check records in order to give the most complete and correct answer.

DISADVANTAGES OF SURVEYING

Despite its advantages, surveying has some limitations as well. Some of these are inherent in the method. What researchers gain in breadth of sampling and generalizability of results, they often lose in depth of information. The data from a survey are seldom as complex and subtle as those from interview and observation, for example. With a survey, there is little chance to learn about the contexts that may have influenced the respondents' answers. If the survey has only fixed-response questions, there is no chance to probe and learn more about the reasons for answers.

Other drawbacks of surveying are due to the human nature of the respondents. There is a chance that the respondents may either purposefully or inadvertently report something that is false. They may give answers they think the researcher wants, or they may change their answers in order to project a more favorable image of themselves. They may choose not to answer some of the questions. If the survey is very long, respondents may become tired or bored toward the end and give rushed or incomplete answers. With a telephone survey, people may simply hang up after answering a few questions or refuse to answer any at all. With a questionnaire mailed to a home or business, the intended respondent may not fill it out, but have someone else answer it instead. Often, mailed questionnaires are simply not returned because taking time to do a favor for an unknown researcher is simply not a priority in most people's lives. Those questionnaires that are returned may represent a somewhat biased sample because they come from respondents who are eager to comply and who want to make their answers known. Many of these limitations can be overcome, however, if the researcher follows some basic principles of survey design and uses care in selecting a sample of people to answer the survey.

DESIGNING A SURVEY

You can design a good survey if you will observe some basic instructions about defining your purpose and writing good questions and clear directions that help you achieve your purpose.

DEFINE YOUR PURPOSE

As with any method, the first step in designing a survey is to define your purpose. You might state it as a question, such as this: "To what extent do people's eating habits and exercise practices coincide with their knowledge about sound nutrition and good exercise habits?" Or you might state it as a hypothesis, such as this: "People who know more about sound nutrition and good exercise habits are more likely than those who don't to eat a balanced diet of daily recommended servings from the food pyramid and exercise for at least 30 minutes 3–4 times a week." Notice that the hypothesis is stated more specifically than the question. Typically, beginning with a hypothesis implies that you will later do some statistical tests to determine whether or not you can confirm or must reject the hypothesis; in order to do the statistical calculations, you must have clearly defined variables to measure and relate. Whether you start with a question or a hypothesis, however, you will find that the way you state your purpose suggests the kinds of questions you must ask. There are basically three kinds of questions you can write.

CREATE DEMOGRAPHIC QUESTIONS

A standard part of almost every survey is questions about what sociologists call the *demographics* of the respondents. These might include questions about the respondent's age, gender, race or ethnicity, occupation, income, education, political and religious affiliation, and so on. Researchers ask about these matters when they want to compare the answers of identifiable groups in order to determine whether or not membership in the group somehow influences the opinions, attitudes, or practices of an individual. So, for example, if political pollsters wanted to find out which gender, which regions of the country, and which income groups vote Democratic more often, they would create questions that allow them to sort the respondents by those categories and compare their overall answers to other questions about voting.

Demographic questions are fairly easy to ask. Normally, they are fixed-response questions because the researcher can usually anticipate accurately all the demographic categories the respondents will fall into. The researcher can then just instruct respondents to check a box or circle a word that corresponds to a particular demographic fact about themselves.

Suppose you wanted to survey students on your campus about how their knowledge compares to their practices in eating and exercising. What demographic groups might you want to compare? It might be interesting to compare men with women, dorm-dwellers with off-campus residents, or juniors and seniors with sophomores and freshmen. If students take a required health and fitness course, it would certainly be interesting to see if students who have already had this course practice better eating and exercise habits than students who haven't had the course. Notice that once you start looking at your respondents by demographic categories, you create sub-questions to answer or additional hypotheses to test. Be sure to write adequate demographic questions that will allow you to sort the responses according to your purposes.

CREATE FIXED-RESPONSE QUESTIONS

As the name implies, a fixed-response question has a limited number of answers a respondent can choose. It is sort of like a multiple-choice question on a test, except it doesn't have one right answer. Instead, you try to think of the range of possible answers that people could give, and you list them all. That way, people only have to check a box or circle the answer that they would give.

Taking our hypothetical survey again as an example, you might ask a question like this to find out how often people exercise.

1. On average, how many times a week do you exercise for at least 30 minutes?
   a. none
   b. 1–2 times
   c. 3–4 times
   d. more than 4 times

Notice that with just four responses you have anticipated all the possible answers respondents could give: In a week, they either exercise or they don't; and if they do, they do it 1 or more times a week. By specifying a range that each respondent would fall into, you make it easy for them to answer quickly. Not only that, but you make it easy for yourself to later tabulate and analyze the responses—a particular advantage of the fixed-response question.

Sometimes you can't anticipate every possible response, but you can still write a mostly fixed-response question by creating categories and offering respondents the option of filling in a blank with answers you can't anticipate. Here is an example:

2. What kind of exercise do you usually do?
   a. individual (e.g., walking, swimming, jogging, biking)
   b. compete against an opponent (e.g., tennis, racquetball)
   c. play a team sport (e.g., basketball, soccer, volleyball)
   d. other (please explain) _____
   e. I don't exercise.

But as you will note, question 2 may be worded ambiguously. Perhaps someone who plays pick-up basketball at the gym three afternoons a week won't be able to decide if that really counts as playing a team sport or if it's just a way of getting a good work-out. Another problem with fixed-response questions is that they may force respondents into a choice that they wouldn't give if the question were open-ended. In that case, respondents may choose the answer that comes closest to the one they want to give, or they may leave the question unanswered. Ideally, fixed-response questions should be pilot-tested so that the researcher can see whether respondents interpret them in ways not intended or otherwise demonstrate that they had difficulty answering the question as it is presently worded.

WRITE OPEN-ENDED QUESTIONS

As the name implies, an open-ended question does not give answers for the respondent to choose. Instead, the questionnaire simply provides a space for the respondent to write what they want to reply; or, if it's an oral survey, the interviewer writes down whatever the respondent says. Here's an example of an open-ended question from our hypothetical survey of knowledge vs. practice in eating and exercise:

> 3. What would motivate you to be more conscientious about following healthy eating and exercise practices?

Questions like this are good for getting qualitative data, with all its nuances. But most surveys use only a few such questions because, as you might guess, they are time-consuming and difficult to analyze and categorize. Sometimes, pilot testing of open-ended questions may reveal that respondents' answers fall into some well-defined categories. In that case, often a fixed-response question can be written to replace an open-ended one.

WRITE UNAMBIGUOUS QUESTIONS

Experienced survey designers have learned to avoid some mistakes in writing questions so that they don't get confusing data. One of these mistakes is the "double-barreled" question. Although such a question appears to be asking for one thing, it is actually asking two things at once. For example, this question at first appears to be about frequency:

> Do you often suffer from anxiety or depression?
> a. yes
> b. no

Suppose it is read by a person who suffers often from anxiety, but not depression. How should they answer it? Suppose they answer it with a "yes." When the investigators analyze the results, they won't know whether the person suffers from anxiety, depression, or both. A muddled question will give muddled results that don't permit you to draw valid conclusions. This double-barreled question would have to be split into two questions—one about anxiety and one about depression.

But you will probably have noted another problem with the question above: How frequently is "often"? Suppose a woman who answers "yes" suffers from depression about three times a year—too often in her opinion. Suppose a man who also suffers from depression about three times a year answers "no" because three times seems infrequent to him. Words referring to time, such as *often, frequently, seldom, occasionally,* and words referring to amounts (*much* or *many*) or degrees (*a lot* or *somewhat*) must be specific enough that people who give the same answer will have similar understandings and will be indicating similar things about themselves. A good way to offer specific choices is to give a range. For example, rather than ask the question about depression this way,

> How frequently do you feel depressed?
> a. never
> b. occasionally
> c. sometimes
> d. frequently

Ask it this way,

> 1. On average, how many days a month do you feel depressed?
>   a. 0–1
>   b. 2–3 days
>   c. 4–7 days
>   d. more than 8

DETERMINE THE ORDER OF QUESTIONS

Another thing you must consider is how to order the questions in your survey. Should you start with demographic questions or end with them? It depends. If the rest of the questionnaire is about sensitive issues or is actually quite dull, you could start with demographic questions because they are usually non-threatening and easy to answer; they get the respondent involved in completing the questionnaire. On the other hand, you could end with them if the main survey questions are on an interesting topic and respondents will be motivated to begin answering them right away. In general, the main questions should follow a sequence that you have reasoned out carefully, rather than being put in a random order.

Sometimes not all questions will apply to all respondents. In that case, you can devise screening questions or directions that tell respondents which question to answer next depending on the answer they have just chosen. For example, suppose in our hypothetical survey on diet and exercise, you planned to ask five questions about exercise, beginning with the example question on frequency of exercise. If respondents chose the answer "never" on question 1, they could be directed to skip to question 6, where the questions on eating habits would begin.

WRITE CLEAR DIRECTIONS

Although directions should come first in your survey, you may wait to write them last. Most people will be curious about what the survey is for, who is conducting it, and how the results will be used; they usually want to be assured also that their answers will remain anonymous. They will be more inclined to cooperate with you if you are open about these matters. You should satisfy their curiosity with a brief, general statement about your purpose and at the same time get their informed consent to use the data they give you (see Chapter 3 and Chapter 10). Your informed consent statement might look something like this:

> We are three students in English 315 conducting this survey to determine students' knowledge and practices in eating and exercise. We will use the data collected to write a paper for the course. You have been chosen to participate because you are a student at BYU. It will take about 5 minutes to complete this survey. There are no known risks or benefits from participation in this study. You may refuse to participate, and you may withdraw at any time without penalty. We will not reveal the identity of any participants in our survey. By completing this survey, you signify your consent to let us use the data in our study. If you have questions about the research, you may contact Dr. Karen Hendriksen at 422-4775; if you have questions about your rights as a research participant, you may contact Dr. William Smith at 422-3987.

Besides writing the initial explanation, you must write clear directions about how you want the respondents to answer questions in each part of your survey. For example, you might write, "Circle the answer that best describes what you do" or "Place an X next to the answer that most closely corresponds to your attitude" or "Fill in the blank with your answer."

FINDING RESPONDENTS

Once you have designed your survey—and, if possible, pilot tested and revised it—the next step is to find respondents for the final study. If you were conducting the study of college students' exercise and eating habits, it wouldn't be practical or necessary to survey every student on campus. Instead, you would need to survey only a sampling of the students. Professionals who conduct surveys place a high priority on getting a *representative sample* of people from the population under investigation. If they can survey a small percentage of the entire population, and if that sample is representative of the whole, then they can save the time and money it would take to survey everyone. And they can confidently generalize the results to the whole—usually allowing, however, for a small margin of error.

Undergraduate students learning how to do survey research, however, are not as likely as professionals to be able to get a representative sample because students generally lack the time and resources to identify and contact a truly representative sample. Because a complete discussion of sampling is beyond the scope of this book, only a brief summary of the main points of sampling is presented here so that you will understand what is involved in getting a representative sample.

RANDOM SAMPLING

A representative sample is a *random sample*. In a random sample, every *unit* (person, family, classroom, etc.) in the entire population has the same chance of being chosen to participate in the survey. To draw a random sample, researchers first must identify all the units in the population. In our example on eating and exercise, the units would be students on your campus. Suppose there are 15,000 students in all. With the proper authorization, you might be able to obtain a master list of every student enrolled at the institution. You might also safely use the student telephone directory. Although not every student may have a telephone, in this case the chances of bias are small. You could then randomly choose a predetermined number of students—say 100—whom you would ask to participate in the survey.

To randomly draw names from the master list or telephone directory, you could use several methods: You could number all the names and use a random number table to select 100 numbers between 1 and 15,000; then you would choose the 100 names that correspond to the random numbers. A faster and easier method would be to draw a systematic sample. Because you need 100 names from 15,000, you could take every one hundred-fiftieth name from the list, after first determining a random starting point. To do this, you would again use a random number table to select a number between 1 and 150. Suppose you selected the number 20; you would take the 20th name; then you would choose the 170th name, the 320th name, and so on, until you had chosen 100 names. After randomly selecting names, you would be ready to contact the people chosen to ask them to participate in your survey.

As you can see, if you used random sampling, you would spend a fair amount of time identifying respondents; then you would have to spend more time phoning, writing, or visiting them to see if they would participate in your survey. If the results of your survey are to be published or if an important decision will be made based on the results, it is crucial for you to use random sampling. If time is short, however, and your purpose is mainly to gather data for the experience of analyzing it and writing a report for a class, random sampling may not be as critical.

CONVENIENCE SAMPLING

Depending on your purpose and your teacher's instructions, you may be able to conduct survey research using a non-random sample. This kind of sample is also called a "convenience sample." As the name implies, you would survey respondents who are conveniently available during the time you must gather your data. You could simply survey your friends or all of your neighbors in a single apartment building or dorm. However, doing so might give you very similar answers to your questions, if you choose your friends or neighbors on the basis of their similarity to you. It might be better to survey a broader cross-section of the population you are interested in, one that would represent more variety than just the people you associate with most often.

For example, suppose you were conducting the eating and exercise habits survey; you could try to get a sample of students that is likely to include students from both genders and from various classes, majors, and ages. To avoid choosing mostly physical education majors for your survey, you shouldn't hand out your survey only in the engineering building. Instead, you could approach students in the various buildings on campus to increase the likelihood of surveying students in fine arts, humanities, social sciences, P.E., and so forth. If you know some professors who would permit you to, you could pass out a questionnaire in courses that are likely to include various kinds of students. Although you couldn't be confident that your results are generalizable from a convenience sample, you could still have the experience of collecting data from a broad sample of people, then analyzing and writing about it.

SAMPLE SIZE

How big a sample do you need? There is no pat answer to this question. The size depends on several factors, including how diverse the population is, the purpose of the research, the available time and resources, and the degree of accuracy needed. The more heterogeneous a population is, usually the bigger the sample size needed to include representatives of each type. The more important the research is and the more it must be accurate and generalizable, the more it should be based on a large enough sample to minimize the margin of error. After determining an appropriate sample size for your study, you should increase the number by five or ten to insure that you will have enough after you set aside incomplete or improperly completed surveys.

CONDUCTING THE SURVEY

Once you have determined how to select respondents, how you actually obtain answers from them depends on whether you have planned an oral or a written survey. A written survey can be printed or it can be electronic. An oral survey can be conducted by telephone or face-to-face.

If you conduct the survey orally, either on the telephone or face-to-face, you ask your respondents to listen to you read each question. If you have written fixed-response questions, you also read the answers and then write down the answer the respondent chooses. For open-ended questions, you write down whatever the respondent says, abbreviating parts of the answer to save time. When reading questions to the respondent, you must take care not to indicate by your tone of voice or body language a preference for a certain answer. The respondent may be able to sense the answer you favor and choose it just to please you. You should also not reveal your approval if the answer is one that you like or your disapproval when a respondent gives a reply that you find unappealing. You must make every effort to remain neutral about the topic during the entire process of reading the survey questions.

If you hand respondents a written copy of your survey, you don't have to worry about unduly influencing them by your intonation or body language. You should, however, not hover about, looking over their shoulders while they fill it out. Create an atmosphere in which they feel free to answer candidly. Be prepared to give simple, clear directions about the purposes of the survey and how to answer the questions when you hand the copy to the respondents. If they ask for clarification during the time they are filling it out, try to give simple answers that focus on the meaning of the question, not on how you expect or want them to answer.

If you want to survey a broader sample of people than you can get in your local area, you can either mail written surveys to potential respondents or you can post an electronic survey on a Web site and contact potential respondents via e-mail. You can give the potential respondents a URL and ask them to click on it and fill out the survey. To create an electronic survey, you can use commercially available software, usually for a fee, or you can use your own computer know-how to create the instrument. Commercial services also provide the option of tabulating the data electronically and making tables and graphs from the results.

ANALYZING THE DATA

When you have collected your data, you can begin tabulating it. If you have asked mostly fixed-response questions, it is not difficult to simply count the number of respondents who chose a given answer on each question. You can use a computer spreadsheet to enter the raw data. If you have asked some open-ended questions, you should read through the answers once quickly to get a sense of the range of answers. You may discern repeated or similar answers immediately that suggest categories you can sort the open-ended answers into. However, it may take more than one reading to see a pattern in the data provided by the open-ended questions. Perhaps only a very faint pattern will be evident, if respondents' ideas or opinions are quite diverse.

The more questions you have asked and the more respondents you have included in your survey, obviously the more time you will need to spend consolidating the data into categories of answers. Once you have total figures, you can use the spreadsheet to calculate percentages of respondents who chose each answer; your readers will find percentages more meaningful than raw numbers. If your aim is simply to describe what you found, the numerical operations you need to perform can stop with percentages and averages. However, if you want to compare numbers to see if they are significantly different, or if you want to compare responses from different sub-groups in your sample, you will have to have some statistical expertise. If you know how, or if you know someone who will help you, you can enter your data into computer programs designed to cross-tabulate data, perform different statistical tests, and determine the statistical significance of your findings. You can also use computer software to create tables and graphs presenting your results. It is beyond the scope of this book to explain statistics, but if you have learned how to use inferential statistics in other courses, by all means try to do a more sophisticated analysis of your data.

WRITING THE REPORT

Survey research is frequently, but not always, reported in the four-part format characteristic of the research report genre, which typically uses the headings "Introduction," "Methods," "Results," and "Discussion." In the readings section at the end of this book, you will find a report of survey research entitled "An Analysis of Career and Educational Goals of BYU Music Majors" which mainly takes this form. However, the authors, Joseph Hoffman and Crystal Young, use additional subheadings in the Results section to break down the goals of the music majors they surveyed. Also, the final section of their report is called "Recommendations" rather than "Discussion," and it also uses additional subheadings that indicate the nature of the recommendations.

The form you present your findings in will depend on your purpose and your audience. Even if you don't choose the standard form, however, your report should still provide a context for the problem you've investigated, then describe who your respondents were and how you collected data from them. It should also present and discuss your results, either separately or together. If your survey elicits quantitative data, you will almost certainly want to present results in tables and graphs, as these make comparisons and trends much more obvious than words do (see Chapter 16). If your results are complex and fall into different categories, consider creating unique headings and subheadings for each section of your report in which you describe a new category of findings.

In the readings section at the end of this book, you will also find selections from *Soul Searching: The Religious and Spiritual Lives of American Teenagers*, written by Christian Smith with Melinda Lundquist Denton. This book reports the findings of the National Study of Youth and Religion (NSYR), the most comprehensive and specific study ever undertaken of American teenagers' religious beliefs, attitudes, and practices. The results come mainly from a nationwide telephone survey of teens and their parents conducted between July 2002 and April 2003 at the University of North Carolina, Chapel Hill. The researchers used a random-digit-dialing method (RDD) to contact a representative sample of 3,290 US households in which there was at least one teen between the ages of 13 and 17. (About 14 percent of all US households have a teen in this age group.) The method assured that there was equal representation of unlisted, listed, and not-yet-listed telephone numbers. In each household, the parent who had the most recent birthday was asked questions for 30 minutes, and one randomly selected teen was questioned for 50 minutes. Following the survey in the spring and summer of 2003, seventeen trained researchers from the NSYR selected a sub-sample of 267 of the telephone respondents for in-depth face-to-face interviews, which were conducted in 45 states. The interview sample was calculated to represent a broad range of difference in teens' religious affiliation, age, race, sex, socioeconomic status, place of residence (urban, suburban, rural), region of the country, and language (English or Spanish). The researchers claim that, using their methods, "the data collected provide for a dependable, representative description and analysis of the contours and character of adolescent religion and spirituality in the United States today" (7). The selections you will read come from Chapter 2, "Mapping the Big Picture," which contains many tables showing the demographics of the sample and comparing religious influences, practices, and beliefs of teens from various denominations.

SUGGESTIONS FOR RESEARCH AND WRITING

1. There is frequently a gap between what people know they should do and what they actually do. In this chapter one of those possible gaps concerned what students know about a healthy diet and exercise regimen and what they actually do. There are many other such gaps between knowledge and action, for example in recycling and conserving resources, in time management and study habits, in smoking, or in drinking alcohol. Working with one or two classmates, identify a potential gap between knowledge and action that you would like to study and plan a survey to gather data that will help you learn whether the gap exists in a population of interest to you.

2. What do students at your institution think about administrative or social and cultural issues on your campus? For example, what is their attitude toward administrative policies on admissions, enrollment, tuition and fees, grading, parking, and so forth? Or what do students think of trends in music, fashion, dating, dance, cinema, and so on? Design and conduct a survey that will identify student attitudes.

3. One of the complaints leveled at the American educational system is that students learn so little of world geography. How informed are students on your campus about geography and its relationship to international politics? To find out, you could give a students a kind of survey that tests how many would be able to locate correctly on a map countries that are currently in the news. Or, taking a different approach, you could find out how many would be able to specify the continent a particular country is on.

4. What is a currently debated state or national political issue? How informed are students on your campus about this issue? What opinions do they hold about a given political candidate or a proposal that will be on the ballot? Design and conduct a survey to answer one or more questions of interest. What conclusions can you draw about the political knowledge of students on your campus?

REFERENCE

Smith, Christian, with Melinda Lundquist Denton. 2005. *Soul searching: The religious and spiritual lives of American teenagers*. New York: Oxford University Press.

8

EXPERIMENTING

CHAPTER OVERVIEW

After reading this chapter, you should be able to answer the following questions:

1. What does it mean to say that an experiment is a "designed event"? What is the goal of most experiments?
2. What is an independent variable? What is a dependent variable? What is a hypothesis?
3. What are the steps in designing an experiment?
4. What is validity? What is reliability?

THE PURPOSE OF EXPERIMENTS

It could well be said that the ultimate goal of science is to explain what causes things to happen. In the biological and physical sciences, humans have made great strides in understanding such things as what happens when various elements are combined under certain conditions of temperature and pressure, how plants can be cross-bred or fertilized to produce better crop yields, or how genetic flaws cause certain diseases. Understanding causes and effects in nature puts humans in the favorable position of being able to partially control their environment, to produce better foods and medicines, and even to intervene in some natural processes to engineer more desirable results. Many of these achievements have been made possible through the method of inquiry known as experimenting.

Not surprisingly, the experiment is also widely used in the social sciences with the goal of establishing firm results that will help us to better understand how individuals and groups function and to create more productive and healthful social environments. The experiment is sometimes considered the most scientific of methods because it aims to determine the cause-and-effect relationship, if any, between a *dependent variable* and one or more *independent variables*. One way to keep these two kinds of variables straight is to think of the independent variable as a possible cause and the dependent variable as an effect. The independent variable is manipulated; the dependent variable follows from this manipulation.

As an illustration of how an experiment can determine the relationship between two variables, consider a famous example from the social sciences, Stanley Milgram's (1974) experiments on obedience. It is important to understand that Milgram's experiments would today likely be considered unethical, but they provide a useful paradigm for describing the experimental method. Milgram chose willingness to obey authority as the dependent variable that he wanted to measure. He devised experiments in which he led participants to believe that they must obey a researcher's orders to administer 30 electric shocks of increasing levels of intensity to another person. (The person supposedly receiving the shocks was actually a knowledgeable confederate in the experiment, but none of the participants knew it at the time.) Milgram designed one series of experiments to see if willingness to obey varied as he manipulated an independent variable, closeness of the "victim" to the person administering the shocks.

Milgram designed four different states of proximity between participants and victim—remote feedback, voice feedback, proximity, and touch-proximity—so that the auditory and visible evidence of the victim's "pain" would vary. He found that willingness to obey decreased as the distance between the participant and the victim also decreased. That is, when the participants could actually see and even touch the confederate, they were more likely to refuse to continue administering the shocks, and the experiment ended sooner. Milgram concluded there is a cause-and-effect relationship between people's willingness to obey morally questionable orders and their ability to have an immediate and clear perception of what happens to those victimized by their obedience.

Perhaps to you Milgram's experiment simply verifies common sense or confirms your experience. It seems to stand to reason that most people would not willingly inflict great harm on others. But the fact that the participants in Milgram's experiments would obey orders up to a certain point under all four proximity conditions may tell you something you wouldn't have thought about human nature—something that believers in the experimental method would say has now been demonstrated conclusively. This cause-and-effect demonstration confers on Milgram's conclusion the status of being more definitive than a hunch, more scientific than common sense. When conclusions have this scientific status, theoretically it becomes possible to explain human nature, to make some predictions about it, and to devise ways to enhance desirable behavior and to mitigate or eliminate undesirable behavior.

For these reasons, experimenting is an important method of social science research, one that has become increasingly sophisticated, generally requiring a budget and a knowledge of intricate statistical procedures to determine the nature and the significance of relationships between variables. It's not possible in a book of this size and scope to give anything more than a basic understanding of the steps in the experimental method. These include creating hypotheses and operational definitions, designing the experiment and implementing controls, selecting participants, establishing validity and reliability, and meeting ethical standards. As you read the following, consider the usefulness of the experimental method and the scope of its applicability in social science research. Think about whether or not an experiment would be an appropriate method to answer a research question you have.

STEPS AND CONSIDERATIONS IN CONDUCTING EXPERIMENTS

CREATING HYPOTHESES

Experimenters usually begin with a hypothesis—a prediction about the outcome of the experiment that can be accepted or rejected. A hypothesis is described as either directional or null. A directional hypothesis predicts that there will be a difference between two or more groups or treatments. For example, in an experiment on a new learning technique, researchers might hypothesize that there will be significantly better learning in the group that tries the technique than in a similar group that does not try it. If the researchers found that the experimental group did learn significantly better, their hypothesis would be confirmed. The same experiment could also be conducted with a null hypothesis, which would predict no difference between the two groups. If a difference were found, the null hypothesis would be rejected. Stating in advance what claim you want to confirm or reject allows you to design your experiment accordingly.

CREATING OPERATIONAL DEFINITIONS

A key factor in being able to eventually accept or reject a hypothesis is the way you operationally define the variables in your experiment. In his experiments, Milgram had to define the abstract concept of *obedience* operationally; that is, he had to have a way to observe and measure obedience. He devised a simulated shock generator with thirty switches on it, each switch apparently corresponding to a different level of voltage (no electricity was actually used, however). In the experiment participants were ordered to "shock" a victim by pressing switches on the control panel, starting with the lowest voltage and moving toward the highest. The number of switches each participant activated was observable and measurable, so, for the purposes of this experiment, the number of switches pressed was the operational definition of obedience. The more switches a participant pressed, the more obedient to authority he was. In any experiment you design, you will have to define the variables in such a way that you can observe them and quantify them. This means that you will have to devise a task in which the independent variable(s) and dependent variable can interact so you can determine their relationship, if any.

DESIGNING THE EXPERIMENT AND IMPLEMENTING CONTROLS

Because experiments are meant to determine cause-and-effect relationships, experiments are, as far as possible, designed events. That is, an experiment doesn't just happen of its own accord in a normally occurring setting; instead, the researcher must somehow manipulate the setting and, to some extent, the people in it in order to test a hypothesis about the relationship between a dependent variable and one or more independent variables. The experimenter designs a study that is suited to the research hypothesis and to the population being studied. The design helps the researcher control for the effect of other possible variables on the dependent variable because, in the end, the experimenter wants to attribute any change in the dependent variable to the independent variable(s) instead of to some other possible cause. Control over other variables is difficult to achieve in a naturally existing setting, so the experimenter designs procedures and creates settings that will permit a restricted focus on just the variables of interest. There are various kinds of designs possible for experiments; they have become so standard that they have names. Here are three very common experimental designs:

- *Classical design,* in which participants are randomly assigned to the experimental and control groups, and members of the experimental group are exposed to the independent variable(s) one or more times, then compared with the control group on measures of the dependent variable;

- *One-group pretest-posttest design,* in which there is only an experimental group, which is pretested before the introduction of the independent variable(s), then tested again after the treatment to see if there is a significant change in the dependent variable;

- *The ABA or time series design,* in which the researchers collect baseline data about the participants' behavior on the dependent variable during an initial time specified as "A," after which they introduce the independent variable during time "B"; then they withdraw the independent variable to see whether the behavior induced by it during time "B" persists during the second time "A."

There are several other basic designs that you can read about in research methods handbooks. Because various statistical procedures can be used with these designs, it is helpful to get the advice of a statistician at the time you plan an experiment so that you will choose the right design and record the right kind of data to use in statistical tests at the end of your study.

As a result of the need for control, some experiments take place in a laboratory setting where necessary equipment is available and experimental conditions are easy to achieve. As has often been noted, however, the laboratory setting isn't a natural context and therefore might itself introduce a variable into the experiment that could cause the participants to behave in a way they wouldn't behave in a more natural setting. For this reason, some cause-and-effect relationships demonstrated in a laboratory may cause suspicion, with readers wondering if the same result would hold in a naturally occurring setting.

Sometimes researchers conduct experiments in "the field"—not in a laboratory but wherever the variables they are interested in can be studied. They might go to a school, for example, or a hospital or workplace. By giving up their ability to control the environment, however, the researchers also give up some of their ability to control some variables. A variable that can't be completely controlled is sometimes called a *confound* to the design. That is, such a variable confounds the researchers' efforts to make an unambiguous inference about the cause-and-effect relationship between an independent and dependent variable. A number of possible confounds have been identified and categorized, including the following:

- **Maturation**—the possibility that a change in the dependent variable is simply due to the participants' maturing during the course of the experiment, not due to the introduction of the independent variable;

- **Attrition**—the possibility that a difference between experimental and control groups is due to some of the participants dropping out during the course of the research;

- **Instrument decay**—the possibility that the instruments the researchers are using to measure change are not as effective at the end of the experiment as at the beginning ("instrument" has a very broad meaning in this context and can include such things as the researchers' observations of the participants' behavior);

- **Testing effect**—in a pretest-posttest design, the effect of taking an initial test may be to familiarize participants with the nature of the posttest so that they will appear to have changed as a result of the independent variable, when in fact they have just become more skillful at test taking;

- **History**—the possibility that an uncontrollable event (e.g., a fire alarm sounding) affects the participants in such a way that the outcome of the experiment is changed;

- **Experimenter bias**—characteristics of the researcher, such as age, race, sex, clothing, or personality traits, that may affect how participants perform in the experiment.

It is important for researchers to be aware of these and other possible threats to validity when designing an experiment. Although they can't always be controlled completely, these confounds can sometimes be minimized if the researchers plan for and take steps to reduce their effect.

Selecting Participants

Experiments are a type of research that aim to permit broad generalization of the results. When researchers find a cause-and-effect relationship, they want to claim that the relationship will hold true for other similar people and events in other times and places. In order to generalize results, however, the researcher must select participants for an experiment who are representative of the entire population that the results will apply to. This means that, where possible, the researcher should select participants randomly. In random selection, every unit (a unit could be individuals, groups, families, classes, etc.) in the entire population being studied has an equal chance of being chosen for participation. The researcher should never intentionally select participants in such a way that the hypothesis will be verified or rejected according to the researcher's desires or prejudices.

Random samples are not always easy to achieve, however. In a study of children learning math with computers, for example, it would not be easy to randomly sort children into experimental and control groups because, in elementary schools, children are already grouped in classes that usually can't be broken up. A researcher could randomly sort whole classes of students into one treatment or the other, however, and could take other steps to estimate the comparability of the two groups. For example, by using personal data about the children and scores from earlier achievement and aptitude tests, the researcher could determine whether or not the classes sorted into the two treatment groups were roughly equal in all pertinent respects at the time the experiment began.

Sometimes, however, even this kind of random assignment of roughly equal groups isn't possible. Many social scientists working on college campuses recruit students as participants in their experiments. These students may participate because of various incentives: course requirements, the promise of extra credit, or small financial or material rewards. In these cases, the experimental results may not be generalizable to populations beyond college students; and sometimes they may not even generalize to all students. Often participants may simply volunteer, which could skew the results because people who like to volunteer for projects are usually different in personality traits from people who don't volunteer. The participants in Milgram's obedience experiments were volunteers who answered a newspaper ad. They represented a fairly good distribution of ages and social class, but they were mostly men, so perhaps the results cannot be generalized to women. Even when participants are representative, some experiments don't include enough participants to have a solid foundation for generalizing.

As a reader of experimental research, you should take note of sample selection techniques and sample size, using them to help you judge the reliability of the conclusions drawn. You may sometimes note that experimental research is still published even when the sample of participants isn't ideal in size or representativeness. You will probably also note that the authors of this research frequently hedge their conclusions with a number of qualifiers (e.g., "suggests," "seems to indicate," "given the constraints noted," "under these limited conditions," etc.) so as not to make their generalizations too sweeping.

ESTABLISHING VALIDITY AND RELIABILITY

Validity is a crucially important concept in experimental research. Briefly, validity means that a given research study has actually demonstrated what it purports to demonstrate. In other words, it means a claim is well supported by the evidence. As noted, the goal of experimental research is to claim precise cause-and-effect relationships between a limited number of variables. The experimenter achieves validity by carefully taking some of the steps already discussed: defining the variables operationally, designing the experiment appropriately, controlling for possible confounds, selecting participants as randomly as possible, assigning participants randomly to experimental or control conditions, and using appropriate statistical tests to analyze the data. But even with all these steps, the relationships between variables are not always so obvious that they immediately compel everyone's assent; instead, the relationships must usually be inferred from the data the experiment has generated. In every inference there is at least a slight "leap of faith" from the evidence to the conclusion, and there is seldom anything like 100 percent assurance that the leap is justified. The experimenter's goal is not only to make the leap as small as possible but also to show that a leap in only one direction is possible—one cause to one effect. Making this inference carefully will persuade others that the conclusion drawn is a valid one.

Reliability is another vitally important concept, one that contributes to validity. Reliability refers to the consistency and strength of a relationship between variables. One way to show that a perceived relationship between two variables is consistent is to replicate the experiment—that is, to do it again under similar conditions. When experimenters write about their research, they give many details about the methods they used—including who the subjects were, what instruments they used, and what procedures they followed—so that other experimenters can repeat the experiment if they choose to. If the same results can be obtained by researchers working independently, confidence in the first results is strengthened, and they are considered reliable.

Another way the experimenter demonstrates reliability is through two kinds of statistics: (1) measures of association and (2) measures of significance. A *measure of association* is a statistic that shows the strength or size of the relationship between any two variables. For example, one measure of association is a statistic called the Pearson product-moment correlation; when this correlation approaches 1.0, the researcher can be confident that there is a strong relationship between two variables. Another measure of association is analysis of variance; when this statistic shows that independent variable X explains 30% of the variation of dependent variable Y, for example, the researcher can be confident that X helps to cause Y.

A *measure of significance* shows how confident the researcher is that the results obtained were not due to chance. It is usually expressed as a confidence level, denoted by p, and is typically set at 0.05 or less. A p-value of 0.05 would mean that the researcher is 95% confident the observed relationship is significant—that is, due to a "real" causal relationship, not simply due to a chance association of the variables.

MEETING ETHICAL STANDARDS

Conducting research according to high ethical standards is important with any method of inquiry, but its importance seems to become more obvious with experimental inquiry. One reason is that experiments often require a temporary deception of participants so that they won't guess what the researcher's hypothesis is or what variables are being studied. When participants figure out what the experiment is about—or *think* they have it figured out—they may behave in the way they think the researcher wants them to, or, just to be perverse, in the exact opposite way they think the researcher wants them to. In either case, the validity of the study would be compromised because the relationship between the variables would be artificial rather than "real." Think for a moment about Milgram's experiments: If the participants hadn't believed they were really administering electric shocks to an innocent person, could Milgram have reported anything significant about obedience to authority?

There has been some debate about whether or not deception is justified. As noted in Chapter 3, using a ruse in an experiment to get participants to cooperate has generally been deemed acceptable if the deception is temporary and of a kind that is not likely to produce any lasting harmful effects on the participants. To ensure that deception is temporary, it has become standard practice to debrief participants immediately after a study to inform them of the purposes of the research; and to ensure that the participants will suffer no continuing distress from the experiment, the debriefing can also calm fears or soothe a ruffled ego. Even though the participants in Milgram's experiments were debriefed, it is still possible that they could have been upset by what happened during the experiment and haunted later by memories of themselves administering what they really believed were high voltage shocks to a person who apparently was suffering great pain.

Since institutional review boards were implemented, standards now require that human participants give their informed consent before they can take part in an experiment (see Chapter 3). Imagine how an IRB approval process and an informed consent form would have changed Milgram's experiment. An IRB, foreseeing the possible traumatic effects of the deception on the participants, would likely not have approved the study. And if each participant had signed an informed consent prior to beginning the experiment, they might have been easily able to figure out what the experiment was about, and then the results would not have been as valid or reliable.

As you can see, experiments may give the best data about real cause-and-effect relationships when the participants are kept somewhat in the dark about the experiment's purpose. Informed consent, however, means that the participants must know enough about the goal of the experiment that they can choose intelligently whether or not they want to be a part of it. The researcher has to strike a careful balance here in order to meet ethical standards yet also produce results that will be considered valid and reliable. If you plan an experiment, you will have to create an informed consent document that adequately reveals the general nature of what you are trying to study, and you will have to submit your informed consent document and a thorough description of your planned experiment for IRB approval before you can proceed. How to do all of this is explained in detail in Chapter 10.

WRITING ABOUT EXPERIMENTS

When professionals write reports of experiments, they usually organize the report in four main parts, most often signaled by these headings: Introduction, Methods, Results, Discussion. In addition to these four main parts, there is often an abstract (a summary) at the beginning of an article, immediately after the title, and a bibliographic list of references to related literature at the end of the report. These divisions typify a genre that is part of a long tradition in the sciences. Using the genre conventions of the experimental report is part of writing persuasively about the experiment, part of establishing validity. Readers have come to expect that experimental results will be communicated in a certain way, and meeting these expectations is one way researchers can enhance the persuasiveness of their conclusions.

In the introduction, the writer usually begins by focusing on the general topic of investigation and by reviewing what previous research on this topic has already shown. The writer next typically shows how there is a need for a certain kind of additional research on this topic by stating what previous research hasn't found. The writer then states the hypothesis that was tested in the present study.

In the methods section, the writer describes the participants and tells how they were selected, identifies any instruments used, and describes the procedures that were followed to gather data. As noted earlier in the chapter, the details in this section are meant to help any reader who wanted to replicate the experiment. Even if no one replicates the experiment, however, readers want to know how the experiment was done because methodological correctness contributes to the validity and reliability of the findings.

In the results section, the writer presents the findings, showing the numerical values for the variables that were studied and the results of the statistical tests that were performed. This part of the report often uses tables and figures to present results in a compact visual form that is easy to understand at a glance. Providing statistical evidence that the variables were measured reliably is an important part of the rhetoric of experimental research. The right numbers, achieved by correct procedures and calculated accurately, are highly persuasive to readers who accept the assumptions of experimental research.

Finally, in the discussion section, the writer interprets the findings, showing how they do or do not support the hypothesis. Frequently, the discussion refers again to previous research, showing how the present study corroborates, contradicts, extends, or modifies what previous researchers have already demonstrated. In this section, too, the writer might note ambiguities and problems with the present research or additional questions that the research now raises, then propose further research that would resolve these problems and answer these questions.

Given this lengthy description of the typical experimental article, it may surprise you to note that there is no example of just such an experimental article in this book. One reason for that is that experimental reports are often full of difficult theoretical and statistical jargon that make them hard for relatively young social scientists from many different fields to understand. So it is very difficult to find an experimental report on a topic that appeals to a broad audience and is simple and short enough to include. Instead, in the readings section at the end of this book, you will find a rather unusual retrospective discussion of an experiment known as the Stanford Prison Experiment, or SPE. This experiment was conducted by Philip Zimbardo and his associates in 1971. The experimenters wrote several articles based on this experiment, at least one of which was a standard scientific report. But because of the nature of the research and the shocking findings (which were similar to Milgram's), the researchers wrote about it for general audiences in a way lay readers could understand. They did this, Zimbardo (2000) explains, because it is important "for psychological researchers who are concerned about the utility of their findings and the practical applications of their methods or conclusions to go beyond the role constraints of academic researcher to become advocates for social change. We must acknowledge the value-laden nature of some kinds of research that force investigators out of their stance of objective neutrality into the realm of activism as partisans for spreading the word of their research to the public and to those who might be able to implement its recommendations through policy actions" (209). What was learned from the Stanford Prison Experiment is probably much more valuable than the intricacies of the methods employed. This reading is a good example of how social scientists can write in such a way that their work really matters to the public, rather than just adding to the length of their resume.

SUGGESTIONS FOR RESEARCH AND WRITING

1. What foods do college students generally consume often? How important is price to them? Peanut butter, pizza, chips, and soft drinks are all possible candidates for an experimental taste test. Design an experiment that would let you conclude whether or not students on your campus judge the more expensive product as better-tasting than the inexpensive one in a blind taste test.

2. Do students automatically assume that male professors are more competent than female professors who work in the same discipline and have the same qualifications and rank? Design an experiment in which you test the hypothesis that students do make this assumption. One way to do this would be to find or write a brief article on an academic topic and reproduce it for a selected number of participants. On half of the copies of the article you could attach a description of a hypothetical male professor who you would say wrote it; on the other half, you could attach the same description, but say that a female professor wrote it. You could randomly assign participants to read a version of the article and then rate it on a list of qualities related to academic competence. By comparing the ratings, you could determine whether or not your hypothesis was supported.

3. To what extent do an attractive face and figure influence people's judgments of someone's qualifications for a job? Design an experiment in which you could test the hypothesis that when other qualifications are equal, the more attractive person in a pair of people will be preferred for a job. (This experiment could be done by having participants look at pairs of pictures, in which one member of the pair is more attractive than the other, but accompanying descriptions of each one's qualifications show them to be equally suited for the hypothetical job.)

4. Look in the professional journals in your major field to find a simple experiment that you could replicate—one that doesn't require a lot of expertise, time, equipment, or money to do. Conduct the experiment and write a report, using the earlier study as a model.

REFERENCES

Milgram, Stanley. 1974. *Obedience to authority: An experimental view.* New York: Harper & Row.

Zimbardo, Philip G., Christina Maslach, and Craig Haney. 2000. Reflections on the Stanford Prison Experiment: Genesis, transformations, consequences. In *Obedience to authority: Current perspectives on the Milgram paradigm,* ed. Thomas Blass, 193–237. Mahwah, NJ: Lawrence Erlbaum Associates.

9

RESEARCHING IN THE LIBRARY AND ON THE INTERNET

CHAPTER OVERVIEW

After reading this chapter, you should be able to answer the following questions:

1. What are directional sources? How do you use directional sources in the library to help you find informational sources?
2. What kinds of informational sources can you find in a library?
3. How can you use search engines and subject directories to retrieve information from the World Wide Web?
4. How do you evaluate the reliability of library sources? Of World Wide Web sources?
5. How can you quickly determine whether a print source will be useful to you in your research?

The development of libraries as places for categorizing, storing, and retrieving information has been of immense importance in the progress of human civilization, allowing today's scholars to build on the work of past ones. Without libraries to organize and store the bodies of knowledge each discipline develops, the collaborative enterprise of science would be more difficult to carry out. In the last 100 years, libraries have had to cope with an amazing explosion of knowledge as various university disciplines have become increasingly specialized and as technologies for producing printed texts have improved. The proliferation of publications has increased costs for libraries, as they have attempted to continue buying the latest books, subscribing to the ever-increasing number of periodicals, and adding to their shelf space.

Now, as digital information is starting to supersede printed texts in some ways, libraries are no longer places that simply catalog and shelve books, journals, and other documents. Increasingly, they are places where you can use computerized catalogs and databases to help you locate and retrieve information that may not even be on the library's shelves. The library spends thousands of dollars annually to subscribe to databases, i.e., indexes to periodicals and other documents, that were formerly available only in print but are now supplied via the Internet. These databases have been carefully compiled to help you retrieve peer-reviewed information from reputable sources. They have made research both easier and more sophisticated: easier because you can search in a matter of minutes for relevant documents by typing keywords into a computer and getting multiple "hits" from your search, and more sophisticated because the software tools allow you to search combined databases and quickly narrow or broaden your search as needed.

Even though you use the Internet to access the library's databases and catalogs, you should not confuse searching them with using search engines to locate information on the World Wide Web. (Note that although the word "Internet" is often used synonymously with "World Wide Web," the Internet is the navigation system by which you can access the World Wide Web. The Internet is like the US Interstate system of highways, while the sites that make up the World Wide Web are like all the cities and towns that are connected by the information highway, as the Internet is sometimes called.) True, some sites on the Web are created and maintained by researchers and organizations that aim to share the latest findings, statistics, evidence, or data, but the Web should generally be last place you look, not the first, when you have an assignment to do academic research. Much of what you retrieve using a Web search engine on the Internet will be of questionable value. By turning to the library first, you increase your chances of finding information that is of high quality; by turning to the World Wide Web second, you will be able to judge the quality of the information you find there in light of what you have first located by searching library indexes.

Because computer technologies change so rapidly, this chapter will focus more on principles and processes than on naming various databases or other research tools you should know about. After reading this chapter to gain an understanding of steps to follow when researching in the library and on the Internet, you should attend the library mini-course that is offered in your field. The subject specialist librarian who teaches the mini-course will teach you how to locate and use the latest research tools in your field.

WHY DO LIBRARY RESEARCH?

Professors frequently assign a library research paper in order to involve students more deeply in the subject matter of a particular course. Completing a library paper requires you to read books and periodicals that are likely very different from the textbooks you read for your courses. The reading you do for a library research paper can also acquaint you more intimately than a textbook does with the community of scholars in your field, with the kinds of knowledge your field values, the methods it uses to create knowledge, and its ways of organizing and expressing that knowledge in written form. As you read the articles published in your field's latest journals, you will begin to see what important questions are driving the current research; you will notice who the major researchers are; you will begin to discern how one study incorporates findings from other studies and then spawns even more studies; and you will notice the rhetoric typical of your field. In short, if you are observant as you do library research—if you think of it as getting acquainted with the members and practices of an intellectual community you want to join, instead of as a hoop you must jump through for a grade—you can learn much about becoming a professional in your field.

Library research is a kind of prewriting, but because it is much more involved and time-consuming than other prewriting techniques such as brainstorming, clustering, or freewriting, this entire chapter is devoted to how to do it. Library research papers always require you to take these five steps: (1) *find*, (2) *evaluate*, (3) *plan*, (4) *record*, and (5) *synthesize* information from sources. In this chapter you will learn about what is involved in the first two steps. You will learn about the other three steps in Chapter 11.

FINDING INFORMATION IN THE LIBRARY

Good library research starts with a question you want to answer. At first your question might be rather broad and ill-defined, but you will be able to narrow and focus it as you learn more through your research. To answer your question, you must first locate sources that contain pertinent information. Library sources can be categorized into two broad classes:

- *directional sources,* such as thesauruses, databases, online catalogs, indexes, and bibliographies
- *informational sources,* such as books and periodicals, but sometimes also databases and other reference works

Directional sources point you to informational sources. There is often some overlap between these two categories; for example, a specialized encyclopedia can be both an informational source about a topic like psychotherapy and a directional source if the entry on psychotherapy includes a bibliography of works you could consult for more information. Likewise, a database can direct you to a source and sometimes help you retrieve the full text at the same time. Because you ultimately want to locate the best informational sources for your question, you must first understand the following steps in using the directional sources available.

LOCATE SEARCH TERMS

A productive search for information begins with defining the terms that will help you locate sources. After you have chosen your topic and have broken it down into key concepts, you need to identify keywords in those concepts that you can use to search databases, catalogs, and other indexes. To do this you should use subject headings lists and thesauruses to find the terms used by professionals to refer to the concepts you want to research. Taking the time to consult these sources will provide you with richer, more in-depth results. For example, you could waste a lot of time and turn up very few sources using "nervous breakdown" as a search term because in the professional literature the concept you want to learn about is described by the term "mental disorders."

A very authoritative directional source that provides you with search terminology is the *Library of Congress Subject Headings List* (*LCSH*). The volumes of this large, red-bound book can be found in the reference area of the library. Say, for example, that your overall goal is to answer the question, "What are the factors that predispose teenagers to join gangs?" As you look in the *LCSH* under such headings as "crime" and "gangs" you will see other terms that you can use to locate information that will answer your question.

The *LCSH* uses several abbreviations to classify the terms it lists. Some of the most important ones include the following:

UF means "use for"

BT stands for "broader topic(s)"

RT stands for "related topic(s)"

NT stands for "narrower topic(s)"

SA directs you to "see also"

So, under the subject "crime," for example, the abbreviation UF tells you that "crime" is used for the terms *crime and criminals, delinquency,* and *urban crime.* Under BT, the *LCSH* lists *social problems.* Under RT, it lists *criminals* and *criminology.* And under NT it lists such terms as *juvenile delinquency, organized crime, drug abuse and crime,* and *education and crime.* All of these other terms would be useful starting places for researching your question on teenagers and gangs.

In addition to the *LCSH*, most disciplines (for example, education, psychology, sociology, and political science) have specialized thesauruses that you can use to define search terms. You can ask your librarian where to locate print thesauruses for your field, but many databases in the social sciences, such as PsycInfo and ERIC, have an online thesaurus in the database. Using an online thesaurus will save you time and effort.

SEARCH DATABASES AND ONLINE CATALOGS WITH BOOLEAN OPERATORS

Once you have located the professionally used keywords you need to research the concepts embedded in your research question, you can use these terms to search databases and online catalogs. Each of these is explained below.

A database is a tool that helps you find periodical literature, i.e., information from newspapers, magazines, professional journals, and other publications that are issued on a regular or periodic basis—daily, weekly, monthly, quarterly, semi-annually, etc. The BYU library spends thousands of dollars annually to subscribe to online professional databases that have indexed the periodical literature in various fields. These databases are carefully organized to help you quickly find reliable, peer-reviewed information. Searching these databases for information will save you hours of work as compared to searching the Internet for reliable information. As you log on to the BYU libraries' home page, you will see that it offers you several options for using its services. If you choose the option "Find Articles," you can then choose from a menu a general subject area that you are interested in. After choosing an area such as "sociology," you will next see a menu of databases recommended by the subject librarian for that subject area. Or, if you already know the name of the database you want to search, you can click on "Databases A to Z," and choose the one you want. You can search a database all by itself, or you can search multiple databases at the same time. You can sometimes have a search of the online library catalog performed simultaneously.

The online library catalog is what you will get if you choose "Find Books," from the libraries' home page. Online catalogs are often called OPACs—short for Online Public Access Catalogs. You are probably familiar enough with these catalogs that you know you can search them by author, title, or subject, because every item the library owns will be listed under all three headings. Library catalogs used to contain only records of printed materials, but now you can find electronic books, videos, CDs, and journal titles via the catalog. (Even though you can find the titles of journals, you can't find the titles of the articles the journals contain, and that is why you need to search databases as well.) Just as you can search databases with keywords you have found, you can search the catalog for any documents that contain the same keywords. When your results are displayed, if you look at the details screen, you will find LCSH subject headings linked to other materials on the same topic. By clicking on these links, you can quickly expand the number of sources you retrieve.

In order to do effective searches it is important to understand Boolean operators. They are named after George Boole, an English mathematician who invented a system of logic in the mid-nineteenth century that later became the basis for the electronic circuitry of computers. An ingenious part of his logic was to show that different combinations of concepts could be represented by just three "operators":

AND

OR

NOT (sometimes called AND NOT)

You can use these operators in searching a database or online catalog as shown in the following examples:

1. Typing *anorexia AND bulimia* in the search window would return a list of all sources that contain both terms. You can use the AND operator more than once in the same search. So you could type *anorexia AND bulimia AND obesity* to get a list of sources that contain all three terms.

2. Typing *anorexia OR bulimia* in the search window would return a list of all sources that contain one term or the other, but not necessarily both.

3. Typing *anorexia NOT bulimia* in the search window would return a list of all sources that contain only anorexia and not bulimia. Sometimes you have to type NOT as AND NOT.

Technically, the three operators above are the only Boolean operators, but the name is sometimes extended to include other operations you can perform to retrieve information. Other techniques to make your search more productive include the following:

*   **Truncation:** Typing *child** will retrieve sources that include the words "child," "children," and "childhood."
*   **Wild Cards:** Typing ? to replace a character in a word will retrieve sources in which the ? could be replaced by any of several characters.

Both the online catalog and databases have advanced search options. Using the advanced search option is generally preferable to the basic search option because the advanced search already includes ways to select the Boolean operators with various windows for you to fill in. In some of these windows you will type words, and for others you will select from menus. You can also limit your search in various ways. For example, you can ask that the results be limited to only those that include a linked full text; only those that are peer reviewed; only those published in a certain time period, in a certain type of publication, or for a given audience; or only those studies that employed a certain method. The options in advanced search menus will prompt you to think about how you can enhance your search and retrieve the best information and the most useful number of sources.

SEARCH FOR GOVERNMENT PUBLICATIONS

Besides periodicals, books, e-books, CDs, and videos, you may need to locate government publications, statistics, maps, and the like. Most university libraries have an area devoted to government resources, usually staffed by librarians who specialize in government research and who are your best resource as you prepare to search for information available from the government. For general research of government resources, you can consult both print and computer indexes. The most widely used print index for government research is the *Monthly Catalog of U.S. Government Publications*. This index is similar to other print indexes you may have used: it indexes government documents by author, title, and subject. You should use it if you are interested in locating government documents older than 1976.

Government documents produced since 1976 are also indexed on computer databases. You'll find hundreds of official U.S. government Web pages and databases, and both governmental and commercial indexes of online materials will help you find what you're looking for. For example, if you needed to know the student-teacher ratio of the high school you attended, you can use www.fedstats.gov to find a link to the National Center for Education Statistics. Or, you can use www.census.gov to find the projected U.S. population for the year 2025. Government Web sites hold vast amounts of information and are usually reliable and respectable sources. Using these computer databases, you can perform searches with author names, titles, subjects, and keywords. The databases are an easy way to search government documents if you are not interested in anything older than 1976.

USE INTERLIBRARY LOAN

No library can afford to buy all the new books printed or to subscribe to all the periodicals issued. By agreeing to share their holdings through interlibrary loans, libraries in a given region can still serve their patrons effectively. If you need a book or journal article that is not available in your library, consider requesting it through interlibrary loan. Usually, interlibrary loans can be made in just a few days, and often the needed material comes to you electronically in an attachment to an e-mail. However, some loans may take longer, depending on what you need and how far away the lending university is. So you should determine if the item will still be useful to you by the time you would get it.

ASK THE LIBRARIAN

With all of the technology for locating sources in today's libraries, it is sometimes easy to overlook the most valuable directional source available to you—the librarian. Librarians are thoroughly trained and highly skilled at locating information. After listening to you describe your research question for just a few minutes, they can often help you define your search terms better and point you to the databases, indexes, and other resources that can best help you answer your question. Don't be shy about asking for a librarian's help. They actually want you to request their services.

FINDING INFORMATION ON THE INTERNET

Most college students are familiar with many uses of the Internet, such as e-mailing, shopping for textbooks, and finding cheap airfares, but they start to feel unsure when it comes to using the Internet for academic research. Above, you learned how the Internet can be your link to the search tools of professional databases, online catalogs, and government resources, but you may wonder what the best strategies are for locating high quality information on the World Wide Web. With hundreds of millions of sites on the Web, the amount of information available online is simply overwhelming, and knowing how to find useful sites and judge their quality for a specific research purpose demands skill, awareness, and even some creativity. Learning the ins and outs of effective Internet research is probably more complicated than learning to do effective library research because there are so many more variables in the mix.

Although Internet research often means faster access to information and sometimes access to unique information, it does not follow that all research for a paper should be gathered from online sources, nor that all online sources are appropriate for academic and professional research. Usually information gathered via the Internet should be used *in addition to* not *instead of* traditional print and online information available at the library. It is unlikely that your professor (or a scholarly journal you might submit an article to) would be pleased with a paper that cites *only* sources available on the World Wide Web; most information posted there isn't reliable because so little of it is peer-reviewed in the way that professional journals and books are. The Web is a medium where anyone, including cranks and crackpots, can post their opinions as if they were the truth. However, you can find useful information from credible, unbiased researchers by using the Internet, and that will likely become even more the case in the future. Your task at this time is to evaluate carefully what you do find so that you can feel confident of its value before you use it in an academic research paper.

Following is an overview of how to search the World Wide Web. Because the Web is constantly changing and expanding, some of this information may be out of date by the time you read it. However, many of the principles that underlie successful Web research will generally remain the same, so this section should be useful to all students, inexperienced and proficient Internet users alike. The following section is built on the assumption that you have a basic understanding of how to use a Web browser.

USE SEARCH ENGINES AND SUBJECT DIRECTORIES

The easiest way to locate information on the Internet is to know the Uniform Resource Locator—the URL, or address—of the site you want to visit. Usually, however, researchers are not aware of where they can find the information they are seeking. Sometimes researchers are not even sure *what* information they are seeking. To help in these situations, two search tools, search engines and subject directories, were created.

Search Engines. Search engines are both powerful and precarious. They can help researchers find a broad sampling of ideas or a specific statistic, but, by themselves, they do not guarantee "good" research. Search engines have three main problems when it comes to research: first, the results list can be too large and unpredictable to be useful; second, search engines in general are not designed for scholarly research, as they generally focus more on commercial topics and do not evaluate the reliability of Web sites; and third, although there are many search engines available, there is no universal code of operating commands.

Additionally, different search engines use different computer programs to index Web sites. Because this technology is changing rapidly, each search engine visits and indexes sites differently. This means that the results for searches using the same keywords will produce different lists of results on different search engines. For example, at the time this book was published, a search for the keyword "narcolepsy" generated a list of over two million sites on the search engine Altavista but nearly four million on Google.

It takes time, thought, and even some trial and error to learn to use search engines effectively. Visiting a search engine homepage, typing a topic into the search field, and receiving thousands of hits is usually not smart—or useful— research. You may have experienced the frustration that accompanies this search engine scenario, and you probably already know some searching strategies to help ease the frustration. Here are a few tips to remember that will help you generate more effective searches:

First, remember that not all search engines have the same reason for existing. Some engines are commercially motivated while others lean more toward scholarly research. Therefore, not all search engines are equally helpful to researchers. While students tend to turn first to Google or Yahoo!, they should realize that some engines, such as Northern Light, deliberately try to index scholarly sites instead of commercial or general sites. Other search engines that the BYU librarians recommend for help with academic research are INFOMINE, Internet Public Library, Librarians' Index to the Internet, Libraryspot, Refdesk.com, and Search Engine Showdown. If you are aware of the general strengths and weaknesses of various search engines, you can use the engine that is appropriate to your needs for a given project. Spend some time experimenting with different search engines to learn their peculiar strengths and weaknesses.

Next, once you have chosen a search engine, experiment with several search terms and combinations, especially if you're not getting the results list you want. Type in your topic, look at your results list, and then decide if you need to try a more specific term, a more general term, or a synonym (this is where a list of related terms from the LCSH could come in handy). Or you may need to combine your search term with something else. For example, if you're looking for a policy analysis of Title IX, you might start with just "Title IX." If the results list links to the text of the law itself, you could type in "Title IX AND policy." Providing the search engines with limits will generate result lists that are more closely tailored to your particular research needs and are smaller in size. Learn to identify which results will be most helpful by skimming through the short descriptions next to each result.

Use Boolean operators (AND, OR, NOT) along with NEAR to limit your searches. NEAR between two keywords can help you retrieve any sources that include the two concepts in proximity to each other. For example, you could type *overeating* NEAR *heart disease* in order to retrieve sources that include both concepts. You can also use quotation marks around a phrase to look for words in the exact order you type them in and not as separate words that may just both happen to be in the retrieved document. For example, typing "multiple personality disorder" will give you a shorter results list than you would get if you typed those three words without the quotation marks. Some search engines allow you to use truncation, often represented by an asterisk. Even with the help of Boolean operators, the search results may be huge. Using the Boolean operators to combine search terms in different orders may yield surprising results. Here's an example from Google that shows some search possibilities (obtained in 2006) for the keywords *orange, grapefruit,* and *juice*:

orange juice OR grapefruit juice	22,000,000 hits
grapefruit juice OR orange juice	3,730,000
(orange AND grapefruit) juice	1,750,000
(grapefruit AND orange) juice	1,750,000
"orange juice" AND "grapefruit juice"	296,000
(orange AND grapefruit) juice*	42,500

Most search engines have an advanced search option. This will allow you to search more specifically for pertinent sites and information. You can find a link to the advanced search option directly from the search engine's homepage.

These advanced searches generally allow you to search under options such as these:

Find results	with **all** of the words
	with the **exact phrase**
	with **at least one** of the words
	without the words
Specify	language
	date
	domains (e.g. .com, .edu, .gov, etc.)
	file format
Find pages	similar to a given page
	that link to a given page
Sort by	date
	number of keyword occurrences

You can look at the "search helps" or "search tips" page for specifics and hints to using advanced search options. Most of these concepts also apply to searching an online database in the library.

Meta-searches, or searches that use more than one search engine at a time, are becoming more widely available, but as yet they are not very reliable. Often a meta-search option will give you fewer results than a search of a single engine alone. While it might be nice to have fewer results, there is no guarantee that they will be quality results. Also, you need to know that no search engine covers more than 25 percent of the sites on the Web, so any time you do a search you should look at the first twenty results for the same search on two or three different search engines (Hock 2001, 21–22). If you only search with one engine, you are likely to miss the key sites on your topic. If you search with two or three, you're much more likely to find the sites that will help you most.

There is a large portion of the Web that no search engine covers, the so-called invisible Web. This consists of sites that are not easily indexed by search engines' indexing mechanisms, such as those that require user input before its pages can be entered and those that display video information. If you are looking for these kinds of sites, search engines will not be your best option. You can, however, use a search engine to find a directory to the invisible Web.

Keep in mind that a search results list is not a bibliography of scholarly books and articles—for that, you need to go to BYU's online catalogue and use the electronic databases the library subscribes to. Very few search engine results are for scholarly books or articles; that is why Internet research usually supplements library research instead of replacing it. However, as this book goes to press in late 2006, the Internet giant Google is developing a new search engine called Google Scholar. It will be a tool for searching scholarly literature, including books, peer-reviewed articles, theses, dissertations, abstracts, technical reports and other kinds of documents from all fields of inquiry. The beta version of the Google Scholar search engine allows for advanced searches similar to those you can use to search professional databases such as ERIC or PsycInfo. Perhaps by the time you read this chapter, the BYU library will be recommending Google Scholar as a search tool, just as it now recommends the professional databases to which it subscribes.

Finally, as you search the Web, remember to bookmark or add to your "favorites" list any useful sites so that you can find them again. If you do cite a Web source in your research paper, you have to give the URL, so be sure that you have noted it in some way.

Subject Directories. Much like search engines, the result of using a subject directory is a list of specific Web sites relevant to your topic. However, subject directories use a slightly different approach. These directories, such as the subject directory on the Yahoo! home page, help you move from broad topics to more specific areas of study and finally to specific Web sites on that specific topic. For example, the Yahoo! Web site lists the broad topics "Business & Economy" and "Society and Culture" (and others) that you can click on to get to more specific subcategories. If you were doing a research paper on game theory in economics, you would click on the "Social Sciences" link, which would take you to a screen with over 40 topics, including economics, women's studies, psychology, conference reports, and social work. In this case you would click on the "economics" link, which would bring you to yet another screen with more specific topics. One of the topics on this third screen is "game theory," which, if you click on it, gives you a list of Web sites that were hand-picked by Yahoo! employees for their value or uniqueness. As you explore these sites, they will give you links to additional sites, which you can examine if you need to. Browsing these sites might help you further refine your topic.

As you can see, subject directories could be helpful in several ways that are essential to effective research, understanding, and writing:

- Choosing a topic
- Narrowing a topic
- Finding the "right" keywords to search with
- Finding Web sites that are guaranteed to relate to your topic
- Gaining a broad picture of how your topic and research fit into the field as a whole

USE THE INTERNET FOR OTHER KINDS OF RESEARCH

In addition to using the Internet to search the Web for material to include in a paper, you can use it to gather data; for example, you could query people by e-mail, conduct an online interview, do an online survey, participate in listserv discussions, and search the archives of discussion groups.

Since e-mail is one of the primary communication tools of our time, it can be helpful whenever you need to coordinate research. Here are some possible research uses:

- To discuss or brainstorm project details with group members or research advisors
- To clarify assignment details with an instructor
- To conduct surveys
- To contact interviewees (and possibly interview them online)

Like all research tools, however, you need to know the unspoken rules of using e-mail, and you need to know its limitations. Most of us are used to using e-mail regularly in very informal contexts—with friends and family—but informal language may not be appropriate when you are communicating with colleagues, research advisors, or interview subjects. Academic research is a serious business, and people will take you more seriously if you are professional in your approach to writing them. Obviously, you do not want to be unnecessarily stiff in your e-mail language, but it's probably good to avoid "lol," "imho," etc. You must also be aware of the demands on someone's time your request will make and allow adequate time for them to respond.

Also, be aware that e-mail does not ensure privacy. McGuire et al. (2001) warn that every message you send "winds up on at least four computers—your own, your company's (or Internet service provider's) server, your friend's computer, and his or her company's server. Those messages can stay on those servers a long time, and as Oliver North and Monica Lewinsky discovered, they can be retrieved years later and used against you" (99). McGuire et al. (2001) therefore suggest that you "don't put anything in a message that you wouldn't be willing to have published or broadcast" (99).

Listservs, newsgroups, or discussion lists can also help you make contacts and find information, but they are not "official" research tools; the information is not necessarily reliable, and it is often very opinionated. However, if you have a research question that these sources could help you answer, there is no research rule against using them. Just be aware that including in a paper the answers to queries you have put to users of a listserv might not be viewed as the most valid kind of evidence to support a point.

EVALUATING SOURCES

Once you have identified the books, periodical articles, government documents, other printed material, audio and visual media, and scholarly Web sites that may help you answer your research question, you begin the process of sifting through everything you have located to judge its reliability and its usefulness to you. These two qualities—reliability and usefulness—are related but distinct. Reliability refers to the quality of the source, whereas usefulness refers to the extent to which it helps you answer your question. A source might be reliable but not useful. Conversely, a source might at first appear to be useful, but if you determined it was unreliable, its usefulness would be questionable. Obviously, you want to use sources that are both reliable and useful, so following are some criteria to use in judging each.

How to Evaluate Reliability of Print Sources

By this point in your education you have no doubt come to realize that not everything in print must be true. As Chapter 1 explained, the production of knowledge in academic disciplines is a social process that uses peer review frequently throughout the process to ensure that the most valid and reliable knowledge is created and disseminated. But not all books, articles, Web sites, and other sources are peer reviewed, and some are not as rigorously reviewed as others. There are also political and ideological dimensions of peer review that should make you a little cautious even of peer-reviewed information.

Political Dimensions of Peer Review. Even when rigorous peer review takes place, it is carried out by humans, who can't entirely escape the way their background, education, and values influence their reading of a manuscript. Peer review therefore has a political dimension because politics, simply defined, is the use of power to gain or offer advantage. There are various points in the process of producing knowledge where some people—particularly reviewers, editors, and publishers—have the power to advance or stall the publication of someone else's ideas. Reviewers, editors, and publishers have the power to decide what ideas will gain the stamp of approval in a particular discipline and therefore to help determine which researchers will come to be considered authorities.

Ideological Dimensions of Research Funding. It is also important to remember that much social scientific research requires funding before it can even be started. Social scientists seek funding from universities, government agencies, and private foundations or institutes. These funding agencies also exercise power in determining what counts as knowledge because they may favor some kinds of research projects and not others. In fact, some foundations and institutes have been established to support research that certain groups believe is needed because this research isn't likely to be supported by other funding agencies. For example, *The Bell Curve* by Richard Herrnstein and Charles Murray (1994) argued that African Americans have lower average IQs because of genetic predisposition—a claim that was very controversial when the book was published. Carey (1994) reported that some of the data used to support the book's main argument came from research supported by the Pioneer Fund Inc., which was established in 1937 to finance studies of human genetics and to "encourage reproduction of 'white persons who settled in the original thirteen colonies'" (36). If you question the ideology of a research fund that exists to help "'conserve the population quality of the U.S.'" (Weyher, as cited by Carey 1994, 36), you might also question the reliability of the data used in *The Bell Curve.*

Considering the political and ideological dimensions of the funding and publishing processes should make you properly cautious of swallowing whole the arguments of any documents you locate in the library. You should evaluate the reliability of every document you locate by considering each of the following.

1. The author's credentials and reputation. Most books and articles give brief biographical information about the author. In books, this information is often given at the back of the book. In periodicals, it is frequently given in a note on the first or last page of the article. By scanning this information, you can often assess the author's education and current status and learn something of his or her research interests and previous publications. As you gather more documents to answer your research question, you can also check to see if a particular author is cited by others writing on the same topic. If an author's research has earned the respect of his or her peers, you can be more confident about using it yourself.

2. The publisher's reputation, aims, and emphases. There are many kinds of publishers, each having different aims and emphases. University presses are among the foremost publishers of academic research; that is usually their reason for being. However, some commercial publishers also define themselves as outlets for certain kinds of academic books. Books from either university presses or academic commercial presses are generally peer-reviewed and likely to be reliable sources. In contrast, many other large commercial publishers are interested in serving the everyday interests of the public and in marketing books that will attract large numbers of readers. Other small commercial presses want to fill niches by publishing books that might not otherwise be printed and that meet the special needs of different groups of readers. Books from either of these two kinds of publishers may be reliable sources for academic research, but you should be aware they are not primary publishers of academic research.

There is one kind of publisher you should especially watch out for—the vanity press. As the name implies, these publishers satisfy the vanity of some authors who want to see their books in print but have not been successful in publishing with a commercial or university press that requires favorable peer review. These authors then pay to have their own books published. Even though a university library may have some books from vanity presses on the shelves, their reliability is questionable because they have not been subjected to rigorous peer criticism.

It's impossible to list all the reputable publishers for the social sciences, but you can start to form impressions of who they are by noticing names of publishers that crop up again and again in the bibliographies of your research sources. You can also ask a professor in your major to name some of the most reputable publishers in your field.

3. Date of publication. In most of the social sciences, the publication date can be an important factor in determining the reliability of a source. As research methods are refined and new questions are investigated in a discipline, new findings frequently replace or at least modify older ones, and the general theories of a particular field change accordingly. Therefore, in order to make your own research as reliable as possible, you may want to restrict your research to the most recent publications—or at least view older documents through the perspective of more recent ones.

If, however, your research is about the historical development of a particular theory, you would want to deliberately choose older sources because they would be considered reliable—even essential—for your purposes. Also, some landmark texts by great innovators in a discipline maintain their relevance over the years, and it is often important to show familiarity with these texts in your writing. (For example, even though the theories of Sigmund Freud are not uniformly regarded as credible today, because his theories were groundbreaking and highly influential, people in many social science disciplines still learn about Freud's work and mention it in their writing.) So you must make decisions about the reliability of older documents based on your purpose, your audience's expectations, and the general regard in which the documents are held.

4. Type of publication. There are basically three types of documents you will use to do research in the social sciences: books, periodicals (in both print and electronic formats), and government documents. These will not be equally pertinent for a given topic. Because recency of publication is frequently an important indicator of reliability, periodicals are likely to be the type of publication you draw on most. But not all periodicals are equal; in most cases, you will want to use professional journals rather than popular magazines and newspapers. Professional journals are refereed, and they contain accounts of original research written by the researchers themselves. Popular magazines and newspapers, on the other hand, contain secondhand information about the latest findings in the social sciences and are usually written by lay reporters. They frequently omit discussion of the methods, and they do not usually qualify and hedge the conclusions the way the authors of the original research do. (There are certainly occasions to use popular magazines and newspapers for research, however; for example, if you were investigating how the news is reported to the public or public reaction to current events, you would have to use popular magazines and newspapers.)

While periodicals are an important source, you should not overlook the potential of books from reputable publishers that serve academic interests. Books may not be as current as periodicals, since it takes longer for a book to be written and published than it does for a journal article. But authors of books have the advantage of being able to take a wider perspective on their subject and more space in which to develop it. One kind of book that you should particularly consider is the edited volume. Edited volumes, as the name implies, have one or more general editors who assemble a collection of articles on related topics. Each article is written by an expert on the particular topic. Edited volumes can be an excellent resource if the information in them is still timely.

Government documents can also be important sources for research questions in several of the social sciences, particularly political science, economics, sociology, and history. Government documents are generally considered reliable because various government agencies have methods and networks for data-gathering that can't usually be duplicated by private entities.

5. *Soundness of research.* Even when you have determined that a particular document comes from a credible researcher and reputable publisher and that it is scholarly and up-to-date, you must still read it critically. Consider the definitions of key terms and note the methods the author used to create his or her findings: Are they sound and rigorous? Are they well-chosen for the question or hypothesis? Have the right statistical tests been used? Scrutinize as well the conclusions the author comes to: Are the conclusions justified on the basis of the evidence? Has the author overlooked other possible interpretations? Is any bias evident? As you read your sources critically, you will be able to judge how much weight to give them in constructing your own argument.

6. *Reviews and citations.* If you feel somewhat unqualified to judge the reliability of sources, you can relax knowing that people more experienced than you have often made those judgments. Most new books in a field are not only peer-reviewed during the pre-publication process, but shortly after publication as well. Most journals print brief reviews of new books, and there are special bibliographies for locating these reviews. Reading the reviews of a book will at least alert you to what reviewers saw as the book's strengths and weaknesses, and it will also make you familiar with the criteria that experts use to judge each other's work.

By paying attention to which books and articles are cited in the bibliographies of the sources you locate, you will also see what others have considered to be good research. Articles and books that are frequently cited are generally well-regarded. There is even an index, the *Social Sciences Citation Index,* which gives you information about how many times articles and even some books have been cited in a given year. This index will also lead you to the authors who are citing those articles or books.

HOW TO EVALUATE RELIABILITY OF WEB SOURCES

Here are a few tips for evaluating Web sites that you turn up in your research. The first tip is to think like a reporter when evaluating a source. Ask the following questions:

- Who is the author of the source? If you've never heard of the author or authors before, check up on them. See if they have authored other information that has been deemed credible. See if there is any information on the site under a link called "About Us." Reliable sites usually provide contact information for the authors and/or sponsors.
- Where is the information located? Take a look at the publisher or sponsor of the site. Pay attention to information in the URL that tells you what sort of organization the author is connected with:

.edu	stands for educational institutions
.gov	stands for U.S. government
.mil	stands for military
.org	stands for nonprofit organization
.net	stands for network
.com	stands for a commercial business

Information from a commercial organization is likely to be highly selective to encourage you to buy a product or service; information from a government agency or educational institution is more likely to be objective. Scam artists can set up .com and .org sites so beware of possible hoaxes. A URL with a tilde or cedilla—"~"—in it usually designates a personal home page and therefore likely a biased site. If you can't determine the sponsor of a site, there are agencies online that can tell you who owns and operates a site.

- When was the source written or last updated? Many Web sites have the copyright or last update recorded at the bottom of the homepage. The

Internet can make new information available faster than regular print sources, which is a good thing to keep in mind while researching a developing topic. But information that is posted in haste or before peer review processes have been completed may sometimes have to be revised as more or newer information becomes available. Credible news organizations, which do the best they can to meet frequent deadlines, will take care to correct earlier mistakes that come to light.

- What does the site tell you? Does the information there accord with information you have gotten from sources you trust, especially credible print sources? Has the information undergone some kind of peer review? Are there citations and archives that suggest careful research? Is there a table of contents and search features that make the site easy to navigate? Are there fallacies or an obviously slanted tone in the writing? Clicking on the links that a site connects to may sometimes help you detect a bias, especially if you can gather information about the originators and sponsors of the links from their home pages. A site that is full of grammar, spelling, and formatting mistakes is likely to be unreliable: if the author is careless about these matters, why should you trust the content of the site? Be aware that some sites plagiarize from other sites. Most importantly, use common sense: if the information sounds ridiculous, over the top, or impossible, look to verify it elsewhere. *Web of Deception: Misinformation on the Internet* (2002) is a good book for learning about the ways that unscrupulous people have misled people looking online for information.

- Why did the author write the information? Why did he or she publish it on the Internet? Does the author have some product to sell or cause to further? Is it evident that the author has an ideology or bias to promote?

Besides the above tips, two more cautions are in order. First, all teachers know that Wikipedia.org is a very popular research tool that many students turn to when researching because it is so convenient to look up information online. While Wikipedia may give you quick, interesting, and often credible information, you should know that it is based on a policy of open authorship. That is, the sponsors of this online encyclopedia allow almost anyone to write or edit any of the entries in the encyclopedia. This policy seems very democratic, but that is not necessarily a good thing for scholarship because sometimes people without adequate credentials or people with a certain ideology can insert their own ideas about a topic into the encyclopedia, and readers may not realize that the objectivity and credibility of the information may be questionable. You should therefore cross-reference information that you gain from Wikipedia with information in an encyclopedia that you know to be peer-reviewed.

Second, teachers also know that students love to use Google for research. In fact, this search engine has become so popular that a new verb has been created in the English language: "to google" means to do an online search. While Google is unquestionably a useful tool for answering all kinds of questions, it should also be used with caution. A Google search will rank sites according to their popularity, so sites that appear at the top of a list of results are the ones most frequently accessed by people looking for similar information. While this lets you know what other readers have found most useful to them, it is not always a good measure of a site's reliability and appropriateness for academic research. Also, the sponsored searches that Google often gives you to click on are not reliable and will usually be a waste of your time to use. When Google Scholar has been thoroughly tested and running for a while, it will likely be a more reliable tool than its parent; until then, use Google with full understanding of its limitations.

SOURCE USEFULNESS

While you are determining the reliability of your sources, you should also check their usefulness to you. You do this by skimming the sources to judge whether or not they contain information that will help you answer your research question. This is not to say that you will already have definite ideas of what your paper will be like. You probably won't, and you should remain open to all points of view rather than automatically rejecting certain ones at the outset. Nevertheless, you can begin making decisions about the scope and content of your paper by noting which of your sources contain the facts, evidence, data, and reasoning that seem most pertinent.

Evaluating Books. As you scan the books you've located, check each of the following:

The book's index. Look in the book's index for the same terms with which you began your search in the online catalog and computer databases. Look for synonyms and related terms as well. Then turn to the pages the index directs you to and skim them to see if they have the kind of information you are seeking.

The preface or introduction. The author of a book frequently gives an overview or summary of the entire book at its beginning, usually in the preface or introduction. Reading this overview can be very helpful to you in judging whether it will be worth your time to read more of the book. Sometimes a book's title sounds very promising, but on closer inspection, you find that the book's focus is too narrow or too broad to be helpful to you.

The table of contents. Look at the chapter titles to determine which ones most closely relate to your topic. Turn to those chapters and skim them quickly.

Headings within chapters. If the author has used them, headings within chapters may allow you to scan even more quickly to locate the kind of information you are seeking.

Evaluating Articles. There are also some quick methods of sizing up a journal article's usefulness to you. Pay attention to the following:

The abstract. Many social science journals require articles to have an abstract, which is simply a summary of the article's contents. The abstract is usually printed directly below the article's title. By reading it you know the purpose or hypothesis of the study, often something about the methods, and the major findings and their implications.

The headings. Most articles are divided into sections with descriptive headings that allow you to find what you are seeking. Typical headings are *Introduction, Methods, Results,* and *Discussion.* The *introduction* will tell you the aims of the research and summarize related studies. The *methods* section will tell you how the investigation was conducted. The *results* section describes the findings in words and often includes tables and graphs as well. The *discussion* section interprets the results and makes generalizations about their implications. Sometimes results and discussion sections are combined. After reading the abstract, you should probably read the discussion section next to see whether the article has implications relevant to your own research. You may also find that it is easier to scan the discussion than the results, where the findings can be presented in language and numbers so technical and complex that you may lack the necessary training to read them easily. Because the discussion interprets the results, you will find that it gives you a grasp of the significance of the research more quickly.

The references. Check the bibliography at the end of the article. From this you can see whether the author of the article has drawn on reputable sources and also whether sources are mentioned you haven't uncovered in your own research. By considering the sources your sources cite, you improve your chances of finding something useful.

Evaluating Web Sites. Once you have determined that a Web site is reliable, finding out if it will be useful to you can be more problematic. Sometimes Web pages are organized in sections with a list of navigational links at the top that you can click on to go to a specific part of the document. Using these links can save you time in skimming the entire site. Some sites also have a search function, so that you can type a keyword in a window and then quickly locate all points in the document where that word is used. Sometimes you can also copy text from a site, then paste it into a word processor and search it with the "find" function. The more complex a site is, the more likely it is that you will be able to use one of these aids. Other times, however, you simply have to start reading at the top and keep moving to see if anything useful is present.

As all of the ideas above suggest, when you are evaluating sources, you should generally not read them straight through from beginning to end. Rather, you should try to focus on those parts that will help you judge the usefulness of each source. After skimming the books, articles, and other sources you've turned up, you may reject half or more of them as not useful. So it's best to start with a longer list of potential sources than you can really use, given the time and length constraints your teacher has imposed on your paper. For example, if your teacher has assigned a 15-page paper that must be based on a minimum of ten sources, try to locate twenty or more sources at the start, as you will surely find some of them not useful or reliable. You should aim to make your paper one that includes the best information you can find, not one that merely meets the minimum requirements for a certain number of sources.

REFERENCES

Carey, John. 1994. Behind the bell curve. *Business Week*, 7 November, 36.

Herrnstein, Richard J., and Charles Murray. 1994. *The bell curve: Intelligence and class structure in American life*. New York: Free Press.

Hock, Randolph. 2001. *The extreme searcher's guide to Web search engines*. 2nd ed. Medford, NJ: Cyberage Books.

McGuire, Mary, Linda Stilborne, Melinda McAdams, and Laurel Hyatt. 2001. *The Internet handbook for writers, researchers, and journalists*. New York: Guilford.

Mintz, Anne P. 2002. *Web of deception: Misinformation on the Internet*. Medford, NJ: Cyberage Books.

PART

III

ACADEMIC AND PROFESSIONAL GENRES

In Part 3 of this book, you will learn about some common genres that are related to the main genres (illustrated in Part 2) that social scientists write in to present their research findings. In Chapter 10, you will learn about proposals, which social scientists write to seek funding or permission to carry out their research. You will also learn about prospectuses, detailed and formal rationales and outlines of what will be included in a long document.

Chapter 11 explains some of the widely applicable processes and principles involved in writing a research paper, whether it is a review of literature, an argumentative source-based paper, or a report of empirical research. Writing any kind of research paper first involves formulating a research question and then finding information or creating data to answer it. Next, the writer must plan and build the paper through outlining the parts and recording borrowed information carefully and ethically. Drafting, revising, and formatting the paper round out the process.

Chapter 12 presents examples of two kinds of writing social scientists sometimes do for a public audience, rather than the specialized audience of their peers. These are position papers and opinion pieces. In these genres, the writers draw on their specialized knowledge to offer the general public a solution to a problem or a professionally informed opinion about a current issue. Instead of following the rhetorical conventions of their more scholarly genres, the authors use a simpler, more general vocabulary and write in a form that will keep their audience's interest and hopefully persuade them to act for the general good.

Chapter 13 describes and illustrates abstracts, critiques, and reviews. Knowing how to write in each of these genres is important because each one plays an important role in constructing the shared body of knowledge in any field. Writers of critiques evaluate documents for their peers to help improve them before they are published. Abstracts and reviews, written after documents are complete, offer members of a field an efficient way to keep up with the endless flow of new books and articles as well as a way to evaluate their usefulness.

Chapters 14 and 15 will help you as you prepare to enter careers or continue your education in graduate or professional schools. Focusing on the preparation of resumes and the writing of letters and memos, these chapters describe contemporary practices and illustrate successful writing in these genres.

10

PROPOSALS AND PROSPECTUSES

CHAPTER OVERVIEW

After reading this chapter, you should be able to answer the following questions:

1. What is a proposal? What is a prospectus?
2. What are the required elements of an IRB (Institutional Review Board) proposal? Why does the IRB require each of these?
3. How does an ORCA proposal differ from an IRB proposal?
4. What are the typical elements of a prospectus?
5. How can a prospectus help you be more successful in completing a long research and writing project?

Planning ahead is crucial to success in any kind of venture, including writing. Sometimes your plans for completing a writing assignment are so brief and simple that you can work them out and store them all mentally. Other times, you may need to at least scribble a brief list or informal outline to remind yourself of the things you want to include in your paper and the order you want to follow. Sometimes your planning may extend to making a formal outline of what you intend to write; your professors may even require that you submit such an outline. The longer and more complex the writing task is, the less likely you are to be able to succeed with simple mental planning. In such cases, prior planning becomes especially important and sometimes very complex itself.

For example, if you have ever tried to write a fifteen-page library research paper just two days before it is due, you know that the best-laid mental plans can be frustrated: You find the books and articles you hoped to use are still checked out or they've simply disappeared from the library shelves. Or you discover that so few people have written on your chosen topic that you can't find enough information to write even five pages, let alone fifteen. Or, even if you have enough sources, you find at the eleventh hour that you are still struggling to understand them and to figure out how to integrate them into a focused, coherent paper. Or you realize at 2 a.m., when the library is closed, that you don't have all the information you need to write the bibliography for a paper that is due six hours later. Any number of other things could also go wrong. By systematically planning several weeks before the paper's due date, you could avoid most of these problems.

An excellent way of planning long, complex research and writing tasks is to write a proposal or prospectus. While these two words are often used interchangeably, a distinction will be made in this chapter. The word *proposal* will be used for research plans that primarily involve methods other than library research and for other kinds of formal written plans, such as bids and grant proposals. The word *prospectus* will be used for plans to write a paper based primarily on library research. Prospectuses contain mainly information that helps the reader imagine a finished written product—a research paper, a dissertation, a book. While proposals also typically promise an eventual written document, it is usually not described in much detail. With proposals, something else besides your plans for a document is usually at stake—money, permission to go ahead with a project, or an invitation to be included in a conference or a publication.

PROPOSALS

Proposals are a very common genre in the worlds of academe, business, and government. In academic professions, calls are routinely issued for people to propose conference presentations, articles for a special issue of a journal, chapters for a book, and other such opportunities to share knowledge and advance one's career. Corporations, philanthropic organizations, and government agencies that grant research funds also announce calls for proposals to compete for a share of the available money. In the business world, proposals may be sought for innovative solutions. Because funds and other resources are limited and must be used in the wisest way, the managers of a business want to be persuaded that the investment will be worthwhile before committing money, time, personnel or other resources to a project. In government, proposals often take the form of a competitive bid for a contract that will be let to the person or company submitting the best proposal to provide a product or service.

Even proposals that are not in competition with others must usually comply with various specifications or measure up to standards predetermined by those with power to approve the proposal. Therefore, proposals stress the researcher's qualifications and preparation to complete the proposed task. They frequently include information that allows the reviewers of the proposal to determine whether the researcher has the necessary expertise to accomplish the task. One way of judging expertise is to scrutinize the proposal author's description of the methods or procedures that will be followed. If the proposal is for a grant, it will include a detailed budget. Often, a proposal will present a reasonable timeline for completing the project.

Because proposals can be written for many diverse purposes and can take many different forms, it is not possible in this chapter to describe or illustrate all kinds of proposals. In the course of your education, your career, and your civic involvement, you may have to write many different kinds of proposals. Teachers and co-workers will be able to help you with some aspects of preparing individual proposals. Beyond that, the best things you can do are to ask a lot of questions about what the organization is looking for in the proposal and study other proposals that were successful in situations similar to yours.

The first half of this chapter will illustrate and discuss two kinds of proposals that, as a student in the social sciences, you are likely to write: (1) an IRB proposal, which seeks permission to conduct research with human participants (see Chapter 3 for more on the ethics of research); and (2) an ORCA proposal, which seeks funding for an undergraduate research project. You will see how one research project proposed by Colleen Johnson, a social science teaching major, was presented in two different formats for the purposes of getting IRB approval and of getting funding. By noticing how Colleen described her research and complied with requirements for each proposal, you should be able to plan and write similar proposals, either for conducting your own research with human participants or applying for an ORCA scholarship—or possibly another type of grant.

THE IRB PROPOSAL

For her honors thesis, Colleen decided to study the reasons why black South African women were marrying less frequently and later in life. Since Colleen wanted to interview young unmarried women in South Africa, she had to get permission first from BYU's IRB. The first step in getting this permission was to retrieve the instructions and forms that the IRB has posted on its Web site at http://orca.byu.edu/. The second step was to read the instructions and fill out the forms precisely, attaching necessary documents described in the instructions. The third step was to submit the proposal and wait to hear if the project had been approved. This entire process took Colleen about two months, as she worked first with her faculty advisor to draft and revise the required documents before submitting them. The review itself took about a month, since her research qualified for expedited review (see Chapter 3).

As you will note from studying Figure 10-1 on the following pages, an IRB proposal is made up of five parts. The first one is Part A, the application information (see Figure 10-1), which simply calls for filling in the blanks and checking boxes. The second is Part B, the research study synopsis, which answers questions about the planned study. The third is Part C, a document that the investigator signs, promising to adhere to IRB policies and procedures. For the fourth part, Part D, the researcher composes a document that summarizes the study in detail. There are 12 required subdivisions in Part D, as you will see from looking at Colleen's proposal. She had to state the aim of her research and then the hypothesis or question she wanted to answer. Then she had to briefly review the literature related to her question to show how previous research had not yet answered the question she intended to answer. By doing this, she was able to demonstrate the significance of her proposed research. Next, she described who would participate in her research and how she would recruit them and keep their identity confidential. Then she had to describe the research methods and the way she intended to analyze the data. She next had to describe the risks and benefits of the research. She inserted references to related literature, written in APA style. Finally, she described her qualifications to carry out the proposed research.

The fifth part of an IRB proposal is all necessary appendixes. All IRB proposals must include Appendix E, an informed consent document that research participants will read and, in many cases, sign before the research proceeds (see Chapter 3 for more about informed consent). If the research involves an interview or a survey, the questions to be asked must be submitted in Appendix F. Appendix G is the certificate that first-time researchers must submit to verify that they completed the online tutorial offered by BYU's Office of Research and Creative Activities. Appendix H includes any related material necessary for the research to proceed. As you will see from looking at the appendixes Colleen submitted, she had a well-organized informed consent statement that her interviewees would read and sign. She submitted all the questions she intended to ask so that the IRB could determine whether the proposal dealt with any sensitive or private issues. She attached her tutorial completion certificate. Finally, she included the script she would use to recruit participants and a copy of an e-mail she had received from a professor in South Africa who agreed to help her gain access to young women who might cooperate in the research.

As you can see from studying Figure 10-1, completing an IRB proposal involves a great number of steps, so careful planning is essential. You want to be sure that you include everything necessary in your application so that permission to perform your research will not be delayed unnecessarily. The IRB reviewers want to be assured that the proposed research will meet the highest standards of ethical practice, so they pay particular attention to the statements about who the participants will be and how they are chosen, as well as to the risks and benefits to the participants. While the reviewers do not focus as much on methodological rigor, they do pay attention to the description of methods, data analysis, and the researcher's qualifications. If the proposed research showed evidence of slipshod planning and the researcher's lack of qualifications, it could be denied. The reviewers would not want to put the university in the embarrassing position of allowing one of its students to waste the participants' time with poorly conceived and sloppily executed research.

FIGURE 10-1. Colleen Johnson's IRB Proposal

Application for the Use of Human Subjects
Part A
Application Information

Title of the Study: <u>Current Attitudes of Young, Black South African Women Towards Marriage and How</u>
<u>These Attitudes Affect the Marriage Rate</u>

Principal Investigator: <u>Colleen Johnson</u>   <u>Student</u>   <u>Sociology</u>
                                       Name   Title   Department

Address (+ ZIP): <u>8819 W. Brown St., Peoria, AZ   85345</u>

Phone: <u>(623) 979-4626</u>   E-mail: <u>colleen7@email.byu.edu</u>

Contact Person: (if different from PI):

Title: _____   Department: _____   Address (+ Zip): _____   Phone: _____   E-mail: _____

Co-Investigator(s): _____
              (Name & Affiliation)   Student   Sociology

Research Originated By: (Check One)   ☐ Faculty   X Student   ☐ Staff

Research Purpose: ☐ Grant   ☐ Dissertation   ☐ Thesis   ☐ ORCA
Scholarship

(Check All that Apply)   X Other: IAS field study   X Honors Thesis   X Course
Project: SOC 399R

Correspondence Request: X Mail   ☐ Call for Pick-Up

Part B   Research Study Synopsis

1. Short Study Description:

    The research will take place during a BYU field study conducted in East London, South Africa, for three months. The PI will be conducting interviews to gather qualitative research to determine the current attitudes of unmarried women of the marriageable age towards the marital relationship. Interviews will include questions about gender and family roles and questions about tradition versus modernization and westernization. Results will be analyzed to determine how these attitudes are affecting the marriage and divorce rate.

2. Study Length

    What is the duration of the study? 9/05–12/05

3. Location of Research

    a. Where will the research take place? Border Technikon College and Rhodes College, East London, South Africa

    b. Will the PI be conducting and/or supervising research activity at any sites not under the jurisdiction of the BYU

    IRB? X Yes   ☐ No   If Yes, please list sites: Border Technikon College and Rhodes College, East London, South Africa

4. Subject Information:

    a. Number of Subjects: 12–18   b. Gender of Subjects: Female   c. Ages of Subjects: 18–28

FIGURE 10-1. Colleen Johnson's IRB Proposal (continued)

5. Potentially Vulnerable Populations: (Check All that Apply)
   ☐ Children   ☐ Pregnant Women   ☐ Cognitively Impaired   ☐ Prisoners
   ☐ Institutionalized   ☐ Faculty's Own Students   ☐ Other. Please describe:

6. Non-English Speaking Subjects
   a. Will subjects who do not understand English participate in the research?   ☐ Yes   X No
   b. If yes describe your resources to communicate with the subjects:

   c. Into what language(s) will the consent form be translated:

7. Additional Subject Concerns
   a. Are there cultural attitudes/beliefs that may affect subjects in this study?   X Yes   ☐ No
   b. If yes, please describe attitudes and how they may affect subjects.
   Women may be reluctant to speak about sensitive issues surrounding marriage and gender roles because the society is traditionally patriarchal.

8. Dissemination of Research Findings
   a. Will the research be published?   X Yes   ☐ No If yes, where if known? Honors Thesis
   b. Will the research be presented?   X Yes   ☐ No If yes, where if known? Honors
   Thesis Defense

9. External Funding
   a. Are you seeking external funding?   X Yes   ☐ No What agency? ORCA grant,
   BYU Women's Research Institute
   b. Have you received funding?   X Yes   ☐ No c. Dollar amount? $1,000 from Honors
   Program

10. Method of Recruitment: (Check All that Apply)
    ☐ Flyer   X Classroom Announcement   ☐ Letter to Subjects   ☐ Third Party
    ☐ Random   ☐ Other

11. Payment to Subjects
    a. Will subjects be compensated for participation?   ☐ Yes   X No   If yes, please
    indicate amount:
    b. Form of Payment: ☐ Cash   ☐ Check   ☐ Gift Certificate   ☐ Voucher
        ☐ 1099   ☐ Other
    c. Will Payment be prorated?   ☐ Yes   ☐ No   If yes, please explain:
    d. When will the subject be paid?   ☐ Each Visit   ☐ Study Completion   ☐ Other

12. Extra Credit
    a. Will subjects be offered extra credit?   ☐ Yes   X No
    b. If yes, describe the alternative:

13. Risks: Identify all potential risks/discomforts to subjects.
    Emotional discomfort at the personal nature of the questions.

14. Benefits:
    a. Are there direct benefits to participants?   ☐ Yes   X No   If yes, please list.

    b. Are there potential benefits to society?   X Yes   ☐ No   If yes, please list.
    Information for researchers on gender issues and role expectations in marriage and family living in South Africa and how changing attitudes are affecting marriage rates.

FIGURE 10-1. Colleen Johnson's IRB Proposal (continued)

15. Study Procedures:
    a. What will be the duration of the subjects' participation? Two days
    b. Will the subjects be followed after their participation ends?   ☐ Yes   X No
       If yes, please describe.

    c. Describe the number, duration and nature of visits/encounters.
       One group interview lasting approximately one hour and one individual interview lasting approximately one hour preceded by a questionnaire determining demographics of participant.
    d. Is the study   ☐ Therapeutic?   X Non-therapeutic?
    e. List all procedures that will be performed to generate data for the research.
       Subjects will be recruited from the Life Skills class at the Border Technikon University and will first participate in a six-person group discussion interview for about an hour. They will be asked to return for individual interviews on the same topic, and they will fill out a questionnaire about their individual demographics so that responses can be analyzed based on demographics.
    f. List all procedures/questionnaires done solely for the purpose of the research study. All interviews and demographic questionnaires.
    g. List all procedures/questionnaires participants already do regardless of research. None
16. Informed Consent:
    a. Are you requesting Waiver or Alteration of Informed Consent?   ☐ Yes X No   If yes, please fill out the waiver of informed consent and attach it.
    b. Briefly describe your process to obtain consent: Participants will read and sign an approved informed consent form before interviews, which the PI will confidentially retain for records.
17. Confidentiality:
    a. Are the subject's social security number, BYU ID number or any identifier (other than study number and initials) being sent off site?   ☐ Yes   X No   If yes, describe and explain reasons.

    b. Will any entity other than the investigative staff have access to medical, health or psychological information about the subject?   ☐ Yes   X No   If yes, please indicate who.

    c. Briefly describe provisions made to maintain confidentiality of data, including who will have access to raw data, what will be done with the tapes, etc.
       Only the PI will have access to raw data including tapes of interviews/transcripts and demographics questionnaires. These will be kept in a locked cabinet. Tapes and questionnaires will be destroyed after research is concluded and data have been analyzed.
    d. Will raw data be made available to anyone other than the PI and immediate study personnel?
       ☐ Yes   X No
       If yes, describe the procedure for sharing data. Include with whom it will be shared, how and why.

FIGURE 10-1. Colleen Johnson's IRB Proposal (continued)

Part C

The attached investigation involves the use of human subjects. I understand the university's policy concerning research involving human subjects and I agree:

1. To obtain voluntary and informed consent of subjects who are to participate in this project.
2. To report to the IRB any unanticipated effects on subjects which become apparent during the course of, or as a result of, the experimentation and the actions taken.
3. To cooperate with members of the committee charged with continuing review of this project.
4. To obtain prior approval from the committee before amending or altering the scope of the project or implementing changes in the approved consent document.
5. To maintain the documentation of consent forms and progress reports as required by institutional policy.
6. To safeguard the confidentiality of research subjects and the data collected when the approved level of research requires it.

Signature* of the Principal Investigator: _electronic_____

      Date: _7/18/05_

Faculty Sponsor Signature <u>Required</u> for All Student Submissions (<u>will not be process without this</u>)
"I have read and reviewed this proposal and certify that it is ready for review by the IRB Board. I have worked with the student to prepare this research protocol. I agree to mentor the student during the research project."
Faculty Sponsor (Please sign and print):   _emailed consent to IRB_____

Thesis/Dissertation – Date of Approval <u>**Required**</u> by the Proposal Review Committee:
approval pending
Committee Chair/Faculty Sponsor <u>**Required**</u> (Please sign and print):   _NA_

* If submitting by email, please check this box to verify that you are the PI listed on this application and agree to follow the items listed above.   **X I agree**

FIGURE 10-1. Colleen Johnson's IRB Proposal (continued)

Synopsis of the Proposal
Part D

1. **Specific Aims.** My honors thesis will answer the question, "What structures of society currently affect unmarried, college-age Xhosa women's attitudes towards marriage?" Most of my research will be conducted during a field study in South Africa where I will interview approximately 18 young women to determine their current attitudes. My thesis will begin with an introduction to the history of marriage in Xhosa culture, including the traditional practices, cultural attitudes and historical events that have contributed to its current state. I will then discuss my findings on the present attitudes and social structure causes, incorporating quotes from the interviews and secondary research as proof of these trends. Through my research, I hope to contribute to the understanding of how changing social structures affect the institution of marriage by altering women's attitudes and practices.

2. **Hypothesis/ Question.** My main question in the field will be, "What are the current attitudes of unmarried women of marriageable age towards the marital relationship?" Through my research I hope to contribute to the understanding of how the current attitude of women towards marriage will affect the future of marriage and family life in South Africa.

3. **Background and Significance.** Current census and survey data on marriage in South Africa indicate that marriage trends in South Africa are changing. Amoateng (2004) states that compared to other African countries, black South African women are getting married less frequently and later in life. In South Africa only 50% of women are married by age 24, whereas 95% of women in Ghana are married by age 25. Using census data, Amoateng also postulates that the more rural and uneducated a woman is the more likely she is to marry and to marry younger. She claims that modernizing forces, which raise the levels of education and urbanization of women, have contributed to the declining marriage rate. She also attributes the increase in popularity of cohabitation among the younger generation to the decrease in marriage.

    While Amoateng does not analyze why modernizing factors affect the marriage rate, Makiwane (2004) claims that with increased education women no longer need men to provide for them, so marriage is no longer an economic necessity; therefore, fewer women are getting married. His explanation for the appeal of cohabitation is that unmarried couples can increasingly receive the same legal benefits that married couples can, so marriage is no longer perceived as a benefit; therefore, the marriage rate is decreasing. Makiwane also cites colonization, apartheid, and the migrant labor system as causes of the decline in marriage.

    While Makiwane's article attempts to explain the historical and current issues that are affecting the marriage trends in South Africa, no consensus exists yet for the decline. Research on trends in marriage is almost exclusively quantitative, but even the data

FIGURE 10-1. Colleen Johnson's IRB Proposal (continued)

available are not very accurate. The present data mostly document official civil marriages, while a large number of blacks marry only in traditional ceremonies. Through qualitative research, I will be able to analyze the current attitudes towards marriage and try to infer what social causes motivate these changes. My data will give a more descriptive account of why the marriage rate is changing because qualitative research can take into account a multitude of variables that quantitative research cannot.

4. **Description of Subjects.** I will select my subjects from among unmarried, female students between the ages of 18 and 28 enrolled in the Life Skills Class at the Border Technikon University in East London, South Africa. I have received permission from the professor of the Life Skills class there to make announcements that I am looking for volunteers for the interviews. I will also recruit students from Rhodes College in East London, South Africa. This will be an ideal place to conduct interviews because it will give me access to unmarried women of marriageable age. Because most of the women in East London are Xhosa, this will naturally limit my study to that particular cultural group. I will get information about their socioeconomic, educational, religious, and cultural backgrounds in a demographics questionnaire so that I can make sure to keep their background in mind in my analyses of the data. Knowing their backgrounds will help me analyze variables that might contribute to differences in women's attitudes toward marriage. Before the interviews students will read and sign the consent forms.

5. **Confidentiality.** Only the PI will have access to raw data including tapes of interviews/transcripts and demographics questionnaires. These will be kept in a locked cabinet. Tapes and questionnaires will be destroyed after research is concluded and data have been analyzed, unless the participant has granted permission to use her data in other ways.

6. **Method or Procedures.** I will use qualitative methods, particularly interviews, to help explain the background and causes of quantitative statistics regarding marriage rates and trends in black South Africa. I will conduct IRB-approved group discussion interviews by asking groups of six women to participate in a guided discussion about marriage. I will interview 3 groups of women, for a total of 18 participants. Before the interviews students will read and sign IRB-approved consent forms, and they will fill out a demographics questionnaire about their socioeconomic, educational, religious, and cultural backgrounds. After the group interviews, I will conduct individual interviews where I can take into account the informant's socioeconomic, educational, religious, and cultural background according to the demographics survey. I will then be able to keep those variables in mind as I analyze any differences in the data.

7. **Data Analysis.** I will be using inductive analysis or the "grounded theory" of sociology to analyze the data my research produces. This analytical technique is useful in qualitative research conducted in field studies because it is flexible enough to allow the data to guide the research and propositions. Throughout the research and interview process I will narrow down my propositions according to the patterns in my research and my expanding

FIGURE 10-1. Colleen Johnson's IRB Proposal (continued)

knowledge of the cultural and historical background. I will also use secondary research from sociological and marriage and family journals to help perform and supplement my analyses.

8. **Risks.** Risks are minimal but do include emotional discomfort at the personal nature of the questions. If the participant displays emotional discomfort, she will be asked if she would like to continue at a later date or discontinue the interview completely.

9. **Benefits.** There are no direct benefits to the participants in the research. Benefits to society include new information for researchers on gender issues regarding attitudes toward and role expectations in marriage and family living in South Africa and how these attitudes and expectations are affecting marriage rates.

10. **Compensation.** No compensation will be offered to the participants.

11. **References**

Amoateng, A. Y. (2004, August). The South African family: Continuity or change? *HSRC Ten Years of Democracy Seminar Series*, 1–27. Retrieved June 10, 2005, from www.hsrc.ac.za

Budlender, D., Chobokoane, N., & Simelane, S. (June, n.y.) Marriage patterns in South Africa: Methodological and substantive issues. *The Southern African Journal of Demography, 9(1)*, 1–25.

Hamon, R. R., & Ingoldsby, B. B. (2003). *Mate selection across cultures.* New Delhi: Sage Publications.

International Defense and Aid Fund for South Africa. (1981). *Women under apartheid.* London: A G Bishop and Sons.

Lawson, Lesley. (1986). *Working women in South Africa.* Oxford, UK: Alden Press.

Makiwane, M. (2004). Demise of marriage. *ChildrenFIRST, 58.* Retrieved June 10, 2005, from http://www.childrenfirst.org.za

Mathabane, M. (1994). *African women: Three generations.* New York: HarperCollins.

12. **Qualifications.** My duties in this project will include conducting interviews and analyzing data according to the guidelines of sociological qualitative research. I have completed the field study preparation course for South Africa, IAS 360, where I learned how to conduct interviews, participant observation, and other kinds of research. This class covered relevant background information including South Africa's history, politics and economics, social and cultural issues. I will complete all the requirements for a sociology internship, SOC 399, before and during my field study, which includes literature on gathering, focusing, and analyzing data.

FIGURE 10-1. Colleen Johnson's IRB Proposal (continued)

Appendix E
Consent to be a Research Subject

Introduction
This research is being conducted by Colleen Johnson, an undergraduate student at Brigham Young University, to determine young South African women's current attitudes towards marriage and gender roles and the effect of these attitudes on marriage rates. You were selected to be a subject because you are a young, unmarried South African woman.

Procedures
You will participate in a group interview with other participants on the subject of marriage and gender roles. This will last approximately one hour. You will then be asked to return on a later date for an individual interview in which you will first fill out a questionnaire about your age, race, culture, religious affiliation, and economic and educational background. Then you will be asked more in-depth questions of a nature similar to those in the group interview. Both interviews will be tape recorded and transcribed.

Risks/Discomforts
There are minimal risks for participation in this study. You may, however, experience discomfort at the personal nature of the questions and may be embarrassed to express your beliefs in front of others at the group interview. The interviewer will be sensitive to the participants who may become uncomfortable.

Benefits
There are no direct benefits to participants. It is hoped that your participation will help researchers learn more about changing attitudes towards marriage, family, and gender roles and how these attitudes affect the marriage rate.

Confidentiality
Information will be reported as group data and will remain confidential unless you agree to be identified. Only those involved with the research will have access to the data, which will be kept in a locked file cabinet. The data, including interview transcripts and tapes, will be destroyed at the conclusion of the research unless you have granted permission for it to be used otherwise.

Participation
Participation in this research study is voluntary. You have the right to withdraw at any time or refuse to participate entirely without jeopardy to your grades or standing with the university.

Questions about the Research
If you have any questions about this research you can contact Colleen Johnson at colleen7@email.byu.edu.

Questions about your Rights as Research Participants
If you have questions you do not feel comfortable asking the researcher, you may contact Dr. Renea Beckstrand, IRB Chair, 1-801-422-3873, 422 SWKT, renea_beckstrand@byu.edu.

Signature:_____   Date:_____

FIGURE 10-1. Colleen Johnson's IRB Proposal (continued)

Appendix F
Demographics Questionnaire

1. What is your age?

2. What is your tribal or ethnic origin?

3. Were you raised in an urban or rural setting?

4. What is your religious affiliation, if any?

5. What level of education have you received?

6. What level of education do you plan on receiving?

7. What is your household income?

Interview Questions

1. What is your definition of marriage? Does it require a civil ceremony, traditional ceremony, both or neither?

2. Does marriage require the payment of labola? How do you feel about labola? Would you want your husband to pay labola for you? Do you think the tradition of labola will continue as South Africa modernizes?

3. What are your family's expectations for you concerning marriage? What are your culture's expectations for you concerning marriage? What are your expectations for yourself concerning marriage?

4. What are the benefits of marriage economically, culturally, religiously, etc.?

5. What are your perceptions of the disadvantages of marriage?

6. What are the advantages of cohabitation versus marriage? What are the disadvantages of cohabitation versus marriage?

7. Do you expect your husband to be monogamous? Do you expect to be monogamous?

8. What do you believe is the role of a wife and mother? What are your culture's expectations of wives and mothers? Do you agree with them?

FIGURE 10-1. Colleen Johnson's IRB Proposal (continued)

9. What do you believe is the role of a husband and father? What are your culture's expectations of husbands and fathers? Do you agree with them?

10. Do you expect to marry for love, economic stability, religious or cultural reasons, etc? Do you expect to marry someone for romantic reasons, someone who is your best friend, someone who is financially stable and a good provider, someone your family approves of, or a combination of all? Which aspect is most important to you? Would you settle for someone who lacked one of these aspects?

11. What actions on your husband's part would warrant a divorce? What actions on your part would warrant a divorce?

12. How do your attitudes towards marriage differ from those of your mother's generation? Your grandmother's generation?

13. How do you think modernization and globalization have affected the marriage rate?

14. What do you think is the future of marriage in South Africa? Do you think the marriage rate will drop, rise or stay the same? Why?

FIGURE 10-1. Colleen Johnson's IRB Proposal (continued)

Appendix G
Certificate of Completion

The BYU Office of Research and Creative Activities

certifies that

Colleen Johnson

has completed the computer-based training course on the

Protection of Human Research Subjects

Certificate #: 15786   Date: 7/12/2005 5:21:25 PM

FIGURE 10-1. Colleen Johnson's IRB Proposal (continued)

Appendix H
Supporting Documents

Script Requesting Subjects' Participation

Colleen Johnson, an undergraduate student at Brigham Young University, is researching young South African women's current attitudes towards marriage and gender roles and their effect on marriage rates. She is looking for subjects who are young, unmarried South African women. Volunteers will participate in a group interview with other participants on the subject of marriage and gender roles. This will last approximately one hour. You will then be asked to return on a later date for an individual interview in which you will first fill out a questionnaire about your demographics including age, race, culture, religious affiliation and economic and educational background. Then you will be asked more in-depth questions similar to those in the group interview. Both interviews will be tape recorded and transcribed. This activity is completely voluntary and the information will be kept confidential. Please sign up if you are interested in participating.

Consent from Linda Smith, Professor of Life Skills at Border Technikon, South Africa

From: "LINDA (DR) SMITH" <lsmith@wsu.ac.za>

To: <colleen7@byu.edu>

Date: Wed, 13 Jul 2005 15:11:57 +0200

Subject: Re: BYU field study

Hello, Colleen.

It's fine for you to conduct your research at Border Technikon. You could work with my Life Skills students. I teach Tuesday through Friday. For some groups I could give you one class period to talk to them, after which you'd set up separate times to see them.

Good luck with your plans.

Linda Smith

AN ORCA PROPOSAL

At BYU every year, undergraduate students have the opportunity to apply for funds to conduct research projects. The proposals they submit are judged in the various colleges and schools by faculty members, and the funds are awarded to the top proposals by the ORCA office. Colleen Johnson applied for funds to support her Honors thesis project. The proposal she wrote is in Figure 10-2. You will note familiar information in it, but since this proposal was for a different audience and purpose, it has new information in it as well, and it is organized differently from her IRB proposal.

THE PROSPECTUS

Publishers typically ask for a prospectus, rather than a complete manuscript, when an author contacts them with an idea for a book. By writing a prospectus, authors are forced to be as clear as possible about their plans, distilling their ideas persuasively in a very few pages. After reading a prospectus (and often having it reviewed by others), publishers can determine whether a project is interesting and promising enough to encourage the author to complete the manuscript. Often, on the strength of a rhetorically effective prospectus, the publisher will offer the author a contract. Similarly, a prospectus for a long academic paper helps both the student writer and his or her instructor come to an agreement about the worth and feasibility of the student's plans. Rather than being offered a contract, however, a student either receives permission and encouragement to proceed with the planned paper or receives advice on how to strengthen or redirect the prospectus.

A prospectus is commonly required in graduate school for a master's thesis or doctoral dissertation. Its primary audience is a committee of professors who must approve the project before the student can proceed. The committee members are not likely to approve a project that is trivial or uninteresting, one that would merely plow over old ground, or one that would be too difficult or even impossible to complete. So the graduate student typically must persuade the committee that he or she has answered these questions:

- What is proposed?
- Why is it proposed? What contribution to knowledge will the student make?
- What will the finished work include?
- How, where, and when will the proposed work be accomplished?
- What qualifications are required to accomplish the proposed project?
- Are the necessary resources available?

FIGURE 10-2. Colleen Johnson's ORCA Application

Fall 2005 ORCA Mentoring Grant Application	
South African Marriage: A Changing Institution	
First applicant name:	**Colleen Johnson**
First applicant email and Route Y login:	**colleen7@email.byu.edu**
Mentor name and department:	**Cardell Jacobson, Sociology**

Importance of Project

The results of this project will help researchers who study gender and family issues understand how and why attitudes towards marriage and family are changing among black South Africans. This information would help sociologists understand why marriage rates among black South African women are declining so that marriage and family social workers can develop appropriate strategies to encourage healthy marriages and family life. Because the family is the basic unit of society, preventing the further decline of marriage and families in South Africa will promote a more stable society in a country that has experienced a great deal of social upheaval in the past 20 years.

Main Proposal Body

I. Project Summary

I plan to write an honors thesis exploring unmarried black South African women's attitudes towards marriage, the possible reasons for those attitudes, and how they are affecting the institution of marriage. Most of my research will be conducted during a field study in South Africa where I will interview young black South African women. My thesis will begin with an introduction about the institution of marriage and the changes it has been undergoing since South Africa has become more westernized and has expanded women's rights. Then, using interview data, I will explain how South African women feel about these changes and what effect the changes have had on the women's aspirations and their attitudes towards marriage. I will interpret the interviewees' perspectives with references to secondary literature.

II. Background and Significance

Data from censuses and surveys conducted in South Africa indicate that marriage trends are changing. Compared to other African countries, black South African women are getting married less frequently and later in life. In South Africa only 50% of women are married by age 24 whereas 95% of women in Ghana are married by age 25 (Amoateng). It is postulated that modernizing forces, which raise the levels of education and urbanization of women, have contributed to the declining marriage rate. With increased education, women no longer need men to provide for them. Marriage is no longer an economic necessity and thus fewer women are getting married (Makiwane). While many researchers (e.g., Budlender et al.; Hamon and Ingoldsby; Lawson; Mathabane) have attempted to explain the historical and current issues that are affecting the marriage trends in South Africa, there is as yet no

FIGURE 10-2. Colleen Johnson's ORCA Application (continued)

consensus on the reason for the new trend (Makiwane). I postulate that marriage is declining not only because of greater economic opportunity for women but also because women are dissatisfied with the traditional institution of marriage in South Africa. Through qualitative research, including interviews, I will be able to analyze and describe the reasons why women are marrying less often and later. My research will not only help support predictions about the future of marriage and family life in South Africa but may enable interventions to prevent the further decline of marriage.

III.   Methods

I will use qualitative methods, particularly interviews, to help explain the background and causes of statistics regarding marriage rates and trends in black South Africa. I will conduct IRB-approved group discussion interviews by asking groups of six women to participate in a guided discussion about marriage. I will interview 3 groups of women, for a total of 18 participants. The participants will be unmarried female students, aged 18 to 28, enrolled in the Border Technikon University Life Skills Class. I have received permission from the professor to recruit volunteer participants from among her students. This will be an ideal place to conduct interviews because it will give me access to unmarried women of marriageable age. The Border Technikon University is in East London, South Africa, where most of the women are Xhosa, so this demographic fact will naturally limit my study to that particular cultural group.

Before the interviews students will read and sign IRB-approved consent forms, and they will fill out a demographics questionnaire about their socioeconomic, educational, religious, and cultural backgrounds. After the group interviews, I will conduct individual interviews where I can take into account the informant's socioeconomic, educational, religious, and cultural background according to the demographics survey. I will then be able to keep those variables in mind as I analyze any differences in the data regarding attitudes toward marriage.

I will be using inductive analysis or the "grounded theory" of sociology to analyze the data my research produces. This analytical technique is useful in qualitative research conducted in field studies because it is flexible enough to allow the data to guide the research and propositions. Throughout the research and interview process I will narrow down my propositions according to the patterns in my research and my expanding knowledge of the cultural and historical background.

Anticipated Academic Outcome

My research will be published as an honors thesis, a copy of which will be available in the BYU library. I will also submit my findings to sociology journals with the help of my mentor.

Qualifications

My duties in this project will include conducting interviews and analyzing data according to the guidelines of sociological qualitative research. I have completed the field study preparation course for South Africa, IAS 360, where I learned how to conduct interviews, participant observation, and other kinds of research. This class covered relevant background information including South Africa's history, politics and economics, social and cultural issues. I will

FIGURE 10-2. Colleen Johnson's ORCA Application (continued)

complete all the requirements for a sociology internship, SOC 399, before and during my field study which includes literature on gathering, focusing, and analyzing data according to the field of sociology.

Dr. Cardell Jacobson, Professor of Sociology at BYU, will be my mentor. Dr. Jacobson has conducted quantitative research on marriage in South Africa and has collaborated with top South African researchers in this field. Along with Acheampong Yaw Amoateng and Tim B. Heaton, he published an article entitled "Interracial Marriages in South Africa" in the *Journal of Comparative Family Studies*. Prof. Jacobson has the knowledge of my topic and practical experience necessary to act as my mentor.

Project Timetable

I have already devoted approximately 100 hours to this project during my International Field Study preparation course. I will devote at least an additional 300 hours to researching my thesis during my field study in South Africa, Fall Semester of 2005, when I will be enrolled in 9 credit hours of Sociology 399. I will continue my research during Winter Semester 2006 and will complete the final draft by April 2006.

Fit With BYU's Mission [optional]

Through this project I hope to contribute to BYU's mission of strengthening families, applying revealed knowledge to secular problems, and promoting morality in law and society. I firmly believe that the family is the core of the gospel and of society and that by strengthening families we can solve many of our societal problems. By understanding women's attitudes towards marriage we can understand what needs to change culturally so that marriage will be a positive institution for both partners. Marriage needs to be viewed as beneficial to women so that the institution of marriage does not disintegrate as women have the option of not marrying because of the increased rights and opportunities brought by westernization. I hope that the results of this research can be used by people and institutions promoting the family to create programs that strengthen marriage.

Sources

Amoateng, A. Y. (2004, August). The South African family: Continuity or change? *HSRC Ten Years of Democracy Seminar Series*, 1–27. Retrieved June 10, 2005, from www.hsrc.ac.za

Budlender, D., Chobokoane, N. & Simelane, S. (June, n.y.) Marriage patterns in South Africa: Methodological and substantive issues. *The Southern African Journal of Demography, 9(1)*, 1–25.

Hamon, R. R., & Ingoldsby, B. B. (2003). *Mate selection across cultures.* New Delhi: Sage Publications.

International Defense and Aid Fund for South Africa. (1981). *Women under apartheid.* London: A G Bishop and Sons.

Lawson, Lesley. (1986). *Working women in South Africa.* Oxford, UK: Alden Press.

Makiwane, M. (2004). Demise of marriage. *ChildrenFIRST, 58.* Retrieved June 10, 2005, from http://www.childrenfirst.org.za

Mathabane, M. (1994). *African women: Three generations.* New York: HarperCollins.

By answering these questions well, the student assures the committee that he or she will undertake a project that is worthwhile, original, well-planned, and feasible. For the same reasons that a prospectus is desirable in graduate school, it is advisable for undergraduates to write one before completing an extended research project.

PARTS OF THE PROSPECTUS

Exploring what is involved in answering the above questions will help you better understand what a typical prospectus contains.

What is proposed? You undertake a research project in order to answer a question or a set of related questions, solve a problem, or address an issue in a new way—perhaps because it has been addressed inadequately in the past or perhaps because there are new methods to be applied or new evidence to be examined. In a prospectus, then, you should state at the outset what the purpose of your research will be—what question, problem, or need your research will resolve. It is also helpful to locate the problem in a context, for example to show what historical, social, or individual issues it relates to. Providing this context will also help you establish a rationale.

At the time you write the prospectus, you may not know exactly what answer you will find to your question, what solution you might propose to a problem, or all the new information you might turn up about your topic. But you should know enough to state very clearly the aim and the scope of the research you want to undertake. For example, suppose a new therapy, validation therapy, has been created for helping elderly persons with dementia, and you wish to know more about it. After considering how little you know about it, you determine that some good questions to start with would be, "How does validation therapy differ from reality orientation, the standard therapy used in hospitals and residential care facilities? What are the merits of validation therapy? What evidence is there that it has been used successfully?" These questions already imply a scope for the paper—limits that will make it manageable because you will focus on answering these questions and not any of several related questions you could also answer.

Why is it proposed? Always intertwined with the *what* of any prospectus is the *why*. Explaining why it is important to research the topic you have chosen constitutes giving a rationale or justification for your project. Your reasons may be partly personal. Continuing the example above, you may have a grandparent who suffers from a form of dementia. Or you may have worked with such persons or plan to work with them in the future. You will no doubt be more interested in researching a topic that draws you personally, and that alone is a good justification.

But remember that you will be writing your paper for an audience too, so you should be able to come up with some more "public" reasons. What will help your readers believe that it is important to do this research? What other reasons justify the time and effort you will spend researching it? What will be the value to your audience and others of the knowledge you will collect and write about? You don't want your audience to read your prospectus and say, "So what?"

For the therapy project mentioned above, for example, you could justify your research by noting the widespread incidence of dementia among elderly people, its debilitating effects on them, and the difficulties that caregivers face in responding adequately to the confusion and disorientation that these patients experience. Perhaps the current therapy is based on faulty premises or it is unsatisfactory in the way it works for some patients. Any research that promises to shed some light on a vexing health issue should be welcome to most audiences because it is possible that many people or their loved ones may be affected by such problems.

The rationale of a prospectus doesn't have to be long, but it ought to be presented carefully. You want your project to be approved, so give some good reasons why it should be. Check with your instructor, however, to learn whether he or she deems it appropriate to bring up personal reasons in the rationale. No doubt all researchers have a personal interest in the research they conduct, but sometimes they do not expressly state their personal reasons in their justification for the research.

What will the finished work include? Your prospectus should give evidence that you have thought about the paper you will eventually write. Because you have already stated the question or the problem and rationale in the introduction of your prospectus, in this part you can show how you plan to present the answer or the solution that meets the need implied in the rationale. To write this part, ask yourself these questions:

- What overall thesis will you argue for?
- What parts will you divide your finished research into?
- What order will you put these parts in? What should come first, second, or third? Last?
- How much space will you devote to each part—how much emphasis will each receive?

In prospectuses for graduate theses, this part of the prospectus usually takes the form of a list of chapters and a summary of what each chapter will cover. In an undergraduate prospectus, a more suitable form might be a preliminary outline of the eventual paper. This outline is usually done in the traditional way, with Roman numerals and indented subheadings. But it could be less formal, in paragraph form, with sentences describing the subtopics you intend to address. Check with your instructor regarding the outline.

Obviously, to write this part of the prospectus you will have to locate at least some of the library sources you plan to use and become familiar with what is in them. It won't do to simply imagine what your eventual paper will contain, hoping that you will later find just the sources you need to fill in the projected parts. What if no such sources exist or they are difficult to get? By going to the library as you prepare your prospectus, you can determine if your project is even feasible and avoid a last-minute attempt to find useable, reliable sources. And by skimming several of your sources weeks before your paper is due, you will already have begun your research, eliminating the need for frantic, late-night reading.

As you can see, a prospectus demands that you "get serious" about your topic early enough to explore it meaningfully. By showing your reader how you have limited the scope and contents of your project, the overview of your proposed research adds greatly to the persuasiveness of your prospectus and enhances the possibility that your project will be approved.

How, where, and when will the work be accomplished? In addition to describing the eventual paper you will write, for many audiences you may need to describe the process you will go through to write it. This description can take the form of a task breakdown showing how and where you will conduct the research. This task breakdown can also include a timeline showing what phases of the work you will have completed by intermediate dates before the final deadline. Including a task breakdown in your prospectus can be very helpful if you plan to conduct complicated research, requiring you to travel to more than one library, for example, or to procure documents through interlibrary loan, or to interview an authority on your topic. Also, if you need to manage your time carefully because of other commitments, planning a reasonable schedule and then sticking to it can help you meet the ultimate deadline without panic. Here are some intermediate steps you could use to create a timeline that will help you finish your research project on time:

- Begin research
- Create preliminary bibliography
- Start notetaking
- End notetaking
- Write first draft of research paper
- Get feedback from peers, teacher, or others
- Write final draft of research paper

The task breakdown in your prospectus might be very brief if your research will be limited to simply reading in your campus library. Similarly, creating a timeline might be a perfunctory step if your instructor has already imposed intermediate deadlines. However, you should not underestimate the time that will be required to do good work, and you should make careful plans for fitting each step of the research process into your personal schedule.

What qualifications are required to accomplish the proposed project? In addition to showing that you can complete the work within the constraints of time and location, you may need to persuade your readers that you have the required background, expertise, and training to accomplish the goal of your research. This would be especially true if you were planning to supplement your library research, say, with some interviews or with statistical data that you would need to collect, analyze, and interpret. Briefly describing your education, your previous experience with your proposed methods, and your other qualifications for completing the task is sufficient for this part of a prospectus. In cases where no especially difficult or unusual research techniques are involved, however, your readers are likely to take for granted your ability to complete the project, and you won't need to demonstrate it.

Are the necessary resources available? Beyond time and expertise, research often requires materials, instruments, and sometimes money to be completed. In more elaborate prospectuses, you would have to make the case that these necessary resources are available. A library research paper, however, typically requires only access to documents. You can usually use library materials at no or very little cost, so the important point to argue in this part of your prospectus is that the documents you need are relevant to your purpose and available for your use. You should also demonstrate that they are reliable and useful (see Chapter 9).

Together with the part of your prospectus that outlines the eventual form and contents of your paper, this part is probably the most important in persuading your audience to approve your project. It usually takes the form of a review of literature—so named because it surveys and summarizes the sources (the "literature") you have already located and shows how they can help you accomplish your research goals.

One possible way to organize the review of literature is to follow the preliminary outline you have already created. For example, if you have planned a paper that has four main divisions, you could similarly divide your review into four parts and summarize the sources that will help you write each part of your proposed paper.

Since your research and reading will continue after the time you write and submit the prospectus, your readers do not expect the review of the literature to be extensive or detailed. In fact, it might be appropriate to indicate that you intend to read sources you haven't yet been able to check out from the library. Your goal in writing this part of your prospectus is to persuade your audience that you have made significant progress toward finding, reading, and organizing information that will eventually be a part of your final paper. It is usually not necessary at this point to quote or paraphrase your sources extensively; instead, you should summarize in a sentence or two the main points of the books and articles you've skimmed, explaining how they will contribute to your project.

Another part of the prospectus that shows available resources is a selected bibliography of works you have identified as relevant to your research. This selected bibliography is usually attached as a separate section at the end of the prospectus, and it should be labeled and formatted according to the documentation style used in your discipline. It should include documents you have reviewed in the prospectus as well as documents you still intend to review. If you are required to use a minimum number of sources, obviously your list should contain at least that many. If no minimum was specified, you ought to list as many sources as you can find that show real promise of contributing to your project, without padding the bibliography just to make it impressive.

Note that any readers of your prospectus will review your selected bibliography carefully to determine whether you have used sound criteria to select your sources. These criteria include the following:

- Are the sources relevant to the proposed purpose?
- Are the authors and publishers of the sources credible and scholarly?
- Are the publication dates of the sources appropriate? For some topics, recency of publication is vital; for other topics, older sources may be particularly relevant.
- Are the authors and sources sufficiently varied so that the biases of individual works are balanced by works with different assumptions and approaches?
- Have you included all potentially useful sources?
- If appropriate, does the list contain a variety of kinds of publications? For example, does it include journal articles, particularly in fields where articles are the primary medium for disseminating information?

As you can see, preparing a prospectus that has all these parts will carry you far along the road toward a finished research paper. Your final paper will be stronger because of the careful planning you will have to do to prepare the prospectus. By starting early and answering the questions outlined above, you will avoid the stress of trying to write your paper in a few rushed days. You might even experience the pleasure—and relief—of finishing your paper ahead of schedule.

ORGANIZATION OF THE PROSPECTUS

Although the parts of a prospectus described above don't vary much, how they are organized in a particular prospectus can vary a great deal, depending on the requirements of the professor or department you are writing for. In most cases, the purpose and rationale of the proposed research project comprise the introduction. After that you may be required to use prescribed headings and subheadings in a specified order so that readers can check the completeness of the prospectus and read or reread parts as they desire. If you are required to follow an organizational plan, it is likely based on current genre conventions in your field. The organization below is suggested mainly for pedagogical reasons—to teach you one way of writing a prospectus that includes the necessary parts. Your instructor may ask you to modify this organizational scheme to meet other objectives he or she has for you. A complete prospectus can be divided into these four main sections:

1. *Purpose and Rationale.* In this section, you describe the general context of the problem, state the narrowly defined question, problem, or issue you propose to research, and justify its importance.

2. *Plan of Work.* In this section, you outline the thesis, organization, and contents of the eventual paper you will write; you provide your qualifications as a researcher (if required); and you outline the schedule you will follow, including how, where, and when you will accomplish the various phases of your research (if necessary).

3. *Review of Literature.* Finally, you summarize what you have learned from your research so far, showing how the sources you have read can help you achieve your purpose and fit into your plans for the eventual research paper.

4. *Selected Bibliography.* Attach to your prospectus a list of the works you have consulted so far and still intend to consult. Write this list according to the specifications of your field's documentation style. Label it appropriately (that is, the APA style and Turabian parenthetical reference style call it "References"; the Turabian note style calls it "Selected Bibliography.")

In addition to following this suggested organizational pattern, remember that the proposal is a formal document; therefore, you should take care to do the following as you compose it:

- *Make the tone formal to match that of the proposed paper.* The prospectus is not like a chatty letter to your teacher, so avoid writing in a casual tone.

- *Revise and edit your prospectus carefully.* Its purpose is to persuade your audience that you have the ability to conduct the proposed research and write the research paper, so you should demonstrate that you can write well.

- *Write the bibliographic citations in the correct format.* Getting the bibliographic citations right at this point will save you time as you prepare the final draft of your paper. If you are using the APA style or the Turabian reference list style, note that when you write the titles of books and articles within the *body* of the prospectus, the titles should be capitalized according to standard conventions, even though they are capitalized sentence style at the end in the list of references.

- *Follow principles of good document design when formatting your prospectus.* Use headings that correspond to the parts of a prospectus described here; or use other headings that your instructor may specify. Use letter-quality printing and a good grade of paper. The professional appearance of the prospectus should enhance its persuasiveness and indicate that you take pride in your work.

SAMPLE PROSPECTUS

The prospectus reproduced in Figure 10-3, by Kemarie Campbell, was written in her English 315 class for a research paper on the causes of obesity. As you will see, this prospectus contains information about the organization and contents of the paper Kemarie planned to write. After submitting a prospectus for your research paper and continuing to do further research, you may discover materials that alter your initial focus and plans. Or you may begin to think differently about the topic and want to change your basic position. If either of these happens, you should change your research paper accordingly rather than adhere rigidly to your previous outline. It would be a good idea to consult with your instructor, however, about any substantive changes in your plans. If you find that very broad changes become necessary, your instructor may advise you to write a new prospectus.

FIGURE 10-3. Kemarie Campbell's Prospectus

Kemarie Campbell
English 315, Section 9
Research Paper Prospectus
March 17, 2006

Obesity and Health Psychology

Purpose and Rationale

It is no secret that obesity is a problem in the United States. In fact, never in the recorded history of man has a nation been so fat—over 30% of the US population is obese (Hellmich, 2005). At the same time, there have never been so many diet and/or exercise programs to help people slim down. But obesity rates continue to rise.

Researchers have attributed the perpetual rise in obesity to a number of factors that all have to do with American lifestyle: quality of food intake, quantity of food intake, sedentary living, etc. We see the proposed solutions to these problems every day in magazine articles and television commercials that advertise the latest discovery on how to get thin fast. With the exception of a few eccentric outliers, each new diet program says the same thing the research has shown: in order to lose fat, you must eat less and exercise more. So, if we have identified the cause of obesity, and we know the solution to the problem, why isn't America slimming down?

I believe that the reason for the rising rates of obesity in the US is two-fold. First, obesity has been misinterpreted as *the* problem when it is really just a symptom of the real problem Americans face—which is a trend of unhealthy lifestyle. Second, while the basic issues of energy intake and expenditure have been addressed by the plethora of diet and exercise programs that are swamping the nation, one very important factor has been overlooked: the psychology of healthy living. In my research paper, I hope to address the importance of these two points in relation to developing a long-term health program that works to fight the problem of obesity.

Plan of Work

Since the science of dieting and fighting obesity has been a big part of US culture for at least the past forty years, I have limited my research to journals that were published in 1995 or later, and books

FIGURE 10-3. Kemarie Campbell's Prospectus (continued)

that were published no earlier than 1988. I will try to obtain the most current information possible. I will not go into detail on the exact regimens of popular diets or fitness/wellness programs, but I will discuss the common threads of American lifestyle in terms of health, how those threads affect American physiology and psychology, and the areas of health that current fitness programs are failing to address.

The main focus of my paper will be on the importance of health psychology, of recognizing obesity as a part of the health problem in the United States, rather than the sole problem, and of using a holistic approach in combating the big problem—one that includes the physical *and* psychological aspects of health. I envision my paper as follows.

Outline of Proposed Paper

I. Introduction

II. Obesity in the United States

    A. Facts about obesity

    B. Fighting obesity

        1. Dieting—effects and effectiveness

        2. Exercise—effects and effectiveness

III. Identifying the real culprit

    A. American lifestyle

        1. Eating in the U.S.

        2. Exercise in the U.S.

        3. Stress in the U.S.

    B. Obesity as a symptom

        1. Obesity in relation to eating habits

        2. Obesity in relation to exercise habits

        3. Obesity in relation to stress

FIGURE 10-3. Kemarie Campbell's Prospectus (continued)

IV. The Psychological Thread

    A. Psychology of dieting

    B. Psychology of exercise

    C. Psychology of stress

 V. Conclusion

<u>Timeline</u>

    I have made the following timeline of completion dates in order to finish a well-organized, well-written research paper by April 17, 2006:

    Begin note-taking—March 9

    Have a working outline—March 17

    Complete prospectus—March 17

    All references collected—March 22

    Write first draft—March 23–April 4

    Submit first draft for peer review—April 7

    Revise first draft—April 8

    Second revision—April 14

    Submit final draft—April 17

Review of Literature

    I have not yet gathered all of the information I will need to write this paper, but the articles and books I have reviewed thus far provide a strong foundation for my paper. They offer information about obesity, lifestyle problems within the US, and how psychology is related to health.

<u>Obesity in the United States</u>

    Nanci Hellmich (2005) gives gender and race-specific statistics on obesity in the United States as well as potential numbers for the future if current trends continue. Tibole and Resch (1995) talk about

---

FIGURE 10-3. Kemarie Campbell's Prospectus (continued)

dieting and the impact it has had in the US. Curioni and Lourenco (2005) discuss the effects of exercise on obesity and the effectiveness of implemented exercise programs over a long-term period. Stambor (2006) illustrates the effects of negative stress on the health of Americans.

Identifying the Real Culprit

Professor Aldana of BYU (2005) introduces the idea of American lifestyle as being the real culprit in the poor health of US citizens (eating, exercise, and relaxation habits) and also discusses the need for a holistic approach to health as a cure. Hirschmann and Munter (1988) discuss American eating habits and offer solutions to overcoming overeating. Smith, Baum, and Wing (2005), along with Michel, Levin, and Dunn-Meynell (2003) assess the effects of stress in relation to obesity. Their findings indicate that prolonged stress plays a role in weight gain.

The Psychological Thread

Cabyoglu and Ergene (2006) write about the ability to reduce obesity by reducing stress through acupuncture. Stice, Presnell, Groesz, and Shaw (2005) reveal the psychological effects of restrained eating (dieting) on teenage girls and how psychology plays a role in the development of bulimia. Urbszat, Herman and Polivy (2002) offer further evidence that psychology plays a large role in eating habits and that restrained eating ultimately leads to binge-eating due to psychological processes. Kamigaki (2005) reports on new findings that show stress as being related to obesity disorders. Tribole and Resch (1995) suggest methods of adopting healthy thinking patterns in order to overcome unhealthy habits. Sobel and Ornstein (1996) discuss specific actions and thought patterns that help one to develop a healthier lifestyle.

References

Aldana, S.G. (2005). *The culprit and the cure.* Mapleton, UT: Maple Mountain Press.

Cabyoglu, M.T., Ergene, N. & Tan U. (2006). The treatment of obesity by acupuncture. *The International Journal of Neuroscience, 116,* 165–75.

Curioni, C.C. & Lourenco, P.M. (2005). Long-term weight loss after diet and exercise: A systematic review. *International Journal of Obesity, 29,* 1168–74.

FIGURE 10-3. Kemarie Campbell's Prospectus (continued)

Hellmich, N. (2005, Oct. 9). Obesity in America is worse than ever [Electronic version]. *USA Today*. Retrieved March 13, 2006 from http://www.diabetichelp.com/ obesity_in_america_is_worse_than%20ever.htm.

Hirschmann, J.R. & Munter, C.H. (1988). *Overcoming overeating*. New York: Fawcett Books.

Kamigaki, M., Sakuae, S., Tsujino, I., Ohira, H., Ideda, D., Itoh, N., Ishimaru, S., Ohtsuka, Y. & Nishimura, M. (2005). Oxidative stress provokes atherogenic changes in adipokine gene expression in 3T3-L1 adipocyte. *Biochemical and Biophysical Research Communications, 339*, 624–32.

Michel, C., Levin, B.E. & Dunn-Meynell, A.A. (2003). Stress facilitates body weight gain in genetically predisposed rats on medium-fat diet. *American Journal of Physiology: Regulatory, Integrative & Comparative, 54*, 791–99.

Smith, A.W., Baum, A. & Wing, R.R. (2005). Stress and weight gain in parents of cancer patients. *International Journal of Obesity, 29*, 244–250.

Sobel, D.S. & Ornstein, R. (1996). *The healthy mind, healthy body handbook*. New York: Patient Education Media, Inc.

Stambor, Zak (2006, Apr. 4). Stressed out nation. *Monitor on Psychology*. Retrieved April 8, 2006 from http://www.apa.org/monitor/apr/06/nation.html

Stice, E., Presnell, K., Groesz, L. & Shaw, H. (2005). Effects of a weight maintenance diet on bulimic symptoms in adolescent girls: An experimental test of the dietary restraint theory. *Health Psychology, 24*, 402–12.

Tribole, E. & Resch, E. (1995). *Intuitive eating*. New York: St. Martin's Griffin.

Urbszat, D., Herman, P.C. & Polivy, J. (2002). Eat, drink, and be merry, for tomorrow we diet: Effects of anticipated deprivation on food intake in restrained and unrestrained eaters. *Journal of Abnormal Psychology, 111*, 396–401.

SUGGESTIONS FOR WRITING

1. After reading Chapters 3 through 8, plan a research project you could carry out using one or a combination of the methods described. Write an IRB proposal using the forms available at the following URL: http://orca.byu.edu/. Comply with all instructions, including the requirement to create a consent form. If you are planning an interview or a survey, attach the questions you will ask. If you do not plan to carry out the research, submit your proposal to your teacher for evaluation and feedback. If you plan to carry out the research, submit your proposal to the IRB or a department committee designated by the IRB to approve research projects.

2. Find out when the next deadline is for ORCA grants or for another granting process that funds undergraduate research. Ask what specifications you must meet in writing the proposal. Then write a proposal applying for funds.

3. After reading Chapter 9, write a prospectus for a research paper you have been assigned to complete during the current academic term. Describe your purpose and tell why it is important to research the topic you have chosen. Describe what the eventual research paper will contain by telling how you have limited the scope of your topic and by outlining the eventual contents of the paper. Summarize the library and Internet sources you have located that will help you write your planned paper. Attach a bibliography of sources, formatted in the style appropriate to your field. Submit the prospectus to your instructor to get approval and advice before proceeding to write your research paper.

11

RESEARCH PAPERS

CHAPTER OVERVIEW

After reading this chapter, you should be able to answer the following questions:

1. What are three general types of research writing?
2. Why is it important to begin research with a well-defined question?
3. Why is outlining an invaluable aid in conducting research and drafting a research paper?
4. What are three ways of incorporating source material into your research paper?
5. What changes are you allowed to make to quotations, and how do you represent those changes in your writing?
6. What are some techniques for writing smooth transitions to make your paper coherent?

No doubt you have written a number of research papers by this point in your education. And no doubt you have noticed that each teacher who has assigned a research paper has had somewhat different purposes and requirements than other teachers as well as a different way of evaluating your work. Some teachers prescribe the topic and make your grade depend heavily on following precise instructions for process and formatting the final draft a certain way. Others are more laissez-faire about such matters, letting you choose the topic, valuing mainly the content and originality of your paper, and grading you more on your demonstration of significant learning. Your work has probably been made more difficult as you have attempted to discern exactly what your teachers expect. While it might seem desirable for all teachers to agree on processes, formats, and evaluation standards for academic research papers, it is not likely ever to happen. The research paper as an academic genre is more variable than it is as a professional genre in a particular field of inquiry simply because professors have their own notions of what an academic research paper should do and be. Likely they are influenced as well by the kind of research writing they do for their own field. Unfortunately, this chapter can't completely overcome that variability.

Even though a major aim of this book is to prepare you for writing in graduate school and/or the workplace, it is impossible to model all the genres of research writing that any student reading this book might need to know now or in the future. Also, because you are still an undergraduate, the research paper you will write in this course is more likely to be an instrument for instruction and practice than it is a new contribution to knowledge that could be published in a professional journal. So this chapter will emphasize fundamental principles that are likely to be true across disciplinary boundaries, thus preparing you broadly for many types of research writing in the academy, the workplace, or graduate school.

One such general principle is that a research paper is fundamentally an argument, not simply an exercise in finding and stringing together information from a certain number of sources your teacher has assigned you to locate and use. The process of creating an argument from research—whether in the library, on the Internet, or from empirical data—includes these steps: (1) identifying the type of research writing you are expected to do; (2) formulating a research question and finding information or creating data to answer it; (3) planning and building your argument through outlining the parts and recording borrowed information carefully and ethically; (4) drafting your paper; and (5) formatting the final draft. Each step in this process will be discussed below except step 2, as that is discussed exhaustively in Chapters 4 through 9. Other chapters in this book also complement what will be said here, and you will be referred to those chapters as appropriate.

IDENTIFYING TYPES OF RESEARCH WRITING

Research writing can be thought of as a continuum: At one end is writing based on information retrieved from libraries and the Internet (which you learned about in Chapter 9) and at the other is writing about data gathered through empirical methods (which you learned about in Chapters 3 through 8). These are not mutually exclusive categories because nearly all empirical research papers include some information from library and Internet research, and sometimes papers based mainly on secondary sources may also include bits of information from primary sources, observations, interviews, and perhaps even casual surveys and experiments. But for clarity's sake, the following discussion will distinguish some of the characteristics of three types of writing that can be found in research papers: reviews of literature, argumentative source-based writing, and writing based on empirical data. All three kinds of writing can be said to advance answers in response to an initial question asked by the researcher.

Reviews of Literature

In the phrase "review of literature," the term "literature" does not refer to poetry and fiction but simply to whatever has been published on a given topic. A review of literature is a standard part of the introduction of almost every paper written to present new empirical data. It answers the question, "What is already known about this topic?" Writers review the existing literature for several reasons: A researcher investigating a given problem doesn't want to reinvent the wheel, so he or she would be foolish not to learn how others have already answered the same or similar questions. The researcher can learn from the successes and shortcomings of previous research how to conceptualize the problem and also how to improve the methods of the present investigation. Further, the researcher wants to understand the prevailing consensus, if there is one, about the question at issue. Above all, the researcher wants to learn what previous investigators have either neglected to study or studied incompletely because he or she has to define a space in the existing literature that the new research will fill. By reviewing or summarizing what all previous research has contributed to the problem, the researcher not only shows readers that the latest investigation is well-grounded conceptually and methodologically, but also that new research is needed to enlarge the boundaries of knowledge on the particular issue. Finally, the researcher can use the conclusions of previous research to interpret and/or bolster conclusions drawn from the results of his or her own study.

The research paper by Heather Bahlmann, "Exploring the Open-Response Task as a Tool for Assessing the Understanding of Fifth-Grade Students in the Content Area of Fractions," in the Readings section at the end of this book, contains a brief review of literature that has philosophical importance for the empirical research she presents. It provides a justification for her research by naming respected researchers who agree that personal agency and choice are vital to effective learning. The review also cites some of the previous work using open-response tasks to assess student understanding of mathematics as a way of justifying Heather's choice to use this method in her investigation. Finally, it shows how her research is unique and will contribute to the body of knowledge because it explores "alternative student strategies," or strategies that students chose not to use in solving problems. While this review of literature is likely not comprehensive, it demonstrates how such a review can provide a context and justification for new research.

But a review of literature can be written for its own sake as well, not only as the rationale for new empirical inquiry. In this case, it is meant to be a comprehensive summary of what is known about an issue. The task of writing such a summary entails, first, a careful library search to turn up all relevant articles and books and perhaps a careful Internet search to locate reliable peer-reviewed information. Second, it calls for patient reading of the sources with a critical eye toward the strengths and weaknesses, the contradictions and similarities of the accumulated studies. In other words, a good review of literature should not be a hodge-podge list-style summary of all the information you have uncovered. Instead, it should have a well-defined organizational plan that reveals the size and contours of knowledge on the issue; the various parts of the review should be proportionate to the varying emphases given the issue over time. Such a review of literature may or may not lead readers to see the gap that new research could fill, but it could very well have a thesis or an overall conclusion that you draw from having read the research. Your teacher may assign you to write this type of review of literature in place of or in addition to another kind of research paper this semester.

SOURCE-BASED ARGUMENTS

Many professors want you to learn how to construct not just a summary, but an argument, from reading the literature on a given issue. An argumentative paper based on library sources is usually less comprehensive than a review of literature. It will also have more of an "edge" to it than a review of literature because you, as the writer, will set out to prove a claim that you believe and that you can support with textual evidence. This claim, or thesis, will be the answer to the question that you posed at the beginning of your research process. Although you may have hunches and hypotheses, you shouldn't enter into your research already knowing the answer. Finding the answer to your question does not mean that you are free to pick and choose your sources so that you include only those that favor a certain position and ignore those that work against it. As a would-be scholar, you must give a fair hearing to all sides of any controversial issue, so you also have to read as much literature as is reasonable, given constraints on your time and your paper's length. You need to analyze the logic or methods of each study you look at to determine if they are valid and reliable, and you need to evaluate the results and conclusions to determine if they are justified. Wherever good opposing arguments exist, you must acknowledge and explain them, but you may be able to refute them with better or equally good arguments in such a way as to lend support to your thesis. Or you can modify your thesis so that it is not as sweeping as it may have been before you encountered strong opposing arguments.

The paper by Kemarie Campbell, "Addressing the Causes of Obesity in the United States: American Lifestyle and the Psychology of Health," in the Readings section at the end of this book, illustrates an argumentative source-based research paper. She began her research with this question: "Why, despite numerous diet and exercise programs, are Americans becoming obese in ever greater numbers?" After reading a number of sources and piecing together the information she found in them, she was ready to claim that the increasing level of obesity in the US is a symptom of an unhealthy lifestyle and psychological disposition, so to attack obesity with diet and exercise plans will not attack the root of the problem; instead, Americans need to change their thinking and practices with regard to food choices, exercise, and stress management. The sources Kemarie used to support her thesis may not have originally been written to make that sort of claim, but taken together they allow her to draw this conclusion. Any source-based research paper is a synthesis of pieces of other papers that were written for other purposes and other audiences. But a judiciously chosen body of reliable studies can be used as evidence for a new purpose and a new audience to support claims that their original authors may not have foreseen. Thus, a source-based argument is not merely an exercise in finding enough authors to quote and summarize in order to make a paper long enough to meet a teacher's requirements; instead, it is an opportunity to make and support an original claim about an issue that truly interests you by taking advantage of the work others have already done.

EMPIRICAL RESEARCH PAPERS

A research paper based largely on empirical data also makes an argument in answer to a question, but the strategies for making and supporting the claim are somewhat different. When you do empirical research, you must create, not simply find and synthesize, the knowledge that you will write about. You do this by selecting a method and then collecting data via that method. When your research process is complete, you have to make your argument out of the data you have and not the data you wish you had. You must analyze and interpret the data to determine what conclusions you can draw. When your empirical data are qualitative, you will often use them in much the same way that library and Internet sources are used to create an argumentative paper. That is, you might use descriptions of observations or quotations from interviews much like quotations or summaries from print or digital sources to support a point. Nearly always, you will turn to secondary sources from the library or Internet to help you interpret your findings or to bolster them with the evidence of previous research. When your empirical data are quantitative, you will usually represent them graphically in figures and/or tables. You probably will also apply statistical tests to raw data that reveal whether they are significant, i.e., due to real definable causes, not random variation or chance. Statistical proofs of significance become very important sources of persuasion in an empirical argument based on quantitative data.

You can see many of the above points illustrated in both Colleen Johnson's paper, "The Social Problems that Deter Xhosa Women from Marriage and How Education and Westernization Allow Them to Refuse Marriage," and Heather Bahlmann's paper, "Exploring the Open-Response Task as a Tool for Assessing the Understanding of Fifth-Grade Students in the Content Area of Fractions," reprinted in the Readings section at the end of this book. Colleen knew that quantitative studies of South African women showed a decrease in marriage rates and an increase in age at first marriage, but these studies did not explain why these statistical trends were occurring. So she began her research with this question: "What are the cultural causes of the new trends in marriage rates and ages among South African women?" After planning her research and having it approved by BYU's Institutional Review Board, Colleen went to South Africa, where she interviewed young single Xhosa women to learn why they were not marrying as frequently or as young as previous generations of Xhosa women. As you read Colleen's paper, you will notice that she has woven together many quotations from her informants with references to secondary sources that help her interpret her unique observations and add credibility.

Similarly, Heather Bahlmann uses qualitative and quantitative data with some references to secondary literature to support her claim. Heather, a math education major, wanted answers to these questions: "How can open-response tasks reveal what a student both understands and misunderstands about ways to solve math problems? In turn, how could a teacher's assessment of a student's use or failure to use effective strategies lead to improved instruction?" Her data came from both videotaped observations of fifth-graders solving fraction problems and content analysis of their written work on a test. By analyzing what students did and did not do in solving fraction problems, Heather was able to argue that open-response tasks have the potential to improve instruction, as students' talk, drawings, use of manipulatives, and solutions to problems can help teachers see what concepts and strategies students have and have not fully mastered. Both Heather and Colleen use an organizational strategy for their arguments that is modified from the conventional scientific format of introduction, methods, results, and discussion. They begin by establishing background information and justifications for their research; next they describe their methods; then they present and interpret results. Their arguments are successful to the degree that readers find their methods sound, their results sufficiently detailed and robust, and their analyses and interpretations careful, complete, and justified.

PLANNING AND BUILDING YOUR ARGUMENT

A good argument based on library or empirical research is never the product of an "overnighter" or even a few days' work. The three student papers described above are the end result of a three-month long process the writers undertook to plan, research, draft, and revise their arguments. They began early in the semester to define the questions they wanted to answer. Then they each wrote a formal prospectus (see Chapter 10) in which they proposed and outlined the argument they wanted to make and also proved that they had the library sources and empirical data to provide the building blocks for their argument. After getting their teacher's approval to proceed, they began reading and taking notes in earnest; then they began drafting their papers. When they had a complete first draft, they each received peer feedback (see Chapter 13); then, using their peer critiques and their own judgment about how to improve their arguments, they revised their papers substantially before submitting them for a grade. Several different tasks are important in this process of planning and building an argument: outlining, recording information, and using sources ethically. Each of these tasks is defined and illustrated below.

OUTLINING

Very few people are capable of outlining the final draft of a paper at the very beginning of their writing process, but this does not mean that an outline isn't valuable from the start. You can certainly outline your first draft at the beginning. From skimming your sources in order to write a prospectus (see Chapter 10), you can learn enough to outline a rough vision of the finished project—enough to get you going. Having an outline as you begin work will help you conduct research and take notes in a more focused and organized way. Not having an outline to work with at the beginning would be like starting to build a home without a blueprint: You would be making up your house (or your paper) as you went along, not really sure of what to include or exclude or how to connect things. Having a blueprint doesn't mean that you can't add a window or a closet or move an interior wall as your house is being constructed, nor does it lock you into any way of decorating your home. Outlines and papers are even more changeable than blueprints and houses. As you proceed in your research, you can change your outline to match what you are finding; as you proceed in your writing, you can change your outline to match your sense of the best way to organize your argument.

Knowing the conventions of outlining can help you as you plan and carry out your work. The purpose of an outline is to show how different parts relate to each other and make up the whole. The principles underlying a good outline are these:

1. Division
2. Coordination
3. Subordination
4. Parallelism

If you learned outlining as a child in school, you know that the traditional way is to use Roman numerals, capital letters of the alphabet, Arabic numerals, and lower case letters in alternation to represent the relationships of parts, as illustrated in Figure 11-1.

The four principles underlying good outlines are evident at every level of the outline in Figure 11-1. The first principle, division, is evident in the fact that there are eleven different headings in the outline; the indentations in the headings indicate that the divisions occur at four different levels. Notice that at any

FIGURE 11-1. Illustration of the traditional outline format

I. First Major Division
   A. First subdivision of Part I
   B. Second subdivision of Part I
      1. First subdivision of Part I-B
      2. Second subdivision of Part I-B
         a. First subdivision of Part I-B-2
         b. Second subdivision of Part I-B-2
II. Second Major Division
   A. First subdivision of Part II
   B. Second subdivision of Part II
   C. Third subdivision of Part II

given level, there are at least two divisions. When you divide, you must always divide into at least two parts; therefore, there can never be an *A* without a *B*, a *1* without a *2*, or an *a* without a *b*. The second principle, coordination, results from this principle of division. When you divide one part into at least two sub-parts, the results should be coordinate with each other; i.e., they should be equally important and receive about the same amount of space and emphasis in your paper. To use a simile, coordinate parts should be like twins or triplets—in the same family, each unique, but all equally important. The third principle, subordination, also results from the principle of division. When you divide a more general part into more specific parts, the more specific parts should be subordinate to the part they came from, i.e., at a deeper level of specification than the more abstract concept they follow. To use another simile, they should be like co-workers subordinate to the same supervisor.

The final principle of good outlining is parallelism, which is to be understood in two different ways. First, concepts at the same level within an outline, because they are coordinate, should be conceptually parallel—of the same type and roughly equal in importance. Second, the conceptual parallelism is made evident through grammatical parallelism. Below is a segment of an outline that lacks both kinds of parallelism:

II. Causes of the American Civil War
   A. Slavery
   B. Southern rebels fired on the US Army at Fort Sumter

As you can see, Part II-A is a very large and complex concept that is not conceptually parallel with Part II-B, which refers to a single event that precipitated the Civil War. The two parts are also not grammatically parallel, as "slavery" is a single noun, and "Southern rebels fired on the US Army at Fort Sumter" is a complete sentence.

Using the principles of outlining will help you as you work to impose a structure on the material you gather through your research. As your research and writing near an end, you will eventually stabilize your outline in its final form. Having a solid outline at the end of the process will be helpful because it will then be a simple matter to turn your outline into a table of contents for your paper and use the headings from your outline as headings in your paper. These structural elements will guide your reader in how to understand the overall organization of your paper and the relationships between different sections and ideas in your paper. As you study the research papers by Kemarie Campbell, Colleen Johnson, and Heather Bahlmann, you will see how their headings indicate the main divisions and subdivisions of their papers and also illustrate the principles of coordination, subordination, and parallelism.

RECORDING INFORMATION

Recording information or taking notes is a process that proceeds in tandem with the process of shaping your outline. As noted above, starting with an outline helps you decide what information to seek and what to record. But as you read, collect data, and take notes, you will also change your outline to reflect what you are learning. When you find something useful in your reading, rather than trust your memory, you should have a system to record the information. You will need to record two kinds of information: (1) bibliographic information and (2) notes on the facts and ideas you want to borrow from each source.

As you use directional sources such as indexes, databases, and search engines to locate good informational sources, you will find titles and abstracts of books, articles, and other documents that seem relevant to answering your research question. To keep track of what you find, you will need a system to note authors, titles, call numbers, URLs, or other information in order to keep your information organized and accessible so you can easily retrieve the sources you need. The traditional medium for recording this kind of bibliographic information has been 3x5 note cards, but the growing accessibility of library computers and student laptops brings new possibilities. You can copy and paste sources directly from a library catalog or database index, e-mail them to yourself, type them into a word processing document, or write them down in a research notebook. The important thing is to have a system rather than depend on your memory or scattered scraps of paper on which you jot information.

If you are systematic, you will need to record the bibliographic information only once; then, as you take notes, you can simply indicate that the note comes from a certain author and page number. Some students prefer to number their sources as they record them and then identify where a note comes from by simply writing the number of the source and the page number next to the note. As you find useful information in your sources, you will also need a method of recording what you wish to borrow. Since you must not deface library materials by marking in them, you have basically three options: photocopying, writing on note cards, and taking notes with a computer.

Photocopying. Most libraries have numerous photocopy machines, conveniently permitting you to make your own copies of source material. The advantage of making photocopies is that you may then underline, highlight, or write in the margins. You may even cut up your photocopies to rearrange source information as you organize your paper. One disadvantage is that photocopying can be an expense you would rather avoid. Another disadvantage is that you may head home from the library with a stack of photocopies thinking that you have already accomplished much of your research, when in fact the work of reading and digesting and encapsulating the information in writing still lies ahead of you. Nevertheless, photocopying is a convenient way of gathering information that you can't check out of the library so that you can read it later. Make sure, however, that you get all the information you will need to write a complete citation for the source later, because you must give credit to the author for any material you eventually use.

Writing Note Cards. The time-honored method of writing your notes on 3x5 cards is still a good one, if you have the patience to do it. One advantage of note cards is that you must come to grips with your sources as you write the notes. If you choose what you will summarize, paraphrase, and quote as you read, your notes will be all ready to use when you begin drafting your paper. A second advantage is that, because you put one piece of information on each card, you can then shuffle your cards into the order you will use them when drafting your paper. This is much harder to do if you have written your notes continuously on notebook pages, for example; while you could cut up the notebook pages to organize your notes, this means more work, and paper is flimsier than card stock. Some students combine photocopying with note cards. They cut out of their photocopies pieces of information they want to use and then glue these pieces on the cards. That way, they save the time of hand-copying a source yet still have the information in a form that is easy to organize. Whatever you do with note cards, be sure to indicate on them what source you have borrowed the note from.

Using a Computer. Some students avoid the expense of photocopies and save the time it takes to write note cards by typing notes directly into a computer, saving the notes in clearly labeled files that correspond to the headings in their preliminary outline. (Some word processing programs have note card functions that make this easy to do.) If they have a laptop computer, they can even take it to the library and take notes from sources they are not permitted to check out. Then in the drafting phase of the paper, they simply retrieve their notes from the files and incorporate them into the text of their paper. The advantages of this method are clear: it saves time, and, if you summarize and paraphrase your sources as you take the notes, it will be easy to fit the borrowed information into the paper later.

Regardless of the recording system that you use, you will need to take stock of your notes periodically and assess whether you have enough information to flesh out each part of your intended outline. If you do not, you may need to locate more information and take more notes. Or you may need to change your outline; for example, what you had intended to have as a major division of the paper might now become a smaller subdivision because you don't have enough to say about it. You may also find that you have so much information for an intended part of your outline that you need to divide it into two or more parts and perhaps leave out something else to make room.

USING SOURCES ETHICALLY

Regardless of the recording methods you use and how you present what you borrow, you must be careful to avoid plagiarism and use your sources ethically and professionally.

Avoiding Plagiarism. To plagiarize means to use an author's words or ideas without acknowledging that you have borrowed them, implying that they are your own. The word plagiarize comes from the Latin for "kidnapping." Metaphorically, the etymology is apt because, if you plagiarize, you are kidnapping someone's brain child—claiming to be the originator of something that someone else took the time and trouble to conceive, bring forth, and give their name to. The copyright laws regard plagiarism as the theft of intellectual property, similar to the stealing of real property, such as jewels or furnishings. Legal protection against plagiarism extends not only to written documents but also to sound and video recordings and computer software. There are not only legal penalties for plagiarism, but severe social and professional penalties as well. Occasionally the news media report on government officials, researchers, academics, and others in the public eye who have had past acts of plagiarism revealed, much to their embarrassment. Such revelations result not only in the loss of credibility and damaged reputation but sometimes in the loss of one's job. For students, the discovery of plagiarism is usually grounds for receiving a failing grade for the plagiarized paper and often for the course in which the plagiarism occurred. Extensive and repeated plagiarism may even be grounds for additional disciplinary action from the university.

But fear of repercussions should not be your primary motive for avoiding plagiarism. Your own integrity should motivate you to avoid this form of theft, just as your obligation to the communities you belong to should motivate you to respect the rules that make communal life possible. The temptation to plagiarize will be minimized if you remember that producing knowledge is a social, not solitary, endeavor. By carefully acknowledging what you have borrowed, you demonstrate that you recognize and are grateful for the contributions of earlier researchers. Far from indicating that you are unable to come up with your own ideas, when you document your use of others' ideas, you show that you are well-read in your field. By citing your sources, you also point the way for your readers to locate more information, should they desire to. Finally, a carefully documented paper shows the limits of your borrowing and makes your original contributions stand out more clearly against the ground of previous research that your ideas grow from. Your readers will be better able to recognize the extent and judge the value of your own thoughts as you carefully distinguish them from what you have borrowed.

   Common Knowledge. There is one qualification of the rule against plagiarism: You are not required to cite a source for what is called "common knowledge." Determining what is common knowledge is often difficult, however, as it depends not only on who the writer is but who the audience is as well. The more educated and specialized both a writer and an audience are, the more likely it is that they can draw particular facts and figures from their store of knowledge without looking them up in other sources. Even though those facts originated with someone, after a period of time these ideas have become so commonplace that their origin is seldom mentioned. As you read your sources, you may see some facts mentioned with no source cited. If you see them mentioned repeatedly, you may assume that these are common knowledge for both the writer and the intended audience.

   When you see specific facts mentioned without a citation, however, you should stop to ask yourself whether they are common knowledge for you and your intended audience. Ask yourself these questions: Did you already know these facts before you began your research? Is it likely that your audience already knows them? If so, you may include them in your paper without a citation. But if you find it necessary to take notes on particular facts, the very act of writing notes suggests that they were not common knowledge for you. You ought to cite at least the source where you first learned them, even if you can't cite the original source. When in doubt, it is safer to cite a source than to assume that something is common knowledge.

   A Final Caution. As you take notes, you must be very careful with your sources as you are recording them so that you don't inadvertently plagiarize, misuse, or distort the information in your sources. You can also save time later when drafting by deciding how you would like to incorporate into your paper each item of information that you record. You have three options: (1) you can summarize, (2) you can paraphrase, and (3) you can quote. Each of these options will be explained in more detail and illustrated in the section entitled "Drafting Your Argument." Quoting your sources is not the best option because research papers are much more effective if you translate most of your sources into your own words and later recombine them in a way that allows you to make your own argument in a way that is both logically and stylistically coherent. Here are some rules of thumb to follow as you decide how to use a source at the time you make your notes:

1. Summarize lengthy and detailed information when you want only the main ideas or the essence of that information. Probably half or more of the borrowed information in your paper should be summarized.

2. Paraphrase information which you want to represent entirely in your paper but which you can say just as well in your words. Probably a third or less of the borrowed information in your paper should be paraphrased.

3. Quote information that you don't want to or can't summarize or paraphrase. Only about ten to fifteen percent of your paper should be quoted. You must write down quotes exactly as they are in the original source, so be very careful in transcribing or make photocopies to be sure you do not distort the original. To help you in choosing when to quote, here are some guidelines:

   - When the words of the original are open to several interpretations. For example, the First Amendment to the U.S. Constitution has been interpreted differently by various groups and at different times by the Supreme Court. If you were writing a paper about the disputes surrounding the First Amendment, it would be important to quote it rather than paraphrase it, since by paraphrasing you might inadvertently favor a particular interpretation.

   - When the words of a document are the topic you are writing about. If you are writing about the language of a treaty, a trade agreement, a letter, a diary, or some other primary source, it is essential to quote actual excerpts from it, both to establish what is under discussion and to make your claims about it credible to the audience.

   - When the words of the original are especially striking and a paraphrase or summary would diminish their impact. Occasionally, one of your sources will provide a phrase, sentence, or paragraph that is particularly well-said and memorable. If quoting it verbatim will add strength, insight, and color to your own argument, by all means quote it. But note that you can be selective about how much you choose to quote by paraphrasing or summarizing some of the original and using only those words that are particularly striking.

   - When a quotation will help bolster the authority of the argument you are making. If you are writing about a controversial topic, trying to persuade a hostile audience, you and your argument may gain some credibility if you judiciously choose some quotations from respected sources that support your position. Be sure you don't distort the intentions of the original authors, however, by lifting supportive quotations out of their original context and using them in a way that the original author would find questionable.

DRAFTING YOUR ARGUMENT

Using your outline as the framework and your notes as the material to fill in and enclose the frame, you can begin to draft your paper. You may find it helpful first to turn your outline into headings for your paper. Every Roman numeral division of your outline will become a primary heading; every *A* or *B* division will become a secondary heading; and every *1* or *2* division will become a tertiary heading. (These three levels of headings are illustrated in Chapter 16, so no more will be said here.) Then, if you have handwritten or photocopied notes, sort your notes into piles that correspond to the divisions of your paper. If you have typed your notes in computer files, organize them so that they are easily retrievable to insert into the different parts of your paper. Now you can begin to write paragraphs under each heading that build each part of your argument, and you can incorporate your borrowed information into the paragraphs as needed to support the assertions you are making. You don't necessarily have to start writing at the beginning of your outline, though most people do. If you have a bit of writer's block about what to say first, start in the middle. Often, writing other parts of your paper will help you see more clearly what you need to say at the beginning to set up your main points and the conclusion.

As you are drafting, you will use your borrowed information as explained earlier, in one of three forms: summary, paraphrase, or quotation. Each of these is explained and illustrated next, followed by advice about writing transitions, introductions, and conclusions.

SUMMARIZING

To summarize is to distill the original source down to its essence, by capturing the main points and ignoring the details. A summary is therefore much shorter than the original. It is also written in your own words, though it might include a few quoted words for which you can find no synonyms or which you can't adequately express in your own style. Although you write a summary in your own words and style, you still must attribute the ideas to the author from whom you borrowed them. Here is an example of a summary from Kemarie's paper.

> Sobel and Ornstein (1996) suggest that regular physical activity should be enjoyable and that it doesn't have to be difficult in order to be beneficial (pp. 109–110).

This adequately sums up the original source, which goes into some detail about the benefits of regular, moderate exercise and even lists types of exercise, such as cycling for pleasure and gardening, which can benefit the body without being intense and vigorous.

Here is another summarized passage from Kemarie's paper. You can be sure this is a summary because the reference is to pp. 69–117 of the original source. Obviously, Kemarie has left out a lot of details and captured just the essence of what is said in all those pages:

> Three of the most common mistakes Americans make in their food choices are in choosing to consume white, refined grains and starches instead of whole grains, not eating enough fruits and vegetables, and going to one extreme or the other in their fat intake (Aldana, 2005, pp. 69-117).

Technically, you do not have to give page numbers for summarized material, particularly if you have summed up an entire article in a few sentences. However, it is never wrong to cite the page numbers that you have summarized, and it is very helpful for anyone who wants to locate the information in the original source.

PARAPHRASING

To paraphrase is to restate the original in your own words and syntax, while still capturing the entire meaning of the original. A paraphrase is thus about the same length as the original, and it parallels the original by following the same order and giving the same emphasis to ideas as the original. A paraphrase might contain a few quoted words or phrases you can't find appropriate synonyms for. When you paraphrase, you do not distort the intent of the original by leaving out ideas or by enlarging minor points or downplaying major points. The value of paraphrasing is that you can give your paper a more coherent voice and point of view by putting source information in your own words. But you still must attribute what you have borrowed to the original author, either as you introduce the paraphrase or in a parenthetical reference. Here is an example of a paraphrase from Kemarie's paper. First, the original passage from the source is presented, then Kemarie's paraphrase of it.

Original Passage:

> More than 250,000 deaths per year in the United States (12% of the total) may be due to a lack of regular physical activity.

Kemarie's paraphrase:

> Research shows that about 12 percent of deaths in the US annually occur because people don't routinely get enough exercise (Sobel & Ornstein, 1996, p. 112).

Note that the paraphrase is about as long as the original; it includes all the ideas in the original using Kemarie's own words and syntax; and it cites the source. As with summarizing, you are not obligated to give page numbers for paraphrased material, but again it is desirable that you do so for the sake of readers who want to locate the information in the original for themselves.

QUOTING

When you were younger, you may have "written" research papers by simply finding and quoting the exact words of many different writers. But now you know that quoting is the type of borrowing you should do least. An exception to this rule would occur when you are writing an empirical research paper based on interviews, such as Colleen Johnson's paper in the Readings section at the end of this book; as you will see, Colleen quotes liberally from the transcripts of interviews she conducted. Papers that consist mainly of many quotations strung together with a few transitional sentences tell your reader that you have failed to digest your sources well enough to present the information in your own voice and as support for your unique thesis. But that is only a part of what you need to know about quoting sources. There are many intricate facets to the mechanics of quoting, so how to do it according to accepted conventions is discussed and illustrated next.

Embedded Quotations. Embedded quotations are incorporated within the flow of a paragraph. They are distinguished from your own words by the use of double quotation marks. Generally, a wise thing to do when introducing an embedded quotation is to attribute it to the source, i.e., name the author or authors (and usually the year of publication) as you introduce a quotation, as in the following examples. If you attribute the quotation at the beginning, you do not need to cite the author's name and the year of publication in the parenthetical reference, as you can see in this example from Heather's paper:

> Students must be instructed sufficiently in order for them to make purposeful choices that will allow them to learn. As Walter and Gerson (in press) assert, "The act of making a purposeful choice is a fundamental component of learning" (Ms. p. 8).

Notice that the page number is *always* given in parentheses at the end of the quotation, if it comes from a printed source. You are obligated to give page numbers when you quote. Notice also in the above and following examples that the parenthetical citation comes *before* the sentence period.

> Eating white breads, white rice, and other processed foods puts Americans at a serious health disadvantage. As Dr. Aldana (2005) puts it, "They have an increased risk of many chronic diseases because, although these foods do not *cause* disease, they fail to *prevent* disease" (p. 71, emphasis added).

Another way to use an embedded quotation is to put the entire reference in the parentheses following the quotation. You might do this when it would be awkward to interrupt the flow of your paragraph by attributing the quotation to its source, as in the following example, which quotes only part of a sentence:

> Exercising along with the dieting produced 20% greater weight loss than dieting without the exercise program. However, while the researchers showed that exercise has a significant effect on weight loss, they noted that "in both groups, almost half of the initial weight loss was regained after one year" (Curioni & Lourenco, 2005, p. 1168).

Here is another example of putting the entire reference after the quotation.

> While researchers attempt to explain the historical and current issues that are affecting the marriage trends in South Africa, "consensus on the reason for such changes is yet to be reached" (Makiwane, 2004, ¶ 1).

Notice that when the quoted material comes from an unpaginated electronic source, you should give the paragraph number that is cited, indicated by the symbol ¶ in the parenthetical reference.

Block Quotations. When quotations are less than 40 words (in APA style) or would run to less than four lines of text (in Turabian style), they are always embedded. When they are longer, they are set off by indentation on the left side, as in the following example from Colleen's paper. Such indented quotations are called "block quotations." Notice that this block quotation is introduced, not by using the authors' names, but by using a sentence that helps the reader understand that the quotation will tell about a trend in western societies that is now finding its way to Africa. Particularly for long quotations, introductions such as these are very helpful to the reader, who needs to know the significance of the quotation.

> South African women also view marriage negatively due to Western ideology's influence on men's and women's attitudes toward marital duties. This trend mirrors what has been found in other westernized societies:
>
> > A cultural lag exists between the changing domestic roles of women and men in U.S. society. Specifically, women are positively embracing their new work and family roles, while men are resisting the increasing independence of women in the workplace and the greater demands placed on men in the home. (Hunt & Hunt, 1987, as cited in Ferguson, 2000, p. 140)

Notice that no quotation marks are used around the quoted part because the indentation indicates the words are quoted. Notice also that the parenthetical reference comes *after* the sentence period at the end of the block quotation.

A final important thing to note is that the above quotation is a secondary citation. That is, Colleen located the information in an article by Ferguson

(2000), but Ferguson was citing Hunt and Hunt (1987). You may find something you want to quote in one source that cites another source. Rather than track down the original source, you may cite it in the manner illustrated above. In such a case, you put only the source you read in your list of references.

If you use a long quotation from a non-print source, such as an interview, you also present it as a block quotation, as in the next example from Colleen's paper, which is preceded by information that helps the reader understand the context of the quotation.

> Even though many wives are sexually inactive until married and remain faithful to their husbands, they still run the risk of contracting AIDS due to their husbands' promiscuity. One interviewee claimed that marriage is the highest risk factor for AIDS because women think,
>
> > "This is your husband, what chance are you going to have [to contract AIDS]," and you're never going to think about it. . . . Long relationships are the one relationship that are good for you in terms of contracting AIDS . . . because you feel so trustworthy and you trust that person. So that's why I'm saying if I were to get married—which won't happen first of all—I don't know. I can't put my life in jeopardy with someone else. (Personal communication, 2005)

Notice that this quotation is introduced by an attribution to an anonymous person. Colleen had pledged not to reveal her informants' names, so she referred to this person as "one interviewee."

Quotation within a Quotation. Notice also that, even though the above example is an indented quotation and therefore doesn't normally use quotation marks, Colleen begins it with quotation marks because the first sentence is a quotation within a quotation. The first line quotes what the informant said women often think to themselves when they get married, i.e., that their husband will not infect them with AIDS. Sometimes block quotations will already contain double quotation marks around certain words or phrases. In that case, you simply use them the same way they are used in the original.

You can also have a quotation within an embedded quotation, as in this example, which compares the original passage with Heather's use of it:

Original from Susan J. Lamon (2005):

> The National Council of Teachers of Mathematics asserted in their Curriculum and Evaluation Standards (1989) that proportional reasoning "is of such great importance that it merits whatever time and effort must be expended to assure its careful development" (p. 82).

Heather's quotation:

> Lamon (2005) cites the NCTM's recommendation that teaching "proportional reasoning 'is of such great importance that it merits whatever time and effort must be expended to assure its careful development'" (p. xiii)

Notice that Heather uses double quotation to surround the whole quotation, and that she uses single quotation marks around the part of the quotation that was quoted in Lamon's book. Thus at the end of the quotation, there are three quotation marks in a row.

Here is another example from Heather's paper in which only one word—*holes*—is in single quotation marks. We may safely assume from this that in the original passage that word was in double quotation marks.

> The open-response task requires "students to explain their thinking and thus allow teachers to gain insights into . . . the 'holes' in their understanding" (Moon & Schulman, 1995, p. 30).

Using Brackets to Add to Quotations. At the end of Colleen's quotation within a quotation, she has used brackets to insert information that helps clarify for the reader what the informant was talking about when she referred to a "chance."

> "This is your husband, what chance are you going to have [to contract AIDS],"

Sometimes when you take a quotation from its context, you will need to insert emendations, but you may do this only in brackets—not parentheses—to let the reader know the words come from you, not the original source. After the close quotation marks, the rest of the quotation is what the informant believed about the naïve attitude of some women that they won't get AIDS from their husbands.

Here is another example of the use of brackets from Heather's paper. She has used brackets here, first, to clarify what in the original passage was simply called "them" and then to change pronouns from "they" to "it" and to change the verb to agree with the singular pronouns.

> "The problem with [finding a common denominator] is that many students cling to [it] without understanding why [it] work[s]. So a good classroom strategy is to make finding a way to explain why common denominator works an on-going problem" (NCTM, 2002, p. 11).

Using Ellipsis to Omit Parts of Quotations. Colleen chose to omit some parts of the transcribed interview by using ellipses, as shown below.

> you're never going to think about it. . . . Long relationships are the one
> relationship that are good for you in terms of contracting AIDS . . . because you
> feel so trustworthy and you trust that person.

The first ellipsis represents the omission of a sentence or more. You can tell this because there are four periods in the ellipsis; the first period is the sentence period, and the three spaced periods represent the missing material. The second ellipsis represents the omission of a few words from within the sentence because it is represented by only three periods. Notice that the three final periods in any ellipsis have spaces *both before and after*. (Even if your word processor does not put in the spaces, you should.)

Citing Non-recoverable Sources. Colleen includes in her paper many parenthetical references that cite the source as "personal communication." This is used for a reference whenever the information cited is not recoverable in print form or from an archive. If you cite personal communication, you should first cite the name of the person you communicated with, unless you have promised not to reveal it. At the end you should also cite a date that is as exact as possible. But you do not have to put anything your list of references because the information is not recoverable.

Adding Emphasis to Quotations. Along with using brackets to add words to quotations and using ellipses to omit words, you can use italics to emphasize words in quotations, as in this example from Kemarie's paper:

> Eating white breads, white rice, and other processed foods puts Americans at a serious health disadvantage. As Dr. Aldana (2005) puts it, "They have an increased risk of many chronic diseases because, although these foods do not *cause* disease, they fail to *prevent* disease" (p. 71, emphasis added).

Notice that immediately after the page number, Kemarie has written "emphasis added" in order to let her readers know that the italics were not in the original source. However, if you use a quotation in which the author has used italics for emphasis, it is important to point that out for your reader, so that the reader does not assume you added the italics. You do this in the parenthetical citation by writing "emphasis in original" immediately after the page number.

Changing Capitalization. One more thing you should know about quoting is that you may silently change capitalization to fit the context in which you are using the quotation. You do not have to use brackets to indicate the changes. You are particularly likely to change capitalization when you introduce a quotation with an attribution followed by the word *that*. When you use *that* to connect your attribution to the quotation, you do not capitalize the first word of the quotation, even if it was capitalized in the original. In the following example, Kemarie has quoted a heading in which every word was capitalized, but she puts the entire borrowed sentence in lower case letters:

> Sobel and Ornstein also confirm that "what you tell yourself matters," pointing out that negative or degrading thoughts about exercise or sports performance prohibit one from getting the full benefits of the exercise (p. 115).

However, when you use an attribution without *that*, you capitalize the first word of the quotation if the quotation is a complete sentence, as in this example:

> As Walter and Gerson (2006) assert, "The act of making a purposeful choice is a fundamental component of learning" (p. 8).

As you can see, there are many intricate conventions for using sources in your paper. As you draft, be sure that you follow these rules. If in doubt, refer to a handbook or ask a tutor or your instructor for help.

Including Transitions With Headings

It is important to note that you should write transitions in addition to using headings. Some readers skip rapidly over headings, and they will feel an abruptness in your prose if you don't write explicit transitions that provide a bridge from part to part. Each time you introduce a new major division of your paper, you should foreshadow the divisions within that section by writing something like this from Kemarie's paper:

> Lifestyle encompasses everything we do—our eating and exercise habits, stress and stress management, and even the way we think. So in order to understand the lifestyle culprit, we must examine American food, exercise habits, and stress.

As you would be able to predict, the next three secondary headings after these introductory sentences are "American Food," "American Exercise Habits," and "Stress in the US."

Even as you move to tertiary subdivisions, you should use a transition, as in this example, also from Kemarie's paper:

> Dieting is the solution for anyone who wants to lose weight—or so we've been told. But is dieting really producing the intended results?
>
> **Dieting.** According to Tribole and Resch (1995), as the dieting industry in America has grown (to an annual value of $50 billion), obesity rates have soared right along with it.

Notice that she transitions to the topic of dieting by bringing up a common belief, i.e., that dieting will promote weight loss. Then she asks a rhetorical question that challenges the reader to rethink that assumption and be ready to learn why dieting is ineffective.

Another way to write a good transition is to look back at what you have just said and then forward to what you will say next. Here are two examples of that from Kemarie's paper. In the first she has just written about the health value of eating whole grains, and next she will tell the reader about fruits and vegetables:

> **Fruits and vegetables.** Besides not getting enough whole grains, Americans are not eating enough fruits and vegetables.

In this one, she has just written about grains, fruits, and vegetables, and next she will discuss fats, but she eases the reader into the discussion rather than simply using the heading for a transition.

> **Fats.** While the health value of whole grains, fruits, and vegetables has been advertised and known for quite some time, fats have gotten a bad rap over the past few decades.

Pay attention to the transitions as you read the papers by Kemarie, Colleen, and Heather. They all illustrate very well how to make writing smooth and coherent without making headings do all the work of showing readers the connections between the parts.

WRITING THE INTRODUCTION AND CONCLUSION

In addition to writing smooth transitions, pay special attention to writing your introduction so that it draws the reader in by making the topic interesting and important and so that it lets your reader knows what you intend to argue and how. Notice that in Kemarie's introduction, she tells the story of a man who weighed 750 pounds and who wanted to lose weight but was unable to stop bingeing on unhealthy food. This unusual anecdote is likely to be intriguing to most readers, and Kemarie leads readers from that story to a brief discussion of the seriousness of the problem of obesity and then to her thesis that diet and exercise programs will not solve the problem because obesity is itself only the symptom of a bigger problem. She promises to explain to the reader how healthy lifestyle and healthy psychology, not more diet and exercise programs, are the key to decreasing obesity. With that her paper is launched.

Equally important is a strong conclusion that gives the reader a sense of completeness and closure. Kemarie's conclusion is an excellent example of this, as she reasserts her thesis that changing lifestyle and psychology is the key to battling obesity. By this point she has offered sufficient evidence in the middle of the paper that the reader should have been persuaded to agree with this assertion. She then refers again to the 750-pound man whose story she told in the introduction, noting that he died. She asserts that merely changing his diet and making him start exercising would not have been sufficient to produce lasting weight change because the reasons he ate so much and chose unhealthy foods were related to his lifestyle and his psychological disposition towards food. Referring again to the story she began with gives a feeling of roundedness to the paper as the story makes concrete the argument she has made using more technical and abstract information from her sources. It also engages readers' emotions, as we pity someone whose life has ended prematurely for causes that might have been prevented, and it may motivate us to be wiser in our own behavior so that we can enjoy better health.

FORMATTING THE FINAL DRAFT

Once you have revised your paper sufficiently that you are prepared to submit it, it is time to add the formatting your teacher requires. Formatting guidelines are admittedly arbitrary. Understanding that surface format features can and will change as you write for different audiences and purposes should help prepare you to be flexible about such matters in the future—and maybe even the present, as your teacher this semester may ask you to follow some different formatting rules than are illustrated in the student research papers at the end of this book. For example, your teacher may ask you to format your paper using the APA manuscript style, which includes a running head. I have chosen not to illustrate that style in this book because the *APA Publication Manual* is a submission manual for professionals preparing copy manuscripts for publication in a journal. The copy manuscript is a peculiar genre that has a very short life and is not seen by very many people. It is read only by the editor, the reviewers, and the typesetter. Once the copy manuscript has been turned into a typeset article, the copy manuscript is discarded. The typeset article looks very different from the copy manuscript.

Student papers are usually not copy manuscripts. They are final documents, and they reach their intended audience in the form in which they are submitted. This means that, as the APA manual states, for student papers "a number of variations from the requirements described in the *APA Publication Manual* are not only permissible but also desirable. . . . The *Publication Manual* is not intended to cover scientific writing at an undergraduate level, because preferences for style at that level are diverse" (p. 322). So, while the format of the papers by Kemarie, Colleen, and Heather conform in many ways to the APA manual's guidelines (principally in the abstract, headings, parenthetical references, and list of references), some of their other features (for example, the title page, the table of contents, and the pagination) do not. For any writing assignment you are given, you should learn what special requirements your instructor has for you in addition to following documentation specifications of a professional style manual.

Following are typical elements for a student research paper. These elements correspond to those you would be required to have in an honors thesis or senior thesis at BYU.

1. *Title Page.* Because your paper is a final document, it should have a title page. The minimum elements for a title page are, of course, your title and your name. Your instructor may also want you to list the name of the course, the teacher's name, and the date the paper was finished or submitted.

2. *Table of Contents.* The table of contents, as previously noted, is the hierarchical arrangement of the headings used in the paper, with indentations showing whether each heading is primary, secondary, or tertiary. Following each heading is the page number where the reader can find the section of the paper under each heading. On the table of contents, it is helpful to use dot leaders, a row of dots running from the heading to the page number, as these help the reader's eye move across the page to the right number.

3. *Other Prefatory Pages.* If your paper contains any tables or figures, there should be an additional page following the table of contents entitled "List of Figures and Tables," or simply "List of Figures" or "List of Tables" if you have only one kind of graphic in your paper. The abstract follows these pages, and is headed with the word "Abstract." (For more information on using figures and tables, see Chapter 17; for more on how to write an abstract, see Chapter 13.)

4. *Pagination.* All of the above prefatory pages except the title page are numbered with lower case Roman numerals. The title page is considered to be page i; however, it is not numbered. The table of contents is numbered as ii, with other prefatory pages following in numerical succession. The first page of text is numbered with the Arabic number 1, and other pages are numbered successively. The list of references begins on a new page after the conclusion of the paper and is numbered with Arabic numbers succeeding the last page of text.

5. *Appendixes.* If you have one or more appendixes, they follow the list of references and are paginated with Arabic numbers succeeding the list of references.

6. *Double spacing.* Double space the final draft that you submit to your teacher.

All of the above formatting conventions are illustrated in the research papers by Kemarie, Colleen, and Heather at the end of this book. However, the papers by Colleen and Heather are not double-spaced in order to save paper and printing costs for this book.

CONCLUSION

As you come to the end of this long and detailed chapter, you are probably feeling a bit daunted by all you have to remember and to do as you write your paper. It would be impossible to take all of the steps outlined here in one short burst of work. Writing a strong research paper is a task that must be spread over many weeks if it is to be successful. At the beginning of the semester, the assignment to write a research paper can loom ahead of you like a grueling hike up a tall mountain. But rather than regard the assignment as an enormous obstacle in the path of your comfort and happiness, try to view it as an adventure and an opportunity to learn new and interesting things at each step along the trail. Choose a topic to research that genuinely interests you and set a goal to write a paper that will benefit you and others. Don't procrastinate starting to read, take notes, and write a rough draft. Divide your journey into stages and mark with satisfaction your progress to each milepost along the way. Then when you finally reach the summit by completing your final draft, you can look back with pride on your achievement and savor the view from the heights of your new knowledge.

SUGGESTIONS FOR DISCUSSION AND WRITING

1. What processes have you followed in the past to complete research papers for school?

2. In the past, have you outlined research papers before starting to work on them? If not, how did you decide what you were looking for in your research and how did you decide to organize your paper? If so, how did outlining help you in your research and writing?

3. What is your preferred method of note taking? Why?

4. What did this chapter teach you about using sources that you did not know (and did not do) in the past? How has this chapter helped you to understand and avoid plagiarism?

5. Have you ever written a paper using headings before? What do you find difficult about using headings? What advantages do you find in using headings?

REFERENCE

American Psychological Association. 2001. *Publication manual of the American Psychological Association*. 5th ed. Washington, D.C.: American Psychological Association.

12

PUBLIC POSITION PAPERS AND OPINION PIECES

CHAPTER OVERVIEW

After reading this chapter, you should be able to answer the following questions:

1. What are position papers and opinion pieces? Who are they written for?
2. What are the steps in researching and writing a position paper or opinion piece?
3. How do the organization and style of position papers and opinion pieces usually differ from reports written for professors or for professional peers?
4. What would it take for a position paper or opinion piece to have an impact on public policy-making?

As a student of the social sciences, you are learning about social and cultural institutions such as governments, the justice system, schools, hospitals, churches, charitable organizations, youth groups, and families. In general, these institutions aim to promote a just, harmonious society and the development of productive, healthy individuals. It's probably clear to you by now, however, that these and other institutions are not always successful in reaching these goals. After more than 200 years of government under the United States Constitution, for example, there is still not complete harmony and equity among various groups in the USA. Some well-intended government programs and policies do not always promote justice or help individuals to be productive. Similarly, as hard as they try, schools, churches, and charitable groups do not always succeed in enhancing individual development. Some families can be dysfunctional, too, not fostering the kind of relationships and individual growth that healthy families do.

As social scientists study these and other institutions, they often point to flaws in them that they believe could be corrected through taking some appropriate action. When social scientists make recommendations that affect public life, their purpose for writing changes from informing their peers about their research to participating in civic discourse. They turn from the professional realm that normally absorbs most of their time and interest to the public realm, an openly political realm in which their recommendations might have real consequences in the lives of real people.

There are several genres in which social scientists might write about their opinions and recommendations. One would be an article for a popular magazine (as opposed to a professional journal). Another would be a newspaper article or editorial, often called an "opinion piece." Still another possible genre is called the "position paper," typically written for government officials and sometimes the public to influence them to adopt recommendations the writer might make.

Although position papers are often identified mainly with the writing that political scientists do, other social scientists—including economists, anthropologists, sociologists, social workers, psychologists—all might have occasion to make important contributions to the formation of public policies and programs. For example, suppose a state has the luxury of a budget surplus and its legislature is debating what to do with the extra funds. An economist might prepare a position paper recommending a reduction in the state property tax or sales tax, showing how the reduction would affect future state revenues and the general economy of the state. A social worker might write a position paper recommending increased funding for state agencies serving unemployed and homeless persons and people whose job skills need to be upgraded. A psychologist might argue for creating and staffing more public mental health clinics. An anthropologist could plead for a bigger budget to preserve sites in the state where remnants of prehistoric cultures have been discovered. The expertise of social scientists can sometimes magnify their voices in the political process and persuade legislators and the public to take actions they might not otherwise think of. By writing effective position papers, then, social scientists can use rhetoric in the way that it was first designed to be used—as a way of influencing the body politic.

As you prepare for your career, it is important for you to consider how you could apply your knowledge to the analysis of real problems that we face as members of the various overlapping communities we belong to. As you learn to create solutions to problems and recommend those solutions persuasively to the people who can implement them, you will see how your developing expertise in a field could have an impact in the lives of other people besides yourself and professional peers. In this chapter, you will learn some basic steps for writing position papers and opinion pieces to be read by the general public.

WRITING A POSITION PAPER

DEFINE AND LIMIT THE PROBLEM

The first step in writing a position paper is to define and limit the problem carefully. Most social problems are complex and therefore require multi-faceted solutions. Consider, for example, the problem of violent juvenile gangs in urban areas. The factors that might lead youth to join gangs are many, including lack of strong family ties, low self-esteem, unemployment and economic despair, peer pressure, racial discrimination, learning disabilities or low motivation to succeed in school, and lack of wholesome leisure time activities. Once youths have formed gangs, other factors could contribute to their destructiveness, including such things as too few police officers, easy access to firearms, inadequate detention and reform facilities, crowded court dockets, or laws with lenient penalties for adolescents. When you see how complex the problem of gangs is, you realize that it would probably take volumes to write a comprehensive position paper recommending solutions that would even start to scale back this problem, let alone get rid of it. Making a problem like this manageable obviously will require the efforts of a number of professions, all working together to attack it from different angles.

The complexity and intractability of most social problems means that writing an effective position paper will usually require you to limit your definition of the problem. So, for example, rather than defining the problem as "gangs," you could define it more narrowly by focusing on one of the factors that lead to the formation of gangs or contribute to their destructiveness. It will be most helpful, too, to focus on factors that could be affected by a public policy or program. For instance, you could focus on the shortage of police officers or the easy availability of firearms, since government officials have the power to appropriate money to hire more officers and to write laws regulating access to firearms.

However, if you see these measures as striking at the branch rather than the root of the problem, you might instead focus on factors that make some youth susceptible to the pressure to join gangs, such as low self-esteem, lack of success in school, or lack of constructive leisure time activities. You might choose these because you think it is possible to create educational and civic programs that could ameliorate the factors that predispose youth to join gangs. By selecting one part of this problem to study and take a position on, you would make your task manageable and you would be more likely to propose a clear and workable solution for decision makers to consider and act on.

RESEARCH THE PROBLEM

Once you have defined the problem, the next step is to learn more about it. Your two most likely sources of knowledge are documents and people who are experts on the subject you plan to write about.

Read documents. You may find most of what you need to know about the problem in documents, either at a library or at an institution that has something to do with the problem, such as a government agency, a workplace, or a charitable organization. Since doing research in the library is already covered at length in Chapter 9, little more will be said here, besides reminding you again to establish the reliability of any documents you read as you try to understand the problem or develop solutions. The recency of publication, the carefulness of the research, the generalizability of any findings, and the political agenda of the writer could all be important for you to consider as you determine how much faith to place in any documents you use.

Documents from another institution could well become an important source of information as you work on defining the problem and developing solutions. For example, suppose your city council is debating whether or not to continue contributing a fraction of its budget to a privately run organization in your area that provides food and shelter to homeless persons. In the past, the city has chosen to make a contribution to this private organization rather than establish its own food and shelter operation, but now some citizens have objected that it is not the proper role of city government to contribute to private welfare services. To study this problem in order to write a position paper about it, you could check the records of the food and shelter organization (with permission of course) to determine how much of its total operating budget comes from the city; how many people it serves each year; how many people it could not serve if it didn't have the city's contribution; and who else contributes to the organization and how much. With facts like these, gleaned from the organization's own documents, you would be in a better position to analyze the nature of the problem and to think about possible solutions.

Consult experts. In addition to reading pertinent documents, it is important to learn from people who are close to the problem and therefore know a lot about it from their experience with it. If these experts are local, you may be able to interview them. For example, you could easily interview the directors of the food and shelter organization; you could also interview the mayor and members of the city council to learn about their reasoning in voting funds for the organization in the past. If the experts you would like to interview are more distant, you may still be able to reach them by phone, letter, or e-mail. (See Chapter 5 for more information about planning and carrying out an effective interview.)

EVALUATE POSSIBLE SOLUTIONS

Once you have limited and defined the problem in a manageable way, you are ready to begin formulating solutions. But clearly it won't do to formulate easy "pie-in-the-sky" solutions that have no chance of being accepted. This means you will also have to evaluate the solutions you formulate so that you can offer those that have a good chance of being accepted. Obviously, solutions have a higher chance of being chosen and implemented if they are feasible (that is, they *can* be implemented and are likely to work); if the benefits are worth what it will cost to obtain them; and if the public can be persuaded to go along with implementing the solution. Let's examine these three interrelated criteria for evaluating solutions.

Feasibility. Solutions must actually be workable, given the power and resources that public officials or other administrators possess and are willing to use to solve a problem. If you identify part of the gang problem as poor parenting, you could decide that one solution would be to require all people who plan to have children to take courses in how to be parents, courses like how to teach their children to be able to resist negative peer pressure. Some reflection on this solution, however, would probably lead you to decide that this solution is simply not workable. How would you identify the people who should take the courses? How would you pay for creating and staffing the course? How would you ensure that people took it, or if they did, that they learned what they were supposed to? Even if you could achieve the initial steps, how could you guarantee the course would have the desired effect? This solution simply would not be practical.

If, however, you identify the most important part of the problem as a lack of constructive leisure time activities for children and teens to engage in, you may decide that a solution is locating or constructing more sports facilities, creating more after-school drama, music, and special interest groups for young people to be involved in, and getting people to work as coaches for sports or as leaders and teachers for other activities after school. This solution might be feasible, provided there are funds and people, either paid employees or volunteers, that can be employed in this cause, and provided that the right officials and the public could be persuaded to see the solution as feasible.

Cost-effectiveness. A very good way to demonstrate that a solution is feasible is to determine what it will cost to implement the solution and then to estimate the value of the benefits that should come from the solution. If the value of the benefits is greater than the cost, then the cost of implementing the solution may be attractive to decision-makers. Suppose you decided to propose that your city should provide two recreation facilities where young people could play sports or engage in other activities that would keep them off the streets. After some research, you could calculate the cost of building, renovating, or renting existing facilities, providing them with equipment, and staffing them with leaders, coaches, and teachers. Then you would attempt to determine the monetary benefits of this solution. It would be difficult, but with some research you might determine the city would eventually save money now being spent on police patrols, repairs of vandalized property, the creation of juvenile detention facilities, the juvenile justice system, and social service workers. If you could show that the costs would lead to measurable financial benefits, your solution would probably stand a better chance of being accepted. In this example, you might not be able to show that the city would save a lot of money, but you could argue that the money currently being spent on apprehension and punishment of gang members could be better spent on preventing gang activity in the first place.

Political Persuasiveness. Although it is important to argue for the feasibility and the cost-effectiveness of a solution in a position paper, these arguments may not count for much if you have misjudged the political climate and the attitudes of the people to whom you will be presenting your solution. Many people inside as well as outside government, for example, are simply not convinced that government can do much to prevent the gang problem. They do not view it as part of government's role to sponsor recreational facilities and hire people or seek volunteers to work with youth. They believe such activities are the proper role of churches, schools, private organizations, and the family. With beliefs like these, they are more likely to see solutions to gangs in stricter laws, more police officers to enforce the law, and more public spending for jails and prisons. You must always carefully analyze your audience and determine whether or not your proposal will be persuasive to them, given the political beliefs and assumptions they have.

RECOMMEND ONE OR MORE SOLUTIONS

As you analyze the problem, you will likely think of more than one solution that could be proposed. As you evaluate each solution, you should identify one that you think will be most feasible, most cost-effective, and most likely to win favor in the given political climate. However, you may believe that more than one of your solutions is workable, and you might consider offering ranked recommendations in the event that the audience for your position paper will be able to implement more than one solution. Remember, however, that you should argue forcefully for the solution you deem best. The whole aim of a position paper is to take a position, not to waffle after you have carefully researched the problem and evaluated the possible solutions.

DRAFT THE POSITION PAPER

After you have analyzed the problem carefully and chosen one or more workable solutions, the final step in producing a position paper is to write it. Two considerations are of prime importance in planning the paper: level of language and organization. As with other writing, your purpose and your audience will determine what you should do.

Level of language. Consider your audience carefully as you compose the sentences and paragraphs of your position paper. Remember that they may not share your expertise and the vocabulary that people in your field generally use. You may need to find synonyms for specialized terms or at least define and illustrate terms carefully before using them repeatedly in your paper. Use shorter sentences than you would generally use in writing for peers in your field. If you are writing for the general public, make your tone less formal as well; it may be appropriate to use some anecdotes, even personal ones, in addition to the statistics or other data you use to make your point. You want to move your audience to action, so in some cases it may be helpful to appeal to their emotions as well as their ability to reason, so long as the appeal is not manipulative. After completing a draft of your position paper, seek feedback from someone who knows the intended audience well or is already a part of that audience to see if the language you have chosen is understandable and makes the impact you desire.

Organization. A position paper can take many forms. If it is to be read by the public, a brief, simple, clear organization is probably best, since many will not likely have the patience to puzzle out a long, complex structure. If it is to be published in a magazine or newspaper, the paragraphs should be short because they will be displayed in narrow columns. The scholarly apparatus of footnotes or parenthetical references can usually be omitted for publication in popular periodicals, although you should be prepared to name your sources of information if asked. You may also work them into the text of the paper; for example, you might write, "A recent survey sponsored by a coalition of local businesses has shown. . . ."

For a more formal position paper that will be read by legislators or heads of organizations, the structure might be longer and more complicated, but it should use principles of document design to make the information accessible (see Chapter 16). For example, it would be wise to use headings that increase the accessibility of the desired information. Features such as numbered or bulleted lists or boldface and italic print can also help draw attention to key points. Important numerical data can often be presented in tables or graphs that let the reader quickly grasp relationships between different bits of data (see Chapter 17). The longer the paper is, the more helpful it is to provide a summary of your position and a table of contents to your document at the beginning to help busy readers get an overview of your position. In most cases, if you cite published sources, the position paper should have a list of references giving bibliographic citations for any printed materials you have consulted and names of people you have interviewed or contacted for information. Finally, if there is extra information that you did not put in the body of the paper but that would bolster the argument you make, it is appropriate to include it in one or more appendixes, so that readers who have the time to study your argument carefully can see all the data that led you to the solution you proposed.

In the Readings at the end of this book are two short pieces written by professionals for a public audience. The first, "Consumer Marriage and Modern Covenant Marriage," by William J. Doherty, is a speech that was published in *Marriage and Families*, a periodical issued by the BYU School of Family Life. The goal of this magazine is to make social science research accessible to lay readers so that they can learn ways to strengthen their own marriages and families without having to read the often difficult and technical literature in professional journals. Doherty's article outlines specific steps that individuals, professionals, and government officials could take to strengthen marriage and stem the tide of divorce in the US. The other, "Abolishing Welfare Won't Stop Poverty, Illegitimacy" is a newspaper opinion piece by Elijah Anderson, a professor of sociology who wrote the influential books *Streetwise* and *Code of the Street*. In this editorial Anderson argues that his research does not support the proposal to abolish welfare, contrary to some people's interpretations, but instead shows that some minimal public support is necessary to help those who have not been able to succeed in the new global economy because they lack education and opportunity. His editorial and Doherty's speech both exemplify how social scientists can use their expertise to attempt to influence public opinion and the makers of public policy. You will also find a short, previously unpublished opinion piece by a student, Jordan Cahoon, who uses her knowledge about educational practices and psychology to argue that schools would foster healthier social and psychological development in students if the schools emphasized cooperation rather than competition. As you read all three of these selections, notice how the texts are organized, how the authors have used language to engage the reader and appeal to their readers' emotions, and how the authors present themselves in their writing.

SUGGESTIONS FOR RESEARCH AND WRITING

1. In the 1970s most states enacted "no-fault" divorce laws, which allowed a couple to divorce without proving there were grounds for the divorce, such as adultery or cruelty. Some politicians believe that because these laws made it easier to divorce, the divorce rate climbed, creating a number of undesirable side effects, including displaced homemakers without job skills, children living in poverty, and increased demands on state welfare agencies. Some governors and state legislatures are now considering repealing no-fault divorce laws, making it more difficult for couples to divorce, on the premise that it is in the state's best interest to encourage couples to stay together. After researching this issue, prepare a position paper for the governor of a state considering the repeal of no-fault divorce laws.

2. Some savings-minded legislators in Washington would like to cut federal funding for a number of social programs they deem costly, ineffective, or not part of government's proper role. These are just a few programs they would like to axe or reduce: Headstart; Women, Infants and Children food supplements; Medicare; Medicaid; the National Endowment for the Humanities; the National Endowment for the Arts. Choose one of these or some other program that is related to your field of study and research its effectiveness. Prepare a position paper that you could send to your Congressional representative recommending a solution, such as a complete cut, a partial cutback, or a revision of the program.

3. Bilingual education has been touted as the best way to help youngsters whose native language is not English succeed in school. Critics argue that bilingual education is too costly and unnecessarily delays children's mastery of English. Research the effectiveness of bilingual education programs in your state and write a position paper making a recommendation to the state superintendent of education.

4. A "flat" income tax has been proposed as the best way of revising the complicated federal tax code and simplifying what citizens have to do in paying their income tax each year. Such a tax would require that all citizens earning above a certain amount pay the same percentage of their income in tax. Study what would happen if this proposal were enacted and write a position paper for your Congressional representative making a recommendation for or against the flat tax.

5. Should adoptions be sealed or public? That is, once a child has been adopted, who should have the right to know about the child's biological parents, including their names and how to locate them? Many adopted children are curious to know about their biological parents and spend a lot of time, money, and effort on a search to locate them. However, some biological parents do not want to be contacted by the child they gave up for adoption. Write a position paper to help lawmakers in your state write a fair law.

6. Choose a local problem that you are aware of in your community, your church, or another institution that you are associated with. Study the problem and recommend a solution to your mayor or city council, your clergyman, or the leader of the institution. Or write an opinion piece for about a current issue for the "op–ed" page of your local newspaper.

7. Consider whether your research paper has information in it that is pertinent to the public and that could be adapted for a general audience. Rewrite a section of your research paper for publication on the op-ed page of a newspaper or as a position paper to help a government agency formulate public policy.

13

ABSTRACTS, CRITIQUES, AND REVIEWS

CHAPTER OVERVIEW

After reading this chapter, you should be able to answer the following questions:

1. What is an abstract? Why is an abstract included in much social science writing? What are the characteristics of an abstract?
2. What is a peer review? What is usually included in one? How does a peer review help a writer improve a text?
3. What are book reviews? Why are they written? What are the usual parts of a book review?

The abstract, the critique, and the review are genres that you will have opportunity to write in both as a student and as a professional. These three kinds of writing have one thing in common: Each one requires you to size up and state succinctly what a document is about. In an abstract, that's all you do; no evaluative comments are included. In a critique or a review, however, you not only summarize the parts of an article, book, or other document, you also offer your opinion about their value. Knowing how to write in each of these genres is important because each one plays an important role in constructing the shared body of knowledge in any field. The critique does this by evaluating documents before they are published. Abstracts and reviews do this by offering members of the field an efficient way to keep up with the endless flow of new publications and to evaluate their usefulness. Because of their importance in shaping knowledge and making it accessible, this chapter will show you some examples and give you guidelines for writing abstracts, critiques, and reviews.

WRITING AN ABSTRACT

Abstract is another name for a summary. Most social science journals require the author of an article to submit an abstract with the article. The abstract is not only printed with the article; it is also included in print sources and electronic databases that students and other scholars can search when looking for information on a particular topic. A well-written abstract is

- Brief, usually only a paragraph
- Dense with information encoded in key words
- Comprehensive in scope, summarizing each section of the document
- Impersonal in tone and style

These characteristics make it more likely that a computer will match the user's search terms with key words in the abstract and retrieve it. They also make it more likely that readers will be able to read the abstract and judge at a glance whether or not the entire article is pertinent to their research and worth reading in its entirety.

To write a good abstract, you have to have a good sense of your main point and of the structure of your document; you need to be able to state precisely what each part contributes to the whole. This means that the best time to write an abstract is after you have completed the entire document. If your document is a report of empirical research, it will likely have the following parts:

- An introduction that states a problem, question, or hypothesis to be investigated
- A description of methods, including participants, procedures, and materials
- A description of results
- A discussion of the significance of the results.

For this type of document, the abstract should have one or two sentences that sum up the important points of each section. For an example of such an abstract, see Figure 13-1, which presents the abstract for Heather Bahlmann's paper, reprinted in the Readings at the back of this book. After reading her paper, judge whether or not it presents concisely what you learned about the purpose, the methods, the participants, the results, and the implications of her research.

Another common kind of document that generally has an abstract is a paper that presents an argument based on library research, such as the one written by Kemarie Campbell. An argumentative paper like this usually has the following traits:

- Focus on a limited topic
- Statement of thesis or purpose

FIGURE 13-1. Example of an Abstract for an Empirical Research Report

Inferring student understanding is imperative in mathematics learning and teaching because it helps teachers plan more effective instruction. This research explored the open-response task as a tool for gaining insights into student thinking about fractions. Fifth-grade students were videotaped solving fraction problems in class, and their talk, drawings, use of manipulatives, and problem solutions were analyzed to determine how students both thought and didn't think about the problems. The solutions of 172 fifth-graders to both multiple-choice and open-response questions on an exam were also analyzed. Detailed qualitative and quantitative analysis of two open-response test items indicated that students who have deeper conceptual understanding of fractions are also more proficient and flexible in applying procedures to solve unfamiliar problems. These data corroborate evidence from analysis of in-class video and demonstrate that students' strategies for solving open-response tasks are among a teacher's best tools for assessing and then improving students' conceptual understanding and procedural proficiency.

- Presentation of the findings from review of literature, data, and reasoning
- General conclusions or implications of the findings

An abstract for such a paper would provide at least a sentence about each of the above. You will note that this is the case in the abstract of Kemarie's paper shown in Figure 13-2.

FIGURE 13-2. Abstract for Kemarie Campbell's Paper

Obesity is a growing problem in the United States and contributes to all of the major causes of death in the US. This paper emphasizes that wellness programs focused on reducing obesity should take lifestyle and psychology into consideration in order to be successful. Many attempts have been made to combat obesity, including the implementation of diets and exercise programs geared toward weight loss. Nearly all diets fail and many exercise programs do not have long-term effects on weight loss because they prove unsustainable. Obesity is really just a side-effect of a bigger problem— American lifestyle. Americans make poor food choices, do not exercise regularly, and have difficulty managing stress. Each of these factors contributes to the epidemic of obesity in the US today. Health is not just physical, but also psychological. Psychology plays an important role in obesity and

FIGURE 13-2. Abstract for Kemarie Campbell's Paper (continued)

poor health, but it has been generally ignored in weight-loss programs of the past. By learning to change their lifestyle and their psychological orientation to eating, exercise, and stress, Americans would have a better chance at combating obesity.

In sum, an abstract should do the following:

- Make sense by itself; it should be a miniature version of the paper, not omitting important points, not adding things that aren't in the paper, and not distorting the emphasis given to any part.
- Be specific; it should give details about the purpose, the scope, the methods used or the literature surveyed, the results, and the conclusions or implications.
- Be coherent and concise; it should move from point to point in a way that the reader can follow, with no wasted, empty words.
- Avoid evaluating; the author should present as objectively as possible what the entire paper is about and let the reader draw his or her own conclusions about the usefulness of the research.
- Be impersonal; it should not use the pronouns "I" or "we" or adopt a familiar, conversational tone.

WRITING A CRITIQUE

In Chapter 1, you learned that a researcher's new contribution to the literature of a field generally goes through a process of peer review before it is accepted for publication. The goal of this process is to ensure that writers will meet their disciplines' high standards for following research methods, analyzing and interpreting data, reasoning, and writing. Typically, a manuscript will be reviewed by at least two reviewers in the writer's field as well as by one or more editors at the journal or press that receives the manuscript. After review, the manuscript is usually returned to the writer with suggestions for revision. These suggestions might take the form of both marginal notations on the manuscript and written critiques in which the reviewers and editor describe in some detail the strengths and weaknesses of the manuscript and suggest ways to improve it. These critiques are meant for the writer only, not for a broader audience. After reading the critiques, the writer usually makes substantial revisions, sometimes negotiating details of content, organization, and style with the editor. Criticism of this kind is positive and helpful because it strengthens a document before it is finally published.

While you are still in college, probably very little, if anything, of what you write will be published in professional journals or by academic presses. (However, many campus departments and organizations sponsor undergraduate writing contests and sometimes journals, so you could very well aim to submit some of your best papers for judging or publication in local forums.) Even though most of your academic writing won't be published, it will be made public in the sense that it will be read by others. Your primary audience in most academic writing tasks is the instructor who assigned the writing. Your goal obviously is to submit quality work, and one way you can improve your written work is to solicit feedback from knowledgeable peers—your classmates, for example, or tutors in your campus writing center. Your teachers may even require that you show early drafts of your writing to others to receive feedback that will help you make your final draft stronger.

Just as you may solicit feedback from peers, you should be prepared to give helpful criticism, oral or written, to others about their writing. Because writing assignments vary widely, the kind of criticism you give to a classmate will depend on what the student has been asked to do; it will also depend on the criteria the instructor will use to evaluate each student's performance. The best place to begin any critique, therefore, is with careful scrutiny of the assignment's requirements and the evaluation criteria. If these are unclear, ask the instructor for more information. Most teachers want to get good writing from their students and therefore should be willing to clarify their instructions. Many instructors will also provide models of the kind of writing they are seeking with a given assignment. By studying the model, you can usually answer your own questions about appropriate format, organization, length, level of detail, and style.

As you evaluate an early draft of a classmate's paper, you will usually need to think about the following characteristics of the writing.

1. Focus. Depending on the type of assignment, the focus might be called the "thesis statement," the "purpose," the "claim," the "point," or some other name that indicates that a piece of writing is generally *about* something—it is generally limited to a particular aspect of a broad topic and the writer generally takes a particular position or point of view. No paper can say something about everything, and a paper that just wanders about, touching on this and that, but never asserting anything in particular, leaves you wondering what the reader is supposed to learn from it. To help you criticize the focus of a paper, ask questions such as these:

- Is the writer's focus clearly stated in a prominent position?
- Is the focus limited enough for the kind and length of paper?
- Is the focus evident throughout the paper, or does the paper seem to wander?

- How could the writer sharpen the focus?
- Could you state the thesis in your own words?
- Is the position the writer takes a significant and valid one?

2. Support. Once you have determined the focus of a paper, you should check how the writer supports his or her point of view. Support for a particular focus might take the form of general reasoning, of evidence drawn from authoritative sources, of data created by research methods, or of personal experience. To determine the relevance of the support, ask yourself such questions as these:

- Is the support appropriate for this kind of paper?
- Is the support relevant?
- Is it credible and reliable?
- Is it sufficient to make the writer's point?
- Has the writer taken into account contradictory evidence or simply ignored it?
- Does the support go into enough detail or is it too general?
- How could the writer make the support stronger?

3. Organization. The organization of a paper will depend on a lot of factors, including any directions the instructor gave in the assignment (or implied in the model, if one is given). The organization of a particular paper might be chronological if the paper is about the past or steps in a process. The organization might proceed from a problem to a solution, from a cause to an effect, or from an effect to a cause. It might compare two things point by point, or it might consider all the points related to one before proceeding to the other. It might divide something into its parts or classify a number of related things. Whatever it does, the organization of a paper should be congruent with the purpose and focus of the paper and help to advance the claim the writer is making. The reader should be able to discern the organization and should feel that the paper moves smoothly from part to part. To help you criticize the organization of someone's writing, consider these questions:

- Could you outline the paper?
- If the writer has outlined the paper, does the outline match the text?
- Has the writer chosen the best order to present points in?
- Are major points obscure, not given enough emphasis or space?
- Are less important points given too much emphasis?
- Would some points fit better somewhere else in the paper?
- Should some parts be deleted because they don't really fit in?

- Does the writer show connections between parts?
- Where could the writer strengthen the connections?
- Are headings appropriate? Would they improve the reader's ability to perceive the organization?
- How could the writer improve the organization?

4. Audience. All good academic writing is for somebody, and it is pitched at an appropriate level for the intended reader. All of the preceding elements—focus, support, and organization—must be considered when you evaluate the appropriateness of the writing for the audience. Ask yourself questions such as these:

- What readers does the paper address?
- What are the audience's expectations and needs?
- Has the writer taken the audience's knowledge, background, and experience into account?
- Will the audience find the particular focus appropriate and interesting?
- Will the audience find the support sufficient, relevant, and reliable?
- Will the organization help the audience understand the writing?
- What improvements in the paper would help the audience understand it better?

5. Format, style, and mechanics. The format of a paper includes such things as the overall appearance, the line spacing, the margins, the page numbering, and so forth. The format will vary with the genre assigned and the instructor's requirements. For example, some professors want a cover sheet on each paper with the title, course name, and your name in designated places. Others want your name, the course number, and the date in the upper right-hand (or left-hand) corner of the first page. Some want the pages numbered at the top, others at the bottom; still others don't care. Some professors are sticklers for one-inch margins; others are less fussy. Be sure you understand the instructor's preferences and instructions, if any, before proceeding to criticize the format of a classmate's paper.

If the instructor expresses no preferences and if the particular genre doesn't require any particular changes, check to see if the paper follows these general conventions:

- Is the text double-spaced?
- Does it have one-inch margins? (the default margins on most word processors)

- Does it have a ragged (unjustified) right margin?
- Has the writer paginated according to some consistent plan? (word processors offer several conventional choices)
- Is the body of the text in a 12-point serif font for the body of the paper?
- Are headings used correctly and appropriately?

Style refers mostly to the elements of writing at the sentence level, including choices about usage and punctuation. It can also refer to the institutional style a writer is expected to follow in a particular field (see Chapter 19). Writers have many choices to make in creating the style of a particular paper. Depending on the audience and purpose, some choices are better than others. *Mechanics* refers to those elements of writing that are purely arbitrary. It includes such things as using capitalization, brackets, ellipses, and italics correctly or following a particular style guide's rules for writing numbers, citing sources, and creating bibliographies. In evaluating style and mechanics, once again, you should do all you can to learn the instructor's requirements and preferences. (No checklist of questions will be given here.)

Usually the best way to note problems with format, style, and mechanics is to mark them directly on the draft of the paper you are criticizing, rather than devote a section of a formal written critique to these matters. It's important to note, however, that matters of format and style belong to the part of the writing process called editing, and they may not be as important in the early stages of writing as focus, support, organization, and appropriate adaptation for the audience. There is usually little point in editing writing that still needs a lot of work on focus and organization, for example.

To suggest a delay in criticizing the style, however, is not to imply that correctness in format, style, and mechanics is unimportant. In the final product correctness is very important, because a lot of small mistakes can interfere with the reader's ability to see the focus of a paper and to appreciate its support and organization. So, as a critic of others' writing, be sure that you do point out any serious problems or patterns of error that you notice in your peer's writing, especially if you are criticizing a near-final draft. But it usually isn't necessary to copy-edit someone's paper line by line. Unless you have been asked specifically to edit the paper, in most cases you can simply point out the problems that you see and let the writer assume the major responsibility for correcting them.

A CAUTION ABOUT BEING TACTFUL

The above criteria are intended to describe writing in general—something that doesn't really exist. Writing is always for a *particular* situation: a paper is written by a particular person for an identified audience in response to a specific assignment about a particular topic. So you must always consider the particulars any time you are asked to offer a verbal or written critique of a classmate's work. One thing that will remain constant, however, is the need to offer criticism with grace and tact. Most people feel possessive about their writing, and even when they want to make it better, they sometimes feel attacked and defensive if their critics take a domineering or sarcastic approach. Imagine yourself on the receiving end of your critique. Would you be offended by it, or would you be able to accept it because it is offered in a kindly way? Be as honest as you must in offering criticism, but be as gentle as you can, too.

EXAMPLE OF A STUDENT CRITIQUE

In Figure 13-3 you will read a critique by Warren Brookes of a library research paper written by Bryce Ott. Brookes wrote the critique of Ott's draft to help him improve it before he wrote the final draft for submission. This critique follows an organization suggested by the instructor's evaluation criteria. As you will note, the critique takes the form of a memo addressed to Bryce, with a copy to Warren's teacher. (How to write a memo is explained in Chapter 15.)

Obviously, you would not want to imitate this critique unless you knew that the paper you were criticizing would be evaluated by the same criteria. Any critiques you write of classmates' papers should take into account the particular assignment and grading criteria that are relevant in your case. Nevertheless, this model should help you see how thorough a critique should be and how the tone of a critique can be critical yet still polite and encouraging.

WRITING A REVIEW

The process of peer review that you learned about in Chapter 1 does not end with publication. Once an article or book appears in print or online, it is subject to the scrutiny of all readers who take an interest in the topic. Although an article or book has already successfully passed pre-publication review, it will continue to be reviewed in both indirect and direct ways. The most common indirect way that publications continue to receive peer review is through other writers' references to and citations of the publications. As one writer uses the work of another in creating a new document, the later writer may disagree with the earlier one; they might also praise the work of earlier ones, using it as a foundation for their own work, or extending an idea from the earlier books or articles. In these indirect ways, the writing of an author continues to undergo a type of review.

FIGURE 13-3. A Peer Critique of a Student Research Paper

TO:	Bryce Ott
FROM:	Warren Brookes
DATE:	12 April 2006
SUBJECT:	Peer Critique of "The History, Reasons, and Possible Implications of Changes in Film Editing"

This memo contains a critique of your research paper "The History, Reasons, and Possible Implications of Changes in Film Editing." I enjoyed reading your paper, and although I will be returning an edited copy of your paper to you, I hope to use this memo to recognize some of the particular strengths of your paper and point out a few areas where I felt some revision or clarification might further strengthen your paper.

Focus and Organization

I find that your focus on the development of film editing through its history is clear and understandable. You allow the reader to understand both the importance of film editing and its current trends through the development of its history, which you have researched very thoroughly. I have only one small suggestion. I think it would be more helpful to the reader to provide a more tightly developed thesis at the beginning of your paper and to word your thesis in such a way that it arouses a more general interest. In your thesis, you express interest in understanding the development of editing and its possible implications. But rather than talking about what you want, maybe you could convince the readers why this will be interesting to them.

I think that your thesis is appropriate for the length of your paper and that you provide adequate discussion. The outline for your paper is highly developed and particularly helpful to the unfamiliar reader. You were also very good about keeping the development of your paper consistent with your outline, and the flow of your ideas seemed to be in logical order.

Research and Support

I observed that you have an appropriate number of sources for a paper of this length and provide very persuasive information to support your thesis. The authorities you cite, particularly those whose work I have perused firsthand, are scholarly, reliable leaders in your field. I see no problems with the way you have quoted, paraphrased or summarized your sources. Thus, I have only a few suggestions regarding the support and research of your paper.

- You do an excellent job of developing the history of film editing through your various sources, but I think that you might do one of two things to strengthen your paper: (1) make the history a little more concise and devote more attention to the implications of changes for film editors, or (2) insert more commentary throughout the history explaining the effects of the historical events on film editors today.

FIGURE 13-3. A Peer Critique of a Student Research Paper (continued)

- If possible, find some more recent articles from journals. These articles, in conjunction with your other sources, might lend greater credibility to your research. To be sure, the sources you've already used are excellent and very helpful, but see if you can't find some journal articles that discuss the implications of change in film for editors.

Style and Mechanics

Style and mechanics are the areas where I have the most suggestions. I do realize, however, that you probably haven't had the opportunity to do any thorough editing. Your paper contains a number of spelling and punctuation errors which I'm sure you would have noticed later, but, in an attempt to be helpful, I marked them for you.

I also think that there are two things that you might do to improve the style of your paper. In your paper, you use a very personal tone that makes it more enjoyable to read. I do feel, however, that you have slightly overused the first person. I think that you should try to cut it down in the final draft. Although the first person is clearly better than passive voice, I think that decreasing the use of the first person in your paper will give your tone greater formality while retaining the comfortable familiarity that I mentioned before.

Copy: Kristine Hansen

Another common way of responding to new publications is through directly commenting on them. Many professional journals have a section that is something like the letters to the editor of a newspaper. Readers can write a formal response to a recently published article and submit it to the journal. In their comments they might praise the article, ask for clarifications, or question the methods, analysis, or interpretations of an article. Sometimes journal editors invite the writer whose work is under scrutiny to reply to these critiques. By reading such comments and responses in the current professional journals of your field, you can gain a good sense of what the important issues are and of how scholars disagree with and challenge each other. You will see how writers defend their thinking or concede the validity of their peers' criticisms. This give-and-take illustrates well how knowledge is socially constructed through the process of offering, receiving, and responding to criticism.

Another direct method of evaluating someone's work is the formal review. For recently published books, editors of most journals invite reviews from knowledgeable peers, to be published in a section of the journal devoted just to book reviews. Each reviewer summarizes and evaluates an assigned book in a brief format, often less than 1,000 words. By reading these short reviews, others in the field can learn a little about new books appearing in the field and determine whether or not they should get a copy of a particular book and read it for themselves. Book reviews are a good source of information for students completing research projects as well. By reading a brief review, you can determine at least three things about a book: (1) what the book's topic and basic argument is; (2) whether a professional peer judges the book to be reliable; and (3) whether it will be worth your time to read the book at length for the information it might add to your research project.

As you near graduation and become more familiar with your major field's body of knowledge and its standards for evaluating new knowledge, you may be assigned to write formal reviews of published works. This is a valuable assignment, both because it requires you to read new books in your field and because it gives you practice in writing in a professional genre. You will learn to read for the main ideas, to separate the generalizations from the details, to think critically about what you are reading, and to apply your field's standards in evaluating the importance of new ideas and research. Writing a review takes practice, especially because the genre typically gives you only a small space in which to sum up and evaluate what you have read.

The best way to approach writing a review is to gain an overall conception of what this genre of writing usually includes. If you are writing a review for a class, your instructor will usually outline what your review should include and a maximum length. If you are writing a review for a journal, the editor will supply specifications. In either case, your review would typically have these parts:

- The facts of publication (author, title, publisher, etc.)
- A statement of the book's purpose and scope
- A summary of the book's contents
- An evaluation of some of the book's strengths and weaknesses
- Your general recommendation of the value of the book

It's important to note that, with the exception of the facts of publication, these parts would not necessarily be found in a review in the order given here. They might be intermixed in various ways. For convenience, however, they will be discussed as listed above.

THE FACTS OF PUBLICATION

The first elements in any book review are the title, author, place of publication, publisher, and year of publication for the book. In addition, the total number of pages and the cost of the book are usually included. If the book is available in both hard cover and paperback editions, the price for each may be given. Sometimes the ISBN (International Standard Book Number) is included as well. These details give readers of the review information they can use to order the book if they decide they want to purchase a copy. Or, if they don't plan to buy it, they have enough information to find it in a library.

STATEMENT OF THE BOOK'S PURPOSE AND SCOPE

The usual way of beginning a book review is to describe as objectively as possible what the author or authors of the book have attempted to do. Don't fault the author or authors for not writing the book you would have written. Try to understand the book in terms of what the author stated he or she was attempting to do. A good place to locate a statement of the author's purpose is in the preface or introduction to the book. State for your readers the book's purpose and its major claim or claims. It would also be appropriate to state any assumptions that underlie the claims.

Describing the particular genre the book belongs to can also help readers understand its purpose; for example, if a book is based on a survey or several interviews, saying so at the start of the review will help readers better evaluate the judgments you make later in the review. It is also helpful to describe briefly the major divisions or the general organization of the book. For example, if the book has three main divisions, you might give their titles and briefly tell what each part includes.

SUMMARY OF THE BOOK'S CONTENTS

In summarizing the book's contents you must be selective, mainly because the typical length limit of a book review forces you to be brief. One way to be selective is to summarize the book's main points at a very general level, giving just enough of the details or examples the authors use to illustrate how the points are supported. It may be appropriate to give a few brief quotations that state very clearly important ideas or focuses of the book. Your summary should substantiate your own overall opinion of the book.

Another way of being selective is to focus on summarizing only some parts of the book, describing the rest in only a sentence or two. This kind of selective review is common when the reviewer and the reviewer's audience have an interest in only one or two aspects of the total book. For example, Valerie Hudson and Andrea Den Boer's *Bare Branches*, from which there is an excerpt in the readings at the end of this book, was widely reviewed in various kinds of journals from different fields. Different readers responded to the book in ways that reflected their training, experience, and biases. Some were highly complimentary; others were very critical. A few were quite balanced.

EVALUATION OF STRENGTHS AND WEAKNESSES

The foregoing parts of a review all tell readers what a book is about, but readers will also want to know what the reviewer thinks of the book. They will want to see praise for specific strengths and criticism of identifiable weaknesses—and usually a book has both strengths and weaknesses, though it might have more of one than the other. As you read a book you've been assigned to review, you should be thinking critically about what the author has done in writing it as well as about what the book actually states. Here are some questions that may guide you in evaluating the strengths and weaknesses of a book:

- Is the book based on methodologically sound research?
- Does it deal adequately with the issues it raises?
- Is the book's scope as inclusive as it should be?
- Is it written clearly and persuasively?
- Has the author drawn on credible sources?
- Has the author overlooked information that would have contributed something worthwhile to the book?
- Is the book suitable for the audience it is intended for?

You might devote one or two paragraphs of your review to strengths and another paragraph to weaknesses. Or you might comment on the strong and weak points of the book as you summarize it. If your overall recommendation of the book is positive, it is important not to give undue prominence to its faults. The amount of space you devote to discussing strengths and weaknesses ought to be proportionate to your general assessment of the book's value.

GENERAL RECOMMENDATION

The reviewer's general recommendation usually appears twice in the review: at the beginning and again at the end. Readers want to find out in the first few sentences of the review if your overall evaluation is positive, negative, or mixed. Be forthright in stating an opinion that you will then support through your summary and evaluation of specific strengths and weaknesses. At the end of the review, you can state your overall opinion again, this time knowing you have supported it with the facts you've included in the body of your review. If your overall opinion is a mix of positive and negative feelings, you should write a carefully qualified statement, balancing praise with criticism.

For example, you should let your readers know if the book is technical and difficult to read but would still have value for a certain group of readers who should take the time to struggle through it. If the book largely repeats what is already known but contributes a few important new ideas, then say what those ideas are. Your readers may ultimately disagree with your evaluation, but that is not a problem. By being a responsible critic, you perform a valuable service in perpetuating the conversation about a field's knowledge. Your review is like a turn in the conversation, which itself should invite still other responses.

At the end of this book in the Readings, you will find three book reviews. The first, by Rose McDermott, is a detailed overview and very positive evaluation of *Bare Branches* by Valerie Hudson and Andrea Den Boer. The second, a review by Jeffrey Arnett of *Soul Searching* by Christian Smith, is also highly laudatory but briefer and more succinct in its summary of the contents. The third, by student Bradley Gunnell, reviews Elijah Anderson's *Code of the Street*. Brad is likewise very positive as he summarizes the main ideas of Anderson's book, and he is very gentle in his criticism as he suggests who could benefit from reading this book and why.

SUGGESTIONS FOR WRITING

1. Write an abstract for a library research paper you have written for this course. Or write an abstract for a paper that you have created from primary sources or new data that you gathered using a method described in Part 2 of this book.

2. With a classmate, exchange drafts of your library research papers. Besides writing marginal comments to each other, write a formal critique of each other's research paper. Or do the same with another major paper for this course.

3. Read a recent book that has appeared in your field. Consider choosing one that is on the topic you have chosen for your research paper. Using the guidelines in this chapter, write a formal review of the book. Submit your review to your campus or local newspaper or to a student journal that might publish it. Compare your review to other reviews of the same book written by professionals in your field.

REFERENCES

Anderson, Elijah. 1999. *Code of the street: Decency, violence, and the moral life of the inner city.* New York: W.W. Norton & Company.

Hudson, Valerie, and Andrea Den Boer. 2004. *Bare branches: The security implications of Asia's surplus male population.* Cambridge, MA: MIT Press.

Smith, Christian. 2005. *Soul searching: The religious and spiritual lives of American teenagers.* New York: Oxford University Press.

14

RESUMES

CHAPTER OVERVIEW

After reading this chapter, you should be able to answer the following questions:

1. What is a resume? What is a *curriculum vitae*? How do they differ?
2. What is a one-column resume? What is a two-column resume?
3. What are the typical parts of any resume?
4. What should you keep in mind when formatting a resume?
5. What are some precautions you need to take when posting your resume online?
6. How does a scannable resume differ from a printed one?

TYPES OF RESUMES

A *resume* (from the French word *résumé*) is a summary of pertinent facts about you that you will often be asked to submit with a letter of application or to bring to an interview. In the academic world, a similar kind of summary goes by the Latin name *curriculum vitae* (often simply called *vita*), which means "course of life." Graduate and professional schools may ask you to submit a vita rather than a resume. The vita typically focuses on academic achievements, such as publications and scholarly activities and awards. Since it is a life-long record, it tends to be longer than a resume, especially as a person ages and has more achievements to list. The resume, on the other hand, is kept brief (usually only a page, occasionally two). Businesses and professional schools often ask for a resume. It tends to focus more on work experience and skills, though education and academic honors are included as well. Since the two kinds of documents are rather similar, and since at this point in your life you are more likely to have had the kinds of experiences that are usually recounted in a resume, the name *resume* will be used in the rest of this chapter.

Although employers normally request a traditional paper resume, electronic resumes are becoming common as well. Electronic resumes can speed up the process of being considered for a job. Once you post your resume on the Web, potential employers can search the Web using key words to locate you and other possible employees. Some employers save time by requesting that printed resumes be *scannable*. Then employers use an optical scanner to "read" the contents of each resume they receive into a computer database; in this way they can efficiently store thousands of resumes for months. Then, when they are looking for an employee with certain skills, they can search the database for all resumes that name the desired skills and retrieve the names and addresses of potential employees. Although this chapter will further describe online and scannable resumes, it will focus mainly on traditional printed resumes. Once you create a printed resume, you can reformat it to fit the online or scannable guidelines.

TRADITIONAL RESUMES

In the traditional resume, the design and visual attractiveness of the document matter much more than in most writing you do for college courses. You should refer to the elements of document design discussed in Chapter 16 as you view the examples of traditional resumes in this chapter. This chapter will also help you as you begin to apply the principles of design to your resume. As important as design is, however, you must first plan carefully what to include and how to organize the contents of your resume for the greatest impact.

ORGANIZATION OF THE TRADITIONAL RESUME

The organization you use for each resume depends on the particular job you are applying for. You should research the requirements for each job carefully so that you can tailor your resume to show how your qualifications match its specifications. In any case, your resume should quickly acquaint the reader with your abilities and strengths. An employer going through a stack of resumes typically spends only 15–20 seconds scanning each one, so he or she needs to be able to access your qualifications right away. Careful organization can help an employer notice your most important qualities.

Information in resumes is typically displayed in categories identified by headings. Within these categories, the facts can be displayed in list fashion with bullets drawing attention to particular items. You can also use concise paragraphs to summarize your work and experiences. Some categories of information are fairly standard on resumes, while others may vary according to your background and the immediate goals and audience for the resume. These standard and optional categories, including what each would contain, are described in the next section. The categories often come in the order given here, but this order is not fixed—you should vary your headings according to specific job requirements.

CONTENTS OF THE TRADITIONAL RESUME

Name and Contact Information (Standard). Every resume should display at the top your name, address, E-mail address, and telephone number(s). When listing more than one number, it is helpful to distinguish them as daytime or evening numbers and to note at which a message can be left. Employers might also appreciate a fax number if you have one. Some college students list permanent contact information in this section as well because their local information frequently changes.

Career Objective (Optional). Some people list a career objective immediately after their name and contact information. However, most career experts advise you to omit the objective because it can limit what an employer will consider you qualified to do. Consider whether you want to use precious space for an objective statement. If you choose to include one, you should customize your resume for each job you apply for by stating your career objective so that it matches what the employer has advertised for.

Trying to write a "one-size-fits-all" career objective can be hazardous. For example, stating your career objective too specifically (e.g., "to work as a tax attorney in a major corporate law firm") could backfire if an employer interpreted it to mean that you would not consider a different, but related, position. Stating it too broadly (e.g., "to manage personnel") might make it seem you are too vague about your career goals. Stating it too ambitiously (e.g., "to become Vice-President of International Marketing") may suggest you intend to use the available position as only a quick stop on your move up the corporate ladder. Consider your purpose and audience carefully when deciding whether or not to include this category in your resume at all. It often can be omitted without sacrificing much.

Educational History (Standard). At this stage of your life, your education will likely be the most prominent category of information after the heading. List the schools where you have studied in *reverse chronological order*, beginning with the university that you are now attending. For your current university, include your major (and minor, if you have one), your dates of enrollment, and your expected graduation date. If your GPA is admirable (generally anything over a 3.5), you may want to list it as well. Some students who don't have an impressive cumulative GPA may have a respectable one for the courses they have taken in their major. If that is the case with you, consider listing your major GPA only.

Some students also include relevant coursework, class projects, or research under the education category. You could also list scholarships and academic honors here, or you could list them later in the resume with other awards and achievements. When listing the schools you have attended, do not go further into the past than high school. In fact, if you graduated from high school more than five years ago, consider omitting that part of your education. (As a general rule of thumb for updating your resume over the years, eliminate the older and less significant facts about yourself as you add more recent and more important achievements.)

Work Experience (Standard). You can organize your work experience by time (a *chronological* resume) or by skill sets (a *functional* resume). You may even choose to use a combination of these. Most career counselors recommend writing a chronological resume because it is easier for an employer to see your work history. If you have had steady work experience and several jobs like the one for which you are applying, write a chronological resume. For this type of resume, list your experiences starting with your current or most recent one and moving back in time. A chronological resume concentrates on day-to-day job responsibilities and can show your progress in a certain career field. Brant Ellsworth's resume (Figure 14-1) follows this format. Notice that he lists his experiences according to the job titles in reverse chronological order.

The work experience section of your resume can include full-time jobs, part-time jobs, internships, research or teaching assistantships, and perhaps even volunteer experience. (If you have a great deal of volunteer experience, consider creating a separate category for it in the resume.) Include only the most applicable experiences rather than listing every position you've held since high school. Or group your part-time or summer jobs in a cluster, without giving details about each.

List the following in the order given for each significant job:

- Your job title
- The name of the organization you worked for
- The location of the organization
- The dates of your employment

You could also list your supervisor's name with each job as a way of indicating whom the prospective employer could contact for a reference.

Especially when you have held few or no full-time jobs, it is important to put the best face you can on the jobs you have held but to do so without overstating what you really did. Employers may not be as interested in the number of years you have worked or the prestige of your jobs as they are in the skills and personal attributes your work experience has given you. Emphasize how your employment has instilled in you such things as the ability to relate well with others, to communicate, to accept responsibility and follow through, to organize, to solve problems, to meet deadlines, to work with various kinds of equipment, and so forth. Describing specific tasks you did on each job will show what skills you have acquired.

When you present your information in your resume, you should use telegraph writing style; that is, you will seldom use complete sentences. Rather, you will write words and phrases that present the information about yourself as clearly and concisely as possible. Keep punctuation to a minimum, using mostly commas. Also, make sure that the items you list are conceptually and grammatically parallel. For example, "Developed preschool evaluations," a verb phrase, is not parallel with "Recreational leader," a noun phrase. Capitalization in the resume will vary from capitalization in the accompanying letter. In the resume, you may use capital letters for degrees you've earned or expect to earn, names of courses, job titles, or other significant words. In the cover letter, however, capitalization should conform to standard rules for common and proper nouns.

Skills (Optional). You may have other skills that an employer would value but which you didn't acquire working at specific jobs. For example, through study or travel you may be fluent in speaking, reading, and writing one or more foreign languages. In school or on your own you may have acquired skills in working with various kinds of computer software (if so, list the name of the particular software program and the version, e.g., Adobe Acrobat 7.0 or Excel 11.0). Through school or volunteer projects, you may have developed expertise in various research methods and in statistics or in writing and editing. This kind of information deserves prominence in your resume, and a skills section is one option for presenting it.

Accomplishments and Awards (Optional). When you are writing a resume, it is no time to be modest about your achievements. As Babe Ruth once said, "If you done it, it ain't braggin'." Obviously, you shouldn't seem vain by making more out of accomplishments than is warranted, but do state the facts. In this section, you can list scholarships and academic awards if you haven't already listed them with your educational history. This may also be the place to describe volunteer work if you haven't included it elsewhere. You may also list civic awards, special recognition from employers, memberships and leadership positions you have held in societies and clubs, or any extracurricular activities that distinguish you. Don't go further back than high school and do weigh the merits of listing some of your honors by considering how impressive they are likely to be to a prospective employer. (That you were the Homecoming Queen or the Most Preferred Man in your senior year of high school is probably not relevant for most jobs.) The heading you give this section can vary depending on what it emphasizes.

Personal Information (Optional). If you have space to include some personal information about yourself, and if you think doing so will help set you apart from other applicants, list your interests, favorite pastimes, or hobbies. Be selective, however; don't overwhelm your reader with too much. In the past it was customary to list facts such as one's age, marital status, and even physical condition, including height and weight; sometimes people even included their photo with their resume. But in this age of sensitivity to the various ways employers might discriminate against applicants, it is not advisable to include such highly personal information. Federal law prohibits employers from discriminating in hiring on the basis of age, race, sex, marital status, and religion. A potential employer is not supposed to ask you about these matters in a job interview, either, so it is wise not to volunteer personal information on your resume that might work against your being chosen for an interview or for employment. Also, be very careful about listing personal information on a resume that will be posted online, as you may unwittingly help some unscrupulous person steal your identity.

References (Optional). Once an employer becomes serious about hiring you, he or she will generally want references from at least three people who can vouch for the quality of your work, your skills, and your personal traits. Often the employer will ask you for names after an initial interview has been successful. The employer can also simply phone supervisors you've listed from previous jobs on your resume. Most experts agree it is a waste of space to list references separately on your resume. However, if you do, you should contact former or current supervisors and professors to ask them if they will be willing to recommend you. If they agree, you can list their names, addresses, and telephone numbers on your resume. Or you can simply write "References available upon request." At BYU, you can have your recommenders write letters for you and put the letters on file in the Career Placement Services office. On your resume you can provide the address and phone number of the center. Then when employers contact the center, a copy of your file of letters will be mailed to them, so your recommenders don't have to write new letters for each potential employer.

DESIGN OF THE RESUME

Layout. Think of the resume as being arranged in "chunks" of information with indented "layers" in the chunks to help readers quickly find what they are seeking. The layout should have a more vertical than horizontal feel to it. Horizontal texts, like this page, are intended for you to read from left to right, line by line, straight through from top to bottom. A resume, however, is a document that should permit random access of information; that is, a reader should be able to scan up or down it quickly, reading the headings to locate needed information. Within the major sections, the lines of text should be short and arranged in layered columns, so that left-to-right reading takes very little time. Generally, resumes have two main columns, with the column at the left containing the headings and the column on the right containing the details (see Figure 14-1). In order to keep a resume to one page, however, it may become necessary to use the width of the page for the details, with headings above each category of details in a one-column format (see Figure 14-2).

White space. Whether you use a one- or a two-column format, be sure to use white space to keep the resume from looking too dense or cluttered. Use indentations within columns to show how the most specific information is subordinate to more general information. Avoid creating "windows" of white space (empty spaces surrounded by print on all sides). Most of the white space should be on the sides and top and bottom, but leave some between the sections of the resume as well.

Graphical devices. Use graphical devices sparingly. Typically the only ones you should use on a resume are horizontal or vertical rules and bullets (see Figures 14-1 and 14-2). Consider your audience and purpose carefully before deciding to include other graphics such as icons or text boxes. A neat, simple appearance is preferable to one that aims to show off all your printer's fonts.

Fonts and Point Sizes. Here are some guidelines to remember when choosing fonts and type sizes:

- *Choose a typeset font.* With contemporary word processors, you can achieve a more professional look in your resume by choosing a font that is used in typesetting (e.g., Times New Roman or Garamond) rather than a font that looks like it was produced by a typewriter (e.g., Courier or Letter Gothic).

- *Choose a serif font for the body (you may choose a sans-serif font for headings).* Always choose a serif font for the body of the resume, though you may use a sans serif font for your name and contact information and for the headings, if you wish. Don't use a script or novelty font.

- *Use no more than two fonts.* In general, you should not use more than two fonts on your resume, though you may put some words in boldface or italics. For example, your name and the headings can be put in boldface to give them more weight and thus visual prominence.

- *Use bigger type for name and headings.* Your name and the headings will also appear more prominent if you put them in a bigger point size.

- *Use type sizes between 9 and 12 points.* In general, other than your name and headings, the resume should be in a point size between 9 and 12. If you are faced with using a point size of 8 or smaller to fit all the information on one page, it is time to leave something out. You may also consider making the resume two pages, but you should realize that a busy reader might not have time to look at both pages.

PAPER AND PRINTING

When applying for a job, internship, graduate school, or other opportunity important to your future, be prepared to spend a few extra dollars to make the best impression possible. You should have your resume laser-printed on high quality bond paper that is white or off-white. If your resume is accompanied by a cover letter, or sent in a business-sized envelope, these should be from the same paper stock.

When you think your resume is nearly done, print and proofread a draft of it; then ask a few people to read it for correctness before printing the final draft. If you make any changes from their feedback, proofread your resume again. Remember that a single spelling, grammatical, or typographical error may be enough reason for a would-be employer to eliminate you from consideration. If you make any changes from their feedback, proofread your resume again.

FIGURE 14-1. An Example of a Two-Column Resume

Brant W. Ellsworth

639 W 100 N
PROVO, UT 84601

(801) 318-0850
BRANTELLSWORTH@HOTMAIL.COM

EDUCATION

B.A., *Brigham Young University*, Provo, Utah, with Honors, August 2006
- American Studies major with an emphasis in political science
- Business Management minor
- Dean's List, 2000, 2003
- GPA: 3.74

Georgetown University, Washington D.C., Summer 2005
- Completed nine upper-division credits from the Fund for American Studies

EXPERIENCE

WRITER/EDITOR, *The Embassy of South Korea*, Washington D.C., May 2005 – Present
- Wrote and edited sports articles for Embassy's on-line newspaper, www.dynamic-korea.com
- Interviewed MLB players; wrote a series of articles highlighting their careers, goals, fears
- Contributing writer for religion, politics and current events
- Covered North-South Korean relations, nuclear disarmament, 6-party talks and presidential referendums

TEACHING ASSISTANT, *Brigham Young University*, Provo, Utah, August 2005 – Present
- Taught four recitation labs a week; introduced new material about politics, history and economics; graded tests and papers; held 4 office hours a week.

OWNER, *English Plus*, Seoul, Korea, April 2004 – August 2004
- Created and managed an English tutoring service with over 50 clientele
- Designed a successful advertising campaign to jump-start the business
- Increased revenue by 900% within 4 months

VOLUNTEER REPRESENTATIVE, *The Church of Jesus Christ of Latter-day Saints*, Seoul, Korea January 2001 – February 2003
- Wrote curriculum for an English-language institution teaching over 1200 students
- Created an advertising campaign to begin the English-language institution
- Coordinated and provided training activities for over 140 other volunteers
- Directed humanitarian services for over 140 church representatives

PUBLICATIONS

- "Poe's Narrator from *The Black Cat*: A Man without a Motive," *Americana*, 5, Nov. 2006
- "History of Missionaries in Korea," in series of articles highlighting the rise of Christianity in Asia published in the Embassy of South Korea's "Dynamic Korea"

SKILLS

- Read, write and speak Korean fluently
- Proficient in Microsoft Office programs, Photoshop, Quark and Illustrator

AWARDS

- Sunmark Foundation Scholar, 2005
- University Advertising Competition winner, 2003

FIGURE 14-2. An Example of a One-Column Resume

Ashley Jones Nelson

1060 S. Orem Blvd. #16
Orem, UT 84058
480-734-8906
ashleyjnelson@gmail.com

Education

2000-2001, 2004-present Brigham Young University, Provo, UT
- B.S. in Marriage, Family and Human Development expected August 2006
- Provisional Certified Family Life Educator credential upon graduation

Employment History and Other Experience

Research Assistant to Dr. Craig Israelsen
September 2005-present, Brigham Young University, Provo, UT
- Edited and prepared textbook, *Personal and Family Finance Workbook*, 4th ed., 2006
- Conducted budgeting research on national consumer spending, creating a budgeting program for student use

Research Assistant to Dr. Alan Hawkins
April 2005-August 2005, Brigham Young University, Provo, UT
- Wrote summaries of research journal articles to be posted online through the National Healthy Marriage Resource Center

Research Assistant to Dr. Roberta Magarrell
September 2004-January 2005, Brigham Young University, Provo, UT
- Helped evaluate the internship program through interviewing professors and students
- Revised the curriculum for the internship program in the School of Family Life

Server
February-August 2005, Olive Garden, Provo, UT
- Offered timely service and advice, ensuring full guest satisfaction, helping the restaurant reach Diamond Club status as one of the top five restaurants in the region
- Greeted, seated, served, and aided guests throughout their dining experience

Server
April-August 2004, Joe's Crab Shack, Orem, UT
- Provided outstanding customer service as a host and a server, greeting, seating, serving, and entertaining guests during their stay
- Offered friendly, outspoken service and advice according to company policy

Official Representative for The Church of Jesus Christ of Latter-day Saints
April 2002-September 2003, Rochester, New York
- Taught local and church history to thousands of visitors at historical sites
- Taught church doctrine and theology to hundreds of people in the area
- Volunteered in hospitals and nursing homes

Skills and Interests

Professional Skills: Microsoft Office, Microsoft Windows, filing, editing, multi-line telephone systems, people- and detail-oriented, public speaking, excellent interpersonal communication
Interests: reading, art, singing, family history, religious and world history, scrapbooking, sewing, politics, camping, hiking, volleyball

SCANNABLE RESUMES

A scannable resume contains the same categories of information as a traditional resume, but it differs in two important ways. First, the design of a scannable resume must be very plain so that the optical scanner can "read" it easily and store the information correctly in a database. Second, the focus of the resume is on a list of key words, usually nouns, that name your skills and abilities, since the key words are what a computer search will look for when retrieving resumes from the database.

Design of the Scannable Resume

The design of a scannable resume is in many ways just the opposite of a traditional resume. The following list of things to do when designing a scannable resume contradicts much of what this chapter says you should do to create a traditional print resume. But each of these guidelines helps to ensure that the optical scanner will store the information as you wrote it.

1. **Use a sans-serif font.** Serifs make letters a little more complicated, and the scanner might read the letter sequence *ti* as an *h*, for example.
2. **Use a typesize between 10 and 14 points.** If you use a smaller point size, the scanner may not be able to read it correctly. The optimal point size is 12, even if using it means that you must make your resume longer than one page. Headings should not be bigger than 14 points.
3. **Avoid italics, underline, and boldface type.** Too many fonts and frills will just confuse the scanner.
4. **Do not use bullets, lines, rules, graphics, or shading.** Limit your resume to words and numerals only.
5. **Display information in one column, left justified.** Putting the information in two columns with lots of indentations and white space may cause the scanner to misread the order of information or leave something out. Putting information in one column may cause your resume to run over onto a second page, but a scannable resume of two pages or more is acceptable.
6. **Send a laser-printed original on plain white paper.** The scanner has a more difficult time reading photocopies and from colored paper. Use only one side of the paper.

ORGANIZATION OF THE SCANNABLE RESUME

Like a traditional resume, a scannable resume should have your name, address, E-mail address, and phone number at the top. The next most important thing is a list of key words that name the various kinds of knowledge and skills you have as well as the abilities and personal traits you have developed. These key words should mostly be nouns and should include the names or labels of jobs, skills, tasks, instruments, software, hardware, or other things currently important in the career field you seek to enter. Some of the key words can be adjectives that describe your character traits and personal abilities. You should list any key words that describe you and your qualifications. Because employers search for particular words, you should try to match your key words to the qualities and descriptions listed in the employer's job advertisement. As you use these words, your resume will more likely appear in an employer's search.

After the key word summary, you should present a summary of your experience in your education, jobs, and personal life. Finally, you list the traditional headings of education, work, service, and so on with pertinent facts under each. Figure 14-3 presents an example of Ashley Nelson's resume reformatted as a scannable resume. Comparing Figure 14-3 with Figure 14-2 will help you see how the scannable resume differs from the traditional one.

FIGURE 14-3. An Example of a Scannable Resume

Ashley Jones Nelson

1060 South Orem Boulevard, Apt. 16
Orem, UT 84058
480-734-8906
ashleyjnelson@gmail.com

Marriage, family, human development major. Family life educator certificate. Editor. Writer. Speaker. Teacher. Library research. Interview research. Curriculum revision. Budgets and budgeting programs. Management. Microsoft Office. Microsoft Windows. Multi-line telephone systems. Filing. Interpersonal communication skills. Detail oriented. Achievement oriented. Disciplined.

Education

Brigham Young University, Provo, Utah
B.S. Marriage, Family, and Human Development
Graduation August 2006

Summary of Experience

Edited and prepared textbook on family and personal finance for Dr. Craig Israelsen, Brigham Young University, September 2005-2006.
Wrote summaries of research journal articles to be posted online at National Healthy Marriage Resource Center for Dr. Alan Hawkins, Brigham Young University, April 2005 to August 2005.
Interviewed professors and students to evaluate internship program for Dr. Roberta Magarrell, Brigham Young University, September 2004 to January 2005.
Server at Olive Garden restaurant, Provo, Utah, February to August 2005.
Server at Joe's Crab Shack, Orem, Utah, April to August 2004.
Representative for the Church of Jesus Christ of Latter-day Saints in Rochester, New York, April 2002 to September 2003. Teacher of local and church history, theology and church doctrine. Volunteer at hospitals and nursing homes.

Interests

Reading. Family history. Religious history. World history. Public speaking. Art. Singing. Sewing. Scrapbooking. Camping. Hiking. Volleyball.

ONLINE RESUMES

Online resumes are written to be posted on the Internet. This type of resume might include color, graphics, and links to other Web sites; it can also be updated frequently. Many employers now advertise job openings online, either on their own corporate Web site or on a commercial site that allows companies to post job openings for job-seekers to search. You can search these huge commercial databases by job title and often by location. When you find an interesting prospect, you can send your electronic resume. You can also post your resume on a commercial site so that organizations looking for employees can use a search engine to retrieve any online resumes that contain key words of interest to the organization. By coupling the keyword with a certain ZIP code, the employer can limit the number of resumes retrieved to people who already live in a certain area. As you can see, this method of putting employers in touch with potential employees operates more efficiently than the standard mail or interview processes.

Although posting your resume online is generally safe, you should still use caution. Post your resume only to credible websites—posting directly to an employer should be your first choice. Never include personal information like your social security number or birth date in your online resumes or applications. After you've located a job, remove your resume from all online sources.

Creating an online resume used to require knowledge of HTML (hypertext markup language), but now software programs and Web sites have user-friendly templates that make the process easier. Still, designing a resume for a computer screen is different from designing one for paper. If you are interested in seeing some online resumes, check the Web sites listed here.

http://www.monster.com Monster Board includes notifications of potential jobs, opportunities to post your resume online, and actual online job applications. For safety, Monster.com screens clients to make sure that they are actual employers or recruiters.

http://www.careerbuilder.com Career Builder's Web site also allows you to post your resume for potential employers to view. In this site you can choose to post your resume according to the security that you feel comfortable with: you specify standard, anonymous, or private access.

http://hotjobs.com Yahoo! runs HotJobs, a site that allows you to conduct an advanced job search by your career interests, preferred location, and experience. HotJobs also supports a program that allows you to create your resume using one of its templates.

IN-HOUSE HELP

While many sources can offer help with the job market and resumes, your best resource may lie right around the corner in BYU's Counseling and Career Center (2500 WSC). Tutors and counselors there can help you with just about any needs you have regarding graduate schools or careers. Here are some services that the center offers:

- Tutors teach daily group workshops on interviewing, preparing for tests, choosing a career, managing stress, and other topics. You can also schedule one-on-one appointments.

- Within the CCC, Career Placement Services contains directories with employers' information listed regionally and by job type. Recruiters can also conduct campus interviews through Career Placement Services.

- CCC personnel can teach you how to use eRecruiting, a career search engine that can be accessed through Route Y. BYU staff members heavily screen each employer who posts on eRecruiting. Through eRecruiting, you can upload your ABC report and several resumes (each targeted to a different company or position) for potential employers to view.

- The CCC offers career-interest tests, some free and some for a fee, to help you learn about careers that are suited to your personality and interests.

SUGGESTIONS FOR WRITING

1. Locate an ad for a job for which you are qualified, then create a traditional resume that presents your qualifications for the job. If you haven't yet done so, read Chapter 16 to learn about document design so that you can format your resume in an attractive, readable way. Write a letter of application (see Chapter 15) to accompany your resume. After getting feedback on your drafts, revise both. If now is the right time to send them, print your resume and letter on high quality paper and mail them. Save your letter and resume on a disk so that you can change the format and contents for the next job you apply for.

2. Reformat your traditional resume as a scannable resume. When you inquire about jobs you want to apply for, find out if the employer prefers a traditional or scannable resume.

15

LETTERS AND MEMOS

CHAPTER OVERVIEW

After reading this chapter, you should be able to answer the following questions:

1. How does a letter of application differ from a letter of intent?
2. What are the typical parts of a letter of application?
3. What is full-block style? What is semi-block style?
4. What is involved in writing a letter of intent?
5. Where are memos used? What are they typically like? When would a person choose to write a paper memo rather than send an E-mail?

As you approach the end of your undergraduate years, important decisions await you. Will you seek a job? If so, where? Will you go to graduate school? If so, what is involved in applying? The answers to these questions are likely to involve writing in some form. For example, if you are ready to apply for a job, you will generally send out letters of application. If you plan to apply for graduate or professional school, you will very likely have to compose a letter of intent or personal statement to send with other required materials. This chapter outlines principles of form and content, as well as steps to composing, that will help you create effective letters of application or intent.

The letter of application or intent helps you start on the path toward your professional goals. Once you are established in your profession, you will learn to write in many other genres, one of which is the memorandum. Since the memo is common in virtually all professions, this chapter also gives some brief instruction about the form and content of memos, both print and electronic. Your instructor may have you write some memos as a way of practicing this genre and communicating with teacher or classmates about assignments in your class.

LETTERS OF APPLICATION

A letter of application is usually accompanied by a resume (see Chapter 14). In fact, the letter of application is sometimes called a "cover letter" because it allows you to draw the reader's attention to the resume and to elaborate on some of the facts listed in it. Generally your purpose in sending a letter and resume is to get an interview with the recipient or the chance to take the next step in the application process. Letters of application may be sent not only for a job, but also for internships, scholarships, grants, or other opportunities you want to apply for. Whatever their purpose, they generally take the same form as a standard business letter. That is, they have each of the parts listed below, and they incorporate the design elements described below and illustrated in Figures 15-1 and 15-2. Knowing about the letter's parts and design is not sufficient for creating a successful letter, however, so this chapter also includes advice for composing your letter.

PARTS OF THE LETTER

Heading. Except when you are writing on letterhead stationery (which is already printed with your return address), the first element of a business letter is the heading, which consists of your address and the date. Give your complete street address on the first line; the city, state, and zip code on the next line; and the date on the third line. The name of the state can be abbreviated using the standard two-letter abbreviation used by the U.S. Postal Service. The date should be written out completely, using the full name of the month rather than an abbreviation or a numeral (e.g., September 15, 2006, or 15 September 2006, but not Sept. 15, '06 or 9/15/06). Here are two sample headings:

726 Pleasantview Drive   1703 Auburn Street #202
Cove Village, CA 96346   Richardson, TX 75081
August 31, 2006   31 August 2006

Inside Address. After spacing at least twice (or more, depending on the length of your letter), write the name, title, and complete address of the person who is to receive your letter. If you don't know the name, it is acceptable to use just the title of the person you wish to receive your letter (e.g., Vice-President for Human Resources, or Chair of the Scholarship Committee). Here are two sample inside addresses:

Anthropology Department Chair   Ms. Lisa Tanner-Hawkins
University of Utah   Director of Human Resources
270 South 1400 East Room 102   National Information Systems
Salt Lake City, UT 84112   259 Research Drive
                                  Longbrook, NY 20153

Salutation or Greeting. Space twice after the inside address and write "Dear _____:" (Note that the salutation is punctuated with a colon, not a comma, unless you know the person to whom you are writing.) Fill in the blank with the title and last name of the person you are addressing. If the person goes by a title such as *Dr.*, *Professor*, or *President*, you should use that. If no special title is used, use the standard polite forms of address. For a man, obviously, you will use the title *Mr.*; for a woman, you should use *Ms.*, unless you know the woman prefers to be addressed by *Miss* or *Mrs.* If you know the person well enough, you may use a first name.

Sometimes a person will use only initials or will have a first name that may be given to either sex. If you haven't met the person or can't otherwise determine the person's gender, the best option is to use the complete name in the salutation. For example, if you didn't know whether Taylor Johnston was a man or woman, you could write "Dear Taylor Johnston:"

Companies or graduate programs will recognize applicants who do some research to find the name of a department chair, director, or manager. Using a name is always preferred to using a title or position. If you cannot find the name of the person who will read your letter, however, you may use a title in the salutation, as in "Dear Graduate Coordinator." Or, in place of the greeting, you may write an attention or subject line, such as one of the following:

Attention: Recreational Programs Director
Subject: Advertisement for Summer Interns
Re: Editorial Position

So-called generic greetings of an earlier era, such as "Gentlemen," "Dear Sir," or "Dear Sir or Madam" are no longer used because they don't adequately reflect the realities or the language used in today's business world. The greeting "To Whom it May Concern" is still used sometimes, but it is rather stiff; use it only as a last resort.

The Body. Beginning two lines under the greeting, write the body of the letter. In a letter of application, the body is generally three or four paragraphs long, each with a definite role to play in raising your reader's interest and persuading him or her to consider your application more carefully.

First paragraph. In the first paragraph, you should name the position or opportunity you are seeking and, particularly for a job, how you learned about it. Include the name of a professor, former employer, or other contact if he or she has encouraged you to pursue the job. Mentioning a contact can impress a potential employer. Employers also want to know how the news of an opening becomes known. If you saw an advertisement, mention it; if you heard about it from another person, mention that. If you do not know there is an opening and are writing on the chance that there might be, briefly explain why you want to work for the organization. End this paragraph by stating in a few words why you feel you are qualified for the position or opportunity.

Middle paragraphs. In the middle paragraph or paragraphs, elaborate on your qualifications. You might devote one paragraph to your educational preparation and another to your work or volunteer experience. Be specific. In addition to writing, "I am a well-organized, efficient worker," provide details that *show* the reader that you are. For example, you might write, "During my internship at Clyde Museum, my public relations team increased museum attendance by 30% through our history awareness campaign." You may also want to address possible reservations that your prospective employer may have about hiring you. Put yourself in the reader's position and consider what he or she might be concerned about or interested in.

Of course, be sure to carefully select what you include; you don't want to oversell yourself, and you want to keep the letter to a page. Remember that your letter works in tandem with your resume to give the reader as full a picture as possible of your experience and abilities. By presenting and elaborating on some well-chosen details about yourself in the letter, you hope to interest the employer enough to gain an interview, at which you can elaborate further.

Final paragraphs. In the final paragraph, refer the reader to your resume and politely request further action. Indicate when you will be available for an interview and express hope that you will hear from the employer soon. If the organization is in another city to which you will soon be traveling, ask to have an appointment during your stay. Sound a confident but not too aggressive tone in the closing lines of your letter.

Complimentary Close. Two lines under the body of the letter, you will write one of several common closings that will precede your signature. For a formal letter addressed to someone you are not well acquainted with, the standard complimentary closes are listed below. Note that each is followed by a comma:

- Sincerely,
- Sincerely yours,
- Yours truly,
- Very truly yours,
- Respectfully,

If you are acquainted with the addressee, you could consider using "Cordially," or "Best regards."

Signature and Typed Name. After the complimentary close, space down four lines and type your complete name. Write your signature in the blank space above your typed name.

Enclosure Line. If you have enclosed something with the letter (and with an application letter you will generally enclose your resume) it is common to type the word "Enclosure" two lines after your name, flush with the left margin.

DESIGN OF THE LETTER

Layout. There are two ways to format a business letter: full-block style (illustrated in Figure 15-1) or semi-block style (illustrated in Figure 15-2). In full-block style, all parts of the letter are aligned flush with the left margin. In semi-block style, the heading, complimentary close, and signature are aligned with each other and are placed right of the center of the page. In addition, in the semi-block style, the opening line of each paragraph can be indented five spaces.

The letter should have enough white space in it that it does not look formidable to read. Although paragraphs are single-spaced, you should double-space between paragraphs. To avoid giving the letter a top-heavy appearance, center the printed matter on the page. One way to introduce more white space at the top of the letter is to space several lines between the heading and the inside address. Between all other parts of the letter, however, you should leave only two lines of space. Margins on both sides and at the top and bottom of the letter should be at least one inch. Do *not* justify the right margin because doing so makes the letter more difficult to read.

Unlike a resume, a letter is not designed for random access. It is meant to be read line by line, from left to right, beginning at the top and moving to the bottom. Additional devices to draw attention to layout, such as boldface or headings, are generally not needed. In some cases, additional indentation and bullets might be used in a letter, but not often.

Fonts and Point Sizes. As with the resume, choose a serif font that looks professionally typeset (such as Times New Roman) rather than typewritten (such as Courier). The usual point size for a letter is 12, though you could use 11 or even 10 if doing so would help you keep the letter to one page. But be considerate of your reader and don't strain his or her eyesight! If you would have to use an even smaller point size to make your letter fit on a page, consider cutting parts of your letter. Only in rare cases should you send a two-page letter.

Paper and Printing. Laser print your letter on high quality bond paper of the same stock you use for your resume. Do not use colors other than white, off-white, or ivory. The professional appearance of your letter makes an important first impression on your reader, so this is no time to be cheap or careless.

COMPOSING YOUR LETTER

Business letters have become a highly standardized genre. In a sense, this is good because the conventions to follow are quite clear-cut. However, it also could be detrimental because you may be tempted to lapse into formulaic, clichéd writing. Your application letter is generally your first contact with an employer or someone who has the ability to grant you the internship or scholarship you are seeking, so you want to make a good impression and distinguish yourself from other applicants. You want your own voice and personality to come through in your letter while still observing the conventions the genre entails. Use the letters in this section mainly for formatting guides; your letter's content should be presented in your own voice, not in words duplicated from a good example.

Prewriting. As in other writing tasks, an effective prewriting strategy is the first step to a successful final draft. Use a technique such as brainstorming, listing, or freewriting to generate as many facts about yourself as you can—anything you think might even remotely interest an employer or award committee. Write much more than you can possibly use because the very act of generating material may help you think more carefully about your strengths. With a lot of material to choose from, select the facts that best represent your qualifications. Plan how you can arrange and interpret these details about yourself to show why you would be the best choice for the job, the internship, the scholarship, or other opportunity.

Drafting. Write a longer first draft than you can use, then cut it down to size. Consider the order you present your ideas in: Is it logical and clear? Also consider how your sentences connect with each other; make transitions explicit.

Because the letter is about yourself, you will find that you need to say "I" in it frequently. There is nothing wrong or immodest about this. However, it can become monotonous if you begin every sentence with "I." Find ways to vary your syntax so that you do not need to start every sentence with a reference to yourself.

To make the letter sound like you, use words you would use if you were speaking with the reader face to face. Present your qualifications in a matter-of-fact, but confident tone. You won't necessarily impress the reader by using highfalutin' and superlative language like this:

I am possessed of the conviction that I can make a uniquely and immensely valuable contribution to your organization because my demonstrable academic success in my chosen major of social psychology and my prior assignments and accomplishments in the business field of employment constitute qualifications of a superior nature.

The reader is likely to be put off by such a pompous, wordy sentence and would probably prefer to read something simpler, like this:

I am confident I can contribute to your organization's success because my training in social psychology and my work experience in business qualify me in unique ways.

Revising and proofreading. Revise and edit carefully to make the letter correct and concise. Show a near-final draft to trusted professors, advisers, or tutors in your campus writing center. Incorporate worthwhile suggestions from them and then proofread with the utmost care. As with a resume, a single spelling, grammatical, or typographical mistake in a letter can be your undoing when the reader is looking for a reason to eliminate some contenders from consideration.

FIGURE 15-1. Full-Block Style Letter

1060 South Orem Blvd., Apt. 16
Orem, UT 84057
January 25, 2006

Mikelle Wilcox
Parent Education Resource Center
Westmore Elementary
1150 South Main Street
Orem, UT 84058

Dear Ms. Wilcox:

I recently looked through the BYU School of Family Life Internship Web site and learned of your ongoing need for interns. I remember meeting you at the Certified Family Life Educator Club meeting a few months ago, when you spoke about your center and the availability of internships. I will be graduating with a degree in marriage, family and human development in August 2006, and I am looking for an internship to finish off my last semester at BYU. The skills I have acquired from taking courses to prepare for CFLE certification have given me a solid base to build from. I would like to put my skills to use at the Parent Education Resource Center, contributing to the ongoing tasks of reaching out and educating the community.

I realize you are looking for applicants with a strong background in child development and a family systems understanding, as well as the ability to relate to people. Because of my experiences working as a research assistant for professors at BYU on topics important to education and families and my work experiences serving people of all types and backgrounds, I am confident that I am well prepared for the internship you are offering. My research and writing abilities and my oral communication skills will be of great benefit in serving the parents of Utah Valley. I have excelled in my major coursework, with a 3.75 GPA, and I have continually displayed a strong work ethic throughout my undergraduate career. I am also currently working with the Forever Families Website at BYU, where I am writing articles for online publication to create another resource of outreach material for families in need.

I hope you will consider me for this internship. I am aware of your plans for expansion in the future and would love to be a part of the team that makes that possible. I have enclosed my resume. I look forward to meeting with you soon. You can contact me by phone at (480) 734-8606, or by email at ashleyjnelson@gmail.com.

Sincerely,

Ashley J. Nelson

Ashley J. Nelson

Enclosure

FIGURE 15-2. Semi-Block Style Letter

430 South 300 West
Provo, UT 84601
January 25, 2006

Mr. Anthony G. Greenwald
Admissions Committee
University of Washington
Psychology Graduate Advising
Seattle, WA 98195-1525

Dear Mr. Greenwald:

I am applying for fall 2007 admission to the graduate social psychology program at University of Washington. I learned of the reputation of your social psychology doctoral program after researching to determine which graduate schools strongly emphasize research in mental representation and unconscious process. Because of my interest in this field, I am writing to ask you to consider me for a research position with you, should I be accepted. I have gained many skills in research from my classes and work at Brigham Young University and am eager to use and improve those skills in a graduate school's research setting.

As a psychology major at BYU I have taken many opportunities to gain skills in research and writing. My interest in mental representation and unconscious process was inspired by an honors class on consciousness where I became fascinated with David J. Chalmers' research on conscious and unconscious processes. I feel my course work has prepared me well for the research required for an assistantship with you. I have completed two minors, in German and business, and through those courses I acquired skills in literary analysis and business development. I also fine-tuned my writing skills through classes offered in psychology, English, and German. My skills particularly improved in my critical analysis course, where I grasped the ability to write clearly and effectively address different audiences.

My work experience in the last few years has also prepared me for this position. Since October 2001 I have worked with Dr. Michelle James of BYU's Germanic and Slavic Languages Department on a digital library of early German women's writing posted on the Web (http://sophie.byu.edu). From that time to the present I have transcribed, edited, glossed, and published eighteenth-century texts for scholarly research and preservation. Through this work I have developed not only research and writing skills, but initiative, analytical thinking, resourcefulness, and a strong work ethic.

I would also like to be considered for department funding through research or teaching assistantships. Please feel free to contact my references listed on the enclosed resume for further information. If you would be interested in seeing some of my writing samples, please call or e-mail me, and I would be happy to send my writing and research portfolio.

Sincerely,

Samuel C. Lindsey

Samuel C. Lindsey

Enclosure

LETTERS OF INTENT AND PERSONAL STATEMENTS

A letter of intent or personal statement is usually part of an application for graduate or professional school, but sometimes it is also required for a scholarship or internship application. Despite its name, a letter of intent is usually not formatted as a letter: it has no inside address, salutation, or complimentary close, though it may have a heading and a signature. It is like an essay in both form and content, yet it is like a letter of application in important ways: it is about your qualifications, and its purpose is to persuade readers (usually a committee of professors) to choose you from among many other applicants for a position in the program you want to enter, or for an internship or scholarship.

In this chapter, it's not possible to delve into how letters of intent for law school might differ from those for an MBA program; instead, this chapter provides some general advice on how to make your letter best represent you. You should be able to get more particular advice from five sources:

1. The admissions offices at the schools you plan to apply to will tell you what form your statement must take, how long it can be, and the kinds of information the admissions committee is seeking.

2. BYU's Counseling and Career Center offers workshops specifically about researching and applying for graduate school. Mentors there can help you write genre-specific letters of intent.

3. A number of books available in libraries and bookstores give helpful advice for writing letters for particular kinds of graduate programs.

4. A professor or mentor in the field you want to enter can give you helpful feedback before you print and mail a final draft of your statement.

5. The instructions that accompany the application form for a scholarship or internship may tell you what to include in your letter.

IMPORTANCE OF THE LETTER

The letter of intent is one of the main parts of a typical application for graduate school. The other parts are usually an application form; a transcript of your undergraduate courses and grades; test scores from standardized aptitude and achievement tests such as the GRE, the LSAT, the GMAT, or the MCAT; letters of recommendation (usually three) from professors or others who can attest to your intellectual, social, and personal qualifications for graduate school; and a resume, or at least a list of work experience and extracurricular activities. Because you will be hurrying to submit all of these parts of the application by a certain deadline, you may be tempted to think you can toss off your personal statement in a few hours a couple of days before you have to mail it. Thinking that would be a big mistake.

The letter of intent is often the most important part of the application—in fact, it is the only one you still have some control over as application deadlines loom. By then your GPA is already pretty well determined, your test scores have already been calculated, and your letters of recommendation are beyond your control. But in your personal statement you can still say things about yourself that will not otherwise be apparent to the admissions committee. A strong personal statement, for example, can sometimes salvage an application that isn't distinguished by a high GPA or impressive exam scores. A poor statement, on the other hand, may sabotage an otherwise competitive application. Even when the other indicators of a successful application are strong, a highly effective personal statement may bring a bonus beyond mere admission—a scholarship or tuition waiver, for example. You should therefore plan to start several weeks early, if possible, to draft your letter of intent. Figure 15-3 presents Spencer James' letter, which resulted from several drafts written over a period of several weeks.

A well-written personal statement can also make or break your application for an internship or scholarship. In most cases, you will be competing with other applicants whose qualifications are about as strong as yours, so the statement is often the best chance you have to distinguish yourself from the others and impress the committee to choose you. Figure 15-4 presents a personal statement written by Jenelle Tittelfitz for an undergraduate scholarship. As you can see, she crafted her statement carefully to demonstrate that she has high goals and clear plans for the future, so she would be a deserving recipient for the scholarship.

GENERATING SUBSTANCE THROUGH PREWRITING

Before you begin drafting your statement, generate a lot of possible material that you could use in it. Here are some questions to which you could freewrite answers:

1. What is your motivation for wanting an advanced degree or other award? What events in your life gave you that motivation? What feelings or impulses move you in this direction?

2. What are your strengths? How are they related to succeeding in the career you've chosen? What have you chosen to do in your courses and extracurricular activities to prepare yourself for the kind of career you want?

3. What significant experiences have you had that show you have the talents to succeed in a rigorous graduate program? What unique experiences and abilities would you bring to the school you are applying to? Why would you make the best use of a scholarship? Why do deserve the internship?

FIGURE 15-3. An Example of a Letter of Intent

Letter of Intent for Graduate School
by Spencer L. James

I grew up in a family that was poor, at least as material wealth is measured by American standards. So in 2002, when I was asked to serve a mission in Ivory Coast, Africa, I thought I was prepared to go to one of the world's least developed nations because I knew what it meant to be poor. After arriving in Ivory Coast, I soon realized I did not. I was forced to acknowledge that though I lacked some of the worldly goods owned by my more affluent friends, in comparison to the average Ivorian I possessed significant wealth, particularly personal, social, and educational capital. My goal is to earn a PhD in development sociology from Cornell University because I want to better understand the dynamics of poverty. I want eventually to help alleviate poverty by working as a scholar in an academic setting, a research firm, or a development NGO. Your development sociology program will give me the necessary intellectual and methodological tools to do that by building on the education, experiences, character, and skills I will bring to your program.

As I said, I know now that I have been blessed with an embarrassment of riches, even though I still lack an abundance of money. My parents taught me to work hard, and that ability alone has increased my intellectual wealth a hundredfold. I will graduate in August 2006 with a B.S. in sociology (research and analysis emphasis) and a minor in French. I will have completed more than 95 percent of my coursework in just two and a half years. I recently completed a semester wherein I took 21 credits, worked 20 hours a week, and did research for 15 hours a week, yet I maintained a 4.0 GPA. I have focused my curriculum around core courses in methods, theory, and statistics, and I have a solid foundation in these basic tools of the discipline. I have greatly increased my knowledge of statistics both by taking courses, including one on regression modeling, and by using statistics on the research projects I have been involved in. But I haven't limited my learning to the classroom and research projects, as I have taken the opportunity to develop strong, personal relationships with my professors, who have given me a thorough understanding of what is expected of a sociologist, especially a graduate student. They have recommended books to further my understanding of African sociology, race and ethnicity, and international development, and I have read dozens of books on my own to help prepare for graduate school. I treasure the relationships I have formed and the knowledge I have gained.

Although I found Ivory Coast poor beyond belief, what I learned and experienced there has enriched me immeasurably. There I gained leadership and teaching skills, as I prepared and taught lessons each day, in addition to overseeing the work of up to ten other missionaries. The culture and language were at first foreign to me, but they became familiar as I devoted myself to my work. I became fluent in French and familiar with Baoulé and Lingala, two native languages that are widely spoken in Ivory Coast and the

FIGURE 15-3. An Example of a Letter of Intent (continued)

Democratic Republic of Congo, respectively. I also learned to love the culture and move easily within it. When I returned to the US in 2004, my French professor at BYU asked me to write the Advanced French Grammar course for the distance-learning program. Through designing and writing the curriculum, especially the exams, I have further developed teaching skills, such as how to present material so that others can understand difficult concepts and how to test effectively. I have also learned to coordinate a complex project that has both academic and business dimensions. My knowledge of French and my fluency have also improved. After finishing the French project, I will work on the sociology courses offered via distance education. I will proofread texts for errors in content or expression, verify the references, and ensure that the curriculum is understandable to all students. I believe that these and other experiences will enable me to succeed in your sociology program not only because of the skills I have gained but because of the ways these projects have taught me to manage time, work efficiently, and produce high-quality work that meets deadlines.

I am currently in a research group led by Dr. Ralph B. Brown. In this group, I have participated in conceptualizing and planning research, executing it, and writing about it for publication. I have learned how to do effective literature reviews that enable me to develop informed hypotheses. Data analysis is no longer an abstract idea for me but a concrete reality, as I have created tables from data and have run multiple regression and factor analyses. One of the projects I have worked on deals with race relations in the Mississippi Delta. I am currently collaborating on two papers on this topic that will be submitted to journals in the summer of 2006. Our research group will also present one of these papers at the 2006 Pacific Sociological Association conference. Participation in this research group has taught me many things in addition to research skills. I have learned the importance of working with others and of doing my part of the task on time. I have learned to appreciate the importance of always being willing to help and the value of what I can learn simply by listening.

In graduate school I plan to pursue a research agenda focused on poverty and development generally and on Western Africa specifically. Given my research interests and career goals, I believe Cornell's development sociology program will give me the ideal foundation. In particular, I hope to work with Dr. Parfait Eloundou, with whom I have been in contact via e-mail and telephone for the past year. I was ecstatic to discover that he does the type of research that I plan to pursue. He has made significant contributions in the fields of poverty reduction and education in West Africa. I believe that with my language ability and understanding of West African culture and politics, I could be an asset to him in further researching these and other issues. I am enthusiastic about the prospect of associating with graduate students who have outlooks and goals similar to my own. I look forward to working with them and the professors in the department on development and population issues and applied social theory. I am ready to invest the capital of my education, experience, skills, and work ethic in graduate study, and I am confident that I can succeed. I look forward to the opportunity of pursuing a Ph.D. in development sociology at Cornell University.

FIGURE 15-4. An Example of a Personal Statement

Personal Statement for the Sant Undergraduate Scolarship
by Jenelle R. Tittelfitz

The moment I saw my baby sister lying gently in the arms of my mother, I knew she was ours to keep forever. She was a new member of our family and would always be the only sister I would have. After I was born, my parents learned they would no longer be able to have children of their own, but they felt inspired that their family was not yet complete. They decided to adopt through LDS Family Services only three years after my birth. Both of my parents viewed adoption as the Lord bestowing their children to them through indirect means. In a way, I feel both my sister and brother have always been my siblings since before they were born; they just took different journeys to join our family than I did.

Their journeys into our family have continued through their lives, however, and have taken me along for the emotional ride. Being of African-American descent, my siblings are both minorities in our community and have struggled with the discrimination, stigmas and stereotypes that surround them everyday. It broke my heart the day my sister pinched her broad nose together and through tears told me she didn't understand why she could not just look more like me. At the perceptive age of 12, I was beginning to understand that even though my sister had been with us since her infancy, it was not inborn in her to feel that she was always meant to be part of our family. It became my ambition to help my brother and sister understand that the union of our family would always be stronger than any outlying forces and that the differences in our features or our birth parents would never change how much my family loved and accepted them.

In high school I realized how much broader the reverberation of discrimination was than just in my local community or nation. My high school curriculum was focused on an international perspective, and I was very much intrigued by the geography, history and literature courses on Africa. The history of apartheid in South Africa aroused the deepest curiosity in me. I couldn't keep my mind from wanting to explore the reasons behind the deep-rooted discrimination between whites and blacks in the country. The fact that apartheid had happened so recently and that it continues to have lasting effects on that country still drives my interests in studying South Africa's people and their tribulations. It was also during high school that I became abruptly aware of the effects of the HIV/AIDS epidemic on families and children, many receiving the virus from mother-to-child transmission and being orphaned, without family or sources of treatment to help them. For the past four years it has been in my heart to work towards being part of a cure for the social problems that continue in South Africa.

Once I began attending Brigham Young University I knew I wanted to major in social work, and I started with the prerequisites my first semester. One of the first assignments in my

FIGURE 15-4. An Example of a Personal Satement (continued)

Introduction to Social Work course was a group interview of a member of the community who held a Masters of Social Work degree. Our interview was with a newly appointed adoption counselor at the LDS Family Services in American Fork, the very place my family met my sister the first time eleven years prior. His fresh perspective on the field was reassuring to my insecure aspirations of one day being in his shoes. His words were encouraging and inspiring, saying that no matter where we wanted to go in the field, we could get there if only we had the determination and unfailing desire to work for what we wanted to achieve. I left his office that day with a strong feeling that I would find a means to the end, that I would be part of the social welfare progress in South Africa. That was when I discovered the field study opportunity in South Africa through BYU's International Study Programs. In preparation for the field work I will be doing in South Africa, I decided to concentrate this coming year's studies on preventative HIV/AIDS education programs for youth and relocating HIV-orphaned children back into families. To this end, I am currently enrolled in a seminar course on HIV/AIDS and its prevention, treatment, and care. The Sant Undergraduate Scholarship would allow me to continue focusing my time on these studies and course work this coming academic year by lessening financial stress.

After anticipated graduation from BYU in December 2007, I plan to carry on my studies in social work with a Masters in Social Work from Columbia University's School of Social Work. After much inquiry into their programs and contacting their office of admissions, I learned that I can focus on family, youth, and children's services as well as electives in international social welfare and services for my fields of practice. My goal is to complete an internship with the UNICEF organization, using the experience I will have gained in South Africa as a tool to continue focusing on HIV/AIDS prevention, parent-to-child transmission, and care and support for orphaned children. I know that my undergraduate studies from BYU and the field study to South Africa will provide me with a solid background, extended knowledge, and the experience needed to go forward in the field of social work.

The journeys I will be taking in my future have all been inspired by the distinct learning experiences of my life and by the continuous support and encouragement of my family. Though my journey in life has been quite different from that of my brother and sister, it will soon be quite the same. I will be the minority in Africa and will be trying to find my way into families, uniting children to parents and helping to strengthen their relations, just as my brother and sister have strengthened our family by completing us. Who knows— maybe one day I will be back in the LDS Family Services building for a third time, gently holding in my arms a part of my future family.

DRAFTING AROUND A THEME

Since the personal statement is a brief essay, it should have a clearly defined focus or theme. After generating ideas through prewriting answers to the above questions, you should be able to select a focus from all you've written and begin to draft your essay around that theme. For example, you could narrate a defining event or series of events in your life that helped crystallize a particular career choice for you. Then you can add brief descriptions of how other choices and experiences have prepared you for that career. Notice how Spencer's statement of intent (Figure 15-3) uses the theme of "rich and poor" to show how his education and experiences have prepared him to succeed in graduate school. He sounds humble yet confident. You must be careful neither to oversell yourself nor to sell yourself short. Admissions committees do want to see how you will apply your knowledge in a career, but a "save-the-world-single-handed" approach is not likely to gain favor.

Another way to make an argument for your acceptance is to explain strengths you have that are not measurable by test scores and GPA. Things such as work and volunteer experience, interpersonal skills, bilingual and bicultural abilities, and the ability to be independent and self-motivated count with admissions and scholarship or internship committees, if you can show how these traits are relevant to the course of study you wish to pursue. Resist the temptation to spell out everything about your life, however. There is no need to repeat information that is available in other parts of your application, and there is generally a word limit for the statement anyway. Still another approach is to explain why your particular background and talents are a good match for unique courses the program offers. This means, of course, that you will have to research the various programs you plan to apply to and learn what special emphases they offer.

REVISING AND EDITING

Plan to spend a number of hours working on your statement over a period of two or three weeks. Draft a version, get feedback on it, and let it rest a few days. Then write another version, trying ideas others have given you. Continue seeking feedback and revising until you have a draft that includes particulars that you think best describe you. Work on the organization to make it clear and cohesive; the conceptual links between paragraphs should be apparent but not obtrusive.

As you edit to make your statement the right length, be alert to empty words you could cut and to stilted words or jargon that you would not likely use if you were speaking to the admissions committee. They are not looking to be impressed by a big vocabulary; instead, they want clarity. The importance of correct spelling, usage, and sentence structure can't be overstated. The ability to write well is extremely important in all kinds of graduate work, and the committee will judge your ability to succeed as a writer in graduate school by the quality of the writing in your personal statement. Mistakes can lower your ranking in the list of applicants. You and at least one other person should proof-read your statement carefully before you mail it. As with other letters, laser print the final draft on high quality bond paper either white or off-white in color.

MEMOS

The memorandum (the plural is memoranda), or the memo for short, is a brief written form of communication used within an organization. Brevity, clarity, and efficiency in reading are its hallmarks. Memos differ from letters in that they have no salutation, no complimentary close, and generally no signature (although the writer sometimes writes his or her initials next to the "from" line). Instead, the memo has a heading indicating who the reader is, who the sender is, the date, and what the memo is about. This is a sample heading:

To: All Faculty
From: Travel Office
Date: 6 August 2006
Subject: New Regulations for Travel Per Diem Allowance

In many organizations, special memo paper is printed with the "To," "From," and "Date" components already supplied, each followed by a blank line which the writer can fill in. These institutions also frequently have special memo envelopes designed for routing memos from one office or department to another. Organizations that you have worked for in the past may have had their own practices for creating and sending memos.

As e-mail is fast becoming the preferred medium for communicating within an organization, special memo stationery and envelopes are on the decline. Nevertheless, hard copies of memos (ones printed on paper) are still important in most organizations, particularly when a durable, portable record of the contents is needed. Memos originally composed in e-mail can be printed. Memos composed for paper circulation can also sent by e-mail, either as an attachment or directly within a message. Whether the original medium is paper or electronic, the general purposes for memos and many of the principles for composing them remain the same. This chapter focuses first on printed memos, then offers tips for using e-mail in a professional setting.

COMPOSING A MEMO

As in other rhetorical situations, begin writing a memo by asking yourself who your audience is and what your purpose is. With a memo, you may have multiple readers. Usually, a memo is addressed to just one person, however, and other intended readers are named in a line that may be headed "Copy" or "cc." (The "cc" stands for "carbon copy" and dates back to the days when typewriters were the principal office technology for writing, and carbon paper was what office workers used in place of a photocopy machine.) The "copy" line may come in the memo's heading or it may come after the body of the memo.

The purposes for memos are numerous and various. Here are some typical ones:

- To propose a course of action
- To report on an action
- To report on facts discovered through research
- To give a progress report
- To record and remind others of decisions made in a meeting or conversation
- To inform of a new policy or procedure
- To make announcements of general interest
- To ask questions
- To answer questions
- To summarize something—e.g., a document or meeting—for a busy person

Whatever the purpose, the goal is to say simply and briefly what you have to say. When little is at stake—when you are simply tossing out ideas for a few co-workers, for example—memos can be hastily written. Memos in government agencies, on the other hand, might become part of a paper trail that has legal or historical implications. The more important your audience or purpose, and the more important the contents are, the more carefully you should plan the wording and the design of your memo. For memos with potentially broad significance, it may take many hours of writing to achieve the right wording and the ease of reading that characterize a good memo.

DESIGNING THE MEMO

Memos usually have two parts: the heading and the body. A long memo communicating complex information might have a separate conclusion as well, summarizing the contents, drawing conclusions, or making recommendations.

How much you need to design the visual structure of a memo depends largely on the length and complexity of the information it conveys. In very brief memos of only a paragraph or two, the need for design is minimal since most readers will be able to understand the entire contents in a few minutes. For a brief memo, the most helpful thing you can do is to write a clear and complete "Subject" or "Re" line in the heading. (*Re* is from Latin and means "concerning" or "about.") The subject line should sum up the memo's contents in a few memorable words. Figure 15-5 presents a brief memo that incorporates very few visual design elements.

For long memos, particularly those conveying complex information, a brief opening paragraph that gives an overview of the contents can help the reader significantly. This overview can correspond to internal headings in the memo that help busy readers locate desired information quickly. Another way to help the reader read efficiently is to use principles of document design (see Chapter 16). For example, internal headings can be placed in a separate column to the left of the text. Or they can be in boldface and underlined, then placed above sections of the text, either centered or on the left margin. Within sections of a memo, bulleted or numbered lists can present complex information in a more visual and useful fashion. White space between sections, around lists, and elsewhere also makes a long memo more readable because it relieves the formidable impression of a densely worded page. Figure 15-6 presents a memo that makes good use of some of these design devices. (Note that this memo was written by a student to a teacher to report on an assignment to attend a library mini-course. Your instructor may ask you to write memos as a way of communicating efficiently about assignments in your course.)

FIGURE 15-5. A Short Memo with Few Design Elements

To: All Faculty and Staff
From: University Recycling Center/College of Humanities
Date: 17 September 2006
Re: Recycling Contest

In light of President Christensen's challenge to "reduce, reuse, and recycle," we will be holding a recycling contest this semester. The department with the most pounds of recycled goods by the first day of finals will win a pizza party. Please bring the following items to recycling bins outside of your department's main office:

1. Paper: newspapers, magazines, white office paper
2. Aluminum: cans stripped of any paper labels
3. Plastic: items marked for recycling (numbers one through five)

FIGURE 15-6. A Long Memo with Design Elements

CAMPUS MEMORANDUM BRIGHAM YOUNG UNIVERSITY

To: Dr. Kristine Hansen
From: Emily Adams
Date: 23 February 2006
Re: Library Mini-Course

This memo briefly summarizes the library mini-course I attended. I note the facts of the session I attended, explain the main ideas that were presented, and evaluate the experience. Finally, I recommend some ideas for improvement of the mini-course.

Session Facts
I attended the library mini-course on linguistics that was held on 15 February 2006 and taught by Richard Hacken, the linguistics librarian. He showed us the various online journal databases we could use for our research, and he introduced us to RefWorks.

Session Summary
Mr. Hacken spoke for about 25 minutes. During that time, he walked us through the four main databases used by linguists: ERIC, JSTOR, LLBA, and the MLA International Bibliography. He told us the advantages and disadvantages of the various reference tools. Then he showed us how to store information and how to create bibliographies in RefWorks. After making sure that we understood, he supervised us as we researched our own topics for the remainder of the time.

Evaluation
I felt that the session was quite valuable as I have never done any intense research in the linguistics field before. Therefore, I found it very helpful to be introduced to the databases and learn how to navigate them. Also, I found RefWorks an extremely useful resource that I will use quite frequently in the future. I felt that the time spent teaching, about 25 minutes, was sufficient, and that the time that we were allowed to research on our own was also quite valuable because Mr. Hacken was available to answer individual questions. In sum, the course was a productive and useful experience.

Suggestions for Improvement
The class was efficient and helpful enough that I do not have any suggestions for improvement of that aspect of the mini-course. However, I would find it helpful if an instruction sheet about RefWorks and the various other databases were posted on the library Web site. This would help me remember some of the more detailed aspects of navigating the library databases and would also be a valuable resource.

Copy: Tammy Siebenberg

E-mail Etiquette

Increasingly, e-mail is used rather than paper memos in academic and professional settings to communicate between teacher and student, supervisor and employee, colleague and colleague. While just about everyone knows how to use e-mail for informal communication with friends and family, it's not the case that everyone knows how to use it in a more formal and professional setting. Here are some tips that will help you avoid having your e-mails deleted or misinterpreted as unprofessional, rude, or trivial.

- Be sure that your e-mail address includes your name or a short version of your name that is clear and unambiguous. A cute or suggestive e-mail address is not appropriate in a workplace. If you want to have such an e-mail address for your personal e-mail, you can establish a different e-mail account for that purpose.

- Use the subject line to tell the recipients of your e-mail what you are writing about. Leaving it blank or writing something generic, like "hi," can be dangerous, as someone might assume it is "spam" and delete it.

- The more formal and important the e-mail is, the more you should use proper letter etiquette: Address the recipient by last name, using a title such as "Dr.," "Professor," "Mr.," or "Ms.," especially if you are not well-acquainted or if there is some social distance between you. Be sure to include your name at the end of the e-mail, so the recipient knows who you are. Adding other contact information, such as your address and phone number, can also be helpful.

- Take time when composing an e-mail. The more important the subject, the longer you should take. E-mail should not be less professional than an office memo. Be concise without being brusque or leaving out important information. Use correct grammar and spelling, and correct your typos. Proofread your message before you send it, and think about whether the content says all you want it to.

- Do not write in all capital letters. Do not use excessive punctuation or no punctuation at all. Do not include emoticons or abbreviations (like TTYL and IMHO).

- Don't use the tab key to begin a new paragraph; skip a line instead.

- When sending attachments, be sure to mention in the body of your e-mail that you are doing so, and explain what the attached file contains. This can eliminate fear of viruses.

- When replying to another's e-mail, it can be helpful to use the reply option. This should automatically keep the sender's original subject line, with "Re:" in front. However, be careful that you are only e-mailing the people you want to. Note that some e-mail programs have an option to reply to all people who received the original e-mail. Keep the amount of quoted text in your reply to a minimum: rereading what one has already sent can be tedious.

- Respect the privacy of others and of yourself. E-mail is *never* completely private! Unless the sender indicates otherwise, treat e-mail messages as though they were meant for your eyes only. But don't assume that everyone else will do the same with e-mails that you send. If you have something confidential to say, it may be best to make an appointment with the person you want to talk to, so you don't have to put in writing something that may later embarrass or harm you.

- Be professional and respectful in your writing. Don't make personal attacks. Company e-mail systems are open to employer scrutiny, and e-mails can be forwarded, misdirected, hacked into, and so on. Once you hit the send button, you have no control over where your message goes.

- It can be helpful to postpone filling in the recipient's e-mail address until you are positive that your e-mail is complete and correct. Waiting can ensure you never accidentally send something weren't ready to, even if you hit the wrong button.

SUGGESTIONS FOR WRITING

1. Locate an ad for a part-time or full-time job for which you are qualified. Compose a letter applying for the job, stressing your qualifications that come from your education or previous work experience. Show a draft of your letter to a friend, tutor, or adviser to get feedback on improving it; then revise it. If now is the appropriate time to send your letter, laser print a final copy, enclose your resume (see Chapter 14), and mail it.

2. If you are planning to attend a graduate or professional school, contact the institutions you plan to apply to (even if the time to apply is still several months away) and ask for application forms and instructions about the kind of personal statement they require. Ask also if they require a resume or *curriculum vitae* (see Chapter 14). Begin now to draft a personal statement, seeking feedback from professors and advisers, as well as your peers. When the application deadline draws nearer, take the draft out and revise it. Proofread carefully, then print your personal statement and send it with other application materials.

3. Write a memo to your instructor reporting your progress on a long writing assignment that will soon be due. Or, if you have recently completed an assignment, write a memo to your instructor reporting on what you learned and evaluating the worth of the experience to you.

IV

VISUAL AND ORAL RHETORIC

To speak of visual rhetoric, as many now do, may seem at first to be extending the meaning of rhetoric too far. Yet, in this section of the book, you will learn that you can enhance the persuasiveness of your written documents through their very appearance and through the graphical devices you create to accompany your written words. In Chapter 16 you will learn basic guidelines for designing documents so that readers will find them inviting to the eye and easy to use. "Desktop publishing" is another name often given to the principles taught there. In our computer age, using a few simple options of widely accessible word processing programs, it has become easier than ever to produce attractive documents that look almost as if a professional typesetter had produced them. Increasingly, employers and professors will expect that you know how to use computer functions to design readable documents on the job and at school. Those who don't know how to use them will be at a disadvantage not only in getting good grades and making good impressions at work, but also in persuading their readers.

In Chapter 17 you will learn principles for creating ethical and effective graphics to display data. Computer programs have made graphics easier to produce than ever before, but they have also made it easier to produce distorted graphics, "chartjunk," and frivolous decorations. Chapter 17 will teach you that tables, figures, and other illustrations should never be merely decorative; instead, they should be simple and informative, enhancing your credibility and the persuasiveness of your argument.

If speaking of visual rhetoric seems strange, speaking of oral rhetoric seems redundant, since rhetoric originally was the art of oratory, or public speaking. Yet, with the great emphasis given to writing in college, it is important to be reminded that speech is still a vital form of communication in professional life. The effective speaker does not leave persuasion to chance, but prepares carefully to make a convincing argument and a favorable impression on an audience. Chapter 18 gives you guidelines for planning, organizing, and delivering effective oral presentations.

16

BASIC PRINCIPLES OF DOCUMENT DESIGN

CHAPTER OVERVIEW

After reading this chapter, you should be able to answer the following questions:

1. How does page layout contribute to a document's readability? What are some desirable features of page layout?
2. What is a typeface? What is meant by type weight? How is type size indicated?
3. What should you consider in choosing a font, a type weight, and a type size?
4. How do headings help indicate the structure of a document?
5. How are headings to be used in APA style? In Turabian style?

ENHANCING A DOCUMENT'S READABILITY

A document's readability is either enhanced or impeded by its visual design. Regardless of how eloquent your words are, if your document is visually daunting to the reader, it will be difficult to read. Research indicates that readers use a text's visual design in order to sum up its structure and make sense of the text itself (Huckin 1983; Redish, Battison, and Gold 1985). You should therefore design your documents to be structurally clear and visually easy to navigate. Elements of document design such as page layout, typography, and headings, when used effectively, will help the reader see the structure of your document, and understand and remember it with less effort. Word processing programs have many features that make it easy to create an effective design for most documents.

PAGE LAYOUT

A page that appears crowded distracts and burdens the reader. Compare Figure 16-1 and Figure 16-2 on the following pages. Even though the main text is identical in each, the different layout makes Figure 16-2 more inviting and easier to read and comprehend.

The following paragraphs explain some of the document design principles that will improve the page layout of the documents you write.

Scan zones. The short headings arranged to the left of the text in Figure 16-2 form a "scan zone." By using a zone like this for short, concise headings that describe the corresponding blocks of text, you make it easier for readers to scan your document and skip over the information they do not need. Scan zones are particularly suited for documents that are meant to be read quickly for specific information, documents such as guidelines, instructions, and resumes.

White space. White space is the space on a page that surrounds the text. White space, or the lack of it, shows relationships between items—it sets off one group from another. Whether you use a little or a lot, your goal should be to use white space for effect. In Figure 16-1 there is very little use of white space, and, as a result, the document is visually overwhelming and difficult to read. There are several ways of effectively using white space in a document

Ragged right margins. Notice that the right margins in Figure 16-1 are justified. This justification reduces the white space on the right side of the page, making the text more difficult to read. Researchers have found that ragged right margins, like those in Figure 16-2, are easier to read (Hartley and Burnhill 1971; Gregory and Poulton 1975). As a general rule, you should use ragged rather than justified right margins.

White space as an organizer of ideas. White space should also be used to show the organization and relationships within the text. When the spacing and location of the text follow a consistent pattern, they help the readers see a text's hierarchy and order of ideas. Use white space to separate groups of ideas. Indent your text appropriately to show where different topics or ideas begin and end. Separate sections with white space. Compare Figures 16-1 and 16-2 and notice how the use of white space in 16-2 makes the text less intimidating and easier to comprehend and remember.

Lists. Listing a series of items vertically rather than as regular running text can often make a page more readable and the list items easier to remember. Lists should be set off by white space in order to draw the reader's attention. Be sure to keep all the elements of a list grammatically parallel. Notice how the lists in the last two sections of Figure 16-2 help the reader see at a glance the various

FIGURE 16-1. Memo with a Poor Design

To:	Joellyn Shuster
From:	Tom Valdivias
Subject:	Human participants in research
Date:	12 January 2007

At your request, I have reviewed the laws and ethical policies regarding using human participants in social science research and have summarized them below for you.

First, researchers must ensure the confidentiality of participants. On questionnaires, it is generally not necessary to have respondents give their names, though they may give demographic information about themselves. Most important, researchers must ensure that no answers can be traced to specific respondents. When reporting interviews, the interviewer must make a joint decision with the interviewee about whether it would be appropriate and permissible to reveal the interviewee's name.

Second, human participants involved in research must have sufficient knowledge about the purposes of the study to give their informed consent before they participate. For experiments, written informed consent must be obtained. For surveys and interviews, the subjects' consent is implied if they complete the survey, but they still must be informed about the purposes of the research so that they can choose whether or not to proceed. Unobtrusive observations of people going about their daily lives do not require informed consent.

Third, researchers must be able to show that the participants will not face risks of physical or emotional harm greater than those encountered in daily life. Surveys don't usually pose this type of risk because respondents can ignore sensitive personal questions, and the respondents' answers are kept anonymous anyway. Experiments are the most likely to pose some emotional risk because they sometimes temporarily deceive participants. There is some disagreement on whether temporary deception is justified by the knowledge gained from experiments, but social scientists generally agree that, while researchers should not tell participants something that is untrue, they may temporarily withhold some information regarding the aim of the study. Generally speaking, an ethical experiment is one in which the participants are given general, yet still accurate, information, and in which participation in the study does not pose a risk of significant emotional or physical harm. Researchers must debrief the participants afterward to fully inform them of the purposes of the experiment.

Fourth, the laws carefully regulate and insist on the strict monitoring of research conducted with the following vulnerable groups: the ill or physically disabled; the institutionalized, including people in hospitals, jails, and prisons; the cognitively disabled; those under 18 years of age (minors); and pregnant women.

All research projects involving human participants must be reviewed and approved by the university's Institutional Review Board (IRB) before being initiated. Because most student research projects will qualify for "exempt" status, rather than requiring approval from the entire Board, student proposals will most likely be reviewed and approved by one person appointed by the IRB for such matters. In order for an experiment to receive "exempt" status, it must meet certain criteria: (1) it must be non-therapeutic; (2) the data must be recorded in a way that protects the identities of the subjects; (3) there must be no risk of criminal or civil liability to the investigator and his or her institution, should a participant's responses become known outside the boundaries of the research project itself; and (4) the research must not deal with private aspects of the participants' behavior, e.g., their sexual practices or drug use.

FIGURE 16-2. Memo with a Readable Design

MEMORANDUM
RIVER STATE UNIVERSITY

To: Joellyn Schuster
From: Tom Valdivias
Date: January 12, 2007
Subject: **Guidelines for using human participants in social science research**

At your request, I have reviewed the laws and ethical policies regarding using human participants in social science research and have summarized them below for you:

Confidentiality

Researchers must ensure the confidentiality of human participants. On questionnaires, it is generally not necessary to have respondents give their names, though they may be asked to give demographic information about themselves. Most important, researchers must ensure that no answers can be traced to specific respondents. When reporting interviews, the interviewer must make a joint decision with the interviewee about whether it would be appropriate and permissible to reveal the interviewee's name.

Informed consent

Researchers must help human participants gain sufficient knowledge about the purposes of the study so the participants can give their informed consent before participating. For experiments, researchers must obtain written informed consent. For surveys and interviews, the participants' consent is implied if they complete the survey, but they still must be informed about the purposes of the research so that they can choose whether or not to proceed. Unobtrusive observations of people going about their daily lives do not require informed consent.

Avoiding risks of physical or emotional harm

Researchers must be able to show that the subjects will not risk physical or emotional harm greater than that encountered in daily life. Surveys don't usually pose this type of risk because respondents can ignore sensitive personal questions, and the respondents' answers are kept anonymous anyway. Experiments are the most likely to pose some emotional risk because they sometimes temporarily deceive subjects.

FIGURE 16-2. Memo with a Readable Design (continued)

When withholding information is okay	There is some disagreement on whether temporary deception is justified by the knowledge gained from experiments, but social scientists generally agree that, while researchers should not tell participants something that is untrue, they may temporarily withhold some information regarding the aim of the study. Generally speaking, an ethical experiment is one in which the participants are given general, yet still accurate information, and in which participation in the study does not pose a risk of significant emotional or physical harm. Researchers must debrief participants afterward to fully inform them of the purposes of the experiment.
Vulnerable groups	*Laws provide strict guidelines and limitations on research conducted with certain vulnerable groups, including:* • the ill or physically disabled • the institutionalized, including people in hospitals, jails, and prisons • the cognitively disabled • those under 18 years of age (minors) • pregnant women
Approval from the IRB	*All research projects involving human participants must be reviewed and approved by the university's Institutional Review Board (IRB) before they are initiated.* Because most student research projects will qualify for "exempt" status, rather than requiring approval from the entire Board, student proposals will most likely be reviewed and approved by one person appointed by the IRB for such matters.
Getting "exempt" status from the IRB	In order for an experiment to receive "exempt" status, it must meet four criteria: 1. It must be **non-therapeutic**. 2. The data must be recorded in such a way as to **protect the identities** of the participants. 3. There must be **no risk of criminal or civil liability** to the investigator and his or her institution, should the participant's responses become known outside the boundaries of the research project itself. 4. The research must not deal with **private aspects of the participants' behavior**, e.g., their sexual practices or drug use.

stipulations that researchers must meet to receive exempt status for research with human subjects.

Bullets and other graphic devices. Most word processing programs allow you to add bullets and other graphic devices such as carets, rules, and bars to your document:

- This is a bullet
- Δ This is a caret

Bullets, carets, and other similar graphic devices can be helpful visual organizers, especially in lists where the items have no particular sequence. Numbered lists should be used when the items do have a particular order they should appear in, e.g., as steps in a process. Just because you can insert a bullet doesn't mean you always should. Excessive graphic devices can make a page very busy and visually overwhelming. A good rule to remember when using graphic devices is "less is more." Look again at Figure 16-2 to see how bullets are used to organize the items in a list.

Many word processors allow you to insert small novelty graphics, sometimes called "wingdings" or "dingbats." (Here are some typical ones: ♣✍✗✄). You should keep your audience in mind when you decide whether or not to use wingdings or dingbats. For most academic and professional writing, they are inappropriate. However, they may be appropriate when you are writing for more familiar audiences and for less formal purposes.

TYPOGRAPHY

The term typography refers to the face, size, and weight of "type" or the letters printed on a page. The face, size, and weight of type are all design elements that, if used effectively, will enhance the readability of your document.

Fonts. Most computer word processors allow you to select from a large variety of typefaces, more accurately called fonts.

Serif vs. sans-serif fonts. There are two basic groups of fonts—serif fonts, which have extensions, or tiny lines on the edges of letters, and sans-serif fonts, which do not use extensions. Note the difference in these examples:

This is serif type. Times, Palatino, New Century Schoolbook, and Courier are all examples of serif type.

This is a sans-serif type. Arial, Helvetica, Gill Sans, Berlin, and AvantGarde are all examples of sans-serif type.

Some fonts are neither serif nor sans-serif. These fonts can be generally classified into two categories, script fonts and novelty fonts:

This is an example of a script font.
This is an example of a novelty font.

Use script and novelty fonts sparingly because they draw attention to themselves. You should stick to serif or sans-serif fonts for most academic and professional writing.

Follow these guidelines when selecting and using a font for your documents:

- **Use a serif font as your main font.** Because serif fonts create horizontal base lines, they help the eye move from one word to the next, making reading easier.
- **Use sans-serif fonts for titles and headings.** Because sans-serif fonts have predominantly vertical lines, they accentuate individual words, making them especially appropriate for titles and headings.
- **Select appropriate fonts for headings and text and stick to them.**

Capital letters. Avoid using all capital letters for regular text. Because we read in part by recognizing the shape of a word, capital letters are less legible than lowercase letters or mixed upper- and lowercase letters because they obscure the shape of the word. Words in all capitals are especially difficult to read if they are in a sans-serif font. Compare these two examples:

COMMERCIALS ARE NOW THE DOMINANT MEANS OF CANDIDATE COMMUNICATION IN TODAY'S POLITICAL RACES. VOTERS ARE NOW BOMBARDED WITH MILLIONS OF DOLLARS IN SPOT ADS DURING THE POLITICAL SEASON. THE 1990 ELECTIONS ALONE GENERATED $203 MILLION IN SPENDING ON ADS, ACCORDING TO AN ESTIMATE BY A BROADCASTING GROUP.

Commercials are now the dominant means of candidate communication in today's political races. Voters are now bombarded with millions of dollars in spot ads during the political season. The 1990 elections alone generated $203 million in spending on ads, according to an estimate by a broadcasting group.

The first example, written in all capitals, is more difficult to read than the second example, which varies upper- and lowercase letters.

Type size. Most word processors offer a wide range of type sizes—called "point sizes"—to choose from. The larger a type's point size, the larger the type is. Note these various type sizes:

This is Times 6-point.

This is Times 9-point.

This is Times 12-point.

This is Times 18-point.

This is Times 32-point.

For regular text, you should use a 9- to 12-point type size—point sizes lower than 8 are very difficult to read and are best suited for informal documents. Point sizes larger than 12 are better suited for titles and headings.

Type weight. As a general rule, use medium-weight fonts for regular text. **Very light and very heavy fonts (such as the boldface used for this sentence) are tiring to read.** However, you may want to use boldface type to emphasize words or short passages of text. Research shows that readers notice changes in type weight more readily than they notice changes in font (Spencer, Reynolds, and Coe 1973).

Compare Figures 16-1 and 16-2 to see how font, size, and weight can be used to enhance a document's readability. Notice that the font in 16-1 is sans-serif and is therefore more difficult to read than the font of the main text in 16-2, which is serif. The left column of headings in 16-2 is in sans-serif, however, which causes the reader to pause appropriately. In 16-2, the point size is varied to show different levels of information. Also, in 16-2, boldface type is used to highlight short passages of main text.

VISUAL CUES TO TEXT STRUCTURE

HEADINGS

Headings serve as the "road map" to your document—they help readers scan the document quickly to locate information and they help readers develop a framework within which they can more easily understand and remember the text.

Heading content. Researchers have found that headings that use complete and specific phrasing, especially full statements or questions, are particularly effective in making a text easier to read (Hartley, Morris, and Trueman 1981). Compare the headings from two outlines in Figures 16-3 and 16-4.

Notice how informative and useful the headings in 16-4 are compared to 16-3. The headings in 16-4 are effective because they are descriptive and specific rather than general and vague—for the most part, they contain a verb rather than a single noun or short noun string. They can be read apart from the text and still make sense.

Heading design. Design your headings so that your document's hierarchy of information is visually distinguishable. In other words, design your headings so that the reader can tell if a particular heading pertains to the paper in general, a large section of text, or a small portion of text. Use distinguishing elements consistently so that, at any point in the text, the reader knows which level a particular heading belongs to.

You can distinguish the level of a heading by changing various type features.

You can vary the type size:

Very Large Type

Large Type

Regular type

You can vary the type weight:

Bold-face type

Medium-weight type

You can vary the capitalization:

In This Heading, the First Letter of Each Important Word is Capitalized

In this heading only the first letter is capitalized

You can underline text or put it in italics:

<u>This is an underlined heading</u>

This heading is in italics

FIGURE 16-3. An outline made from vague, generic headings

I.   Introduction
II. History
III. The Pathological Perspective
     A. Definition
     B. Techniques
IV. The Cultural Perspective
     A. Definition
     B. Reforms
V.   Conclusion

FIGURE 16-4. An outline made from specific, informative headings

I.   Introduction
II. Early Deaf History in America
     A. Thomas Gallaudet: American Pioneer in Deaf Education
     B. American Sign Language: A Hybrid of European and Indigenous Sign Languages
     C. Founding of Gallaudet University
     D. 1817–1880: The "Golden Age" of the Deaf
III. The Tendency to Consider Deafness a Disease
     A. The "Pathological" Perspective Defined
     B. 1880–1960: The Pathological Perspective Prevails
     C. Recent Methods of "Treating" Deafness
         1. Oralism: Restoring the Deaf to Society
         2. Imposing English Grammar on Sign Language
IV. An Alternative to the Pathological Perspective: Viewing the Deaf as a Culture
     A. The Cultural Perspective Defined
     B. How Hearing Societies Can Adopt the Cultural Perspective
         1. Treating American Sign Language as a Unique Language
         2. Celebrating the Unique Values of the Deaf Community
         3. Becoming Aware of the Deaf Community's Unique Social Conventions
         4. Celebrating the Deaf Community's Literature and Traditions
V.   Conclusion

You can combine several of these elements:

This Heading is in Initial Capitals, is Underlined, and is in Boldface Type

Or you can use a different font altogether.

This heading is in a sans-serif font

The main text is in a serif font

You can also vary the spacing on the page. You can center a title or heading:

This Heading is Centered

The text starts here and continues. . . .

You can keep a heading flush with the left margin:

This heading is flush left

The text starts here and continues. It keeps going in this example so you can see how it would look. . . .

You can indent the heading above the text:

This heading is indented above the text

The text starts here and continues. These lines of text will help you see how this kind of heading would look. . . .

Or you can indent the heading and place the text adjacent to it:

> **This heading is indented and next to text.** The text continues from
> here and wraps down to additional lines. . . .

You can also use a rule to distinguish a heading:

> ## This Heading is Separated from the Text with a Rule
>
> The text starts here and continues . . .

Notice how, in Figure 16-2, font, size, and weight are used to show different levels of headings. Larger point sizes and bold-faced type are used for major headings, while italics and medium-weight type are used for minor headings.

Additional advice regarding headings. There are a few more things to remember regarding headings: unless your style guide says otherwise, limit the number of heading levels to four or less. If you use more than four levels of headings, your document can become confusing and difficult to read. Also, remember that readers will expect headings in larger point sizes to be more important than headings in smaller ones. And they will expect a heading in all capitals to be more important than a heading in mixed- or lowercase type. Finally, don't leave a heading at the bottom of a page if the text starts on the following page. You should have at least one line of text accompany a heading.

HEADINGS AND PROFESSIONAL STYLE GUIDES

If your document must adhere to a particular style guide, such as APA or Turabian, you should follow its prescriptions for headings. When following the style recommended by the APA *Publication Manual* (2001), you should not use more than five levels of headings. The APA manual prescribes the following formats for each of the five levels (see p. 115):

LEVEL 5 HEADINGS ARE CENTERED IN UPPERCASE

Level 1 Headings are Centered in Uppercase and Lowercase

<u>Level 2 Headings are Centered, Uppercase and Lowercase, and Underlined</u>

<u>Level 3 Headings are Flush Left, Uppercase and Lowercase, and Underlined</u>

<u>Level 4 headings are indented to begin the paragraph, lowercase, and underlined, and they end with a period.</u>

Not every document you write will require all five levels of headings. APA offers the following guidelines for selecting level formats when you use fewer than five heading levels:

One level. When you only have one level of headings, use the format for Level 1 headings described above.

Two levels. When your document has two levels of headings, use Level 1 and Level 3 heading formats.

Three levels. For three levels of headings, use Level 1, Level 3, and Level 4 heading formats.

Four levels. When you have four levels of headings, use the heading formats for Levels 1 through 4.

Five levels. When you have five levels of headings, use Level 5 format for broadest heading, then Levels 1 through 4.

Figure 16-5 is an excerpt from a paper that follows APA guidelines regarding headings. The paper contains three levels of headings. Notice how each heading's level is easily distinguishable through its design.

FIGURE 16-5. Headings in APA Style

Our Tendency to Consider Deafness a Disease

The "Pathological" Perspective Defined

The introduction discussed some facets of the pathological view of deafness. According to this perspective, deafness is seen as something that is missing, or as a handicap (Eldredge, 1994). Padden (1988) states that professionals such as doctors and teachers usually refer to deaf people according to their "pathological condition: hearing loss" (p. 1). They are treated as medical cases, or as people with "disabilities" (Padden, 1988).

Using this perspective, deafness is considered a problem that needs to be fixed. When parents discover that their child is deaf, the first person they usually consult is a medical doctor. Throughout history, physicians have used many techniques to help deaf patients regain their hearing. Eldredge describes some of these methods:

Treatments varied from making a loud noise near the ear in order to open up the ear canal (but probably damaged the ear drum even further!) to pouring liquids down ears to wrapping deaf dog carcasses around sick children's heads. (Eldredge, 1994, p. 1)

It seems that the remedies were worse than the "disease" they were supposed to cure.

1880-1960: The Pathological Perspective Prevails

The years from 1880 to 1960 are known in the deaf community as the "Dark Ages." As Sacks (1990) relates, "What was happening with the deaf and Sign was part of a general (and if one wished, 'political') movement of the time: a trend to Victorian oppressiveness and conformism, intolerance of minorities, and minority usages, of every kind—religious, linguistic, ethnic" (p. 24). Because of this trend to conformity, languages that didn't have a great number of users were under threat of extinction. This sentiment affected the Deaf community in America. During the "Dark Ages" the Deaf community was almost destroyed by three main thrusts—"oralist" philosophy, Alexander Graham Bell's campaign for eugenics, and the Milan Conference.

Oralism: Restoring the Deaf to Society. For two centuries there had been rampant feelings that the goal of deaf education should be teaching the deaf how to speak. . . .

Like APA, Turabian (1996) suggests that no more than five levels of headings be used. According to Turabian, the following formats may be used for each of the five levels.

Level 1 Headings are in Boldface, Italicized, or Underlined, Centered, and Capitalized Headline Style

Level 2 Headings are in Text Type, Centered, and Capitalized Headline Style

Level 3 Headings are in Boldface, Italicized, or Underlined, Flush Left, and Capitalized Headline Style.

Level 4 headings are in text type, flush left, and capitalized sentence style.

Level 5 headings are in boldface, italicized, and/or underlined, are indented to begin a paragraph, and are capitalized sentence style with a period at the end.

If you don't need five levels of headings, Turabian suggests that you select the heading formats you prefer from those shown above, always making sure that you use them in descending order. See Figure 16-6 for an example of headings that follow Turabian guidelines.

There is more to document design than the brief pointers covered in this chapter, but these relatively simple guidelines are ones you can implement with most word processing programs. Using these principles will make the documents you create for school and on the job more readable.

FIGURE 16-6. Headings in Turabian Style

Our Tendency to Consider Deafness a Disease

The "Pathological" Perspective Defined

The introduction discussed some facets of the pathological view of deafness. According to this perspective, deafness is seen as something that is missing, or as a handicap (Eldredge 1994). Padden (1988) states that professionals such as doctors and teachers usually refer to deaf people according to their "pathological condition: hearing loss" (1). They are treated as medical cases, or as people with "disabilities" (Padden 1988).

Using this perspective, deafness is considered a problem that needs to be fixed. When parents discover that their child is deaf, the first person they usually consult is a medical doctor. Throughout history, physicians have used many techniques to help deaf patients regain their hearing. Eldredge describes some of these methods:

> Treatments varied from making a loud noise near the ear in order to open up the ear canal (but probably damaged the ear drum even further!) to pouring liquids down ears to wrapping deaf dog carcasses around sick children's heads. (Eldredge 1994, 1)

It seems that the remedies were worse than the "disease" they were supposed to cure.

1880–1960: The Pathological Perspective Prevails

The years from 1880 to 1960 are known in the deaf community as the "Dark Ages." As Sacks relates, "What was happening with the deaf and Sign was part of a general (and if one wished, 'political') movement of the time: a trend to Victorian oppressiveness and conformism, intolerance of minorities, and minority usages, of every kind—religious, linguistic, ethnic" (1990, 24). Because of this trend to conformity, languages that didn't have large number of users were under threat of extinction. This sentiment affected the Deaf community in America. During the "Dark Ages" the Deaf community was almost destroyed by three main thrusts—"oralist" philosophy, Alexander Graham Bell's campaign for eugenics, and the Milan Conference.

Oralism: restoring the Deaf to society. For two centuries there had been rampant feelings that the goal of deaf education should be teaching the deaf how to speak. . . .

REFERENCES

American Psychological Association. 2001. *Publication manual of the American Psychological Association.* 5th ed. Washington, D.C.: American Psychological Association.

Gregory, M. and E. C. Poulton. 1975. Even versus uneven right-hand margins and the rate of comprehesion in reading. *Applied Ergonomics 6.*

Hartley, J. and P. Burnhill. 1971. Experiments with unjustified text. *Visible Language 5,* 265–278.

Hartley, J., P. Morris, & M. Trueman. 1981. Headings in text. *Remedial Education 15,* 5–6.

Huckin, Thomas N. 1983. A cognitive approach to readability. In *New Essays in Technical and Scientific Communication: Research, Theory, and Practice,* eds. Paul V. Anderson, R. John Brockmann, and Carolyn R. Miller, 90–101. Farmingdale, NY: Baywood.

Redish, Janice C., Robin M. Battison, and Edward S. Gold. 1985. Making information accessible to readers. In *Writing in Nonacademic Settings,* eds. Lee Odell and Dixie Goswami, 129–53. New York: Guilford.

Spencer, H., L. Reynolds, & B. Coe. 1973. *A comparison of the effectiveness of selected typographic variations.* Readability of Print Research Unit, London: Royal College of Art.

Turabian, Kate. 1996. *A manual for writers of term papers, theses, and dissertations.* 6th ed. Chicago: University of Chicago Press.

17

GRAPHICS

CHAPTER OVERVIEW

After reading this chapter, you should be able to answer the following questions:

1. In what sense can graphics be a kind of rhetoric?
2. What are tables? What are figures?
3. What kinds of figures might you include in a written report?
4. Where do you position graphics in a paper? How do you direct the reader to look at them?
5. How should tables and figures be numbered and labeled?
6. What are some of the ethical issues associated with using graphics?

GRAPHICS AS RHETORIC

Graphics are tables and figures that you can add to your writing to clarify and illustrate the ideas or facts you are writing about. *Tables* are rows and columns of data—words or numbers or both—that display the data in a small space so that it is easy for the reader to see relationships among various parts of the entire set of data. *Figures* are all other illustrations that are not tables. Figures include photographs, line drawings, maps, diagrams, flowcharts, and various kinds of graphs—line graphs, circle graphs, and bar graphs (also called column graphs). In this chapter you will learn principles for creating clear, appropriate tables and figures and for integrating them into the texts that you write so that your writing is rhetorically effective.

It may seem that graphics are always so straightforward and neutral that they have no persuasive dimension, hence do not belong to the study of rhetoric. If you recall the definition of rhetoric used in Chapter 1, you may remember this part of it:

Rhetoric is using words and other symbols skillfully to articulate and advocate your beliefs about something you assume to be true, addressing an audience you want to persuade to assent to your beliefs by choice, not by coercion, and possibly to cooperate with you. . . .

Well-made graphics use symbols and design principles skillfully to appeal to the visual sense, enhancing and clarifying a message, making it more persuasive than it might otherwise be. Poorly designed, badly integrated, or incomplete graphics can detract from the effectiveness of a message because they call into question the writer's knowledge. Misleading graphics cast doubt on the writer's trustworthiness, detracting from the ethical appeal of the message.

In today's world, visual rhetoric is very important. Consider the advertisements you see each day on television and billboards or in newspapers and magazines. The ad-makers work very hard to create images and words that will catch your attention and stay in your memory, subtly or not so subtly persuading you to buy a product or try a service. It is fairly easy to see that graphics (usually photographs) in advertising are a form of rhetoric. Unlike academic and professional rhetoric, advertising rhetoric usually relies heavily on appeals to emotion. It someti mes appeals to other aspects of human nature as well, such as our senses and our basic drives and appetites.

As a consumer bombarded daily with advertising rhetoric, you must be alert to the kinds of hidden appeals embedded in the words and images of ads so that you can evaluate their messages rationally and avoid being unconsciously manipulated by this kind of rhetoric. Similarly, as a reader of social science research, you need to evaluate graphics for their clarity, completeness, and appropriateness of design. Probably very few social scientists set out to manipulate their audiences, but they may inadvertently make their writing less effective and credible than it could be by not creating understandable and reliable graphics.

As a student of the social sciences, you should not only learn how to read and judge graphics knowledgeably; you should also be able to create them so that you can display complex data in a concise, readable form. Because graphics are becoming much easier to create with various kinds of computer software, it will be to your advantage to learn to use one or more graphics programs. However, some features of the available software programs are not based on sound communication and design principles, so you need to be aware of the potential flaws and ethical pitfalls in creating graphics with computers—such as needless third dimensions in bar graphs or cute but empty illustrations on tables and graphs. You shouldn't forsake simplicity and clarity for what graphic designer Edward Tufte calls "chartjunk" simply because a computer program allows you to create it. More will be said about chartjunk and the ethics of creating graphics at the end of this chapter.

TABLES

Tables are efficient, compact summaries of large data sets presented in rows and columns. The pattern formed by the rows and columns resembles a grid, even when the rows and columns do not have visible lines subdividing the grid into cells. Whether the lines are there or not, however, it is helpful to think of a table as containing a cell for each item of information that you want to display. Suppose, for example, that you conduct a survey of undergraduate students' reasons for reading the daily campus newspaper. You identify four primary reasons why students read the newspaper, as well as a few miscellaneous reasons you can characterize as "other." So you identify five reasons in all. You also learn that the percentage of students giving each reason varies with year in college—that is, from the freshman to the senior year.

To display these twenty items of data, you would need a 4 x 5 grid. You could create four columns to display the reasons and four rows to display the years in college; the intersection of these rows and columns would create sixteen cells. However, in order for a reader to know what the cells represent, you would also need another row to label the columns and an extra column to label the rows, so you would have to make a 5 x 6 grid. Your table might look like the one in Figure 17-1.

This table permits your audience to read the data horizontally to see what the most important and least important reasons are for each group of students; it also enables your audience to read vertically to see how the importance of a particular reason changes as the average student progresses through college. The table would also permit the reader to quickly compare any two items of information. Besides helping the reader, this table would help you as the writer to draw conclusions about the significance of the survey findings and interpret them. What trends do you notice in the data? What plausible explanations for these trends can you give?

TABLE 17-1. A Simple Table

Students' Reasons for Reading the Campus Newspaper

	Read world and national news	Learn about campus events	Read advertisements	Read about sports	Other Reasons
Freshman	11%	70%	9%	9%	1%
Sophomore	15%	64%	11%	8%	2%
Junior	36%	33%	17%	11%	3%
Senior	45%	10%	30%	10%	5%

TABLE 17-2. A Table Made of Words

Comparison of Quantitative and Qualitative Methods

	Types	Advantages	Limitations
Quantitative methods	Experiments Surveys	Possibility of large sample size Generalizability and breadth High degree of control	Loss of particularity Possibly high costs
Qualitative methods	Interviews Observations Documents	Rich data Particularity and depth Large scope for interpretation	Low generalizability Overwhelming data Time consumption

Imagine how much more difficult it would be for a reader to make comparisons or notice trends if the data in Table 17-1 were to be explained in paragraph form. You would have to write a very long and complex paragraph to present all of this information, and the paragraph would be much more time-consuming and tiresome to read than the table. It would be difficult for the reader to pick out any two items of information for comparison. You can strengthen the credibility of your interpretations if they are based on data that are easy to find, to read, and to understand.

Tables usually present numbers, but they can also consist of words. Table 17-2 (reproduced from Chapter 3) compares the advantages and disadvantages of quantitative and qualitative research methods. It presents a handy summary of information that took several paragraphs to explain.

You can create simple tables with word processing programs. Many of them have special functions to help you create tables. Even without a special tables function, however, it is not difficult to align data in columns and rows simply by setting up tabs or columns with your word processing program. You can also use computer spreadsheets into which you can enter data and then convert the data from the spreadsheet into a table.

FIGURES

As noted above, figures are all graphics that are not tables. (In some fields, these graphics might also go by the name "illustration," "exhibit," "chart," or even "visual." In most social science journals, however, these graphics are usually called figures.) In the next few pages, some of the most common types of figures are described and illustrated, and guidelines are provided for creating these kinds of graphics.

PHOTOGRAPHS

A photograph is an especially useful kind of figure when you are writing about a person—perhaps a famous one—or place and you want the reader to be able to see what the person or place actually looks like. Photographs are also helpful when you are writing about an object or event and it is important to give a realistic and detailed image of it, rather than the abstract, less concrete image provided by a sketch. They can be enlarged to show more detail. Photos can also be cropped to eliminate irrelevant parts of a picture. Because photographs reproduce every detail visible to the camera, however, they may cause the reader to get caught up in the little things and perhaps lose focus on the most important features of the illustration. Also, because photographs are more difficult and expensive to reproduce than drawings, you may need to limit their use.

If you decide that a photo is the best kind of illustration for a particular text, original photos must be of a high quality with high contrast between light and dark to provide the best reproductions. You will need to be skillful with a camera or hire someone to produce original photos. If you use a copyrighted photo, you will have to acknowledge the photographer and the copyright holder in the caption. You will likely have to pay a fee to others for permission to use their photos.

LINE DRAWINGS

Line drawings are simple sketches that eliminate much of the detail included in photos for the sake of simplifying and emphasizing the most important features of the illustration. Figure 17-1 is a line drawing of an archeological dig site showing the types of objects found at each level of the site excavated.

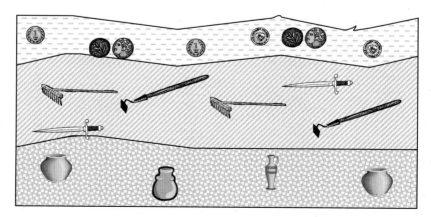

FIGURE 17-1. A Line Drawing

Line drawings to illustrate something like a dig site may be a more rhetorically effective choice than photographs because the simplicity of the drawing allows the writer to abstract from the detail that would be provided in a photo in order to emphasize the critical features of the site. A drawing imposes an interpretation on the raw physical data, so it may be more persuasive to the reader.

If, in your research, you find that line drawings would be the best choice to illustrate your main points, you might consider employing an artist to create the drawings if you don't feel competent to make them yourself, drawing freehand. However, using computer software that is readily available, you should, with some practice, be able to create effective drawings of your own.

MAPS

A map is a type of line drawing because it leaves out a lot of detail that could be included in order to simplify matters and to illustrate the writer's point. For example, a road map usually doesn't include the varying elevations of the terrain that the roads cross. A contour map, however, focuses on elevations and often leaves out roads. Maps such as these, which represent geographic realities, usually include a scale showing how much real distance is represented by each unit of distance (such as an inch or centimeter) on the map. These maps may also include legends (explained later in this chapter) indicating what the various symbols on the map stand for. For example, the legend might show that various kinds of lines represent interstate highways, state highways, improved roads, and unimproved roads.

Maps can also be used as ways of making points about political, economic, or social realities. For example, a simple map of the United States outlining the boundaries of the states is a favorite way used by newspapers and magazines for making various kinds of comparisons among the 50 states. By shading in the states that have capital punishment, for example, a writer can help the reader see at a glance how many and which states have such laws on the books. Figure 17-2 shows the number of interviews Christian Smith and his associates conducted in each state and where for the National Study of Youth and Religion.

DIAGRAMS AND FLOWCHARTS

A diagram is a drawing that simplifies a complex object or concept. Frequently diagrams represent abstract ideas or relationships, such as parts of a theory or a conceptual model. They may consist of both words and graphical elements such as lines, circles, boxes, arrows, etc. A particular kind of diagram is a flowchart, which generally depicts a process or the possible steps in an operation. Diagrams and flowcharts are excellent ways of summarizing visually the main points you make in words, so that the reader has a handy way to remember

FIGURE 17-2. A Map

concepts and how they are related to each other. The diagram in Figure 17-3 is from Kemarie Campbell's paper on causes of obesity in the US (reprinted in the Readings section of this book). This diagram shows the dieter's dilemma, or the cycle of restrained eating followed by cravings and loss of control.

GRAPHS

Graphs are special kinds of figures that allow you to display the relationships between numerical and categorical variables for easy comprehension and comparison. There are three kinds of commonly used graphs: line graphs, bar graphs, circle graphs.

Line graphs. Line graphs show the continuous relationship between at least two variables. The two variables are represented as points in a space defined by two axes—an *x*-axis (horizontal) and a *y*-axis (vertical)—each of which has been divided into meaningful increments. To show the continuous relationship between the two variables, you can draw a line from one point to the next, thus showing the upward and downward trends in the relationship between the variables. For example, the fluctuations of a particular stock price over a period of months can be clearly represented by a line graph, as shown in

Reprinted from *Soul Searching: The Religious and Spiritual Lives of American Teenagers* (2005), Oxford University Press.

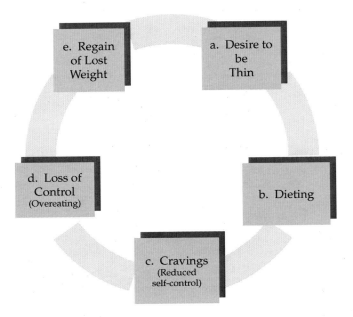

FIGURE 17-3. A Diagram

Figure 17-4. The x-axis names the months in a six-month period; the y-axis shows the prices per share of the stock. The maker of this graph simply plotted a point to represent the price for the stock each month and then connected the points to make a line showing the overall trend.

   More than one line can be plotted on a particular line graph. For example, the line graph in Figure 17-4 could have a second line showing the price fluctuation of a different stock over the same period of time. The second line could be drawn as a broken or a dotted line to differentiate it from the first one. Still more lines could be added as long as each could be clearly distinguished from the others. However, too many lines that cross each other at numerous points would clutter the graph and make it confusing and difficult to read.

   Bar (column) graphs. Like a line graph, a bar graph also plots the relationship between at least two variables by using two clearly labeled and subdivided axes. The difference is that a bar graph is used when the independent variable is categorical, rather than numerical. The data are represented as discrete units, rather than as continuous, the way they are in a line graph. Thus, one axis is not a numbered scale; instead, it is divided into categories of data, and each bar on the graph represent a different amount or number in a particular category. Using bars with different shading or cross-hatching, you can even compare data for different groups within each category.

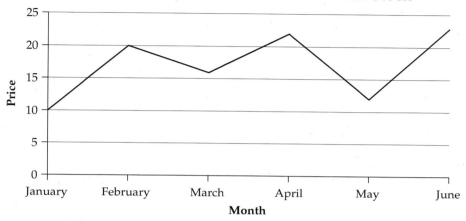

FIGURE 17-4. A Line Graph

Fig. 1 Career Goals of Music Majors

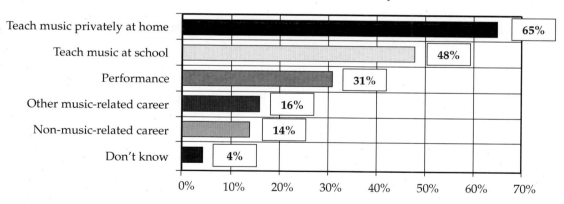

FIGURE 17-5. A Bar Graph

For example, in the bar graph in Figure 17-5 from a student paper on the professional and educational goals of music majors, the *y*-axis shows categories of career goals chosen by participants in the survey. The *x*-axis shows the total percentage of the respondents that chose each career goal.

Another important thing to notice about the bar graph in Figure 17-5 is that each bar is labeled at its end with the exact percentage of respondents who chose each category. Even though the x-axis is divided into increments of ten percent, it is important to let the reader know the exact figure in any category. The standard way to do this is to write the exact figure on the bar or at the end of the bar. Note also that the bars in a bar graph can run either horizontally or vertically. (A graph with vertical bars is sometimes called a column graph.) In the case of Figure 17-5, horizontal bars were a good choice so that the labels for the categories could be written horizontally, making them easier to read than if they were written vertically.

Circle graphs. Circle graphs are also called "pie charts" because they are divided into wedges just as a pie is. They are particularly good for representing percentages and proportions. For example, a budget is commonly represented with a circle graph because the relative size of the wedges makes it easy to see how much money has been allotted to each budget category. Usually, the circle is considered to be like a clock face, and the wedges are put in descending order of size starting at 12 o'clock. Sometimes, however, the convention of descending order is not followed in order to keep wedges that are similar close to each other.

Like a line or bar graph, a circle graph can present too much data and become confusing. If a circle graph has very many wedges, several of the wedges are likely to be very small, and it will become more difficult for a reader to see the relative differences in size. It is also difficult to label very small wedges of a circle graph, so a bar graph might be a better choice when a lot of categories are to be compared. However, if the pie will be cut into only a few wedges, a circle graph can be a good choice to show the divisions of a whole. Figure 17-6 is a simple circle graph from the same student paper showing the percentage of respondents who chose three different answers to a question. Note that a different kind of shading is used in each wedge to help distinguish the wedges and help you see the proportions more clearly. Note also that the responses and the percentages choosing that response are written just outside each of the wedges.

Figure 4. "How interested are you in participating in a career fair?"

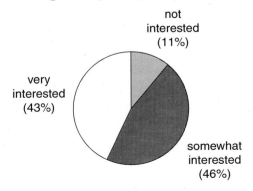

FIGURE 17-6. A Circle Graph

POSITIONING AND LABELING GRAPHICS

POSITION GRAPHICS FOR EASY VIEWING

Once you have decided what kinds of graphics will best illustrate your verbal message, next you must determine where to put the graphics in the text. If graphics are meant to illustrate and clarify a verbal text, it is important to place them as close to the relevant text as you possibly can—on the same or the following page, so that the reader can easily pause while reading to glance at or study the graphic. Sometimes graphics can be made small enough that the text can run in a narrow column right next to the graphic. Sometimes graphics are so big that they must cover two pages or even be printed on extra large paper that can be folded into the document and then unfolded when the reader is ready to look at them. Occasionally, however, graphics present information that is interesting and relevant, but not critical for the reader to see while reading the text. In this case, graphics can be placed in an appendix to the document for readers to look at or not, as they choose.

NUMBER GRAPHICS FOR EASY REFERENCE

Although positioning a graphic in the most advantageous place is an important way to help the reader, position by itself is not enough to make reference to the graphic convenient. Each graphic also needs a number so that you can refer to it without having to write something clumsy like "the bar graph showing the means for each year at the top of page 4" or "the table on page 2 that compares men's and women's responses." Usually tables and figures are numbered separately from each other. So if you created a document that had two tables and three figures, they would be called Table 1 and Table 2, and Figure 1, Figure 2, and Figure 3 respectively.

Giving each graphic a number helps you refer to it conveniently as often as you need to. In the text of your paper, you can refer directly to a graphic by writing something like this: "As Table 1 shows, students in the experimental treatment scored significantly higher on the post-test." Or you can refer more indirectly, using parentheses: "Investments rose as inflation declined (see Figure 1)." But it is important to refer to your graphics and to discuss their significance. Don't simply put them in your paper and expect your reader to figure out why they are there and what they show.

GIVE GRAPHICS DESCRIPTIVE CAPTIONS

Besides numbering your graphics, you should add a descriptive caption that allows a reader who is skimming your document to understand what kind of information the graphic displays without having to read the verbal text. Rather than make your captions vague (e.g., "Comparisons") or cute (e.g., "Sexist Sentencing"), make them long enough to be informative. For example, don't be reluctant to write a long, specific and detailed caption such as the following: "Comparison of Prison Sentences for Males and Females Convicted of the Same Kinds of Crimes."

LABEL PARTS OF TABLES AND FIGURES

Besides positioning, numbering, and labeling graphics, you will have to add other information to make clear what kind of information each part of each graphic shows. For tables, you will have to label the columns and rows, and you may have to add more information in notes, depending on your purpose and audience needs. For drawings, diagrams, and flow charts, you may need to label individual parts. For line and bar graphs, you have to label the axes; for circle graphs, you have to label the wedges. For all of these, you may need to add a legend. Each of these features is explained and illustrated below.

Labeling parts of tables. In addition to a number and a caption, a table needs other information, depending on how complicated the depicted information is. Each column and each row needs a heading so that a reader can tell what particular information is given in each cell. Notice the various kinds of headings and subheadings used in Table 17-3.

As you can see from Table 17-3, a table can have footnotes besides column and row headings and subheadings. A table can also have other information

TABLE 17-3. A Complex Table

Comparison of Male and Female Professors' Job Satisfaction and Job Performance Ratings

Rank	Mean Job Satisfaction Rating[a]		Mean Job Performance Rating by Chair[a]		Mean Self-Performance Rating[a]	
	Male[b]	Female[c]	Male	Female	Male	Female
Assistant Professor	4.3	3.5	4.5	5.3	5.0	4.3
Associate Professor	5.2	4.3	6.0	6.0	5.7	5.4
Professor	6.5	5.4	5.6	5.6	6.7	5.5

[a] All rankings are based on a 7-point scale, where 7 is greatest.
[b] $n = 46$.
[c] $n = 24$.

printed immediately above or under it to help the reader understand the context of the data.

Labeling parts of graphs. On a circle graph, you must make clear what each wedge stands for. You can do this by writing directly on the wedge what it represents. If the wedge is too small, you can write the description outside the circle and draw a line to the wedge the description stands for, as Figure 17-7 shows.

Line graphs and bar graphs plot data along two axes, the *y*-axis (vertical) and the *x*-axis (horizontal). Usually, numerical values are shown on the *y*-axis and any other variable (such as time or a category) on the *x*-axis; however, this convention can be reversed, as it is in Figure 17-5. Remember that your reader needs to know what information you are showing on each axis, so clearly label each one, as Figure 17-8 shows. Figure 17-8 also shows the use of a *legend*. Legends are used when figures present several kinds of data on one grid; the legend helps the reader understand the figure by showing what different kinds of lines, shading, or cross-hatching stand for. For example, if you had a bar graph with several different bars in each category, you could create a legend that helps the reader understand what each bar represents. Figure 17-8 shows how a legend can be incorporated.

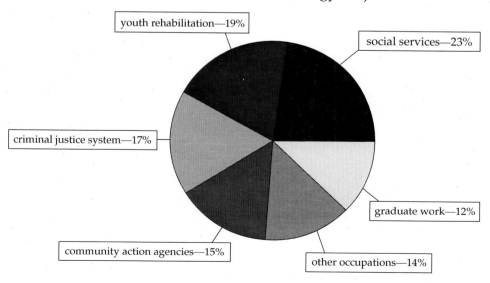

FIGURE 17-7. A Labeled Circle Graph

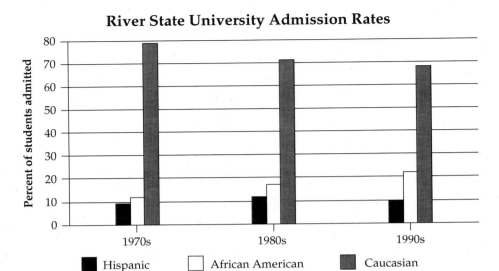

FIGURE 17-8. A Bar Graph with a Legend

ETHICAL ISSUES IN USING GRAPHICS

As you learned in Chapter 1, rhetoric can be used for good or ill. Your ethical stance as a writer will be evident in the choices you make in composing and presenting information to your readers, including how you present graphical information. With graphics there are basically three areas of concern: plagiarism; omitting information or not following reasonable conventions for representing variations in the data; and unfairly manipulating the impression the graphic makes on the reader by using chartjunk or distorting or cluttering the design of the graphic.

PLAGIARISM

Much of the time, graphics in your writing will present original data that you have gathered in your own research. However, graphics could present information that you have borrowed from other people's research and adapted to display in graphic form. Or they could be reproductions of graphics someone else made, which you have recreated, photocopied, or electronically scanned to use in your own documents. In either of the latter two cases—borrowed information or adapted graphics—you would need to give credit to the original source in your paper, just as you would for a quotation, summary, or paraphrase of words you have borrowed. Failing to cite the source of graphical data would be a form of plagiarism. If you create a graphic out of adapted information or reproduce a graphic, the easiest way to attribute it to the source is to put a credit line in small type underneath the graphic. You would also cite the source in the reference list of your paper.

OMITTING OR MISREPRESENTING VARIATIONS IN THE DATA

Graphics can be misleading, and therefore unethical, when they don't show all the pertinent data or they misrepresent the data, making something appear to be the case that isn't actually so. One way that the maker of a graphic might misrepresent is by using an inappropriate scale on the y-axis of a line graph or bar graph or by changing the unit of division in the scale at some point. For example, notice that in Figure 17-9, at first it appears that campus rapes have risen sharply in one year. But then notice the unit of division on the y-axis.

Figure 17-9 uses an inappropriate scale on the y-axis, decimal figures ascending in increments of two-tenths. But it makes no sense to think of two-tenths of a rape. In actuality, there has been one rape in a three-year period, but this graph might at first lead a reader to believe there has been a startling jump. While no one wants to minimize the seriousness of even one rape on any campus, it is important to give readers an accurate rather than misleading depiction of any statistical data.

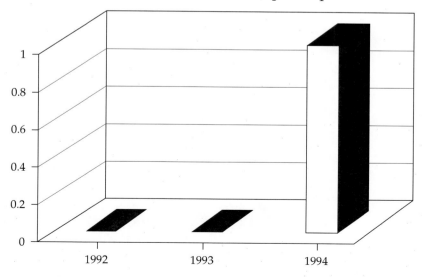

FIGURE 17-9. A Misleading Graph

DISTORTING OR CLUTTERING THE DESIGN

Graphics can also border on unethical if they distort the impression the reader gets from the actual design. There are two common sources for this kind of problem: (1) using three-dimensional bars on a bar graph (as in Figure 17-9) or adding a third dimension to a circle graph can distort the data by changing the viewers' perspective of the graph and causing them to misunderstand the comparative size of the bars or wedges; (2) adding "chartjunk"—cute but unnecessary illustrations, objects, or icons to a graph either draws the viewer's attention away from the real information the graphic has to convey or makes it difficult to find the information. Following are two illustrations that show distortion and clutter. Figure 17-10 distorts by using a needless third dimension in the bars, making it more difficult to compare the heights of the bars. Figure 17-11 shows

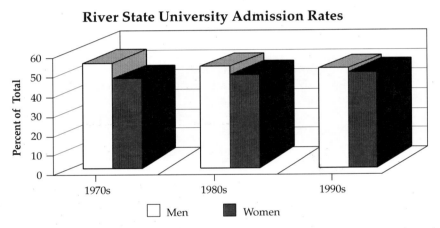

FIGURE 17-10. A Distorted Three-Dimensional Bar Graph

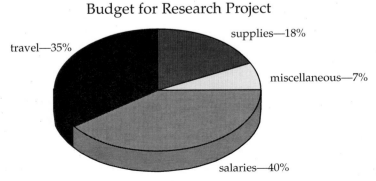

FIGURE 17-11. A Distorted Three-Dimensional Circle Graph

how adding a third dimension to a pie chart makes the wedges in the foreground look bigger than they are.

Figure 17-12 draws attention away from the important information by using chartjunk, perhaps in an attempt to make the chart more entertaining or

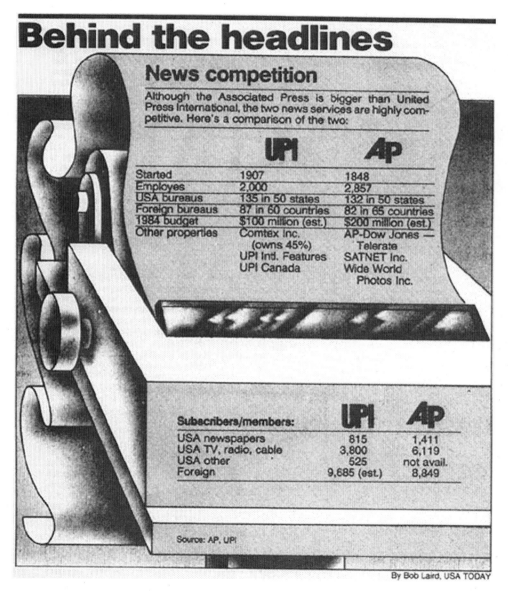

FIGURE 17-12. An Example of Chartjunk

picturesque. When you finally locate the basic information the chart conveys, however, you may feel that the maker of the chart has overwhelmed the data by unnecessarily giving prominence to something that is meant to be a clever illustration. By cluttering the chart, the designer causes you to spend more time searching for and interpreting the basic information.

CONCLUSION

You will frequently see graphics in newspapers and popular magazines that violate the principles this chapter espouses. One reason may be that untrained designers create the graphics to add color and entertainment to an article. Another reason is that many computer programs for graphics actually invite the user to clutter figures with junk, add needless third dimensions, or display information in a type of graph that isn't suited for the data. As you read professional journals in your field, however, you will notice that graphics are usually simpler and clearer than in popular periodicals. You are well advised to study the graphics of professional publications so that you can become both a wise consumer and producer of informative figures and tables.

SUGGESTIONS FOR PRACTICE

1. Using a spreadsheet or the table function of a word processing program, create a table that shows your personal budget for the last five months. Create six rows, one for each month and a final row for totals. Create as many columns as you need to display budget categories such as rent, food, clothing, transportation, entertainment, and school expenses. Give your table a number and an informative caption.

2. Convert the total figures from your budget table into a circle graph that shows what portion of your income went to each category. Label each wedge with the name of the budget category represented. Give your graph a figure number and a title.

3. Display in a table the following 2006 crime statistics from three urban counties: Washington County had 5 homicides, 4 rapes, and 10 armed robberies. Jefferson County had 2 homicides, 5 rapes, and 15 armed robberies. Madison County had 6 homicides, 6 rapes, and 17 armed robberies. Give the table a number and an appropriate caption.

4. Display the above crime statistics in a bar graph that compares the three counties for each type of crime. That is, create three bars side by side to show how they compare on numbers of homicides; three bars to show

how they compare on numbers of rapes; and three more bars to compare numbers of armed robberies. Use shading to distinguish the three counties' bars, and use a legend to show which shade is used for which county. Give your bar graph a number and an appropriate caption.

5. Create an original table or figure to display data that you have collected as part of using one of the research methods described in Part II of this book.

6. In a library research paper display data that you have borrowed from a library source in a table or figure. Give the graphic a number and an appropriate caption. Give a credit line to the original source and give a complete bibliographic citation at the end of your paper.

REFERENCE

Tufte, Edward. 1990. *Envisioning information*. Cheshire, CN: Graphics Press.

18

ORAL PRESENTATIONS

CHAPTER OVERVIEW

After reading this chapter, you should be able to answer the following questions:

1. How do you evaluate the rhetorical situation when you have to give a speech?
2. What should the opening of a speech do? How can you get the audience's attention?
3. How does speaking differ from writing? What are the implications of the difference for the way you should organize the middle of a speech?
4. What should the ending of an oral presentation do?
5. What are the advantages and disadvantages of various kinds of visual aids?
6. What factors are important to remember in the delivery of an oral presentation?

THE TRADITION OF ORAL RHETORIC

As you learned in the opening chapter of this book, the ancient study of rhetoric focused on analyzing and teaching the art of public speaking. Two of the divisions of classical rhetoric—memory and delivery—taught students mnemonic devices to help them memorize their speeches and the art of using just the right stance, gestures, and voice inflections to make their words emphatic and memorable. In the eighteenth and early nineteenth centuries, the main goal in teaching rhetoric at the university was to produce skilled orators who could take their place in society as ministers, lawyers, judges, legislators, doctors, and professors. The ability to speak eloquently and persuasively was considered a prime requirement for these professions and was the hallmark of an educated man (women did not regularly have access to higher education until the twentieth century). Some of the rituals that are still a part of traditional university life—debates, valedictory addresses, and oral exams—are a result of the strong emphasis on rhetorical training from the Middle Ages until well into the nineteenth century.

Being an effective, persuasive speaker is still vital for success in most avenues of professional life, just as it is for any citizen interested in affecting the course of local government. But in this century, what little rhetorical instruction students receive is usually limited to writing (and then only one or two courses). Courses in public speaking are still taught at most universities and colleges, but they are often no longer required. As a result, it is possible to graduate from college now without having formally studied and practiced the art of oral rhetoric. This is unfortunate because it is valuable to have the ability to get people to listen to you, to take your ideas seriously, and even to join you in action. While this chapter can't take the place of a full course in public speaking, it can offer some pointers that should be useful in your future—whether you present research findings at the meetings of professional organizations, go to a city council meeting to influence the local zoning ordinances, or make presentations to your supervisor or your subordinates on the job. You will learn how to evaluate each rhetorical situation, organize your presentation, use resources wisely, and plan and rehearse your delivery.

EVALUATING THE RHETORICAL SITUATION

Just as you do when you write, the first thing you should do when planning an oral presentation is evaluate your rhetorical situation: What is your purpose? Who is your audience? What do you intend to talk about? Whether you are writing or speaking, these are questions you must always answer when composing a text.

DEFINING YOUR PURPOSE

Your general purposes in any oral presentation will usually be to inform and persuade—though not always in equal measure. Sometimes your purpose may be to entertain (e.g., when serving as master of ceremonies) or respond appropriately on a ceremonial occasion (e.g., when receiving an award, proposing a toast, giving a eulogy). In addition to identifying your general purposes, you also need to define your immediate purpose or goal for the particular speech you are planning. For example, suppose you were presenting your research findings about a new behavior modification therapy to a group of peers. You could formulate your immediate purpose as follows:

> To inform my colleagues about the theory and practice of therapy X and persuade them that it is effective in dealing with people who display behavior Y.

By defining your immediate goal as precisely as you can, you are better able to make decisions about what information and evidence to include in your presentation and how to arrange its parts.

SIZING UP YOUR AUDIENCE

You can hardly think about your immediate purpose without simultaneously thinking about your audience. Here are some questions that will help you decide how to achieve your purpose with a given audience:

- Who are my listeners?
- What do they already know about the subject?
- What position, if any, have they already taken on the subject? Are they likely to be skeptical, favorable, or neutral to my point of view?
- What do they already know about me and how do they feel about me?
- What relationship do they have to me? Are they my peers, my supervisors, my students, my subordinates?

As you can see from these questions, there are many variables to consider as you plan how to address your audience. For example, if your audience knows you already and knows your background, it will not be necessary to have someone introduce you and explain your credentials—or to work that into your talk if no introduction is to be given. If the audience knows little about your subject, you will have to think carefully about ways to give them a quick, basic understanding of it. If the audience already knows something about your subject, but is already inclined to disagree with you about it, you must plan ways to overcome their resistance. And if the audience members are your superiors and have the power to approve your ideas or grant money for a proposal, you must remember their need to be fully informed and to explore all the ramifications of the decisions they might make. You need to anticipate their concerns and be prepared to answer their questions.

ASSESSING THE CONTEXT AND ENVIRONMENT

As you define your immediate purpose and size up your audience, you should also assess the context and environment in which they will they be listening to you. Will you make your presentation to a class? During a board meeting? After dinner? At the end of a two-day conference? How many people will be there? What sort of mental and physical state are they likely to be in? How many minutes will you have to speak? What will the room be like in which you speak? Will it be a small classroom, a large auditorium, or a hotel conference room?

Will you be standing at a podium or seated with your audience around a table? To answer questions such as these, try to learn as much as you can about the context and environment for your presentation, as they will certainly affect the strategy you will want to use. (More will be said later about how to plan for the environment.)

ORGANIZING YOUR PRESENTATION

After you have considered the above aspects of the rhetorical situation, you can begin planning what to include in your presentation and how to organize the parts. Generally, you will not have unlimited time for giving an oral presentation, so you need to limit your focus to a few aspects of the topic that you can present effectively in the allotted time. After you have decided what the focus will be, it's helpful to think about the presentation's organization in terms of the beginning, the middle, and the end.

THE BEGINNING

The beginning or introduction of your presentation should do these three things

1. Establish your credibility.
2. Interest the audience in the topic and make them want to listen.
3. Outline the main point and supporting points you will make.

Some experts estimate that you have about a minute to make a good first impression on your audience and engage their attention. An audience that is bored or confused by the introduction is likely to give less than full attention to the rest of the talk. And they may reject the message if the messenger doesn't seem credible. In the opening sentences, then, you must simultaneously orient the audience to the purpose and scope of your presentation and make them feel you are a trustworthy, credible speaker.

You establish your credibility, your *ethos*, by projecting good will towards the audience, revealing yourself as a person of good character, and being knowledgeable about your topic. You do this in part through nonverbal communication—through your dress, posture, facial expressions, and gestures—so it is important to make these work in your favor (more will be said about how to do so below under "Delivery"). But you can also establish credibility—as well as interest your audience—in the way you choose to introduce the topic. Here are some possibilities:

Begin with an anecdote that sets up a key issue you plan to discuss. Because stories deal with concrete people, places, and events, they are more memorable than abstract generalizations. They also get people's attention better than a dry statement such as, "In this presentation I will compare two therapies for eating disorders." In a well-chosen anecdote you can illustrate a problem or sketch quickly some key points of your presentation. Rather than seeming artificial, the anecdote should lead naturally to a statement of the purpose of your talk and a brief overview of the body of the talk. If you have engaged your audience's attention and shown your wisdom by framing your message through an appropriate story, the audience will credit you with the good sense and good character that wins their trust. And they will be prepared to listen to the statement of your main point before you move to the body of your speech.

Use brief, gentle humor. An audience perks up when a speaker opens with something that everyone can laugh at. A joke or witty remark suggests to them that you are relaxed and confident and that you do not want to bore them. Humorous remarks must be related to the subject of your presentation, however, and must lead easily to a preview of its contents. Gratuitous, unrelated humor might send the wrong message—that you are nervous, for example, or a frustrated comedian, rather than someone to be taken seriously.

Say something startling or unexpected. The audience will likely know the title or topic of your remarks ahead of time and will probably have some expectations of what you will say. You will generate greater interest if you begin with a statement they *aren't* expecting. Offer a little-known statistic that points up something unusual about your topic. Or make a seemingly implausible claim that you'll support in the middle of your presentation. The audience will be curious to see how you will make the startling statistic relevant or the unusual claim plausible. Again, to win their trust, you must be prepared to move deftly from this kind of opening to a statement of the key point of your message and an overview of the facts, examples, or other evidence you will offer. You must show you can say something significant, not merely shock your listeners.

Ask a rhetorical question. A rhetorical question is one that the speaker does not expect anyone to answer out loud. But by asking the question and pausing a moment while the audience members answer it silently in their own minds, you are likely to gain everyone's involvement instantly. As you then proceed to outline and present your own answer to the question, you should have the attention of your listeners. And if your answer differs from the one they would have given, they will be particularly interested to learn why you think as you do.

Give a brief demonstration. Like a story, a demonstration immediately provokes interest and helps to make the abstract concrete. It gives the audience something to watch as well as to hear, and therefore increases the chance they will remember your main point. Granted, it is easier and more appropriate to demonstrate some topics than others, so don't stretch imagination and credulity too thin. But if the presentation is about something that lends itself to a demonstration—for example, equipment, methods, or physical facts—consider a demonstration an excellent way to introduce your presentation. For example, suppose your speech was about the way smoking impairs health. To dramatize one health problem, the loss of lung capacity that smokers experience, you could have someone stand in front of the audience with nose and mouth taped shut, except for a small opening through which a drinking straw is inserted into the mouth. Have the person breathe through the straw for 30 seconds. As the person's face grows redder, the audience will see how difficult it is to get enough oxygen when the lungs can't be inflated fully.

Involve the audience in doing something. Most people learn better when they actually do something during a presentation rather than passively listen. If your audience is small enough, if you have some flexibility with the time allotted, and if your presentation is not supposed to be very formal, consider beginning by having one or more of your listeners do something: Ask a question and then call for volunteers to answer it. Involve a few members of the audience in a simple role play, game, or demonstration that illustrates one of your main points. Have everyone write for one minute about a topic that you give them; then have some of them share what they've written. Be aware, however, that the more you open your presentation up to audience participation, the less control you will have over it because someone may say or do something entirely unexpected or use up more of your precious time than you planned. If you choose this way of beginning, you need to plan carefully for all the eventualities you can think of; then you must be flexible and think quickly on your feet to recover from an unanticipated outcome. But if you are successful in involving the audience, you will earn not only their attention, but their respect and trust as well.

Whatever you choose as an attention-getter, be sure that you keep it relatively short in comparison to the rest of your talk. You can damage your credibility by being too funny or too enchanted by your method of getting attention or by taking so long to get to the point that people begin to wonder if you have one. Always follow your introduction with a clear and succinct statement of your main point and a quick overview of the middle of your presentation. It is usually a good idea to have some kind of visual aid that outlines your main point and the supporting points you intend to cover (visual aids will be discussed later in this chapter). Your audience will be able to listen for the key supporting points in the presentation if you outline them in advance.

THE MIDDLE

In the middle or body of your presentation, you elaborate on the points you previewed in your introduction. The number of points you should plan to cover depends on the time you have. In five minutes, you probably can do justice to only one; in fifteen minutes, only two or three. Even if you have been given 45-60 minutes to make your presentation, you would be wise not to elaborate on more than five points.

As you compose your presentation beforehand, think carefully about the best way to order the parts of your talk. For example, if your topic is historical, a chronological order might be the most appropriate. Or, for a topic that speculates on the future, it might be useful to discuss causes and then effects. But discussing effects first and causes second might be a good way to answer a question like "How did we get to the situation we're in now?"

Because your audience is listening to, not reading, your presentation, they won't have the benefit of headings, paragraph indentations, or boldfaced type to let them know what the main ideas are. You will need to draw their attention to the fact that you are stating a main point by saying something like, "My second point is. . . ." If you have created visual aids to supplement your speaking, you can use these to indicate that you are moving on to a new point.

You will need to give adequate illustrations, reasons, or other concrete data supporting each point. Because your audience can't re-read your text, repetitions and variations of supporting evidence will help them grasp the points more firmly. For example, you might give some statistics and then make an analogy showing the significance of these statistics in a more concrete context. Once again, visual aids are a big help with illustration of a point, particularly if a long quotation or numerical data are involved.

Avoid dwelling on a point too long, and don't assume that all of your points need the same emphasis. You might, for example, spend two minutes elaborating on a simple idea so that you can have ten minutes to spend on a more complex one. You should plan the relative amount of emphasis for each point ahead of time by carefully analyzing your audience's needs. Then you can adjust your emphasis during the presentation as you notice your audience's reaction. If they seem bored and fidgety, they are probably ready for you to move on. If they seem a bit confused or anxious, they may be hoping you will say something more to clarify the matter.

THE ENDING

Rather than assuming your conclusion will just take care of itself, or that you will simply stop talking when your time is up, you should plan the ending of your presentation as carefully as the beginning, The ending is the ideal time to reassert your main points, because research shows people remember beginnings and endings better than middles. If someone missed a point or two that you made in the middle, you can still hope to reach that person with an effective summary of your points.

Although summarizing is an important part of the conclusion, you can aim to do even more. In the conclusion you can relate the significance of your presentation to a broader context, perhaps even personalize the message for audience members so that they feel its significance more strongly. For example, if you have just spoken on the 1950-era McCarthy hearings in the US Senate, you could draw some comparisons between those events and current events of a similar nature. If the topic warrants it, at the end you can also issue a sort of challenge or call to action that inspires your listeners to do something with the information you have given them.

Whatever you do at the end of your presentation, provide a sense of closure that makes the audience feel they have come full circle with you in the minutes you've been talking. For example, you may allude to the anecdote, the joke, the rhetorical question, or the demonstration you began with. Say something to help the audience understand how the expectations you aroused with your introduction have now been fulfilled. In that way, they will sense that you have given the topic a full and satisfying treatment and not simply run out of time.

USING RESOURCES WISELY

Because there are important differences between listening to and reading a text, you should consider these differences as you prepare an oral presentation. Unlike written words, which are more or less permanent, spoken words vanish almost immediately. While readers can pause and reread parts of a text that aren't clear at first, in a formal setting listeners usually don't have the luxury of interrupting and asking the speaker to repeat things. As you understand the differences between writing and speaking, you can prepare to capitalize on the advantages of face-to-face communication as well as compensate for the transitory nature of speech. In planning your presentation, you should consider each of three resources that can enhance your oral message if used properly—or detract from it if you fail to take them into account. These resources are time, the environment for your talk, and visual aids.

TIME

In most cases, you will be told early on that you can speak a specific number of minutes. (If you are not told, be sure to ask how much time you'll have.) But be aware that the amount of time you are promised and what you may actually get are often not the same. For example, at meetings of professional organizations, you may be one member of a panel of three or four speakers, each of whom is supposed to talk for 20 minutes. But if you are the last speaker and the speaker just before you takes 30 minutes, you may be forced to cut your presentation. Or if one of the speakers fails to show up, you may suddenly have the dubious luxury of speaking ten minutes longer than planned. Because of unexpected events like these, you should plan in advance where you could condense or expand your presentation if you had to. Rather than adding another point or extra detail to your talk, one good way of using additional time is to ask for questions and comments from the audience. Try to anticipate how the audience might react to your presentation so you can be prepared with good responses.

ENVIRONMENT

Before planning your presentation, it is wise to learn as much as you can about the place where you will be speaking. If you can, visit the place ahead of time to evaluate its size and other features. If it is a large auditorium, you will want to know if the acoustics are good and if a powerful enough microphone will be provided. If it is a small room, you may want to know if the chairs are fixed to the floor in rows, or if they can be moved into another arrangement. If you plan to show slides or overhead transparencies, you will need to know if the room has a projector and screen, and if the windows, if any, can be darkened with drapes or blinds. In short, what you can do in your presentation may be constrained by the physical limitations of the environment. It's better to know what those limitations are ahead of time rather than be embarrassed by not having planned for them.

VISUAL AIDS

Experts on learning agree that people will understand something better and remember it longer if you appeal to more than one of their senses. So, for important points in your presentation, it's wise to use a visual aid so that your listeners can *see* the point as well as *hear* it. The hallmarks of a good visual aid are visibility, clarity, and simplicity.

Visibility is largely a function of size, so if you plan to put a list on a posterboard, for example, the lettering must be big enough to be read easily by people in the back row. For a large audience in a large auditorium, a posterboard would be a poor choice of visual aid simply because it would have to be enormous to be visible to people in the last row. A slide of the same information would be a better choice because it could be projected onto a large screen.

Visibility can also be related to color choices. Using black lettering on a dark green or dark blue background is not a good idea, for example, because there won't be enough contrast between the two colors. You also need to take care when using contrasting colors to emphasize a contrast in ideas because some people are colorblind, and they may not be able to discern the contrasts you intend.

Clarity and simplicity in visual aids are inextricably related. Generally, the simpler and less cluttered a visual is, the clearer it will be. Rather than try to put a lot of information into a few visuals, use more visuals with just one or two items of information on each. Don't use so many visuals, however, that you are constantly revealing a new one; your audience will start to feel overwhelmed with information and distracted by the rapid succession of visual aids.

A good visual aid should be largely self-explanatory; that is, even if a listener momentarily loses track of what you are saying, he or she should be able to pick up the thread by looking at the visual aid you have displayed. Each visual should therefore have a clear label and other cues about how to read it. On a bar graph, for example, the x-axis and y-axis should be clearly labeled.

In an era of sophisticated computer presentations, it seems almost old-fashioned to list other kinds of visual aids. But computer technology is not one hundred percent reliable, so even when you are prepared with your laptop, projector, and disk or CD, it's good to know how to use other technology in case you have to use it. Here is a list of some common visual aids with suggestions about how and when to use them.

Chalkboards, Whiteboards, and Sketchpads. The venerable chalkboard, the more modern whiteboard, and the portable sketchpad on an easel are all useful tools for an interactive presentation or one in which you want to present a developing progression of ideas. The physical act of portraying ideas visually on these surfaces can add energy and interest to your presentation, making you and the ideas seem more dynamic. But because you have to turn your back to the audience to write on a board or pad, and because you may have to erase the board or turn the page on the sketchpad, you will lose some time and audience contact while writing on them. It's important, therefore, to limit the length or complexity of what you write or draw. If you are a weak speller, you may want to forego these options, since a number of spelling errors may decrease your credibility. Also, because what you write or draw may seem spontaneous and rough, using the chalkboard, whiteboard, or sketchpad may make your presentation seem less polished than one in which the visuals are prepared ahead of time. It's probably best to use these kinds of visual aids only for interactive presentations that you want to seem quite spontaneous.

Posterboards. Lists, diagrams, graphs, and tables can be prepared on sturdy posterboards in advance and displayed on an easel at the right moment in your presentation. You can use a pointer to draw the audience's attention to specific parts. If you have very many posters, it is a good idea to ask an assistant to help you with them—to remove one and reveal another as you nod your readiness.

Overhead Transparencies. Transparencies are in some ways like posterboards, and they may be easier to prepare for those whose hand lettering skills are not very good. Using a word processing program and a printer with variable fonts and point sizes, you can produce neat, legible lists, tables, graphs, and figures on a computer. You could also photocopy tables, figures, or sketches from published sources (giving credit of course). Then, using a thermal process, you can transfer the images from paper onto transparent sheets of film (any shop that specializes in making photocopies should be able to do this for you). You then lay these transparencies on an overhead projector and a large image will be projected onto a screen. You can even overlay one transparency on another, building up a series of images so that your audience can see a progression of steps in a process, for example. You can also switch the projector on to focus audience attention on the visual aid, then switch if off again to return their focus to you.

Transparencies can also function like a chalkboard, as you can write directly onto blank transparencies with special pens. This method has some drawbacks, however, as the silhouette image of your hand and arm will also be projected onto the screen, and your body may block some people's view of the screen. For a small audience, writing directly onto transparencies may be a good way to keep audience attention. For a large audience, however, transparencies are probably best used like posterboards, with you standing to the side of the screen, using a pointer to draw attention to the words and images. If you have more than two or three transparencies, you may wish to have an assistant position the transparencies on the projector and then remove them so that you can concentrate on speaking.

Computer presentations can be converted to transparencies quite easily, and it is usually a good idea to have a back-up set of transparencies to use in case a planned computer presentation goes awry.

Handouts. A printed handout distributed to each audience member can serve at least two functions. One is to provide an outline of your presentation so that listeners can follow along, perhaps taking notes on their outlines, and carry away a detailed record of what you have said. Computer presentation software allows you to easily make a handout of your slides with spaces for notes, and many audience members appreciate receiving such a handout. Another function of handouts is to supplement your presentation with visual or written information that fills in information you cannot cover completely during your presentation. Though handouts might be potentially enriching, they can also have the effect of drawing your listeners' attention away from what you are saying as they become engrossed in reading your visual aid, so be judicious in how you use them. You might want to distribute a supplemental kind of handout at the end of your talk.

Photos. Still photographs of objects may be appropriate for some topics. They work best with small audiences, where the photos can be passed from person to person. To be visible to a large audience, a photo would have to be enlarged many times, and the process of enlargement usually degrades the quality of the details in a photo. But a photo can be made into a slide or incorporated in a computer presentation without losing detail.

Slides. Slides overcome the drawback of photos because a tiny 35-mm slide can be projected onto a screen and be visible to all in the room. Slides are very versatile and can be made of photographs, tables, graphs, lists, words, etc. Using a remote-control slide projector, you can then introduce your visuals at the right moments in your presentation. You can also use a light pointer to highlight certain parts of a slide. Some of the disadvantages of slides are the time and cost of preparation and the potential for an equipment failure. Also, because you must darken the room, you may lose eye contact with your audience. And some people may fall asleep during a slide presentation. On the other hand, a polished slide presentation can lend a very professional tone to an oral presentation.

Videos. You can use professionally produced, custom-made videotapes or CDs to create interest, illustrate a point, or analyze something in your presentation. If you use a segment from a commercially available video, be sure that you comply with any copyright restrictions. Before turning on a video, you should prepare your audience to notice the relevant details. Since videos are normally projected via an ordinary TV screen, they are best used with small groups unless you know there will be a big screen for projection. And like other visual aids, videos should be chosen for their relevance and not simply for their novelty or to create a change of pace. If you decide to use a video clip, you also need to make sure ahead of time that the equipment is working properly and that you know where to start and stop the videotape. This means watching it ahead of time so that you have it cued to the right starting point and know when the end point is coming.

Objects and models. If your presentation centers around some physical object, the actual object or a model of it can be very helpful in focusing attention and helping your listeners understand your main points. An object or model would best be used with a small group, so that all can see it clearly and perhaps even hold it. While small, inexpensive objects might be easy to bring along, a large or expensive piece of equipment may not be a practical visual aid. Models can be time-consuming and expensive to construct, too, so you need to weigh their advantages against the costs.

Computer presentations software. If you have access to the necessary equipment and software, you can incorporate audio and visual aids into your presentation with computer presentations software. This software allows you to create a sophisticated slide presentation. You can make black and white or color overheads, 35-mm photographic slides, or on-line slides that include outlines, tables, figures, diagrams, and charts. You can also embed animated graphics and audio or video clips into your presentation. The software often provides clip-art or allows you to create your own figures to illustrate text. Using this software, you can prepare each component of a presentation—for example, your notes, audience handouts, and slides—and everything you create will be in a consistent format. Be careful, however, to observe good design principles and good taste in planning your presentation. The software programs offer you a dizzying array of fonts, background colors, and options for introducing and erasing text, some of which would not be good choices for particular occasions, subjects, and audiences. As with any other medium, you should aim at communicating an idea clearly and simply rather than just producing a "gee whiz" effect. Keep your audience focused on your message more than on the medium. Because computer presentation software has become so widely used, a few pointers about using it wisely are in order. Remember the following:

- A fancy computer presentation will not disguise a lack of research and preparation. Focus on the content first before the packaging.

- Choose the colors for your presentation carefully. The background should contribute to the subject matter and "feel" of your presentation, not distract from it. Colors can evoke emotions; for example, consider the difference between a blue background and a yellow background. "Cool" colors, especially blues, are popular because they suggest detachment and objectivity. "Warm" colors, such as bright yellow and deep red, suggest a high degree of emotion and are harder to look at for a sustained period of time. Slightly textured or patterned backgrounds can be pleasant, but you should avoid "busy" backgrounds, such as a photograph or a complicated, highly defined pattern.

- Once you have chosen a background, find a color for your text that will contrast with the background. Some common combinations are dark blue background with white or yellow text, and beige with dark blue or green text. You should definitely avoid combinations such as red and green (which can be indistinguishable to colorblind individuals), orange and blue, and red and blue. Also, avoid choosing two very similar colors for background and text, as there will not be enough contrast between them.

- Select fonts and text sizes that are clear and easy to read on your background. Again, don't sacrifice clarity for cuteness.

- Maintain unity within your presentation. Don't switch backgrounds or fonts from slide to slide. Generally, the entire presentation should use the same background and font.

- Create a hierarchy of points, just as you would in an outline (see Chapter 11).

- Limit the number of points you make on each slide, and keep each point brief and succinct. A common rule is "sixes and sevens": no more than six points on a slide, and no more than seven words per point. Two or three points per slide would be much better than five or six.

- Don't distract the audience with excessive special effects, transitions, sounds, and so forth. These can be helpful if used sparingly and wisely, and annoying if not.

- Don't overload your audience with a complicated visual aid all at once. Start simple, and add pieces as you go along, explaining each one and how it fits in with the rest.

- Don't put everything you intend to say on your slides and then simply read your slides to the audience. Your audience will feel bored and be tempted to tune you out. You, not your slides, should be the focal point in your presentation most of the time.

- Preview your presentation before you deliver it. Ask some trusted friends to watch it with you and give you pointers so that it will look as good to your audience as it does on your computer screen.

PLANNING FOR DELIVERY

Once you have analyzed your rhetorical situation, organized your presentation, and considered how to use the resources available, you are ready to prepare for the moment of truth—the time when you actually deliver your message.

Delivery is the most important part of an oral presentation. Even if you have prepared thoroughly, all of your hard work may come to naught if you can't deliver your message effectively. To be successful you should consider how presenting a message orally differs from giving a reader a written text. As a speaker, you can capitalize on important differences in these two types of rhetorical situations. In the oral situation, listeners have the advantage of hearing your actual voice and watching you deliver your message. You can use your voice, appearance, personal traits, gestures and body language to enhance the reception of your message in a way that you can't when you write. Planning and practicing your delivery involves the following: (1) deciding what method of memory support to use, (2) choosing appropriate dress and grooming, and (3) rehearsing to make your voice and body movements support your message.

MEMORY SUPPORT

Although you may occasionally be called on without warning to give an impromptu speech, usually you are given time to prepare. As you look ahead to the time when you will speak, you should decide whether you will speak from memory, from notes, or from a complete manuscript. Memorizing your presentation is good mental discipline; it can also make you so familiar with your material that you feel more confident and poised. For some people, however, memorizing a speech can lead to a colorless, rote presentation and inflexibility in adapting to the occasion and the audience. Others may freeze if their minds suddenly go blank and they aren't able to improvise with words other than the ones they memorized. Because of these potential pitfalls, memorizing an entire presentation is usually not the best option.

Speaking from notes is probably far more common in today's academic and professional world than is speaking from memory. Using notes permits you to sound natural and to maintain good eye contact; it may also make you feel free to move about naturally. Your notes might take the form of a simple one-page outline of your presentation that you can set in front of you and glance at, or some 3x5 cards on which you have written key words and which you can hold discreetly in one hand. Focusing your mind on concepts and key words rather than entire sentences allows you to speak extemporaneously, using the words that seem appropriate for the purpose and audience. If you are inter-rupted while speaking extemporaneously from notes, you can recover easily, without having to worry about exact wording. If you prepare a computer pre-sentation, a handout, or transparencies, these often take the place of notes, as you simply need to look at what you have written on your visual aids to prompt you in your speaking.

For more formal occasions, reading from a prepared manuscript may be the best option, particularly if the audience is large and you will have to remain at a lectern with a microphone. Reading from a text is also helpful if you are trying to communicate something delicate, and you have worked very carefully beforehand to find just the right words for your message. Also, if you want to create a certain mood and images with your words, you may want to read from a prepared manuscript. Reading from a manuscript is often the man-ner of delivery used at professional conferences where social scientists share their research findings. The scripts of their oral presentations may become the basis for eventual publications.

Reading your speech doesn't have to be monotonous and boring if you practice your delivery enough times that you can say your sentences effectively while still looking up frequently to maintain eye contact with the audience. To facilitate finding your place again easily after you look up, prepare your manu-script in a large font with wide margins and triple spacing. Don't feel so tied to what you have written that you don't feel comfortable improvising a little—tossing off a spontaneous comment related to the occasion or pausing to offer a simple explanation for something your audience seems puzzled about.

APPROPRIATE DRESS

Dressing and grooming yourself appropriately on the day of your presentation can't be overemphasized. People form first impressions about you based on your appearance, and, as unfair as it may seem, if they form negative impressions, your audience will probably not be able to judge the merits of your presentation objectively. Even though you may view your clothing, hairstyle, and jewelry as your way of making a statement about your personality, putting your individuality as your first priority can distract or even alienate your audience. Celebrities may be able to get away with eccentric dress, unusual hairstyles, and excessive jewelry, but because you are trying to establish your credibility, you would be wise to conform to the style that others follow in a given setting.

You should not dress less formally than your audience because your prominence as the speaker will make your casual clothing even more conspicuous than it would otherwise be. On the other hand, if you are dressed up a bit more than the audience, they may take it as a compliment to them; they certainly won't judge you as being careless about your dress. Often, you can adjust your clothing in simple ways to fit in. If the other men in the audience are all tie-less and in shirtsleeves, for example, a man may be able to remove his jacket and tie to be like them. Women can also remove accessories to achieve a more relaxed, understated look and blend in with how other women in the audience are dressed. If you are unsure about what to wear, ask ahead of time.

VOICE QUALITIES

Just as you want your appearance to enhance your delivery, you need to consider how you can use your voice to have the right impact on your audience. The first thing to consider is the *volume*, or loudness, of your voice. If you will be speaking into a microphone, you will merely need to be sure that you are close enough to it and that it is amplifying your voice adequately for everyone in the room. When there is no microphone, you need to speak loudly enough for people in the rear to hear you without straining. If you have a naturally quiet voice, you will need to make a conscious effort to project your voice more than usual. You can practice by rehearsing your speech for a friend in a room the size of the one you'll be speaking in.

You also need to consider the *pitch*, or high and low tones, of your voice. Interesting speakers vary their pitch rather than droning on at the same level all the time. Lowering the pitch of your voice can add a sense of drama and solemnity to what you say, while raising it can impart a sense of urgency.

The *pace* of your delivery is also important for achieving the effect you want to have on your audience. Pace is simply the speed you speak at. Most speakers average between 125 and 150 words per minute. At this rate, it takes you about two minutes to read a standard page of typewritten text. You can slow your pace down to emphasize points or to discuss complex ideas, or you can speed it up a bit to show excitement or cover some simple ideas quickly. Talking too slow or too fast all the time, however, will make it difficult for your audience to listen: Their minds will start to wander if you are too slow, and they will become confused and frustrated if you race through your presentation faster than they can comprehend it.

Finally, you must take care to articulate your words clearly, pronouncing them according to common standards, and to use correct grammar. Articulating "did you eat yet?" as "jeetyet?" may be acceptable in a conversation with friends, but it will convey excessive casualness in a presentation to an audience. Similarly, if you pronounce "exactly" as "ezackly," your audience may believe you are not well educated. Likewise, making grammatical errors such as "He done it" or "Me and him went" will seriously detract from your credibility. As with your dress and grooming, you risk conveying the wrong impression if you insist on using idiosyncratic speech or a dialect that is considered non-standard.

Nonverbal Communication

Although using your voice carefully can help make your delivery memorable, equally important are the nonverbal ways you communicate your message. A key factor here is eye contact. Speakers who seldom look into the eyes of their audience members convey the impression of being painfully shy and nervous or, perhaps worse, indifferent to the audience. On the other hand, a speaker who makes frequent eye contact with individuals in the audience reassures them that he or she is poised and prepared, keeps their attention, can assess how they are receiving the message, and can make subtle corrections as needed. Making eye contact means that you actually look into the eyes of different people in different parts of the room. You should hold one person's gaze for 3-5 seconds before moving on to someone else.

Gestures are another form of nonverbal communication that can enhance or detract from a message. Gestures are movements, both voluntary and involuntary, that can illustrate or emphasize a point, such as striking the podium with your fist to demonstrate your determination. (Admittedly, this particular gesture may be overdramatic, and it is certainly not one to use often.) Many people gesture naturally, using their fingers to point or to enumerate, or spreading their hands to indicate size. Others find it difficult to "talk with their hands." Too much gesturing may make you seem a bit frantic and distract your audience; too little gesturing may make you seem wooden and unnatural. As you rehearse your presentation, have a friend pay attention to your natural gestures; then make a conscious effort to eliminate distracting ones and to make the remaining ones smooth and effective. If you don't make many gestures naturally, think of appropriate ones you could make and practice them until they become natural. It is important to have some animated gestures during your presentation because they will help keep your audience alert and involved.

Your other movements, posture, and facial expressions also communicate your attitude and emotional state to your audience. Even though you may feel butterflies in your stomach, if your talk is well-focused and organized, there's really nothing to dread. Move confidently to the position you will occupy as speaker. If you will be standing, keep your feet about 10-12 inches apart, relax your knees, then keep them slightly bent. Take a deep breath and let your shoulders drop naturally rather than keeping them hunched up around your neck. Pause a moment to survey your audience and smile at them. If you are not tied by necessity to a lectern, move about a little in front of your audience, but avoid pacing. Channeling your nervousness into appropriate movements as you speak will help dissipate your anxiety and will make you seem animated and at ease.

REHEARSING YOUR DELIVERY

Just as actors and singers rehearse before performing, good speakers do too. You need to practice integrating all the things you've learned in this chapter, and make your presentation a seamless whole. The better rehearsed your presentation is, the more confident you will feel and the more poised you will appear to your audience. If you practice using your visual aids, you will be able to control them and any necessary equipment smoothly, without unduly interrupting your talk and losing audience attention. Finally, if you rehearse your presentation several times you will be able to judge how well your presentation fits into the time limits you've been given and be more able to adjust its length as needed.

Asking a friend to listen to you and watch you has already been mentioned as one effective rehearsal strategy. Be sure to ask a friend who will be honest with you and critical enough of your performance to offer helpful feedback rather than simply reassure you that you're doing fine. Another rehearsal method is to practice in front of a full-length mirror. Still another is to have someone videotape you as you give a dress rehearsal; then watch the videotape several times to see where you can improve your performance.

Though all of these preparations may seem extensive and elaborate for just a few minutes on stage, after you successfully deliver your first oral presentations, you will find that you can prepare more quickly and easily for succeeding ones. Following many of the steps detailed here will become second nature, and you will become a more confident and polished public speaker.

SUGGESTIONS FOR DISCUSSION AND APPLICATION

1. Think of effective and ineffective speeches you have heard. What were the deficiencies of the ineffective speeches? What did the effective speakers do very well that made their speeches memorable?

2. Attend a special lecture given by a guest on your campus or an important person in your community. Pay attention to how the speaker presents his or her message and make notes of what is done well and what could be improved. Report your findings to the class.

3. Prepare a ten-minute oral presentation based on the library research paper you complete for this class. Deliver your presentation to other members of your class and then listen as they give you feedback on your performance.

V

STYLE IN THE SOCIAL SCIENCES

Style is such an important part of rhetoric that in the past it has sometimes been the main focus of writing instruction. Although this book does not emphasize style as much as it could if there were space to do so, learning to use the right style for a given purpose and audience is one of the most important things you can do to make your rhetoric persuasive. Some elements of style are common to virtually all fields that write in the English language. Other elements of style, however, are limited to particular fields; they are an identifiable feature of the rhetoric of that field. To learn more about the elements of style common to all fields, you should consult a current handbook; there you will find guidelines for correct punctuation and mechanics and for effective sentence construction. In Chapter 19 you will find some guidelines to help you with a few elements of style that are more particular to the social sciences, such as current guidelines for referring to yourself in your writing, for using the specialized terminology of your field, and for using unbiased language.

19

INSTITUTIONAL STYLE

CHAPTER OVERVIEW

After reading this chapter, you should be able to answer the following questions:

1. What is meant by institutional style? Why do institutions adopt style guidelines?
2. What is the detached persona? How does one achieve this effect in writing?
3. When is jargon not objectionable?
4. What are operational definitions? Acronyms? Initialisms? Neologisms? Multiple noun strings?
5. What are the latest APA guidelines for inclusive and unbiased language?

WHY DO STYLES DIFFER?

Style can refer to a distinctive or characteristic way of expressing oneself. For example, Mark Twain's style is very different from Jane Austen's, and both are different from Stephen King's. Novelists are not the only writers with a noticeable style; poets, playwrights, essayists, journalists, and other writers also are often noted for their unique styles. Political columnist William F. Buckley has a very erudite style that bespeaks his Ivy League education, for example, while Molly Ivins, also a political columnist, has a down-home, folksy style in which you can almost hear a Texas drawl. A writer's style is the result of all the many choices the writer make, from deciding what to write about to selecting words, constructing and punctuating sentences, and organizing the text. Writers make their choices for many reasons, some of which they might not even be aware of, but their personal styles result at least in part from their language background, education, personal preferences, interests, goals, even their politics.

A style can be institutional as well as personal. For example, a particular publishing company, journal, newspaper, business, or professional organization will specify certain choices that a writer must make in selecting words, constructing and punctuating sentences, writing headings, documenting sources, and so on. Institutions don't specify everything a writer must do, however. Two writers writing for the same journal won't necessarily sound just alike, because institutional guidelines still leave room for individual expression. But if the writer doesn't adhere to those matters prescribed by the institution, usually an editor will change the writer's text to make it conform to the specifications before it is printed.

While it may seem that writing would be much easier if everyone, including institutions, could just agree on a common set of rules, it's not that simple. Although there are a number of commonly shared rules for good style that transcend the boundaries of institutions (any current handbook of style and usage will inform you of these), like individuals, institutions have histories that have shaped their assumptions about language. They also have an image they want to project and even ideologies and political stances that their chosen style may help to further. A group's institutional style is, in part, its way of creating an identity and pursuing its goals. Styles differ because people and institutions differ and because language is an extremely flexible tool.

In this chapter you will learn about particular aspects of institutional style in the social sciences. Though it may seem that much is prescribed for you, you will find that there is also some room to develop your own personal style. Indeed, as you develop expertise as a researcher in your field, you will find you can make a more enduring mark in your profession if you also develop a mature and confident command of the English language, which will allow you to put your personal stamp on your prose.

STYLE IN THE SOCIAL SCIENCES

It's somewhat hazardous to generalize about the style of the social sciences, because the social sciences do not all sanction the same styles. For instance, the writing style of an anthropologist might vary considerably from that of an economist. In fact, two economists may write rather differently because of different focuses in their field. Furthermore, the social sciences do not equally emphasize conformity to a style. One field that does emphasize conformity to a style, however, is psychology. Over the years since 1929, through issuing increasingly specific editions of its *Publication Manual*, the American Psychological Association (APA) has significantly influenced the style of not only psychology but many other social sciences as well. The APA style manual has been adopted in many fields, including communications, education, family science, linguistics, sociology, and social work. Professionals seeking to publish in many social science publications, including more than thirty sponsored by the APA, must conform to the manual's prescriptions. So despite the hazards of generalizing, it is worth noting some features of the writing style that are authorized by the fifth edition of the APA *Publication Manual* (2001) and that are also characteristic of other social sciences, even though they may not have adopted the APA style manual.

It is important to note here that characteristics of any institutional style can and do change. The goal of this chapter is to help you realize that style is not a constant in any field; it is always the product of choices based on assumptions about knowledge—what knowledge is, how it is created, and how it should be represented in language (see, for example, Madigan, Johnson, and Linton 1995). As these assumptions change, style usually changes as well.

THE DETACHED PERSONA

Until recently, one of the most recognizable features of the social scientific style was the detached persona. A writer's *persona* is his or her *ethos*—how the self is presented in the writing as a voice or character that the reader can judge as reliable, credible, and knowledgeable. For at least a century, the hallmark of good scientific writing was to project this authoritative ethos without revealing much about oneself. This stylistic trait is now changing, but because it has been so pervasive—and still is considered good style by many older professors who learned it in their graduate school eduction—it is necessary to understand what it was in order to understand how it is changing.

To create the detached persona, a writer avoided using first-person pronouns like "I" and "we." Presumably, this style gave the impression that the writer was objective and emotionally uninvolved in the subject matter. Also, by effacing him- or herself, a writer conveyed the impression that knowledge is self-existent, an object that is discovered rather than at least partially created through researchers' methods of collecting and interpreting evidence. There are two major ways writers have achieved this detached style. Both involve *not* putting human agents in the subject position of sentences (usually the first part of English sentences).

The first way of achieving the detached persona was to put nonhuman nouns in the subject position. For example, in social science writing you may still find sentences like this:

> This study investigates the relationship between marital satisfaction and the wife's employment status.

Note that "this study" is in the subject position, implying that it does the action of the verb "investigates." But only in a metaphorical sense can an inanimate thing like a study investigate something else. The APA *Publication Manual* (2001) calls this use of "study" as a subject "anthropomorphic" because it gives human characteristics to a nonhuman thing. In reality, the researcher investigates the relationship, yet only recently has the social science style begun to include sentences like this:

> In this study I investigate the relationship between marital satisfaction and the wife's employment status.

By leaving out the human agent who actually investigates, the first sentence with the nonhuman subject contributes to the impression that knowledge is objective, impersonal, and disembodied, existing apart from people who know it. By contrast, the second sentence acknowledges the role the investigator played in creating the knowledge.

Sometimes writers used sentences that acknowledged the human role in the investigation, but they used a third person noun rather than a first-person pronoun:

> The researcher investigated the relationship between marital satisfaction and the wife's employment status.

While this sentence at least puts a human agent in the subject position, it can be ambiguous because the reader can't be sure if "the researcher" refers to the writer or to someone else. The fifth edition of the APA *Publication Manual* (2001), specifically advises writers not to use anthropomorphic nouns or to refer to oneself in the third person. Instead, it tells the writer to use the appropriate first-person pronoun and simply write, "In this study *I* investigated the relationship between marital satisfaction and the wife's employment status." Or, if you collaborated in your research, you would write, "In this study, *we* investigated the relationship between marital satisfaction and the wife's employment status."

The second way of creating the detached persona was to use the passive voice. For example, instead of writing the active voice sentence,

> I conducted an experiment.

in which the pronoun "I" is in the subject position, the researcher would write instead,

> An experiment was conducted.

This second sentence is in passive voice with the words "an experiment" in the subject position. Although the researcher might have added *"by me"* at the end of the second sentence, doing so acknowledges human agency in conducting the experiment. Because passive voice allows writers to omit the agent of an action, social scientists have in the past often used passive voice, perhaps to imply that they are writing about knowledge that is objective, impersonal, and self-existent. Using this particular strategy, a writer could avoid claiming responsibility for actions performed. The APA *Publication Manual* (2001) advises against the use of passive voice unless "you want to focus on the object or recipient of the action rather than on the actor" (42). For example, if you wanted to describe your procedures in survey research, you might write, "Copies of the questionnaire were mailed to 100 people chosen randomly from the telephone directory," because this sentence would emphasize the questionnaires, not who mailed them.

The detached persona is not necessarily "bad," either in a moral or a grammatical sense. People still understand sentences with impersonal subjects and sentences in passive voice, and probably no one imagines that experiments simply happen or that studies investigate things without humans being present. Still, this style reflects an assumption about scientific knowledge—that it exists apart from people who know it, and therefore it is not necessary to refer to the human agents who invent it. This assumption is changing, however, as more scientists agree that knowledge is something humans create as much as discover, and that therefore the style of scientific language ought to openly acknowledge the role humans play in their own research.

JARGON: WHEN IT IS AND WHEN IT ISN'T

Another major characteristic of the social science style is the prevalent use of jargon. The word *jargon* generally has negative connotations, suggesting writing that is practically unintelligible because of its technical vocabulary. But the same writing that a lay reader might label "jargon" may be completely accessible to and communicate very efficiently with readers who share the writer's assumptions, training, and knowledge. So jargon can be positive as well, when it means using specialized vocabulary and following other conventions that permit a community of trained people to communicate effectively with each other. Whether jargon is appropriate or inappropriate, then, depends to some extent on the reader. "Borderline personality disorder" may sound merely intimidating to the lay reader, but to the psychologist it communicates a concept clearly.

It must be acknowledged, however, that much writing in many fields, not just the social sciences, is needlessly difficult, even pompous, using too many unfamiliar, multi-syllable words and a complex style with no gains in efficient communication to any audience. This use of unnecessary jargon often goes by such names as "gobbledygook," "bureaucratese," or "academese." In this kind of jargon, a simple sentence like "Too many cooks spoil the broth" becomes "A superfluity of culinary experts degrade the quality of the beef or poultry extract." If we agree that writing such gobbledygook is unnecessary anytime, we must still consider when there are good reasons in the social sciences (and other fields as well) to use jargon. Four kinds of sometimes necessary jargon are listed below.

New combinations of words to create operational definitions. Scientists of all kinds attempt to explain the phenomena they study as precisely as they can. Often, when they have formulated a new concept that they believe explains things well, they may create new phrases to name it. Since the social sciences are often concerned with measurements, scientists need names for their concepts that will allow them to perform precise observations and numerical operations. In other words, they must make the definition of a new concept operational. An operational definition is one that permits scientists to observe the concept with their methods (observation, experiments, surveys, and so on) and quantify it with their instruments, such as scales and tests. For this reason, social scientists don't want names with existing connotations that will make it difficult for others to accept them as operational definitions.

For example, a sociologist may want to learn something about how "happy" people are in their families or with their jobs. But "happiness" is such an emotionally loaded term that it can't be defined as precisely as needed for the kinds of measurements and statistical tests the sociologist might need to do. Therefore, the sociologist will create a more neutral name for the concept, such as "life satisfaction." While this invented phrase may seem puzzling to a lay reader, it actually increases the precision of the definition the sociologist can give to the term and allows the sociologist to measure life satisfaction, for example on a scale from one to six. And among professional peers, the term works as an efficient way of discussing an important concept.

Acronyms and Initialisms. The social sciences are rich sources of *acronyms*—words made of the initial letters in a phrase, usually spelled in all upper-case letters. You already know and use acronyms such as AIDS, a short and pronounceable name for Acquired Immune Deficiency Syndrome that increases efficiency in writing and speaking because of its brevity. In the social sciences, acronyms like this gain currency among groups of researchers interested in the same phenomena. For example, those who study the deaf culture needed a convenient way to refer to the children of deaf adults. In order to save the time of constantly saying or writing four words, they created the acronym CODA. While that acronym may not have widespread use in the general population, it does make communication more efficient for the initiated.

Initialisms are like acronyms, shortening the way of referring to a multi-word phrase. The difference is that initialisms can't be pronounced as a word; instead, the initial letters of the phrase are read off. For example, "borderline personality disorder" is often shortened to BPD in order to avoid continually writing or saying the entire phrase. And the Minnesota Multiphasic Personality Inventory is usually shortened to MMPI, with corresponding savings of space and time. With both acronyms and initialisms, however, the first use of the abbreviation should be spelled out entirely, with the short form given in parentheses immediately following, so that any uninitiated reader can learn what the letters stand for.

Sometimes an acronym becomes so common that we even forget its origin as an acronym, and it becomes, for all intents and purposes, a single word which we needn't expand into the longer phrase it stands for in order to comprehend it. *Radar* and *sonar* are such words. Most people have forgotten—if they ever knew—that radar stands for "*ra*dio *d*etection *a*nd *r*anging" and sonar for "*so*und *n*avigation *a*nd *r*anging." *Laser* is another such word. (Do you know what each of its letters stands for?) Note that these words are not written in all capital letters anymore. The initialism HIV (for "human immunodeficiency virus") is fast becoming a term that people don't stop to recall the component words for any longer. The same assimilation of acronyms and initialisms to single words may happen in your field, though their use may not become widespread beyond the members of your field.

Neologisms. The word *neologism* may itself look like unnecessary jargon, but when you consider its Greek roots, it's not so difficult. The prefix *neo* simply means "new," and the root comes from *logos*, Greek for "word." So a neologism is simply a new word or phrase coined to represent a concept that can't be adequately represented with existing words. An example of a neologism in psychology is *affect*, a noun to refer to an emotional state as opposed to a cognitive or perceptual state. Though it has been in use for several decades now, the term is not used widely by the general public. But it has come to be a very useful name for an important concept in psychology, education, and related fields. Another neologism from the social sciences is *eustress*, which someone invented to attempt to describe a good kind of stress that produces desirable results rather than the negative outcomes we usually associate with *stress*. Two neologisms that have caught on in wider spheres are *Reaganomics*, which stands for the kind of economic policy President Ronald Reagan espoused, and *webliography*, a neologism based on *bibliography* that means a list of Web sites instead of a list of books and articles. Can you think of other neologisms?

Multiple noun strings. One of the interesting things about the English language is that it can use a noun to modify another noun. For example, we all understand that the noun *headache* in the phrase *headache remedy* tells us what kind of remedy. Every field takes advantage of this characteristic of English and uses groups of nouns to create names for the concepts it studies; for example, psychologists speak of "attention deficit hyperactivity disorder"—a string of four nouns in a row, in which *attention* tells what kind of *deficit,* and together with *hyperactivity*, they all tell what kind of *disorder*. But when the jargon of a field begins to string four, five, and sometimes even six nouns in a row, the result is often sentences that are almost unreadable—even for the initiated. Here is an example quoted in the fifth edition of the APA *Publication Manual* (2001, p. 33):

commonly used investigative expanded issue control question technique

It's a safe bet that only a few insiders would understand that string of four modifiers and four nouns—and they might not be sure! When that many words are strung together in this fashion it is almost impossible to tell which ones modify which other ones and in what way. It could be rewritten more clearly in any of three ways depending on what is meant: "a control question technique that is commonly used to expand issues in investigations"; "a common technique of using control questions to investigate expanded issues"; or "a common investigative technique of using expanded issues in control questions" (APA *Publication Manual* 2001, 34).

Even though stringing nouns together makes information more compact, it also makes it less understandable. "Unpacking" the noun strings makes sentences easier to read. In general, the way to go about unpacking a noun string is to start with the last noun in the string (the base noun) and then put the other nouns in prepositional phrases or relative clauses that modify the base noun. For example, suppose you encountered this multiple-noun string:

a five-year hiring needs assessment plan

Starting with *plan*, you could arrange the other words as modifiers like this:

a plan that assesses hiring needs [relative clause] for the next five years [prepositional phrase]

In your writing, particularly when your audience is not likely to understand the jargon, you should not use multiple-noun strings. For example, don't write this sentence for a lay audience:

Although individuals typically have little difficulty in successfully monitoring the sources of their affective reality, errors or equivocations in their cognitive reality monitoring process sometimes occur.

Instead write this one:

Although people can usually monitor the sources of their affections, they may make mistakes or equivocate when monitoring their cognitive reality.

When you are writing about the subject matter of your discipline, always consider your audience. If your readers are likely to know the jargon you wish to use, or if they can be helped to understand it with brief, simple definitions, you may feel safe in using it. When you are writing for an audience of all or mostly lay readers, however, it is important to reduce the amount of jargon you use, as the sheer abundance of it may bewilder your readers. This means that you may actually have to write five pages to say what you could say to your peers in three; paradoxically, in some cases, increased length results in more efficient communication.

INCLUSIVE AND UNBIASED LANGUAGE

Perhaps because they often study marginalized groups and unusual individuals and their behaviors, social scientists are sensitive to the processes of prejudice and exclusion that can lead to the demeaning of individuals and groups and even to discrimination against them. Perhaps also because of their quest for precise ways of describing the individuals and groups they study, the social sciences have often been leaders in using language that reduces stereotyping, eradicates bias, and promotes fairness. For example, the American Psychological Association states the following in its *Publication Manual* (2001):

> As an organization, APA is committed both to science and to the fair treatment of individuals and groups, and policy requires authors of APA publications to avoid perpetuating demeaning attitudes and biased assumptions about people in their writing. Constructions that might imply bias against persons on the basis of gender, sexual orientation, racial or ethnic group, disability, or age should be avoided. Scientific writing should be free of implied or irrelevant evaluation of the group or groups being studied. (61)

"Political Correctness." In recent years, the phrase "political correctness" has been used rather loosely to characterize efforts such as the APA's to encourage language that respects differences and speaks of differences in nonjudgmental language. The phrase is accurate in acknowledging that language choices can indicate a political stance. But too often the label "political correctness" seems to be used negatively to mean a coercive movement to change the language of the majority to language that a minority wants to enforce as "correct." While it may be true that some efforts to change the language have been excessive or unproductive, the underlying motive in most cases has been to promote language that shows sensitivity and respect. Therefore, even though you may find some proposed language changes unnecessary or even foolish, you ought not to automatically reject efforts like those of the APA as "mere political correctness." These proposed changes only ask people to think carefully about the attitudes their language may reveal and to use words and names that avoid stereotyping or offending. Considering the professional and social penalties you might pay for ignoring such prescriptions, you should realize that compliance is often a safer choice than resistance, especially when you understand that the goal is clear communication that avoids offending others or treating them as

objects. Though some terms suggested below may at first seem awkward to you, they will seem less so after you use or read them repeatedly.

References to Gender. Some of the most important changes in professional language concern the way the genders are referred to. Until a couple of decades ago, it was common to refer to human beings in general with such terms as "man," "men," and "mankind." While a few people still insist that these words are generic—that is, that they include both genders—such a claim is less credible now. Because words get their meaning from the way people use them, not from the dictionary or from some invisible authority, their meanings can and do change (for example, *fond* once meant "foolish," not "affectionate" as it does now). Today's usage and many research studies demonstrate that most people no longer regard "man" and related words as generic. To insist on using them in a generic sense can create ambiguity, since "man" also refers to a male person and "men" refers to more than one male person. Readers and listeners may not know when the specific sense or the so-called generic sense is intended. The simplest way of avoiding this confusion is to say "men and women" when you mean both genders, or to say "humankind" or "humans" rather than "mankind." Using these terms is important for greater precision. These usages also acknowledge that women constitute half the human race, and they accord women the dignity of being included in categories that are accurately named.

The increasing presence of women in the workforce, specifically in jobs that were once exclusively the domain of men, means that the suffix *-man* in certain job titles is also no longer thought to be inclusive or accurate. A number of titles have been adapted to avoid conveying the impression that only men hold these jobs and to include the women who do, too. For example, a policeman is now called a police officer; a mailman, a mail carrier; a fireman, a firefighter; a chairman, a chair or chairperson; and so on. In references to other jobs previously dominated by one gender, it is considered unnecessary and condescending to point out that a person holding a particular job is unusual because of her or his gender. For example, it is not appropriate to say or write "lady lawyer" or "woman doctor" any more than it is to say or write "male nurse" or "gentleman secretary." Qualifications such as these are generally irrelevant. The only time they are relevant is when research makes gender a variable, as, for example, in a study that compares female lawyers' attitudes with those of male lawyers. In such a case, it would be important to add distinguishing adjectives, and "female" and "male" would be the best choices because they have neutral overtones, and they are parallel grammatically and conceptually.

In general, when referring to individuals or groups who are alike in all ways but gender, it is important to refer to the genders in a parallel way. For example, to call a group of twenty-one-year-old male college students "men" but call an identically aged group of female students "girls" would not acknowledge their parallel status. Similarly, to refer to men by their professional titles but to women who hold equal credentials by their first names or their husbands' names is to imply that an important difference exists. Although no disrespect may be intended, readers may infer a subtle disparagement of individuals or groups whose equal status is not acknowledged.

Disparagement also comes from language that evokes cultural stereotypes; too often, these stereotypes are grossly inaccurate and unexamined. To use the phrase "woman driver," for example, is simply unfair to all the women whose driving ability is normal and whose behavior behind the steering wheel is safe and characteristic of that of most drivers on the road. Similarly, to say that someone behaved "like a typical man" doesn't offer any helpful information; it merely leaves the reader wondering what "typical" means. Stereotypes are usually generalizations based on insufficient or skewed data, and using them is inappropriate for anyone who would claim to be a scientist.

References to Racial, Ethnic, and Other Groups. Stereotypes and inaccurate labels can also be applied unfairly to other groups—racial and ethnic groups, for example, as well as elderly persons, people with disabilities, or people with homosexual orientation. The APA *Publication Manual's* (2001) advice on referring to these groups is as follows:

> Respect people's preferences; call people what they prefer to be called. . . . Accept that preferences will change with time and that individuals within groups often disagree about the designations they prefer. . . . Make an effort to determine what is appropriate for your situation; you may need to ask your participants which designations they prefer, particularly when preferred designations are being debated within groups. (63)

As you are no doubt aware, the names that some groups prefer to be called have changed more than once over the last twenty years. These name changes are often due to a linguistic process called "pejoration," in which a new word or a new name will start its life with positive or at least neutral connotations, but after a period of time, it will start to have negative connotations, often for prejudicial reasons, and will then be considered a "pejorative"—a name that is disparaging or degrading. Obviously, since no group wants to have a name that is a pejorative, the group often creates a new name for itself. Rather than look upon this process of renaming as an unnecessary nuisance, consider that each individual and group wants to be respected and take pride in their identity.

At the time this book went to press, according to the APA *Publication Manual* (2001), the accepted way of identifying major racial and ethnic groups in the United States was to use the following terms:

African American or *Black*
Asian American or *Asian*
Mexican American, Hispanic, Latino, or *Chicano*
Native American or *American Indian*   (pp. 68–69)

Another useful rule of thumb for showing respect for others is to avoid turning adjectives into nouns that become labels, suggesting that you have objectified the people you are referring to. For example, rather than write about "the elderly," "gays," and "the mentally retarded," write instead about "elderly people," "gay men," or "mentally retarded persons." In this way you acknowledge the humanity of the individuals. Another way of following this rule is to put the person first, not their condition or disability. So, rather than write "paraplegic" or even "paraplegic patient," write "person with paraplegia." This kind of phrasing separates the person from the disability, rather than identifying him or her as only the disability. Finally, avoid language that unnecessarily expresses emotion about a person's condition or disability. For example, write "persons with schizophrenia" rather than "victims of schizophrenia," which suggests that these people are doomed to a hopeless life.

REFERENCES TO PARTICIPANTS IN RESEARCH

In accord with this same line of thought, the APA *Publication Manual* (2001) also encourages writers not to think of the people who participate in their research as *subjects*. The word "subject" implies that people who agree to participate in an experiment, answer a survey, or otherwise cooperate with researchers are acted upon, rather than acting freely according to their own agency. Preferred names for those who take part in research are *participants, respondents, informants, individuals,* or some other name that accurately describes their status, such as *children, teens, college students,* or *patients.*

The APA style manual (2001) suggests further that, to show that individuals in research studies are actors, not subjects who are acted upon, writers should construct sentences in the active rather than the passive voice when describing what the participants did. For example, rather than write, "Subjects were administered a questionnaire," researchers should write, "Respondents completed a questionnaire." Writers should also avoid using verbs that, although not passive voice in the grammatical sense, still suggest that the participants are passive rather than active. For example, writers should not say, "The participants *showed* distress"; they should write instead, "The participants *reported* they felt distress."

CONCLUSION

These recommendations of the APA *Publication Manual* (2001) indicate a significant shift in thinking for the fields that subscribe to that manual. However, you should be aware that the changes the manual advocates will take place gradually. Some social scientists, editors of some journals, or some of your professors may still prefer that you use the passive voice or impersonal and anthropomorphic subjects. As in other rhetorical matters, you should always learn what your audience expects and adapt your writing as necessary to achieve your goals in submitting your work. One of the most important things you can do as a fledgling social scientist, however, is to examine the prevailing style of your field for the assumptions it reveals and make informed choices rather than simply comply without thinking. If APA is not the relevant style manual for you to follow, you may need to find out what other guides you should consult. Some professional journals publish or will mail to you upon request the style guidelines they require authors to comply with. You can also learn a lot about style by simply observing what authors do in the books and journals that you read for your own research. Finally, you can ask a professor in your major what guidelines have been published for your field.

This chapter began with the assertion that an institutional style is, in part, a group's way of creating an identity and pursuing its goals. At this point, you may feel that in some ways you are asked to give up your individuality or your personal convictions and simply submit to rules that you didn't help create. In a way, that's so: No one asked you what you thought, but that's because you weren't a part of the field when the institutional style was being formulated. But like styles in clothing, styles in language also change. By understanding and complying with the style guidelines of your field, you can become an insider and then have the chance to influence future changes in the style. Those with the most persuasive voices will exert the most influence. Until you have the stature to influence change, take the opportunity to observe, to learn, and to reflect on the assumptions underlying the institutional style of your field.

SUGGESTIONS FOR WRITING OR DISCUSSION

Directions: Imagine that you are the editor of a professional journal, and you find the following sentences in various manuscripts that scholars have sent to you. Edit the sentences to comply with the style guidelines given in this chapter. Be prepared to defend your choices by discussing how a given context and audience would affect your decisions.

1. The following professors collaborated in this study: Dr. Robert Jackson, Dr. Michael Parmenian, Dr. Octavio Salazar, and Mrs. David Schuster.

2. The depressives were assigned to a treatment regimen that included four doses of the experimental drug each day for two weeks.

3. This article describes and evaluates the opinions of the elderly about nursing home care.

4. In sessions with the therapist, the client acted like a typical man.

5. Mankind's quest for knowledge has led to some revolutionary discoveries in sociobiology.

6. The study included six physicians, including one woman doctor.

7. The personality is a unique configuration of life history identity items that differentiate the self from the other.

8. The 30 college-aged subjects in this experiment were all US citizens; they included 10 Orientals, 15 Negroes, and 5 Indians.

9. Interviews were conducted with 10 learning disabled students, one of whom was additionally afflicted with muscular dystrophy.

10. Tom Schwartz is a male nurse.

11. While building up her clinical practice clientele, she supplements her salary by teaching a community college general education introductory psychology course.

12. The client, Mrs. Daniel Johnson, works as a foreman in a software production plant.

13. The African American subjects were randomly assigned to one of the two treatments.

14. Ironically, busy family therapists often don't spend enough time with their own wives and children.

15. The university was persuaded by faculty advocates to create a women's resource center as part of the Counseling Service.

16. The respondents were 25 men and 25 women young professionals just starting in business. The businessmen tended to rate themselves as satisfied with their jobs significantly more often than the girls did.

17. The first two informants, Joshua and Elaine Carmichael, were man and wife.

18. I would like to thank Dr. Gloria Brunetti, the chairman of my department, for her careful reading of the first draft of this manuscript.

19. The subjects were 50 male homosexuals.

20. Since the major oil companies began using fast-pay credit card reader gasoline purchase systems, they have been able to decrease labor costs by as much as 10%.

21. It has been shown in clinical drug trials that these new medications are effective in alleviating symptoms for schizophrenics.

22. Stereotyping the elderly can be seen as serving an ego protection function for youth.

23. It was argued by the defense attorneys that the crime lab had contaminated the evidence.

24. The AIDS victims attributed their long survival to their optimistic outlook on life.

25. Determination of veteran's benefits payments eligibility is decided by the SPE (Standards, Procedures and Exceptions) committee during its monthly analysis and review meeting.

REFERENCES

American Psychological Association. 2001. *Publication manual.* 5th ed. Washington, D.C.: American Psychological Association.

Madigan, Robert, Susan Johnson, and Patricia Linton. 1995. The language of psychology: APA style as epistemology. *American Psychologist* 50 (June): 428–436.

THE READINGS

Journal Article Review

by
Michelle Pomeroy

Michelle Pomeroy is majoring in marriage, family, and human development at Brigham Young University. After graduation, she plans to be a great mother while her husband, Miles, earns his Ph.D. Michelle's hobbies include jigsaw puzzles, cross-stitching, cooking, and reading. She is from St. George, UT.

1. The article in review was coauthored by Lori A. Francis and Leann L. Birch, both from Pennsylvania State University. I assume Dr. Francis and Dr. Birch are professors at PSU because both have been members of the Department of Human Development and Family Studies, and Dr. Francis is currently in the Department of Biobehavioral Health. It is noted in the article that this research was supported by grants from the National Institutes of Health. Given the authors' current positions and their ability to earn prestigious grants, Francis and Birch seem to have the credentials to research and write a persuasive article.

2. The title of this article is "Maternal Influences on Daughters' Restrained Eating Behavior." This article comes from the journal *Health Psychology*. The title is a good summation of what is discussed in the article because Francis and Birch discuss how mothers' attitudes toward their own weight correlate with restrained eating behavior in their daughters.

3. The article has an abstract that summarizes the content well; however, it seems to be a little more elementary than professional. The methods and findings seem to be stated in a simplistic style. However, this style helps even novices understand clearly what the article is about.

4. Within the introduction of the article, previous research is cited. The research is put in a family context by highlighting the mother-daughter association. The overall objective or purpose for this study is clearly given, as the authors state they had three questions: (a) whether mothers' preoccupation with weight influences daughters' weight and eating, (b) whether attempted influence was linked to daughters' retrained eating, and (c) whether these influences were mediated by daughters' perceptions of maternal pressure to lose weight. I found this explanation to be the closest thing to a concrete thesis. The thesis is clearer in the conclusion of the article.

5. Within the methods section the participants are defined: 173 non-Hispanic, White mother-daughter dyads living in central Pennsylvania. Middle class mothers and their daughters were studied. Francis and Birch used different scales to measure the results of various surveys given to the mothers and daughters, including the Weight Concerns Scale and the Three-Factor Eating Questionnaire. The Weight Concerns Scale measures fear of weight gain, worry about weight and body shape, and the importance of weight, diet history, and perceived fatness. The Three-Factor Eating Questionnaire consists of 51 true-false questions that ask

about dietary restraint, dietary disinhibition, and susceptibility to hunger. Six items overall were measured between the mothers and daughters. The mothers were evaluated for preoccupation with own weight and eating, attempts to influence daughters' weight and eating, and concern for daughters' weight. The daughters' measures included retrained eating behavior, perceptions of maternal pressure to lose weight, and weight concerns. The methods Francis and Birch used are described in detail. The measures taken seem to be valid for answering the research questions. Relationships between the different variables are tested thoroughly and the statistical inference is sound. However, the participants volunteered for the study rather than being selected randomly. This may imply that mothers interested in weight and eating issues were more willing to participate, so the method of recruitment may have introduced volunteer bias.

6. The findings of this study are given in the results and discussion sections of the article. The findings of the article are as follows: maternal preoccupation with weight and eating is associated with mothers' restriction of daughters eating energy-dense foods. Daughters' perception of maternal pressure to lose weight is correlated with mothers who encourage weight-loss, but it is not correlated with maternal restriction of high-energy food intake. Pressure from mothers to lose weight is correlated with daughters' restrained eating behavior. These findings are illustrated in an easy-to-follow flowchart. The chart helps clarify the concepts being explained and the association between the tested variables.

7. The findings of this study are reported in the results section. They are summarized as follows: "Mothers who were more preoccupied with their own weight and eating made more attempts to influence their daughters' weight and eating by restricting daughters' intake of energy-dense foods and encouraging daughters to lose weight. These weight- and eating-focused parenting behaviors were in turn associated with daughters' restrained eating" (Francis & Birch, 2005). These findings are justified because a statistically significant correlation is shown between the variables. The authors, however, do mention that the study was done with a demographically homogenous sample, which limits possible generalizations. It is suggested that many of these issues are prevalent in boys as well as across cultures. In conclusion, the authors suggest that the findings of this study indicate one possible point of intervention in decreasing poor eating behavior in young girls.

8. The article is concise and well organized. With my educational background I was able to understand the flow of the article. I do believe this research to be well supported and reliable. However, I would have been more impressed if the authors had used a random sample from a larger population. Nevertheless, I did appreciate the fact that the authors recognized the need for a broader study. The findings were relevant, but were unable to be generalized. I believe the authors were knowledgeable and professional in their research. This was shown by their referring to past research that they themselves have done.

9. The audience for this article seems to be a cross between the general public and professionals. I suggest this because the language used in the abstract as well as throughout the article is somewhat elementary, but the methodology is detailed and complex. I am a

person who fell right into this audience. I am not yet a professional, but I do have some background education which allows me to understand the methods used and the conclusions.

Reference

Francis, F.A., & Birch L.L. (2005). Maternal influences on daughters' restrained eating behavior. *Health Psychology, 24,* 548–554.

Bare Branches: The Security Implications
of Asia's Surplus Male Population

by
Valerie M. Hudson and Andrea M. den Boer

Valerie M. Hudson is Professor of Political Science and a faculty affiliate of the David M. Kennedy Center for International and Area Studies at Brigham Young University. She earned a BA in political science with minors in Russian and international relations at BYU in 1978. Her PhD, from Ohio State University in 1983, is in political science with emphasis in international relations, methodology, and policy analysis. Her research focuses on decision-making in foreign policy, national security policy, international politics, and women and the developing world. Andrea M. den Boer received her bachelor's degree at the University of Manitoba and her master's degree at BYU. She earned her PhD at the University of Kent in Canterbury, England, where she is currently a Lecturer in International Relations and Director of the Master of Arts in Human Rights, Ethics and International Relations. In 2006, their book, Bare Branches, *won the Association of American Publishers' award for Best Professional/Scholarly Book in Government and Political Science, and Dr. Hudson appeared on CBS's* 60 Minutes *to discuss the implications of their argument. The following are excerpts from Chapter 4, "China's 'Missing Females'" and Chapter 5, "Bare Branches of High-Sex-Ratio Societies: Theory and Cases."*

The One-Child Policy and Son Preference

China's first national census, taken in 1953, recorded a population of 583 million, but by 1975, the population was estimated to be more than 900 million. The following factors caused the government to reexamine Mao's assertion that more children would lead to a stronger nation: the large increase in population between the 1950s and early 1970s; the famine of the early 1960s; a lack of housing, food, and jobs; and the declining health of the population.[1] In the early 1970s, the government adopted a policy known as *wan, xi, shao* ("later, farther apart, and fewer") and encouraged couples to limit the number of children to two (in urban areas) or three (in rural areas).[2] This policy was then adapted in 1979, when China introduced the strategic demographic initiative known as the "one-child policy," which aimed to reduce population growth. The one-child policy was part of a family planning law to be presented to the Fifth National People's Congress in 1980, but it was not formally enacted until the twenty-fifth session of the Standing Committee of the National People's Congress in December 2001. Although the one-child policy did not become a law until September 2002, from 1979 on government at all levels throughout China acted as though the policy were law and attempted to enforce its rules and penalties. Family planning has become a fundamental part of Chinese life and is even written into the constitution, which states that it is the duty of a husband and wife to practice family planning, and that their rights may not infringe on the interests of the state, the society, or the collective.[3]

The 2002 Population and Family Planning Law states that couples can have only one child. A second child, if requested, may be arranged but is "subject to law and regulation."[4]

Reprinted from *Bare Branches: The Security Implications of Asia's Surplus Male Population* (2005), by permission of MIT Press.

The circumstances under which couples may actually be permitted to have a second child are unclear. Under the previous one-child policy, regulations regarding fertility varied in rural and urban areas. In urban areas, the one-child policy was applied with strictness, whereas in rural areas the policy was to encourage one birth, control second births, and prevent third births. Even this policy varied depending on the gender of the births. A woman with two daughters was often permitted the chance to have a third child in the hope that it would be a boy. Other exceptions to the rule of the one-child policy were made for parents whose first child had a nonhereditary disability, for parents who were both the only child of their parents, for spouses who had both returned from overseas, for minorities, and for residents of regions where there was a shortage of labor.[5] The legal marriage age in China is 20 for women and 22 for men; in rural areas, however, men were not permitted to marry until age 25, and women could marry only when they reached 23. Also in rural areas, first children could follow immediately after marriage, but subsequent children had to be spaced four years apart.[6] Most universities prohibited undergraduates from marrying and placed limits even on the marriage of graduate students. Failure to follow these rules resulted in heavy fines, ranging from a one-time payment to payments over several years.[7] Couples who had unauthorized children could also be denied government aid, such as poverty assistance, access to farming materials, technology training programs, and even health care and education for the children.[8] It is too early to determine whether the penalties under the new family planning law will be the same as those in the past.

Since the one-child initiative was introduced, China's birth rate has decreased and the use of birth control, including sterilizations, intrauterine devices, and abortions, has greatly increased.[9] The number of killed or abandoned infants, particularly female infants, however, has also risen, so much so that the 2001 Marriage Law and the 2002 Population and Family Planning Law both contain prohibitions against infanticide.[10] Li Xiaorong argues that local government policies and campaigns have exacerbated the problem of female infanticide and abandonment of infant girls by forcibly detaining women for abortions and sterilizations, demolishing houses, and generally terrorizing women.[11] It is not simply parents who are making decisions regarding family planning; in some cases, local family planning officials have the last word. Article 22 of the Population and Family Planning Law in fact points to the mistreatment of even the mothers who give birth to females: "Discrimination against and mistreatment of women who give birth to female children or who suffer from infertility are prohibited. Discrimination against, mistreatment, and abandonment of female infants are prohibited."

The one-child policy has reinforced the tradition of son preference. To understand the people's response to China's family planning policies, we must understand the role of children—in particular, sons—within the Chinese family, and examine the politics surrounding the difficult reproductive decisions of parents.

In Chinese culture, children are viewed as the means of family continuity, the basis of prosperity, and the source of care for the aged. Caring for the financial needs of parents is one of the primary roles of sons. Daughters do not play a role in carrying on the family name, nor is their labor thought to be equally valuable, although in some cases women produce and earn more than men.

The need to produce sons is particularly evident in rural areas, where males are considered more valuable as laborers. The system of farming adopted in the 1970s changed the focus from the collective to the family. Families with sons seem to have an economic advantage because males are given tasks of heavy agricultural work and also handle disputes over land boundaries or allocation of resources. Females, on the other hand, are given less strenuous farming jobs not considered as valuable to the family's welfare.[12] As H. Yuan Tien notes, "This preference for male children, contrary to the explanation offered most often by scholars and others in China, is not simply an expression of feudalistic mentality. It is very much dictated by highly labor-intensive agricultural and related pursuits. Even during the days of collective farming under the People's Commune, more males enabled a family to earn more work points and, hence, to better its standard of living."[13]

There are additional economic advantages to having sons in rural areas: At least 90 percent of rural populations are pensionless and must rely on sons to meet the economic needs of aged parents.[14] A daughter typically marries and then moves into the home of her husband's family, where she becomes responsible for the care of her in-laws. Anthropologist Sulamith Heins Potter describes living conditions for those without children who rely on government support as "pitiable," adding that these old men and women live in decrepit buildings with little food and must depend on the goodwill of neighbors to provide water and fuel.[15]

The Rising Sex Ratio at Birth

As a result of the one-child policy and the politics surrounding it, sex ratios at birth in China have increased greatly. As discussed previously, the sex ratios at birth between 1936 and 1989 reported in the 1982 and 1988 fertility surveys stayed above the expected norm of 105–107 [boys born for every 100 girls born]. According to Chinese demographers, the sex ratio at birth between 1970 and 1980 remained close to normal levels; since that time, however, sex ratios have risen well above the norm and are still increasing. Yet the precise sex ratio at birth is difficult to ascertain. Unlike India, where data on number and sex of births are not collected by census surveyors, they are collected in China. Unlike India, however, where each member of the population is counted, censuses in China are actually samplings of the population. The Fourth National Population Census of July 1, 1990, was merely a 10 percent sample, as was the 2000 census. Figures for 1995 are based on a 1.04 percent sample survey, and 1994 figures are taken from a 0.63 percent sample survey. Because these small sample surveys may not accurately represent the population of China, calculations based on them are imprecise.

Figure 1, based on calculations by Chinese demographers Gu Baochang and Li Yongping, depicts the rising sex ratio at birth for the total population of China. Since 1980 and the implementation of the one-child policy, sex ratios at birth have continued to rise. In some areas, the sex ratio is rising to much higher levels than the figure suggests, and in other areas, the sex ratio at birth is closer to the norm.

Table 1 shows a breakdown of the sex ratio at birth in the years 1982, 1989, and 1995, according to province, autonomous region, and municipality. As the table shows, the birth sex ratios in China have increased from 108.5 to 115.6, with sex ratios exhibited as high as 130.3 in one province in 1995. Unlike India, where there was a marked difference between north and south, the only difference we find in China is in the outlying autonomous regions of Guizhou, Tibet, and Xinjiang, which, for reasons we discuss later, consistently exhibit birth sex ratios within or below the norm.

FIGURE 1 Sex Ratio at Birth in China 1980–95.

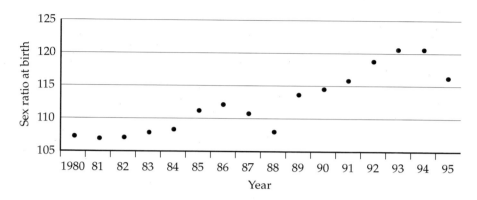

Sources: 1980–91: Gu Baochang and Krishna Roy, "Sex Ratio at Birth in China, with Reference to Other Areas in East Asia: What We Know," *Asia Pacific Population Journal*, Vol. 10, No. 3 (September 1995), p. 20, Table 1; 1992-95: China, State Family Planning Commission, *China Birth Planning Yearbook*, Beijing, 1996, p. 483, reported in William Lavely, "Unintended Consequences of China's Birth Planning Policy," University of Washington, July 14, 1997.

Using the sex ratios at birth and the totals for male and female births, it is possible to calculate and then compare the number of missing females from China's birth population (see Table 2). For example, in 1985 the overall sex ratio at birth was 111.4, and there were 11.6 million male births and 10.42 million female births. Using an expected birth sex ratio of 105, 11.05 million females should have been born, suggesting that there are 628,000 females missing from the population that year. Between 1985 and 1995, the number of missing females ranges from 342,000 to 1.47 million, which represents 3 to 15 percent of female births. In total, 10.68 million females are missing from China's birth population during this period.

The number of births in China has remained relatively constant since 1981, with 20–25 million births each year, but because the sex ratio has increased steadily in this same period, the number of missing females has also increased. In Tables 3 and 4, the missing female population is examined for 1989 and 1995 births, showing the increase in the number of missing females from 700,000 to 800,000. Based on the data available since 1995, an average of more than 1 million females are "missing" each year from the birth population alone.

A strong regional pattern of high sex ratios and missing females emerges from the north coastal province of Liaoning to the southern coastal province of Guangxi, and to the south-central province of Sichuan. All the provinces covered in this area exhibit high sex ratios at birth and also contribute the greater percentages to the total missing female population in China. In addition to geographic variations in sex ratios at birth, other factors, including education and ethnicity, play a role in sex ratio variations among localities. In their analysis of 1990 figures, Gu Baochang and Xu Yi suggest that the regions that exhibit normal sex ratios are at opposite poles: either economically and socially advanced for a long time with more modern attitudes about gender or economically and socially backward.[16]

TABLE 1. Sex Ratios at Birth in China by Region, 1982–95.

Region	1982	1989	1995
China	**108.5**	**111.3**	**115.6**
Beijing	107.0	107.1	112.4
Tianjin	107.7	110.4	110.5
Hebei	108.2	110.9	115.2
Shanxi	109.4	110.1	112.0
Inner Mongolia	106.8	108.5	110.0
Liaoning	107.1	110.5	111.4
Jilin	107.8	107.8	109.6
Heilongjiang	106.9	107.3	110.0
Shanghai	105.4	104.1	104.8
Jiangsu	107.9	113.8	123.4
Zhejiang	108.8	116.7	115.2
Anhui	112.5	111.3	116.4
Fujian	108.6	109.9	122.3
Jiangxi	107.9	110.4	115.4
Shandong	109.9	115.0	118.8
Henan	110.3	116.2	126.7
Hubei	107.0	109.5	130.3
Hunan	107.6	110.1	116.4
Guangdong	110.5	111.3	123.1
Guangxi	110.7	117.4	119.1
Hainan	—	116.1	124.5
Sichuan	108.0	112.1	110.1
Guizhou	106.8	103.4	99.1
Yunnan	106.2	107.3	108.5
Tibet	101.3	103.6	100.7
Shaanxi	109.2	110.3	123.1
Gansu	106.3	108.4	108.6
Qinghai	106.2	104.6	107.1
Ningxia	106.2	109.7	107.4
Xinjiang	106.1	104.1	102.0

SOURCES: 1982—China, Population Census Office under the State Council and the Department of Population Statistics of the State Statistical Bureau, *The 1982 Population Census of China (Major Figures)* (Hong Kong: Economic Information Agency, 1982); 1989—China, State Statistical Bureau, *10 Percent Sampling Tabulation on the 1990 Population Census of the People's Republic of China* (Beijing: China Statistics Press, 1991); 1995 sex ratio at birth for China is from China, State Statistical Bureau, *China Population Statistical Yearbook, 1996* (Beijing: China Statistics Press, 1996); and regional figures are from the 1995 1 Percent Population Sample Survey in China, State Statistical Bureau, *China Population Statistical Yearbook*, 1997 (Beijing: China Statistics Press, 1997), Table 2-32.

TABLE 2. Missing Females in China's Birth Population, 1985–95.

Year	Sex Ratio at Birth	Numbers of Births	Males	Females	Expected Females	Missing Females	Missing Females (%)
1985	111.4	22,020,000	11,600,000	10,420,000	11,047,000	627,619	6.0
1986	112.3	23,840,000	12,610,000	11,230,000	12,009,524	779,524	6.9
1987	111.0	25,220,000	13,270,000	11,950,000	12,638,095	688,095	5.8
1988	108.1	24,570,000	12,760,000	11,810,000	12,152,381	342,381	2.9
1989	113.9	24,070,000	12,820,000	11,250,000	12,209,524	959,524	8.5
1990	114.7	23,910,000	12,770,000	11,140,000	12,161,905	1,021,905	9.2
1991	116.1	22,580,000	12,130,000	10,450,000	11,552,381	1,102,381	10.5
1992	119.0	21,190,000	11,510,000	9,680,000	10,961,905	1,281,905	13.2
1993	121.0	21,260,000	11,640,000	9,620,000	11,085,714	1,465,714	15.2
1994	121.0	21,040,000	11,520,000	9,520,000	10,971,429	1,451,429	15.2
1995	115.6	20,630,000	11,060,000	9,570,000	10,533,333	963,333	10.1
1985–95	114.7	250,330,000	133,690,000	116,640,000	127,323,810	10,683,810	9.2

SOURCES: 1985–90 sex ratios at birth are from Gu Baochang and Krishna Roy, "Sex Ratio at Birth in China, with Reference to Other Areas in Asia: What we Know," *Asian-Pacific Population Journal*, Vol. 10, No. 3 (September 1995), p. 20; 1991–94 sex ratios at birth are from William Lavely, "Unintended Consequences of China's Birth Planning Policy," University of Washington, July 14, 1997; and 1985–95 birth totals and 1995 sex ratios at birth are from China, State Statistical Bureau, *China Population Statistical Yearbook, 1996* (Beijing: China Statistics Press, 1996), p. 372.

TABLE 3. Missing Females among China's Birth Population by Province, 1989 (a 10 percent sample of the population).

Region	Males	Females	Sex Ratio	Expected Females	Missing Females	Contribution to Missing Females (%)	Missing Females (%)
China	**1,299,880**	**1,168,165**	**111.28**	**1,238,032**	**69,867**	**100.0**	**6.0**
Beijing	8,003	7,469	107.15	7,622	153	0.2	2.0
Tianjin	7,682	6,959	110.39	7,316	357	0.5	5.1
Hebei	69,616	62,756	110.93	66,300	3,544	5.1	5.6
Shanxi	34,039	30,904	110.14	32,417	1,513	2.2	4.9
Inner Mongolia	21,878	20,156	108.54	20,836	680	1.0	3.4
Liaoning	33,261	30,104	110.49	31,678	1,574	2.3	5.2
Jilin	25,355	23,524	107.78	24,147	623	0.9	2.6
Heilongjiang	33,055	30,797	107.33	31,480	683	1.0	2.2
Shanghai	8,224	7,897	104.14	7,832	−65	−0.1	−0.8
Jiangsu	74,182	65,185	113.80	70,648	5,463	7.8	8.4
Zhejiang	33,623	28,805	116.73	32,023	3,218	4.6	11.2
Anhui	73,090	65,642	111.35	69,612	3,970	5.7	6.0
Fujian	38,353	34,905	109.88	36,527	1,622	2.3	4.6

Continued

TABLE 3. Missing Females among China's Birth Population by Province, 1989 (a 10 percent sample of the population) (continued)

Region	Males	Females	Sex Ratio	Expected Females	Missing Females	Contribution to Missing Females (%)	Missing Females (%)
Jiangxi	48,024	43,516	110.36	45,737	2,221	3.2	5.1
Shandong	90,205	78,444	114.99	85,907	7,463	10.7	9.5
Henan	121,502	104,553	116.21	115,715	11,162	16.0	10.7
Hubei	70,131	64,019	109.55	66,793	2,774	4.0	4.3
Hunan	76,482	69,490	110.06	72,839	3,349	4.8	4.8
Guangdong	76,047	68,352	111.26	72,427	4,075	5.8	6.0
Guangxi	52,194	44,447	117.43	49,709	5,262	7.5	11.8
Hainan	8,608	7,417	116.06	8,198	781	1.1	10.5
Sichuan	102,953	91,817	112.13	98,052	6,235	8.9	6.8
Guizhou	40,482	39,139	103.43	38,554	−585	−0.8	−1.5
Yunnan	45,194	42,126	107.28	43,041	915	1.3	2.2
Tibet	3,478	3,356	103.64	3,313	−43	−0.1	−1.3
Shaanxi	42,429	38,484	110.25	40,408	1,924	2.8	5.0
Gansu	29,461	27,183	108.38	28,058	875	1.3	3.2
Qinghai	5,337	5,102	104.61	5,083	−19	0.0	−0.4
Ningxia	6,174	5,628	109.70	5,880	252	0.4	4.5
Xinjiang	20,818	19,989	104.15	19,827	−162	−0.2	−0.8

SOURCE: Figures are based on the 10 percent Fourth National Population Census on July 1, 1990—China, State Statistical Bureau, *China Population Statistical Yearbook, 1991* (Beijing: China Statistics Press, 1991).

TABLE 4. Missing Females among China's Birth Population by Province, 1995 (a 1.04 percent sample of the population).

Region	Males	Females	Sex Ratio	Expected Females	Missing Females	Contribution to Missing Females (%)	Missing Females (%)
China	**95,144**	**82,293**	**115.62**	**90,616**	**8,323**	**100.0**	**10.1**
Beijing	562	459	122.44	535	76	0.9	16.6
Tianjin	496	449	110.47	472	23	0.3	5.2
Hebei	4,249	3,687	115.24	4,047	360	4.3	9.8
Shanxi	2,760	2,464	112.01	2,629	165	2.0	6.7
Inner Mongolia	1,917	1,743	109.98	1,826	83	1.0	4.7
Liaoning	2,720	2,441	111.43	2,590	149	1.8	6.1
Jilin	1,794	1,637	109.59	1,709	72	0.9	4.4
Heilongjiang	2,627	2,389	109.96	2,502	113	1.4	4.7
Shanghai	455	434	104.84	433	−1	0.0	−0.2

Continued

TABLE 4. (continued)

Region	Males	Females	Sex Ratio	Expected Females	Missing Females	Contribution to Missing Females (%)	Missing Females (%)
Jiangsu	4,832	3,915	123.42	4,602	687	8.3	17.5
Zhejiang	3,003	2,607	115.19	2,860	253	3.0	9.7
Anhui	5,116	4,396	116.38	4,872	476	5.7	10.8
Fujian	2,485	2,032	122.29	2,367	335	4.0	16.5
Jiangxi	4,200	3,641	115.35	4,000	359	4.3	9.9
Shandong	4,342	3,655	118.80	4,135	480	5.8	13.1
Henan	6,230	4,918	126.68	5,933	1,015	12.2	20.6
Hubei	5,091	3,907	130.30	4,848	941	11.3	24.1
Hunan	4,123	3,542	116.40	3,927	385	4.6	10.9
Guangdong	7,033	5,714	123.08	6,698	984	11.8	17.2
Guangxi	3,998	3,356	119.13	3,808	452	5.4	13.5
Hainan	768	617	124.47	731	114	1.4	18.5
Sichuan	9,881	8,979	110.05	9,411	432	5.2	4.8
Guizhou	3,901	3,938	99.06	3,715	−223	−2.7	−5.7
Yunnan	4,192	3,864	108.49	3,992	128	1.5	3.3
Tibet	293	291	100.69	279	−12	−0.1	−4.1
Shaanxi	2,943	2,391	123.09	2,803	412	4.9	17.2
Gansu	2,565	2,362	108.59	2,443	81	1.0	3.4
Qinghai	525	490	107.14	500	10	0.1	2.0
Ningxia	521	485	107.42	496	11	0.1	2.3
Xinjiang	1,521	1,491	102.01	1,449	−42	−0.5	−2.8

SOURCE: Figures are based on the 1 Percent Population Sample Survey of 1995. China, State Statistical Bureau, *China Population Statistical Yearbook, 1997* (Beijing: China Statistics Press, 1997), p. 183, Table 2-32. Births are from October 1, 1994 to September 30, 1995.

The China Population Information and Research Center, through its examination of the 1990 census, found that there was also a difference in the sex ratio at birth according to nationality. Differences in culture and religious practices may affect attitudes toward gender and practices of offspring sex selection. The Han nationality, which comprises more than 90 percent of the Chinese population, recorded a high average birth sex ratio of 111.71. Minority nationalities, on the other hand, exhibited a sex ratio at birth of 107.5, no doubt due to the more lenient family planning quotas for minorities. (For example, Inner Mongolians may have three children, Uighurs five, and Tibetans an unlimited number.) Within these nationalities, the sex ratio at birth also varies, with some groups exhibiting stronger son preference through higher sex ratios; among the eighteen nationalities with more than 1 million people, Dong, Hani, Man, and Xhuang have birth sex ratios above 110.[17]

Explaining the Rising Sex Ratios

Most researchers do not agree on the extent of sex selection in China. Despite recent claims of large numbers of females missing from the population, some demographers suggest that undercounting of females in general and a failure to count adopted females in particular explains the statistical discrepancy. Other social scientists, meanwhile, trace what they view as an accurate report of skewed ratios to sex-selective abortion and female infanticide.

Undercounting of Females

Zeng Yi, Tu Ping, Gu Baochang, Xu Yi, Li Bohua, and Li Yongping, of Beijing University's Population Institute and the China Population Information and Research Center, claim that undercounting of females is responsible for China's skewed sex ratios—that parents are more willing to report the birth of a son, regardless of his birth order and any penalties that may be inflicted on them, to produce a legal heir. According to this argument, parents will not consider it worthwhile to report a female birth and risk penalty. The parents will then "hide" the female infant from the authorities by putting her up for adoption, reporting her later as an immigrant, or simply not reporting her at all.[18] In his study of the fertility survey responses for the provinces of Hebei and Shaanxi, Wen Xingyan argued that because most births occurred outside of a hospital, unassisted by doctors, nurses, or midwives, it would be easy to hide births of females.[19]

Gu and Xu offer a variation on the theme of underreporting: Not only will parents withhold the truth from officials, but officials will also mislead local political leaders.[20] There is ample opportunity for parents to hide births from family planning cadres, and for the cadres to hide them from other family planning officials. But do they? The findings of Zeng and his colleagues are representative of the official Chinese position on the problem of China's missing females: Their calculations of 1989 census data led them to conclude that errors in birth statistics (i.e., under-reporting of females) account for 50–75 percent of the abnormal sex ratio at birth.[21]

As Gu and Xu note, however, statistical factors cannot explain the missing females in all regions and areas of the country. Data from Zhejiang and Shandong Provinces show that underreporting of infants occurs equally for both male and female births, and that it occurs with greater frequency in reports by local leaders than in reports by parents. Although local leaders suggest that underreporting of male births actually exceeds that of female births, Gu and Xu dispute this claim. Parents are more likely to underreport the birth of a female "for fear of having an 'oviduct ligation' committed on women who have only girls."[22] Against claims that underreporting does not occur, Zeng and his coauthors use a reverse survival method to estimate that underreporting of births does occur for 2.26 percent of male births and 5.94 percent of female births.[23] Western demographers Ansley Coale and Judith Banister disagree, however, stating that figures from the 1990 census point to an equal under-counting of males and females in the 1982 census.[24] Undercounting in the 1990 and 1995 censuses, however, has not yet been examined in a comprehensive manner. There may have been some undercounting of female births between 1985 and 1989, but statistics appear to be accurate for births after 1990.

It should also be noted that parents' underreporting of females born is accompanied by local officials' overreporting of females born. William Lavely, comparing micro data from the 1990 Chinese census with published tabulations, found credible evidence of significant overreporting of infant females in one locale.[25] If this case is indicative of a national trend, then the underreporting of female infants by families may in some cases be exceeded by official overreporting of female infants. For all of these reasons, we argue that underreporting cannot account in large part for the skewness, and the increase in skewness, of China's sex ratios.

Adoption

Sten Johansson and Ola Nygren estimate that half of the missing females in China in the 1980s were adopted children and thus were not reported as live births by their mothers.[26] This conclusion parallels that of Sten Johansson, Zhao Xuan, and Ola Nygren, who calculate that the number of children adopted in 1987 was approximately 500,000, with 80 percent of those adoptees being female.[27] This would account for more than half of the missing girl births that year. In their study of infants abandoned between 1995 and 1996, Kay Johnson, Huang Banghan, and Wang Liyao find that gender, birth order, and gender composition of siblings were the key determinants in abandonment. Of the 237 abandoned infants in their study, 90 percent were female, 87 percent had no brothers, and 95 percent were second, third, or fourth daughters.[28] Thus the typical profile of an abandoned child is a healthy newborn girl who has one or more older sisters and no brothers. She is abandoned because her birthparents already have daughters and want a son. These birth parents routinely say they did not want to abandon the child but that given their desire for a son, birth planning policies left them "no choice."[29]

This matter is difficult to clarify, however. The fertility surveys did ask questions about adopted children but did not ask the date of adoption; thus demographers have not been able to conclude whether some of these adoptions correspond to underreported births. As one demographer notes, more female than male babies were adopted in the provinces of Hebei and Shaanxi (sex ratios of adopted children were 38.9 and 73.6, respectively); the number of adopted children, however, was small (75 for Hebei and 158 for Shaanxi), suggesting that even adopted children are underreported or that adopted children cannot account for the numbers of missing girls in these, or perhaps other, provinces.[30] Coale and Banister agree that child adoption cannot explain the missing females in census data because "they are members of the adopting household and presumably would be listed in the household to qualify for benefits."[31]

Sex-Selective Abortion and Infanticide

Underreporting and adoption are no doubt occurring in China, but the steady increase in sex ratios since 1980 seems to imply that something more is going on. As Coale and Banister note, "Foreign demographers had not widely accepted conjectures that the sex ratio at birth increased in the 1980s because of increased recourse to sex-selective abortion. It was believed that the technical means for identifying the sex of the fetus were not available, except perhaps in major cities. In 1992, however, the Chinese government and Chinese scholars revealed previously unreported evidence that adequate technology may be widely available, and that the sex ratio at birth has risen."[32] China began importing ultrasound machines in the late 1970s and imported them on a massive scale in the 1980s, when it also started to manufacture its own machines, according to Chinese demographers.[33] Moreover, by the end of 1991, 2,227 county-level family planning facilities had been established; in addition, there were 29,000 planning clinics in townships and towns, with an average of 12 ultrasound machines per county in some areas. Gu and Xu estimated that in 1994 there were more than 100,000 ultrasound machines throughout China. If only a small number of facilities use these to determine the gender of a fetus—despite the fact that the use of ultrasound to determine fetal sex, and sex-selective abortion itself, are both illegal in China—the effect could be huge.[34]

Judging from data collected for seven Chinese provinces, cities, townships, and counties in 1989, ultrasound machines are already having a huge impact on the population. Sex ratios for Shandong, Henan, Guangdong, Jiangsu, Fujian, Jiangxi, and Shanxi climbed to a range from 109.40 to 115.60.[35] In 1993 Nicholas Kristof reported that the sex ratio at birth in China rose to 118.5 in 1992, a statistic he claims is based on an official survey of 385,000 births that the government kept secret.[36] While in Xiamen, China, Kristof recorded villagers' accounts of sex-selective abortion: "'Last year we had only one girl born in the village—everybody else had boys,' villager Y.H. Chen said in a tone of awe, as the others nodded agreement." He explained that "for a bribe of $35 to $50, a doctor will tell whether a woman is pregnant with a boy or a girl. Then, if it's a girl, 'you get an abortion.'" In fact, Kristof discovered that the gift of a carton of cigarettes would encourage a physician to say whether a fetus is male or female.[37]

Xu Song points to hospital surveys to estimate the effects of ultrasound technology on the sex ratio. Asserting that a hospital survey precludes underreporting, abandonment, or infanticide, Xu notes that the Huaxi Medical Hospital found a birth sex ratio across twenty-nine provinces and 945 hospitals of 108.0 in 1986–87, rising to 109.7 in 1991.[38] Of course, it could be argued that women who knew through ultrasound they were carrying daughters declined to give birth in hospitals so that underreporting, abandonment, or infanticide could take place away from the scrutiny of officials. But that would not easily explain the *rise* in the birth sex ratio over the five-year period that Xu studied.

Although the number of ultrasound machines and abortions performed each year in China suggests that sex selection through testing and abortion is occurring, hard data are difficult to obtain. According to Gu and Xu, "The areas with high birth ratios are also areas with the greatest popularity of ultra-sound equipment."[39] Banister estimates that between the mid-1980s and 1990, 1.5 million female fetuses were selectively aborted in China.[40] This figure is low when compared with the numbers of missing females among the birth population in any given year in the 1980s.

In addition to sex-selective abortion, infanticide—active or passive—contributes to China's high sex ratios. The China Population and Information Research Center acknowledges that drowning is still a problem, despite being strictly forbidden by law. Abandonment also contributes to the high sex ratios for male infants, because the victims are primarily female. Many abandoned female infants are placed in orphanages, but because of the poor care received in these "dying rooms," few survive.

Although female infanticide received little attention in the first three decades following the 1949 communist revolution, it gained recognition again in 1982 when newspapers throughout China published articles informing the public of the practice.[41] In 1983 China's Central Committee's Propaganda Department called for "the protection of infant girls, and also of women who had given birth to daughters, from social ostracism and physical cruelty at the hands of husbands, parents-in-law, or other kinfolk."[42] The practice of infanticide is not always confined to the female gender: Reports of doctors killing third children or any infant born without permission from the mother's work unit are common.[43] Women with unauthorized pregnancies often have little choice but to undergo an abortion, even when the pregnancy is well advanced. When the fetuses survive a late abortion, physicians or health-care workers will smother and kill the babies to avoid punishment of "refusing to carry out family-planning policy."[44] The risk of punishment for not killing the child can be much greater than the risk of punishment for killing it. Laws regarding female infanticide generally vary from province to province and are often left to the discretion of the working unit of those accused of the crime. As Li Xiaorong notes, the government has generally failed to carry out punishment for female infanticide.[45]

Bare Branches of High-Sex-Ratio Societies: Theory and Cases

Artificially high sex ratios pose potentially grave problems for society.[46] They also create vexing policy dilemmas for governments. James Boone explains, "Reproductive strategies have an important effect on the development of state political organization, and . . . there is a fundamental contradiction between individual (or familial) reproductive interests and the social reproduction of the state political structure."[47] It is to this contradiction that we now turn.

The sex ratios in the world's two most populous countries, China and India, are increasing as sex-selective practices continue to produce unprecedented numbers of surplus males. A confluence of factors—including female infanticide, sex-selective abortion, higher female mortality in youth, and a rise in female suicide rates—have helped to create this outcome. These variables are contributing to a larger syndrome of exaggerated gender inequality in both countries.

In this chapter, we outline a theory of surplus young adult male behavior that synthesizes theoretical insights and empirical findings from a variety of disciplines. In keeping with the Chinese vernacular of the nineteenth century, we refer to surplus young adult males as "bare branches," or *guang gun-er*. Bare branches are males who will never have families because they cannot find spouses.[48] As one contemporary Chinese citizen put it: "This is a metaphor, which indicates that the unmarried men have nothing attached, just like bare branches. Bare branches give people an impression of bleakness and loneliness. It is quite similar to the lives of the unmarried men. They have no warm families, which can give them support and comfort; they have no children, who can take care of them when they become old."[49]

Characteristics of Bare Branches

In high-sex-ratio societies, surplus males share several characteristics. First, they belong predominantly to the lowest socioeconomic class. Unlike men of higher standing, surplus males have little or no bargaining power in the marriage market and thus frequently end up alone. The evidence for this assertion is ample: Beginning with nonhuman primate studies and moving up the evolutionary chain to humans, when females are scarce, the only reproductive failures are low-status males.[50] As noted in chapter 1, the upward movement of women who marry—hypergyny—results because men with greater status and wealth are better able to attract mates. Indeed the phrase "bachelor herd," originating in the study of mammals, refers to low-status males who lack access to females and who congregate at the outer edges of society waiting for their chance to overthrow the group's alpha male.[51] As Martin Daly and Margo Wilson put it, "Top males keep other males down—underdeveloped, out of circulation, out of the breeding population. In song birds, for example, there are always 'floater' males ready to take the place of any territory holder that should disappear. In many monkey species there are solitary males and all-male groups ever eager to break into the mixed-sex groups in which breeding occurs."[52]

Second, in economies with market features, bare branches are more likely to be underemployed or unemployed. They are also more likely to be chosen for low-status jobs that are dangerous, menial, labor intensive, or seasonal.[53] A 1990 Chinese survey indicates that of the 94 percent of Chinese unmarried adults who were male, 73.8 percent had failed to graduate from high school.[54]

In nonmarket economies, bare branches generally do not have land or other resources that would increase their chances of marrying. For this reason, second, third, and higher birth-order sons in primogeniture societies are likely to become bare branches. Even in nonprimogeniture societies, such as China's, eldest sons are more likely to have access to the resources needed to attract wives. Like those at the bottom of the socioeconomic ladder, higher birth-order sons of the upper classes frequently engage in risky ventures to acquire the resources and status they lack. The most common route is through military service, a path also taken by low-status bare branches. According to Boone, "Many males at the lower end of the scale lead lives of enforced celibacy in what for them is a seller's market and are furthermore engaged in production, construction, and military occupations that tend to raise their mortality rates through occupational hazards and unhealthful conditions. Their poor socio-economics [*sic*] position and reproductive prospects make them perennial aspirants in large-scale expansionist and insurgent military campaigns through which they might hope to achieve higher positions."[55]

Third, bare branches are typically transients with few ties to the communities in which they look for work. Because they move repeatedly to find jobs, they possess a high degree of anonymity.[56] This anonymity and lack of community attachment combine to loosen the psychological constraints of bare branches against engaging in criminal behavior. Also, they have a lower probability of being identified or apprehended in the event they do commit a crime. Two criminologists explain this dynamic in modern China:

[China's] stable social order before economic reform was built upon the interaction of three factors: a strict restriction on population movements; efficient informal control mechanisms, including the resident committee, where one lives (the *danwei*), where one works, and the school where one studies; and an ideological and moral consensus in conjunction with the three mechanisms. However, the massive movement of [the] transient population has directly disrupted this arrangement. Criminal opportunities have greatly increased due to the disturbance of the neighborhoods by the introduction of temporary workers. Eighty million people, who are on the move, have left their villages, work units, and communities, where they are deeply attached, and become free persons who are subject to no supervision in a new environment. Ideological and moral norms have seriously declined in that they were built upon collective brainwashing and reinforced education, which are difficult to continue among mobile population[s]. All these changes have drastically undercut the control mechanisms that functioned effectively in the past. As the external control weakened, increase in crime became inevitable.[57]

Fourth, bare branches live and socialize with other bare branches, creating distinctive bachelor subcultures.[58] Predictably, the rest of the community treats them as social outcasts. Historically, James Rooney argues, "the continuous development of a distinctive single man's culture was associated with increasing differentiation, isolation, and opposition from the stable, family-oriented community. The unattached men could not be included in the status groups of the resident community because of the differences of values stemming from the former's lack of structured responsibility, particularly as expressed in the lack of restraint in recreation, pursuit of immediate pleasure, and lack of concern for the future."[59]

These four features are classic hallmarks of surplus male behavior in high-sex-ratio societies. Interestingly, these features may also be found among the lowest-status males in other kinds of communities, including: frontier outposts,[60] male labor colonies,[61] and itinerant male "societies" in which females never amount to more than 3–5 percent of the population.[62]

In sum, most bare branches in high-sex-ratio societies historically did not choose their bachelorhood. Some, though, did make this choice, among them, men in celibate religious orders and many of China's eunuchs. The status of these men was higher—much higher in some cases—than that of the involuntary bachelor.

Behavioral Tendencies of Bare Branches
Typically, bare branches are more likely than other males to turn to vice and violence.[63] Unable to achieve satisfaction in socially approved ways, they spend their meager wages on gambling, alcohol, drugs, and prostitutes in short (but intense) sprees.[64] The disorder created during these sprees predictably has a negative impact on society, but it is the violence that surplus males engage in during these episodes that arguably has the greatest negative effect. Consider the following [four] facts.

First, males are more violent than females. One of the few social science verities, confirmed through experiments and anthropological observation over the last 100 years, is that males are more aggressive than females. This is also one of the few sex differences that has a firm biological basis. In addition, male sex hormone levels can be manipulated to increase or decrease the intensity of male aggression.[65] Sex differences in aggression appear early in life, arguably before socialization.

Although in some instances females may be as aggressive as males (e.g., when their offspring are threatened), males generally inflict more serious injuries. Indeed males are responsible for the vast majority of violent deaths.[66] As Richard Wrangham and Dale Peterson note, "Male criminals specialize in violent crime. In the U.S., for example, a man is about nine times as likely as a woman to commit murder, seventy-eight times as likely to commit forcible rape, ten times as likely to commit armed robbery, and almost six and a half times as likely to commit aggravated assault. Altogether, American men are almost eight times as likely as women to commit violent crime."[67]

Second, males engage more often than females in other types of antisocial behavior. For example, in the American case,

> Men are nearly thirteen and a half times as likely to commit fraud, thirteen times as likely to be arrested for carrying or possessing a weapon, more than ten times as likely to burgle, nine times as likely to steal a car, eight and a half times as likely to find themselves collared for drunkenness, and well over eight times as likely to be pinched for vagrancy. They are eight times as likely to vandalize, nearly seven and a half times as likely to fence stolen property, seven times as likely to commit arson, six and a half times as likely to be arrested for gambling offenses, six and a half times as likely to be stopped for drunk driving, and some five and a half times as likely to be hauled in for sex offenses (excluding prostitution and forcible rape). And they are five times as likely to be taken in for drug abuse offenses, four and a half times as likely for offenses against children and the family, over twice as likely for larceny, almost twice as likely for forgery or counterfeiting, and one and a half times as likely for embezzlement.[68]

In addition, younger males exhibit more antisocial behavior than older males. The ages of greatest commission of violence are 15 to 35, with violent criminal behavior (indeed all criminal behavior) peaking in late adolescence and early adulthood, then declining to a low plateau around age 40.[69] Younger males are also responsible for the vast majority of crimes that result in violent death.[70] In China, perhaps more than 80 percent of incarcerated males in the 1990s were younger than 30.[71] Young men in all societies monopolize violence and violent crime.[72] The higher potential of young males to commit violent acts exists at both the individual and collective levels. In their analyses of interstate and intrastate episodes of collective aggression since the 1960s, Christian Mesquida and Neil Wiener write, "[There is] a consistent correlation between the ratio of males 15 to 29 years of age per 100 males 30 years of age and older, and the level of coalitional aggression as measured by the number of reported conflict-related deaths."[73]

Third, unmarried males commit more violence than married males.[74] As David Courtwright notes, "It is when young men cannot or do not marry that socially disruptive behavior is intensified."[75] According to Robert Wright,

> Womanless men . . . compete with special ferocity. An unmarried man between twenty-four and thirty-five years of age is about three times as likely to murder another male as is a married man the same age. Some of this difference no doubt reflects the kinds of men that do and don't get married to begin with, but . . . a good part of the difference may lie in "the pacifying effect" of marriage. Murder isn't the only thing an "unpacified" man is more likely to do. He is also more likely to incur various risks—committing robbery, for example—to gain the resources that may attract women. He is more likely to rape. Abuse of drugs and alcohol . . . compound the problem by further diminishing his chances of ever earning enough money to attract women by legitimate means.[76]

Allan Mazur and Joel Michalek have determined that T (serum testosterone) levels in men who marry drop relative to men who are single: "Changing T levels may explain the low criminality found among married men. . . . Married men, living stably with their wives, are less prone to crime than unmarried men. Married men are less likely than single men of the same age to kill an unrelated male."[77] According to Mazur and Alan Booth, T has been found to be significantly related to antisocial behavior, including criminal activity and alcohol and substance abuse. When T falls, so does the propensity to engage in this kind of behavior.[78]

Psychologist Satoshi Kanazawa argues that men's psychology is attuned to marriage as a cue to cease criminal behavior: "Criminologists have known that one of the strongest predictors of desistance from criminal careers is a good marriage. Criminals who get married, and especially those who maintain strong marital bonds to their wives, subsequently stop committing crime, whereas criminals at the same age who remain unmarried tend to continue their criminal careers."[79]

Mazur and Michalek suggest some of the dynamics that underlie this tendency:

Single men spend more time in male company than do married men, and they are more likely than married men to encounter confrontations and challenges. Lacking the social support of a wife, they are more likely to face situations where they must protect their social prestige in competitive encounters with other males. These are precisely the kinds of situations in which T elevates. The marriage ceremony is the culmination of a more gradual period of courtship and engagement, in which a man accepts the support and consortship of his partner, removing himself from competition with other men for sexual partners. As a result, according to the reciprocal model, his T declines.[80]

Thus, according to the analyses of Mazur and his colleagues, the larger the number of men who are unable to marry, the higher their circulating T, and the greater amount of violent and antisocial behavior they will exhibit. Kanazawa concurs: "The sudden drop in testosterone after their marriage and the birth of their children might provide the biochemical reason why men's psychological mechanism to commit crime . . . 'turns off' when they get married and become fathers and simultaneously why the same mechanism does not 'turn off' when the men do not get married."[81] As George Gilder puts it, "Individual life assumes a higher value within the monogamous marriage than it does in the male group."[82] This is not a new phenomenon: The scriptural *Ben Sira* in Jewish tradition, for example, declares, "Without a hedge, the vineyard is laid waste, and without a wife, a man is a hopeless wanderer. Who trusts an armed band of vagabonds?"[83]

Fourth, low-status males commit more violence than high-status males. Again, this empirical finding has found wide confirmation in human societies.[84] As Theodore Kemper notes, "A careful examination of the social science literature supports the view that the lower class is physically more aggressive and more violent in its social relations than the middle class, whether one looks at child rearing, adolescent and young adult peer groups, street encounters, domestic relations, conflict resolution, or crime."[85] In a study by Wilson and Daly, unemployed males, when compared with employed males, were more than four times as likely to commit homicide.[86] Courtwright finds the correlation between unemployment and violent death to be 0.73, and the correlation with homicide to be 0.65; both are statistically significant.[87] In addition, Mazur and Booth cite a study in which unemployed males had the highest T levels among males categorized according to occupation.[88]

Endnotes

[1] Mao reasoned that "every mouth comes with two hands." Cited in Lisa B. Gregory, "Examining the Economic Component of China's One-Child Family Policy under International Law," *Journal of Chinese Law*, Vol. 6, No. 1 (Spring 1992), p. 48. Another popular slogan following the 1949 revolution was, "The more babies the more glorious are their mothers." Cited in Li Xiaorong, "License to Coerce: Violence against Women, State Responsibility, and Legal Failures in China's Family-Planning Program," *Yale Journal of Law and Feminism*, Vol. 8, No. 1 (Summer 1996), p. 148.

[2] Li, "License to Coerce," p. 148.

[3] Lisa B. Gregory, "Examining the Economic Component of China's One-Child Family Policy under International Law: Your Money or Your Life," *Journal of Chinese Law*, Vol. 6, No. 1 (Spring 1992), pp. 50–51.

[4] Article 18 of the 2002 Population and Family Planning Law declares: "The state shall maintain its current fertility policy encouraging late marriage and child bearing and advocating one child per couple; arrangements for a second child, if requested, being subject to law and regulation. Specific measures shall be enacted by the People's Congress or its standing committee in each province, autonomous region, and municipality. Ethnic minorities shall also practice family planning. Population and Family Planning Law of the People's Republic of China, http://www.unescap.org/pop/database/law china/chrecord052.htm.

[5] Li, "License to Coerce," p. 154.

[6] Sulamith Heins Potter, "Birth Planning in Rural China: A Cultural Account," in Nancy Scheper-Hughes, ed., *Child Survival: Anthropological Perspectives on the Treatment and Maltreatment of Children* (Dordrecht, Netherlands: D. Reidel, 1987), pp. 41–42.

[7] Nicholas D. Kristof and Sheryl WuDunn provide the following example of a man who failed to space his children four years apart. In 1983, following the birth of a second child three years after his first child was born, a grade school teacher was fined $2,456 by the government. This fine was seventeen times the teacher's annual salary at the time. For the next ten years, 80 percent of the teacher's salary was deducted to pay the fine. For similar stories, see Kristof and WuDunn, *China Wakes: The Struggle for the Soul of a Rising Power* (New York: Vintage, 1994), pp. 237–239.

[8] Li, "License to Coerce," pp. 158–159.

[9] For a discussion of the increase in abortion rates, sterilizations, and birth control, see H. Yuan Tien, Zhang Tianlu, Ping Yu, Li Jingneng, and Liang Zhongtang, "China's Demographic Dilemmas," *Population Bulletin*, Vol. 47, No. 1 (June 1992), p. 12. The central government's resolutions regarding the one-child policy outline the following: Couples must apply for a birth permit before trying to conceive; following the birth of the permitted number of children, at least one spouse has to use contraception and women are required to use an intrauterine device; and any unauthorized pregnancies, especially after the birth of the permitted number

of children, must be terminated, or, if the birth occurs, one spouse must be sterilized. See Li, "License to Coerce," pp. 152–53.

[10]   Article 21 of the 2002 Marriage Law states that "infant drowning, deserting and any other acts causing serious harm to infants and infanticide shall be prohibited." Marriage Law of the People's Republic of China, http://www.fmprc.gov.cn/eng/28840.html. Population and Family Planning Law of the People's Republic of China, *http://www.unescap.org/pop/database/law china/ch* record052. htm.

[11]   Li, "License to Coerce," pp. 145–191.

[12]   See ibid., p. 173. In their research in rural China, Susan Greenhalgh and Li Jiali also found that because "village culture continued to see women and girls as lesser beings, girls were restricted from engaging in some crucial agricultural activities, making sons prized members of the family labor force." See Greenhalgh and Li, "Engendering Reproductive Practice in Peasant China: The Political Roots of the Rising Sex Ratios at Birth," Working Paper No. 57 (Beijing: Population Council Research Division, 1993), p. 15.

[13]   H. Yuan Tien, *China's Strategic Demographic Initiative* (New York: Praeger, 1991), p. 202.

[14]   Potter, "Birth Planning in Rural China," p. 35.

[15]   Ibid.

[16]   Gu Baochang and Xu Yi, "A Comprehensive Discussion of the Birth Gender Ratio in China," *Chinese Journal of Population Science,* Vol. 6, No. 4 (1994), p. 423.

[17]   Ibid.

[18]   Zeng Yi, Tu Ping, Gu Baochang, Xu Yi, Li Bohua, and Li Yongping, "Causes and Implications of the Recent Increase in the Reported Sex Ratio at Birth in China," *Population and Development Review,* Vol. 19, No. 2 (June 1993), p. 290.

[19]   Wen Xingyan, "Effect of Son Preference and Population Policy on Sex Ratios at Birth in Two Provinces of China," *Journal of Biosocial Science,* Vol. 25, No. 4 (October 1993), p. 518.

[20]   Gu and Xu, "A Comprehensive Discussion of the Birth Gender Ratio in China," p. 424.

[21]   The findings of the team from Beijing University and the China Population Information and Research Center were first presented at the Fourth Population Census Beijing International Conference, October 19–23, 1992, and later published as Zeng Yi, Gu Baochang, Tu Ping, Xu Yi, Li Bohua, and Li Yongping, "Analyses on the Origins and Consequences of the Increase in China's Gender Ratio at Birth," *Population and Economy,* Vol. 1 (1993). Another article presenting their findings was published in *Population and Development Review* under the title "Causes and Implications of the Recent Increase in the Reported Sex Ratio at Birth in China," Vol. 19, No. 2 (June 1993), pp. 283–301. It was also published in the *Economist* as "The Lost Girls," September 18, 1993, pp. 38–41. As Gu and Xu note, the Chinese researchers sought to correct the biases in international opinion regarding the causes of the increasing birth sex ratio. See Gu and Xu, "A Comprehensive Discussion of the Birth Gender Ratio in China," p. 429. This article represents the first Chinese attempt to address the problem of birth sex ratios to a Western audience.

[22]   Gu and Xu, "A Comprehensive Discussion of the Birth Gender Ratio in China," p. 424.

[23]   Zeng et al., "Causes and Implications of the Recent Increase in the Reported Sex Ratio at Birth in China," p. 285.

24   Ansley J. Coale and Judith Banister, "Five Decades of Missing Females in China," *Demography*, Vol. 31, No. 3 (August 1994), p. 476.

25   William Lavely, communication with Valerie Hudson, September 26, 2000.

26   Sten Johansson and Ola Nygren, "The Missing Girls of China: A New Demographic Account," *Population and Development Review*, Vol. 17, No. 1 (March 1991), pp. 35–51.

27   Sten Johansson, Zhao Xuan, and Ola Nygren, "On Intriguing Sex Ratios among Live Births in China in the 1980s," *Journal of Official Statistics*, Vol. 7, No. 1 (1991), http://www.jos.nu/Articles/abstract.asp?article=7125.

28   Kay Johnson, Huang Banghan, and Wang Liyao, "Infant Abandonment and Adoption in China," *Population and Development Review*, Vol. 24, No. 3 (September 1998), pp. 469–481, at p. 475.

29   Ibid., p. 477.

30   Wen, "Effect of Son Preference and Population Policy on Sex Ratios," p. 51.

31   Coale and Banister, "Five Decades of Missing Females in China," p. 475.

32   Ibid.

33   Gu and Xu, "A Comprehensive Discussion of the Birth Gender Ratio in China," p. 425.

34   Ibid.

35   Ibid., p. 427. In the first few years of the one-child policy, abortion rates also soared. In 1978, 5,391,000 abortions were performed, but that number increased to 12,412,000 by 1982. The number of abortions throughout the 1980s remained fairly constant, averaging 11,010,000 abortions per year. By 1989, 632 abortions were being performed for every 1,000 live births in China, ranging from a low of 181 for the province of Liaoning to a high of 2,022 for Shanghai.

36   Kristof, "Chinese Turn to Ultrasound," p. A4.

37   Ibid.

38   Xu, "A Quest on the Causes of Gender Imbalance in China."

39   Gu and Xu, "Comprehensive Discussion of the Birth Gender Ratio in China," p. 426.

40   Quoted in Rick Weiss, "Anti-Girl Bias Rises in Asia, Studies Show: Abortion Augmenting Infanticide, Neglect," *Washington Post*, May 11, 1996, p. A1.

41   Article titles included the following (translated into English): "Young Worker Wan Chuwen Sentenced to 13 Years in Prison for Murdering His Own Infant Daughter"; "Strictly Prohibit the Killing of Girl Babies"; "Cases of Abandoning of Girl Babies Occur Frequently in Yancheng, Jiangsu"; and "Phenomenon of Discarding Baby Girls Becomes Serious in Fujian." Cited in John S. Aird, *Slaughter of the Innocents: Coercive Birth Control in China* (Washington, D.C.: AEI Press, 1990).

42   H. Yuan Tien, "Provincial Fertility Trends and Patterns," in Elisabeth Croll, Delia Davin, and Penny Kane, eds., *China's One-Child Family Policy* (New York: St. Martin's Press, 1985), p. 131.

43   See Aird, *Slaughter of the Innocents*, pp. 91–92.

44   Li, "License to Coerce," p. 163.

45   Ibid., pp. 167–168.

[46] This volume addresses the problems of high-sex-ratio societies; a case can be made, however, that there are negative societal consequences to very low-sex-ratio societies as well.

[47] James L. Boone, "Parental Investment and Elite Family Structure in Preindustrial States: A Case Study of Late Medieval—Early Modern Portuguese Genealogies," *American Anthropologist*, Vol. 88, No. 4 (December 1986), p. 859.

[48] Elizabeth Perry, *Rebels and Revolutionaries in North China, 1845–1945* (Stanford, Calif.: Stanford University Press, 1980). *Guang* means shiny/bare/naked/bald/crazy; *gun-er* means branch/club/stick/truncheon/rascal/villain/ruffian. To this day, *guang gun-er* is slang for a bachelor, and *lao guang gun-er* is slang for an old bachelor. We are indebted to David Wright of Brigham Young University for this linguistic explication.

[49] Quoted in Ren Feng, "Bare Branches among Rural Migrant Laborers in China: Causes, Social Implications, and Policy Proposal," Foreign Affairs College, Beijing, March 1999, p. 6.

[50] See, for example, John H. Crook, "Sexual Selection, Dimorphism, and Social Organization in the Primates," in Bernard Campbell, ed., *Sexual Selection and the Descent of Man* (Chicago: Aldine de Gruyter, 1972), pp. 231–281; Irven deVore, "Male Dominance and Mating Behavior in Baboons," in Frank Ambrose Beach, ed., *Sex and Behavior* (New York: Wiley and Sons, 1965), pp. 266–289; Mildred Dickemann, "The Ecology of Mating Systems in Hypergynous Dowry Societies," *Social Science Information*, Vol. 18, No. 2 (May 1979), pp. 163–195; Mildred Dickemann, "Female Infanticide, Reproductive Strategies, and Social Stratification: A Preliminary Model," in Napoleon A. Chagnon and William Irons, eds., *Evolutionary Biology and Human Social Behavior: An Anthropological Perspective* (North Scituate, Mass.: Duxbury, 1979), pp. 321–367.

[51] See, for example, S.M. Mohnot, "Peripheralization of Weaned Male Juveniles in Presbytis entellus," in David John Chivers and J. Herbert, eds., *Recent Advances in Primatology*, Vol. 1: *Behavior* (London: Academic Press, 1978), pp. 87–91; J.K. Russell, "Exclusion of Adult Male Coatis from Social Groups: Protection from Predation," *Journal of Mammalogy*, Vol. 62, No. 1 (February 1981), pp. 206–208; and Thad Q. Bartlett, Robert W. Sussman, and James M. Cheverud, "Infant Killing in Primates: A Review of Observed Cases with Specific Reference to the Sexual Selection Hypothesis," *American Anthropologist*, Vol. 95, No. 4 (December 1993), pp. 958–990.

[52] Martin Daly and Margo Wilson, *Sex, Evolution, and Behavior: Adaptations for Reproduction* (North Scituate, Mass.: Duxbury, 1978), p. 201.

[53] See David T. Courtwright, *Violent Land: Single Men and Social Disorder from the Frontier to the Inner City* (Cambridge, Mass.: Harvard University Press, 1996).

[54] That is, they either were illiterate (17.24 percent), had received only an elementary education (23.13 percent), or had graduated only from junior high school (33.36 percent). Figures refer to 1987 and are from Zhang Ping, "Issues and Characteristics of the Unmarried Population" *Chinese Journal of Population Science*, Vol. 2, No. 1 (1990), pp. 87–97.

[55] Boone, "Parental Investment and Elite Family Structure in Preindustrial States," p. 862.

[56] See Courtwright, *Violent Land*; Joan M. Nelson, "Migrants, Urban Poverty, and Instability in Developing Nations," Occasional Papers in International Affairs No. 22 (Cambridge, Mass.: Center for International Affairs, Harvard University, September 1969); Howard M. Bahr, ed., *Disaffiliated Man: Essays and Bibliography on Skid Row, Vagrancy, and Outsiders* (Toronto: University of Toronto Press, 1970); and Gregory R. Woirol, *In the Floating Army* (Chicago:

University of Illinois Press, 1992). The mobility of low-status male laborers was also a common theme in medieval Europe.

57   Yingyi Situ and Liu Weizheng, "Transient Population, Crime, and Solution: The Chinese Experience," *International Journal of Offender Therapy and Comparative Criminology*, Vol. 40, No. 4 (December 1996), p. 297.

58   See Lionel Tiger, *Men in Groups* (London: Marion Boyars, 1984); Courtwright, *Violent Land*; John C. Burnham, *Bad Habits: Drinking, Smoking, Taking Drugs, Gambling, Sexual Misbehavior, and Swearing in American History* (New York: New York University Press, 1993); George Gilder, *Naked Nomads: Unmarried Men in America* (New York: Quadrangle, 1974); Bell I. Wiley, *The Life of Billy Yank: The Common Soldier of the Union* (Baton Rouge: Louisiana State University Press, 1978); J.S. Holliday, *The World Rushed In: The California Gold Rush Experience* (New York: Simon and Schuster, 1981); Joe B. Frantz and Julian Ernest Choate Jr., *The American Cowboy* (Norman: University of Oklahoma Press, 1960); Murray Melbin, "Night as Frontier," *American Sociological Review*, Vol. 43, No. 1 (February 1978), pp. 3–22; Murray Melbin, *Night as Frontier: Colonizing the World after Dark* (New York: Free Press, 1987); and Sanyika Shakur, *Monster: The Autobiography of an L.A. Gang Member* (New York: Atlantic Monthly Press, 1993).

59 See James F. Rooney, "Societal Forces and the Unattached Male," in Bahr, *Disaffiliated Man*, p. 18.

60   Courtwright, *Violent Land*, is arguably the definitive work on this matter. See also David Dary, *Cowboy Culture: A Saga of Five Centuries* (Lawrence: University Press of Kansas, 1989); Frantz and Choate, *The American Cowboy*; David H. Breen, *The Canadian Prairie West and the Ranching Frontier: 1874–1924* (Toronto: University of Toronto Press, 1983); Robert Wooster, *Soldiers, Sutlers, and Settlers: Garrison Life on the Texas Frontier* (College Station: Texas A&M University Press, 1987); and Ray A. Billington, *America's Frontier Culture* (College Station: Texas A&M University Press, 1977). The Argentine gaucho era is also a case in point.

61   Australia started out as one such colony; other examples include the California Gold Rush labor camps, the labor camps involved in the construction of the transcontinental railroad in the United States, and the Chinatown male labor camps of early California. See, for example, Ged Martin, ed., *The Founding of Australia: The Argument About Australia's Origins* (Sydney: Hale and Iremonger, 1978); Holliday, *The World Rushed In*; Charles Ross Parke, *Dreams to Dust: A Diary of the California Gold Rush, 1849–1850*, ed. James E. Davis (Lincoln: University of Nebraska Press, 1989); James McCague, *Moguls and Iron Men: The Story of the First Transcontinental Railroad* (New York: Harper and Row, 1964), Gunter Barth, *Bitter Strength: A History of the Chinese in the United States, 1850–1870* (Cambridge, Mass.: Harvard University Press, 1964); Lucie Cheng and Edna Bonacich, eds., *Labor Immigration under Capitalism: Asian Workers in the United States before World War II* (Berkeley: University of California Press, 1984); and Sian Rees, *The Floating Brothel: The Extraordinary True Story of an Eighteenth-Century Ship and Its Cargo of Female Convicts* (New York: Theia/Hyperion, 2002).

62   Itinerant males, usually former soldiers, were common in both medieval and Renaissance Europe. Indeed many of the central characters in Anderson's and Grimms' fairy tales are bare branches. See, for example, "The Tinder Box," "The Twelve Dancing Princesses," and "The Robber Bridegroom." For the situation in the Middle Ages, see James L. Boone, "Noble Family Structure and Expansionist Warfare in the Late Middle Ages," in Rada Dyson-Hudson and

Michael A. Little, ed., *Rethinking Human Adaptation: Biological and Cultural Models* (Boulder, Colo.: Westview, 1983), pp. 79–96. Itinerant males were also commonplace in the United States until World War I. See, for example, Eric H. Monkkonen, *Walking to Work: Tramps in America, 1790–1935* (Lincoln: University of Nebraska Press, 1984); Roger Bruns, *Knights of the Road: A Hobo History* (New York: Methuen, 1980); and Woirol, *In the Floating Army*. This category of itinerant male groups includes mobile armies. See, for example, Olive Knight, *Life and Manners in the Frontier Army* (Norman: University of Oklahoma Press, 1978).

63   Theodore D. Kemper has constructed an elegant theory of this dynamic. He discusses how low-status, unmarried young males have few opportunities to achieve dominance or eminence, and thus engage in behavior that will bring them the "T surge" that they cannot achieve any other way. See Kemper, *Social Structure and Testosterone: Explorations of the Socio-Bio-Social Chain* (New Brunswick, N.J.: Rutgers University Press, 1990). Such behavior includes physical aggression, drug and alcohol abuse, risk taking, and sexual misconduct.

64   See Courtwright, *Violent Land*, especially chap. 5.

65   Eleanor Emmons Maccoby and Carol Nagy Jacklin, *The Psychology of Sex Differences* (Stanford, Calif.: Stanford University Press, 1974), pp. 227–247.

66   The literature here is immense. Illustrative works include D. Benton, "Do Animal Studies Tell Us Anything about the Relationships between Testosterone and Human Aggression?" in Graham C.L. Davey, ed., *Animal Models of Human Behavior* (Chichester, U.K.: Wiley, 1983), pp. 281–298; Marie-France Bouissou, "Androgens, Aggressive Behaviour, and Social Relationships in Higher Mammals," *Hormone Research*, Vol. 18, Nos. 1–3 (1983), pp. 43–61; John M.W. Bradford and D. McLean, "Sexual Offenders, Violence, and Testosterone: A Clinical Study," *Canadian Journal of Psychiatry*, Vol. 29, No. 4 (June 1984), pp. 335–343; Kerrin Christiansen and Rainier Knussmann, "Androgen Levels and Components of Aggressive Behavior in Men," *Hormones and Behavior*, Vol. 21, No. 2 (June 1987), pp. 170–180; James M. Dabbs Jr. and Robin Morris, "Testosterone, Social Class, and Antisocial Behavior in a Sample of 4,462 Men," *Psychological Science*, Vol. 1, No. 3 (May 1990), pp. 209–211; Bruce B. Svare, ed., *Hormones and Aggressive Behavior* (New York: Plenum, 1983); Janet Shibley Hyde, "Gender Differences in Aggression," in Janet Shibley Hyde and Marcia C. Linn, eds., *The Psychology of Gender: Advances through Meta-Analysis* (Baltimore, Md.: Johns Hopkins University Press, 1986); Kenneth E. Moyer, "Sex Differences in Aggression," in Richard C. Friedman, Ralph M. Richart, and Raymond L. Vande Wiele, eds., *Sex Differences in Behavior* (New York: Wiley, 1974), pp. 335–372; and Dolt Zillmann, *Connections between Sex and Aggression* (Hillsdale, N.J.: Lawrence Erlbaum, 1984).

67   Richard Wrangham and Dale Peterson, *Demonic Males: Apes and the Origins of Human Violence* (New York: Houghton Mifflin, 1996), p. 113.

68   Ibid., pp. 113–114.

69   Travis Hirschi and Michael Gottfredson, "Age and the Explanation of Crime," *American Journal of Sociology* (November 1983), pp. 552–584.

70   See, for example, Dan Olweus, Ake Mattsson, Daisy Schalling, and Hans Loew, "Circulating Testosterone Levels and Aggression in Adolescent Males: A Causal Analysis," *Psychosomatic Medicine*, Vol. 50, No. 3 (May–June 1988), pp. 261–272; Margo Wilson and Martin Daly, "Competitiveness, Risk Taking, and Violence: The Young Male Syndrome," *Ethology and*

Sociobiology, Vol. 6, No. 1 (1985), pp. 59–73; Derral Cheatwood and Kathleen J. Block, "Youth and Homicide: An Investigation of the Age Factor in Criminal Homicide," *Justice Quarterly*, Vol. 7, No. 2 (June 1990), pp. 265–292; and Christian G. Mesquida and Neil I. Wiener, "Human Collective Aggression: A Behavioral Ecology Perspective," *Ethology and Sociobiology*, Vol. 17, No. 4 (July 1996), pp. 247–262. Males aged 15–35 are responsible for the vast majority of homicides. Within that age group, males between 20 and 29 commit most of the homicides. See Wilson and Daly, "Competitiveness, Risk Taking, and Violence."

71   James D. Seymour and Richard Anderson, *New Ghosts, Old Ghosts: Prisons and Labor Reform Camps in China* (London: M.E. Sharpe, 1998), p. 115. These figures can only be approximated from representative cases for which data are available.

72   Satoshi Kanazawa and March C. Still, "Why Men Commit Crimes (and Why They Desist)," *Sociological Theory*, Vol. 18, No. 3 (2000), pp. 434–447.

73   Mesquida and Wiener, "Human Collective Aggression," p. 247.

74   See ibid.; John H. Laub, Daniel S. Nagin, and Robert J. Sampson, "Trajectories of Change in Criminal Offending: Good Marriages and the Desistance Process," *American Sociological Review*, Vol. 63, No. 2 (April 1998), pp. 225–238; Robert J. Sampson and John H. Laub, Crime *in the Making: Pathways and Turning Points through Life* (Cambridge, Mass.: Harvard University Press); Daly and Wilson, *Sex, Evolution, and Behavior*; Courtwright, *Violent Land*; Kemper, *Social Structure and Testosterone*; Robert Wright, *The Moral Animal* (New York: Pantheon, 1994); Laura Betzig, "Despotism and Differential Reproduction: A Cross-Cultural Correlation of Conflict Asymmetry, Hierarchy, and Degree of Polygny," *Ethology and Sociobiology*, Vol. 3, No. 4 (1982), pp. 209–221; Martin Daly and Margo Wilson, *Homicide* (Hawthorne, N.Y.: Aldine de Gruyter, 1988); Martin Daly and Margo Wilson, "Killing the Competition: Female/Female and Male/Male Homicide," *Human Nature*, Vol. 1, No. 1 (1990), pp. 81–107; Napoleon A. Chagnon, "Is Reproductive Success Equal in Egalitarian Societies?" in Chagnon and Irons, *Evolutionary Biology and Human Social Behavior*, pp. 374–401; David Buss, *The Evolution of Desire: Strategies of Human Mating* (New York: Basic Books, 1994); Frank A. Pedersen, "Secular Trends in Human Sex Ratios: Their Influence on Individual and Family Behavior," *Human Nature*, Vol. 2, No. 3 (1991), pp. 271–291; and Randy Thornhill and Nancy Thornhill, "Human Rape: An Evolutionary Analysis," *Ethology and Sociobiology*, Vol. 4, No. 3 (1983), pp. 137–173.

75   Courtwright, *Violent Land*, p. 202.

76   Wright, *The Moral Animal*, p. 100.

77   Allan Mazur and Joel Michalek, "Marriage, Divorce, and Male Testosterone," *Social Forces*, Vol. 77, No. 1 (September 1998), p. 315.

78   See Allan Mazur and Alan Booth, "Testosterone and Dominance in Men," *Behavioral and Brain Sciences*, Vol. 21, No. 3 (June 1998), pp. 353–397. The debates over the effects of testosterone on behavior have been numerous. Some suggest that it is testosterone's transformation into estradiol that provides the effect. Others dispute that any effect exists at all. See, for example, David France, "Testosterone, the Rogue Hormone, Is Getting a Makeover," *New York Times*, February 17, 1999, p. G3.

79   Satoshi Kanazawa, "Why Productivity Fades with Age: The Crime-Genius Connection," *Journal of Research in Personality*, Vol. 37 (2003), pp. 257–272, at p. 269.

80 Mazur and Michalek, "Marriage, Divorce, and Male Testosterone," p. 327.

81 Kanazawa, "Why Productivity Fades with Age," p. 270.

82 Gilder, *Naked Nomads*, p. 152.

83 We are indebted to Theodore Kemper for bringing this to our attention. *Ben Sira* is the book of Ecclesiastes. The language of the King James version does not, however, accurately reflect the Hebrew nuances of this passage in chapter 36.

84 The literature on this subject is immense, so we provide only a sampling here: Wilson and Daly, "Competitiveness, Risk Taking, and Violence"; Mesquida and Wiener, "Human Collective Aggression"; Kemper, *Social Structure and Testosterone*; Courtwright, *Violent Land*; Betzig, "Despotism and Differential Reproduction"; Laura Betzig, *Despotism and Differential Reproduction: A Darwinian View of History* (New York: Aldine de Gruyter, 1986); Daly and Wilson, *Sex, Evolution, and Behavior*; and William H. Durham, "Resource Competition and Human Aggression," *Quarterly Review of Biology*, Vol. 51, No. 3 (September 1976), pp. 385–415.

85 Kemper, *Social Structure and Testosterone*, p. 73.

86 Wilson and Daly, "Competitiveness, Risk Taking, and Violence."

87 Courtwright, *Violent Land*.

88 Mazur and Booth, "Testosterone and Dominance in Men," p. 361.

QUESTIONS FOR DISCUSSION

1. In your own words, what is the main claim that Hudson and den Boer are making? Does the evidence they provide support this conclusion?

2. What do you think the reception of this book would be in China? How would Hudson and den Boer want to change the tone, rhetorical appeals, or other characteristics of their book if they were to publish there?

3. How do the tables and figures in this piece add to your understanding of the problem? How could they be more effective? What other information would you like to see in them?

4. Would you say that unmarried males in the US face the same conditions and problems as the bare branches in China? Do you think the rising age of first marriage and the rising disinclination to marry in the US will bring problems similar to those the authors describe for China?

5. How, if at all, does the opinion editorial by Elijah Anderson (reprinted later in this book) support the argument that Hudson and Den Boer make?

6. How do the extensive endnotes contribute to the credibility of the researchers and the logic of their argument?

7. What to you would be the best solution to the problems of China's missing females and resulting bare branches?

Harlem Town

by
Sarah and A. Elizabeth Delany with Amy Hill Hearth

Amy Hill Hearth is a journalist who discovered the reclusive sisters Sarah and Elizabeth Delany, the daughters of a man born into slavery, and wrote an article about them for the Sunday New York Times *in 1991. She was asked by a book publisher who read her article to expand it into book form. The result was* Having Our Say, *an enormously successful oral history that stayed on* The New York Times *bestseller list for more than two years. The excerpt that follows is from Chapters 18 and 19 of that book. The book won several prestigious awards, including an ABBY Honor Book (American Association of Booksellers) and a spot on the coveted American Library Association's "Best Books of the Year." Ms. Hearth also co-authored* The Delany Sisters' Book of Everyday Wisdom *with the late Sarah and Elizabeth Delany and* On My Own at 107: Reflections on Life Without Bessie *with the late Sarah Delany. In 2003, Ms. Hearth wrote a children's illustrated biography of the sisters called* The Delany Sisters Reach High, *which received national attention and critical acclaim. Ms. Hearth is a member of the Authors Guild and the American Society of Journalists and Authors.*

From the Preface to *Having Our Say,* by Amy Hill Hearth

When I met Sadie Delany and her sister, Bessie, in September 1991, I was on assignment for *The New York Times,* hoping to write a story on these two elderly but reclusive sisters who had just celebrated their one-hundred-and-second and one-hundredth birthdays. In my hand I carried a letter written by their neighbor in Mount Vernon, New York, who had extended an invitation to come by and meet them. The Delany sisters had no phone, so I wasn't entirely sure they knew I was coming. I was prepared to be turned away.

I knocked on the door. I waited and raised my hand to knock again, when suddenly the door swung open. The woman who answered, with her head held high, her eyes intense and penetrating, extended her hand in formal greeting. "I am Dr. Delany," she said elegantly.

She ushered me into the house, and from across the room, another elderly woman said sweetly, "Please come in, child. Won't you sit down?" This was the elder sister, Sadie Delany.

I must have hesitated for a moment. "Go on, sit down," Bessie urged. "Sit down as long as you like. We won't charge you rent!" Then they both laughed uproariously at this little joke.

Over the next three hours, I was charmed by their vivaciousness and playfulness. They seemed to have conquered old age, or to have come as close to it as anyone ever will. It was clear that they had found the source of their vitality in each other's company, and in the tales they told and retold each other from a century of living.

When my piece was published, the reaction was swift. Readers fell in love with the Delany sisters. There were letters from all over the country, demands for television interviews, requests for guest appearances at schools and at political functions. The sisters declined nearly all of the invitations.

Among those who read my article were editors at Kodansha America, Inc., who felt that the Delanys' story deserved to be a book. At first the sisters demurred, unsure that their life

Sarah and A. Elizabeth Delany with Amy Hill Hearth, *Having Our Say: The Delany Sisters' First 100 Years.* Reprinted from *Kodansha International,* (1993), Kodansha America.

stories were sufficiently interesting or significant. But they came to see that by recording their story, they were participating in a tradition as old as time: the passing of knowledge and experience from one generation to the next.

The daughters of a man born into slavery and a mother of mixed racial parentage who was born free, the sisters recall what it meant to be "colored" children in the late nineteenth century in the South. Their early lives were sheltered: They grew up on a college campus, Saint Augustine's School in Raleigh, North Carolina, where their father was an Episcopal priest and vice principal. Despite their privileged status, they suffered the insult of Jim Crow when it first became law.

After years of teaching in the rural South to raise money, the Delany sisters joined the great wave of black Americans who headed north in search of opportunity during the early part of this century. Bessie became only the second black woman licensed to practice dentistry in New York, and Sadie was the first black person ever to teach domestic science on the high school level in New York City public schools.

The sisters lived in Harlem, and were acquainted with such legendary figures as the statesman and poet James Weldon Johnson and the entertainer Cab Calloway. During an era when hearth and home defined the place of women, the Delany sisters spurned marriage opportunities for careers. In the 1950s they were in the vanguard of middle-class black Americans who integrated the suburbs and faced a new and difficult set of challenges. Already elderly in the 1960s, they cheered from the sidelines as the civil rights movement flourished, praying and worrying about younger relatives who were getting caught up in the protests.

Each sister developed her own way of coping within a racist society. Sadie expertly "played dumb" and manipulated the system, and Bessie believed in confrontation, regardless of the cost. This difference in personal styles has brought balance—and occasionally fireworks—to their hundred-year companionship. "We are living proof that you don't change one bit from cradle to grave," Bessie likes to say.

This book is woven from thousands of anecdotes that I coaxed from the Delany sisters during an eighteen-month period (September 1991 to April 1993). The sequence of stories is mine but the words are all theirs. At times the sisters' versions of particular events were almost identical or told in a joint fashion—with one sister beginning a sentence, and the other finishing it—and so some chapters bear both of their names. In the others, either Sadie or Bessie chronicles their life together, each with her own distinct spin, voice, and viewpoint. Their story, as the Delany sisters like to say, is not meant as "black" or "women's" history, but American history. It belongs to all of us.

Sadie

When Papa became bishop in 1918, people were mighty impressed. His accomplishment was so extraordinary, I still wonder how he did it. He put up with a lot to get where he got. One time, not long after Papa was consecrated to the bishopric, he did a service at Christ Church in Raleigh. It was a white, segregated church. Our family attended, and do you know what happened? We had to sit in the balcony, which was built for slaves! And we were not given the privilege of Communion. Ooooh, that makes Bessie mad. At the time, she wanted to make a fuss, but she did not, because she did not want to embarrass Papa.

Somehow, Papa always endured this kind of degradation. He saw the hypocrisy, but he felt that gently, slowly, he was making true progress for himself and his people, and he was at peace with that. I learned a lot from my Papa about coping with institutionalized racism. The way to succeed was simple: You had to be better at what you did than any of your white competition. That was the main thing. But you couldn't be too smug about it, or white folks would feel threatened.

I'll tell you a story. Before I could get my teaching license in New York City, a supervisor named Miss Schermerhorn had come to observe me while I taught a domestic science class. There were three of us student teachers and the assignment was to take a class of young girls and teach them to bake a batch of cookies—how to follow a recipe, and so on. Well, Miss Schermerhorn didn't have time for each of us to go through the whole lesson. So she split up the lesson and I got stuck with the last piece—how to serve and clean up the kitchen efficiently. This was bad because I was dependent on the other girls meeting their deadline ahead of me. I probably got the "cleaning up" part of the assignment because I was colored.

Well, the first girl was a disaster. She panicked, and forgot to halve the recipe. There was enough flour and butter flying around that room to make cookies for the whole world. She also forgot to preheat the ovens. The second girl was supposed to see that the cookies got baked perfectly, but she was so behind because of the first girl that they just made a mess.

Well, then it was my turn. It was clear the first two girls had failed. I thought to myself, now how am I going to land on my feet here? I just sat those students down and said, "Listen, we have to work together as a team. We only have ten minutes to make the most of this." So we took the rest of the batter and we made those cookies. And while some of the girls were watching them and taking them out to cool, I had the others lined up to scrub the pans. Then I had them lined up to scrub up themselves.

When my ten minutes were up, we had several dozen perfect cookies, a clean kitchen, and those girls were washed up and ready to go on to their next class. Miss Schermerhorn said to me, "Miss Delany, I don't know how you did that." And she not only passed me, she offered me a substitute teacher's license on the spot. So you see, my way to get ahead was to be better than my white competition. Papa had set a good example for me of how to work within the system.

I got my first teaching job in New York in the fall of 1920. I think I was paid $1,500 for the year. It was at P.S. 119 in Harlem, which was an elementary school, mostly colored. This was a typical assignment for a colored teacher. They most certainly did not want us in schools where the children were white. The parents would object. One way that the principals kept us out was to say they could not hire anyone with a Southern accent because it would be damaging to the children. Well, most of us colored teachers at the time had Southern accents. So it was just a way of keeping us out.

When my Southern accent was considered a problem, I found a way around that. I signed up with a speech coach—a woman in Manhattan. She was a white woman, a lovely woman. I don't think she had too many colored clients. I remember that when I would go to her apartment for the lessons, the doorman made me take the freight elevator. I didn't make a fuss because I wanted those speech lessons.

You had to decide: Am I going to change the world, or am I going to change me? Or maybe change the world a little bit, just by changing me? If I can get ahead, doesn't that help my people?

I was very ambitious. Much of the time that I taught at P.S. 119 I made money on the side by baking cakes and selling them for a nickel a slice to the teachers at school. I would make a cake and cut it into twenty slices, and make a dollar. The ingredients didn't cost me anywhere near that much to buy, so I made a neat profit. Another thing I would do is make lollipops at home and sell them in the school cafeteria for a penny each. Sometimes I'd make lemon; other times I'd make cinnamon, or something else. You might think that making lollipops and cakes is an awful slow way to get money, but I liked doing it. Besides, you'd be surprised at how it adds up—a penny here, a nickel there—after a few years. I never let a nickel get by me, that's what Bessie always says. Why, for several years during the 1920s I even made good money!

You see, Miss Larson, the principal at P.S. 119, got this idea that her boyfriend could peddle my candy. He had trouble holding onto a job and she was looking for something for him to do. So I rented a loft at 121st Street, in the business district. We called the candy "Delany's Delights" and had tins made up with that name. The candy was hand-dipped chocolate fondant and we had three sizes: a half-pound, a pound, and two pounds. We charged two dollars per pound and we just sold that stuff all over New York, even at Abraham & Straus, the department store! I made it and he sold it.

Eventually, I gave up the candy business. The Depression came along and people had no money for chocolate fondant, that's for sure. Also, I had begun teaching at a high school, and it was a more demanding schedule than elementary school.

I had wanted to teach at a high school because it was considered a promotion, and it paid better. But I had to be a little clever—Bessie would say sneaky—to find ways to get around these brick walls they set up for colored folks. So I asked around quietly for some advice. A friend of my brother Hubert's who worked for the Board of Education suggested a plan, which I followed.

This is what I did: I applied for a high school position, and when I reached the top of the seniority list after three years, I received a letter in the mail saying they wished to meet with me in person. At the appointment, they would have seen I was colored and found some excuse to bounce me down the list. So I skipped the appointment and sent them a letter, acting like there was a mix-up. Then I just showed up on the first day of classes. It was risky, but I knew what a bureaucracy it was, and that in a bureaucracy it's easier to keep people out than to push them back down.

Child, when I showed up that day—at Theodore Roosevelt High School, a white high school—they just about died when they saw me. A colored woman! But my name was on the list to teach there, and it was too late for them to send me someplace else. The plan had worked! Once I was in, they couldn't figure out how to get rid of me.

So I became the first colored teacher in the New York City system to teach domestic science on the high school level. I spent the rest of my career teaching at excellent high schools! Between 1930 and 1960, when I retired, I taught at Theodore Roosevelt High School, which is on Fordham Road in the Bronx, then at Girls' High School in Brooklyn, and finally at Evander Childs High School, which is on Gun Hill Road in the Bronx.

Plus, I got a night job—at Washington Irving High School in lower Manhattan—teaching adults who had dropped out of school. This was something I really wanted to do. The way I got the job was that the girl who had it before me complained a lot, was late a lot, and would ask me to substitute for her. Eventually, they just hired me instead of her! But that's the way you get ahead, child. Even if you're colored, if you're good enough, you'll get the job. As long as they need you, you've got that job.

Meanwhile, I was studying for my master's degree in education at Columbia, which I completed in 1925. I was a busy gal, but I was happy being busy. My classes were usually very demanding because as a colored teacher, I always got the meanest kids. Except once. That was the year they had me mixed up with a white woman whose name also was Delany. It was kind of funny. She was just furious, because she got all these tough girls, and I got the easy ones—college-bound and motivated. Tell you the truth, I did not mind the tough kids. I loved them all.

It was lonely being about the only colored teacher around. Sometimes the white teachers were friendly, but you couldn't count on any of them being your real friends. There was one woman I was friendly with, and we decided to meet on a Saturday and go swimming at a public pool in the Bronx. I remember that when she saw me in my bathing suit, she looked at my legs and said, "Why, Sarah, you are very white!" And I said, "So what?" I guess she was surprised that I didn't try to pass for white.

Personally, I never had any desire to be white. I am absolutely comfortable with who I am. I used to laugh at how both races seem to hate their hair. All these Negro ladies would run out and get their hair *straightened*, and all these white ladies would run out and get their hair *curled*. My hair was in-between, with a little kink in it, just enough to give it body. I had no desire to change it. I had no desire to change me. I guess I owe that to my Mama and Papa.

This same teacher who seemed to wonder why I didn't just try to "pass" turned out to be a fair-weather friend. Once, she and I had planned to go swimming, and she said to wait under the clock at noon, and so I did. But coincidentally, some other white girls she knew showed up right when she arrived. So she just snubbed me. She didn't want them to know we were friends, so she left me standing there and walked on past, with them. She was so obvious that there really wasn't anything to do but laugh it off and forget about it.

I remained on friendly terms with that woman. Bessie says, "I wouldn't have had nothing more to do with her this side of Glory!" This is the kind of thing that drives Bessie wild. Bessie would have given her a piece of her mind. Sure, it annoyed me. But I didn't let it ruin my day. Life is short, and it's up to you to make it sweet.

Bessie

I was known in the Negro community as "Dr. Bessie" to distinguish me from my brother Hap, who was known as "Dr. Delany." There was a time, in the 1920s, '30s, and '40s in Harlem when just about every living soul knew of Dr. Bessie. My patients would go on vacation and send postcards addressed only to "Dr. Bessie, New York City" and I would get those cards.

In those days, folks were probably more attached to their dentists than today. They saw more of their dentists because their teeth were worse, generally. Today there's fluoride in the water, and better toothbrushes and floss, plus people are better educated about oral hygiene than they used to be.

When we were children, we had no toothbrushes. We would take little switches from a peach tree and rub them on our teeth. Actually, it did a pretty good job. Sadie and I still brush our teeth with equal parts of baking soda and salt, mixed into a paste with a little water in the palm of your hand. And once a week, we wash our teeth with our homemade soap. Hap used to say there was nothing that made for a gleaming smile more than homemade soap! Sounds funny, but it's true.

Hap was four years younger than me but he was already finishing school and starting his practice by the time I got to dental school. When I graduated, he invited me to share an office with him and another dentist, Dr. Chester Booth, at 2305 Seventh Avenue—that's the corner of Seventh Avenue and 135th Street. We were on the second floor, above the Corn Exchange Bank, which later became the Chemical Bank.

This was the center of Harlem! From the office window you could see everything that was going on. Harlem was like a beehive, with people running every which way, going to work, school, or to entertainment. It was a positive place.

There were some colorful folks, like this peculiar man that people called the Barefoot Prophet. In actuality, I suppose he was a hobo, but he looked like Jesus Christ. He had long hair, and wore long, flowing robes, and he'd march around barefoot in Harlem. And there was this fella named Father Divine. He was a Negro minister whose background was a mystery. People said he could do supernatural things, like perform miracles and heal the sick. At his church, which was across from St. Martin's Church at 122nd Street and Lenox Avenue, they had a great big dining hall, where they fed all the hungry in Harlem. At that time, Father Divine had a huge following. His followers thought he was God. Now, those are the fellas you have to watch out for, the ones who think they are God. Look out!

Hap and I loved having our offices in the middle of everything. After awhile, we moved next door—to 2303 Seventh Avenue—where we shared a suite of offices with our brother Lucius, who was an attorney, along with a Negro real estate agent, and Dr. MacDonald, a Negro dentist from Trinidad who had gone to Saint Aug's. We had our own X-ray lab, a technician, and two mechanics who were hired by me and Hap to make dentures and bridges. I was the only woman among the bunch of us, and I ran the show. On the day the rent was due, I'd say, "OK, fellas, pay up!" Somehow, among all those men, I ended up being the boss.

In those days, many people simply would not go to a woman dentist. There were so very few women dentists at all, never mind colored women dentists. Why, I was only the second Negro woman licensed to practice in New York. I was also only the second Negro woman to get a dental license in North Carolina. (I got my license there, thinking I might go back someday.)

It was bad enough to be discriminated against by white people because I was colored. But then, my own people would discriminate against me because I was a woman! Two times I remember that men patients of mine insisted that Hap come and pull their teeth. I remember one man said to me, "Can you pull teeth with those little hands?" and I said, "Do you really want to find out?" It made me mad. I could take those forceps and pull just as hard as any man. That sexism was a nasty thing to deal with. But once a person had been my patient, they'd always come back. The word got out: That colored woman dentist has a gentle touch.

Every colored person in New York knew that I would take any patient, no matter how sick. We had the same concerns then about contagious diseases as there are today about this new disease, AIDS. It was a human reaction that dentists had; we were afraid of getting infectious diseases from our patients. It was human, but it wasn't professional.

Back in dental school, I treated a little white girl with syphilis who came to the school clinic. I imagine she was born with it. It just about broke my heart. She was sitting in the hallway alone, crying, and my classmates just about broke their legs trying to run away from her. Not one of them would touch her, so I volunteered. I said to them, "What do you think it's going to be like in the real world, when we graduate? Are you just going to run away from people who need your help?"

In those days, we did not wear gloves. But I always took care of my hands. I was careful to avoid getting cuts and I kept my nails very short. Now, I am almost embarrassed when I go to the dentist—embarrassed for my profession, I mean. They come at you with these masks and gowns; they look like they're from outer space. When I went to school, you became a doctor or dentist in order to help people. Society respected you for taking risks.

Even then, of course, there were those who wanted society's respect but did not earn that esteem. For instance, there were many dentists in my day who would not take colored patients. That was why it was so important that there were colored dentists! One time, after graduation, a white classmate of mine from Columbia called me up and said he was sending over a patient. At first, I thought he was doing me a favor, but then he mentioned that it was his maid. And I realized he didn't want to work on her mouth because she was colored. So I said to him, "You are not a doctor of dentistry! You are a doctor of segregation!" I yelled at him so loud he hung up. Well, his maid came over and of course I helped her. But I never spoke to him again.

And there were those who only wanted the money. Some dentists would even do poor quality work, just to make the patient uncomfortable so that he'd have to come back. It would never have occurred to me to do that. No, sir! When I started my practice in 1923, I charged two dollars for a cleaning, two dollars for an extraction, five dollars for a silver filling, and ten dollars for a gold filling. When I retired in 1950, I was still charging the same rate. I never raised my rates because I was getting by OK. I was always very proud of my work, and that was enough for me.

I never turned anyone away because they couldn't pay me. Back when I was a young dentist, a child could not enroll in New York City public schools without a dental exam. This was tricky for a lot of poor, colored parents because they couldn't afford it. Honey, I must have done thousands of those dental exams without charge. But it was rare that someone outright stole my services. One time comes to mind, when I worked on a man's teeth, and he said he had to run down the street to do something and would be right back, and he never came back. So I never got paid. But usually, people would find a way to pay me, or they paid me eventually.

Not all the patients were poor. Hap and I had separate practices, and he had a large number of famous people, such as Walter White[1] of the NAACP and entertainers like Bojangles Robinson and Alberta Hunter, who was one of the nicest women I ever knew. But some of Hap's jazz friends were annoying because they always wanted to use the phone. I still remember the number. It was the most well-used phone in Harlem! Once, the bill was $100 and I nearly fainted dead on the floor. That was a lot of money in those days and those jazz folks never did chip in to pay us back, even though they had more cash than anybody. So you know what I did? I went and had a pay phone put in.

I had a few famous patients of my own, including Ed Small, the nightclub owner, and Dr. Louis T. Wright[2]—I was also *his* patient—and Dr. Wright's family. I also took care of James

Weldon Johnson,[3] and once he gave me a signed copy of a book of poetry he had just published, and there were only five hundred copies printed. My patients were as nice to me as I was to them.

But there were people who couldn't stand the very idea of a colored woman being a dentist, and they weren't shy about letting me know. Once, about 1925, I went to a medical conference at the Hotel Pennsylvania in Manhattan. I remember I had borrowed Sadie's horsehair turban, and I thought I looked very attractive, very professional. I went up to the front desk and identified myself as a dentist who was to attend the meeting, and this white fella looked at me like I was some little monkey that had just fallen out of a tree and landed in his soup and ruined his day. I asked him for directions to my meeting. Yes, he gave me directions—to the *men's toilet.*

When I found myself standing in front of the men's room instead of the conference room, I was so filled with rage that I couldn't move. Fortunately, one of my former classmates—he happened to be white—saved me from total humiliation. He saw me standing there and said, "Bessie Delany, what in the world are you doing *here*?" And he just took my arm and escorted me to the conference like I was the queen of England.

That day was one of the lowest points of my life, but I didn't have time to dwell on it. I often worked about fifteen hours a day. The only time I ever closed my office early was when one of my patients died, because I would go to the funeral. Wednesday was supposed to be my day off, but often I spent it covering for Hap while he and Dr. Chester Booth ran the Harlem Dental Clinic, which they founded with the help of the Urban League.

During the week, I had no free time for myself. I had to get up at daybreak and go to the office and clean and disinfect it, since I was always too exhausted at the end of the day to sterilize things properly, and I couldn't afford a cleaning lady. To save money, I walked ten blocks to work rather than ride the trolley or the subway, which cost five cents. I'd walk home again after cleaning the office, then bathe, and walk back to the office in time to open up at nine o'clock, looking fresh out of a bandbox.

For a while, I had a beau who would drive me to work. He was the brother of a dentist I knew. One day, I went on a date with this man and we drove to the Palisades in New Jersey. We were parked, looking over the edge of these cliffs, when this fella got crazy on me. He said: "I could just hit the gas, and we'd go right over the edge and we'd both be dead. We would both *die.*"

And I thought, Oh, Bessie Delany, you have got yourself in a fine mess. But I just said, "Now, what would you want to do that for?" as calmly as possible, like it was a joke. But it wasn't a joke. This fella was nuts.

Finally, after threatening me for a while longer, he quieted down and drove me home. But would you believe the next morning that fella was parked at the curb, as if nothing had happened, ready to give me a ride to work? I felt like yelling at him, "You are crazy!" but for once in my life, I kept my mouth shut and just said, "No, thanks, I'd rather walk" in a friendly way. Still, that fella followed me to my office every day for weeks.

I know it sounds like I *lived* at my office, but I did make room in my life for relaxation. If I hadn't, I wouldn't have lived this long! Saturday was often a day for fun, and sometimes I'd go shopping with Sadie, or on a picnic with a beau. Occasionally, I'd be real naughty and go to the horse races on Long Island. I would bet a little money, say, five dollars. But I always won! So did Sadie. Our men friends would ask, "How do y'all always know which horse to pick?" Well, we studied the horses carefully before the race, and since we grew up around animals, we knew which ones were winners. And of course, I was a little psychic about these things.

I guess our most favorite pastime of all was baseball. We weren't too far away from the team which became the Yankees, but they were slow to integrate so we weren't interested in them. Sadie and I loved Walter Johnson, a pitcher for the Washington team. If he was pitching in New York, we were there! But we were really Giants fans. The day I heard they were moving out to San Francisco, well, I was beside myself with sorrow. I said, "How can they do this to me?" I was a-carrying on like somebody had up and died.

Another thing we used to do was go to the Old Bronx Opera house, where they used to preview Broadway plays. You could go there real cheap and see the best musicals New York had to offer. It only cost fifty cents if you sat in the balcony.

I remember being at the Old Bronx Opera house once with Papa, who must have come up from Raleigh with Mama to see us. This must have been about 1925. Well, Papa was nervous because it was Lent and he didn't think he should be at the Old Bronx Opera house. He said, "What if someone sees me?" Papa always did care about appearances. But I think it was because he had to; it was part of getting ahead. White people were watching you all the time, just waiting for you to make a mistake. So we not only *lived* a clean life, we wanted to be sure people *knew* that we did.

This is a burden that white people do not have, I think. It always seemed to me that white people were judged as individuals. But if a Negro did something stupid or wrong, it was held against *all* of us. Negroes were always representing the whole race.

All I ever wanted in my life was to be treated as an individual. I have succeeded, to some extent. At least I'm sure that in the Lord's eyes, I am an individual. I am not a "colored" person, or a "Negro" person, in God's eyes. I am just me! The Lord won't hold it against me that I'm colored because He made me that way! He thinks I am beautiful! And so do I, even with all my wrinkles! I am beautiful!

Endnotes

1   Walter White (1892–1955) was the executive secretary of the National Association for the Advancement of Colored People from 1931 to 1955. Born in Atlanta of mixed black and white parentage, White used his light complexion to investigate and write exposes about lynchings and race riots.

2   Dr. Louis T. Wright (1891–1952) was a New York surgeon and civil rights leader who served as chairman of the board of the NAACP from 1935 to 1952. He often combined his two passions—medicine and civil rights—by promoting better health care for black Americans.

3   James Weldon Johnson (1871–1938) was the first executive secretary of the NAACP, as well as a diplomat, poet, and anthologist of black American literature. With his brother, John Rosamond Johnson, a composer, he wrote "Lift Every Voice and Sing," which is often called the Negro national anthem.

SUGGESTIONS FOR DISCUSSION

1. This oral history is based on many interviews. Can you see any evidences in the text of its being "pieced together" by Amy Hill Hearth? How do you imagine she created this text?

2. What is the advantage of having the stories told in the sisters' own words rather than Hearth retelling them in her words?

3. Oral history does not typically make a claim or state a thesis. But can you infer a claim or a main point from Sadie's and Bessie's stories? If so, how would you state the main point of each?

4. What research similar in either topic or method does this reading make you think of?

5. The Delany sisters were about a century old when their stories were collected. Whose oral histories do you think ought to be collected and published before the informants die?

Watching the English: The Hidden Rules of English Behaviour

by
Kate Fox

Anthropologist Kate Fox has studied and written about many types of human social interaction, from flirting to violence to celebrations. Although she was born in England (her father, Robin Fox, was also an anthropologist), Fox spent years in the United States, Ireland, and France, leaving her with an "erratic education" and an interest in social behavior. Fox studied anthropology and philosophy at Cambridge, and now works as Director of the Social Issues Research Centre in the United Kingdom. The following excerpts from her book Watching the English: The Hidden Rules of English Behaviour *come from the Introduction and Chapter 8, "Rules of the Road." British spelling and punctuation have been retained, and unfamiliar vocabulary items have been glossed with American equivalents in brackets.*

The 'Grammar' of Englishness

We are constantly being told that the English have lost their national identity—that there is no such thing as 'Englishness'. There has been a spate of books bemoaning this alleged identity crisis, with titles ranging from the plaintive *Anyone for England?* to the inconsolable *England: An Elegy*. Having spent much of the past twelve years doing research on various aspects of English culture and social behaviour—in pubs, at racecourses, in shops, in night-clubs, on trains, on street corners—I am convinced that there *is* such a thing as 'Englishness', and that reports of its demise have been greatly exaggerated. In the research for this book, I set out to discover the hidden, unspoken rules of English behaviour, and what these rules tell us about our national identity.

The object was to identify the *commonalities* in rules governing English behaviour—the unofficial codes of conduct that cut across class, age, sex, region, sub-cultures and other social boundaries. For example, Women's Institute members and leather-clad bikers may seem, on the surface, to have very little in common, but by looking beyond the 'ethnographic dazzle'[1] of superficial differences, I found that Women's Institute members and bikers, and other groups, all behave in accordance with the same unwritten rules—rules that define our national identity and character. I would also maintain, with George Orwell, that this identity 'is continuous, it stretches into the future and the past, there is something in it that persists, as in a living creature'.

My aim, if you like, was to provide a 'grammar' of English behaviour. Native speakers can rarely explain the grammatical rules of their own language. In the same way, those who are most 'fluent' in the rituals, customs and traditions of a particular culture generally lack the detachment necessary to explain the 'grammar' of these practices in an intelligible manner. This is why we have anthropologists.

Reprinted from *Watching the English: The Hidden Rules of English Behaviour* (2005), Hodder Headline PLC.

Participant Observation and Its Discontents

Anthropologists are trained to use a research method known as 'participant observation', which essentially means participating in the life and culture of the people one is studying, to gain a true insider's perspective on their customs and behaviour, while simultaneously observing them as a detached, objective scientist. Well, that's the theory. In practice it often feels rather like that children's game where you try to pat your head and rub your tummy at the same time. It is perhaps not surprising that anthropologists are notorious for their frequent bouts of 'field-blindness'—becoming so involved and enmeshed in the native culture that they fail to maintain the necessary scientific detachment. The most famous example of such rose-tinted ethnography was of course Margaret Mead, but there was also Elizabeth Marshall Thomas, who wrote a book entitled *The Harmless People,* about a tribe who turned out to have a homicide rate higher than that of Chicago.

There is a great deal of agonizing and hair-splitting among anthropologists over the participant-observation method and the role of the participant observer. In my last book, *The Racing Tribe*, I made a joke of this, borrowing the language of self-help psychobabble and expressing the problem as an ongoing battle between my Inner Participant and my Inner Observer. I described the bitchy squabbles in which these two Inner voices engaged every time a conflict arose between my roles as honorary member of the tribe and detached scientist. (Given the deadly serious tones in which this subject is normally debated, my irreverence bordered on heresy, so I was surprised and rather unreasonably annoyed to receive a letter from a university lecturer saying that he was using *The Racing Tribe* to *teach* the participant-observation method. You try your best to be a maverick iconoclast, and they turn you into a textbook.)

The more usual, or at least currently fashionable, practice is to devote at least a chapter of your book or Ph.D. thesis to a tortured, self-flagellating disquisition on the ethical and methodological difficulties of participant observation. Although the whole point of the participant element is to understand the culture from a 'native' perspective, you must spend a good three pages explaining that your unconscious ethnocentric prejudices, and various other cultural barriers, probably make this impossible. It is then customary to question the entire moral basis of the observation element, and, ideally, to express grave reservations about the validity of modern Western 'science' as a means of understanding anything at all.

At this point, the uninitiated reader might legitimately wonder why we continue to use a research method which is clearly either morally questionable or unreliable or both. I wondered this myself, until I realized that these doleful recitations of the dangers and evils of participant observation are a form of protective mantra, a ritual chant similar to the rather charming practice of some Native American tribes who, before setting out on a hunt or chopping down a tree, would sing apologetic laments to appease the spirits of the animals they were about to kill or the tree they were about to fell. A less charitable interpretation would see anthropologists' ritual self-abasements as a disingenuous attempt to deflect criticism by pre-emptive confession of their failings—like the selfish and neglectful lover who says 'Oh, I'm so selfish and neglectful, I don't know why you put up with me,' relying on our belief that such awareness and candid acknowledgement of a fault is almost as virtuous as not having it.

But whatever the motives, conscious or otherwise, the ritual chapter agonizing over the role of the participant observer tends to be mind-numbingly tedious, so I will forgo whatever pre-emptive absolution might be gained by this, and simply say that while participant observation has its limitations, this rather uneasy combination of involvement and detachment is still the best method we have for exploring the complexities of human cultures, so it will have to do.

The Good, the Bad and the Uncomfortable
In my case, the difficulties of the participant element are somewhat reduced, as I have chosen to study the complexities of my own native culture. This is not because I consider the English to be intrinsically more interesting than other cultures, but because I have a rather wimpish aversion to the dirt, dysentery, killer insects, ghastly food and primitive sanitation that characterize the mud-hut 'tribal' societies studied by my more intrepid colleagues.

In the macho field of ethnography, my avoidance of discomfort and irrational preference for cultures with indoor plumbing are regarded as quite unacceptably feeble, so I have, until recently, tried to redeem myself a bit by studying the less salubrious aspects of English life: conducting research in violent pubs, seedy nightclubs, run-down betting shops and the like. Yet after years of research on aggression, disorder, violence, crime and other forms of deviance and dysfunction, all of which invariably take place in disagreeable locations and at inconvenient times, I still seemed to have risen no higher in the estimation of mud-hut ethnographers accustomed to much harsher conditions.

So, having failed my trial-by-fieldwork initiation test, I reasoned that I might as well turn my attention to the subject that really interests me, namely: the causes of *good* behaviour. This is a fascinating field of enquiry, which has been almost entirely neglected by social scientists. With a few notable exceptions,[2] social scientists tend to be obsessed with the dysfunctional, rather than the desirable, devoting all their energies to researching the causes of behaviours our society wishes to prevent, rather than those we might wish to encourage.

My Co-Director at the Social Issues Research Centre (SIRC), Peter Marsh, had become equally disillusioned and frustrated by the problem-oriented nature of social science, and we resolved to concentrate as much as possible on studying positive aspects of human interaction. With this new focus, we were now no longer obliged to seek out violent pubs, but could spend time in pleasant ones (the latter also had the advantage of being much easier to find, as the vast majority of pubs are congenial and trouble-free). We could observe ordinary, law-abiding people doing their shopping, instead of interviewing security guards and store detectives about the activities of shoplifters and vandals. We went to nightclubs to study flirting rather than fighting. When I noticed some unusually sociable and courteous interaction among the crowds at a racecourse, I immediately began what turned out to be three years of research on the factors influencing the good behaviour of racegoers. We also conducted research on celebration, cyber-dating, summer holidays, embarrassment, corporate hospitality, van drivers, risk taking, the London Marathon, sex, mobile-phone gossip and the relationship between tea-drinking and DIY (this last dealing with burning social issues such as 'how many cups of tea does it take the average Englishman to put up a shelf?').

Over the past twelve years, my time has thus been divided roughly equally between studying the problematic aspects of English society and its more appealing, positive elements (along with cross-cultural, comparative research in other parts of the world), so I suppose I can safely claim to have embarked on the specific research for this book with the advantage of a reasonably balanced overview.

Boring but Important
This book is not written for other social scientists, but rather for that elusive creature publishers used to call 'the intelligent layman'. My nonacademic approach cannot, however, be used as a convenient excuse for woolly thinking, sloppy use of language, or failing to define my terms. This is a book about the 'rules' of Englishness, and I cannot simply assert that we all know what we mean by a 'rule', without attempting to explain the sense or senses in which I am using the term.

I am using a rather broad interpretation of the concept of a rule, based on four of the definitions allowed by the *Oxford English Dictionary*, namely:

- a principle, regulation or maxim governing individual conduct;
- a standard of discrimination or estimation; a criterion, a test, a measure;
- an exemplary person or thing; a guiding example;
- a fact, or the statement of a fact, which holds generally good; the normal or usual state of things.

Thus, my quest to identify the rules of Englishness is not confined to a search for specific rules of conduct, but will include rules in the wider sense of standards, norms, ideals, guiding principles and 'facts' about 'normal or usual' English behaviour.

This last is the sense of 'rule' we are using when we say: 'As a rule, the English tend to be X (or prefer Y, or dislike Z).' When we use the term rule in this way, we do not mean—and this is important—that all English people always or invariably exhibit the characteristic in question, only that it is a quality or behaviour pattern which is common enough, or marked enough, to be noticeable and significant. Indeed, it is a fundamental requirement of a social rule—by whatever definition—that it can be broken. Rules of conduct (or standards, or principles) of this kind are not like scientific or mathematical laws, statements of a necessary state of affairs; they are by definition contingent. If it were, for example, utterly inconceivable and impossible that anyone would ever jump a queue [cut in line], there would be no need for a rule prohibiting queue jumping.[3]

When I speak of the unwritten rules of Englishness, therefore, I am clearly not suggesting that such rules are universally obeyed in English society, or that no exceptions or deviations will be found. That would be ludicrous. My claim is only that these rules are 'normal and usual' enough to be helpful in understanding and defining our national character.

Rules of the Road

If home is what the insular, inhibited English have instead of social skills, how do we cope when we venture outside our castles? The quick answer, as you might expect, is 'not very well'. But after more than ten years of participant observation in train stations, on buses and on the streets, I should be a bit more specific than that, and try to decipher the unwritten codes of conduct involved. I'm calling these 'rules of the road' for shorthand, but I'm really talking about every kind of transport—cars, trains, aeroplanes, taxis, buses, bicycles, motorbikes, feet, etc.—and every aspect of the process of getting from a to b.

Speaking of cars, I should mention that I can't drive. I did try to learn, once, but after a few lessons the driving instructor and I agreed that it was not a good idea, and that I could save a lot of innocent lives by sticking to public transport. From a research point of view, this apparent handicap has proved a blessing in disguise, as it means that I get to spend a lot of time observing English behaviour and conducting devious little field-experiments on trains and buses, and interviewing captive taxi drivers about the quirks and habits of their passengers. And whenever I do travel by car, some long-suffering friend or relative is always doing the driving, which leaves me free to scrutinize their behaviour and that of other road users.

Public Transport Rules

But I'll start with the rules of behaviour on public transport, as these more graphically illustrate the problems faced by the English when we step outside the security and privacy of our homes.

The Denial Rule

Our main coping mechanism on public transport is a form of what psychologists call 'denial': we try to avoid acknowledging that we are among a scary crowd of strangers, and to maintain as much privacy as possible, by pretending that they do not exist—and, much of the time, pretending that we do not exist either. The denial rule requires us to avoid talking to strangers, or even making eye contact with them, or indeed acknowledging their presence in any way unless absolutely necessary. At the same time, the rule imposes an obligation to avoid drawing attention to oneself and to mind one's own business.

It is common, and considered entirely normal, for English commuters to make their morning and evening train journeys with the same group of people for many years without ever exchanging a word. The more you think about this, the more utterly incredible it seems, yet everyone I spoke to confirmed the story.

'After a while,' one commuter told me, 'if you see the same person every morning on the platform, and maybe quite often sit opposite them on the train, you might start to just nod to each other when you arrive, but that's about as far as it goes.' 'How long is "a while"?' I asked. 'Oh, maybe a year or so—it depends; some people are more outgoing than others, you know?' 'Right,' I said (wondering what definition of "outgoing" she could possibly have in mind). 'So, a particularly "outgoing" person might start to greet you with a nod after seeing you every morning for say, what, a couple of months?' 'Mmm, well, maybe,' my informant sounded doubtful, 'but actually that would be a bit, um, forward—a bit pushy; that would make me a bit uncomfortable.'

This informant—a young woman working as a secretary for a PR agency in London— was not an especially shy or retiring person. In fact, I would have described her as quite the opposite: friendly, lively and gregarious. I am quoting her here because her responses are typical—almost all of the commuters I interviewed said that even a brief nod constituted a fairly drastic escalation of intimacy, and most were highly cautious about progressing to this stage, because, as another typical commuter explained, 'Once you start greeting people like that—nodding, I mean—unless you're very careful, you might end up starting to say "good morning" or something, and then you could end up actually having to *talk* to them.' I recorded other commuters using expressions such as 'tip of the iceberg' and 'slippery slope' to explain their avoidance of premature nodding, or even making eye contact with other commuters (eye contact in public places in England is never more than a fraction of a second: if you do accidentally meet a stranger's eye, you must look away immediately—to maintain eye contact for even a full second may be interpreted as either flirtation or aggression).

But what would be so awful, I asked each of my informants, about a brief friendly chat with a fellow commuter? This was clearly regarded as an exceptionally stupid question. Obviously, the problem with actually speaking to a fellow commuter was that if you did it once, you might be expected to do it again—and again, and again: having acknowledged the person's existence, you could not go back to pretending that they did not exist, and you could end up having to exchange polite words with them *every day*. You would almost certainly have nothing in common, so these conversations would be highly awkward and embarrassing. Or else you would have to find ways of avoiding the person—standing at the other end of the platform, for example, or hiding behind the coffee kiosk, and deliberately choosing a different compartment on the train, which would be rude and equally embarrassing. The whole thing would become a nightmare; it didn't bear thinking about.

I laughed at all this at first, of course, but after a little soul-searching realised that I have often practised much the same kind of contact-avoidance myself, and actually with rather less justification. How can I laugh at the fears and elaborate avoidance strategies of English commuters, when I employ much the same tactics to save myself from a mere half-hour or so of uncomfortable interaction on a one-off [one-time] journey? They could be 'stuck with' someone *every day* for *years*. They're right: it doesn't bear thinking about. Best not even to nod for at least a year, definitely.

The one exception to my utterly typical English behaviour on public transport is when I am in 'fieldwork mode'—that is, when I have burning questions to ask or hypotheses to test, and I am actively looking for 'subjects' to interview or upon whom to conduct experiments. Other forms of fieldwork, such as simple observation, are entirely compatible with squeamishly English contact-avoidance—in fact, the researcher's notebook serves as a useful barrier-signal. But to interview people or conduct field-experiments, I have to take a deep breath and try to overcome my fears and inhibitions. When interviewing the English on public transport, I have to overcome their inhibitions as well. In a sense, all my field-interviews with commuters and other bus, train and tube passengers were also experiments in rule-breaking, as by speaking to them at all I was automatically in breach of the denial rule. Whenever possible, therefore, I tried to minimize the distress (for both of us) by taking advantage of one of the exceptions to the denial rule.

Exceptions to the Denial Rule

There are three situations in which one is allowed to break the denial rule, acknowledge the existence of other passengers, and actually speak directly to them.

The Politeness Exception

The first situation is one I call the 'politeness exception': when not speaking would constitute a greater rudeness than the invasion of privacy by speaking—such as when one accidentally bumps into people and must apologize, or when one must say 'excuse me' to get past them, or ask if the seat next to them is free, or if they mind having the window open. It is important to note, however, that these politenesses are *not* regarded as ice-breakers or legitimate preludes to any further conversation: having made your necessary apology or request, you must immediately revert to the denial state, both parties pretending that the other does not exist. The politeness exception is therefore not of much use for research purposes, except as a means of gauging the degree of distress or irritation likely to be caused by any attempt at further interaction: if the response to my polite apology or request was grudgingly monosyllabic, or a mere non-verbal signal such as a curt nod, I would be less inclined to regard the person as a potential informant.

The Information Exception

Somewhat more helpful was the 'information exception', whereby one may break the denial rule to ask for vital information, such as 'Is this the right train for Paddington?' or 'Does this one stop at Reading?' or 'Do you know if this is the right platform for Clapham Junction?' The responses to such questions are often mildly humorous: I've lost count of the number of times my panicky 'Is this the right train for Paddington?' has prompted replies such as 'Well, I certainly hope so!' or 'If it's not, I'm in trouble!' When I ask: 'Is this the fast train to London?' (meaning the direct train, as opposed to the 'stopping' train that calls at lots of small stations), some Eeyorish wit is sure to respond with 'Well, depends what you mean by "fast" . . .' Although technically the same principle applies as with the politeness exception, in that one is supposed to revert to the denial state once the necessary information has been imparted, the more humorous responses can sometimes indicate a greater willingness to exchange at least a few more words—particularly if one can subtly engineer the conversation towards the 'moan exception' category.

The Moan Exception

The 'moan exception' to the denial rule normally only occurs when something goes wrong—such as an announcement over the loudspeakers that the train or plane will be delayed or cancelled, or the train or tube stopping in the middle of nowhere or in a tunnel for no apparent reason, or an inordinately long wait for the bus to change drivers, or some other unforeseen problem or disruption.

On these occasions, English passengers appear suddenly to become aware of each other's existence. Our reactions are always the same and minutely predictable, almost as though they had been choreographed. A loudspeaker platform announcement of a delayed train, or an abrupt jerking stop in the middle of the countryside, prompts an immediate outbreak of sociable body language: people make eye contact; sigh noisily; exchange long-suffering smiles, shrugs, raised eyebrows and eye-rolling grimaces—invariably followed or accompanied by snide or weary comments on the dire state of the railway system. Someone will always say 'Huh, *typical!*' [or] another will say 'Oh, *now* what?' . . .

Nowadays, you will also nearly always hear at least one comment containing the phrase 'the wrong sort of leaves', a reference to a now legendary excuse offered by the railway operators when 'leaves on the track' caused extensive disruption to a large part of the railway system. When it was pointed out to them that fallen leaves were a perfectly normal feature of autumn and had never previously brought the railways to a halt, they responded plaintively that these were 'the wrong sort of leaves'. This admittedly daft [crazy or stupid] remark made headlines in all the newspapers and news broadcasts at the time, and has been a standing joke ever since. It is often adapted to suit the circumstances of the delay or disruption in question: if the loudspeaker announcement blames snow for the delay, someone will invariably say: 'The wrong sort of snow, I suppose!' I was once waiting for a train at my local station in Oxford when the loudspeaker announced a delay due to 'a cow on the line outside Banbury"[4]: three people on the platform simultaneously piped up: 'The wrong sort of cow!'

Such problems seem to have an instant bonding effect on English passengers, clearly based on the 'them and us' principle. The opportunity to moan or, even better, the opportunity to indulge in *witty* moaning, is irresistible. The moan-rests prompted by delayed trains or other public-transport disruptions are very much like weather-moaning: utterly pointless, in that we all know and stoically accept that nothing can or will be done to remedy the situation, but enjoyable and highly effective as facilitators of social interaction.

The moan exception turns out, however, to be yet another of those 'exceptions that prove the rule'. Although we appear to break the denial rule to indulge in this favourite pastime, and may even engage in quite prolonged discussion of the flaws and failings of the relevant public-transport system (and by extension the incompetence of the authorities, companies or government departments deemed responsible for its inadequacies) it is universally understood that such conversations are a 'one-off'. What is involved is not a true breach of the denial rule, but a temporary suspension. Commuters know that they can share an enjoyable moan about a delayed train without incurring any obligation to talk to their fellow moaners again the next morning, or even to acknowledge their existence. The denial rule is suspended only for the duration of the collective whinge [whining]. Once we have completed our moan, silence is resumed, and we can go back to ignoring each other for another year or so—or until the next plague of delinquent leaves or suicidal cows. The moan exception proves the rule precisely because it is specifically recognized as an exception.

The temporary suspension of the denial rule during moaning-opportunities does, however, offer the intrepid researcher a little chink in the privacy armour of the English commuter—a brief chance to ask a few pertinent questions without seeming to pry or intrude. I had to be quick, though, to avoid giving the impression that I had misunderstood the strictly temporary nature of the moan exception and was settling in for a long chat.

Waiting for moan-worthy mishaps and disruptions may sound like a rather unsatisfactory and unreliable way to conduct field-research interviews—if you are unfamiliar with the vagaries of English public transport, that is. Anyone who lives here will know that few journeys are completed without at least one delay or interruption, and if you are English (and generous-spirited), you will no doubt be pleased to hear that there is one person in the country who actively benefits from all those leaves, cows, floods, engine troubles, bottlenecks, AWOL drivers, signal faults, points failures and other obscure malfunctions and obstructions.

Apart from moan-exception interview opportunities, public transport was one of the field locations in which I was often obliged to conduct 'formal' interviews, by which I mean interviews where the subjects knew that they were being interviewed. My preferred method of disguising interviews as casual, ordinary conversations—a highly effective technique at pub bar counters, at the races, at parties and other locations where conversation between strangers is permitted (although regulated by strict protocols)—was not suitable in environments subject to the denial rule. Under these conditions, it was less threatening to come clean and tell people that I was doing research for a book, asking politely if they would mind answering 'just a couple of questions', rather than attempting to break the denial rule and engage them in spontaneous chat. A researcher with a notebook is a nuisance, of course, but much less scary than a random stranger trying to start a conversation for no apparent reason. If you simply start chatting to English people on trains or buses, they tend to assume that you are either drunk, drugged or deranged.[5] Social scientists are not universally liked or appreciated, but we are still marginally more acceptable than alcoholics and escaped lunatics.

This formal approach was not necessary with foreigners, however, as they do not suffer from English fears, inhibitions and privacy obsessions, and seemed generally quite happy to engage in casual chat. In fact, many tourists were positively delighted to encounter, at last, a 'sociable', 'friendly' native, especially one who expressed genuine interest in their impressions of England and the English. Quite apart from my preference for informal, incognito interviews, I could not bring myself to dispel their illusions and spoil their holiday by revealing my ulterior motives— although I must admit to an occasional twinge of conscience when effusive visitors confided that I had caused them to revise their view of the English as a cold and standoffish race. Whenever possible, I did my best to explain that most English people observe the denial rule on public transport, and tried to direct them towards more sociable environments such as pub bar counters—but if you are one of the hapless tourists who were misled by my 'interviews', I can only apologize, thank you for your contribution to my research, and hope that this book will clear up any confusions I may have caused.

The Mobile-phone Ostrich Exception

I mentioned earlier that there are two aspects to the denial rule: pretending that other people do not exist, and also, much of the time, pretending that we do not exist either. On public transport, it is considered unseemly to draw attention to oneself. There are people who violate this rule, talking and laughing loudly with each other instead of hiding quietly behind their newspapers in the approved manner, but they have always been a much-frowned-upon minority.

Until the advent of the mobile phone, which brings out the ostrich in us: just as the dimwit ostrich with its head in the sand believes that it is invisible, the dimwit English passenger on a mobile phone imagines that he or she is inaudible. People on mobiles often seem to go about in a little personal bubble, oblivious to the crowds around them, connected only to the person at the other end of the phone. They will happily discuss the details of their domestic or business affairs, matters that would normally be considered private or confidential, in tones loud enough for half a train carriage to hear. Tremendously useful for eavesdropping nosey researchers—I get a lot of data from mobile-phone ostriches—but irritating for all the other passengers. Not that they would actually *do* anything about it, of course, except tut and sigh and roll their eyes and shake their heads.

We are not all ostriches. Many English passengers—the majority, even—are smart enough to realise that other people can in fact hear what you are saying on your mobile, and we do our best to keep our voices down. The oblivious loudmouths are still a minority, but they are a highly noticeable and annoying minority. Part of the problem is that the English will not complain—not directly, to the person making the noise, only quietly to each other, or to colleagues when they get to work, or to their spouse when they get home, or in letters to the newspapers. Our television and radio comedy programmes are full of amusing sketches about the infuriating stupidity of noisy mobile-phone ostriches, and the banality or utter pointlessness of their 'I'm on a train!' conversations. Newspaper columnists are equally witty on the subject.

In typically English fashion, we channel our anger into endless clever jokes and ritual moans, reams of print and hours of airtime, but fail to address the real source of the problem. Not one of us is brave or blunt enough to go up to a mobile-phone ostrich and simply ask him or her to keep it down. The train companies are aware of the issue, and some have designated certain sections of their trains as 'quiet' carriages, where the use of mobile phones is prohibited. Most people observe this rule, but when an occasional rogue ostrich ignores the signs, nobody dares to confront the offender. Even in a designated 'quiet' carriage, the worst an ostrich can expect is a lot of glares and pointed looks.

Courtesy Rules

Although many of the foreign visitors I interviewed complained about English reserve, they all tended to be impressed by our courtesy. This apparent contradiction is accurately expressed by Bill Bryson, who is amazed and somewhat spooked by the 'orderly quiet' of the London Underground: 'All these thousands of people passing on stairs and escalators, stepping on and off crowded trains, sliding off into the darkness with wobbling heads, and never speaking, like characters from *Night of the Living Dead*.' A few pages later, at another train station, he is full of praise for the courteous behaviour of a large crowd of rugby fans: 'They boarded with patience and without pushing, and said "sorry" when they bumped or inadvertently impinged on someone's space. I admired this instinctive consideration for others, and was struck by what a regular thing that is in Britain and how little it is noticed.'

'Negative-politeness' Rules

But our much-maligned reserve and our much-admired courtesy are, it seems to me, two sides of the same coin. In fact, at one level, our reserve is a *form* of courtesy—the kind of courtesy that the sociolinguists Brown and Levinson call 'negative politeness', meaning that it is concerned with other people's need not to be intruded or imposed upon (as opposed to 'positive politeness', which is concerned with their need for inclusion and social approval). The restraint, cautiousness and contact-avoidance of English public-transport passengers—the standoffishness that foreigners complain about—are all characteristic features of 'negative politeness'. What looks like unfriendliness is really a kind of consideration: we judge others by ourselves, and assume that everyone shares our obsessive need for privacy—so we mind our own business and politely ignore them.

All cultures practise both forms of politeness, but most incline somewhat more towards one than the other. The English are a predominantly 'negative-politeness' culture, while the Americans, for example, tend to favour the more warm, inclusive 'positive-politeness' mode. Although these are crude distinctions, and there are class and other sub-cultural variations in both types of culture, it seems probable that visitors from 'positive-politeness' cultures are more likely to misunderstand and be offended by the 'polite' aloofness of the English than those from cultures that are similar to our own in this respect (according to Brown and Levinson, these 'negative-politeness' cultures include Japan, Madagascar and certain sections of Indian society).

Bumping Experiments and the Reflex-apology Rule
Which brings me to the bumping experiments. I spent several amusing afternoons in busy, crowded public places (train stations, tube stations, bus stations, shopping centres, street corners, etc.) accidentally-on-purpose bumping into people to see if they would say 'sorry'. A number of my informants, both natives and visitors, had cited this 'reflex apology' as a particularly striking example of English courtesy, and I was fairly sure I had experienced it myself—but I felt obliged to do the proper scientific thing and actually test the theory in a field-experiment or two.

My bumping got off to a rather poor start. The first few bumps were technically successful, in that I managed to make them seem convincingly accidental[6], but I kept messing up the experiment by blurting out an apology before the other person had a chance to speak. As usual, this turned out to be a test of my own Englishness: I found that I could not bump into someone, however gently, without automatically saying 'sorry'. After several of these false starts, I finally managed to control my knee-jerk apologies by biting my lip—firmly and rather painfully—as I did the bumps. Having perfected the technique, I tried to make my experiments as scientific as possible by bumping into a representative cross-section of the English population, in a representative sample of locations. Somewhat to my surprise, the English lived up to their reputation: about 80 per cent of my victims said 'sorry' when I lurched into them, even though the collisions were quite clearly my fault.

There were some minor variations in the response: I found that older people were slightly more likely to apologize than younger people (late-teenage males were the least apologetic, particularly when in groups), and British Asians seemed to have a somewhat stronger sorry-reflex than British Afro-Caribbeans (possibly a reflection of the negative-politeness tendency in Indian culture—such apologies being a clear example of politeness that is primarily concerned with the avoidance of imposition or intrusion). But these differences were marginal: the vast majority of the bumped, of all ages, classes and ethnic origin, apologized when I 'accidentally' jostled them.

These experiments would tell us little or nothing about Englishness if exactly the same results were obtained in other countries, so by way of 'controls' I diligently bumped into as many people as I could in France, Belgium, Italy, Russia, Poland and Lebanon. Recognising that this would not constitute a representative international sample, I also bumped into tourists of different nationalities (American, German, Japanese, Spanish, Australian,

Scandinavian) at tourist-trap locations in London and Oxford. Only the Japanese (surprise, surprise) seemed to have anything even approaching the English sorry-reflex, and they were frustratingly difficult to experiment on, as they appeared to be remarkably adept at sidestepping my attempted collisions[7]. This is not to say that my bumpees of other nationalities were discourteous or unpleasant—most just said 'Careful!' or 'Watch out!' (or the equivalent in their own language), and many reacted in a positively friendly manner, putting out a helpful arm to steady me, sometimes even solicitously checking that I was unhurt before moving on—but the automatic 'sorry' did seem to be a peculiarly English response.

George Orwell said that the English are 'inveterate gamblers, drink as much beer as their wages will permit, are devoted to bawdy jokes and use probably the foulest language in the world', but he nevertheless concluded, without contradiction, that 'The gentleness of the English civilization is perhaps its most marked characteristic'. As evidence of this, along with the good-temperedness of bus-conductors and unarmed policemen, he cited the fact that 'In no country inhabited by white men is it easier to shove people off the pavement [sidewalk]'. Quite so, and if your shove appears to be genuinely accidental, they might even apologize as they stumble into the gutter.

You may be wondering why the English seem to assume that any accidental collision is our fault, and immediately accept the blame for it by apologizing. If so, you are making a mistake. The reflex apology is just that: a reflex—an automatic, knee-jerk response, not a considered admission of guilt. This is a deeply ingrained rule: when any inadvertent, undesired contact occurs (and to the English, almost any contact is by definition undesired), we say 'sorry'.

In fact, any intrusion, impingement or imposition of any kind, however minimal or innocuous, generally requires an apology. We use the word 'sorry' as a prefix to almost any request or question: 'Sorry, but do you know if this train stops at Banbury?' 'Sorry, but is this seat free?' 'Sorry—do you have the time?' 'Sorry, but you seem to be sitting on my coat.' We say 'sorry' if our arm accidentally brushes against someone else's when passing through a crowded doorway; even a 'near miss', where no actual physical contact takes place, can often prompt an automatic 'sorry' from both parties. We often say 'sorry' when we mean 'excuse me' (or 'get out of my way'), such as when asking someone to move so we can get past them. An interrogative 'sorry?' means 'I didn't quite hear what you said—could you repeat it?' (or 'what?'). Clearly, all these sorries are not heartfelt, sincere apologies. Like 'nice', 'sorry' is a useful, versatile, all-purpose word, suitable for all occasions and circumstances. When in doubt, say 'sorry'. Englishness means *always* having to say you're sorry.

Endnotes

[1] A term coined by my father, the anthropologist Robin Fox, meaning blindness to underlying similarities between human groups and cultures because one is dazzled by the more highly visible surface differences.

[2] Such as the social psychologist Michael Argyle, who studied happiness, and the anthropologist Lionel Tiger, who has written books on optimism and pleasure, and teaches a course entitled 'The Anthropology of Fun and Games'.

3   We do, in fact, have some rules prohibiting behaviours which, while not inconceivable, are unlikely or even unnatural—see Robin Fox's work on the incest taboo, for example—cases where a factual 'it isn't done' becomes formalized as a prescriptive 'thou shalt not do it' (despite the claims of philosophers who hold that it is logically impossible to derive an 'ought' from an 'is'), but these tend to be universal rules, rather than the culture-specific rules that concern us here.

4   This is not as improbable as it might sound: cows on the line are quite a frequent problem in this country, and most regular rail passengers will have heard a similar announcement at least once.

5   If you are female, lone males may instead assume that you are chatting them up [i.e., flirting]. They are therefore more than willing to break the denial rule and talk to you, but it can then be difficult to extricate yourself from the conversation. Even the 'formal interview' approach can be misinterpreted, so I tended to avoid speaking to unaccompanied males unless I was (a) surrounded by other passengers and (b) getting out at the next stop.

6   If you would like to try this yourself, I found that the best method was to pretend to be searching for something in my shoulder-bag: with my head down and hair over my eyes, I could actually still see my 'target' and calculate my trajectory to achieve a relatively gentle bump, while giving the impression that I was genuinely distracted by my bag-rumblings.

7   I have since been told about a cross-cultural study of pedestrians which showed that the Japanese are indeed much more skilled than other nations at avoiding bumping into each other in crowded public places—so this was not just my imagination.

QUESTIONS FOR DISCUSSION

1.   What do you think of Fox's introductory remarks about participant observation as a method of inquiry? How does she justify her choice to study her own people and culture? What does she mean by "rule"? Do you think a participant observer who is a native of a given culture can extract the rules of behavior in that culture?

2.   What is Fox's main claim about British behavior on public transport? How does she support this claim? Do you believe she has given enough evidence to support her claim?

3.   What exceptions apply to the general rule about behavior on public transport? How does Fox support her contention that these exceptions exist? Do you accept her evidence that these are exceptions to the rule?

4.   If you have spent any time in England or know any British people, does your perception of this particular rule of British behavior square with Fox's? If not, how does it differ?

5.   Fox quotes George Orwell and Bill Bryson to support the claim that the British are a very gentle and polite people. Does this claim hold up given what she reports about their pretending not to notice others? What do you think of the theory of "negative politeness"? Do you ever find yourself acting in some of the negatively polite ways she describes?

6. What would you say are the rules of behavior for Americans riding buses, subways, and trains?

7. Is there anything about Fox's methods that you find questionable or unethical? What do you think an institutional review board would have said to a proposal to conduct the kind of research that Fox did?

8. How does the style of Fox's writing differ from that in Hudson and den Boer's article or in Smith and Denton's? Did you like the style? Why or why not? How often do you find this style in writing you read for your courses?

Soul Searching: The Religious
and Spiritual Lives of American Teenagers

by
Christian Smith with Melinda Lundquist Denton

Christian Smith is the author of several books and numerous articles about morality and religion. Previously the Stuart Chapin Distinguished Professor of Sociology at the University of North Carolina, Chapel Hill, Smith joined the faculty of Notre Dame University in 2006, where he is the William R. Kenan Professor of Sociology and Director of the Center for the Sociology of Religion. He received his bachelor's degree from Gordon College in Massachusetts, then studied one year at the Harvard Divinity School before earning both his master's and doctoral degrees in sociology from Harvard University. Dr. Smith directs the National Study of Youth and Religion (NSYR). Melinda Lundquist Denton, an assistant professor of sociology at Clemson University, was the project manager for Wave I of the NSYR. The following excerpts from the book Soul Searching: The Religious and Spiritual Lives of American Teenagers *come from Chapter 2, "Mapping the Big Picture."*

Maps are great for providing a big picture sense of the proportions and contours of the spaces that we occupy. Maps help us to understand the geography through which we move, so that we know where we stand in the world and what the world is like beyond our immediate field of vision. Maps do this by simplifying relevant features of the actual world we live in with visual symbols, such as lines, colors, dots, and shapes depicting roads, rivers, cities, and altitudes. Sociological research can also descriptively map the contours and proportions of social life by simplifying features of the social world relevant to a particular interest and representing them with symbols. But instead of using lines, colors, and dots for its symbolic representations, sociological research often uses numbers—such as frequencies, percentages, averages—to represent through numeric abstraction the social world's dimensions and qualities. All such descriptions oversimplify the complexity of the real social world in which we live. And maps as abstractions are never as interesting as, say, personal stories. But, as with maps generally, such simplified descriptions can help to provide an overarching sense of our social world, where we stand within it, and what it looks like beyond our immediate field of vision.

In this chapter, we descriptively map the world of contemporary U.S. adolescent religion and spirituality by presenting statistical findings from the National Survey of Youth and Religion. Following chapters explore some of the cultural meanings, textures, and complexities of U.S. adolescent faith. But before getting to such meanings and complexities, we outline some of the major dimensions of adolescent religion and spirituality to build a general framework of knowledge about the proportions and distributions of the matter in question. This chapter is full of numbers and percentages, which take some effort to digest. But working through the abstract statistics pays off in providing us with a clear overview of the religious and spiritual lives of U.S. teenagers.[1] Even so, those who are less interested in detailed statistics but are intrigued by the cultural meanings of religion can easily skim this chapter, read its conclusion, and come back to the details later.

Reprinted from *Soul Searching: The Religious and Spiritual Lives of American Teenagers* (2005), Oxford University Press.

Religious Affiliations and Identities

We begin with some basic statistics about U.S. adolescent religious affiliations and identities. What kind of religious people do U.S. teens consider themselves to be? In which religious denominations are they located? According to NSYR data presented in table 1, three quarters of U.S. teens between 13 and 17 years old are Christians. About one-half of teens are Protestant and one-quarter are Catholic. Christianity, in other words, still very much dominates American religion numerically at the level of teenage affiliation. The next largest group is the 16 percent of U.S. teens who consider themselves to be not religious. Note that not all of this 16 percent *acts* not religious. As we will see in the next chapter, many nonreligious U.S. teens believe in God, attend church, and pray; thus, there must be something in the way they understand the term "religious" that causes them to identify themselves as not religious on surveys. Seven percent of U.S. teens affiliate with one of the many minority U.S. religions, particularly Mormonism (2.5 percent) and Judaism (1.5 percent). Finally, nearly 2 percent do not know what their religion is or refused to answer the question.

TABLE 1. Religious Affiliations of U.S. Adolescents, Ages 13–17 (Percentages)

	U.S.
Teen religious affiliation	
Protestant	52.0
Catholic	23.0
Mormon	2.5
Jewish	1.5
Jehovah's Witness	0.6
Muslim	0.5
Eastern Orthodox	0.3
Buddhist	0.3
Pagan or Wiccan	0.3
Hindu	0.1
Christian Science	0.1
Native American	0.1
Unitarian Universalist	0.1
Miscellaneous other	0.2
Don't know/refused	1.8
Teen not religious	16.0
Teen affiliates with two different faiths	2.8

SOURCE: National Survey of Youth and Religion, 2002–3.

NOTE: Percentages may not add to 100 due to rounding.

Some interesting findings are immediately apparent in table 1. First, U.S. youth are not flocking in droves to "alternative" religions and spiritualities such as paganism and Wicca. Teenagers who are pagan or Wiccan represent fewer than one-third of 1 percent of U.S. teens. There are thus twice the number of Jehovah's Witness teens as there are pagan and Wiccan teens. Second, it does not appear that American religion, at the adolescent level at least, is being profoundly diversified by new immigrant groups. Harvard's Diana Eck asserts that the United States is the most religiously diverse nation in the world.[2] That simply is not true. The vast majority of U.S. teens (like adults) are Christian or not religious. The so-called new immigrant religions are tiny fractions of adolescent religion. Muslim teens represent one-half of 1 percent of U.S. teens, Buddhists less than one-third of 1 percent, and Hindu a mere one-tenth of 1 percent.[3] For every one Muslim teen in the United States there are five in the home-grown American religion of Mormonism.[4] For every Buddhist teen there are five Jewish teens. The case for rapid numeric diversification and pluralization of U.S. religions seems to have been overstated. The country has indeed seen a great deal of immigration in recent decades, but many of those immigrants came to the United States as Christians, such as Catholic Latinos from Mexico, the Caribbean, and Central America, and Christian believers from a variety of non-Christian nations seeking refuge from anti-Christian persecution in their home countries. In addition, some immigrant youth become Christians in the process of assimilating to U.S. culture.

The third finding worth noting in table 1 is that relatively few U.S. teens (2.8 percent) affiliate with more than one religion. Numerous scholarly and journalistic voices have recently called attention to an alleged rise in an eclectic, mix-and-match approach to religion among youth. We do not find evidence for this in our data. Nearly all U.S. teens affiliate with one religion or no religion. Very few adhere to two religions, and that small minority apparently does so not because they are on some syncretistic spiritual quest, but because their parents affiliate with two different religions which they wish to honor. Even more telling, only *one* of our 3,290 survey respondents (0.0003 percent of all U.S. teens) professed to affiliate with three religions, in this case, Catholicism, Judaism, and Buddhism. U.S. teenagers as a whole are thus not religiously promiscuous faith mixers. Almost all stick with one religious faith, if any.

Table 2 unpacks the 52 percent of Protestants seen in table 1, specifying the various denominational families and traditions that teens call their religious homes.[5] The proportions seen in table 2 roughly mirror the distribution of U.S. adults into these groups. Clearly, the Baptists have the largest proportion of teens here (17.3 percent), followed by other traditions with notable numbers, including Methodists (4.7 percent), Lutherans (3.5 percent), and nondenominational churches (3 percent). Most of the remainder are scattered across the vast variety of denominations and traditions that constitute U.S. Protestantism. Note, however, that nearly 16 percent of youth do not appear familiar enough with any specific group they may be affiliated with and so answer[ed] this question as "Just Christian," "Just Protestant," or "Don't know" or refused to answer the question.

How similar to or different from their parents are U.S. religious teens? One popular stereotype of American youth casts them as religious dissidents who find their parents' religious beliefs and practices old and meaningless and want to have little to do with any of it. Is this so? According to NSYR data shown in table 3, about three in four religious teens in the United States consider their own religious beliefs somewhat or very similar to their parents; they are more

TABLE 2. Protestant Denominations of the Congregations Teens Attend, Protestant U.S. Adolescents, Ages 13–17 (Percentages)

Adventist	0.43	Free Methodist Church	0.03
Assemblies of God	0.71	Friends/Quaker	0.11
Baptist	17.3	Holiness	0.34
Bible Church	0.22	Independent/Nondenominational	3.02
Brethren	0.21	Lutheran	3.54
Charismatic	0.04	Mennonite	0.12
Christian and Missionary Alliance	0.03	Methodist	4.74
Church of Christ	1.21	Missionary Church	0.04
Church of God	0.46	Nazarene, Church of the	0.09
Calvary Chapel	0.02	Pentecostal	1.82
Congregationalist	0.2	Presbyterian/Reformed	1.83
Disciples of Christ	0.06	United Church of Christ	0.09
Episcopalian	0.82	Vineyard Fellowship	0.02
Evangelical, Independent	0.31	Wesleyan Church	0.16
Evangelical Covenant	0.02	Just Protestant	0.18
Evangelical Free Church	0.07	Just Christian	12.58
Four Square	0.08	Don't know/refused	3.01

SOURCE: National Survey of Youth and Religion, 2002–3.

NOTE: Percentages may not add to 100 due to rounding.

similar to mother's than to father's beliefs (teen similarity to parent religion for nonreligious teens is examined in chapter 3). Only 6 percent of teens consider their religious beliefs very different from that of their mother and 11 percent very different from that of their father. And not all who reported "very different" for this question are rebellious, antireligious teens of religiously devout parents. Fully 37 percent of teens whose beliefs are very different from their mother's and 45 percent whose beliefs are very different from their father's report on another question that their own religious faith is very or extremely important to them in their daily lives. They appear to hold firm to their own faith but apparently simply don't agree with their parents on most religious matters.

Religious similarity to parents varies somewhat by the religious tradition the teen belongs to, as do many of the other religion variables we examine in this chapter. Therefore, table 4 and most of the tables below split out all U.S. teens for comparisons into six religious traditions by the denominations with which they affiliate (Appendix D explains the methods used to categorize teens into these groups by religious denomination):

- Conservative Protestant (CP)
- Mainline Protestant (MP)

TABLE 3. Belief Similarity of Religious U.S. Adolescents, Ages 13–17, to Mother and Father (Percentages)

	U.S. Religious Teens	Teen Religious Tradition					
		CP	MP	BP	RC	J	LDS
Religious belief similarity to mother's							
Very similar	41	48	36	39	33	41	73
Somewhat similar	37	34	43	37	41	27	18
Somewhat different	15	12	14	15	20	24	5
Very different	6	5	6	7	6	8	4
Religious belief similarity to father's							
Very similar	36	42	30	32	31	38	75
Somewhat similar	36	34	40	34	39	22	17
Somewhat different	16	15	19	20	17	35	4
Very different	11	8	9	13	13	5	4

SOURCE: National Survey of Youth and Religion, 2002–3.

NOTES: Percentages may not add to 100 due to rounding and unreported don't know and refused answers. Jewish respondents include only religiously Jewish, not culturally Jewish only respondents.

- Black Protestant (BP)
- Catholic (RC)
- Jewish (J)
- Mormon/Latter-day Saint (LDS)

Here we see that Mormon teens are the most likely among all U.S. teens to hold religious beliefs similar to their parents', followed by conservative Protestant, mainline Protestant, Catholic, and black Protestant teens. Jewish teens are comparatively the least likely to say they share the beliefs of their parents, although, to keep it in perspective, still an impressive majority of them do. If anything, then, U.S. teens lean strongly toward similarity with their parents in religious belief.

Personal Religious Practices

[A]nother important dimension of religious life worth examining is religious practices: specific actions in which religious believers engage over time that embody spiritual meaning and foster personal formation toward excellence in religious faith and works. Religious practices are spiritually significant habits intentionally engaged in for the purpose of being shaped by them toward the good as known by a religious faith. Prayer, scripture reading, meditation, and tithing are well-known religious practices, but there are many other possibilities.[6] Not all religious traditions encourage or require observing the same religious practices, obviously, but the NSYR survey asked all teens about many practices anyway, simply to map out proportions. Inclusion in table 4, however, does not imply that all teens should be engaging all of these practices. In any case, table 4 shows their reported engagement in a great variety of religious practices, with the first cluster of measures listed in order of participation, from least to greatest. What we see is that significant minorities of U.S. teenagers report having engaged in most of a long list of religious practices in the previous year. Fewer than 20 percent have meditated, served as acolytes, or participated in a religious group meeting at school. Between 20 and 29 percent have taught Sunday school, burned candles or incense for religious reasons, engaged in the spiritual disciplines of fasting or self-denial, and participated in a scripture study or prayer or religious music group. About one-third of teens report having read a religious book, spoken at a religious service, practiced a religious day of rest, and attended a religious music concert, and nearly half have worn clothing or jewelry with religious meaning, shared their faith with another person, and listened to religious music outside of a concert. (Nearly 60 percent of teens report having worked toward relational reconciliation, although whether or not this was religiously motivated was not specified by the survey question.)

Differences across religious traditions for many of these practices are notable, although not consistent across them all. Mormon teens, for instance, are strong on sharing their faith and teaching Sunday school, among other practices, but seem to avoid burning candles and incense and are less likely than other groups to wear jewelry or clothing that expresses spiritual meaning. Black Protestant teens are big on playing or singing in religious music groups and choirs but come out on the lower end on spiritual meditation. Similar comparative observations could be made for teens in other religious traditions, although space does not allow for specific mention of all interesting differences, which readers will have to study in greater depth. Suffice it to say here that significant minorities of U.S. teens of all religious traditions examined profess in their survey answers to have in the previous year engaged in nearly all of the different religious practices we asked about. Furthermore, although the NSYR did not ask all religious practice questions of nonreligious teens, for obvious reasons, more than trivial numbers of them report having engaged in the previous year in most of the religious practices about which the survey did ask. Twenty percent of nonreligious teens, for instance, listen to religious music, 15 percent wore religious jewelry or clothing, 11 percent burned candles or incense for spiritual reasons, 11 percent practiced spiritual meditation, and 9 percent attended a religious music concert. Thus, while the majority of nonreligious U.S. teenagers refrain from religious practices, not all do.

Table 3 also explores the reported personal prayer practices of U.S. teens. Nearly 40 percent report that they pray daily or more often; nearly 30 percent pray once or a few times a week; 20 percent pray more sporadically than that; and 15 percent of U.S. teens never pray. Again, the variance in frequency of personal prayer across all U.S. teens is impressive. Mormon teens appear to pray the most often, followed by black Protestant and conservative Protestant teens. Catholics and mainline Protestants pray alone with comparative moderate frequency. Jewish and nonreligious teens are the least likely to engage in the regular practice of personal prayer. At 5 percent, the nonreligious are the most likely never to pray, but they are also slightly more likely than Jewish youth to pray once a week or more. Social location in

TABLE 4. Personal Religious Practices of U.S. Adolescents, Ages 13–17 (Percentages)

	U.S.	Religious Tradition						
		CP	MP	BP	RC	J	LDS	NR
In prior year, teen:								
Practiced religious or spiritual meditation not including prayer	10	8	10	7	10	7	9	11
Served as an acolyte or altar server	11	7	25	10	16	1	13	—
Been part of a religious support of evangelism or prayer group that meets at school	15	25	17	17	8	7	17	—
Taught a Sunday School or religious education class	20	28	26	22	15	16	42	—
Burned candles or incense that had religious or spiritual meaning	21	14	24	12	35	43	7	11
Fasted or denied self something as spiritual discipline	24	22	25	20	29	49	68	4
Been part of any other scripture study or prayer group	27	42	31	35	17	26	50	—
Played or sang in a religious music group or choir	28	37	35	52	18	14	49	—
Read a devotional, religious, or spiritual book other than the scriptures	30	45	28	29	22	28	68	—
Spoke publicly about own faith in a religious service or meeting (not including bar/bat mitzvah)	30	42	33	34	20	21	65	—
Tried to practice a weekly day of rest or Sabbath	31	40	27	35	30	25	67	5
Attended a religious music concert	34	51	51	41	20	16	42	9
Chose to wear jewelry or clothing expressing religious or spiritual meaning	41	49	47	41	42	37	37	15
Shared own religious faith with someone not of faith	43	56	51	41	37	58	72	—
Listened to religious radio programs, or CDs or tapes by a religious music group	51	70	52	79	35	18	59	20
Worked hard to reconcile a broken relationship	59	61	63	50	61	57	55	53

Continued

TABLE 4. (Continued)

	U.S.	Religious Tradition						
		CP	MP	BP	RC	J	LDS	NR
Frequency of teen praying alone								
Many times a day	16	22	13	30	10	1	33	4
About once a day	22	27	19	25	23	8	24	7
A few times a week	15	18	18	14	16	4	11	8
About once a week	12	11	16	13	13	7	7	8
1-2 times a month	13	12	14	10	16	28	4	10
Less than once a month	7	5	8	3	9	18	9	10
Never	15	5	11	5	13	34	12	51
Public professions of faith								
Of all Christians: been confirmed or baptized as public affirmation of faith (not infant baptism)	46	54	59	53	—	—	—	—
Of all Jewish: had a bar or bat mitzvah						73		
Of all Mormons: been confirmed or baptized as public affirmation of faith (not infant baptism)							79	
Of all other religions: done any religious rite of passage or public affirmation of religious faith: 15 percent								

SOURCE: National Survey of Youth and Religion, 2002–3.

NOTE: Percentages may not add to 100 due to rounding and unreported don't know and refused answers; cells of <1 are reported as ~.

a particular U.S. religious tradition thus strongly influences the likelihood of teens engaging in the practice of personal prayer.

The NSYR also asked teens of different religious groups whether they have ever completed the religious rite of passage or public affirmation of faith appropriate to their tradition (table 4). On the high end, 79 percent of Mormon teens had been baptized. Fewer than half of all Christian teens together (46 percent) had been confirmed or baptized as youth, with the spread among those traditions ranging from 59 percent of mainline Protestant teens to 41 percent of Catholic teens on the high and low ends, respectively. Only 15 percent of teens in other religions (not Christian, Jewish, or Mormon) appear to have performed a religious rite of passage or public affirmation of faith.

Religious Group Activities

For many American teenagers, religious involvement means more than simply attending church, synagogue, mosque, or temple. A variety of other religious activities are often also available for their participation. Table 5 begins our examination of these activities by focusing in depth on U.S. teens' involvement in religious youth groups. According to NSYR data, 38 percent of all U.S. teenagers are currently involved in a religious youth group, and 69 percent are now or previously have been involved in a religious youth group.

The lives of the majority of young Americans, then, connect to religious youth groups at some time during the teenage years. Nearly 70 percent of all teens attend a religious congregation that also sponsors a youth group; fully 85 percent of teens who attend religious services belong to congregations with youth groups. The vast majority of religious congregations with teens present, then, appear to offer youth groups for their teenagers. Furthermore, 30 percent of all teens have available to them youth group programs overseen by full-time youth ministers (whether or not the teens participate in them), according to teen reports, and nearly the same number have youth groups with part-time or volunteer youth ministers (again, whether or not they participate). Slightly more than one-third of U.S. teens (36 percent) either do not attend services at a religious congregation where they might encounter a youth group or do attend a congregation that does not sponsor any youth group. Of teens involved in religious youth groups, the vast majority (32 percent of all teens, 84 percent of youth group-involved teens) participate in a youth group from their own religious congregation. Only 4 percent of all teens participating in a youth group attend youth groups at religious congregations other than their own, and fewer than one-half of 1 percent participate in religious youth groups from another religious faith altogether.

TABLE 5. Religious Youth Group Experiences of U.S. Adolescents, Ages 13–17 (Percentages)

	U.S.	Religious Tradition						
		CP	MP	BP	RC	J	LDS	NR
Currently involved in a religious youth group	38	56	55	38	24	27	72	1
Ever in life involved in a religious youth group	69	86	86	76	59	58	87	31
Involved in a congregation with a youth group (of religious service-attending teens: 85 percent)	69	86	84	81	67	63	90	—
Youth group participation rate (currently involved in YG/YG available in congregation)	52	64	64	44	32	41	75	—
Congregation has a designated youth minister								
Full-time	30	44	37	41	21	21	7	—
Part-time	9	8	12	11	11	10	2	—
Volunteer	20	18	17	21	23	12	85	—
Don't know	5	4	2	7	8	5	1	—
Not attending congregation or no youth minister	36	26	32	20	37	52	5	—

Continued

TABLE 5. (Continued)

	U.S.	Religious Tradition						
		CP	MP	BP	RC	J	LDS	NR
Youth group teen is involved with is								
Part of teen's religious congregation	32	49	49	32	20	22	66	—
Part of another religious congregation	4	6	5	5	3	4	5	—
Of another religious faith	0.4	0.5	0.5	0.4	0.5	~	~	—
Teen not in youth group	62	43	45	62	76	73	28	—
Frequency of current youth group attendance								
More than once a week	8	14	9	8	2	1	24	1
About once a week	18	29	26	15	11	11	33	~
2–3 times a month	6	7	11	7	4	5	6	~
About once a month	4	4	6	3	4	8	6	~
A few times a year	2	3	3	4	3	2	3	~
Never	62	44	45	62	76	73	28	99
Number of years currently involved teen in youth group								
8–10	5	7	4	9	4	4	15	~
5–7	7	11	13	8	3	2	15	~
2–4	19	30	32	14	11	17	42	1
1	5	7	5	5	5	4	~	~
<1	1	1	1	1	1	~	~	~
Zero	62	44	45	62	76	73	28	99
Type of youth group involvement								
Teen is a leader	13	19	19	15	5	7	36	~
Teen is just a participant	24	35	35	22	18	19	35	~
Both (leader and participant)	1	2	2	~	~	~	1	~
Not involved	62	44	45	62	76	73	28	99

SOURCE: National Survey of Youth and Religion, 2002–3.

NOTE: Percentages may not add to 100 due to rounding and unreported don't know and refused answers; cells of <1 are reported as ~.

Teen involvement with religious youth groups is highly variable by tradition. The majority of Mormon and conservative and mainline Protestant teens are currently involved in youth groups. But only about one-quarter of Catholic and Jewish youth participate in religious youth groups. Nearly one-third of currently nonreligious teens were once involved in a religious youth group, but all but 1 percent have dropped that involvement, presumably in the process of having become not religious. By dividing the percentage of teens currently involved in a religious youth group by the percentage attending congregations sponsoring youth groups, we can estimate the youth group participation rate of teens in various traditions. Mormons have the highest participation rate (75 percent), followed by mainline and conservative Protestants (64 percent each). Black Protestant and Jewish teens have participation rates of 44 and 41 percent, respectively (in many black churches, participation in youth choir functions as the equivalent of involvement in a religious youth group, about which see table 4). Of all the religious groups examined, Catholic teens have the lowest youth group participation rate, thus calculated, at 32 percent; in other words, two-thirds of Catholic teens who attend churches that sponsor youth groups do not participate in them.

But how deeply are U.S. teens involved in religious youth groups? According to table 9, nearly one-third of all teens (32 percent) report attending youth group two to three times a month or more often. Only a handful attend more sporadically. The remaining teens simply do not attend. Youth group attendance thus appears to be something teens do regularly or not do at all. Youth group attendance varies by religious tradition as well. Fifty-seven percent of Mormon teens, 43 percent of conservative Protestant teens, and 35 percent of mainline Protestant teens attend youth group weekly or more often. By contrast, only 13 percent of Catholic and 12 percent of Jewish teens attend youth group weekly or more often, and about three-quarters of those groups never attend youth group, a number surpassed only by the 99 percent of nonreligious teens who also never attend. As to years spent in youth groups, of those teens participating in religious youth groups, the majority have been involved for more than one year, with 31 percent of all U.S. teens involved for two or more years. Mormon teens tend to have been involved in youth group for more years, as have conservative and mainline Protestant teens, compared to black Protestant, Catholic, and Jewish teens. Finally, overall, one in three teens in youth groups appear to think of themselves as leaders and not merely participants. Mormon youth are the most likely to claim to be leaders in their youth groups and Catholic youth the least likely.

Table 6 examines U.S. teens' participation in a number of other kinds of organized religious group activities. Here we see, first, that 36 percent of U.S. teenagers report attending Sunday school or CCD (Confraternity of Christian Doctrine) classes almost every week or more often; 34 percent attend sporadically, between a few times a year and a few times a month; and 29 percent never attend Sunday school or CCD. Again, the variance across all U.S. teens is great. Mormon and conservative Protestant teens attend such religious education classes the most, and nonreligious and Catholic teens attend the least.

Nearly half (45 percent) of U.S. teens have attended religious youth retreats, conferences, rallies, or congresses; 39 percent have attended religious summer camps as campers; and 30 percent have participated in a religious missions team or service project. Substantial numbers of U.S. teenagers, in other words, have at least been exposed to if not significantly involved in a variety of youth-oriented religious group learning and service activities beyond religious service attendance and religious education classes. Indeed, when answers for these three questions are combined, 60 percent of all U.S. teens have participated in at least one of these religious group activities at least once; only 40 percent have done none of these activities. Mormon and conservative and mainline Protestant teens were much more likely than the average teen to be involved in youth retreats, camps, and missions and service projects; while nonreligious and Catholic youth were much less likely

TABLE 6. Religious Group Activities of U.S. Adolescents, Ages 13–17 (Percentages)

	U.S.	Religious Tradition						
		CP	MP	BP	RC	J	LDS	NR
Frequency of religious Sunday School or CCD attendance								
More than once a week	7	12	7	9	2	3	35	1
Once a week	18	24	18	18	17	19	27	1
Almost every week	11	15	17	14	9	5	11	1
A few times a month	10	12	9	20	10	9	5	1
Once a month	6	8	10	4	3	10	2	2
A few times a year	18	15	19	22	19	16	8	19
Never	29	13	19	12	40	35	9	74
Number of religious youth retreats, conferences, rallies, or congresses participated in								
0	55	42	39	57	63	59	24	85
1	12	13	14	11	13	11	11	7
2–4	19	22	28	18	18	15	22	5
5–7	6	10	10	7	3	7	17	2
8+	6	10	8	6	2	8	26	1
Number of times attended religious summer camp as a camper								
0	61	44	47	67	76	50	18	87
1	13	17	18	12	11	14	13	7
2–4	17	25	23	15	10	25	43	5
5–7	6	8	9	4	3	5	17	2
8+	3	4	3	2	1	7	8	~
Number of times gone on a religious missions team or service project								
0	70	65	55	70	77	74	30	92
1	11	13	18	10	9	8	9	4
2–4	13	16	19	13	12	3	22	2
5–7	2	2	2	2	1	6	10	~
8+	3	2	3	3	1	5	29	~

SOURCE: National Survey of Youth and Religion, 2002–3.

NOTE: Percentages may not add to 100 due to rounding and unreported don't know and refused answers.

than the average. Even so, fully 24 percent of nonreligious teens have participated in at least one of these religious group activities. Jewish teens are somewhat less likely than the average teen to be involved in religious retreats and missions and service projects, but they are also more likely to have attended a religious summer camp as a camper. Taken altogether, the numbers in table 6 suggest that the means by which U.S. teenagers connect to religion through organized group activities are many and significant, even if the effects of such involvements remain to be explored.

Religion in Relationships: Family, Friends, School, and Other Adults

Religious faith and spiritual practice are not simply matters of individual experience and institutional involvements. They are also embedded in and sometimes draw much of their life from personal relationships in families, with friends, at school, and with other adults. The NSYR asked its sample of U.S. teenagers how religion connected through and interacted with these kinds of personal social ties. Table 7 examines religious expression and interaction in the teens' families. There we see that about one-third of families (34 percent) talk together about God, the scriptures, prayer, or other religious or spiritual matters a few times a week or more; 28 percent talk about these matters a few times a month or weekly; and 38 percent a few times a year or never. Thus, in their family conversations about matters of faith, U.S.

TABLE 7. Religious Life in Families of U.S. Adolescents, Ages 13–17 (Percentages)

	U.S.	Religious Tradition						
		CP	MP	BP	RC	J	LDS	NR
Family talks about God, the scriptures, prayer, or other religious or spiritual things together								
Every day	14	19	8	27	6	~	50	4
A few times a week	20	27	15	29	18	9	24	5
About once a week	11	14	11	12	10	8	6	5
A few times a month	17	16	26	17	22	16	3	10
A few times a year	19	14	19	10	25	22	5	26
Never	19	10	20	5	19	44	11	48
Family gives thanks before or after mealtimes	54	67	54	79	45	13	84	18
Teen prays out loud or silently with one or both parents, other than at mealtimes or religious services	41	53	35	56	36	22	79	11

SOURCE: National Survey of Youth and Religion, 2002–3.

NOTE: Percentages may not add to 100 due to rounding and unreported don't know and refused answers; cells of <1 are reported as ~.

families of teenagers are split roughly into thirds between high, medium, and low levels of discussion. Families of Mormon teens appear to talk about religious and spiritual matters the most, followed next in frequency by families of black and conservative Protestant teens. Families of nonreligious and Jewish teens talk about religion the least, with only 9 percent each talking a few times a week or more often. Families of mainline Protestant and Catholic teenagers fall between those groups. Overall, however, it is a minority of every type of household that never talks about religious or spiritual matters.

A slight majority of all U.S. families with teenagers (54 percent) is reported by teens as regularly praying to give thanks before or after mealtimes. Families of Mormon, black Protestant, and conservative Protestant teens are more likely than the average family with teens to pray to give thanks at meals. They are followed in frequency by Catholic (45 percent) and nonreligious teen families (18 percent). Jewish teen families are, at 13 percent, the least likely to give thanks at meals, which, like some of the other measures in this chapter, is not an expected or required religious observance for Jews anyway. Mainline Protestant teen families pray at meals at the national average. But praying to give thanks at family mealtimes, one might think, is a rather easy and costless habit that can be as perfunctory and rote as sincere and meaningful. What about more obviously significant family religious practices? Table 7 also presents the percentage of teens whose parents in the previous year prayed together with them, out loud or silently, at times other than at meals or religious services. Forty-one percent of all teenagers report praying in this way with their parents in the previous year. Again, Mormon, black Protestant, and conservative Protestant teens are most likely to pray with their parents, and nonreligious, Jewish, mainline Protestant, and Catholic teens are less likely than the national average to pray with their parents. The overall large minorities and sometimes majorities of teens across the religious groups whose parents pray together with them other than at mealtimes or religious services is notable and perhaps even surprising, given the intimacy that can be involved in such experiences. More generally, table 7 tells us that for a significant number of U.S. teens, religion and spirituality are not simply compartmentalized in church, synagogue, mosque, or temple, but are also expressed and shared in the family life of the home.

One of the key themes of this book is that parents are normally very important in shaping the religious and spiritual lives of their teenage children, even though they may not realize it. It seems that many parents of teens rely primarily on the immediate evidence of the overt attitudes, statements, and sometimes behaviors that their teenage children dole out to them on a daily basis in order to estimate their current level of parental influence. Many of the attitudes and statements that teenagers communicate to their parents do not exactly express great admiration and gratitude for and readiness to listen to, emulate, or freely obey their parents. Many parents therefore appear to come to the conclusion that they have lost their influence in shaping the lives of their teenage children, that they no longer make any significant difference. But for most, this conclusion is mistaken. Teenagers' attitudes, verbal utterances, and immediate behaviors are often not the best evidence with which to estimate parental influence in their lives. For better or worse, most parents in fact still do profoundly influence their adolescents—often more than do their peers—their children's apparent resistance and lack of appreciation notwithstanding. This influence often also includes parental influence in adolescents' religious and spiritual lives. Simply by living and interacting with their children, most parents establish expectations, define normalcy, model life practices, set boundaries, and make demands—all of which cannot help but influence teenagers, for good or ill. Most teenagers and their parents may not realize it, but a lot of research in the sociology of religion suggests that the most important social influence in shaping young people's religious lives is the religious life modeled and taught to them by their parents.[7]

These findings in prior research are also evident in NSYR data. Take, for instance, the figures presented in table 8, which cross-tabulates differences in the importance of faith in the daily life of U.S. teenagers (in columns) by the importance of faith for their parents (in rows). Table 8 shows clearly that the importance of faith for teenagers fairly closely tracks the importance of faith for their parents. Parents for whom religious faith is quite important are thus likely to be raising teenagers for whom faith is quite important, while parents whose faith is not important are likely to be raising teenagers for whom faith is also not important. The fit is not perfect. None of this is guaranteed or determined, and sometimes, in specific instances, things turn out otherwise. But the overall positive association is clear. Hence, of parents who report that their faith is extremely important in their daily lives, 67 percent of their teens report that faith is extremely or very important in their daily lives; only 8 percent of those parents' teens report that faith is not very or not at all important in their lives. Likewise, of parents for whom faith is somewhat important in their daily lives, 61 percent of their teens also report that faith is somewhat or not very important in their daily lives; only 8 percent of those parents' teens report that faith is extremely important in their lives. Finally, of parents for whom faith is not at all important in their daily lives, 47 percent of their teens also report that religious faith is not at all or not very important in their lives; only 2 percent report that faith is extremely important in their lives. In sum, therefore, we think that the best general rule of thumb that parents might use to reckon their children's most likely religious outcomes is this: "We'll get what we are." By normal processes of socialization, and unless other significant forces intervene, more than what parents might *say* they *want* as religious outcomes in their children, most parents most likely will end up getting religiously of their children what they themselves *are*.

TABLE 8. Association of the Importance of Faith in Daily Life for U.S. Parents of Teenagers and of Their Adolescent Children, Ages 13–17 (Row percentages)

Parent importance of faith	Teen Importance of Faith					
	Extremely	Very	Somewhat	Not Very	Not at All	*Percent Total*
Extremely important	30	37	24	5	3	*100*
Very important	14	32	36	12	5	*100*
Fairly important	7	23	38	21	10	*100*
Somewhat important	8	15	41	20	16	*100*
Not very important	3	11	37	22	26	*100*
Not important at all	2	15	37	19	28	*100*

SOURCE: National Survey of Youth and Religion, 2002–3.

NOTE: Percentages may not add to 100 due to rounding and unreported don't know and refused answers.

Conclusion

Surveys cannot tell us everything or perhaps even the most important and interesting things there are to know about people and their lives. Surveys do have real limits in the insights they can render about the social world and personal experiences, perhaps especially about the lives of adolescents and perhaps especially about faith and spiritual practices. All of this is important to bear in mind. Nevertheless, survey research findings can provide an important, general starting point for further understanding of what we want to know about people's lives. We began this chapter by suggesting that, although survey data may oversimplify the complexity of the real social world, they can also help to draw a kind of map that provides an overarching sense of our social world, where we stand within it, and what it looks like beyond our immediate field of vision. We believe the NSYR findings presented in this chapter have done precisely this.

Endnotes

[1]   In trying to make sense of the findings of this book, it is essential that readers be aware of the qualifications and limitations of our research data and therefore of the conclusions we can draw from them. The findings of our telephone survey, for example, represent only teenage household with telephones, not the few percent of definitely poorer and more transient families who do not have household telephones. Our survey findings also represent only teen households where one parent and the eligible teen speak either English or Spanish; those families who speak other languages exclusively are omitted from our sample. Furthermore, survey questions themselves involve some amount of inevitable superficiality and misrepresentation. Forced-choice survey questions written to be useful for an entire population of respondents are limited, for example, in their ability to measure the ambivalences, contradictions, and complexities of people's beliefs, experiences, and feelings. To better get at these, we employed personal, in-depth, face-to-face interviews with a sample of teenage survey respondents. Yet even the most honest and in-depth interviews have limits in their ability to comprehend and represent a person's life in fullness. An ideal research project would also bring in significant linked elements of ethnographic participant observation, but this was beyond the scope of our project. Some of the limitations inherent in our research methods and subject matter we cannot fully assess. For instance, it may be that some teen interview respondents refrained from fully elaborating on their religious and spiritual beliefs and experiences because they viewed us as academic researchers from a secular state university and felt the need to be circumspect or polite in company whose religious commitments they did not know. We can know none of this with certainty precisely because of the very limitations intrinsic to such academic social research. Readers must recognize, therefore, the bounded value of our findings, which we think are rich and informative but know are not flawless, exhaustive, or absolutely definitive. More research using alternative methods from different perspectives is needed to move us closer to an even more complete understanding of the issue at hand.

[2]   Diana Eck, *A New Religious America: How a "Christian Country" Has Become the World's Most Religiously Diverse Nation* (New York: HarperCollins, 2001).

[3]   It is possible that we slightly undersampled certain Asian minority religions by not offering our survey in various Asian languages, but, given the relatively minuscule size of

only-Asian-language-speaking minority religion U.S. residents, the marginal differences here are extremely slight.

4   Many Latter-day Saints consider themselves Christians. But for purposes of clear analytical distinctions, in this book, we refer to Catholic and Protestant groups as Christian and Mormons distinctly as Mormons.

5   We do not disaggregate all of the many specific denominations under the Baptist, Methodist, and Lutheran umbrellas. Statistics on many specific major U.S. denominations, however, can be found in the 2005 NSYR-published report, *Portraits of Protestant Teens: A Report on Teenagers in Major U.S. Denominations*, by Phil Schwadel and Christian Smith (Chapel Hill, NC: National Study of Youth and Religion). See www.youthandreligion.org for more information.

6   See, for example, Dorothy Bass, ed., *Practicing Our Faith: A Way of Life for Searching People* (San Francisco: Jossey-Bass, 1997); Dorothy Bass and Don Richter, eds., *Way to Live: Christian Practices for Teens* (Nashville: Upper Room Books, 2002). Also see Craig Dykstra, *Vision and Character* (New York: Paulist Press, 1981).

7   This confirms what a significant body of research literature on religious retention has shown. See, for instance, Scott Myers, "An Interactive Model of Religiosity Inheritance: The Importance of Family Context," *American Sociological Review* 61 (October 1996): 858–866; Dianne Kieren and Brenda Munro, "Following the Leaders: Parents' Influence on Adolescent Religious Activity," *Journal for the Scientific Study of Religion* 26, no. 2 (1987): 249–255; Hart Nelson, "Religious Transmission versus Religious Formation: Preadolescent-Parent Interaction," *Sociological Quarterly* 21 (spring 1980): 207–218; Elizabeth Weiss Ozorak, "Social and Cognitive Influences on the Development of Religious Beliefs and Commitment in Adolescence," *Journal for the Scientific Study of Religion* 28, no. 4 (1989): 448–463; Gerald Stott, "Familial Influence on Religious Involvement," *The Religion and Family Connection: Social Science Perspectives* 3 (1988): 258–271. For a larger review and analysis, see Christain Smith and David Sikkink, "Social Predictors of Retention in and Switching from the Religious Faith of Family of Origin," *Review of Religious Research* 45, no. 2 (2003): 188–206.

QUESTIONS FOR DISCUSSION

1.   What do Smith and Denton say in their introduction and conclusion about the advantages and limitations of survey research? Would you agree? Why or why not?

2.   If you were to state an overall conclusion from reading this excerpt from Smith and Denton's book, what would it be and why?

3.   Do any of the numbers in this study surprise you? If so, which ones? What had you previously believed about the statistics that surprised you? What were your beliefs about the religiosity of American teenagers prior to reading this excerpt?

4.   Consider the first endnote. Do you think that the findings are necessarily limited because of the sampling methods and decisions made or because of the forced choice questions that were asked? Is there some better way that you can think of to inquire into the true religious feelings of teens more accurately?

5. What do you think of the authors' fourth endnote, in which they explain that they will not include Mormons with other Christians? In what ways was this decision helpful to you as a reader and in what ways was it a hindrance?

6. Look again at Table 2. How many Protestant denominations in the sample have a higher percentage of teenagers than the LDS Church (see Table 1)? Does this fact surprise you?

7. Look at the personal religious practices detailed in Table 7. If you had been telephoned when you were about 15 years old and asked which of these practices you engaged in, how would you have answered? Were you surprised at how some of the LDS teens answered?

8. This reading includes numerous tables which the authors often summarize and interpret in adjacent paragraphs. Which—reading the tables or reading the paragraphs—was more helpful to you? Why?

The SPE: What It Was, Where It Came From, and What Came Out of It

by
Philip G. Zimbardo

Philip G. Zimbardo has been Professor of Psychology at Stanford University since 1968. He earned his BS degree in 1954 at Brooklyn College, where he majored in psychology and minored in sociology and anthropology. After earning a PhD from Yale in 1959, he taught at Columbia, Barnard, and New York University. He has won numerous awards for his research and writing but also for his teaching and media productions. He created a popular PBS-TV series, Discovering Psychology, *and he authored the nation's oldest continuously selling textbook in psychology,* Psychology and Life, *now in its sixteenth edition. In 2002, he was President of the American Psychological Association. He is an internationally recognized researcher on various topics, including shyness, persuasion, cults, hypnosis, violence, evil, and madness. Perhaps his best known research is the Stanford Prison Experiment, in which students played the roles of prisoners and guards in a simulated prison that became all too real, so the experiment had to be ended prematurely. The excerpt below is Zimbardo's description of what happened, why he did the experiment, and his provocative analysis of what was learned from it.*

The serenity of a summer Sunday morning in Palo Alto, California, was suddenly shattered by the sirens of a police squad car sweeping through town in a surprise mass arrest of college students for a variety of felony code violations. They were handcuffed, searched, warned of their legal rights, and then taken to police headquarters for a formal booking procedure. Let's return to that scene on August 14, 1971, to recall what those arrests were all about.

Synopsis of the Research

The police had agreed to cooperate with our research team in order to increase the "mundane realism" of having one's freedom suddenly taken away by the police rather than surrendering it voluntarily as a research participant who had volunteered for an experiment. The city police chief was in a cooperative and conciliatory mood after tensions had run high on Stanford's campus following violent confrontations between his police and student anti-Vietnam War protesters. I capitalized on these positive emotions to help defuse these tensions between police and college students and thereby to solicit the invaluable assistance of police officers in dramatizing our study from the outset.

These college students had answered an ad in the local newspaper inviting volunteers for a study of prison life that would run up to 2 weeks for the pay of $15 a day. They were students from all over the United States, most of whom had just completed summer school courses at Stanford or the University of California, Berkeley. Seventy of those who had called

Philip G. Zimbardo, Christina Maslach, and Craig Haney, "The SPE: What It was, Where it Came From and What Came Out of It." Reprinted from *Obedience to Authority,* edited by Thomas Blass, (2000), Lawrence Erlbaum Associates, Inc.

our office were invited to take a battery of psychological tests (the California Personality Inventory) and engage in interviews conducted by Craig Haney and Curtis Banks, who were graduate students at that time. We were assisted by David Jaffe, an undergraduate who played the role of prison warden. I played the role of prison superintendent, in addition to being the principal investigator, which would later prove to be a serious error in judgment.

Two dozen of those judged most normal, average, and healthy on all dimensions we assessed were selected to be the participants in our experiment. They were randomly assigned to the two treatments of mock prisoner and mock guard. Thus there were no systematic differences between them initially nor systematic preferences for role assignments. Virtually all had indicated a preference for being a prisoner because they could not imagine going to college and ending up as a prison guard. On the other hand, they could imagine being imprisoned for a driving violation or some act of civil disobedience and thus felt they might learn something of value from this experience should that ever happen.

The guards helped us to complete the final stages in the construction of the mock prison in the basement of the Stanford University psychology department. The setting was a barren hallway, without windows or natural light. Office doors were fitted with iron bars, and closets were converted to dark, solitary confinement areas. The "yard" was the 30-foot-long hallway in front of the three prison cells—converted from small staff offices. Three offices were set up in an adjacent hallway for the staff: one for the guards to change into and out of their uniforms, one for the warden, and the third for the superintendent. Provision was made for space in the hallway to accommodate visitors on visitors' nights. There was only a single door for access and exit, the other end of the corridor having been closed off by a wall we erected. A small opening in that wall was provided for a video camera and for inconspicuous observation. The cells were bugged with microphones so that prisoner conversations could be secretly monitored.

The guards were invited also to select their own military-style uniforms at a local army surplus store and met as a group for a general orientation and to formulate rules for proper prisoner behavior on the Saturday before the next day's arrests. We wanted the guards to feel as if it were "their prison" and that soon they would be hosting a group of prisoner-guests.

The would-be prisoners were told to wait at home or at the address they provided us, and we would contact them on Sunday. After the surprise arrest by the police, they were brought to our simulated prison environment, where they underwent a degradation ceremony as part of the initiation into their new role. This is standard operating procedure in many prisons and military institutions, according to our prison consultant, a recently paroled ex-convict, Carlo Prescott. Nine prisoners filled three cells, and three guards staffed each of the 8-hour shifts, supplemented by backups on standby call. Additional participants were also on standby as replacements if need be, one of whom was called on midweek to take the place of a released prisoner. The prisoners wore uniforms that consisted of smocks with numbers sewn on front and back, ankle chains, nylon stocking caps (to simulate the uniform appearance from having one's hair cut off), and rubber thongs on their feet, but no underwear. Among the coercive rules formulated by the guards were those requiring the prisoners to refer to themselves and each other only by their prison number and to the guards as "Mr. Correctional Officer."

Much of the daily chronology of behavioral actions was videotaped for later analysis, along with a variety of other observations, interviews, tests, diaries, daily reports, and follow-up surveys that together constituted the empirical data of the study. Of course, we were studying both guard and prisoner behavior, so neither group was given any instructions on how to behave. The guards were merely told to maintain law and order, to use their billy clubs as only symbolic weapons and not actual ones, and to realize that if the prisoners escaped the study would be terminated.

It is important to realize that both groups had completed informed-consent forms indicating that some of their basic civil rights would have to be violated if they were selected for the prisoner role and that only minimally adequate diet and health care would be provided. The university Human Subjects Review Board approved of the study with only minor limitations that we followed, such as alerting Student Health Services of our research and also providing fire extinguishers because there was minimal access to this space. Ironically, the guards later used these extinguishers as weapons to subdue the prisoners with their forceful blasts.

It took a full day for most of the guards to adapt to their new, unfamiliar roles as dominating, powerful, and coercive. Initial encounters were marked by awkwardness between both groups of participants. However, the situation was radically changed on the second day, when several prisoners led all the others in a rebellion against the coercive rules and restraints of the situation. They tried to individuate themselves, ripped off their sewn-on prisoner numbers, locked themselves into their cells, and taunted the guards. I told the guards that they had to handle this surprising turn of events on their own. They called in all the standby guards, and the night shift stayed overtime. Together, they crushed the prisoner rebellion and developed a greater sense of guard camaraderie, along with a personal dislike of some of the prisoners who had insulted them to their face. The prisoners were punished in a variety of ways. They were stripped naked, put in solitary confinement for hours on end, deprived of meals and blankets or pillows, and forced to do push-ups, jumping jacks, and meaningless activities. The guards also generated a psychological tactic of dividing and conquering their enemy by creating a "privilege cell" in which the least rebellious prisoners were put to enjoy the privilege of a good meal or a bed to sleep on. This tactic did have the immediate effect of creating suspicion and distrust among the prisoners.

We observed and documented on videotape that the guards steadily increased their coercive and aggressive tactics, humiliation, and dehumanization of the prisoners day by day. The staff had to remind the guards frequently to refrain from such abuses. However, the guards' hostile treatment of the prisoners, together with arbitrary and capricious displays of their dominating power and authority, soon began to have adverse effects on the prisoners. Within 36 hours after being arrested, the first prisoner had to be released because of extreme stress reactions of crying, screaming, cursing, and irrational actions that seemed to be pathological. The guards were most sadistic in waking prisoners from their sleep several times a night for "counts," supposedly designed for prisoners to learn their identification numbers but actually to use the occasion to taunt them, punish them, and play games with them, or rather on them. Deprivation of sleep, particularly REM sleep, also gradually took a toll on the prisoners. Interestingly, the worst abuses by the guards came on the late-night shift, when they thought the staff was asleep and they were not being monitored.

That first prisoner to be released, Prisoner 8612, had been one of the ringleaders of the earlier rebellion, and he jolted his fellow prisoners by announcing that they would not be allowed to quit the experiment even if they requested it. The shock waves from this false assertion reverberated through all of the prisoners and converted the simulated experiment into "a real prison run by psychologists instead of run by the state," according to one of the prisoners. After that, some prisoners decided to become "good prisoners," obeying every rule and following all prison procedures faithfully in zombie-like fashion. Powerful conformity pressures eliminated individual differences among the prisoners. But another generalized reaction was to imitate the behavior of Prisoner 8612 and passively escape by acting "crazy" and forcing the staff to release them prematurely. On each of the next three days a prisoner took that path out of the SPE. A fifth prisoner was released after he broke out in a full body rash following the rejection of his appeal for parole by our mock parole board. The parole board heard prisoner requests for early parole and refutations by the guards. The board consisted of secretaries, graduate students, and others, headed by our prison consultant, who was familiar with such hearings because his own parole requests had been turned down at least 16 times.

Although most of the time during the day and night the only interactions that took place were between prisoners and guards, it should be noted that probably as many as 100 other people came down to our basement prison to play some role in this drama. On Visitors' Night, about two dozen parents and friends came to see their prisoners. A former prison chaplain visited, interviewed all but one of the inmates, and reported that their reactions were very much like those of first-time offenders he had observed in real prisons. Our two parole boards consisted of another 10 outsiders. Perhaps as many as 20 psychology graduate students and faculty looked in from the observation window or at the video monitor during the experiment or played more direct roles inadvertently. Others helped with interviews and various chores during the study. Finally, a public defender came to interview the remaining inmates on the last day. He came at the request of the mother of one of the prisoners, who had been informed by the Catholic priest (who had visited our prison earlier) that her son wanted legal counsel to help him get out of the detention facility in which he was being held. He too likened their mental and behavioral state to those of real prisoners and jailed citizens awaiting trial.

We had to call off the experiment and close down our prison after only 6 days of what might have been a 2-week long study of the psychological dynamics of prison life. We had to do so because too many normal young men were behaving pathologically as powerless prisoners or as sadistic, all-powerful guards. Recall that we had spent much time and effort in a selection process that chose only the most normal, healthy, well-adjusted college students as our sample of research participants. At the beginning of the study there were no differences between those assigned randomly to guard and prisoner roles. In less than a week, there were no similarities among them; they had become totally different creatures. Guard behavior varied from being fully sadistic to occasionally acting so to being a tough guard who "went by the book" and, for a few, to being "good guards" by default. That is, they did not degrade or harass the prisoners, and even did small favors for them from time to time, but never, not once, did any of the so-called good guards ever contest an order by a sadistic guard, intervene to stop or prevent despicable behavior by another guard, or come to work late or leave early. In a real sense, it was the good guards who most kept the prisoners in line because the prisoners wanted their approval and feared things would get worse if those good guards quit or ever took a dislike to them.

Building on this brief synopsis of an intensely profound and complex experience, I next want to outline why this study was conducted as it was and what we learned from it. Before doing so, I should preview the next section of this chapter by noting that the immediate impetus for terminating the study came from an unexpected source, a young woman, recently graduated with a PhD from our department, who had agreed to assist us with some interviews on Friday. She came in from the cold and saw the raw, full-blown madness of this place that we all had gradually accommodated to day by day. She got emotionally upset, angry, and confused. But in the end, she challenged us to examine the madness she observed that we had created. If we allowed it to continue further, she reminded us of our ethical responsibility for the consequences and well-being of the young men entrusted to our care as research participants.

Genesis of the Experiment: Why Did We Do This Study?

There were three reasons for conducting this study, two conceptual and one pedagogical. I had been conducting research for some years earlier on deindividuation, vandalism, and dehumanization that illustrated the ease with which ordinary people could be led to engage in antisocial acts by putting them into situations in which they felt anonymous or in which they could perceive others in ways that made them less than human, as enemies or objects. This research is summarized in Zimbardo (1970). I wondered, along with my research associates, Craig Haney and Curt Banks, what would happen if we aggregated all of these processes, making some participants feel deindividuated and others dehumanized within an anonymous environment, that constituted a "total environment" (see Lifton, 1969) in a controlled experimental setting. That was the primary reason for conducting this study.

A related second conceptual reason was to generate another test of the power of social situations over individual dispositions without relying on the kind of face-to-face imposition of authority surveillance that was central in Stanley Milgram's obedience studies (see Milgram, 1992). In many real-life situations, people are seduced to behave in evil ways without the coercive control of an authority figure demanding their compliance or obedience. In the SPE, we focused on the power of roles, rules, symbols, group identity, and situational validation of ordinarily ego-alien behaviors and behavioral styles. We were influenced here by earlier reports of "brainwashing" and "milieu control" coming out of accounts of the Korean War and Chinese Communist indoctrination methods (Schein, 1956).

Pedagogically, the study had its roots in a social psychology course I had taught the previous spring, after the student strikes against the university as part of anti-Vietnam War activities. I invited students to reverse roles and instruct me on 10 topics that interested me but that I had not had the time to investigate. They were primarily topics and issues that were at the interface of sociology and psychology or of institutions and individuals, such as the effects of being put into an old-age home, media distortion of information, and the psychology of imprisonment. The group of students, headed by David Jaffe, who chose the prison topic conducted a mock prison experiential learning session over a weekend just before they were to make their class presentation. The dramatically powerful impact this brief experience had on many of them surprised me and forced us to consider whether such a situation could really generate so much distress and role identification or whether the students who chose to study prisons, among the many other options available to the class, were in some way more "pathological" than the rest of the ordinary students. The only way to resolve that ambiguity was to conduct a controlled experiment that eliminated self-selection factors, and so we did.

Ten Lessons Learned From the SPE

1.   Some situations can exert powerful influences over individuals, causing them to behave in ways they would not, could not, predict in advance (see Ross & Nisbett, 1991). In trying to understand the causes of complex, puzzling behavior, it is best to start with a situational analysis and yield to the dispositional only when the situational fails to do a satisfactory causal job.

2.   Situational power is most salient in novel settings in which the participants cannot call on previous guidelines for their new behavior and have no historical references to rely on and in which their habitual ways of behaving and coping are not reinforced. Under such circumstances, personality variables have little predictive utility because they depend on estimations of future actions based on characteristic past reactions in certain situations but rarely in the kind of situation currently being encountered. Personality tests simply do not assess such behaviors but rely on asking about typical reactions to known situations—namely, a historical account of the self.

3.   Situational power involves ambiguity of role boundaries, authoritative or institutionalized permission to behave in prescribed ways or to disinhibit traditionally disapproved ways of responding. It requires situational validation of playing new roles, following new rules, and taking actions that ordinarily would be constrained by laws, norms, morals, and ethics. Such validation usually comes cloaked in the mantle of ideology; value systems considered to be sacred and based on apparently good, virtuous, valued moral imperatives (for social psychologists, ideology equals their experimental "cover story").

4.   Role playing even when acknowledged to be artificial, temporary, and situationally bound can still come to exert a profoundly realistic impact on the actors. Private attitudes, values, and beliefs are likely to be modified to bring them in line with the role enactment, as shown by many experiments in dissonance theory (Festinger, 1957; see Zimbardo & Leippe, 1991). This dissonance effect becomes greater as the justification for such role enactment decreases—for example, when it is carried out for less money, under less threat, or with only minimally sufficient justification or adequate rationale provided. That is one of the motivational mechanisms for the changes we observed in our guards. They had to work long, hard shifts for a small wage of less than $2 an hour and were given minimal direction on how to play the role of guard, but they had to sustain the role consistently over days whenever they were in uniform, on the yard, or in the presence of others, whether prisoners, parents, or other visitors. Such dissonance forces are likely to have been major causes for the internalization of the public role behaviors into private supporting cognitive and affective response styles. We also have to add that the group pressures from other guards had a significant impact on being a "team player," on conforming to or at least not challenging what seemed to be the emergent norm of dehumanizing the prisoners in various ways. Finally, let

us take into account that the initial script for guard or prisoner role playing came from the participants' own experiences with power and powerlessness, of seeing parental interactions, of dealing with authority, and of seeing movies and reading accounts of prison life. As in Milgram's research, we did not have to teach the actors how to play their roles. Society had done that for us. We had only to record the extent of their improvisation within these roles as our data.

5.   Good people can be induced, seduced, initiated into behaving in evil (irrational, stupid, self-destructive, antisocial) ways by immersion in "total situations" that can transform human nature in ways that challenge our sense of the stability and consistency of individual personality, character, and morality (Lifton, 1969). It is a lesson seen in the Nazi concentration camp guards; among destructive cults, such as Jim Jones' Peoples Temple or more recently the Japanese Aum cult; and in the atrocities committed in Bosnia, Kosovo, Rwanda, and Burundi, among others. Thus any deed that any human being has ever done, however horrible, is possible for any of us to do under the right or wrong situational pressures. That knowledge does not excuse evil; rather, it democratizes it, shares its blame among ordinary participants, rather than demonizes it. Recently, a program at the U.S. Air Force Academy (code-named SERE) that was designed to train cadets for survival and escape from enemy capture had to be terminated early because it got out of control. As part of a "sexual exploitation scenario," women cadets were beaten repeatedly, degraded, humiliated, put in solitary confinement, deprived of sleep, and made to wear hoods over their heads all much like the SPE. But in addition, the women cadets in this course were subjected to simulated rapes by interrogators that were realistic enough to cause posttraumatic stress disorder. These "rapes" were videotaped and also watched by other cadets, none of whom ever intervened. The grandfather of one abused female cadet, himself a World War II hero, said, "I can't believe that all these men, these elite boys, could stand around and watch a young woman get degraded and not one had enough guts to stop it" (Palmer, 1995, p. 24). After watching our "good guards" be similarly immobilized when witnessing SPE abuses, I can now understand how that could happen.

6.   Human nature can be transformed within certain powerful social settings in ways as dramatic as the chemical transformation in the captivating fable of Dr. Jekyll and Mr. Hyde. I think it is that *transformation of character* that accounts for the enduring interest in this experiment for more than a quarter of a century. A recent analysis of the SPE by an Australian psychologist (Carr, 1995) reports that undergraduate students in that country who learn about the study are left surprised, disturbed, and mystified by it. He notes:

> Judging by the reactions of our own students, it has even more impact than either Asch's "line-length" study (Asch, 1951) or Milgram's (1963) obedience study. What seems to strike home is that Zimbardo's situation impacted much more deeply on his subjects, reportedly corrupting their own innermost beliefs and feelings and all this without involving the direct pressure to change which runs through the classic conformity and obedience studies. (Carr, 1995, p. 31)

7.   Despite the artificiality of controlled experimental research such as the SPE or any of Milgram's many variations on the obedience paradigm, when such research is conducted in a way that captures essential features of "mundane realism," the results do have

considerable generalizability power. In recent years, it has become customary to deride such research as limited by context-specific considerations, as not really credible to the research participants, or as not tapping the vital dimensions of the naturalistic equivalent. If this were so, there would be no reason to ever go through the enormous efforts involved in doing such research well. We believe that much of that criticism is misguided and comes from colleagues who don't know how to do such research or how to make it work or who misunderstand the value of a psychologically *functional* equivalent of a real-world process or phenomenon. Several previous chapters in this volume document eloquently the generalizability of Milgram's experiments.

I would like to call attention to two parallels to the SPE: one recent, the other from an earlier era. On July 22, 1995, news headlines chronicled, "Guards abused inmates in immigration center" (Dunn, 1995, p. A6). The article, reprinted in the San Francisco Chronicle from the New York Times, reported on an investigation of a New Jersey detention center holding immigrants awaiting deportation. It outlined "a culture of abuse that had quickly developed at the detention center," in which "underpaid and poorly trained guards had beaten detainees, singling out the midnight shift as particularly abusive." Investigators found that "guards routinely participated in acts meant to degrade and harass, such as locking detainees in isolation and repeatedly waking them in the middle of the night." This was all possible in part because "the detention center had become a closed and private world." Such an account mirrors exactly what transpired in the SPE: The worst abuses were by guards on our midnight shift, who thought they were not being monitored by the research team; they degraded, harassed, and woke the prisoners repeatedly every night, and at times hit them and locked them in isolation and they were also underpaid and poorly trained to be guards.

Historian Christopher Browning (1992) provides a chilling account of a little-known series of mass murders during the Holocaust. A group of older reserve policemen from Hamburg, Germany, was sent to Poland to round up and execute all the Jews living in rural areas because it was too costly and inconvenient to ship them to the concentration camps for extermination. In his book, appropriately titled *Ordinary Men,* Browning documents how these men were induced to commit the atrocities of shooting Jewish men, women, and children, doing the killing up close and personal, without the technology of the gas chambers to distance the crimes against humanity. The author goes on to note, "Zimbardo's spectrum of guard behavior bears an uncanny resemblance to the groupings that emerged within Reserve Police Battalion 101" (p. 168). He shows how some became sadistically "cruel and tough, "enjoying the killings, whereas others were "tough, but fair" in "playing the rules," and a minority qualified as "good guards" who refused to kill and did small favors for the Jews.

So we side with Kurt Lewin, who argued decades ago for the science of experimental social psychology. Lewin asserted that it is possible to take conceptually and practically significant issues from the real world into the experimental laboratory, where it is possible to establish certain causal relationships in a way not possible in field studies and then to use that information to understand or make changes in the real world (Lewin, 1951; Lewin, Lippitt, & White, 1939). In fact, in his presidential speech to the American Psychological Association, psycholinguist George Miller (1969) startled his audience by advocating a radical idea for that time, that we should "give psychology away to the public." The exemplars he later used, in a *Psychology Today* (1980) interview, as being ideal for public consumption of psychological research were the Stanford Prison Experiment and Milgram's obedience studies.

From another perspective, the SPE does not tell us anything new about prisons that sociologists and narratives of prisoners have not already revealed about the evils of prison life. What is different is that by virtue of the experimental protocol, we put selected good people, randomly assigned to be either guard or prisoner, and observed the ways in which they were changed for the worse by their daily experiences in the evil place.

8.   Selection procedures for special tasks, such as being prison guards—especially those that are relatively new to the applicants—might benefit from engaging the participants in simulated role playing rather than, or in addition to, screening on the basis of personality testing. As far as I know, current training for the very difficult job of prison guard, or correctional officer, involves minimal training in the psychological dimensions of this position.

9.   It is necessary for psychological researchers who are concerned about the utility of their findings and the practical application of their methods or conclusions to go beyond the role constraints of academic researcher to become advocates for social change. We must acknowledge the value-laden nature of some kinds of research that force investigators out of their stance of objective neutrality into the realm of activism as partisans for spreading the word of their research to the public and to those who might be able to implement its recommendations through policy actions. Craig Haney and I have tried to do so collectively and individually in many ways with our writings, public testimonies, and development of special media to communicate to a wider audience than the academic readers of psychology journals.

For starters, we published the SPE first to U.S. audiences in articles in the *New York Times Magazine* (Zimbardo, Haney, Banks, & Jaffe, 1973) and in *Society* (Zimbardo, 1972), as well as to international audiences (Haney, Banks, & Zimbardo, 1973; Zimbardo & Haney, 1978); we extended the implications to education in a *Psychology Today* magazine piece (Haney & Zimbardo, 1975) and in an educational journal (Haney & Zimbardo, 1973); and we related psychology to legal change (Haney, 1993b). I have also specified how the SPE gives rise to considering new role requirements for social advocacy by psychologists (Zimbardo, 1975). Most recently, we have just published an article in *American Psychologist* on how the lessons learned from the SPE could improve the ill health of America's out-of-control correctional system (Haney & Zimbardo, 1998). Appearances on national television and radio shows, such as *The Phil Donahue Show* and *That's Incredible,* in which I discussed the SPE, have also extended the audience for this research. In each case, some of the participants from our prison study were involved. We have carried the message to college and high school students and also to civic groups through colloquia and distribution of a dramatic slide-tape show (Zimbardo & White, 1972; available on the INTERNET, http://www.ZIMBARDO.COM/PRISONEXP) and the provocative video *Quiet Rage* (1992), as well as in the PBS video series *Discovering Psychology* (1989; Program #19, "The Power of the Situation"). Finally, I have given invited testimony relating the SPE to various prison conditions before Congressional Subcommittees on the Judiciary (The Power and Pathology, 1970; The Detention and Jailing, 1973).

10. Prisons are places that demean humanity, destroy the nobility of human nature, and bring out the worst in social relations among people. They are as bad for the guards as the prisoners in terms of their destructive impact on self-esteem, sense of justice, and human compassion. They are designed to isolate people from all others and even from the self. Nothing is worse for the health of an individual or a society than to have millions of people who are without social support, social worth, or social connections to their kin. Prisons are failed social-political experiments that continue to be places of evil and even to multiply, like the bad deeds of the sorcerer's apprentice, because the public is indifferent to what takes place in secret there and because politicians use them and fill them up as much as they can to demonstrate only that they are "tougher on crime" than their political opponents. At present, such misguided thinking has led to the "three strikes" laws in California and a few other states. Meant to curtail violent crime, the statute was so broadly written as to include drug offenses as "serious felonies," thus filling prisons with a disproportionate number of nonviolent, young minority drug offenders—for a minimum of 25 years to a maximum life term. The cost to taxpayers figures to be about one million dollars per inmate for 25 years of warehousing and medical care and to be even greater for older inmates (see Zimbardo, 1994). The costs of extensive prison construction and of hiring many guards to oversee the many prisoners starting to fill these new prisons is already diminishing the limited state and county funds available for health, education, and welfare. A "mean-spirited" value system pervades many correctional operations, reducing programs for job training, rehabilitation, and physical exercise, and even limiting any individuality in appearance. Projections are dire at best for the future of corrections in the United States.

I was able to terminate my failed prison experiment, but every citizen is paying for, and will continue to pay an enormous price in taxes for, the failed experiments taking place in every state of this union—the failed U.S. prison system. This system has failed by any criteria: of recidivism, of prison violence, of illegal activities practiced in prisons, of second offenders often committing more serious second-time-around crimes than initially, of low morale of corrections staff, and of deadly prison riots. Among the most outrageous examples of the evil that prison settings can generate come from the recent reports of guards "staging fights among inmates and then shooting the combatants," 50 of whom have been shot and 7 killed in the past 8 years (Holding, 1996). Federal investigators have been checking out such reports (*Los Angeles Times*, 1998). Obviously, sometimes it is the guards we must be protected from, as we saw in the SPE.

Ethics of the SPE

Was the SPE study unethical? No and Yes. No, because it followed the guidelines of the Human Subjects Research Review Board that reviewed it and approved it (see Zimbardo, 1973). There was no deception; all participants were told in advance that, if they became prisoners, many of their usual rights would be suspended and they would have only minimally adequate diet and health care during the study. Their rights should have been protected by any of the many citizens who came to that mock prison, saw the deteriorated condition of those young men, and yet did nothing to intervene—among them, their own parents and friends on visiting nights, a Catholic priest, a public defender, many professional psychologists, graduate students, secretaries, and staff of the psychology department, all of whom watched live action videos of part of the study unfold or took part in parole board hearings or spoke to participants and looked at them directly. We might also add another no, because we ended the study earlier than planned, ended it against the wishes of the guards, who felt they finally had the situation under their control and there would be no more disturbance or challenge by the prisoners.

Yes, it was unethical because people suffered and others were allowed to inflict pain and humiliation on their fellows over an extended period of time. This was not the distress of Milgram's participants imagining the pain their shocks were having on the remote victim-learner.

This was the pain of seeing and hearing the suffering you as a guard were causing in peers, who, like you, had done nothing to deserve such punishment and abuse. And yes, we did not end the study soon enough. We should have terminated it as soon as the first prisoner suffered a severe stress disorder on Day 2. One reason we did not was because of the conflicts created by my dual roles as principal investigator, thus guardian of the research ethics of the experiment, and as prison superintendent, thus eager to maintain the integrity of my prison.

Positive Consequences

1. The study has become a model of the "power of the situation" in textbooks and in the public mind. Along with Milgram's obedience studies, the SPE has challenged people's views that behavior is primarily under the influence of dispositional factors, which is the view promoted by much of psychology, psychiatry, religion, and law.

2. The study's results, as presented in my testimony before a Congressional Judiciary Committee, influenced federal lawmakers to change a law so that juveniles jailed in a pretrial detention (as was the case in our study) would not be housed with adult prisoners because of the anticipated violence against them, according to Congressman Birch Bayh.

3. The study has been presented to a great many civic, judicial, military, and law enforcement groups to enlighten them and arouse concern about prison life and has influenced guard training in some instances (see Newton & Zimbardo, 1975; Pogash, 1976). Its role-playing procedures have been used to demonstrate to mental health staff how their mental patients perceive and respond to situational features of the ward and staff insensitivity toward them (see Orlando, 1973). Its results have been generally replicated in another culture, New South Wales, Australia (Lovibond, Mithiran, & Adams, 1979).

4. Ideas from the SPE have been the source of three research programs that I have carried out in the past 20 or more years, most notably on the psychology of shyness and ways of treating it—first in the unique Shyness Clinic that I started at Stanford and now in the local community—to liberate shy people from their self-imposed silent prisons (see Zimbardo, 1977, 1986; Zimbardo, Pilkonis, & Norwood, 1975). The second long-standing research program influenced by my personal experience in the SPE is the study of time perspective,

how people come to develop temporal frames to partition their experiences but then come to be controlled by their overuse of past, present, or future time frames (see Gonzalez & Zimbardo, 1985; Zimbardo & Boyd, in press). Temporal distortion was a fact of life in the SPE, with 80% of the conversations (monitored secretly) among mock prisoners focused around the immediate present and little about the past or future. Also apparent in the SPE was the fact that many healthy, normal young men began behaving pathologically in a short time period. Thus I began to study the social and cognitive bases of "madness" in normal, healthy people in controlled laboratory experiments (see Zimbardo, Andersen, & Kabat, 1981; Zimbardo, LaBerge, & Butler, 1993). We have found that pathological symptoms may develop in up to one third of participants in the process of trying to make sense of their unexplained sources of arousal (Zimbardo, 1999).

References

Browning, C.R. (1992). *Ordinary men: Reserve Police Battalion 101 and the final solution in Poland.* New York: HarperCollins.

Carr, S. (1995). Demystifying the Stanford Prison Study. *British Psychological Society, Social Psychology Section, Newsletter No. 33,* 31–34.

Dunn, A. (1995, July 22). Guards abused inmates in immigration center. *San Francisco Chronicle,* p. A6.

Festinger, L. (1957). *A theory of cognitive dissonance.* Stanford, CA: Stanford University Press.

Gonzalez, A., & Zimbardo, P.G. (1985, March). Time in perspective: The time sense we learn early affects how we do our jobs and enjoy our pleasures. *Psychology Today,* pp. 21–26.

Haney, C. (1993). Infamous punishment: The psychological effects of isolation. *National Prison Project Journal, 8,* 3–21.

Haney, C., & Zimbardo, P.G. (1973). Social roles, role-playing, and education. *Behavioral and Social Science Teacher, 1,* 24–45.

Haney, C., & Zimbardo, P.G. (1975, June). Stimulus/Response: The blackboard penitentiary: It's tough to tell a high school from a prison. *Psychology Today,* pp. 26, 29–30, 106.

Haney, C., & Zimbardo, P.G. (1998). The past and future of U.S. prison policy: Twenty-five years after the Stanford Prison Experiment. *American Psychologist, 53,* 709–727.

Holding, R. (1996, November 8). State sends investigators to Corcoran. *San Francisco Chronicle,* pp. A1, A19.

Lewin, K. (1951). *Field theory in social science.* New York: Harper.

Lewin, K., Lippitt, R., & White, R.K. (1939). Patterns of aggressive behavior in experimentally created "social climates." *Journal of Social Psychology, 10,* 271–299.

Lifton, R.J. (1969). *Thought reform and the psychology of totalism.* New York: Norton.

Los Angeles Times. (1998, March 19). FBI probes slayings at state prisons: Civil rights inquiry at Pelican Bay, Susanville.

Lovibond, S.H., Mithiran, X, & Adams, W.G. (1979). The effects of three experimental prison environments on the behavior of non-convict volunteer subjects. *Australian Psychologist, 14*, 273–287.

Milgram, S. (1992). *The individual in a social world: Essays and experiments* (2nd ed.). New York: McGraw-Hill.

Miller, G.A. (1969). Psychology as a means of promoting human welfare. *American Psychologist, 24*, 1063–1075.

Miller, G.A. (1980, January). Giving psychology away in the 80s (An interview with E. Hall). *Psychology Today*, pp. 38ff.

Newton, J.W., & Zimbardo, P.G. (1975). *Corrections: Perspectives on research, policy, and impact.* (ONR Technical Report No. Z-13). Summary of proceedings of the third annual conference on Correcations in the United States Military, Stanford, CA. June 1974. Stanford University: Stanford, CA.

Orlando, N.J. (1973). The mock ward: A study in simulation. In O. Milton & R.G. Wahler (Eds.), *Behavior disorders: Perspectives and trends* (3rd ed., pp. 167–170). Philadelphia: Lippincott.

Palmer, L. (1995, May 28). Her own private Tailhook. *New York Times Magazine*, 23–26.

Pogash, C. (1976, March 25). Life behind bars turns sour quickly for a few well-meaning Napa citizens. *San Francisco Chronicle*, pp. 10–11.

Ross, L., & Nisbett, R. (1991). *The person and the situation.* New York: McGraw-Hill.

Schein, E.H. (1956). The Chinese indoctrination program for prisoners of war: A study of attempted brainwashing. *Psychiatry, 19*, 149–172.

Zimbardo, P.G. (1970). The human choice: Individuation, reason, and order versus deindividuation, impulse, and chaos. In W.J. Arnold & D. Levine, (Eds.) *1969 Nebraska Symposium on Motivation* Vol. 27, (pp. 237–307). Lincoln, NE: University of Nebraska Press.

Zimbardo, P.G. (1972). Pathology of imprisonment. *Society, 6, 4, 6,* 8.

Zimbardo, P.G. (1973). On the ethics of intervention in human psychological research: With special reference to the Stanford Prison Experiment. *Cognition, 2,* 243–256.

Zimbardo, P.G. (1975). On transforming experimental research into advocacy for social change. In M. Deutsch & H. Hornstein (Eds.), *Applying social psychology: Implications for research, practice, and training* (pp. 33–66). Hillsdale, NJ: Lawrence Erlbaum Associates.

Zimbardo, P.G. (1977). *Shyness: What it is, What to do about it.* Reading, MA: Addison-Wesley.

Zimbardo, P.G. (1986). The Stanford shyness project. In W.H. Jones, J.M. Cheek, & R. Briggs (Eds.), *Shyness: Perspectives on research and treatment* (pp. 17–25). New York: Plenum Press.

Zimbardo, P.G. (1994). *Transforming California's prisons into expensive old age homes for felons: Enormous hidden costs and consequences for California's taxpayers.* San Francisco, CA: Center for Juvenile and Criminal Justice.

Zimbardo, P.G. (1999). Discontinuity theory: Cognitive and social searches for rationality and normality may lead to madness. In M. Zanna (Ed.), *Advances in experimental social psychology* (Vol. 31, pp. 345–486). San Diego, CA: Academic Press.

Zimbardo, P.G., Andersen, S., & Kabat, L.G. (1981). Induced hearing deficit generates experimental paranoia. *Science, 212,* 1529–1531.

Zimbardo, P.G., & Boyd, J.N. (in press). Putting time in perspective: A new individual differences metric. *Journal of Personality and Social Psychology.*

Zimbardo, P.G., & Haney, C. (1978). Prison behavior. In B.B. Wolman (Ed.), *International encyclopedia of psychiatry, psychology, and neurology* (Vol. 4, pp. 52–53). New York: Human Sciences Press.

Zimbardo, P.G., Haney, C., Banks, W.C., & Jaffe, D. (1973, April 8). The mind is a formidable jailer: A Pirandellian prison. *New York Times Magazine,* pp. 36ff.

Zimbardo, P.G., LaBerge, S. & Butler, L. (1993). Physiological consequences of unexpected arousal: A posthypnotic suggestion paradigm. *Journal of Abnormal Psychology, 102,* 466–473.

Zimbardo, P.G., & Leippe, M.R. (1991). *The psychology of attitude change and social influence.* New York: McGraw-Hill.

Zimbardo, P.G., Pilkonis, P., & Norwood, R. (1975, May). The silent prison of shyness. *Psychology Today,* pp. 69–70, 72.

Zimbardo, P.G., & White, G. (1972). *The Stanford Prison Experiment slide-tape show,* Stanford University.

SUGGESTIONS FOR DISCUSSION

1. This article reports on an experiment but not in the standard four-part form. What would it look like if it were organized as reports of experiments usually are? Why do you think the author chose not to report the experiment in the standard fashion?

2. There is no section called "Methods," but what can you infer from this report about the procedures the experimenters followed?

3. Zimbardo credits a young woman who was part of the research team with challenging the other researchers to call off the experiment. In light of what you read in Hudson and Den Boer's article about the potential for violence in all-male environments, what significance do you see in this fact? Why do you think Zimbardo relates this information to the reader?

4. Did it surprise you that this experiment had been approved by the Stanford University IRB before it was undertaken? What conclusions can you draw from the fact that the participants signed informed consent forms and then became part of a situation that very likely caused them some possibly temporary but nevertheless real psychological and physical harm? Who, if anyone, should be blamed for that harm?

5. In the seventh lesson drawn from the SPE, Zimbardo refutes those who argue that experimental conclusions are not generalizable because they derive from artificial situations. How does he refute this argument? Do you agree with him? Why or why not?

Three Student Research Papers

About the Papers

Following are three student research papers written by students who took English 315 in Winter 2006. These papers are noteworthy for several reasons. First, they exemplify writing from research gathered not only in the library and on the Internet but also from such methods as observation of classroom videos, analysis of fifth-graders' test papers, and interviews with young Xhosa women in South Africa. Second, they each represent a carefully planned argument with a clearly stated thesis supported by sufficient evidence organized according to a logical plan. Third, the papers represent good writing for the field each student comes from and illustrate many general principles of research writing in the way the papers summarize, paraphrase, and quote primary and secondary sources. Fourth, each one is carefully and accurately documented using APA style. They are meant to be models of successful papers that you can emulate as you plan and write your own research paper.

About the Authors

Heather Bahlmann is an honors student majoring in mathematics education with a minor in Spanish education. She plans to earn her master's degree in mathematics education from Brigham Young University and then teach mathematics at a high school. She was involved in a group of professors and students who conducted a large research project, part of which she reports in her paper. Heather is from Orem, UT, and she enjoys running, camping, playing the piano, and spending time with her family.

Colleen Johnson is a social science teaching major at Brigham Young University, and she plans to become a professor of applied sociology. She completed an internship at the Family and Marriage Society of South Africa in East London, South Africa, in 2005. Colleen is from Peoria, AZ, and her interests include photography, international affairs, accordions, and gardening.

Kemarie Campbell is a health science major with a minor in international development. Born in California, she has lived in Utah and Colorado. Her future goals include receiving an MBA, establishing a health organization for women, and improving the health of families in impoverished nations by teaching mothers about healthy living. Kemarie enjoys sports, music, and learning languages.

Exploring the Open-Response Task as a Tool for Assessing the Understanding of Fifth-Grade Students in the Content Area of Fractions

by
Heather Bahlmann

English Department
Brigham Young University
April 17, 2006

Table of Contents

List of Figures and Tables iii

Abstract iv

Introduction 1

Literature Review 1

    Theoretical Perspective on Learning 1

        Personal Agency 1

        Definition and Characteristics of the Open-Response Task 2

    Examining Student Strategies 2

Research Questions 3

Methods 3

Data and Analysis 4

    Open-Response Question #1 4

        Student Strategies 4

        Teaching Implications 11

    Open-Response Question #2 13

        Student Strategies 13

        Teaching Implications 15

Conclusions 15

References 17

Appendix (Assessment) 18

List of Figures and Tables

Figure 1 4
Figure 2 5
Figure 3 5
Figure 4 6
Figure 5 9
Figure 6 10
Figure 7 11
Figure 8 13
Figure 9 14
Figure 10 14
Figure 11 14
Figure 12 14
Table 1 11
Table 2 15

Abstract

Inferring student understanding is imperative in mathematics learning and teaching because it helps teachers plan more effective instruction. This research explored the open-response task as a tool for gaining insights into student thinking about fractions. Fifth-grade students were videotaped solving fraction problems in class, and their talk, drawings, use of manipulatives, and problem solutions were analyzed to determine how students both thought and didn't think about the problems. The solutions of 172 fifth-graders to both multiple-choice and open-response questions on an exam were also analyzed. Detailed qualitative and quantitative analysis of two open-response test items indicated that students who have deeper conceptual understanding of fractions are also more proficient and flexible in applying procedures to solve unfamiliar problems. These data corroborate evidence from analysis of in-class video and demonstrate that students' strategies for solving open-response tasks are among a teacher's best tools for assessing and then improving students' conceptual understanding and procedural proficiency.

Exploring the Open-Response Task as a Tool for Assessing the Understanding of Fifth-Grade Students in the Content Area of Fractions

Introduction

Inferring student understanding is at the heart of improvement in mathematics learning and teaching; it has been described by the Mathematical National Research Council (1993) as a "lever for propelling reform forward" (p. 30). Assessment of student understanding provides valuable information that can be used, according to the National Council of Teachers of Mathematics (hereafter called NCTM), to "promote growth, modify programs, recognize student accomplishments, and improve instruction" (1995, p. 27). Because inferring student understanding serves such significant purposes, it is imperative that methods for assessing student understanding be constantly explored and evaluated. Regarding the growing need to explore and evaluate assessment tools, the Mathematics Learning and Study Committee (2001) comments that not enough attention

> appears to have been paid to how teachers' assessments might help improve mathematics learning. According to one analysis, "Aside from teacher-made classroom tests, the integration of assessment and learning as an interacting system has been too little explored." (as cited in Kilpatrick, 2001, p. 40)

Given the current need for researching assessment, in this paper I will present my analysis of open-response tasks as tools for gaining insights into student thinking. Through detailed analysis of the solutions of 172 fifth-graders to two open-response tasks on an exam, I studied how students' strategy choices indicate their mathematical understanding and proficiency in the content area of fractions. Quantitative and qualitative data from post-tests corroborate evidence from analysis of in-class videos to show that the various strategies students use to solve open-response tasks can be used as tools to assess students' understanding of concepts and their procedural proficiency.

Literature Review

Theoretical Perspective on Learning

Before discussing my exploration of open-response tasks as assessment tools, it is necessary to explain my beliefs about mathematics learning and teaching because these beliefs guide my research. These beliefs, along with previous research, also justify my decision to examine student strategies for evidence of learning.

Personal Agency. I identify my theoretical perspective on learning with that which Walter & Gerson (in press) have said concerning personal agency, i.e., that students learn mathematics by exercising their personal agency as they make sense of mathematics individually and as they participate in communities of inquiry. Teachers play a vital role because they help guide and inform students' personal agency and provide appropriate opportunities for students to exercise their agency. Students must be instructed sufficiently so they can make purposeful choices that will allow them to learn. Walter and Gerson (in press) assert, "The act of making a purposeful choice is a fundamental component of learning" (Ms. p. 8).

Assessment is also a component of learning. The NCTM (2000) explains that effective assessment should not only provide teachers with the opportunity to infer student understanding, but it should also provide students the opportunity to learn mathematics. Because assessment is linked to learning, assessment should allow students to exercise personal agency.

Definition and Characteristics of the Open-Response Task. My decision to research the open-response task as an assessment tool is a result of my belief of how students learn mathematics; the open-response task allows students to exercise their personal agency. Unlike process-constrained problems, open-response tasks are characterized as "open" because using a specified procedure is not required to solve the problem (Cai, 2001). Open-response tasks focus on eliciting not only *what* students know, but also *how* students explore concepts that can be thought about in a variety of ways. Student responses are therefore unique to the individual and provide significant insight into how a student is thinking about mathematics. For this reason open-response tasks are considered a useful tool to assess a student's "mathematical power" because they require "students to explain their thinking and thus allow teachers to gain insights into . . . the 'holes' in their understanding" (Moon & Schulman, 1995, p. 30). Hence, open-response tasks provide opportunities for teachers to recognize where students lack understanding because they have incomplete or incongruous solution strategies.

Examining Student Strategies

A brief review of literature on examining student strategies provides support for my decision to use open-response tasks. Investigation of student strategies has provided invaluable information for mathematics educators. An early study on a sixth grader's strategy choices in solving fraction problems led to the discovery of his belief about mathematics: It is a set of rules for "every type of problem" (Erlwanger, 1973, p. 12). Recent research on student strategies in solving open-response or process-open, and process-constrained tasks suggests that "examining solution strategies provides information regarding students' mathematical thinking and reasoning" (Cai, 2001, p. 402). Gaining insights into students' mathematical thinking and reasoning is a prerequisite for making effective instructional decisions. Lamon (2006) suggests steps that teachers can take to increase student understanding of fractions after a careful review of children's strategies in making sense of part-whole comparisons.

Although past studies have proven that examining student strategies is helpful in assessing student understanding, the present study evaluated and further supported the usefulness of open-response tasks as assessment tools. This study not only examined student strategies, but also considered how alternative student strategies (i.e., strategies that students did not use to solve open-response tasks) provide insight into student thinking. Considering "alternative student strategies" has not, to my knowledge, been explored before. Thus, this study provides a new perspective on exploring assessment.

Research Questions

This research was designed to answer the following questions: Does analysis of solutions to open-response tasks provide evidence that "holes" in student understanding may be inferred from the student's choice of one correct method? In other words, does a student's strategy choice indicate a lack of proficiency or conceptual understanding that may be evidenced in alternative strategies? If so, the open-response task may have yet another powerful role in influencing instructional decisions that affect student learning. It could impel teachers to ask the question, "How was the student *not* thinking about this problem?" Answers to that question could provide ways to encourage students to use alternative strategies to build deeper understandings of multiple concepts in a particular open-response task, thus improving their reasoning and problem-solving skills.

Methods

A mixed method employing qualitative and quantitative research procedures was used to infer student understanding and establish the role of strategy choices in solving open-response tasks. Pre- and post-tests were administered to 774 elementary students as part of a larger mathematics education professional development project with practicing elementary teachers. The exams assessed content knowledge of probability and fractions by using a combination of multiple-choice and open-response questions. A detailed test-item analysis was conducted on two open-response questions (problems 13 and 21) and a combination of 15 related multiple-choice and additional open-response questions on 172 post-tests given to fifth graders at two elementary schools. (See Appendix 1 for a copy of the test.) Each open-response task was graded individually by two research team members using a rubric developed by principal investigators in the larger study. Any discrepancies in grading were discussed and resolved before a final score was given. Qualitative analysis was performed by reviewing all student solutions to the open-response tasks and assigning a code to those solutions according to the strategy or strategies used by the student (i.e., how the student thought about the problem was interpreted). Quantitative analysis was performed by evaluating each student's performance on related questions; the related questions answered incorrectly by each student were quantified. Correlations were noted between the alternative student solution and the incorrect question dealing with the concepts addressed by the alternative solution.

Further evidence of the fifth graders' conceptual understanding and mathematical proficiency was inferred from analyzing videotapes of student learning in classroom sessions on fractions. A focus on two different students as they participated in learning activities produced evidence of the strengths and deficiencies in their content knowledge.

This inferred understanding was substantiated by the students' strategy choices in solving open-response tasks on their respective exams. These qualitative findings combined with the number of correlations found between the alternative student solution and the incorrect related questions suggest that the open-response task has an important role to play in inferring the fifth grade students' conceptual knowledge of fractions.

Data and Analysis

The 172 fifth graders' exam scores improved significantly ($p < 0.01$) from their pre-test to their post-test performance. Because the pre-tests and the post-tests were identical, this result establishes the validity of the assessment and justifies the conclusion that the students learned the content the exams addressed. Thus, the hypothesis that the students did not learn the content presented in the exams was rejected because their learning can only be explained by classroom instruction they received. The following data and analysis are therefore based on a valid assessment.

Open-Response Question #1

The first open-response question, problem 13 on the assessment, asks students to identify the larger of two fractions (2/3 or 3/2) and to use words or pictures to explain their answer. Of the 172 students who took the exam, 63 students received full credit for this problem. The requirement to receive full credit could be fulfilled in a variety of ways: comparing both 2/3 and 3/2 to one whole (a picture or explanation was necessary here), finding a common denominator (including showing work or a picture), reasoning by using the definitions of numerator and denominator, and subtracting 2/3 from 3/2 and identifying a remainder. After carefully reviewing the student solutions that employed correct strategies, I suggest teaching implications that can be supported by the data.

Student Strategies. Here I will discuss three different strategies that received full credit: comparing 2/3 and 3/2 to one whole by using a picture or explanation; comparing 2/3 and 3/2 to one whole by using a picture or explanation and representing 3/2 as a mixed number; and finding a common denominator. (At the end of this discussion, Table 1 summarizes the percentage of students who used each of these strategies.) Figures 1, 2, and 3 are examples of student solutions that were coded for these strategies respectively.

FIGURE 1. Student solution coded as comparing 2/3 and 3/2 to one-whole using a picture or explanation.

13. Which is larger $\frac{2}{3}$ or $\frac{3}{2}$? Use words and pictures to explain your answer.

$\frac{3}{2}$ because it is realy $1\frac{1}{2}$ and $\frac{2}{3}$ isnot even a hole

FIGURE 2. Student solution coded as comparing 2/3 and 3/2 to one-whole using a picture or explanation and representing 3/2 as a mixed number.

FIGURE 3. Student solution coded as finding a common denominator by drawing a picture or providing work.

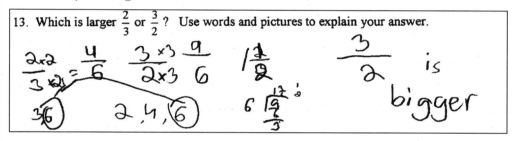

Of the 63 students who received full credit for this problem, 35 students employed the strategy of comparing both 2/3 and 3/2 through the use of a picture or explanation. Of these 35 students, 57% missed two or more questions involving finding a common denominator, and 29% of the students missed multiple-choice question number 5 dealing with representing a top-heavy fraction as a mixed number. The performance of these 35 students on the exams can be separated into two groups—one group that demonstrates both an intuitive understanding and procedural proficiency, and another group that uses an intuitive approach but performs poorly on process-constrained problems such as those dealing with finding a common denominator or representing fractions as mixed numbers.

Twenty-two of the 63 students who received full credit represented 3/2 as a mixed number in addition to comparing both 2/3 and 3/2 through the use of a picture or explanation. These students performed better on question number 5 than the previously discussed group of students (those who did not represent 3/2 as a mixed number) with only 1 of the 22 students missing number 5. However, 63% of these students missed 2 or more questions involving finding a common denominator.

Seven students (11%) used the procedural strategy of comparing 2/3 and 3/2 by finding a common denominator. However, only two of these students provided evidence that finding a common denominator is accomplished by re-unitizing each fraction so that each unit is divided into the same size of pieces (see Figure 4). These were the only two students that did not miss a single problem involving finding a common denominator.

FIGURE 4. Student solution that evidences a deep understanding of using a common denominator as a strategy.

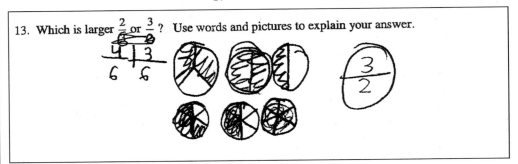

Four of the 7 students (or 57%) who employed finding a common denominator as a strategy missed 2 or more questions dealing with finding a common denominator. Although this result seems counter-intuitive, since the strategy of finding a common denominator gives each fraction meaning in terms of the other, the approach is less economical. Students who use economical strategies with regard to partitioning fractions have "a more mature approach" (Lamon, 2006, p. 142). Students' ability to recognize 3/2 as a fraction greater than one-whole and 2/3 as a fraction less than one-whole results in a more economical strategy. Evidence for this comment from Lamon can be seen from a detailed analysis of in-class video where one fifth-grade student, Spencer, demonstrates both procedural proficiency and conceptual understanding as he solves a task dealing with fractions in multiple ways. Ms. W, the fifth grade teacher introduces the task (note that the teacher is represented by "Ms. W" and Spencer is represented by "S" in the following transcript).

> **Ms. W:** I'm going to give you your first worthwhile mathematical task. Like I said, I want you to do it on your own, by yourself , for a minute. I'm going to come around and ask you some questions. . . . And then, um, we'll work together as teams and we'll work on it. O.K., um, before we get started, remember the first time we did our first worthwhile mathematical task, one of our big ones, we were talking about our class party, right? And we decided what we were going to do, we decided what pops we were going to have for our party, right? Well, today we're going to talk about our party because we're going to plan that and that's coming up really soon. So, um, for the class party

6

I brought three and one sixth pepperoni pizzas to school. I got hungry that morning and had a couple pieces for breakfast. I had three and one sixth. I brought them to school and I put them in the faculty room because I didn't know where else to put it. But, guess what? When I went back to get them, Mr. B had eaten one and five-sixth of the pizza, of our class party pizza. Can you believe that? Um, so I want to know how much pizza we have left for our party. Is it going to be enough?. . . . So, go ahead on your paper, take a minute by yourself, to figure it out and then we'll talk about it as a class later. So, your information is here, if you need to refer to it, you've got it. Okay?

While Ms. W is introducing the task, Spencer begins to work out the problem procedurally on his paper. He writes 1 and 5/6 below 3 and 1/6. He crosses out the 3, changes it to a 2 and adds 6 sixths to the 1/6 that he had before—borrowing the whole. He subtracts the 5/6 from his now 7/6 leaving him 2/6. He then subtracts the whole numbers—2 from 3 which leaves him with 1. So, he's left with an answer of 1 and 2/6. About 30 seconds after Ms. W introduces the task, she comments:

> **Ms. W:** By the way, if you notice, on your desk you have anything you could possibly need. If you want to do it with manipulatives, do. If you want to do it with a picture, do it. If you want to do it, any way you want to do it, do it. And I also want it in multiple ways. . . . So, when you're done, do it another way and use whatever you need to complete it.

As Ms. W makes this comment, Spencer immediately puts down his pencil and looks at the blocks, fraction tiles, and transparencies on his table. He picks up a transparency and a marker and draws four circles, divides them into sixths, and shades 3 and 1/6 of the circles. He draws a horizontal line beneath the circles on the upper portion of his paper and then draws two circles below the horizontal line, divides them into sixths, and shades 1 and 5/6. He labels the portion of his paper above the horizontal line "in all" and below the horizontal line "eaten by Mr. B." He crosses out one whole pizza from each side of the line. He then crosses out the 1/6 in the fourth pizza on the upper half of his paper, and then crosses out four more sixths in one of the other whole pizzas he had drawn. This leaves him with everything crossed out on the portion of his paper below the horizontal line, and everything crossed out except one whole pizza and 2/6 of a pizza left above the horizontal line.

After solving the problem using a picture, Spencer uses manipulatives to solve the problem. He first solves the problem with blocks and then again solves the problem with fraction tiles. Ms. W interrupts the students:

> **Ms. W:** Boys and girls, can you stop for just one second? What I would like you to do now, is I want you to discuss at your table what you're doing. I want you to ask each other questions, I want you to, I want discourse. I want you to talk about what you are

7

doing to each other and say, "You know what? This is how I saw it, what did you do? Let me listen to your way. I don't understand that, will you explain that to me?" So, I want you to use what you know about fractions to discuss it and teach each other. So, right now I'm going to give you some time to work in your tables, in your small groups. So, talk about it. Explain it to each other. And if you need to, come up with a new way that all of you agree on.

Spencer explains to his group how he solves the problem using fraction tiles:

S: This is my three and one-sixth.

Spencer points to the three equally sized whole cardstock circles and one-sixth of a circle. These whole circles vary in that they are made up of different sized pieces: 2 halves, 3 thirds, and one-whole (there is only one circle for each representation, so in order to work with circles that involve sixths, Spencer must be creative and use equal sized wholes composed of different sized pieces for each whole). Ms. W walks over to Spencer's table just as he begins his explanation.

Ms. W: I have a question, how do you know that's a sixth?

S: Because I took all of these [Spencer takes 6 sixths and puts them together to equal one-whole circle] and they all went into one.

Ms. W: Okay. [To the other students at the table] Do you guys agree with him?

S: And then it's negative one, so I take off one. [Spencer removes one circle] And then five-sixths, so I could, since I know that two-sixths equal one-third [Spencer places two-sixths on top of one-third in one of the circles on his table that is divided into thirds].

Ms. W: Wait. What is that called?

S: Equivalent fraction.

Ms. W: Oh. You're brilliant! I love this! Keep it coming. Go.

S: So then I take off four [Spencer takes away two "one-thirds" of the whole circle, each overlaid with other fraction tiles—two sixths] and then I can take off this [Spencer takes away the one-sixth that he had in his original representation of 3 and 1/6] and I'm left with one and two sixths [Spencer places two-sixths on top of the one-third of a circle he had remaining].

8

Ms. W: Interesting. Wow. Do you guys have questions for him? Did that make crystal-clear sense? Or, do you guys have questions?

Student: That was cool.

Ms. W: That was awesome, huh? Can you believe that!

Spencer demonstrated conceptual and procedural understanding by choosing to solve the problem in four unique ways. The Mathematics Learning Study Committee (2001) has said that "a significant indicator of conceptual understanding is being able to represent mathematical situations in different ways and knowing how different representations can be useful for different purposes" (as cited in Kilpatrick, 2001, p. 119). Spencer's intuitive and conceptual understanding allows him to recognize 5/6 as a fraction bigger than 1/6, which causes him to borrow by re-unitizing a whole (giving a fraction another name while preserving its identity, e.g., changing one-whole to six sixths), and to carry out the procedure correctly. Given that Spencer demonstrates conceptual understanding and procedural fluency (he scores 100% on the post-test), it is important to note that he solves the open-response task, problem 13 on the exam, using an economical/intuitive approach even though he is very capable of solving problems using a common denominator strategy (see Figure 5). To summarize, students with a mature understanding of fractions are probably more likely to use an economical approach (for problem 13, drawing a simple picture or recognizing that 2/3 is less than one-whole and 3/2 is larger than one whole) rather using a common denominator as a strategy without interpretation.

FIGURE 5. Spencer's solution to open-response question #1 (problem 13)—an intuitive approach.

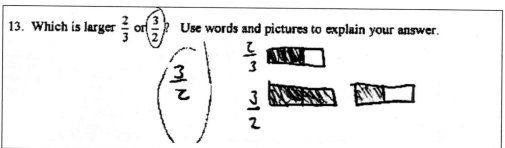

It seems counter-intuitive that students who use a common denominator strategy to solve problem 13 miss questions dealing with finding a common denominator, but they may lack intuition in knowing when to use this strategy. For example, analysis of Joshua's exam (see Figure 6), a student who used finding a common denominator as a strategy, suggests that when comparing fractions he employed finding a common denominator (see Figure 6.1a and 6.1b), but when using a common denominator would be the most useful for solving certain addition or subtraction problems, he added or subtracted across the numerators and denominators (see Figure 6.2).

FIGURE 6. Portions of Joshua's exam.

FIGURE 6.1a   FIGURE 6.2

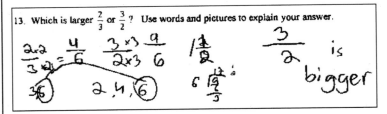

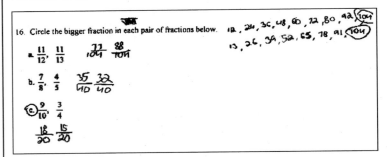

Evidence that the students who employed finding a common denominator as a strategy need to build their intuitive understanding can be inferred from the fact that 71% of these students missed an intuitive problem, question 14 on the exam (see Figure 7). This question assesses an intuitive sense of fractions because a procedure can not be used to solve the problem. It is interesting to note that only 37% and 45% of the students who used an intuitive approach (similar to those strategies in Figures 1 and 2 respectively) missed problem 14. Also interesting is that the only two students among those who employed a common denominator strategy who did not also miss problem 14 were those two students who demonstrated their understanding as shown in Figure 4. These students interpreted what finding a common denominator meant and therefore demonstrated their intuitive understanding.

FIGURE 7. Problem which requires intuitive understanding, problem 1.

14. In the picture below, a brownie is cut into 4 pieces. Some people think that the pieces are **not** equal shares. Do you agree that they are **not** equal? Explain your answer.

The preceding solutions illustrate some of the findings summarized in Table 1, i.e., that percentages are greater for the number of students who missed questions assessing understanding of those concepts that are evident in alternative strategies. For example, the percentage of students who missed question 5 and who did not include a mixed number (mn) in their solution was higher than those who did include a mixed number.

TABLE 1. Summary of data for 3 strategies on open-response question 13.*

Strategy	Percentage of students who used this strategy	Missed 2 or more common denominator questions (procedural cd)	Missed question #5 (procedural mn)	Missed question #14 (intuitive)
Comparison, Picture, Explanation(intuitive)	56%	57%	29%	37%
Comparison, Picture, Explanation, with Mixed Number (intuitive/ procedural mn)	35%	63%	4%	45%
Common Denominator (procedural cd)	11%	57%	14%	71%

*Key for concepts that the questions address and the strategies demonstrate knowledge of (listed in parentheses under the question or strategy): cd = common denominator, mn = mixed number.

Teaching Implications. Students who compared 2/3 to 3/2 to one-whole through a picture or explanation and who missed questions dealing with finding a common denominator might be encouraged to consider how finding a common denominator would help them solve problem 13. The students who did not include a mixed number in their solution could be encouraged to develop their procedural fluency in representing mixed numbers. The seven students who employed a common denominator strategy might be encouraged to develop their intuitive understanding and explore the meaning of part-whole comparisons in greater depth by drawing pictures or using manipulatives to solve problem 13. These facts support the idea presented by the National Research Council (2003) that students should learn with understanding:

> Learning with understanding is often harder to accomplish than simply memorizing and it takes more time. Many curricula fail to support learning with understanding because they present too many disconnected facts in too short a time—the 'mile wide, inch deep' problem. Tests often reinforce memorizing rather than understanding. The knowledge-centered environment provides the necessary depth of study, assessing student understanding rather than factual memory. It incorporates the teaching of meta-cognitive strategies that further facilitate future learning. (p. 21)

The open response task gives opportunities for students to learn with understanding as a teacher supervises and encourages students to explore the alternative "meta-cognitive strategies that further facilitate future learning." Though it takes time to allow for this deeper learning, Lamon (2006) cites the NCTM's recommendation that teaching "proportional reasoning 'is of such great importance that it merits whatever time and effort must be expended to assure its careful development'" (p. xiii).

Another teaching implication that can be drawn from the data is explained by the Mathematics Learning and Study Committee (2001): "Procedural fluency and conceptual understanding are often seen as competing for attention in school mathematics. But pitting skill against understanding creates a false dichotomy. . . . The two are interwoven" (as cited in Kilpatrick, 2001, p. 123). As proven by the two students who demonstrated their understanding as shown in Figure 4, conceptual and procedural understandings are not disjoint; an increase in one area should result in an increase in the other. This is so because

> as a child gains conceptual understanding, computational procedures are remembered better and used more flexibly to solve new problems. In turn, as a procedure becomes more automatic, the child is enabled to think about other aspects of a problem and to tackle new kinds of problems, which leads to new understanding. (Kilpatrick, 2001, p. 134)

Students need to know how to perform procedures, when to carry out a procedure, and why that procedure works. However, a push toward the use of an algorithm should not be accelerated above a student's capacity to develop conceptual understanding (NCTM, 2002, p. 26). The algorithm of finding a common denominator is not an exception. "The problem with [finding a common denominator] is that many students cling to [it] without understanding why [it] work[s]. So a good classroom strategy is to make finding a way to explain why a common denominator works an on-going problem" (NCTM, 2002, p. 11).

The Mathematics Learning and Study Committee (2001) comments on the consequences of learning procedures without conceptual understanding: "When skills are learned without understanding, they are learned as isolated bits of knowledge. . . . This practice leads to a compartmentalization of procedures that can become quite extreme, so that students believe that even slightly different problems require different procedures" (as cited in Kilpatrick, 2001, p. 123). Evidence of compartmentalization can be seen from Joshua's exam (Figure 6). Knowing that Joshua did not solve problem 13 without interpretation might be worrisome based on the previous quotations from current research. Thus, considering how Joshua and the other students did not solve the open-response task provided insight into their understanding. This adds a promising perspective on open-response tasks as assessment tools.

Open-Response Question #2

Open-response question #2, problem 21 on the exam, asks students to list three fractions equivalent to 9/12. This open-response task is not as involved as problem 13 and does not ask students to "use words and pictures to explain" their answer. Therefore, because the question does not ask for an explanation or picture, the opportunity to infer student *understanding* (both conceptual and procedural) is not as great. However, because there is not one "right answer," I include some data that might suggest how the open-response task can provide insights into student understanding. The open-response task allows teachers to encourage their students to explore alternative strategies in solving a problem.

Student Strategies. I will discuss two strategies that can be used to find equivalent fractions. One of these is to multiply by a fraction equivalent to one, thus making the numerator and denominator bigger (from here on, I will refer to this strategy as "enlarging" a fraction—see Figure 8). Another strategy is to divide both the numerator and denominator by a common divisor (note that some answers may be of the form k·f where f is the smallest fraction that is found by dividing by the greatest common divisor and k is a fraction equivalent to one where the numerator and the denominator are the same integer greater than one, e.g., $9/12 = k \cdot f = 2/2 \cdot 3/4 = 6/8$. From here on, I will refer to this strategy as "reducing" a fraction—see Figure 9). The students received full credit if they listed three equivalent fractions, and partial credit if they listed less than three (see Figures 10, 11, 12). Of the 172 students who took the post-test, 143 students received full or partial credit. Referring back to my research questions, I carefully examined students' strategies to determine if those students who chose to enlarge the fraction had difficulty reducing and vice-versa.

FIGURE 8. Student solution coded as enlarging three times.

21. List three fractions equivalent to $\frac{9}{12}$. $\frac{18}{24}$ $\frac{27}{36}$ $\frac{36}{48}$

FIGURE 9. Student solution coded as reducing three times.

21.   List three fractions equivalent to $\frac{9}{12}$: $\frac{3}{4}$ $\frac{6}{8}$ $\frac{1\frac{1}{2}}{2}$

FIGURE 10. Student solution that received partial credit coded as reducing twice.

21.   List three fractions equivalent to $\frac{9}{12}$.

$\frac{3}{4}$ $\frac{6}{8}$

FIGURE 11. Student solution that received partial credit coded as enlarging once.

21.   List three fractions equivalent to $\frac{9}{12}$. $\frac{18}{12}$ $\frac{1}{4}$ $\frac{27}{36}$

FIGURE 12. Student solution that received full credit coded as writing three equivalent fractions (they both enlarged and reduced).

21.   List three fractions equivalent to $\frac{9}{12}$. $\frac{3}{4}$ $\frac{18}{24}$ $\frac{36}{48}$

A summary of the number of students who used each strategy is given in Table 2. While it is clear that the students who wrote one reduced fraction had more difficulty in reducing fractions, the table suggests the general trend that the more equivalent fractions the student can write, the better they perform in both enlarging and reducing fractions. This is most likely due to a strong conceptual understanding. "Conceptual knowledge . . . provides a base on which to develop procedural knowledge" (NCTM, 2002, p. 26). Building conceptual knowledge is a result of children "[engaging] in meaningful thinking about fractions when the contexts relate to their personal situations" (NCTM, 2002, p. 26). Evidence for this idea can be seen in an in-class video of a student, Carly, as she develops a conceptual understanding of equivalent fractions. By comparing rods of different lengths, she discovers that 2/10 equals 1/5. She assigns the orange rod as "one-whole" and finds that 10 white rods equal one orange rod. She calls the white rods "1/10." She compares green rods with the orange rod and discovers that five green rods equal one orange rod. She calls the green rods "1/5." She finally compares the white rods with the green rods and discovers that two white rods equal one green rod. She comes to the conclusion that 2/10 equal 1/5. It is important to note that she received full credit for problem 21 by writing three equivalent fractions after she developed this conceptual understanding.

TABLE 2. Summary of data from open-response question 21.*

Strategy	Percentage of students who used this strategy	Missed 2 or more Questions Enlarging	Missed 2 or more Questions Reducing
1 Reduced	18%	37%	19%
2 Reduced	3%	0%	0%
3 Reduced	Less than 1%	0%	0%
1 Enlarged	3%	25%	0%
2 Enlarged	5%	0%	0%
3 Enlarged	5%	0%	0%
2 Equivalent	13%	11%	0%
3 Equivalent	52%	0%	0%

* The strategies listed include the number of fractions the student wrote. Enlarged or reduced referred to what type of equivalent fractions they listed. The strategies that include the word "Equivalent" mean that the student did a combination of reducing and enlarging.

Teaching Implications. Students who wrote less than 3 equivalent fractions might be encouraged to explore in greater depth the meaning of equivalent fractions and could be given more opportunities to practice writing equivalent fractions. The number of students who missed questions dealing with enlarging fractions (those who only wrote one reduced equivalent fraction) suggests that these students might have difficulty with concepts addressed by the alternative strategy of reducing. Given the opportunity, like Carly, to see concrete representations of equivalent fractions, students might be able to carry out procedures correctly because they have developed conceptual understanding.

Conclusions

A careful review of student strategies on open-response tasks warrants a new interpretation of the open-response task as an assessment tool. Open-response tasks provide the opportunity for teachers to consider how students did *not* solve the problems; teachers can then encourage their students to develop their understanding of the concepts addressed by using alternative strategies because students might not be proficient in those concepts. Of these fifth grade students, those who worked procedurally on open-response problems to find common denominators did not provide evidence of intuitive understanding through drawings or explanations. Students who demonstrated limited intuitive understanding by comparing fractions directly without prior interpretation may not have procedural fluency. Students may be able to solve open-response problems, such as those involving finding common denominators, but when similar problems are placed in another context, they may be unsuccessful in demonstrating their content knowledge or mathematical skills. Implications for teaching include discovering whether or not students can flexibly use their understanding of fractions in multiple contexts. Students also should be encouraged to practice using algorithms once they have developed a conceptual understanding. The more knowledge they are able to demonstrate on open-response tasks exploring equivalent fractions, the greater the probability is that they are more proficient finding equivalent fractions. Through the use of open-response tasks, teachers can gain greater insight into student thinking and provide opportunities for their students to learn as they exercise their agency. By using this assessment tool, teachers can "promote growth, modify programs, recognize student accomplishments, and improve instruction" (NCTM, 1995, p. 27).

References

Cai, J. (2001). Improving mathematics learning: Lessons from cross-national studies of Chinese and U.S. students. *Phi Delta Kappan, 82,* 400–404.

Erlwanger, S.H. (1973). Benny's conception of rules and answers in IPI mathematics, *The Journal of Children's Mathematical Behavior, 1,* 7–26.

Kilpatrick, J. (Ed.). (2001). *Adding it up: Helping children learn mathematics.* Washington, D.C.: National Academies Press.

Lamon, S.J. (2006). *Teaching fractions and ratios for understanding.* 2nd ed. Mahwah, New Jersey: Lawrence Erlbaum Associates.

Mathematical National Research Council. (1993). *Measuring what counts: A conceptual guide for mathematics assessment.* Washington, D.C.: National Academy Press.

Moon, J., & Schulman, L. (1995). *Finding the connections: Linking assessment, instruction and curriculum in elementary mathematics.* Portsmouth, NH: Heinemann.

National Research Council. (2003). *How people learn: Bridging research and practice.* Washington D.C.: National Academy Press.

National Council of Teachers of Mathematics. (1995). *Assessment standards for school mathematics.* Reston, VA: NCTM.

National Council of Teachers of Mathematics. (2000). *Principles and standards for school mathematics.* Reston, VA: NCTM.

National Council of Teachers of Mathematics. (2002). *Making sense of fractions, ratios, and proportions.* Reston, VA: NCTM.

Walter, J., & Gerson, H. (in press). Teachers' personal agency: Making sense of slope through additive structures. *Educational Studies in Mathematics.*

Appendix
(Assessment)

NAME_____   TEACHER_____   Grade 5

1. If a line that is 40 inches long is divided into fifths, how long is each segment?

    a.   6 inches

    b.   7.5 inches

    c.   8 inches

    d.   10.5 inches

2. What fraction of the rectangle is shaded?

    a. $\dfrac{5}{7}$

    b. $\dfrac{5}{8}$

    c. $\dfrac{5}{10}$

    d. $\dfrac{5}{12}$

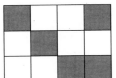

3. What is the simplest form of the fraction $\dfrac{9}{15}$?

    a. $\dfrac{2}{3}$

    b. $\dfrac{3}{4}$

    c. $\dfrac{3}{5}$

    d. $\dfrac{9}{15}$

18

4. The fraction $\frac{7}{10}$ is equivalent to which decimal number?

   a. 0.1

   b. 0.3

   c. 0.7

   d. 1.7

5. Which fraction is equivalent to 7?

   a. $\frac{7}{10}$

   b. $\frac{10}{3}$

   c. $\frac{7}{7}$

   d. $\frac{21}{3}$

6. Which fraction is equivalent to $\frac{2}{5}$?

   a. $\frac{2}{10}$

   b. $\frac{4}{10}$

   c. $\frac{3}{7}$

   d. $\frac{4}{7}$

19

7. Which of the fraction below is equivalent to $\frac{1}{4}$?

    a. $\frac{1}{8}$

    b. $\frac{2}{8}$

    c. $\frac{3}{8}$

    d. $\frac{4}{8}$

8. Use twelfths to write a fraction equivalent to $\frac{2}{3}$.

9. The weather channel wants to let you know that there is very little chance of it freezing today. From the options below, what is the lowest possible probability they might report?

    a.   1/10

    b.   1/100

    c. -10

    d. -100

10. What is probability of spinning a 2?

    a. 1 out of 4

    b. 1 out of 8

    c. 2 out of 4

    d. 3 out of 8

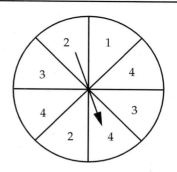

11. If 9 marbels represent $\frac{3}{4}$ of the marbles in a bag, how many total marbles are in the bag? Use words or pictures to explain your answer.

12. The picture is $\frac{3}{5}$ of a rectangle. Draw a picture that shows the whole rectangle.

21

13. Which is larger $\frac{2}{3}$ or $\frac{3}{2}$? Use words and pictures to explain your answer.

14. In the picture below, a brownie is cut into 4 pieces. Some people think that the pieces are **not** equal shares. Do you agree that they are **not** equal? Explain your answer.

15. Write the following fractions in order from smallest to largest.

$$\frac{3}{8}, \frac{3}{5}, \frac{11}{12}, \frac{1}{2}, \frac{2}{7}$$

16. Circle the bigger fraction in each pair of fractions below.

a. $\frac{11}{12}, \frac{11}{13}$

b. $\frac{7}{8}, \frac{4}{5}$

c. $\frac{9}{10}, \frac{3}{4}$

17. $\dfrac{4}{7} + \dfrac{2}{7} =$

18. $\dfrac{1}{4} + \dfrac{7}{6} =$

19. $2\dfrac{3}{5} - \dfrac{1}{5} =$

20. $\dfrac{3}{4} - \dfrac{2}{3} =$

21. List three fractions equivalent to $\dfrac{9}{12}$.

(Candice) Keisha and James each bought fruit punch for the class party. Keisha paid $2.00 for a 16 oz. bootle and James paid $1.60 for a 12 oz. bottle. Who got the most fruit punch for their money? Who paid the most per ounce for their fruit punch?

The Social Problems that Deter Xhosa Women from Marriage and How Education and Westernization Allow Them to Refuse Marriage

by
Colleen Rebecca Johnson

English 315
Brigham Young University
April 10, 2006

Table of Contents

Abstract iii

Introduction 1

    Previous Attitudes toward Marriage 1

    Current Trends in Marriage 3

Methods 3

Findings 4

    New Attitudes toward Marriage 4

    Social Problems Contributing to the Undesirability of Marriage 5

        Infidelity and AIDS 5

        Abuse and Subordination 6

    The Influence of Western Ideology 7

    Factors Allowing Women to Refuse Marriage 8

        Education 8

        Westernization and Women's Rights 9

Conclusion 10

References 12

Abstract

Twenty years ago in South Africa, despite a Xhosa woman's dissatisfaction with marriage, she was unable to refuse it due to cultural expectations and a lack of education. For many women marriage meant deficient amounts of money because of the husband's alcoholism and gambling and the migrant labor system, lack of support in parenting and housekeeping, and extreme physical and emotional abuse. This paper reports young, contemporary Xhosa women's attitudes toward marriage now that they are able to refuse the associated social problems because of increased education and women's rights. The current data indicate that compared to other African countries, black South African women are getting married less and later. Qualitative research, including the interviewing of 13 unmarried, college-enrolled Xhosa women, was conducted to determine the attitudes behind this change. From these interviews, it was found that women have negative attitudes toward marriage because of husbands' infidelity and the resulting risk of AIDS, and because of potential abuse and subordination by their husbands. Now that women have acquired through education and Westernization the economic and social freedom to refuse marriage, they are increasingly foregoing marriage and the social problems they associate with it, despite their belief that marriage is potentially a positive institution.

The Social Problems that Deter Xhosa Women from Marriage and How Education and Westernization Allow Them to Refuse Marriage

Introduction

Twenty years ago in South Africa, the ability of Xhosa women to refuse marriage was vastly different than it is today. Then, women were culturally expected and even forced to marry young and quickly bear children (Mathabane, 1994). The worth of a woman to her family was based on her ability to get married and produce posterity (Holden, 1963, p. 189). Even if a woman was dissatisfied with marriage, she was also unable to refuse it due to a lack of education and the economic independence education provides. Before apartheid ended, most black women were denied access to higher education. Legally, the education system of apartheid limited what women could learn and therefore limited what occupations they could hold and how much they could earn (Ross, 1999, pp. 161–162). These two factors—cultural pressure and lack of education—prevented many women from acting on any negative feelings they may have had toward marriage. Today, however, many young Xhosa women of marriageable age are not marrying. By comparing the results of interviews with South African women from the 1980's with the results of interviews conducted in 2005, this paper will illustrate how women's attitudes have changed with changing social conditions in South Africa that have caused the marriage rate to decline. The results show that women's increasing levels of education and the Westernization of South Africa since the fall of apartheid now allow women to refuse marriage.

Previous Attitudes Toward Marriage

In an interview conducted in 1984, a South African woman named Rose Modise from Soweto said, "I don't want my daughters to get married. If they are educated, it's better that they earn a living wage. Marriage, I don't care for it. I'd like them to stay with me. They can have children and support them. They will have a better life" (quoted in Lawson, 1986, p. 12). This attitude toward the institution of marriage was not limited to just a few black women living in apartheid South Africa. Interview after interview confirms that to these women the cost of a marital relationship far exceeded the benefit. For many women, having a husband meant deficient income because of the husband's alcoholism and gambling and the migrant labor system, as well as extreme physical and emotional abuse and a lack of support in parenting and housekeeping.

To Rose, who lost her husband eight years after they were married, "life was easier after he died. Because he was the one who was wasting money—drinking too much. He used to go and use my wages and go and get drunk" (quoted in Lawson, 1986, p. 10). Many men would use all the money they were supposedly earning to help support their family to support their alcohol and gambling habits instead. Because apartheid also

1

enforced a migrant labor system, many women were neglected and abandoned by their husbands, making it necessary for them to find alternative means for financial support (Schapera, 1947, p. 177). Having a husband no longer meant financial stability for many women.

More often than not, marriage meant that women were forced to obtain menial jobs, such as factory work and domestic service, which kept them from home long hours and paid them barely enough to buy food for their children. When the women came home their second shift of housekeeping and childrearing started. In another interview, a woman named Nomvula described her struggle managing her family and home without the support of her husband: "When he comes home he sleeps—because he's got no children to watch. . . . He doesn't help at home. No! (laughs) Because you know they say a husband is a big man. He shouldn't do anything at home—the woman must work. We both work at night but he can't help me with anything" (quoted in Lawson, 1986, p. 22). Having a husband did not mean receiving help raising a family and sustaining a home.

Many times marriage meant that women feared for their physical safety. In some instances husbands beat their wives bloody at the slightest sign of independence or resistance. Because of societal expectations and cultural practices, such as *lobola* (the payment for brides), many women were forced to remain in abusive relationships they did not necessarily choose. Once their parents received the *lobola*, the bride's rights were transferred from her family to her husband's family (Mathabane, 1994). If, to South African women, marriage meant nothing but abuse, neglect, and poverty with no way out, it is no wonder many women began to feel they were better off single.

During apartheid most women were still expected to get married, but some women already resisted it. Alfie was one of these women. "I'm afraid to get married. . . . Because men are so hard when you are married. Men drink and they hit you. I see it everywhere. . . . I don't like men. Life would be harder if I was married—yes" (quoted in Lawson, 1986, p. 86). Was Alfie's decision not to get married the foreshadowing of a great future trend? At the end of her interview Rose Modise declared, "Women have just decided not to get married. . . . They're tired of it. Soon there will be no more marriage. Just boyfriends and girlfriends!" (quoted in Lawson, 1986, p. 12). Yet because of cultural expectations and their economic dependence on men, most women during this time were not yet able to make good this threat.

Today, 22 years after the interviews cited above were conducted, the daughters of these women have reached marriageable age. They now have greater access to education and financial independence. As South Africa becomes more involved in the world, "indigenous knowledge and skills are giving way to Western knowledge and skills" (Chepyator-Thomas, 2005, p. 11). Due to Westernization, cultural expectations to get married have also changed. Now that the ability to refuse marriage has increased, is Rose Modise's prophecy correct? Are young black women in South Africa increasingly choosing to forego marriage? How have recent cultural changes related to education and Westernization affected Xhosa women's ability to refuse marriage and its associated social problems?

2

Current Trends in Marriage

The current data from censuses and surveys on marriage in South Africa indicate that marriage trends are indeed changing. Compared to other African countries, black South African women are getting married less frequently and later in life. In South Africa, only 50% of women are married by age 24, whereas 95% of women in Ghana are married by age 25 (Amoateng, 2004, p. 10). Researchers postulate that the more rural and uneducated a woman is the more likely she is to marry, and to marry younger. Modernizing forces, which raise the level of education and urbanization of women, have contributed to the declining marriage rate (Amoateng, 2004, p. 12) With an increase in education and financial freedom women no longer need men to provide for them; marriage is no longer an economic necessity, so fewer women are getting married (Makiwane, 2004, ¶ 8).

While researchers attempt to explain the historical and current issues that are affecting the marriage trends in South Africa, "consensus on the reason for such changes is yet to be reached" (Makiwane, 2004, ¶ 1). Research on trends in marriage is almost exclusively quantitative, but even this research is not very accurate because it mostly documents official civil marriages while a large number of blacks marry only traditionally in ceremonies not recorded by civil records. According to the *Southern African Journal of Demography*, the problems involving accurate census information "are particularly acute in South Africa as a result of the wide diversity in marriage forms, cultures, religions and languages. Inadequacies in coverage of large segments of the population during the apartheid years add to the difficulties" (Budlender, Chobokoane, & Simelane, n.d., p. 1). Qualitative data can take into account a multitude of variables that quantitative research cannot on this subject. Through qualitative research, including interviews, current attitudes about marriage can be analyzed in order to give a more descriptive account of why the rate is changing and the role that education and Westernization play in this change. The research presented here is an attempt to provide that description.

Methods

I conducted qualitative research to help researchers understand the cultural causes of statistics indicating declining marriage rates in black South Africa. I conducted interviews in the urbanized city of East London, South Africa. Because most of the women in East London are Xhosa, this naturally limited my study to that particular cultural group. I conducted interviews by asking groups of two to three women to participate in guided discussions about marriage. I did this with 5 groups for a total of 13 women. I selected my subjects from among unmarried female Xhosa students at Border Technikon University and Rhodes College. I recorded information about their socioeconomic, educational, religious, and cultural backgrounds in a demographics questionnaire and kept their circumstances in mind while analyzing the data.[1] Because of the small size of this sample the following results are not meant to be representative; rather they are meant to demonstrate common themes in greater depth. I supplemented the interview information with secondary

3

research from sociological and marriage and family journals to show how my analysis is congruent with modern theories and research findings.

Findings

With the end of apartheid, globalization and the spread of western ideology are having a significant effect on the culture of the Xhosas of South Africa. Television, radio and the Internet are now readily available, and the influence these media have on the rising generation is clear to anyone who visits a college campus. This influence has instigated a great transition from tribal culture to a modern western culture. The western culture of individual economic and social rights has begun to resonate with young Xhosa women, who now have a greater opportunity to gain higher education. The cultural effects of greater women's rights and opportunities are especially apparent in young women's attitudes toward marriage. The decline in the marriage rate is caused by the new attitudes learned from Westernization and higher education combined with the social problems that make marriage undesirable.

New Attitudes Toward Marriage

The South African women interviewed believe that the institution of marriage was originally good for women and society. According to one informant, marriage is beneficial "spiritually as well, because it's a God-ordained institution and if you are doing it you get a blessing from God" (personal communication, October 2005). The majority of the women interviewed had very positive attitudes toward marriage when it is practiced correctly: respectfully and lovingly, without infidelity and abuse. However, most of the women believe that marriage has become distorted and they are therefore unwilling to participate in it. For example, one interviewee stated,

> Marriage was a very good thing, a beautiful thing, but today it's no longer. You would like to get married, but as you see the world outside you look at the married people. Sometimes you see people get married this year and next year they're divorced, and you wonder what's happening. What is it that's special about me that will make me reach goal point? It's either my husband will commit adultery, or I will commit adultery. Or if not, my husband will abuse me. If not, he won't be responsible. (personal communication, October 2005)

Despite the belief that marriage can be beneficial, many of these Xhosa women do not believe that they will be able to find someone to enter into a healthy union with. When asked what one respondent believed the chances were of finding a respectable South African man, she replied, "I believe that really there are like 44 million people living in South Africa, so, like, one in 44 million" (personal communication, October 2005). The undesirability of marriage increases when women's positive perception of potential partners decreases.

4

Social Problems Contributing to the Undesirability of Marriage

Attitudes toward marriage are affected not only by women's increasing opportunities to be educated and employed, but also by social conditions that make marriage undesirable. These include infidelity, risk of HIV infection, abuse, and the demeaning subordination of women to men.

Infidelity and AIDS. When asked about the disadvantages of marriage, the women most often cited the high occurrence of infidelity and the resulting risk of contracting AIDS from one's husband. This more than anything else makes marriage undesirable for young Xhosa women. As one woman put it,

> There is HIV, so if you get married before you are even infected by that, then it's like, "Wow, thank God! At least now she's got someone she can be stable with and chances of her getting HIV are very slim," you know? But that's not the case because husbands cheat sometimes. It's the norm. (personal communication, October 2005)

According to the interviewees, infidelity has become a way of life for the majority of South African men, and this has dangerous consequences.

Even though many wives are sexually inactive until married and remain faithful to their husbands, they still run the risk of contracting AIDS due to their husbands' promiscuity. One interviewed woman claimed that marriage is the highest risk factor for AIDS because women think,

> "This is your husband, what chance are you going to have [to contract AIDS]," and you're never going to think about it. . . . Long relationships are the one relationship that are good for you in terms of contracting AIDS . . . because you feel so trustworthy and you trust that person. So that's why I'm saying if I were to get married—which won't happen first of all—I don't know. I can't put my life in jeopardy with someone else. (personal communication, October 2005)

Her fear is well founded as many recent studies show that a large and growing number of AIDS cases were contracted from spouses as a result of infidelity (Maharaj & Cleland, 2004, p. 116).

The fear of infidelity and AIDS has led many South African women to demand change or else refuse marriage. One respondent explained, "I'm to a certain extent anti-marriage. . . . I know the infidelity issue is big. . . . And women here in South Africa, they keep quiet about it. They have accepted it and I think they need to start a revolution of some sort" (personal communication, October 2005). This issue, combined with the problem of abuse, is enough to convince many women to avoid marriage.

5

Abuse and subordination. For many Xhosa women abuse is one of the associated outcomes of marriage. South Africa has the highest rate of domestic abuse in the world as "one in four women in South Africa is in an abusive relationship—while one woman is killed every six days by a male partner" (Ndura, 2005, p. 1). This abuse stems from a tradition of violence as a means of conflict resolution during apartheid, the emasculation of Xhosa men by the apartheid regime, widespread poverty and unemployment, and tribal practices in which women are subordinate to male dominion (Malley-Morrison, 2004, p. 254).

The majority of domestic abuse goes unreported in South Africa because many women are afraid of the social and economic consequences. The subject of domestic abuse is taboo and complaints to family often fall on unsympathetic ears (Malley-Morrison, 2004, p. 254). Due to tradition, women are often told by other women to keep silent. One participant reported,

> Abuse will happen. It is high, but people are keeping quiet about it. . . . The older women come and tell you the behavior you have to show in the family, and you find that now when your husband is abusing you, you'll think of the *iziyalo*—when you are telling the women when she's getting married how she must behave in the new family she's in—and now you will remind yourself of all those things they told you, and you'll keep quiet when your husband is abusing you. (personal communication, October 2005)

Women also won't report abuse due to the economic consequences. The higher earning power and greater control of money by men makes "women dependent on husbands and likely to stay with husbands despite abuse" (Malley-Morrison, 2004, p. 248). As a result of this potential abuse and subordination, many young women are afraid to get married. One informant recalled that

> During the old days, they tell you, "You have to tolerate. You have to [bow] down to your in-laws and to your husband. You have to do whatever they tell you to do whether you like it or not." Whether it's something very bad or not, you have to because you're married. . . . Looking at what is happening right now I don't think I'll ever get married; it might happen to me. (personal communication, October 2005)

Another informant told of her disgust with traditional subordination:

> This one time I was hiding behind the *kraal*, because that's where they give them all the rules and stuff, like on how to live like a man, and I was just hiding and I was listening to what they were telling them. They were telling them, "From now on you are a man. You never ever listen to a woman. Whatever you say goes in the house. You are the one who makes the rules. A woman doesn't tell you what to do. You are the man; you can have as many women as you want." And they were telling them all

6

these things, and I was saying to myself, *"Oh my word, so that's why they become so ignorant in everything they do!"* (personal communication, October 2005)

Apparently, many young women of this generation feel this way. They would rather face the prospect of remaining single and raising children on their own than entering into the potentially dangerous institution that marriage has become. And now they have the option to refuse marriage because of changing social conditions in South Africa.

The Influence of Western Ideology

These South African women view marriage negatively due to Western ideology's influence on men's and women's attitudes toward marital duties. This trend mirrors what has been found in other westernized societies:

A cultural lag exists between the changing domestic roles of women and men in U.S. society. Specifically, women are positively embracing their new work and family roles, while men are resisting the increasing independence of women in the workplace and the greater demands placed on men in the home. (Hunt & Hunt, 1987, as cited in Ferguson, 2000, p. 140)

Many young South African women feel that this cultural lag applies to them as well. Like their mothers' generation, these women are tired of the lack of support in caring for the home and children and would like roles to change. One participant said that, for example, she would like to see men help more with child care and household duties:

If you [women] get off late, then you [men] can take the child so that you can watch him in the night, diaper change and everything. Maybe make supper or buy supper, or whatever, and try and make things be equal. . . . Not just the man works and that's the only thing he does, and going to bed. (personal communication, October 2005)

Due to the influence of western ideology, women are now eager to work outside the home and expect greater help from their husbands with familial duties. This expectation is often not met, however, because of men's more traditional ideals as illustrated by one participant:

The expectations [of men] are always old-fashioned. . . . The husband will be like "when I get married my wife will stay at home with the kids and I'm going to come home with the bear and I'm going to kill the bull." The woman will be like "I'm a working woman and I'm independent. I'm making my own money." (personal communication, October 2005)

7

While women are becoming more progressive in gender ideology, South African men still have difficulty accepting the independence of women. "Despite their education and modernity, many males still hold to traditional ideas regarding male dominance over their wife" (Anderson, 1997, p. 156). This disparity caused by Westernization is yet another reason many women choose to forego marriage. The increase in education and the adoption of Western attitudes have now made it possible for them to refuse marriage.

Factors Allowing Women to Refuse Marriage

The declining marriage rate appears to be due not only to the fears women have about marrying an irresponsible and abusive partner, but also to increasing opportunities for women to be educated and to enjoy rights that women in Western societies have had for some time.

Education. According to resource theory, people with the most economic resources naturally exhibit the most power in relationships. In the instance of uneducated women, "the economic dependence of wives on husbands limits wives' influence and leaves them vulnerable to the wants and needs of their husbands" (Stets & Hammons, 2002, p. 6). To young Xhosa women enrolled in college, education is the key to the economic freedom that allows them to be independent and invulnerable. They feel that because of education, women are economically and socially empowered to make known their opinions regarding their own lives. When women aren't economically tied to men, they are safeguarded against abuse. One interviewee made this clear when she stated,

> A woman is no longer expected to stay at home. You can go and do whatever you want. You can own a car and you can buy a house if you want to, instead of your husband. I think most women should work because these guys like taking advantage. If you stay at home they will tell you what to do. (personal communication, October 2005)

This economic freedom directly translates into freedom of choice in regards to marriage. "As a result of economic independence, women can now choose from a variety of lifestyles, including marriage, marriage and motherhood, single hood, unmarried single motherhood, or a career-oriented lifestyle" (Rhoden, 2003, p. 248). Many women are using this freedom to delay or forego marriage as in the case of this participant: "I don't think I'm ready for a relationship right now, and like, the focus is on my career and what I want to do. I've got the freedom. I'm not looking to a guy for support and money and stuff like that" (personal communication, October 2005).

Education and its economic implications are the means by which women are able to resist the social problems they associate with marriage. Women who are educated are more

8

aware of their rights and more confident in their abilities and are therefore more able to make their desires known. Whereas their mothers' generation was not as able to take a stand against such problems as infidelity and abuse, this generation feels empowered, as one informant commented:

> I think that this acceptance of infidelity is more with the older generation. The emerging [generation] is beginning to be like, "Hang on, this is not acceptable! I don't have to do this." They are getting to see that there is life even if you are not married. You don't have to succumb to this sort of lifestyle. You don't have to accept this. . . . Because they were always, in the past, living in the shadow of men or their husband. But now we are getting all these opportunities. Women are able to do things. . . . I think with the younger generation they will be more educated. That's the thing. The minute they become more educated about themselves and they know their rights. (personal communication, October 2005)

Education has opened the way for women to demand more not only because of its economic implications, but also because of the cultural transition it has instigated. Whereas in earlier times most parents wanted their daughters to get married and have children at a young age, now their expectations for their daughters are that they postpone marriage for their education, as one informant stated:

> My dad wants me to be studying and be independent and be off with my studies, and then on to getting married. But the priority right now is the studying. I wouldn't say it's [marriage] expected. We don't really discuss it that much. It's not an issue . . . as long as you study, get higher education, learn to be independent and then get onto marriage. (personal communication, October 2005)

Because of this lack of cultural pressure from their parents, many young women are now free to prioritize education over marriage.

Westernization and women's rights. Cultural pressure to get married has also subsided due to the spread of Western ideology. The Western movement toward greater women's rights greatly appeals to educated Xhosa women and changes their attitudes toward marriage. One informant told of her appreciation for Westernization because of this change:

> It's good that we have our independence, or whatever, because if you look at prior to the whole Westernized culture women didn't really have any rights, you know what I mean. In our days women are, women have, everything. They want to prove to men that "we can do whatever you can do." There's nothing special. There's nothing new

9

that men can do that woman can't do, so they think, "I can live my life the way I want. I don't want any man in my life." If it's a man it must be a boyfriend, not a husband. (personal communication, October 2005)

As women begin to believe that they have greater rights, they begin to demand greater rights, including the right to avoid relationships they deem harmful to themselves.

As Western thought spreads, non-Western women begin to see themselves as individuals who don't need to give in to the expectations of society. While in Western society "individuality is the ideal of life; to the African, the ideal is the right relations and behavior to other people" (Kenyatta as cited in Chepyator-Thomas, 2005, p. 14). Many African women therefore used to enter into marriage to please their family and society. One informant added, "It's a family culture. It's not individualistic. Marriage is not individualistic in our culture" (personal communication, October 2005). Now, however, women are being influenced by Western media to assert their individuality, as another informant stated:

I think it's influenced women to be more independent. . . . On TV you see white people in America. They seem to be, like, independent. They have their own lives, like they are not really married, you know. . . . I'd say that other cultures have influenced what we do and what we can get without marriage. (personal communication, October 2005)

This individualistic attitude has caused many women to believe that they can be happy without society's approval. They are therefore socially able to refuse marriage when they believe its effects are negative.

Conclusion

So it seems that Rose Modise's prophesy is correct. More and more women are rejecting marriage, not because they believe it is in itself a negative institution, but because they are tired of the social problems associated with it. In the words of one interviewee, "I think women are waking and saying, 'Sorry, I can't take this crap no more'" (personal communication, October 2005). Added to the known risk of abuse, neglect, and infidelity rampant during their mothers' generation is now an even greater threat: AIDS. This life-threatening danger is enough to make anyone break with tradition. As one participant put it, "Again in my tradition you're supposed to get married. Today I'm not considering tradition, in the life I'm living in today. Today, in the life we're living now, there's viruses" (personal communication, October 2005).

Unlike Rose's generation, young women are now empowered to forego marriage because of higher education and an increase in women's rights. According to one interviewee,

On face value my mother's generation was more accepting of marriage. But I believe that underneath it all, it's always been unstable. It's only now that we are talking about it. Women now are becoming more educated; they are able to learn about what their rights are. Before, they just had to accept. (personal communication, October 2005)

When compared with the interviews from twenty years ago, her interpretation is correct.

Even though women are now able to forego marriage, refusing to enter into it is the last resort, not their primary choice, as expressed by this informant:

I think most people would love to get married; it's just the things that have happened which make them think "No." It's not to say they hate marriage. . . . They would love to be in there, but they are sick and tired of those things. . . . I should think it's nice being with someone, sharing your life with someone, the ideal, you know, the picture that one thinks of marriage. But things are happening and people change their minds about it. (personal communication, October 2005)

According to the informants I interviewed, if South African women believed that a marriage without abuse and infidelity were possible, they would gladly accept it, because they believe that it is a positive institution. But rather than entering into a harmful relationship, many young Xhosa women are employing their newfound independence to call for reform:

I think it's up to the women to demand change, but at the same time the men need to realize that what they are doing is not [right], to change their attitudes. . . . I think as a whole, society needs to just change. (personal communication, October 2005)

As Westernization has increased women's rights and women have been empowered through education, more and more South African women are willing and able to hold out for something better than the social problems they associate with marriage.

References

Anderson, G.L. (Ed.). (1997). *The family in global transition*. St. Paul: Professors World Peace Academy.

Amoateng, A.Y. (2004, August). The South African family: Continuity or change? *HSRC Ten Years of Democracy Seminar Series*, 1–27. Retrieved April 10, 2006, from www.hsrc.ac.za

Budlender, D., Chobokoane, N., & Simelane, S. (June, n.y.) Marriage patterns in South Africa: Methodological and substantive issues. *The Southern African Journal of Demography, 9(1)*, 1–25.

Chepyator-Thomas, J.R. (Ed.) (2005). *African women and globalization: Dawn of the 21st century*. Trenton, NJ: Africa World Press.

Ferguson, S.J. (2000). Challenging traditional marriage: Never married Chinese-American and Japanese-American women. *Gender and Society, 14*, 136–159.

Lawson, L. (1986). *Working women in South Africa*. Oxford, UK: Alden Press.

Holden, W.C. (1963). *The past and future of the Kaffir races*. Cape Town: Gothic Printing Company.

Maharaj, P., & Cleland, J. (2004). Condom use within marital and cohabitating partnerships in KwaZula-Natal. *Studies in Family Planning, 35, 2*, 116–124.

Makiwane, M. (2004). Demise of marriage. *ChildrenFIRST, 58*. Retrieved April 10, 2006, from http://www.childrenfirst.org.za

Malley-Morrison, K. (Ed.) (2004). *International perspectives on family violence and abuse: A cognitive ecological approach*. Mahwah, NJ: Lawrence Erlbaum Associates.

Mathabane, M. (1994). *African women: Three generations*. New York: HarperCollins.

Ndura, M. (2005, November 25). Rights—South Africa: Domestic violence afflicts one woman in four. *Global Information Network*, p. 1.

Rhoden, J. (2003). Marital cohesion, flexibility, and communication in the marriages of nontraditional and traditional women. *Family Journal: Counseling and Therapy for Couples and Families, 11(3)*, 248–256.

Ross, R. (1999). *A concise history of South Africa*. London: Cambridge University Press.

Schapera, I. (1947). *Migrant labor and tribal life*. London: Oxford University Press.

Stets, J.E., & Hammons, S.A. (2002). Gender, control, and marital commitment. *Journal of Family Issues, 23*, 3–25.

Endnotes

[1] For a copy of interview transcripts, please contact Colleen Johnson at colleen7@byu.net.

Addressing the Causes of Obesity in the United States:
American Lifestyle and the Psychology of Health

by

Kemarie Ann Campbell

English 315

Brigham Young University

April 10, 2006

Table of Contents

List of Figures iii

Abstract iv

Introduction 1

Obesity in the United States 2

    Facts about Obesity 2

    Fighting Obesity 2

        Dieting 3

        Exercise 4

    Summary and Analysis 6

Identifying the Real Culpri 7

    American Food 7

        Refined vs. Whole Grains 7

        Fruits and Vegetables 8

        Fats 8

        Summary and Analysis 9

    American Exercise Habits 9

    Stress in the US 10

    Summary and Analysis 11

The Psychological Thread of Obesity 11

    The Psychology of Dieting 12

    The Psychology of Exercise 13

    The Psychology of Stress 13

Conclusion: Tying the Threads all Together 14

References 16

List of Figures

Figure 1: The Dieter's Dilemma 3

Abstract

Obesity is a growing problem in the United States and contributes to all of the major causes of death in the US. This paper emphasizes that wellness programs focused on reducing obesity should take lifestyle and psychology into consideration in order to be successful. Many attempts have been made to combat obesity, including the implementation of diets and exercise programs geared toward weight loss. Nearly all diets fail and many exercise programs do not have long-term effects on weight loss because they prove unsustainable. Obesity is really just a side-effect of a bigger problem—American lifestyle. Americans make poor food choices, do not exercise regularly, and have difficulty managing stress. Each of these factors contributes to the epidemic of obesity in the US today. Health is not just physical, but also psychological. Psychology plays an important role in obesity and poor health, but it has been generally ignored in weight-loss programs of the past. By learning to change their lifestyle and their psychological orientation to eating, exercise, and stress, Americans would have a better chance at combating obesity.

Addressing the Causes of Obesity in the United States:
American Lifestyle and the Psychology of Health

Introduction

I recently turned on the television and was shocked to see a report about a man who weighed 750 pounds. After being bed-ridden for seven years in his home, he was moved to a specialized care facility for the morbidly obese. His face was tiny in comparison with the discolored rolls of skin and flab that were his chest and shoulders; he looked like he was suffocating in his own flesh. So disturbing was the image that my roommate begged me to turn the channel. But as a health scientist I was fascinated. I watched awhile longer as he stared unbelievingly at the lunch a health care worker brought him—a chef's salad and a bowl of vegetable soup. He mumbled something about doing what he had to do to lose the weight, but he'd really rather have a hamburger. The next scene was intriguing. Apparently, Mr. 750 had smuggled some illegal snacks into the facility and took the liberty of bingeing to the extreme on chips and cupcakes. I turned off the TV as the health care workers at the facility were cleaning out his closet, making sure to rid the place of any more hidden snacks. This man's story is just one example—admittedly an extreme one—of a situation that is fast becoming a tremendous health threat in the United States: obesity.

It is no mystery that obesity is a problem in the US. Never in the recorded history of man has a nation been so fat (Hellmich, 2005). Not coincidentally, there have never been so many diet and/or exercise programs to help people slim down, either (Tribole & Resch, 1995). But obesity rates continue to rise. With the exception of a few eccentric outliers, each new diet program says the same thing the research has shown: in order to lose fat, you must burn more calories than you consume (i.e., eat less and exercise more). However, knowledge of the cure has done little to combat the fat problem in America. This fact suggests that US citizens are facing a problem much bigger than obesity.

1

I believe that the reason behind the high rate of obesity in the US is two-fold. First, obesity has been mislabeled—it isn't *the* problem. Obesity is only a symptom of the real problem, which is a trend of unhealthy living in America. Second, while the basic issues of energy intake and expenditure have been addressed (and then over-addressed) by the plethora of diet and exercise programs that are swamping the nation, one very important factor has been overlooked: the psychology of healthy living. These two factors—healthy lifestyle and healthy psychology—are indispensable in developing long-term health programs, and the fact that they have not been taken seriously is why obesity is such a big problem today.

Obesity in the United States

Facts about Obesity

According to recent studies, 40% of adults in the US are obese (Aldana, 2005). *USA Today's* Nanci Hellmich (2005) reported that 64.5% of adults are overweight. This is a serious problem, since obesity is a contributing factor to the leading causes of death in the United States—heart disease, cancer, respiratory disease, and diabetes (Aldana, 2005). If rates of obesity continue to increase as they have over the past decade, the number of heart disease and diabetes cases will skyrocket (Hellmich, 2005). With over half of the population qualifying as overweight or obese, this is an issue that concerns everyone in the US. Many efforts have been made to fight obesity, with little to show for it. It is important to understand these efforts and why they're not working.

Fighting Obesity

Someone who struggles with weight problems should go on a diet. At least this is a commonly held point of view among Americans. The word "diet" has become as American as baseball and apple pie. Dieting is the solution for anyone who wants to lose weight—or so we've been told. But is dieting really producing the intended results?

Dieting. According to Tribole and Resch (1995), as the dieting industry in America has grown (to an annual value of $50 billion), obesity rates have soared right along with it. This isn't surprising when one considers the fact that 90 to 95 percent of all diets fail because they are impossible to maintain for an extended period of time (Tribole & Resch, 1995). A person might successfully follow a strict diet for a short period of time and achieve the desired result of quick weight loss, but once the dieter "breaks" the diet and returns to normal eating patterns, the lost weight comes back—usually with a vengeance (Hirschmann & Munter, 1988). Figure 1 illustrates this concept, which is referred to as the *dieter's dilemma* by Tribole and Resch (1995). The dieter's dilemma is a harmful cycle that wears on the dieter emotionally and physically as the body goes up and down in weight (Tribole & Resch, 1995).

FIGURE 1. The Dieter's Dilemma.

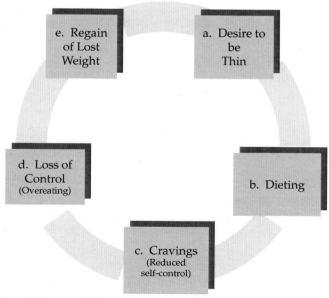

Source: Adapted from Tribole & Resch (1995).

3

Unfortunately, dieters believe *they* are the ones with the problem, rather than the diet, so they continue going from one diet to another in a cycle known as chronic dieting, searching for the one diet that will finally work (Tribole & Resch, 1995). The effects of chronic dieting are harmful. They include:

- The body retaining more fat once the dieter starts eating normally again

- A decreased rate of weight loss with each new diet attempt

- A decrease in metabolism

- An increase in binges and cravings

- An increased risk of premature death and heart disease

- An inability to identify natural biological hunger and fullness cues

- A change in body shape

- Headaches, menstrual irregularities, fatigue, dry skin, and hair loss (Tribole & Resch, 1995, pp. 48–49)

This list only identifies the physical damage that dieting can do. Diets also have serious psychological consequences, including the development of eating disorder mentalities, stress, feelings of failure, low self-esteem and anxiety, diminished confidence and self-trust, loss of control over eating habits, and feelings of having a "fundamental character deficit" (Tribole & Resch, 1995, p. 50).

The knowledge we now have about the effectiveness of dieting does not correlate with dieting trends in the US. Either Americans do not realize that diets are ineffective and harmful or they choose to deny it, as they eagerly lay down their money in exchange for the latest diet books, videos, and magazines that flood the market each year.

Exercise. Happily, dieting has not been the only suggested solution for losing weight. Science has proven that in order to shed pounds, a person needs to either decrease their energy consumption (eat less), increase their energy expenditure (exercise more), or do both

(Aldana, 2005). That is why personal fitness programs have also increased in number. Public health workers are encouraged to stress the importance of regular exercise in a weight loss program. The question is, are exercise programs making a difference in the health of the nation?

The benefits of regular exercise are inarguable: it can reduce the risk of heart disease and stroke, increase levels of HDL cholesterol (the good kind that helps clear arteries), control blood pressure, lower the risk of osteoporosis and diabetes, contribute to weight maintenance, protect against certain kinds of cancer, help with stress and anxiety, and improve mood (Sobel & Ornstein, 1996, pp. 111–113). Research shows that about 12 percent of deaths in the US annually occur because people don't routinely get enough exercise (Sobel & Ornstein, 1996, p. 112). Clearly, exercise makes a difference.

However, even when people do slim down as a result of a weight-loss exercise program, their chances of gaining it back are high. For example, Curioni and Lourenco (2005) researched the effectiveness of exercise and dieting as a long-term weight loss program for overweight and obese individuals. Their studies revealed a significant difference between the combination of diet *and* exercise and just dieting to lose weight. Exercising along with the dieting produced 20% greater weight loss than dieting without the exercise program. However, while the researchers showed that exercise has a significant effect on weight loss, they noted that "in both groups, almost half of the initial weight loss was regained after one year" (Curioni & Lourenco, 2005, p. 1168).

Perhaps the reason these persons regained weight after such a short period of time is that, much like dieting, the exercise program they were using was difficult to sustain because of its extreme intensity. Exercise is very beneficial, but regular high-intensity exercise can lead to burn-out and/or injury (Sobel & Ornstein, 1996). Sobel and Ornstein (1996) suggest that regular physical activity should be *enjoyable* and it doesn't have to be

5

difficult in order to be beneficial (p. 109). They point out that calories burned by normal activities, such as raking leaves, walking up stairs, gardening, and house work, add up throughout the day; these activities thus become beneficial forms of exercise (p. 110).

I have observed in today's society that diet and exercise mentalities are similar. People who exercise for the sole purpose of losing weight may feel that only high-intensity or even painful exercises will help them become slim. A strong determination may motivate them to work hard at an exercise program in the beginning, just as they do while on a diet, but as time goes by, a difficult program wears on initial motivation; control wears thin, and the whole process may lead to complete rejection of any form of exercise for a period of time. The would-be exerciser goes back and forth between intense exercise and almost no physical activity at all. Sobel and Ornstein point out that both of these extremes are harmful (1996, p. 109).

Summary and Analysis

Obesity is inarguably a serious problem in the United States. In response to this problem, the dieting industry has grown, but has been ineffective in combating obesity. Rather, dieting has many negative effects, including the inability to maintain the diet, that actually impede one's ability to lose weight. Many exercise programs have also been launched in response to high obesity rates. High-intensity exercise programs can lead to burn-out and/or injury. From this we can gather that in order to maintain a sustained exercise program, physical activity should be enjoyable. We can therefore conclude that there is a prevailing flaw in today's weight loss programs: that is, they focus on weight loss. Any doctor knows that treating a symptom will not cure the disease. Obesity has been treated as if it were a disease in and of itself, when it is really just a symptom of a much more serious disease.

Identifying the *Real* Culprit

Dr. Steven Aldana, a professor of health science at Brigham Young University, identifies lifestyle as the disease or *culprit* that is causing obesity and other diseases in America (Aldana, 2005, pp. 13–15). Lifestyle encompasses everything we do—our eating and exercise habits, stress and stress management, and even the way we think. So in order to understand the lifestyle culprit, we must examine American food, exercise habits, and stress.

American Food

Three of the most common mistakes Americans make in their food choices are choosing to consume white, refined grains and starches instead of whole grains, not eating enough fruits and vegetables, and going to one extreme or the other in their fat intake (Aldana, 2005, pp. 69–117). Outlined below are the reasons why each one of these consumption choices contributes to obesity.

Refined vs. whole grains. A century ago, bleached white flour and refined starches were uncommon and expensive, so most people ate whole grain foods. Today, most Americans eat white flour and refined starches because modern technology has made them cheaper and more accessible (Aldana, 2005, p. 69). Whole grain foods contain every part of the grain—the bran, germ, and flour—while refined flours have had the bran and germ removed. Yet the bran and the germ contain most of the grain's fiber and nutrients (Aldana, 2005, pp 69–71). Thus, refined flours don't really have much nutritional value. Eating white breads, white rice, and other processed foods puts Americans at a serious health disadvantage. As Dr. Aldana (2005) puts it, "They have an increased risk of many chronic diseases because, although these foods do not *cause* disease, they fail to *prevent* disease" (p. 71, emphasis added).

7

Fruits and vegetables. Besides not getting enough whole grains, Americans are not eating enough fruits and vegetables. The National Cancer Institute recommends that a person eat at least 5 servings of fruits and vegetables per day—and the more, the better (Aldana, 2005, p. 90). The average American eats only 2.7 servings per day and the most commonly consumed fruit and vegetable are *ketchup* and *French fries* (Aldana, p. 90)!

All plants contain important disease-fighting agents known as *phytochemicals*. Phytochemicals have been proven to fight cancer at all stages of development (Aldana, 2005, pp. 86–87). Those who eat more fruits and vegetables as a regular part of their diet are at a much lower risk for heart disease, and their risk for cancer is cut in half compared to those who don't eat many fruits and vegetables (pp. 81–86).

Fats. While the health value of whole grains, fruits, and vegetables has been known and advertised for quite some time, fats have gotten a bad rap over the past few decades. Many diets encourage the complete elimination of fats, and a trip to the local grocery store offers ample evidence that fat-free products have become a significant part of the food market. The results of many low-fat diets have actually been positive in terms of weight loss and lowering heart disease risk (Aldana, 2005, p. 100), especially if the kinds of fats that have been eliminated are saturated and trans fats. These fats are unhealthy and contribute to heart disease, high levels of cholesterol, and obesity. They are found in dairy products, fatty meats, fried foods, and anything containing shortening or partially hydrogenated oils (Aldana, 2005, p. 103). Elimination of these fats in a diet is a healthy step, and leads to weight loss, which is probably why low-fat diets have proved more successful than others.

However, not all fats are bad. In fact, our bodies *need* certain kinds of fat. These "good" fats are called monounsaturated and polyunsaturated fats; they are found in plants, nuts, and fish (Aldana, 2005, p.102). They lower blood cholesterol, prevent certain

8

chronic diseases, decrease the risk of heart disease and Alzheimer's disease, and even work to reverse the effects of bad fats (pp. 104–107). Clearly, avoiding fats completely is not a good idea; but Americans definitely need to become more educated about the difference between good and bad fats. Furthermore, they need to act on that knowledge.

Summary and Analysis. Despite all of the benefits that come with the consumption of whole grains, fruits and vegetables, and healthy fats, Americans still don't eat enough of them while they tend to eat too much of less healthy foods (Aldana, 2005, pp. 100–101). We are a fast-paced, fast-food nation, consistently choosing easy-to-make or take-out meals over health. Unfortunately, the eating habits of this culture have a great impact on the number of deaths each year from heart disease, cancer, and diabetes—some of the nation's top killers. And, of course, the American diet has contributed immensely to the amount of obesity in the US. American food choices are definitely one of the biggest culprits in the obesity problem. Americans' exercise habits are the other part of the problem.

American Exercise Habits

It is no secret that Americans, in general, don't exercise enough. Inactivity is one of the greatest contributors to obesity in America. While our ancestors' daily tasks of clearing land, raising and preparing food, and making clothing were necessary for their survival and required a significant amount of exertion, today it takes a concentrated effort in order for most of us to get just an adequate amount of physical activity (Sobel & Ornstein, 1996, p.109). Modern technology has made everything incredibly simple, making movement almost unnecessary. We drive instead of walk; we take the elevator instead of the stairs; we don't even have to get off the couch to turn the channel on the TV! We are much more sedentary than our ancestors; even children, who in past generations expended a lot of energy playing outdoors, now spend their leisure time watching television and playing

9

video games. This lack of strenuous physical activity in the American lifestyle is making

the average American obese—it is literally killing us.

Stress in the US

Another deadly aspect of American lifestyle is the unhealthy way in which Americans

tend to deal with stress. Sobel and Ornstein (1996) explain that, if not dealt with properly,

long-term stress has significant negative effects on the body and mind. Stress results in

increased blood pressure, heart rate, and breathing rate; it causes the digestive system to

slow down or even stop at times; it can cause hypertension (high blood pressure) to

develop; and it can make muscles tighten (p. 81). Stress can also cause anxiety problems,

excessive worrying, and difficulty concentrating (p. 84). About half of all Americans are

concerned about the amount of stress they have in their lives (Stambor, 2006). Although

stress is a natural part of life, Stambor (2006) reports that many Americans don't know how

to deal with stress in healthy ways. Rather than relaxation or counseling, they turn to

smoking, alcohol, or food as sources of comfort.

Considering the negative effects of stress and the typical American response to it, is it

any wonder that Michel, Levin, and Dunn-Meynell (2003) identified stress as a contributor

to obesity? Smith, Baum, and Wing (2005) conducted a study on the effects of chronic stress

(they tested parents with cancer-stricken children) and found that major stressors can have

a significant effect on weight gain. They suggest that this effect is partly due to the way

stress impacts patterns of both eating behavior and physical activity. Kamigaki (2005)

reports that increased stress levels have been related to obesity disorders. Cabyoglu,

Ergene, and Tan (2006) give further evidence that stress contributes to obesity in their

study, which shows that acupuncture used as a stress reliever helps patients lose weight.

They report that acupuncture affects physical factors—such as eating habits and

metabolism—but also emotional factors like stress (Cabyoglu & Ergene, 2006, abstract).

10

While stress is not entirely avoidable, it is important that Americans learn to cope with stress through healthy activities (such as participating in hobbies, taking time to relax, meditation, journaling, etc), rather than developing harmful habits related to consumption of food and drugs. Stress is undoubtedly a significant factor in the obesity epidemic in the United States.

Summary and Analysis

Rather than trying to treat obesity as a problem in and of itself, it is important to recognize that *lifestyle* is the real disease in America, and obesity is simply a result of a culture that fosters unhealthy living. Americans eat unhealthy foods, don't get adequate exercise, and are not very good at managing stress in their lives. All of these factors contribute to obesity, as well as several other diseases in the US.

If the rates of obesity are to go down, it will only be because of a change in the personal lifestyle of each American. Most likely, there will need to be a complete shift in thinking and behavior for this to occur. Americans will need to reevaluate their lives, their priorities and the importance of their health. Changing the way they view and conduct their lives suggests that health goes far beyond simply being physically fit. Health is as much a matter of psychology as anything else. In fact, the answer to dealing with obesity in this nation may very well lie in the psychology of health.

The Psychological Thread of Obesity

Every subject discussed thus far has dealt with psychological issues in some way, but a deeper look at the psychology of dieting, exercise, and stress-management is now required. As noted, people make lifestyle choices for the psychological rewards they derive from them; in order for people to change their lifestyle, they must also be able to change their thinking to desire the new psychological benefits they will derive.

11

The Psychology of Dieting

When one refers again to Figure 1 and the list of the effects of dieting found immediately after Figure 1, it becomes clear that psychology plays a prominent role in the diet-binge cycle. It is, after all, not the body that loses control over dieting, but the mind. Stice, Presnell, Groesz and Shaw (2005) conducted an experiment to discover the psychological effects of dietary restraint (putting restrictions on food concerning what one can and can't eat). Their findings reveal that dietary restraint can lead to bulimic mentalities (thought patterns that lead to restrained eating, followed by bingeing and purging) and increase the risk for onset of obesity. Urbszat, Herman and Polivy (2002) came to similar conclusions, showing that even the *thought* of restrained eating or going on a diet in the future can lead to abnormal psychological behavior. Those subjects who believed they would soon go on a diet began to overeat and display binge-like behaviors.

Hirschmann and Munter (1988) explain that diets are ineffective because they don't address one's psychological *need* to turn to food (p. 12). Diets simply command the dieter to physically stop eating certain foods or certain quantities. This approach doesn't work because compulsive eaters usually run to food in order to cope with stress, anxiety or fears; when faced with difficult situations, compulsive eaters literally feel compelled to eat (p.13). Hirschmann and Munter help compulsive eaters to overcome their food obsessions by helping them learn to identify their emotions, become gentler in their self-talk, accept and love themselves under any condition, and identify real sources of comfort in their lives. This approach demonstrates just how great a part psychology plays in healthy living and weight loss.

Diet program planners go wrong when they fail to take psychology into consideration; rather, they outline a plan that addresses only the purely physical aspects of eating. Failure to understand the psychological reasons for eating is the true reason why

12

diets will never be the cure for obesity. They simply don't offer what it takes to solve the problem.

The Psychology of Exercise

Just like diets, many exercise programs do not address the psychological implications of staying physically active. But the importance of psychology in physical fitness is demonstrated by the fact that many college and professional teams now have sports psychologists. With the help of these professionals, athletes have been able to improve and enhance their game performance by visualizing themselves succeeding on the track, court, or field.

Sobel and Ornstein (1996) stress the importance of finding an exercise that is enjoyable (p. 114). If a person considers exercise painful or boring, they probably won't sustain it for long. Sobel and Ornstein also confirm that "what you tell yourself matters," pointing out that negative or degrading thoughts about exercise or sports performance prohibit one from getting the full benefits of the exercise (p. 115). Therefore, a truly effective exercise program should allow for creativity and flexibility, taking into account psychological factors and helping people find activities that suit them, as well as teaching them the power of positive thinking.

The Psychology of Stress

Dr. Keith Karren, a BYU professor, points out that most stress in the United States comes from the human mind (class lecture). Sobel and Ornstein (1996) explain that stress occurs when the mind perceives any psychological or physical danger or threat, *real or imagined* (pp. 143–144). Stress can therefore be reduced and sometimes even eliminated by retraining the mind's thought processes and perceptions of fear. By working to counter negative or anxious self-talk with positive affirmations, stress and anxiety can be greatly reduced (Sobel & Ornstein, 1996, p. 149).

13

Developing a positive, confident attitude and a faithful outlook on life has been proven to reduce the effects of stress (Sobel & Ornstein, 1996, pp. 35–41). Such thought patterns have been shown to boost immunity, help fight cancer and other illnesses, contribute to longer life, and speed recovery from surgery (pp. 40–41). Clearly, the mind has a powerful effect on stress level and duration. Since stress has been proven as a contributor to obesity, it follows that people who learn to manage stress through developing different thought patterns will be more protected from the psychological processes that may lead to obesity.

Conclusion: Tying the Threads All Together

Obviously, there are many factors to be considered in developing a wellness program for people struggling with obesity. But changes in at least two factors—lifestyle and psychology—are indispensable in any successful effort to fight obesity. Obesity itself is not the problem; rather it is the result of underlying causes that must be identified and addressed.

A century ago, it would most likely have been inconceivable to anyone in America that there could be a 750-pound man. But today, in a nation where nearly half the population suffers from obesity, the idea is not so shocking—and that is a sobering thought indeed. I learned later that the man I had seen on television had passed away due to the complications of his obesity. Years of inactivity and unhealthy food choices got him to where he was. Enforcing healthy meals and exercises on him didn't prove successful in curing him.

Perhaps health care workers could have gone one step further than forcing him to eat salads or confiscating his smuggled-in snacks; perhaps they should have looked into the *why* of his behaviors. His comment that he'd "rather have a hamburger" demonstrated that, although he wanted to lose weight, he did not understand that it was his *lifestyle* that

14

had landed him in a special care facility for the morbidly obese, and his lifestyle is what needed to change in order for him to recover. The fact that he was bingeing on unhealthy snacks in the middle of the night suggests that he had real emotional issues that were not being addressed—and so he sought solace in the form of cupcakes and chips.

When someone weighs 750 pounds, contemplating a change in lifestyle may seem too late. But it is never too late to work toward better health; it is not too late for Americans to turn the tide of obesity in the US today. The answer lies in a change of lifestyle and a greater focus on the psychology of health.

References

Aldana, S.G. (2005). *The culprit and the cure.* Mapleton, UT: Maple Mountain Press.

Cabyoglu, M.T., Ergene, N., & Tan U. (2006). The treatment of obesity by acupuncture. *The International Journal of Neuroscience, 116,* 165–75.

Curioni, C.C. & Lourenco, P.M. (2005). Long-term weight loss after diet and exercise: A systematic review. *International Journal of Obesity, 29,* 1168–74.

Hellmich, N. (2005, Oct. 9). Obesity in America is worse than ever [Electronic version]. *USA Today.* Retreived March 13, 2006 from http://www.diabetic.help.com/obesity_in_ america_is_worse_than%20ever.htm

Hirschmann, J.R., & Munter, C.H. (1988). *Overcoming overeating.* New York: Fawcett Books.

Kamigaki, M., Sakuae, S., Tsujino, I., Ohira, H., Ideda, D. Itoh, N. Ishimaru, S., Ohtsuka, Y., & Nishimura, M. (2005). Oxidative stress provokes atherogenic changes in adipokine gene expression in 3T3-L1 adipocyte. *Biochemical And Biophysical Research Communications, 339,* 624–32.

Michel, C., Levin, B.E., & Dunn-Meynell, A.A. (2003). Stress facilitates body weight gain in genetically predisposed rats on medium-fat diet. *American Journal of Physiology: Regulatory, Integrative & Comparitive, 54,* 791–99.

Smith, A.W., Baum, A. & Wing, R.R. (2005). Stress and weight gain in parents of cancer patients. *International Journal of Obesity, 29,* 244–250.

Sobel, D.S. & Ornstein, R. (1996). *The healthy mind, healthy body handbook.* New York: Patient Education Media, Inc.

Stambor, Z. (2006, Apr. 4). Stressed out nation. *Monitor on Psychology.* Retrieved April 8, 2006 from http://www.apa.org/monitor/apr/06/ nation.html

16

Stice, E., Presnell, K., Groesz, L., & Shaw, H. (2005). Effects of a weight maintenance diet on bulimic symptoms in adolescent girls: An experimental test of the dietary restraint theory. *Health Psychology, 24,* 402–12.

Tribole, E. & Resch, E. (1995). *Intuitive eating.* New York: St. Martin's Griffin.

Urbszat, D., Herman, P.C., & Polivy, J. (2002). Eat, drink, and be merry, for tomorrow we diet: Effects of anticipated deprivation on food intake in restrained and unrestrained eaters. *Journal of Abnormal Psychology, 111,* 396–401.

Consumer Marriage and Modern Covenant Marriage

by
William J. Doherty

William J. Doherty is the author of several books, articles, and programs focused on improving marriages and family relationships. He has been a therapist and psychologist for over 25 years, and he advocates great changes in order to restore lasting marriages to a position of social importance. Doherty aided the development of "Putting Family First," a grass roots movement designed to help parents get communities involved in prioritizing family time. The titles of his books, such as Take Back Your Kids *and* Take Back Your Marriage, *demonstrate his focus on action. Doherty is the Director of the Marriage and Family Therapy Program in the Department of Family Social Science of the University of Minnesota, Twin Cities. The following are excerpts from an article adapted from a talk presented at a conference entitled "Revitalizing the Institution of Marriage for the 21st Century" held at Brigham Young University in March 2000.*

Advertisers know a cultural trend when they see one. A recent magazine ad pictures a new Honda Civic with the headline, "The sad thing is, it'll probably be the healthiest relationship of your adult life." Honda explains: "You've tried the personals, blind dates, even one of those online chat rooms. Why? The Civic Sedan is smart, fun, reliable and good-looking. Not to mention, it's ready to commit, today." Then, lest the reader feel suddenly commitment-shy, the ad ends in the wink of a headlight: "Looking for a good time?"[1]

Apparently we must seek "healthy adult relationships" with cars because, as an ad for Levi's jeans has recognized, marriage can't be counted on anymore. In a lavish six-page spread we see happy dating couples, with captions announcing how long they were together before breaking up. The final page shows two female roommates, one consoling the other about a recent breakup. Just behind the two roommates, on the kitchen wall, is an art poster with the Spanish words, *Mis padres se divorcian*: "My parents are divorced." The caption underneath delivers the ad's take-home message: "At least some things last forever—Levi's: they go on."

The message is that we can only count on what we buy, not on what we share or the people to whom we commit ourselves. And the only role that endures is that of consumer. Companies that want our business will do whatever it takes to meet our needs, unlike our spouses, who sometimes put their own needs, or the children's needs, before ours. Levi's will be there for us, even if our parents divorce and our lovers leave us. How comforting. . . .

Consumer culture has always been based on individuals pursuing their personal desires. But in the late twentieth century, advertisers began to emphasize desire for desire's sake. An example is Nike's slogan: "Just do it!" Or Sprite's: "Obey your thirst." A Toyota ad campaign has a voiceover saying to a father, "Your kids always get what they want; now it's your turn." Consumer culture has always been one of self-gratification, but the entitlement dimension is more prominent now.

. . . My concern is less with consumer culture in the marketplace, but with how it has invaded the family. Consumer culture teaches us that we never have enough of anything we

Reprinted from *Marriage & Families*, August 2000.

want, that the new is always better than the old—unless something old becomes trendy again. It teaches us not be loyal to anything or anyone that does not continue to meet our needs at the right price. Customers are inherently disloyal. I want to support American workers, but have always bought Japanese cars because I see them as superior to American cars for the price. I eat Cheerios for breakfast every day, but if the price gets too much higher than Special K, my second choice, I will abandon Cheerios. Or if they change the recipe, I might jump ship. I owe nothing to those who sell to me except my money, which I can stop giving at any time.

We Americans are also less loyal to our neighborhoods and communities than in the past; we move where there are jobs and where we can afford to live. Who asks nowadays whether you should not move because the neighborhood needs you? We are less loyal to particular religious denominations, churches, and other faith communities; we shop for the best religious experience.

Is it surprising that in this new consumer world, we are less loyal to our spouses, to our marriages? And when a marriage breaks up, is it surprising that one of the parents, often the father, exits from the children's lives to create a new life and a new family?

The sociologist Arlie Hochschild observed that in the new American lifestyle, rootlessness occurs on a global scale. "We move not only from one job to another, but from one spouse—and sometimes one set of children—to the next. We are changing from a society that values employment and marriage to one that values employability and marriageability."[2] This reminds me of a line from the huge 1970s best-selling book, *Passages*, by Gail Sheehy: "Though loved ones move in and out of our lives, the capacity to love remains."[3] You see, it is your ability to love, not the people you love, that counts as a permanent asset in the consumer culture of relationships.

What happens when we approach marriage and family life as entrepreneurs? When the initial glow fades and the tough times come, we are prepared to cut our losses, to take what we want from our old marriages in order to forge new, more perfect unions until they also must be dissolved. Where does it end? Even worse than the results of business layoffs, there are few soft landings after marital downsizing.

How did we get there? Until the twentieth century, marriage all over the world could be called "Institutional Marriage." It was based on economic security, raising children, and men as the head of the household representing the couple in the world. Families were large and expectations for emotional intimacy between the spouses were low. Husband and wife roles were separate. Divorce was rare, and couples expected to stay together unless someone did quite awful things. The key value in the Institutional Marriage was responsibility. Marriage existed for the welfare of children and families, not primarily for the personal happiness of the spouses.

The social changes of the twentieth century in the United States and other Western nations brought on the "Psychological Marriage."[4] Here the emphasis was on the emotional satisfactions of marriage relationships based on friendship, intimacy, sexual satisfaction, and gender equality. For the first time in history, families existed for individuals rather than vice versa. The key value of the Psychological Marriage was personal satisfaction. Commitment in marriage was a "given," as seen by the low divorce rates at the high-water mark of the Psychological Marriage during the post-World War II era.

The social revolutions of the 1960s and 1970s changed the face of marriage again by bringing in a powerful form of me-first individualism combined with a call for far more gender equality than the Psychological Family had delivered. Expectations for marital closeness and happiness skyrocketed along with the divorce rate. For the first time, the "soft" reasons for getting divorced became both acceptable and common, supported by legal changes to "no-fault" divorce. For the first time in human history, marriages could be ended by one of the spouses saying, "It's not working for me anymore." The era of Consumer Marriage was dawning.

During the go-go economic years of the 1980s and 1990s, when market economies triumphed over socialist economies all over the world, the consumer culture captured the hearts—and marriages—of Americans in new ways. Psychological Marriage mutated into Consumer Marriage, marriage with high psychological expectations but now spiced with a sense of entitlement and impermanence. The chief value of the Consumer Marriage is making sure that one's needs are being met and that one's spouse is doing a good job.

In practice, most couples embrace a variety of values for their marriage, including the values of responsibility and commitment emphasized by the Institutional Family. But these values are always in danger of being trumped by the consumer values of personal gain, low cost, entitlement, and keeping one's options open. In consumer culture, the exit door is always available. Commitments are always provisional, as long as the other person is meeting our needs. In some circumstances, we manage to convince ourselves that we need only provide money to keep the relationship intact, as when a noncustodial parent considers the payment of child support his only parental obligation. And when the price gets too high or the relationship supplies little or nothing in return, even money may be withdrawn in favor of another "product." The parent owes no loyalty beyond payment, as in the consumer relationship with breakfast cereal or a car.

Has the consumer culture brought some good things into contemporary marriage? Yes. The positive side of being a good consumer is the value of advocating for oneself in the marketplace. Good consumers in the marketplace are well-informed. They insist on high-quality goods and service. They are not patsies for misleading advertising or bad deals. They spend their resources wisely.

When it comes to marriage, good consumers choose their mates carefully rather than impulsively. They take time to get to know a person before making a commitment. They take premarital education classes. They learn what it takes to make a marriage work. And they expect to be treated lovingly and fairly by their spouses. Although these qualities are part of overall psychological well-being, they are supported by the best elements of a culture that emphasizes consumer rights and consumer information. Fewer women nowadays will stand for abuse from their husbands because it's their "fate" as wives. They will use consumer ideas such as "I deserve better" and "I have a right to expect something different." The problem is not that we are constructive consumers in our marriages. The problem arises when that's all we are.

As a culture, we have no new, coherent alternative to Consumer Marriage. The more stable Institutional Marriage is dead, and most contemporary men and women do not want to bring it back. The price in personal freedom and equality for women is too high. We will not turn the clock back to a pre-individualistic era; rather, we must learn to tame individualism. The Psychological Marriage, which assumed commitment but did not work on building it, was not sturdy enough to withstand the me-first consumer world. It's not that most people go into marriage with a full-blown consumer attitude; indeed, most believe that they are fully committed for life. The consumer model kicks in when problems arise and gridlock occurs, as they do in almost every marriage. That's when we begin to ask if what we are getting from the marriage is worth the price of dealing with its problems, whether the costs outweigh the benefits of being with this person.

Towards A New Cultural Ideal Of Marriage

We need a new ideal of marriage that re-emphasizes the commitment and responsibility of the Institutional Marriage while embracing emotional satisfaction elements of the Psychological Marriage and the self-advocacy elements of the Consumer Marriage. We need an ideal of marriage that fosters commitment and individual well-being, both permanence and equality between men and women. An ideal that accepts divorce but sees it as the tragic exception and not the norm. I call this Modern Covenant Marriage, "covenant" to connote the religious sense that marriage is a powerful, sacred commitment, and "modern" to suggest that we need a new way to be in committed marriages in the twenty-first century. This form of marriage is similar to, but more than, Covenant Marriage legislation passed in Louisiana and Arizona and proposed in other states.

Every cultural trend, including consumer culture, has something to teach us. As I suggested before, Modern Covenant Marriage is like Consumer Marriage in one important way. It embraces the importance of spouses advocating their needs and rights in the relationship. It stresses that people should not sit still while being taken advantage of by their spouses. It promotes self-advocacy in marriage for both men and women.

But Modern Covenant Marriage goes beyond Consumer Marriage in most other ways. Covenant marriage involves a commitment not only to the other person but also to the marriage itself. In the consumer economics model, I am committed to a product or service as long as it meets my needs, but I am not committed to the relationship I have with the company that makes it. I eat Cheerios, but I am not committed to General Mills. In a covenant marriage, the spouses have an abiding commitment to the "we" as well as to the other spouse, to the marriage along with the person. The marriage becomes the third party in their couple relationship.

This "third party" commitment is especially easy to see if you have children, because you realize how much your children rely on your marriage relationship, in addition to relying on each of you individually. Kids whose parents divorce may still have two parents to depend on, but not a marriage. It is a huge loss.

Modern Covenant Marriage requires the habits of the heart and mind to cultivate a lifelong relationship that is loving and fair to both partners, where the well-being of your spouse and your marriage is as important as your own well-being, where the soft reasons for divorce are off the table, and where efforts for continued improvement of the marriage are tempered with acceptance of human limitations.

I think that most of us dearly want what I am calling a Modern Covenant Marriage, but don't know how to achieve it or hold onto it. It is not enough to start with a loving commitment, or even with a religiously grounded commitment. Most divorces occur to people who start with heartfelt commitment, backed by religious convictions. The battlefields of divorce are strewn with the carcasses of couples who started out with love, commitment, and good intentions. As stresses and dissatisfactions mount, and they inevitably do, the seductive forces of consumer culture are too strong to resist without an alternative model of marriage. I am offering Modern Covenant Marriage as an alternative.

. . . Modern Covenant Marriage puts high demands for self-awareness, empathetic understanding, and negotiation skills. Researchers have found that the ability to deal constructively with conflict is a key factor in long-term successful marriage. But skills are not enough, as evidenced by the fact that male therapists, who presumably have good communication skills, have higher-than average divorce rates. Knowing what to do to help your marriage, although necessary, is not enough to see you through the hardest of times. A covenantal commitment is needed, but with a modern sensibility that recognizes the dignity and worth of both spouses along with the abiding importance of the bond they have created.

Specific Actions

I propose several courses of action based on the foregoing analysis. The most obvious implication of this proposal is to support Covenant Marriage laws in the United States. Covenant Marriage laws generally give couples, newly marrying or already married, the option of a legal marriage arrangement that requires premarital education, marriage counseling in times of trouble, and a two-year separation period before a divorce can be decreed, unless there is abuse, adultery, abandonment, or a felony conviction. Covenant Marriage initiatives are an intervention aimed at creating a new cultural conversation about marriage commitment.[5]

Second, I propose that we form state and national associations of couples in covenant marriages, in order to provide mutual support and affirmation for one another and to be a public force for promoting the ideal of Modern Covenant Marriage. We need a grassroots movement of couples, not led by professionals, to fight Consumer Marriage on behalf of higher ideals.

Third, I propose that we engage the professionals who practice psychotherapy and marriage therapy in a discussion of Consumer Marriage and Modern Covenant Marriage.[6] Towards this end, I have drafted a values statement for therapists who wish to identify themselves as pro-commitment in today's complex world. It can also be used by consumers and referring professionals to seek out pro-commitment therapists.

We have to find the way together, as husbands and wives, as a community. We have to find a new way to be married in a new century, or else I fear that nothing we do for the generations that follow us—no technological or medical breakthroughs—will offset the debilitating losses that failed marriages will inflict on our children and their world. We have to name the problem of consumer marriage before we can fight it. And we have to unleash the human capacity for sustained moral commitment from the tentacles of a marketplace that is slowly choking it, generation by generation. The stakes could not be higher.

Endnotes

1   *Entertainment Weekly* 539 (March 12, 2000) 36–37.

2   Arlie R. Hochschild, "How has 'the organization man' aged: A need to belong." *The New York Times* (January 17, 1999) 17.

3   Gail Sheehy, *Passages* (New York: Bantam, 1976) 513.

4   J. Stacey, *Brave New Families* (New York: Basic Books, 1990)

5   Alan J. Hawkins, "Perspectives on covenant marriage." *Marriage, Family & Society* Spring/Summer 1999, 14–20; Steven L. Nock, J. D. Wright, and L. Sanchez. "America's divorce problem." *Society* 36: 43–52, 1999.

6   William J. Doherty, "How therapists threaten marriage." *The Responsive Community* 7:31–42, 1999.

QUESTIONS FOR DISCUSSION

1. How does Doherty make his point that many people today take a consumer approach toward marriage? Does he substantiate his point sufficiently, in your opinion? How does the fact that he presented this text as a speech affect the way he makes his points?

2. What is Institutional Marriage? What is Psychological Marriage? How did Institutional Marriage differ from Psychological Marriage? How did Psychological Marriage mutate into Consumer Marriage?

3. What does Doherty mean by "modern covenant marriage"? How does it differ from the other three kinds of marriage he describes?

4. What specific recommendations does Doherty make to reclaim marriage as a stable and enduring institution of society? Do you think his recommendations are feasible? Why or why not?

5. How did the style of Doherty's writing impress you? How would it have been different if he had written this argument for a peer-reviewed journal?

6. Do you think social scientists have any obligation to try to address general audiences in speaking or writing? Why or why not?

Abolishing Welfare Won't Stop Poverty, Illegitimacy

by
Elijah Anderson

Elijah Anderson is a noted sociologist whose research focuses on black America. Anderson received degrees from Indiana University and the University of Chicago; his Ph.D. is from Northwestern University. He is a professor of sociology at the University of Pennsylvania, where he is the Charles and William L. Day Distinguished Professor in the Social Sciences. He has been a visiting professor at both Yale and Princeton universities. His book The Code of the Street: Decency, Violence, and the Moral Life of the Inner City *has received a great deal of attention, and it won the Karmarovsky Award from the Eastern Sociological Society.*

Those who have been calling recently for an end to welfare, seeing this as a way of solving poverty and illegitimacy, are wrong. Eliminating the program would only make things much worse. As an ethnographer and sociologist who has worked in poor, inner-city neighborhoods, I welcome the debate and the search for solutions to these problems. But the proposals to abolish welfare outright espoused by such people as syndicated columnist Charles Krauthammer and Charles Murray are dangerously shortsighted.

Krauthammer, in fact, cites my research in one inner-city neighborhood in support of his thinking. Since welfare provides economic support to illegitimate babies and their mothers—a fact of inner-city life my research has indeed shown to be one consideration in the sexual game that leads to illegitimate births—he argues that eliminating welfare will eliminate the interest in having babies. This reasoning is seriously flawed precisely because it ignores all the other considerations bearing down on inner-city adolescents, thereby exaggerating the role played by welfare.

In "Sex Codes and Family Life Among Poor Inner-City Youths," a chapter in my book *Streetwise*, I describe ethnographically the perspectives and experiences of young black men and women in one community.

I found that the lack of family-sustaining jobs denies many young men the possibility of forming an economically self-reliant family, the traditional American mark of manhood. Partially in response, the young men's peer groups emphasize sexual prowess as a sign of manhood, with babies as evidence. A sexual game emerges as girls are lured by the (usually older) boys' vague but convincing promises of love and marriage. When the girls submit, they often end up pregnant and abandoned. I also noted that these new mothers become eligible for a limited but steady welfare income that may allow them to establish their own households and at times attract other men who need money. But it is simplistic and wrongheaded to suggest that if you stop welfare, you will stop this behavior. A fundamental question is: Why do people behave in the ways I have described?

A significant part of the answer is: Because of the unraveling of the economy in their communities, which results in hopelessness. The lack of responsibility shown by the men, the "wantonness," is exacerbated by the very bad economic conditions—the exodus of jobs and

Reprinted from the *Seattle Times*, Jan. 6, 1994.

the inability of people to get the jobs still available because of a lack of education, skills and training.

Illegitimacy is not caused by welfare, but it is, in part, an outgrowth of the failure of the welfare system to achieve its purpose—to alleviate the human problems inherent in the vicissitudes of capitalism, enabling people temporarily (according to theory) displaced by changes in the economic marketplace to survive. Yet I see that what so many people in the inner city are up against are, in fact, the vicissitudes of the economy and an economy now global in scope that has left them behind.

The situation I describe in the "Sex Codes" chapter springs from alienation and despair— which then creates nihilism. This is born of a lack of hope and the inability to form a positive view of the future. So many of the young men I got to know don't get married because they don't feel they can "play house." What they mean is they can't play the roles of men in families in the way they would like.

Their assumption is that men in middle- and upper-class families that they see as models control their households. To be that upstanding husband and father, you need resources, you need money. Facing persistent discrimination, a lot of the men I interviewed believe they can't get the money, can't get the family-sustaining jobs. This has a profound impact on how they see their future.

As we move from a manufacturing to a service and high-tech economy, great numbers of inner-city poor people are not making an effective adjustment to the change. The service jobs they are able to obtain often don't pay them enough money to live, and so some of the most enterprising young people have opted for the underground economy of drugs and crime. One of the results is the social disorganization that contributes not only to increasing violence and alienation but also to a syndrome of abuse, in which people are bent on getting what they can out of other people—including sex and money—without any real concern for those they victimize.

Buffeted by the global economy, communities such as this one find themselves with fewer and fewer dependable sources of capital. Welfare is one relatively small but reliable source. To eliminate welfare is to destroy an important source of capital in the community. If welfare suddenly ceased to exist, many people would be forced to look elsewhere for resources. Some would seek the low-paying jobs available, but the hard reality is that others would be driven to more desperate measures. The nihilism that you now see among inner-city people would only increase and spread further beyond the bounds of ghetto communities. Cities would become almost unlivable. Blacks would continue to be the primary victims, though; illegitimacy rates would rise, not diminish.

The welfare system is in need of an overhaul, but it does not follow that we should throw meager income supports overboard. We need to maintain the support at the same time that we create opportunity for independent income. The way to make real headway is to create jobs and job opportunities and build hope through education and job training.

When a sense of the future exists, we will see more responsible behavior, sexual and otherwise. To take welfare away without replacing it with such opportunities would effectively remove a lifeline for the very poor but also what has become a safety valve protecting both inner-city communities and the rest of society from the consequences of steadily escalating frustration.

QUESTIONS FOR DISCUSSION

1. Why does Anderson believe that abolishing welfare would not halt poverty and illegitimacy?

2. According to Anderson, why do so many young black men in inner cities engage in illicit sexual behavior? Why do young women?

3. What to Anderson is the legitimate purpose of welfare? Why has welfare not served as an effective bridge for many people in inner cities today? What does Anderson predict would happen if welfare were removed as a means of support for people who are unemployed and possibly unemployable in today's economy?

4. Do you agree with Anderson's argument? Why or why not?

5. Do you find the style of Anderson's writing appropriate for the opinion page of a major newspaper? Why or why not?

6. Do you think that social scientists have an obligation to write for public forums about public policy when they believe their research has something to contribute? Why or why not?

Competition in the Classroom: Are We Teaching Kids to be Insecure?

by
Jordan Richardson Cahoon

In April 2006 Jordan Cahoon graduated with a degree in sociology from Brigham Young University. After attending graduate school, Jordan plans to work with refugees, the homeless, and the incarcerated, helping them to live productive and socially acceptable lives. Jordan is from Boyds, Maryland.

Jules Henry once said, "A competitive culture endures by tearing people down." This poses a problem to American education, which works to increase the self-esteem of the rising generation while at the same time pitting students against each other in classroom competitions. A staggering amount of competition in education today undermines both a student's sense of control and self-esteem. Changes in the structure of education can help solve the self-esteem crisis experienced by many of today's youth.

American education could almost be defined by what Alfie Kohn calls *mutually exclusive goal attainment*, which means the success of one student requires the failure of another—two individuals' fates are negatively linked. If both Susan and Bob want to win the spelling bee, the victory of one means the defeat of the other. *Both* cannot win the spelling bee. All too often classrooms are set up this way: curved grades, student of the month awards, valedictorian. But at what cost?

Sociologist Elliot Aronson wrote, "The American mind in particular has been trained to equate success with victory, to equate doing well with beating someone." Success and victory are not the same thing: success is achieving a goal, while victory results only when one person keeps others from reaching a goal. This distinction makes a considerable difference in behavior, each producing a different kind of attitude in a student. Forced to compete for best speller, students are not concerned with doing their best, increasing knowledge, or improving skills: they are concerned with knowing enough to do better than others, to achieve victory—to win. Working towards success would mean a student sets a goal and works hard to achieve it by improving skills and increasing knowledge.

The above motivations and behaviors each correspond to a different locus of control, which is simply what a person believes is in control of his or her life. An individual with an external locus of control believes outside factors have more control than internal factors, while an individual with an internal locus of control believes life is under his or her own control. Thus, when a student's *victory* depends on the performance of other students, he or she will be more likely to have an external locus of control. But when a student's *success* depends only on how much effort is put into the performance, that student will have an internal locus of control. Alfie Kohn argues that competition encourages an external locus of control: it forces children to think of achievements in terms of victory instead of success, convincing them that they have no control over their lives.

The above factors—competition, the locus of control, and behavior that results—influence the self-esteem of students. First, it should be understood that the importance of self-esteem cannot be overstated. It can be considered the basis of a healthy personality, a respect for and faith in oneself that does not depend on approval from others. A person with high self-esteem has an internal locus of control: things that are not going well can be changed through hard work. Low self-esteem contributes to a wide number of problems: it makes it hard to have good feelings towards other people; life seems out of control; and depression, alienation, and feelings of inadequacy result because the person does not think he or she can change. School is a place to learn about oneself and how to interact with peers, and without good self-esteem, a child will encounter emotional and social difficulties.

Butler says that students who have been trained to fight for victory define their ability in relation to their peers' abilities: success depends on relative strength and thus personal evaluations of competence depend on the performance of others (external factors). Therefore, a student's self-evaluation of ability fluctuates with the outcome of a competition: ability is high after winning but low after losing. Losing will likely lead to less effort because the student believes that effort doesn't matter. A student who defines ability in terms of success, or how hard he or she works, has a much more stable self-evaluation. Failures do not decrease self-esteem if the student tried his or her hardest; instead, failures often increase motivation to try harder next time.

The interconnection of these three factors can be better understood through the following examples. Mary has always been at the top of her class and asks other students what they got on a test to make sure she is still the smartest. This year her grades have not been as good, and she thinks it is because her teacher does not like her as much as other students. Mary believes an external factor (the opinion of her teacher) controls the grades she receives. There is nothing she can do to change her teacher's opinion, and Mary feels sorry for herself and stops trying to do well—it doesn't matter anyway. In contrast, Jack has always been told by his parents to work his hardest, no matter how other students do. He receives a poor grade on a test and thinks it is because he stayed up late watching television instead of studying. Jack knows that it was internal factors (his decision to not study) that affected his grade, and does not feel too bad because next time he will try harder. For the next test he studies extra hard and goes to bed early. Of these two, Jack will have higher self-esteem because he knows he can study harder next time, while Mary feels that she will fail as long as she has a teacher who does not like her.

Kohn says that cooperation, unlike competition, promotes an internal locus of control. Without the drive to outperform others, students feel more in control of their lives, as other students and teachers do not change how hard they work. Researchers Johnson, Johnson and Maruyama concluded that cooperative learning promotes higher levels of self-esteem than competitive learning that stresses individualism. Thus, students who cooperate have better psychological health.

Though the modem American educational system is overrun by competition, it does not have to be this way. Cooperative learning has been implemented with much success in classrooms around the country, including Johns Hopkins University. But cooperative learning is not just seating students together and telling them to work with each other; it is, as Kohn says, working toward a common goal in the context of positive interdependence. Positive interdependence is sometimes seen as the opposite of mutually exclusive goal attainment.

When two people are working interdependently, neither is denied success by the success of another, and with each student working his or her hardest, both can reach success.

Cooperation in the classroom is one way to help children increase self-esteem, which is so important for future success. Kohn believes that learning in groups gives children social support and increases their likelihood of success because children develop more self-confidence, greater resilience, and a feeling that they control their own destiny. Instead of spelling bees, student of the month awards, and curved grades, cooperation should fill classrooms. If Steve is good at math, he should be encouraged to help Rebecca, who is not; Rebecca should be encouraged to help Steve with art. Students should edit each others' papers, engage in lively discussion without mention of who is "right" or "wrong," and applaud the efforts of others.

Changing the competitive nature of schools will not guarantee that every student who graduates from high school will be confident and successful. But when children face so many situations that can make them insecure, they should have at least one place that will build their confidence to face challenges with heads held high. In a world where competition, winners, and losers are the norm, a school could be a place to learn how to build each other up. If our society founds schools on ideals of cooperation rather than competition, the rising generation will learn that while one person can achieve victory, everyone can achieve success.

SUGGESTIONS FOR DISCUSSION

1. What distinction does Cahoon make between victory and success?

2. Why does Cahoon believe cooperation is a better principle to found school on than competition? What is the main kind of support she offers to make her point? Does she offer sufficient evidence?

3. This position paper is derived from a longer research paper that Cahoon wrote. In what ways does it differ from the typical academic research paper?

4. Do you think this position paper would be persuasive to an audience such as a school board or a group of parents? Why or why not?

Book Review

by
Rose McDermott

Rose McDermott is a professor of political science at the University of California, Santa Barbara. Her main focus is on political psychology in international relations, and she has written several books on the subject, including Risk Taking in International Relations. *She has also written on the effects of medical and psychological illness on foreign policy decisions. McDermott received her Ph.D. from Stanford University, and she has been appointed a fellow of Harvard University.*

Bare Branches: The Security Implications of Asia's Surplus Male Population. By Valerie Hudson and Andrea den Boer. Cambridge, MA: MIT Press. 2004. 400 pp.

In a time when nontraditional threats to international relations, including environmental degradation, pandemic disease, and drug and sex trafficking, are increasingly coming to the forefront of national concern and academic debate, Valerie Hudson and Andrea den Boer's book squarely confronts the security problems raised by sex ratio imbalances in Asia. Focusing extensively on India and China, which currently compose almost 40% of the world's population, *Bare Branches: The Security Implications of Asia's Surplus Male Population* argues that the surplus of men in these regions poses a serious threat to both domestic political stability and international security. As such, this book represents a groundbreaking contribution to the literature on both gender and security studies.

For those familiar with the earlier article of the same title by these authors, which appeared in *International Security* in April 2002, this book expands on the article in substantive, creative and novel ways. Both the article and the book are well-written and well-organized, persuasively and carefully argued, and methodically supported by rich empirical data. In the opening chapter, Hudson and den Boer carefully and thoroughly categorize the literature on the biological bases of sex differences in aggression. The overall argument concerning the potential danger presented to these societies by such highly skewed sex ratios appears quite compelling. Beginning with the widespread use of ultrasound technology in these areas in the mid-1980s, more and more people could get access to information about the sex of their unborn child. In the wake of such knowledge, sex-selected abortion rates catapulted, particularly in areas of China where families were limited by government policy to one child. But other mechanisms have helped to skew sex ratios as well, including high rates of female infanticide, poor health care for young girls as opposed to young boys, and high rates of maternal death in childbirth. Such factors have produced extremely imbalanced sex ratios throughout much of the Asian continent. Specifically, under normal circumstances, approximately 105 boys will be born for every 100 girls. This number tends to equal out in the first few years of life, as boys tend to die more frequently in childhood accidents, and do not appear as robust in response to illness, all other things being equal. Greater female endurance continues throughout life, resulting in women living longer everywhere. Yet in China, for

Reprinted from *Political Psychology* 27, no. 2 (April 2006), by permission of Blackwell Publishing, Ltd.

example, the official birth ratio is 117 boys per 100 girls, but the reality is well over 120 in many regions. In India, the official rate is 114 boys per 100 girls, but specific regions report up to 156 boys per 100 girls.

These large sex ratio imbalances pose tremendous societal consequences. For example, Hudson and den Boer document the large percentage of men in China who are known as *tiudong renkou*, or the floating population. About 80% of this population is men under the age of 35. These men are often known by the name *"guang gun-er"* or "bare branches" on their family tree, because they will never produce children due to the lack of potential female mates. Because men who are wealthy and educated are more likely to be able to attract wives, bare branches come disproportionately from the poor, uneducated, and unemployed elements of society. In China and India, this group constitutes almost 15% of the young male adults. China now reports increasing crime rates, where between 50–90% of the crimes committed in big cities can be attributed to these bare branch populations.

Drawing on historical examples, Hudson and den Boer demonstrate that the Chinese leadership, in particular, has recognized the threat posed by groups of young men who exist without the strong social bonds provided by family. Traditionally, such men have united into either monastic or militant groups for mutual strength and support. In the past, such groups, including the Shaolin fighting monks, have played a part in numerous uprisings and rebellions in Chinese history, including the Nien and Boxer rebellions. The Chinese government, in turn, has tended to use these men in external military campaigns and high-risk public work projects in order to ensure that they do not turn on the leadership. Indeed, Hudson and den Boer note that societies with large bare branch populations have typically required authoritarian political structures in order to keep control. They argue that the large surplus of men in India and China poses a threat for the successful maintenance and creation of democracy, respectively, as well as leading to pessimistic prospects for peace in Kashmir between India and Pakistan and between China and Taiwan.

Hudson and den Boer's book has already achieved resonance in the popular media and imagination. Felicia Lee of the *New York Times* and Mike Schmidt of the *Boston Globe* have interviewed various political scientists including Steve Fish and Joshua Goldstein for articles that report the findings and implications of this book. The television program *60 Minutes* is planning a segment on the book. Clearly, *Bare Branches* has already generated a broad-based public intellectual debate on the impact of sex imbalances on the prospects for peace and security.

The book has also generated a great deal of scholarly acclaim. It won the 2004 Association of American Publishers Award for Best Professional/Scholarly Book in Government and Political Science and the American Sociological Association's 2004 Otis Dudley Duncan Award for best book on social demography.

Indeed, Hudson and den Boer make a significant and convincing case which is worthy of widespread academic attention. If one buys the central argument that sex ratio imbalances pose a large and underrecognized threat to international security—then the authors are raising a critically important, timely, and vastly understudied threat to the stability of international relations in the future, particularly in the Asian region. This topic, and its security implications, cannot help but become increasingly important as these sex ratios become increasingly skewed over time. The political implications of this book should serve as a . . . clarion call for greater attention and analysis to this problem and its potential resolutions.

While the whole book makes a creative, important, and interesting case about the significance of imbalanced sex ratios, chapters five and six remain the most theoretically captivating, compelling, and persuasive. Hudson and den Boer describe the bare branches as men who derive disproportionately from the lowest socioeconomic groups, are more likely to be unemployed, remain largely transient, and bond together in groups of similar males. These men are more violent and engage in more antisocial behavior than women. They are more likely to commit violent crimes than their married peers. Since, in addition, single men abuse substances more often than their married counterparts, and men commit more violence under the influence of alcohol and drugs than their sober mates, bare branches here too show a greater proclivity toward increased violence. Finally, men given to risky behavior exaggerate this tendency under the influence of like minded others. These specific points about who the bare branches are, and what their behavioral propensities are, and why, is simply dead-on accurate from a biological perspective. Some people may not like the political implications of these findings, but there is no question that this is an authentic and compelling portrait of the consensus opinion on the relationships between age, testosterone, marriage, violence, and other social forces such as employment and transience by those biologists, anthropologists, sociologists, and psychologists who have done extensive basic and cross-cultural work in this area. Similarly, the work in chapter five on the consequences for women of these sex ratio imbalances is fascinating, clever, creative, and quite provocative: counterintuitively, women lose more status as male control becomes more assertive; the incentives for sex-trafficking increase; the age of female consent drops as older, richer men marry younger in order to find brides; birth rates rise in proportion to female loss of control over their destiny under male dominion; and prostitution increases. In this regard, the statistics on female suicide in China are simply stunning: "Nearly 56% of female suicides worldwide are Chinese women, making this the highest female suicide rate in the world. The overwhelming majority of these women are of childbearing age. In addition, twice as many women as men under the age of 45 commit suicide in China" (p. 205).

The chapter on policy options seems reasonable and thoughtful, especially in light of the evidence presented earlier. The authors suggest such options as outsourcing men for labor, opening new frontiers for settlement, providing social safety nets, increasing the status of women in society and providing different incentive structures for sex selection in child bearing. Overall, *Bare Branches* tackles the issue of sex ratio imbalances in a creative and timely manner, with meticulous data collection, careful and thoughtful analysis, and compelling argument. It constitutes a seminal achievement and a unique contribution to the literature.

QUESTIONS FOR DISCUSSION

1. What is McDermott's overall assessment of the book? Where do you find her most general claims about it?
2. How does McDermott's review enhance what you already know about *Bare Branches* from having read the excerpt in this book?

3. What specific things does McDermott praise about the book? What does she find fault with?

4. Why do you think McDermott draws attention to the popular and scholarly acclaim the book has met with?

5. How does McDermott's summary of the book's argument differ from the summary of *Soul Searching* given by Jeffrey Arnett in his review?

6. What do you notice about the style of McDermott's writing?

Book Review

by
Jeffrey Jensen Arnett

Jeffrey Jensen Arnett is a research professor at Clark University in Massachusetts. His specialty is emerging adulthood, and he has edited the Journal of Adolescent Research *along with several encyclopedias on adolescence. Arnett has spent time at Stanford University and the University of Jena in Germany as a visiting scholar, and he was a Fulbright Scholar at the University of Copenhagen. He has published three books, and several of his articles have appeared in* American Psychologist. *Arnett received his Ph.D. from the University of Virginia.*

Soul Searching: The Religious and Spiritual Lives of American Teenagers. Smith, Christian. (2005). New York: Oxford University Press.

This book is, quite simply, the best book ever on the best study ever on the topic of adolescents and religion. It is exemplary social science, combining the best of qualitative and quantitative methods, not only empirically strong but theoretically rich.

The book is based on the National Study of Youth and Religion conducted from 2001 to 2005 at the University of North Carolina at Chapel Hill (see www.youthandreligion.org). The main data from the study are from a nationally representative telephone survey of 3,290 American adolescents and (for 96% of them) their parents. In addition, 247 in-depth face-to-face interviews were conducted with a subsample of the telephone survey respondents, selected to represent a broad range of adolescents in terms of religion, age, ethnicity, gender, socioeconomic class, and region.

The principal investigator of the study and the author of the book, sociologist Christian Smith, demonstrated an exceptional level of involvement in the data collection for a principal investigator on a large research project, conducting many of the interviews himself, and it shows. His first-hand knowledge of the participants enabled him to present the qualitative portions of the book with a great degree of personal insight. As a result, the adolescents in his book have a vitality that is all too rare in accounts of large-scale social science research on adolescents.

Chapter 1 presents case examples of two Baptist girls Smith interviewed. The focus is on their religious beliefs and experiences, but these are presented in the context of the rest of their lives, so that we can see how religious beliefs and experiences are connected to the whole person. Chapter 2, "Mapping the Big Picture," does just that, presenting the overall framework of the survey results, on topics such as adolescents' religious self-identities (Presbyterian, Baptist, Catholic, Mormon, Jewish, etc.), self-reported religious practices (attendance at religious services, participation in religious youth group, etc.), and beliefs (in God, angels, life after death, etc.).

Chapter 3 focuses on three distinct groups of adolescents—spiritual seekers, the disengaged, and religiously devoted teens—and explores the reasons for their differences in religiosity. Parents' and friends' religiosity are, not surprising, related to adolescents'

Reprinted from *Journal of Adolescent Research* 21, no. 2 (March 2006), by permission of Sage Periodicals Press.

religiosity, but a more striking finding in this chapter is that some religious traditions are more successful than others in promoting religious devotion among adolescents, with Conservative Protestants and Mormons most successful and Catholics least. This appears to be due in part to the establishment, in the successful groups, of well-developed youth programs with full-time, paid adult leaders.

Chapter 4, "God, Religion, Whatever: On Moralistic Therapeutic Deism," is perhaps the best in the book. Here Smith goes deeper than the survey results to present insights into what American adolescents really believe on religious questions. On the surface of it—from the survey results in Chapter 2—American adolescents appear to be highly religious, overall. Nearly all believe in God, and strong majorities say they feel close to God, believe in angels, pray at least once a week, and have been involved in a religious youth group. Yet Smith shows in Chapter 4 that when you actually talk to them about their religious beliefs and practices, the picture you get is quite different. First, although most adolescents say that religion is important in their lives, Smith finds that it is of secondary importance to many other priorities, "competing for time, energy, and attention and often losing against other, more dominant demands and commitments, particularly school, sports, television, and other electronic media" (p. 161).

Second, adolescents typically have little understanding of the traditions and doctrines of their religious affiliations. They may call themselves Baptist or Methodist or Catholic or "whatever," but they have little knowledge of the content traditionally associated with those faiths, and they rarely talk about their beliefs in terms of the language of their religious tradition—for example, Christian adolescents rarely mention concepts such as the Trinity, sin, grace, and salvation. Instead, American adolescents mostly believe in what Smith terms *moralistic therapeutic deism*, meaning that they value religion as something that gives people a strong moral foundation and value their own religious beliefs as something that: makes them feel happy and provides a source of strength when they feel troubled. Tolerance is among their highest values; few believers think that nonbelievers are less favored by God than they are, either in this world or after death, despite the importance of this distinction in traditional religion. It is in this chapter that the importance of the interviews especially shows, because the interviews allowed Smith to gain deeper insights than would have been possible on the basis of the survey alone.

Chapter 5 seeks to explain the origins and wider cultural context of moralistic therapeutic deism, drawing on a rich sociological tradition of religious theorizing, from scholars like Peter Berger, Philip Rieff, and Robert Bellah. Chapter 6 focuses on Catholic adolescents, in an effort to explain their relative religious laxity and concludes that it is due primarily to the decline of institutional frameworks such as Catholic schools and the low priority that youth programs appear to have within the Catholic church.

Chapter 7 returns to the overall survey results to show that religiosity is favorably related to a wide range of positive outcomes, from lower rates of risk behavior to higher well-being and better relationships with parents. Most of this is well-known from other surveys, but in the second half of the chapter, Smith provides an extensive interpretation of the relations between religiosity and life outcomes. He acknowledges the role of self-selection (adolescents who have more conventional personalities tend to be more religious) and reverse causation (adolescents who get into trouble of various kinds tend to reduce their religious participation), but he also provides a persuasive argument that religiosity does have genuinely positive effects on adolescents' development. This chapter is followed by a brief summary conclusion and then a part Smith disarmingly calls a "Concluding Unscientific Postscript" that presents the implications of this research for religious communities and youth workers.

In sum, this is a book that should be read by everyone who researches or works with adolescents in America. It is essential reading for anyone who seeks a full understanding of the lives of adolescents in our time.

QUESTIONS FOR DISCUSSION

1. How does Arnett's review enhance what you already know about *Soul Searching* from the excerpt you read in this book?
2. What specific things does Arnett praise about the book? What does he criticize?
3. Why do you think Arnett describes the methods used in the National Study of Youth and Religion?
4. How does this review compare to McDermott's review of *Bare Branches*?
5. How would you characterize Arnett's tone? His style?

Book Review

by
Brad Gunnell

Bradley Gunnell is from Beavercreek, Ohio. He is a sociology major with a business management minor student at Brigham Young University. He intends to work as a project manager in the oil and gas industry after graduation. Brad enjoys sports and camping.

Code of the Street: Decency, Violence, and the Moral Life of the Inner City. Elijah Anderson. New York: W.W. Norton & Company, 1999. 352 pp. $16.95.

Code of the Street offers a unique and much needed perspective on the culture of violence that operates within inner-city America. Elijah Anderson, Professor of Sociology at the University of Pennsylvania, effectively uses his ethnographic study of blighted neighborhoods in Philadelphia as a tool to educate not only about the rules of violence in the rough-and-tumble urban neighborhoods of America but also about the social roots and necessities of such behavior. The code of the street is based upon the principles of mutual respect and the willingness to be violent in defense of that respect. Though to the outsider they may appear one and the same, Anderson accurately identifies the distinctions between the "street" and "decent" families that share tough urban neighborhoods and how both are forced into the culture of violence. The author then evaluates the effects of this culture in the drug trade, crime, dating behaviors and other urban phenomena. To close, Anderson properly illustrates how traditional roles of the decent life—moral fathers and moral grandmothers—are falling victim to the code of the street and thereby limiting our opportunities to reverse the trend.

In the poorest of the inner-city neighborhoods mainstream society has passed the residents by, Anderson shows. These neighborhoods are inhabited by those without the educational or material means to live elsewhere. Residents here have the distinct feeling— reinforced by police behavior—that they are alone and that they must deal with their own problems. In such neighborhoods a code of behaviors emerges based upon the principle of respect. As the outer world is hesitant to intervene, residents must enforce this code the best they can with the means they have. This leads to an eye-for-an-eye approach resulting in violent behaviors. This code of the street is so pervasive that otherwise decent persons must learn to live by it as a matter of necessity rather than choice. If they are not violent persons, they must show a willingness to act violently if challenged as a way to deter attacks. Those who are disrespected (dissed) lose status in the community and feel a need to regain that status by exacting revenge or dissing another. Through a deliberate use of case studies and personal narratives Anderson powerfully illustrates the day-to-day violent consequences of the code of the street.

The code of the street, as Anderson effectively labels it, lends itself to the drug trade. Those most feared in the community are the drug dealers, as they are those who have shown the greatest tendency to react violently. Material possessions become a symbol of the code as the act of wearing something new shows that an individual is unafraid of another person stealing from

Reprinted by permission of the author.

them. Hence, he argues, we see well dressed black youth arguing over arbitrary amounts of money. Despite poverty many youth will spend any money they get to try and attain the drug dealer image and the status associated with it. Such imitative behavior makes it difficult for police and outsiders to differentiate the drug dealers from decent kids trying to avoid "getting rolled on," and this confusion adds to the perception that the outside world views all poor blacks as the same—worthless and immoral. Often it is this need to dress up that drives young men and women to sell drugs so they can afford the clothes drug dealers wear.

Anderson shows how the code of the street affects all aspects of inner-city life. The dating game becomes part of the quest for respect. Boys learn from their peers that respect is to be garnered through fooling as many girls as possible to sleep with them. The girls dream of a decent boy who will take them away from the street life and are quick to try and attach themselves to any boy with promise. The same imitative behavior in dress makes it difficult for the young women to distinguish the decent boys with promise from the street boys who are trying to notch their belts with another girl. In an effort to pin down a boy, girls will try to become pregnant at a young age to try and secure their future. However, this often fails as street boys feel that being tied down to one girl would lower their opportunities to gain respect.

Anderson finally examines how the very centers of decency in otherwise "street" neighborhoods are becoming extinct. The good fathers who raised decent children are becoming rare as marriage has lost credibility with the boys of the street. The fathers' place is being taken by rappers and drug-dealers. The grandmother used to be the authority figure in the family who would call the collective family to action. It is now becoming more likely that the grandmother will raise the grandchildren herself as the mothers are sucked into the world of the "street." As these institutional roles of the inner-city fade, Anderson argues that the code of the street will grow in strength with little challenge, and reversal of the code and its effects will become difficult.

This book is of tremendous value to sociologists and other persons interested in how social structure can define and limit our choices of behavior. While Anderson does not eliminate personal choice in actions, he illuminates how culture can limit the choices we can make. The book does leave one feeling helpless as Anderson does not suggest any immediate action or policy to confront the problems he has enumerated. However, *Code of the Street* offers profound insight into the often misunderstood world of the black inner-city community and Anderson's writing carries an implicit call for change. Those responsible for policy regarding welfare, education, and other urban problems would be well-served to read Anderson's book to better understand the culture that their policies must deal with.

INDEX

Page numbers followed by f indicate a figure
Page numbers followed by t indicate a table

ABA (time series) design, 114
Abstracts:
    books evaluation and, 142
    definition of, 221
    role of, 224
    samples of, 223f, 224f
    suggestions for writing, 236
    writing an, 222–224
Academic disciplines:
    rhetoric in, 9–10
    social sciences and, 11
Academic writing, prewriting and, 25–26
Accomplishments and awards, in resume, 237
Acronyms, 338–339
Adding, revising and, 27
Addressee, 19
Addresser, 19
Advanced search options, 128
Altavista, 131
America, art and practice of rhetoric in, 7
American Psychological Association (APA) style. *See* APA style
Amounts, words referring to, 102
Analysis:
    of observation data, 92
    of questionnaire data, 107–108
    systematic, 65
Anecdote, presentations and, 315
APA Publication Manual, 284–285
    multiple noun strings, 339
    racial/ethnic/group references, 343
    references to participants in research, 344
    use of passive voice, 336
    using inclusive/unbiased language, 341
APA style, 179, 334, 335
    headings in, 286f
Application sheet, IRB proposal, 151f
Aristotle, 7
    definition of rhetoric, 6
Arrangement, 24
Ashton-Jones, Evelyn, 79, 80
Attributing, library research and, 124–125
Attrition, as confound to a design, 115

Audience(s):
    characteristics of, 30–31
    of critiques, 223
    influence of, 30–31
    lay, 30
    nonverbal communication and, 327–328
    participation in presentations, 316
    role in rhetorical situation, 9
    sizing up in rhetorical situation, 318
    social scientists and, 20–21
    types of, 30
Audiotapes/audiotaping, 62
    interviews, 75
    note taking and, 78
    for recording data, 90
Authenticity, determining sources, 64–65

Background research, for interview, 73
Bar (column) graphs, 291, 298–300
    with a legend, 304
Battison, Robin M., 289
Belenky, Mary Field, 35, 79
Beliefs, rhetoric and, 8, 9
Bell Curve, The:
    (Carey), 137
    (Herrnstein, Murray), 61
Belmont Report, 50–51
Beneficence, as ethical principle, 51
Bibliographies:
    in historical documents, 63
    prospectus and, 163, 164
    as type of directional sources, 125
Books, 125
    evaluating, 136–138
    reliability and publishers, 136–137
    reviews of, 229
Boolean operators, 127–129, 132
"Bowling Alone," excerpt from Bowling Alone, review of, 106, 208, 209
Brace, C. Loring, 62
Brainstorming, as prewriting technique, 25
Brigham Young University (BYU)
    counseling and career center at, 247
    exempt reviews of research at, 54
    Institutional Review Boards at, 51

    levels of IRB review at, 53t
    library online resources, 127
Brown v. Board of Education, 60
Bullets, 278
Burnhill, P., 274
BYU. See Brigham Young University (BYU)

Carey, John, 144
Case studies, 32
    multiple observers and, 91
    strengths of, 49
    as type of observation, 85–86
Cause-and-effect relationship, 111–112
Chalkboards, oral presentations and, 320
Chartjunk, 306
    example of, 307f
Chronological resume, 234
Churchill, Winston, 7
Circle graphs, 300
Citations, reviews and, 139–140
Classical design, 114
Clinchy, Blythe McVicker, 35
Clustering, as prewriting technique, 25
Coding systems, recording data and, 89–90
Coe, B., 280
Collaboration:
    composing and, 34–35
    recording data and, 89
Column graphs. *See* Bar (column) graphs
Common sense, 18
Communication:
    with group members, 38
    rhetoric and, 20
    writing and, 30
Composing:
    as an idiosyncratic act, 28–29
    collaboration and, 34–35
    with computers, 28
    memoranda, 265–267
    as a private act, 29
    as process, 23–24
    social nature of, 29–34
    subprocesses of, 24–28
Computers:
    composing with, 28
    presentation software, 321

Conclusions, reliability and, 91–92
Confidentiality:
    human participants and, 50–51
    of institutional review boards
        (IRBs), 51–52
Confounds to a design, 115
Consent form, IRB proposal, 152–153
Conservatism, science and, 17
Content analysis, 59
Context/environment
    assessment, 313–314
Contextual information, interviews
    and, 78–80
Convenience sampling, 105–106
Credibility, in oral presentations, 316
Credit, 39–40
Critiques:
    audience, 220, 221
    example of student critique, 225
    focus, 218, 219
    format, style, and mechanics,
        223, 224, 227
    organization, 222–223
    suggestions for writing, 231
    support, 222, 226f
    writing, 220–225

Data, omitting/misrepresenting
    variations in, 305
Databases, 124
Data recording, observation and, 89–90
Deception, research and, 54
Degrees, words referring to, 102
Delany, A. Elizabeth, 80, 378–387
Delany, Sarah, 80, 378–387
Deleting, revising and, 27
Demographic questions, 100
Demonstration, in presentations, 316
Den Boer, Andrea, 63, 229, 354–377
Descriptive notes, 89
Design;
    ABA (time series), 114
    distorting/cluttering graphics, 304
    document, 273–288
    of experiments, 114–116
    of letters of application, 250–255
    of memoranda, 265, 267f
    one-group pretest-posttest, 114
    of scannable resume, 243
    of surveys, 99–104
    of traditional resume, 238–240
Detached persona, 335–337
Diagrams/flowcharts, 296–297
Dialogue or edited transcripts, 79
Diaries, 62
Directional sources, 125
Directions, in questionnaires, 103–104
Direct observation, 84
Directories, subject, 131
Discussing, as prewriting technique, 25
Discussion lists, 135
Documentation, 63

Document design, 273–288
    page layout, 274–278
    typography, 278–280
Documents analysis, strengths of, 49
"Double-barreled" question, 102
Drafts/drafting:
    and composing, 24, 26
    letters of application, 254–255
    letters of intent and personal
        statements, 264
    of library research, 124
    organization of data and, 26–27
    position paper, 213–214
    preferences and habits in, 28
    of source documents, 66
    working in groups and, 37
Drawings, line, 295–296
Dressing and grooming, in oral
    presentations, 325–326

Ede, Lisa, 42
Editing, 24, 27
    letters of intent and personal
        statements, 264
    source documents, 67
    transcripts, 79
    working in groups and, 37
Electronic journals, 32
E-mail, 32
    research and, 135–136
    using for research purposes
Endnotes, in historical documents, 63
Environment, oral presentations and, 319
ERIC (Educational Resources
    Information Center), 126
Ethical appeal, 8
Ethical lapses, consequences of, 57
Ethics in research:
    graphics and, 292
    meeting standards in experiments,
        112–113
    participant observation and, 86
    research and, 56
    researchers and, 51
    unobtrusive observation and, 84
Ethnocentrism, 87
Ethnographic research, 86
Ethnographies, 32, 86
Ethos, 8, 314, 335
Europe, art and practice of rhetoric in, 7
Evaluative notes, 89
Evidence, collecting of, 45–46
Exempt reviews, research and, 54–55
Experience, in resume, 236–237
Experimental research method, 47
Experimental research report,
    genres of, 31–32
Experimenter bias, as confound to a
    design, 115
Experiments, 111–122
    ABA (time series) design, 114
    classical design, 114

conducting, 113–119
    controls, implementing, 114–116
    designing, 114–116
    ethical standards,
        meeting, 118–119
    hypotheses, creating, 113
    operational definitions,
        creating, 113–114
    participants, selecting, 116–117
    validity/reliability,
        establishing, 117–118
    one-group pretest-posttest, 114
    purpose of, 111–113
    suggestions for research and writing,
        121
Experts, consulting in position papers,
    210
Eyewitnesses, 62

Facial expressions, 314
Figures, 293, 294–300
    diagrams/flowcharts, 296–297
    graphs, 297–300
    line drawings, 295–296
    maps, 296
    photographs, 295
Fixed response questions, 99
Focus group research, 72
Fonts:
    document design and, 279
    letters of application, 253
    resume, 239–240
Footnotes, in historical documents, 63
Format, critiques, 223–224
Fraud, 56
    avoiding, 57
Fraudulent research, 56, 57
Freewriting, as prewriting technique, 25
Freud, Sigmund, 138
Full-block style, letters of application,
    253, 256f
Functional resume, 236f

Gender references, 342–343
Genres:
    influence on writers, 33–34
    social evolution and influence of,
        31–32
Gestures, 311
Gold, Edward S., 292, 309
Goldberger, Nancy Rule, 35
Google, 131, 132
Gorgias (Plato), 7
Gould, Stephen J., 62
Government research resources, 129
    reliability of, 139
Graphical devices, 239
Graphics:
    ethical issues in using graphics,
        304–308

distorting/cluttering the design, 306
omitting/misrepresenting variations in the data, 305
plagiarism, 305
figures, 294–300
labeling, 301–304
positioning, 301–304
as rhetoric, 291–292
suggestions for practice, 308–309
tables, 293–294
Graphs, 297–300
bar (column) graphs, 298–300
circle, 300
labeling parts of, 303, 303f
line, 297–298
Gregory, M., 274
Group(s):
guidelines for working in, 36–38
interview, 72
vulnerable, protection of, 53

Handouts, oral presentations and, 321
Haney, Craig, 420
Haring-Smith, Tori, 35
"Harlem Town," 80, 378–387
Hartley, J., 274, 281
Headings, 280–288
in APA style, 286f
books evaluation and, 136
content, 281
design, 281
letters of application, 250
and professional style guides, 284–288
in Turabian style, 284, 288f
Hearth, Amy Hill, 80, 378
Heckman, James J., 62
Herrnstein, Richard J., 61, 137
Historical documents, 62–63
Historical narrative, 63
History:
as confound to a design, 115
of social sciences, 11
Hock, Randolph, 133
Hoffman, Joseph M., 108
Huckin, Thomas N., 273
Hudson, Valerie, 63, 229, 354–377
Human participants, research and, 50–51
Humor, in presentations, 315
Hyatt, Laurel, 144
Hypotheses, experiments and, 113

Inclusive and unbiased language, 341–344
Incubating, as prewriting technique, 25
Indexes:
as directional sources, 125
Individual guidelines for collaboration, 38–40
communication, 38
cooperation, 39

listening, 38
negotiation, 39
Informants:
contacting, 73
finding, 72–73
and the interview, 76–77
Information, synthesizing, 125
Informational sources, 125
Informed consent:
human participants and, 52–53
sample of, 104
Initialism, 338–339
Inquiry:
genres and method of, 32
rhetorical genres and methods of, 33
Institutional review boards (IRBs), 51–54
confidentiality of, 51–52
informed consent, 52–53
proposal, 149–150
qualifying for exempt review, 54–55
reviews not required by, 55–56
risk and, 53–54
vulnerable groups, protection of, 53
Institutional style, 333–345
acronyms, 338–339
detached persona, 335–337
inclusive and unbiased language, 341–344
gender references, 342–343
political correctness, 341–342
racial/ethnic/group references, 343–344
research participant references, 344
initialism, 338–339
jargon, 337–338
multiple noun strings, 339–341
neologisms, 339
operational definitions, new combination of words to create, 338
suggestions for writing/discussion, 345–347
Instrument decay, as confound to a design, 115
Internet, 124
evaluating sources, 136
finding information
BYU library online resources, 127
finding information, 130–135
E-mail, 129–135
government resources, 136
research, 130
search engines, 131–134
sources vs. printed sources, 136
subject directories, 131
print vs. Internet sources, 136
Interpretation:
of documents,
on prior knowledge/assumptions, 60–61
"Interrater reliability," 76, 92

Inter subjectivity, 17
Intertextual, 63
Interview:
conducting, 72–81
interview summary, 80
length, 77
as a method in the social sciences, 71–72
observation and, 84
preparing for, 72–78
background research, 73
contacting informants, 73
finding informants, 72–73
material needed, 74
planning your questions, 74
recording, 74–78
audiotaping, 75
note taking, 74–75
videotaping, 76
reports of, 52
schedule, 97
strengths of, 47
synthesis, and elaboration, 80–81
transcripts, 78–81
completeness, 78
dialogue/edited, 79
Introduction, books evaluation and, 142
Invention, 23
Investigator's assurance form, IRB proposal, 154f
IQ tests, 61
IRBs. See Institutional review boards (IRBs)
Isocrates, use of rhetoric and, 6–7
Ives, Edward D., 75, 76, 77

Jakobson, Roman, 22
Jakobson's Model of the Rhetorical Situation, 19f
Jargon, 337–341
Johnson, Susan, 347
Journals, 59
Justice, as ethical principle, 51

King, Martin Luther Jr., 7
Knowledge:
common, 141
establishing claims, 14, 18
and methods and instruments, 15–16
and observation, 15
and peer review, 16–17
and questions, 14
and science, 43
social construction of, 12–13
social dimension of, 13, 22

Labeling graphics:
301
with descriptive labels, 301

with numbers, 308
with parts of tables and figures, 302
Language:
    inclusive and unbiased, 341
    rhetoric and, 6
    as a social medium, 29–30
Lay audiences, 30
Layout:
    of document, 271, 273
    letters of application, 249
    resume, 233
LCSH. *See* Library of Congress Subject
    Headings List (LCSH)
Legends, 296, 303
Letters, to informants, 72
Letters of application, 249–250
    composing, 254
        drafting, 254
        prewriting, 254
        revising/proofreading, 255
    design of
        fonts/point sizes, 253
        layout, 253
        paper/printing, 253
    full-block style, letters of application,
        250, 256f
    parts of
        body, 251
        complimentary close, 252
        enclosure line, 253
        heading, 250
        inside address, 256
        salutation/greeting, 251
        signature/typed name, 253
    semi-block style, letters of
        application, 253, 257f
Letters of intent and personal
    statements, 258
    drafting, 264
    importance of, 258
    revising/editing, 264
Librarian, 129
Libraries, twentieth century, 123
Library of Congress Subject Headings
    List (LCSH), 126
Library research:
    examples, 128
    evaluating Internet sources, 136
    finding information in the library,
        125
        government publications, 129
        interlibrary loan, 129
        Online catalogs, 127
        periodical indexes, 124
        subject headings lists, 126
    finding information on the Internet,
        130–131
        BYU library online resources, 127
        E-mail, 129, 130
        government research resources,
            129

print sources *vs.* Internet sources,
    141
    search engines, 131
    subject directories, 134
methods of recording notes, 143
purpose of, 130, 138
recording notes and the computer,
    124, 127
source reliability, 136
source usefulness, 142
synthesizing information, 125
Lincoln, Abraham, 7
Line drawings, 295–296
Line graphs, 297–298
Linton, Patricia, 347
Listening, to group members, 38
Lists, 274
Listservs, 32, 135
Log:
    keeping and observation, 84
    prewriting and, 24
Logos, 8
Lunsford, Andrea, 34, 42

Madigan, Robert, 347
Maps, 296
Maslach, Christina, 420
Maturation, as confound to a design, 115
McAdams, Melinda, 144
McGuire, Mary, 144
Measure of association, 118
Measure of significance, 118
Mechanical recording devices, 90
Mechanics, of critiques, 223
Meetings, working in groups and, 36
Memoirs, 62
Memoranda, 265
    composing, 266
    poor design, 275
    purposes of, 275
    readable design, 276f
    suggestions for writing, 270
Memory support, 324–325
Meta-searches, 129, 133
Method(s):
    definition of, 46
    as disciplined inquiry, 46–47
Methods and instruments, 15–16
Milgram, Stanley, 110, 112, 114, 116, 122
Miller, Carolyn, 42, 289
*Monthly Catalog of U.S. Government
    Publications*, 126, 129
Morris, P., 257, 281
Multiple noun strings, 339–340
Murray, Charles, 61, 137

Narratives, 32
National Center for Education Statistics,
    129
Negotiation, group members and, 39
Neologisms, 339

Newsgroups, 135
Northern Light, 131
Notebook keeping, observation and, 89
Note cards, writing, 190
Notes:
    evaluating, 136, 142
    interpretation of, 60
    methods of recording, 125, 138
    recording after the interview, 74
    types of, 94
Numerical data, 48
Nuremberg Code, 50

Obedience, concept of, 113
Objectivity, 17
Objects and models, oral presentations
    and, 322, 325
Observation, 83–94
    analyzing and writing about, 92–93
    defining purpose, 88
    direct, 84
    kinds of, 84, 87
        case studies, 85–86
        participant observation, 86–87, 88
        structured observation, 85
        unobtrusive observation, 84–85
    and knowledge, 12
    methods and instruments, 15–16
    in natural settings, 48
    people selection and, 88
    recording data, 89–90
        coding system, 90
        mechanical recording devices, 90
        notebooks/logs, 89
    as scientific method, 83
    selecting behavior for
        observation, 88
    setting selection and, 88
    strengths of, 49
    suggestions for research and writing,
        94–95
Observation journal, 25
Observers, observational research and,
    91–92
Office of Research and Creative
    Activities (ORCA), 51
One-group pretest-posttest design, 114
Online catalogs, 127, 128
Online Public Access Catalogs (OPACs),
    127
Online resume, 246
OPACs. *See* Online Public Access
    Catalogs (OPACs)
Open-ended questions, 101–102
Operational definitions, new combina-
    tion of words to create, 338
Opinion piece, 207
Oral presentations, 311
    delivery
        pace of, 326
        rehearsing, 328

environment, 319
evaluating rhetorical situation, 312–314
organizing, 314
    beginning, 314
    ending, 317–318
    middle, 317
planning for delivery, 324
    appropriate dress, 325–326
    memory support, 324–325
    nonverbal communication, 327–328
    voice qualities, 326–327
rehearsing, 328
resources in, 318
suggestions for discussion and application, 328–329
time, 318–319
visual aids, 319–320
Oral rhetoric, 311–312
Oral surveys, 97
Oratory, 7
ORCA. *See* Office of Research and Creative Activities (ORCA)
Organization:
    of critiques, 217
    of data and drafts, 26–27
    of oral presentations, 311
    of position papers, 207, 208
    of the prospectus, 163
    of scannable resume, 243
    of traditional resume, 234
Organizations, working in groups and, 36
Outlining:
    of library research, 124–125
    as prewriting technique, 24, 25
    prospectus, sample of, 173, 174f
Overhead transparencies, oral presentations and, 321

Page layout, documents, 274
    bullets, 278
    graphic devices, 278
    lists, 274
    ragged right margins, 274
    resumes, 233
    scan zones, 274
    white spaces, 274
Paper and printing, for resume, 240
Participant observation, 86–87
    defining purpose and, 88
    multiple observers and, 91–92
Pathos, 8
Peer review. *See also* Review(s)
    feedback and, 40
    and knowledge, 12
    political dimensions of, 136
    research and, 3, 10
Performance, working in groups and evaluation, 38

Periodical indexes, 124–125
    general computer, 135
    in print, 136, 138
    specialized computer databases, 123, 125
Periodicals, 123, 129
Personal information, in a resume, 238
Persuasion:
    and change in social sciences, 17–18
    rhetoric and, 6, 7
Phaedrus (Plato), 7
Photographs, 62
    as kind of figure, 297
    oral presentations and, 311
Phrenology, 12
Pioneer Fund Inc., 137
Plagiarism, 56
    avoiding, 39–40
    graphics and, 291
Plato, 7, 11, 18
Political correctness, 341–342
Pope John Paul II, 7
Positioning graphics, 301
Position papers, 32, 207
    defining/limiting the problem, 209, 210
    drafting, 213
        level of language, 213
        organization, 191–192, 213
        evaluating possible solutions, 208–209
            cost-effectiveness, 211–212
            feasibility, 212
            political persuasiveness, 212
        recommending solutions, 209
        suggestions for research and writing, 215
Posterboards, oral presentations and, 320
Poulton, E. C., 274
Preface, books, 142
Presentations, oral. *See* Oral presentations
Prewriting:
    common ways of, 24–25
    incubating and, 25
    letters of application, 249
    specialized kinds of, 25–26
    strategy of, 39
Primary sources:
    definition of, 62
    locating, source documents and, 64
Print sources:
    evaluating, 135–138
    vs. Internet sources, 139
Professional audiences, 30
Professional style guides, headings and, 284–288
Propaganda. *See* Rhetoric
Proposal:
    institutional review boards (IRBs), 51
        consent form, 152
        summary, 164

ORCA, 156, 163
    prospectus, 147–151
    research and, 145–179
Prospectus, 145, 159
    organization of, 148–149
    parts of, 145, 149, 157
    sample, 173
Publication:
    date and source reliability, 128
    type and source reliability, 128, 132
Publisher, source reliability and reputation of, 136
Purpose:
    in book review, 227
    in observation, 83
    and rationale in prospectus, 145
    in rhetorical situation, 271–272
    in surveys, 97, 102

Qualitative data, 43
    writing about, 92–93
Qualitative research methods, 43
    compared to quantitative research methods, 43
    limitations, 47
    strengths of, 47–48
Quantitative data
    writing about, 92–93
Quantitative research methods, 43
    compared to qualitative research methods, 93
    limitations, 47
    strengths of, 47–48
Questionnaires, 48, 95–96, 97. *See also* Written surveys, 51, 97, 99
    creating demographic questions in, 100
    creating fixed-response questions in, 100–101
    order of questions in, 103
    writing clear directions, 99, 103
    writing open-ended questions in, 107–108
Questions, 59
    defining, source documents and, 59
    and knowledge, 8
    order in questionnaires, 97
    in presentations, 311
    as prewriting technique, 24
Quintilian, 7

Racial/ethnic/group references, 341–343
Ragged right margins, 274
Randolph, Hock, 144
Random sample, 105
Reader's Guide to Periodical Literature, 127
Reading, social scientists and, 59, 60
Rearranging, revising and, 27
Redish, Janice C., 273, 289

Reliability, 16
    in experiments, 111–119
    in social sciences, 93
    of sources, 62
    observation and, 83
Renaissance, rhetoric changes in, 7
Representative sample, 98
Research:
    background, interview and, 73
    deception and, 54
    definition of, 55
    and ethics, 45, 47, 49
    fraud and, 56
    ideological dimensions of, 136–137
    methods, 47–50
        experimenting, 48, 111–112
        interviewing, 71–82
        observing, 83–94
        surveying, 97–109
    methods, prewriting and, 25, 26
    notebook, prewriting and, 25
    as part of writing, 45–46
    plagiarism and, 45
    soundness of, 139
    suggestions for source documents,
        59, 64, 66
Researchers, ethical principles and, 51
Resources, in oral presentations,
    318–324
Respect, as ethical principle, 51
Respondents to surveys, finding, 104
Resumes, 233–248
    online, 233–234
    scannable, 234–243
        design of, 243
        organization of, 244
    suggestions for writing, 247
    traditional, 234–235
        chronological, 235–236
        contents of, 235, 247
            accomplishments/awards,
                237
            career objective, 235
            educational history, 235–237
            name/contact information,
                237
            personal information, 238
            references, 238
            skills, 238
            work experience, 233, 236
        design of, 238, 243
            fonts and point sizes, 239
            graphical devices, 239
            white space, 239
        functional, 236
        organization, 236, 244
        paper/printing, 240
Reviewers, 16–17
Review(s):
    and citations, 139
    exempt, research and, 53–54
    journal article review, 351

levels of, at Brigham Young
    University (BYU), 51
of literature in prospectus, 145, 150
    sample, 173
    suggestions for writing, 231
    writing, 231
        evaluation of strengths/
            weaknesses, 220
        facts of publication, 228
        scope, 218
Revising, 27
    letters of application, 249
    letters of intent and personal state-
        ments, 258
    preferences and habits in, 28–29
    source documents, 59
    working in groups and, 36
Reynolds, L., 280
Rhetoric, 5–10, 9
    academic disciplines and, 9–10
    and audience, 8
    definition of, 5, 8–9
    graphics as, 291–292
    as language, 5–6
    oral, 311–312
    as potentially positive force, 7
Rhetoric, by Aristotle, 7
Rhetorical situation, 18–21
    defined, 6
    evaluating, 312
Risk:
    human participants and, 50
    and Institutional review boards
        (IRB), 51
    working in groups and, 36

Sample/Sampling:
    convenience, 105–106
    observational research and, 83
    random, 97
    representative, 97
    size, 106
Scannable resume, 233, 234, 243
Scan zones, 274
Science:
    definition of, 6, 9
    and knowledge, 43
Scientists, 3
    goal of, 9
Search engines:
    advanced search options in,
        128
    for locating information on the
        Internet, 130–131
Secondary sources, 62–63
Semi-block style, letters of application,
    249
Serif *vs.* sans-serif fonts, 278
Sketchpads, oral presentations and, 320,
    325
Skills, in resumes, 233, 234
Slides, oral presentations and, 319, 325

Social sciences:
    fields of, 6
    history of, 10
    and human behavior, 10
    persuasion and change in, 17–18
    style in the, 331, 334
    as university disciplines, 11
Social Sciences Citation Index, 140
Social Sciences Index, 126
Social scientists, 3
    prewriting techniques and, 24
    writing of, 207
Source documents:
    interpreting, 59, 62
    suggestions for writing, 68–69
    writing about, 66
Source reliability, 139, 136
    author's credentials/reputation,
        137
    date of publication, 138
    peer review, political dimensions of,
        136
    publication type, 138–139
    publisher's
        reputation/aims/emphases, 137
    research funding, ideological dimen-
        sions of, 136–137
    reviews/citations, 139
Source usefulness, 142
    books, evaluating, 142
Specialized computer databases, 129
Spencer, H., 182f, 280, 444
Stanton, Elizabeth Cady, 7
Statistics:
    interpretation of, 60
    oral presentations and, 311, 325
Stilborne, Linda, 144
Structured observation, 85
Style, 24
    of critiques, 217
    differences, 341
    in the social sciences, 331, 334
Subject directories, 131
Subject headings lists, 126
Summarizing, 143
    interview data, 75, 80
Summary, IRB proposal, 147, 149
Surveys, 97, 102
    advantages of, 97
    conducting, 104, 106
    designing, 97, 99
        clear directions, 103–104
        defining purpose, 99
        demographic questions, 100
        determining order of questions,
            103
        fixed-response questions,
            100–101
        open-ended questions, 101–102
        unambiguous questions, 102
    disadvantages of, 98–99
    instrument, of IRB proposal, 149

suggestions for research and writing, 109
writing the report, 108–109
Synthesis:
information outlining and, 123
interview data, 80

Table of contents, books evaluation and, 141, 142
Tables, 293
and data display, 293
labeling, 302
Tannen Deborah, 85
Tarule, Jill Mattuck, 35
Task analysis, working in groups and, 36, 37
Testing effect, as confound to a design, 115
"The Role of Writing in BYU Economics Education" (Killingbeck), 161f
Thesauruses, 125
Thesis statement, 221
"The SPE: What It Was, Where It Came From, and What Came Out of It" (Zimbardo), 420
"Thick description," in observational research, 91
Thomas, Dene Kay, 79, 80
Time:
case studies and, 85
interview, 71
oral presentations and, 318, 319
words referring to, 102
Traditional resume, 234
Transcripts, interviews and, 71, 78
Triangulation, 92
Truth, Sojourner, 7
Tufte, Edward, 292

Turabian, Kate
heading in Turabian style, 273, 288f
Typography:
capital letters, 279
fonts, 278–279
serif *vs.* sans-serif fonts, 278–279
type size, 280
type weight, 280

U.S. Department of Health, Education, and Welfare, Belmont Report, 50–51
Unambiguous questions, 102–103
Unobtrusive observation, 84–85
defining focus and, 88

Validity, in experiments, 117–118
"Vatican Diplomacy and the Jews During the Holocaust 1939–1943," review of (Loughran), 231–232
Videotapes/videotaping:
interview and, 76
observations, 90
oral presentations and, 322
Visual aids:
oral presentations, 319–324
chalkboards, 320
computer presentation software, 322
handouts, 321
objects and models, 322
overhead transparencies, 321
photos, 321–322
posterboards, 320
sketchpads, 320
slides, 322
videos, 322
whiteboards, 320
Voice qualities, 326–327

Web sites, online resume and, 246
Whiteboards, oral presentations and, 320
White space:
documents, 274
resume, 238–239
Women's Ways of Knowing, 35, 79, 81
Words:
referring to amounts, 102
referring to time, 102
Words of Pain, 79
Writing:
about experiments, 119–121
about observations, 92–93
about qualitative data, 92
an abstract, 218–219
communication and, 30
context of the interview, 78
critiques, 199–203
interpreting texts and, 63
interviewing suggestions for research and, 81–82
memoranda, 265–270
position paper, 209–214
research as part of, 45–46
reviews, 228–231
suggestions for source documents, 67–68
survey report, 108–109
Written surveys, 97, 98

Yahoo, 131
Young, Crystal M., 108

Ziman, John, 14
Zimbardo, Philip G., 120, 420–433